The Daily Office –
Benedictine and Episcopal

Volume III
The Seasons After Epiphany and Pentecost

ISBN 9781686777141

Dedication

To my parents
Gisella Ann De Franco & Peter De Franco, Sr.
I have been sustained by you, O Lord, ever since I was born;
from my mother's womb you have been my strength;
my praise shall be always of you.
Psalm 71:6

To the women in my family
whose wisdom and strength
have continued to build strong families
and a better world.

Anna Mozer Tell, *Great Grandmother*
Eva Tell Mosckvam, *Grandmother*
Teresa De Franco, *Grandmother*
Roseann Shomberg, *Sister*
Melinda Calderon, *Niece*
Jennifer Rosales, *Niece*
Mia Lopez, *Great Niece*
Gisella Rosales, *Great Niece*
Priscilla Lopez, *Great Niece*

She opens her mouth with wisdom,
and the teaching of kindness is on her tongue.
Proverbs 31: 26

With thanks to
Angelina Respoli;
Bro. Anthony Maggiore, O.S.C.O. of St. Joseph's Abbey, Spencer, and
Bro. Michael Morotti, O.S.B. of Conception Abbey,
who assisted in this project.

With Gratitude to
The Rev. Brother Robert Sevensky, O.H.C.,
The Rev. Robert Solon and
The Rev. Diana Wilcox
who graciously reviewed the manuscript.

Table of Contents

Introduction

The Daily Office Benedictine and Episcopal is offered for those who are looking for a form of daily prayer that emerges from the Benedictine and Anglican traditions. It draws on the fourfold structure of the Daily Office as found in the Book of Common Prayer integrated with material from the Sarum Offices, and the Thesaurus Liturgiae Horarum Monasticae developed by the Benedictine Order in response to the reform of the Liturgy called for by the Second Vatican Council. This book stands in the liturgical tradition of The Prayer Book Office.

This book follows the Anglican Tradition which places the main hinges of the office with the hours of Morning Prayer and Evening Prayer. In that tradition, the office of Morning Prayer incorporates elements of the monastic office of Vigils and so it should be the more contemplative office. The contemplative nature of this office can be enhanced with silence after the psalms and the readings. In personal use, a period of Lectio Divina can be included after either reading with the conclusion of the office as the end of personal prayer. To incorporate a more Benedictine character of Vigils, a third reading from a Patristic Source can be included after the Second Biblical Reading. Lectionaries of Patristic Readings are readily available.

The Calendar

Since this book is intended for persons who are looking to celebrate a Benedictine and Anglican cycle of saints, the Anglican saints are mostly drawn from Lesser Feasts and Fasts 2006 of the Episcopal Church, the Benedictine saints are taken from the Calendars of the Swiss American Benedictine Congregation and the Cistercians of the Strict Observance, and the Calendar of the Roman Church for those Benedictine saints included in the universal calendar. Women saints from the Apostolic era and presented in Holy Women Holy Men, A Great Cloud of Witnesses and Lesser Feasts and Fasts 2018 are included to provide a gender balance to the traditional twelve apostles. Founders of Religious Communities in the Episcopal Church are included. Finally, this Calendar incorporates some new saints who are significance for New Monastics. The inclusion of these New Monastic Saints marks the beginning of their local cult as a prelude for their submission in the calendar of the Episcopal Church. Saints not included in Lesser Feasts and Fasts 2006 are printed in italic in the Calendar. Saints from the Benedictine Calendar and other saints not in Lesser Feasts and Fasts 2006 are printed in the calendar in italic.

Three Benedictine feasts are ranked as Principal Feasts: St. Scholastica, the Transitus of St. Benedict and St. Benedict. This calendar retains the traditional dates for the Principal and Major feasts of St. Scholastica, the Transitus of St. Benedict, St. Joseph and the Annunciation of Our Lord Jesus Christ to the Blessed Virgin Mary. When these feasts fall in Holy Week, they are transferred to the week following the Second Sunday of Easter with the following priority: The Annunciation, St. Joseph the Transitus of St. Benedict. All the feasts would begin with Morning Prayer.

Following the classifications of the Episcopal Church, the feasts have three ranks: Principal Feasts and Feasts of Our Lord, Major Feasts and Lesser Feasts. Principal Feasts and Feasts of Our Lord are designated in the Calendar in Bold print. They begin with Evening Prayer I and conclude with Evening Prayer II. The Magnificat Antiphon should be used for both Evening Prayer I and Evening Prayer II. Major feasts begin with Morning Prayer, use proper or common antiphons on the psalms and the Sunday or proper psalmody. Major feasts, such as the Apostles and Evangelists, St. Mary the Virgin and Mary Magdalene may also be celebrated with Evening Prayer I which is provided in either the Proper or the Common of the Saints. Lesser Feasts begin with Morning Prayer and conclude with Compline. Lesser feasts may use the common antiphons for the daily psalter or antiphons taken from the common of the saint but a proper or common antiphon should be used with the Benedictus and Magnificat.

The Psalter

While the Rule of St. Benedict requires that the entire Psalter be recited in one week, this office accommodates itself to those persons living a more active life style and so uses a four week psalter. While ever effort was made to retain the assignment of psalms to the offices suggested in the Rule of St. Benedict, such an arrangement could not be scrupulously followed. The present Psalter is structured around the following themes: Sunday, the Resurrection; Monday, Creation; Tuesday, Zion and the Incarnation; Wednesday, Salvation History; Thursday, the Holy Eucharist; Friday, the Cross, and Saturday, Wisdom and the Burial of Christ. Not all the psalms fit into these categories and some psalms could fit into more than one place. Every effort was made to integrate the major themes of the psalms with the corresponding areas of Christian life and thought. In an effort to integrate the psalms into the Christian life, a short passage from the Christian Scripture is offered before the psalm to direct the prayer around that psalm toward the mystery of Christ. These phrases can be alternately used as antiphons. The assigned antiphons are usually taken from the psalms to show how the major themes of the liturgical year can be found in the psalter. Other antiphons are drawn from the Benedictine Thesauraus. the pages of Scripture, the ancient life of the saint or the Rule of St. Benedict.

How To Use This Work

In using this resource, the reader should use a bible as the source for the readings from the Daily Office Lectionary of the Episcopal Church which is included as a resource at the end of this book. If the reader would like to integrate music into the office, as happens in the best parts of the Benedictine Tradition, suggested hymns are taken from the Hymnal 1982.

This book emerges from the Benedictine Tradition and works well with persons who are engaged in a daily practice of Lectio Divina and contemplative prayer. The Verses and Responses as well as the Responsories are structured into the office as a way to integrate Lectio Divina into the Daily Office as well as take from the offices those short prayers that are used in the course of the day to practice continual prayer. The lectionary could be used as the basis for daily Lectio Divina and the responsories assist in that practice.

The use of this book requires that the user understand some parts of the liturgical cycle of the church. The Revised Common Lectionary uses a three year cycle: Year A, Year B and Year C. During Year A, the readings from the Gospel are taken mostly from Matthew, during Year B mostly from Mark, with an extended passage from the Gospel according to John, and Year C from Luke. Accordingly, the antiphons for the Gospel Canticles on Sunday are taken from the Gospel used for that year. The Episcopal Daily Office Lectionary uses a two year cycle. Advent of the odd numbered years use Year Two and Advent of the even numbered years use Year One.

This Daily Office is structured around a Four Week Psalter. The current week of the Psalter is found in the proper of the Seasons. Week One of the Psalter always begins on the first week of a new liturgical season. The First Week of Advent uses Week 1 of the Psalter. For the Season after Epiphany and the season after Pentecost, the Week of the Psalter is found with the corresponding week of the Season.

The structure of the four offices is found in the Ordinary of the Daily Office beginning on page 95. To use this book, a person should mark the ordinary of the Daily Office since the structure of the Hours is laid out in the Ordinary. The other mark should designate the Week of the Psalter. If a saint's day is being celebrated, the third mark should be placed on the page for that saint's day. If you enjoy a more complete office for a saint with a lesser feast, you can also use the common of that saint with antiphons on the psalms of the day, responsories, a canticle after the first reading for Morning Prayer, antiphons on the Gospel Canticle and a litany.. If a day celebrates a season, a mark should be placed on that day for the season along with a mark on the particular week or day which is being celebrated.

The Common Office for the Dedication of a Church would be used by individual members to celebrate the Dedication of their church.

The Common of the Founding of the Community would be used by those religious communities on their Founding Day. Communities which use this resource should consider adapting at least the Antiphons on the Benedictus and Magnificat with passages which reflect the charism of that community.

The Saturday Common Office of the Blessed Virgin Mary can be used on those Saturdays which do not celebrate a particular saint. This Saturday Common Office of the Blessed Virgin Mary is offered as a devotional office. It includes an Invitatory Antiphon, a Hymn, Antiphons for the Psalms and the Benedictus and a concluding Litany and Collect. While the full office should not be used during the Seasons of Advent, Christmas, Lent and Easter, a person can include the Benedictus antiphon provided for those seasons.

The Office of the Dead is included for use on the Commemoration of All Faithful Departed, for the Faithful Departed of the Benedictine Order and for personal use to pray for a person who has died on the day of their death or the anniversary of their death. The Office for the Dead should never be used on Sundays, the Easter Triduum, or Principle or Major Feasts.

The Common for Rogation Days is retained in this volume to use for celebrations related to the environment.

Unique Qualities of The Office in this Work

This Daily Office attempts to bring a greater simplicity to the office, respecting the intention of the Reformers as well as the structure of the office as presented by St. Benedict. A single Collect concludes each office and devotional elements, such as the General Thanksgiving, are not included.

Many people engage in a practice of intercessory prayer and the Noonday Office is structured to provide opportunity for intercessory prayer for the needs of the World, the Church and personal concerns. These needs can be included in a litany which provides a place for these needs to be raised in spontaneous prayer. Since this office traditionally remembers the hour of the Descent of the Holy Spirit and the Crucifixion of our Lord, the collects and hymns reflect that remembrance.

Compline follows the pattern of the Sarum Office. Proper parts are included for the Gospel Canticle.

St. Benedict urges us to prefer nothing to the work of God. This book is offered as a means of integrating the Benedictine culture with the Anglican Tradition as received by the Episcopal Church. As countless Christians, lay, monastic and ordained, found in the Daily Office a source of the sanctification of the day and an entry into the Mystery of Christ, this book is presented with the prayer that its users may continue to discover the richness of the Daily Office as an integral part of the Benedictine Tradition.

February 26, 2020
Photini, The Samaritan Woman, Equal to the Apostles
Peter De Franco

The Calendar of the Church Year

January

1 A **THE HOLY NAME OF OUR LORD JESUS CHRIST**

2 b

3 c

4 d *Elizabeth Seton, Professed Religious and Founder of the American Sisters of Charity, 1821*

5 e *Sarah, Theodora, and Syncletica of Egypt, Desert Mothers, 4th-5th century*

6 F **THE EPIPHANY OF OUR LORD JESUS CHRIST**

7 g

8 A Harriet Bedell, Deaconess and Missionary, 1969

9 b Julia Chester Emery, 1922

10 c William Laud, Archbishop of Canterbury, 1645

11 d

12 e Aelred, Cistercian Monk, Abbot of Rievaulx, 1167

13 f Hilary, Bishop of Poitiers and Teacher of the Faith, 367

14 g

15 A *Maur and Placid, Disciples of St. Benedict*

16 b *Richard Meux Benson, Religious and Founder of the Society of St. John the Evangelist, 1915 and Charles Gore, Founder of the Community of the Resurrection, Bishop of Worcester, of Birmingham, and of Oxford,1932*

17 c Antony, Abbot in Egypt, 356

18 d ***The Confession of Saint Peter the Apostle***

19 e Wulfstan, Bishop of Worcester, 1095

20 f Fabian, Bishop and Martyr of Rome, 250

21 g Agnes, Martyr at Rome, 304

22 A Vincent, Deacon of Saragossa, Martyr, 304

23 b Phillips Brooks, Bishop of Massachusetts, 1893

24 c Florence Li Tim-Oi, First Woman Priest in the Anglican Communion, 1944

25 d ***The Conversion of Saint Paul the Apostle***

26 e Timothy and Titus, Companions of Saint Paul

26 e *Robert of Molesme, Alberic and Stephen Harding, Abbots and Founders of the Cistercian Order*

27 f John Chrysostom, Bishop of Constantinople and Teacher of the Faith, 407

28 g Thomas Aquinas, Friar, Priest and Teacher of the Faith 1274

29 A

30 b

31 c *Marcella of Rome, Urban Monastic and Scholar, 410*

February

1 d Brigid (Bride), 523

2 E **THE PRESENTATION OF OUR LORD JESUS CHRIST IN THE TEMPLE**

3 f Anskar, Archbishop of Hamburg and Missionary to Denmark and Sweden, 865

4 g Cornelius the Centurion

5 A *Agatha of Sicily, Martyr c. 251*

5 A The Martyrs of Japan, 1597

6 b

7 c

8 d

9 e *Anne Ayers, Religious and Founder of the Sisterhood of the Holy Communion, 1896*

10 F ***SCHOLASTICA, NUN AND SISTER OF BENEDICT, 542***

11 g *Benedict of Aniane, Abbot, 821*

12 A

13 b Absalom Jones, Priest, 1818

14 c Cyril, Monk, and Methodius, Bishop, Missionaries to the Slavs, 869, 885

15 d Thomas Bray, Priest and Missionary, 1730

16 e

17 f Janani Luwum, Archbishop of Uganda and Martyr, 1977

18 g Martin Luther, Reformer, 1546

19 A

20 b

21 c

22 d *Saint Matthias the Apostle*

23 e Polycarp, Bishop and Martyr of Smyrna, 156

24 f

25 g *Walburga, Benedictine Abbess of Double Monastery of Heidenheim, c 777*

26 A *Photini, The Samaritan Woman, Equal to the Apostles*

27 b George Herbert, Priest, 1633

28 c

29

March

1 d David, Bishop of Menevia, Wales, c. 544

2 e Chad, Bishop of Lichfield, 672

3 f John and Charles Wesley, Priests, 1791, 1788

4 g

5 A

6 b

7 c Perpetua, Felicity and their Companions, Martyrs at Carthage, 202

8 d

9e Gregory, Bishop of Nyssa, c. 394

9 e *Frances of Rome, Married Woman, Founder of the Olivetan Oblates of Mary and Benedictine Oblate, 1440*

10 f

11 g

12 A Gregory the Great, Monk, Bishop of Rome and Teacher of the Faith, 604

13 b James Theodore Holly, Bishop of Haiti and of the Dominican Republic, 1911

14 c

15 d

16 e

17 f Patrick, Bishop and Missionary of Ireland, 461

18 g Cyril, Bishop of Jerusalem and Teacher of the Faith, 386

19 A **Saint Joseph**

20 b Cuthbert, Monk and Bishop of Lindisfarne, 687

21 C ***TRANSITUS OF OUR HOLY FATHER SAINT BENEDICT***

22 d James De Koven, Priest, 1879

23 e Gregory the Illuminator, Bishop and Missionary of Armenia, c. 332

24 f Óscar Romero, Archbishop of San Salvador, and the Martyrs of San Salvador, 1980

25 G **THE ANNUNCIATION OF OUR LORD JESUS CHRIST TO THE BLESSED VIRGIN MARY**

26 A *Harriet Monsell, Professsed Religious, Founder of the Community of St. John Baptist, 1883*

27 b Charles Henry Brent, Bishop of the Philippines, and of Western New York, 1929

28 c

29 d John Keble, Priest, 1866

30 e

31 f John Donne, Priest, 1631

April

1 g Frederick Denison Maurice, Priest, 1872

2 A James Lloyd Breck, Priest, 1876

3 b Richard, Bishop of Chichester, 1253

3 b *Mary of Egypt, Monastic c. 421*

4 c Martin Luther King, Jr., Pastor and Civil Rights Leader, 1968

5 d *Harriet Starr Cannon and her companions, Professed Religious, and Founders of the Community of St. Mary, 1896*

6 c

7 f Tikhon, Patriarch of Russia, Confessor and Ecumenist, 1925

8 g William Augustus Muhlenberg, Priest, 1877

9 A Dietrich Bonhoeffer, Theologian and Martyr 1945

10 b William Law, Priest, 1761

11 c George Augustus Selwyn, Bishop of New Zealand, and of Lichfield, 1878

12 d

13 e

14 f

15 g

16 A

17 b

18 c

19 d Alphege, Archbishop of Canterbury, and Martyr, 1012

20 e

21 f Anselm, Monk, Archbishop of Canterbury, and Teacher of the Faith, 1109

22 g *Hadewijch of Brabant, Beguine, Poet and Mystic, 13th Century*

23 A

24 b

25 c **Saint Mark the Evangelist**

26 d

27 e

28 f

29 g Catherine of Siena, Dominican Tertiary, Teacher of the Faith, 1380

30 A

May

1 b *Saint Philip and Saint James, Apostles*

2 c Athanasius, Bishop of Alexandria, and Teacher of the Faith, 373

3 d

4 e Monnica, Mother of Augustine of Hippo, 387

5 f

6 g

7 A

8 b Dame Julian of Norwich, Hermit, and Mystic, c. 1417

9 c Gregory of Nazianzus, Bishop of Constantinople, and Teacher of the Faith, 389

10 d

11 e *The Holy Abbots of Cluny: Odo, Mayeul, Odilo, and Hugh, and Peter the Venerable*

12 f

13 g *Bede Griffiths, Benedictine Monk, Yogi, Priest 1993*

14 A

15 b *Pachomius, Abbot, 348*

16 c *The Martyrs of the Sudan 1983-2011*

17 d

18 e

19 f Dunstan, Monk, Restorer of the Monastic Life and Archbishop of Canterbury, 988

20 g Alcuin, Deacon, and Abbot of Tours, 804

21 A

22 b *Lydia of Thyatira, Coworker of the Apostle Paul*

23 c

24 d Jackson Kemper, First Missionary Bishop in the United States, 1870

25 e Bede, the Venerable, Priest, Monk of Jarrow and Teacher of the Faith, 735

26 f Augustine, Monk and First Archbishop of Canterbury, 605

27 g

28 A *Mechthild of Magdeburg, Mystic, Beguine, Benedictice Nun c.1282*

29 b

30 c

31 D **THE VISITATION OF THE BLESSED VIRGIN MARY**

The First Book of Common Prayer, 1549, is appropriately observed on a weekday following the Day of Pentecost.

June

1 e Justin, Martyr at Rome, c. 167

2 f Blandina and her Companions, Martyrs of Lyons, 173

3 g The Martyrs of Uganda, 1886

4 A

5 b Boniface, Monk, Archbishop of Mainz, Missionary to Germany and Martyr, 754

6 c *Ini Kopuria, Professed Religious, Founder of the Melanesian Brotherhood, 1945*

7 d

8 e *Melania the Elder, Monastic, 410*

9 f Columba, Abbot of Iona, 597

10 g Ephrem of Edessa, Syria, Deacon and Teacher of the Faith 373

11 A **Saint Barnabas the Apostle**

12 b Enmegahbowh, Priest and Missionary, 1902

12 b *Alice of Schaerbeek, Cistercian Nun and Leper, 1250*

13 c

14 d Basil the Great, Monk, Author of a Monastic Rule, Bishop of Caesarea and Teacher of the Faith, 379

15 e Evelyn Underhill, Mystic and Theologian, 1941

16 f Joseph Butler, Bishop of Durham, 1752

16 f *Lutgard, Cistercian Nun, 1246*

17 g

18 A Bernard Mizeki, Catechist and Martyr in Rhodesia, 1896

18 A *Elisabeth of Schönau, Benedictine Abbess and Mystic, 1164*

19 b *Romuald, Abbot and Founder of the Camaldolese Order, 1027*

20 c

21 d

22 e Alban, First Martyr of Britain, c. 304

23 f *Ethelreda, Benedictine Abbess of Double Monastery at Ely, 697*

24 g **THE NATIVITY OF SAINT JOHN THE BAPTIST**

25 A

26 b

27 c

28 d Irenaeus, Bishop of Lyons, c. 202

29 e **Saint Peter and Saint Paul, Apostles**

30 f

July

1 g

2 A

3 b

4 c *Independence Day*

5 d

6 e *Eva Lee Matthews, Professed Religious, Founder of the Sisters of the Transfiguration, 1928*

7 f

8 g *Priscilla and Aquila, Coworkers of the Apostle Paul*

9 A

10 b

11 c **OUR HOLY FATHER SAINT BENEDICT OF NURSIA, ABBOT OF MONTE CASSINO, C. 540**

12 d *John Gualbert, Abbot, Founder of the Vallumbrosan Order*

13 e *Henry, Holy Roman Emperor and Benedictine Oblate, 1023*

14 f

15 g

16 A

17 b William White, Bishop of Pennsylvania, 1836

18 c

19 d Macrina, Monastic and Teacher, 379

20 e Elizabeth Cady Stanton, Amelia Bloomer, Sojourner Truth, and Harriet Ross Tubman

20 e *Maria Skobtsoba, Monastic and Martyr, 1945*

21 f

22 g **Saint Mary Magdalene**

23 A *John Cassian, Abbot at Marseilles, 433*

24 b Thomas a Kempis, Priest, 1471

25 c **Saint James the Apostle**

26 d Joachim and Anne, The Parents of the Blessed Virgin Mary

27 e William Reed Huntington, Priest, 1909

28 f

29 g Mary, Martha and Lazarus of Bethany, Hosts and Friends of our Lord

30 A William Wilberforce, 1833

31 b Ignatius of Loyola, Religious, Priest and Founder of the Society of Jesus, 1556

August

1 c Joseph of Arimathaea

2 d

3 e *Joanna, Mary, and Salome, Myrrh-bearing Women*

4 f

5 g

6 A **THE TRANSFIGURATION OF OUR LORD JESUS CHRIST**

7 b John Mason Neale, Priest, 1866

8 c Dominic, Friar, Priest and Founder of the Order of Preachers, 1221

9 d *Teresa Benedicta of the Cross, Scholar, Carmelite Nun and Martyr, 1942*

10 e Laurence, Deacon, and Martyr at Rome, 258

11 f Clare, Abbess at Assisi and Founder of the Poor Clares, 1253

12 g Florence Nightingale, Nurse and Social Reformer, 1910

13 A Jeremy Taylor, Bishop of Down, Connor, and Dromore, 1667

14 b Jonathan Myrick Daniels, Seminarian, Martyr and Witness for Civil Rights, 1965

15 c **SAINT MARY THE VIRGIN, MOTHER OF OUR LORD JESUS CHRIST**

16 d *Roger Schutz, Monk and Founder of Taize, 2005*

17 e

18 f Artemisia Bowden, Educator, 1969

19 g

20 A Bernard, Abbot of Clairvaux and Teacher of the Faith, 1153

21 b

22 c

23 d

24 e Saint Bartholomew the Apostle

25 f Louis, King of France, 1270

26 g *Raimon Panikkar Priest and Theologian of the New Monasticism, 2010*

27 A Thomas Gallaudet, 1902 with Henry Winter Syle, 1890

28 b Augustine, Bishop of Hippo and Teacher of the Faith, 430

29 c

30 d

31 e Aidan, Monk and Bishop of Lindisfarne, 651

September

1 f David Pendleton Oakerhater, Deacon and Missionary, 1931

2 g The Martyrs of New Guinea, 1942

3 A *Phoebe, Deacon*

4 b Paul Jones, Bishop and Prophetic Witness, 1941

5 c

6 d

7 e

8 f

9 g Constance, Nun, and her Companions, Martyrs 1878

10 A Alexander Crummell, Priest, Prophetic Witness and Founder of the Union of Black Episcopalians 1898

11 b

12 c John Henry Hobart, Bishop of New York, 1830

13 d Cyprian, Bishop and Martyr of Carthage, 258

14 E **HOLY CROSS DAY**

15 f

16 g Ninian, Bishop in Galloway, c. 430

17 A Hildegard, Abbess and Teacher of the Faith, 1179

18 b Edward Bouverie Pusey, Priest, 1882

19 c Theodore of Tarsus, Archbishop of Canterbury, 690

20 d John Coleridge Patteson, Bishop of Melanesia, and his Companions, Martyrs, 1871

21 e *Saint Matthew, Apostle and Evangelist*

22 f Philander Chase, Bishop of Ohio, and of Illinois, 1852

23 g

24 A

25 b Sergius, Abbot of Holy Trinity, Moscow, 1392

26 c Lancelot Andrewes, Bishop of Winchester, 1626

27 d

28 e *Richard Rolle, 1349, Walter Hilton, 1396, and Margery Kempe, c. 1440, Mystics*

28 e *Lioba, Benedictine Abbess of Bischofsheim and Companion of St Boniface, 782*

29 f *Saint Michael and All Angels*

30 g Jerome, Monk of Bethlehem, Priest and Teacher of the Faith, 420

October

1 A Remigius, Bishop of Rheims, c. 530

1 A *Therese of the Child Jesus and the Holy Face, Discalced Carmelite Nun, 1897*

2 b

3 c

4 d Francis of Assisi, Friar, Deacon and Founder of the Friars Minor, 1226

5 e

6 f *Bruno, Hermit, Founder of the Carthusian Order 1101*

7 g William Tyndale, Priest, 1536

8 A

9 b Robert Grosseteste, Bishop of Lincoln, 1253

10 c Vida Dutton Scudder, Educator and Witness for Peace, 1954

11 d Philip, Deacon and Evangelist

11 d *Ethelburga, Benedictine Abbess of double monastery at Barking, 675*

12 e

13 f

14 g Samuel Isaac Joseph Schereschewsky, Bishop of Shanghai, 1906

15 A Teresa of Jesus, Nun, Founder of the Discalced Carmelites, Mystic and Teacher of the Faith, 1582

16 b Hugh Latimer and Nicholas Ridley, Bishops, 1555 and Thomas Cranmer, Archbishop of Canterbury, 1556, Martyrs

17 c Ignatius, Bishop of Antioch, and Martyr, c. 115

18 d **Saint Luke the Evangelist**

19 e Henry Martyn, Priest, and Missionary to India and Persia, 1812

20 f

21 g

22 A

23 b **Saint James of Jerusalem, Brother of Our Lord Jesus Christ, and Martyr, c. 62**

24 c

25 d *Tabitha (Dorcas) of Joppa*

26 e Alfred the Great, King of the West Saxons, 899

27 f

28 g **Saint Simon and Saint Jude, Apostles**

29 A James Hannington, Bishop of Eastern Equatorial Africa, and his Companions, Martyrs, 1885

29 A *Maryam of Qidun, Monastic, 4th century*

30 b

31 c

Responsory Two (Tob. 13:11; Num. 24:17)
A bright light will shine to all the ends of the earth
> **− many nations will come to you from far away.**

A star shall come out of Jacob
> **− many nations will come to you from far away.**

Glory to the Father and to the Son and to the Holy Spirit.
A bright light will shine to all the ends of the earth
> **− many nations will come to you from far away.**

Benedictus Antiphon Where is the child who has been born king of the Jews? For we observed his star at its rising, and have come to pay him homage.

Litany

You are anointed prophet of the new covenant; let us share your prophetic call and challenge the abuses of our day.
Lord, have mercy.
You are anointed priest of the new covenant; let us offer with you the sacrifice of ourselves, our souls and our bodies.
Christ, have mercy.
You are anointed king of the new covenant; let us share your ministry of service and care for those neglected and unseen.
Lord, have mercy.

Invitation to the Lord's Prayer We celebrate the light of Christ and ask the Father to heal the blindness of our hearts and minds.

Collect *From Morning Prayer of January 7*
O God, by the leading of a star you manifested your only Son to the peoples of the earth: Lead us, who know you now by faith, to your presence, where we may see your glory face to face; through Jesus Christ our Lord, who lives and reigns with you and the Holy Spirit, one God, now and for ever. Amen.

The Blessing

May we sing and rejoice, for God has come and dwells in our midst.
Amen.

January 7 Noonday Prayer

Hymn O Light of Light *Hymnal 134*

Reading Deuteronomy 4: 7-9
For what other great nation has a god so near to it as the Lord our God is whenever we call to him? And what other great nation has statutes and ordinances as just as this entire law that I am setting before you today?

Verse and Response
Sing to the Lord a new song. Alleluia.
Sing to the Lord, all the whole earth. Alleluia.

Collect *From Morning Prayer of January 7*

January 7 Evening Prayer

Hymn As with gladness men of old *Hymnal 119*

Responsory (Gen 12:3; Mt. 2:11)
All peoples will be blessed in Christ
  — peoples from every corner of the world.
They will hasten to find the child
  — peoples from every corner of the world.
Glory to the Father and to the Son and to the Holy Spirit.
All peoples will be blessed in Christ
  — peoples from every corner of the world.

Magnificat Antiphon You, Bethlehem, in the land of Judah, are by no means least among the rulers of Judah; for from you shall come a ruler who is to shepherd my people Israel.

Litany
You illumined the night sky with the revelation of the star; draw all people to you through your Word.
Lord, have mercy.
You manifested the mystery of the Trinity in the waters of the Jordan; reveal yourself to us through our Baptism.
Christ, have mercy.
You foretold the mystery of your heavenly banquet in the transformation of water into wine; transform the dead to rejoice at your table.
Lord, have mercy.

Invitation to the Lord's Prayer You continually manifest yourself to us through signs and wonders so open our hearts to behold your present revelation among us.

Collect *From Morning Prayer of January 7*

The Blessing
May we rejoice and sing for the Lord, our God, is in our midst: the God who will rejoice over us with gladness, who will renew us in his love; who will exult over us with loud singing. **Amen.**

January 8 Morning Prayer

Invitatory Alleluia. Christ has manifested himself to the world: Come let us worship. Alleluia.

Hymn When Christ's appearing was made known *Hymnal 131*

Responsory One (Ps. 72:11; Gen. 12:3)
All rulers of the earth bow down before him
— all the nations do him service.
All the nations of the earth shall be blessed in him
— all the nations do him service.
Glory to the Father and to the Son and to the Holy Spirit.
All rulers of the earth bow down before him
— all the nations do him service.

Canticle – Canticle of Jerusalem, My Delight N*on vocaberis*
(Isaiah 62: 4-7)
Antiphon As the bridegroom rejoices over the bride, so shall your God rejoice over you.

You shall no more be termed "Forsaken," *
and your land shall no more be termed "Desolate;"

You shall be called "My Delight," *
and your land "Espoused."

For the Lord delights in you, *
and your land shall be married.

For as a young man marries a young woman, *
so shall your builder marry you.

As the bridegroom rejoices over the bride, *
so shall your God rejoice over you.

Upon your walls, O Jerusalem, *
I have posted sentinels.

All day and all night *
they shall never be silent.

You who remind the Lord, take no rest, *
and give him no rest

Until he establishes Jerusalem *
and makes it renowned throughout the earth.

Antiphon As the bridegroom rejoices over the bride, so shall your God rejoice over you.

Responsory Two (Tob. 13:11; Num. 24:17)
A bright light will shine to all the ends of the earth
        — nations will come to you from far away.
A star shall come out of Jacob
        — many nations will come to you from far away.
Glory to the Father and to the Son and to the Holy Spirit.
A bright light will shine to all the ends of the earth
        — nations will come to you from far away.

Benedictus Antiphon The wise men set out; and there, ahead of them, went the star that they had seen at its rising.

Litany
You broke down the wall dividing Jew and Gentile; unite all people as children of our one Father.
Lord, have mercy.
You fulfilled the promise to Abraham and Sarah that all people may find a blessing in you; bring together people divided by differing theologies.
Christ, have mercy.
You accepted the life of an immigrant and refugee; sustain all without a home and open homes to all who are abandoned.
Lord, have mercy.

Invitation to the Lord's Prayer We acknowledge our unity with all people through Christ and pray that the Father may bring us together under God's gracious rule.

Collect *From Morning Prayer of January 7*

The Blessing
We know that we are God's children, and we know that the Son of God has come and has given us understanding so that we may know him who is true. **Amen.**

January 8 Noonday Prayer
Hymn O Wondrous Type *Hymnal 137*

Reading Ephesian 2: 4-6
God, who is rich in mercy, out of the great love with which he loved us even when we were dead through our trespasses, made us alive together with Christ—by grace you have been saved— and raised us up with him and seated us with him in the heavenly places in Christ Jesus.

Verse and Response
Declare God's glory among the nations. Alleluia.
His wonders among all peoples. Alleluia.

Collect *From Morning Prayer of January 7*

January 8 Evening Prayer
Hymn The people who in darkness walked *Hymnal 126*

Responsory (Gen 12:3; Mt. 2:11)
All peoples will be blessed in Christ
          – peoples from every corner of the world.
They will hasten to find the child
          – peoples from every corner of the world.
Glory to the Father and to the Son and to the Holy Spirit.
All peoples will be blessed in Christ
          – peoples from every corner of the world.

Magnificat Antiphon The star stopped over the place where the child was.

Litany
Deliver us from the way of sin and death and open our hearts to your holy and life-giving Spirit.
Lord, have mercy.
Keep us in the faith and communion of your holy Church and teach us to love others in the power of the Spirit.
Christ, have mercy.
Send us into the world in witness to your love and bring us to the fullness of your peace and glory.
Lord, have mercy.

Invitation to the Lord's Prayer Since we are baptized into the death and resurrection of Jesus Christ, let us ask the Father to open our eyes that we may see Christ come again in glory.

Collect *From Morning Prayer of January 7*

The Blessing
May the grace of the Lord Jesus be with us. Let us love one another in Christ Jesus. **Amen.**

January 9 Morning Prayer

Invitatory Alleluia. Christ has manifested himself to the world: Come let us worship. Alleluia.

Hymn O wondrous type *Hymnal 136*

Responsory One (Ps. 72:11; Gen. 12:3)
All rulers of the earth bow down before him
  – all the nations do him service.
All the nations of the earth shall be blessed in him
  – all the nations do him service.
Glory to the Father and to the Son and to the Holy Spirit.
All rulers of the earth bow down before him
  – all the nations do him service.

Canticle – of Ransomed Jacob *Audite verbum Domini gentes*
(Jeremiah 31: 10-14)

Antiphon The Lord has ransomed Jacob, and has redeemed him from hands too strong for him.

Hear the word of the Lord, O nations, *
  and declare it in the coastlands far away:

"He who scattered Israel will gather him, *
  and will keep him as a shepherd a flock."

For the Lord has ransomed Jacob, *
  and has redeemed him from hands too strong for him.

They shall come and sing aloud on the height of Zion, *
  and they shall be radiant over the goodness of the Lord.

They shall rejoice over the grain, the wine, and the oil, *
  and over the young of the flock and the herd.

Their life shall become like a watered garden, *
  and they shall never languish again.

Then shall the young women rejoice in the dance, *
  and the young men and the old shall be merry.

I will turn their mourning into joy, *
  I will comfort them, and give them gladness for sorrow.

I will give the priests their fill of choice portions, *
  and my people shall be satisfied with my bounty.

Antiphon The Lord has ransomed Jacob, and has redeemed him from hands too strong for him.

Responsory Two (Tob. 13:11; Num. 24:17)
A bright light will shine to all the ends of the earth
     – nations will come to you from far away.
A star shall come out of Jacob
     – nations will come to you from far away.
Glory to the Father and to the Son and to the Holy Spirit.
A bright light will shine to all the ends of the earth
     – nations will come to you from far away.

Benedictus Antiphon The kings of Tarshish and of the isles shall pay tribute, and the kings of Arabia and Saba offer gifts.

Litany
As the morning star illumines the sky, so shine in our hearts with the light of your Spirit.
Lord, have mercy.
As the radiant sun fills the world with light, so inspire all who are desolate and depressed.
Christ, have mercy.
As the moon and stars shin in the evening, so enlighten all who dwell in darkness.
Lord, have mercy.

Invitation to the Lord's Prayer Christ continues to manifest himself to all who seek him so let us ask the Father to reveal the Son to us through the Spirit.

Collect *From Morning Prayer of January 7*

The Blessing
May we rejoice for our light has come, and the glory of the Lord has risen upon us. **Amen.**

January 9 Noonday Prayer
Hymn The Sinless One to Jordan Came *Hymnal 120*

Reading John 3: 19-21
The light has come into the world, and people loved darkness rather than light because their deeds were evil. For all who do evil hate the light and do not come to the light, so that their deeds may not be exposed. But those who do what is true come to the light, so that it may be clearly seen that their deeds have been done in God.

Verse and Response
I am the light of the world. Alleluia.
Whoever follows me will have the light of life. Alleluia.

Collect *From Morning Prayer of January 7*

January 9 Evening Prayer

Hymn All praise to you, O Lord *Hymnal 138*

Responsory (Gen 12:3; Mt. 2:11)
All peoples will be blessed in Christ
    – peoples from every corner of the world.
They will hasten to find the child
    – peoples from every corner of the world.
Glory to the Father and to the Son and to the Holy Spirit.
All peoples will be blessed in Christ
    – peoples from every corner of the world.

Magnificat Antiphon A multitude of camels shall cover you, the young camels of Midian and Ephah; all those from Sheba shall come.

Litany
You illumine the minds and hearts of people seeking you; shine in the hearts of all people and draw them to you.
Lord, have mercy.
You promised to make your people Israel a light to the nations; may your church, faithful to your ancient promise, shine as a lamp pointing to you.
Christ, have mercy.
You shine on the world bringing hope and peace; may your light shine on the dead and give them peace.
Lord, have mercy.

Invitation to the Lord's Prayer As we stand in the light of the star may we pray with the wise ones of every generation who seek Christ and with them we say.

Collect *From Morning Prayer of January 7*

The Blessing
May we be glad and rejoice forever in what God is creating; for God is creating Jerusalem as a joy, and its people as a delight. **Amen.**

January 10 Morning Prayer

Invitatory Alleluia. Christ has manifested himself to the world. Come let us worship. Alleluia.

Hymn Christ upon the mountain peak *Hymnal 129*

Responsory One (Ps. 72:11; Gen. 12:3)
All rulers of the earth bow down before him
　　— all the nations do him service.
All the nations of the earth shall be blessed in him
　　— all the nations do him service.
Glory to the Father and to the Son and to the Holy Spirit.
All rulers of the earth bow down before him
　　— all the nations do him service.

Canticle – Song of God's Light *Quod fuit ab initio*
(1 John 1: 1-7)
Antiphon God is light and in him there is no darkness at all.

We declare to you what was from the beginning, *
　　what we have heard, what we have seen with our eyes.

What we have looked at and touched with our hands, *
　　concerning the word of life.

This life was revealed, and we have seen it and testify to it, *
　　and declare to you the eternal life
　　that was with the Father and was revealed to us.

We declare to you what we have seen and heard *
　　so that you also may have fellowship with us.

Our fellowship is with the Father and with his Son Jesus Christ. *
　　We are writing these things so that our joy may be complete.

This is the message we have heard from him and proclaim to you, *
　　that God is light and in him there is no darkness at all.

If we say that we have fellowship with him
while we are walking in darkness, *
　　we lie and do not do what is true.

But if we walk in the light as he himself is in the light, *
　　we have fellowship with one another,
　　and the blood of Jesus his Son cleanses us from all sin.

Antiphon God is light and in him there is no darkness at all.

Responsory Two (Tob. 13:11; Num. 24:17)
A bright light will shine to all the ends of the earth
　　　　– nations will come to you from far away.
A star shall come out of Jacob
　　　　– nations will come to you from far away.
Glory to the Father and to the Son and to the Holy Spirit.
A bright light will shine to all the ends of the earth
　　　　– nations will come to you from far away.

Benedictus Antiphon They shall bring gold and frankincense, and shall proclaim the praise of the Lord.

Litany
You are anointed prophet of the new covenant; let us share your prophetic call and challenge the abuses of our day.
Lord, have mercy.
You are anointed priest of the new covenant; let us offer with you the sacrifice of ourselves, our souls and our bodies.
Christ, have mercy.
You are anointed king of the new covenant; let us share your ministry of service and care for those neglected and unseen.
Lord, have mercy.

Invitation to the Lord's Prayer We celebrate the light of Christ and ask the Father to heal the blindness of our hearts and minds.

Collect *From Morning Prayer of January 7*

The Blessing
May we shout aloud and sing for joy for great in our midst is the Holy One of Israel. **Amen.**

January 10 Noonday Prayer
Hymn Brightest and best of the stars of the morning *Hymnal 117*

Reading Isaiah 60: 4-5
Lift up your eyes and look around; they all gather together, they come to you; your sons shall come from far away, and your daughters shall be carried on their nurses' arms. Then you shall see and be radiant; your heart shall thrill and rejoice, because the abundance of the sea shall be brought to you, the wealth of the nations shall come to you.

Verse and Response
Nations shall come to your light. Alleluia.
Kings to the brightness of your dawn. Alleluia.

Collect *From Morning Prayer of January 7*

January 10 Evening Prayer
Hymn The people who in darkness walked *Hymnal 125*

Responsory (Gen 12:3; Mt. 2:11)
All peoples will be blessed in Christ
    – **peoples from every corner of the world.**
They will hasten to find the child
    – **peoples from every corner of the world.**
Glory to the Father and to the Son and to the Holy Spirit.
All peoples will be blessed in Christ
    – **peoples from every corner of the world.**

Magnificat Antiphon When the wise men saw that the star had stopped, they were overwhelmed with joy.

Litany
You illumined the night sky with the revelation of the star, so draw all people to you through your Word.
Lord, have mercy.
You manifested the mystery of the Trinity in the waters of the Jordan, so reveal yourself to us through our Baptism.
Christ, have mercy.
You foretold the mystery of your heavenly banquet in the transformation of water into wine, so transform the dead to rejoice at your table.
Lord, have mercy.

Invitation to the Lord's Prayer You continually manifest yourself to us through signs and wonders so open our hearts to behold your present revelation among us.

Collect *From Morning Prayer of January 7*

The Blessing
May we exult in our Lord Jesus Christ, who, though he was rich, yet for our sakes he became poor, so that by his poverty we might become rich.
Amen.

January 11 Morning Prayer

Invitatory Alleluia. Christ has manifested himself to the world. Come let us worship. Alleluia.

Hymn Christ upon the mountain peak *Hymnal 130*

Responsory One (Ps. 72:11; Gen. 12:3)
All rulers of the earth bow down before him
      – all the nations do him service.
All the nations of the earth shall be blessed in him
      – all the nations do him service.
Glory to the Father and to the Son and to the Holy Spirit.
All rulers of the earth bow down before him
      – all the nations do him service.

Canticle – Song of Jerusalem Betrothed *Propter Sion non tacebo*
(Isaiah 62:1-5)
Antiphon You shall be a crown of beauty in the hand of the Lord, and a royal diadem in the hand of your God.

For Zion's sake I will not keep silent, *
      and for Jerusalem's sake I will not rest,

Until her vindication shines out like the dawn, *
      and her salvation like a burning torch.

The nations shall see your vindication, *
      and all the kings your glory.

You shall be called by a new name *
      spoken by the mouth of the Lord.

You shall be a crown of beauty in the hand of the Lord, *
      and a royal diadem in the hand of your God.

You shall no more be termed "Forsaken," *
      and your land shall no more be termed "Desolate;"

You shall be called "My Delight," *
      and your land "Espoused."

For the Lord delights in you, *
      and your land shall be married.

For as a young man marries a young woman, *
      so shall your builder marry you,

And as the bridegroom rejoices over the bride, *
   so shall your God rejoice over you.

Antiphon You shall be a crown of beauty in the hand of the Lord, and a royal diadem in the hand of your God.

Responsory Two (Tob. 13:11; Num. 24:17)
A bright light will shine to all the ends of the earth
   ‒ nations will come to you from far away.
A star shall come out of Jacob
   ‒ nations will come to you from far away.
Glory to the Father and to the Son and to the Holy Spirit.
A bright light will shine to all the ends of the earth
   ‒ nations will come to you from far away.

Benedictus Antiphon On entering the house, the Magi saw the child with Mary his mother.

Litany
You broke down the wall dividing Jew and Gentile; unite all people as children of our one Father.
Lord, have mercy.
You fulfilled the promise to Abraham and Sarah that all people may find a blessing in you; bring together people divided by differing theologies.
Christ, have mercy.
You accepted the life of an immigrant and refugee; sustain all without a home and open homes to all who are abandoned.
Lord, have mercy.

Invitation to the Lord's Prayer We acknowledge our unity with all people through Christ and pray that the Father may bring us together under God's gracious rule.

Collect *From Morning Prayer of January 7*

The Blessing
May we sing aloud, rejoice and exult with all our hearts for the king of Israel, the Lord, is in our midst.
   Amen.

January 11 Noonday Prayer

Hymn Alleluia, song of gladness *Hymnal 122*

Reading Jeremiah 31: 11-12

The Lord has ransomed Jacob, and has redeemed him from hands too strong for him. They shall come and sing aloud on the height of Zion, and they shall be radiant over the goodness of the Lord, over the grain, the wine, and the oil, and over the young of the flock and the herd; their life shall become like a watered garden, and they shall never languish again.

Verse and Response

The young women rejoice in the dance. Alleluia.
The young men and the old shall be merry. Alleluia.

Collect *From Morning Prayer of January 7*

January 11 Evening Prayer

Hymn When Christ's appearing was made known *Hymnal 132*

Responsory (Gen 12:3; Mt. 2:11)
All peoples will be blessed in Christ
      − peoples from every corner of the world.
They will hasten to find the child
      − peoples from every corner of the world.
Glory to the Father and to the Son and to the Holy Spirit.
All peoples will be blessed in Christ
      − peoples from every corner of the world.

Magnificat Antiphon The wise men knelt down before Christ and paid him homage.

Litany

Deliver us from the way of sin and death and open our hearts to your holy and life-giving Spirit.
Lord, have mercy.
Keep us in the faith and communion of your holy Church and teach us to love others in the power of the Spirit.
Christ, have mercy.
Send us into the world in witness to your love and bring us to the fullness of your peace and glory.
Lord, have mercy.

Invitation to the Lord's Prayer Since we are baptized into the death and resurrection of Jesus Christ, let us ask the Father to open our eyes that we may see Christ come again in glory.

Collect *From Morning Prayer of January 7*

The Blessing
May we rejoice greatly and shout aloud for our king has come to us.
Amen.

January 12 Morning Prayer

Invitatory Alleluia. Christ has manifested himself to the world. Come let us worship. Alleluia.

Hymn Alleluia, song of gladness *Hymnal 123*

Responsory One (Ps. 72:11; Gen. 12:3)
All rulers of the earth bow down before him
 − all the nations do him service.
All the nations of the earth shall be blessed in him
 − all the nations do him service.
Glory to the Father and to the Son and to the Holy Spirit.
All rulers of the earth bow down before him
 − all the nations do him service.

Canticle − Song of Amos *Ecce formans montes*
(Amos 4: 13; 5:8; 9: 5-6)
Antiphon The Lord turns deep darkness into the morning, and darkens the day into night.

Behold, the one who forms the mountains, creates the wind, *
 reveals his thoughts to mortals.

The Lord makes the morning darkness, *
 and treads on the heights of the earth—
 the Lord, the God of hosts, is his name!

The Lord made the Pleiades and Orion, *
 and turns deep darkness into the morning,
 and darkens the day into night,

The Lord calls for the waters of the sea, *
 and pours them out on the surface of the earth,
 the Lord is his name,

The Lord, God of hosts, touches the earth and it melts, *
    and all who live in it mourn.

All of it rises like the Nile, *
    and sinks again, like the Nile of Egypt.

The Lord calls for the waters of the sea, *
    and pours them out upon the surface of the earth—
    the LORD is his name.

Antiphon The Lord turns deep darkness into the morning, and darkens the day into night.

Responsory Two (Tob. 13:11; Num. 24:17)
A bright light will shine to all the ends of the earth
    – nations will come to you from far away.
A star shall come out of Jacob
    – nations will come to you from far away.
Glory to the Father and to the Son and to the Holy Spirit.
A bright light will shine to all the ends of the earth
    – nations will come to you from far away.

Benedictus Antiphon Opening their treasure chests, the wise men offered Christ gifts of gold, frankincense, and myrrh.

Litany
As the morning star illumines the sky, so shine in our hearts with the light of your Spirit.
Lord, have mercy.
As the radiant sun fills the world with light, so inspire all who are desolate and depressed.
Christ, have mercy.
As the moon and stars shin in the evening, so enlighten all who dwell in darkness.
Lord, have mercy.

Invitation to the Lord's Prayer Christ continues to manifest himself to all who seek him so let us ask the Father to reveal the Son to us through the Spirit.

Collect *From Morning Prayer of January 7*

The Blessing
May we sing aloud, rejoice and exult with all our hearts for the king of Israel, the Lord, is in our midst. **Amen.**

January 12 Noonday Prayer

Hymn O Light of Light *Hymnal 133*

Reading Ezekiel 34: 11-12

For thus says the Lord God: I myself will search for my sheep, and will seek them out. As shepherds seek out their flocks when they are among their scattered sheep, so I will seek out my sheep. I will rescue them from all the places to which they have been scattered on a day of clouds and thick darkness.

Verse and Response

The Lord is my shepherd. Alleluia.
He leads me beside still waters. Alleluia.

Collect *From Morning Prayer of January 7*

The Baptism of Our Lord
Evening Prayer I

Hymn The Sinless One to Jordan came *Hymnal 120*

Antiphon 1 After me comes a man who ranks ahead of me because he was before me. I am not worthy to untie the thong of his sandal. Alleluia.

Psalms from Sunday Week 1 Evening Prayer I, page 130

Antiphon 2 I baptize you with water; but one who is more powerful than I is coming; I am not worthy to untie the thong of his sandals. He will baptize you with the Holy Spirit and fire. Alleluia.

Antiphon 3 When all the people were baptized, and when Jesus also had been baptized and was praying, the heaven was opened, and the Holy Spirit descended upon him in bodily form like a dove. Alleluia.

Responsory (Rev. 21:6; Is. 55:1)
To the thirsty I will give water
        — from the spring of the water of life.
Let all who are thirsty come, all who desire it, come and drink
        — from the spring of the water of life.
Glory to the Father and to the Son and to the Holy Spirit.
To the thirsty I will give water
        — from the spring of the water of life.

Magnificat Antiphon
Year A "I need to be baptized by you, and do you come to me?" Jesus answered him, "Let it be so now; for it is proper for us in this way to fulfill all righteousness."
Year B The one who is more powerful than I is coming after me; I have baptized you with water; but he will baptize you with the Holy Spirit. Alleluia.
Year C I baptize you with water; but one who is more powerful than I is coming; I am not worthy to untie the thong of his sandals. He will baptize you with the Holy Spirit and fire. Alleluia.

Litany
In Baptism you deliver us from the way of sin and death; open our hearts to your grace and truth.
Lord, have mercy.
In Baptism you fill us with your holy and life-giving Spirit; keep us in the faith and communion of your holy Church.
Christ, have mercy.

In Baptism you teach us to love others in the power of the Spirit; send us into the world in witness of your love.
Lord, have mercy.

Invitation to the Lord's Prayer We are buried with Christ in Baptism and raised with Christ in these waters. Reborn in the Holy Spirit, let us pray as beloved daughters and sons.

Collect Father in heaven, who at the baptism of Jesus in the River Jordan proclaimed him your beloved Son and anointed him with the Holy Spirit: Grant that all who are baptized into his Name may keep the covenant they have made, and boldly confess him as Lord and Savior; who with you and the Holy Spirit lives and reigns, one God, in glory everlasting. Amen.

The Blessing
May we who have entered the household of God confess the faith of Christ crucified, proclaim his resurrection, and share in his eternal priesthood. **Amen.**

The Baptism of Our Lord Morning Prayer
Invitatory Christ is the Beloved Son in whom the Father is well pleased: Come let us adore. Alleluia.

Hymn "I Come," the great Redeemer cries. *Hymnal 116*

Antiphon 1 The warrior baptizes his ruler; the servant his Lord; John his Redeemer. Tremble, O waters of the Jordan for a dove hovers in witness and the Father's voice proclaims: This is my Beloved Son. Alleluia.
Psalms from Sunday Week 1 Morning Prayer, page 134
Antiphon 2 Come, draw water from the springs of the Savior for Christ has sanctified the universe. Alleluia.
Antiphon 3 Seas and rivers, bless the Lord; O fountains, sing a hymn to the Lord. Alleluia.

Responsory One (Lk 18:38)
Christ, Son of the Living God
    – have mercy on us.
Today you appeared in glory
    – have mercy on us.
Glory to the Father and to the Son and to the Holy Spirit.
Christ, Son of the Living God
    – have mercy on us.

Canticle – Song of the Anointed Servant *Spiritus Domini super me*
(Isaiah 61: 1-3)

Antiphon The Holy Spirit descended upon him in bodily form like a dove. Alleluia.

The spirit of the Lord God is upon me, *
    because the Lord has anointed me;

He has sent me to bring good news to the oppressed, *
    to bind up the brokenhearted,

To proclaim liberty to the captives, *
    and release to the prisoners;

To proclaim the year of the Lord's favor, *
    and the day of vengeance of our God;
    to comfort all who mourn;

To provide for those who mourn in Zion *
    to give them a garland instead of ashes,

The oil of gladness instead of mourning, *
    the mantle of praise instead of a faint spirit.

They will be called oaks of righteousness, *
    the planting of the Lord, to display his glory.

They shall build up the ancient ruins, *
    they shall raise up the former devastations;

They shall repair the ruined cities, *
    the devastations of many generations.

Antiphon The Holy Spirit descended upon him in bodily form like a dove. Alleluia.

Responsory Two (Is. 42:1)
Here is my servant, whom I uphold
    – my chosen, in whom my soul delights.
I have put my spirit upon him
    – my chosen, in whom my soul delights.
Glory to the Father and to the Son and to the Holy Spirit.
Here is my servant, whom I uphold
    – my chosen, in whom my soul delights.

Benedictus Antiphon

Year A When Jesus had been baptized suddenly the heavens were opened to him and he saw the Spirit of God descending like a dove and alighting on him. Alleluia.

Year B As Jesus was coming up out of the water, he saw the heavens torn apart and the Spirit descending like a dove on him. Alleluia.

Year C When all the people were baptized, and when Jesus also had been baptized and was praying, the heaven was opened, and the Holy Spirit descended upon him in bodily form like a dove. Alleluia.

Litany

In the waters of the Jordan, you open a path for us to become sons and daughters in God's family, help us to draw the scattered members of your family together.

Lord, have mercy.

In the waters of the Jordan, you sanctify all the waters of the earth help us to honor that holiness by being good stewards of your waters.

Christ, have mercy.

In the waters of the Jordan you continue to draw us into the new life of grace let us desire you with inquiring and discerning hearts.

Lord, have mercy.

Invitation to the Lord's Prayer Anointed with Christ by the Holy Spirit to share in a royal priesthood let us pray in the Spirit with Christ to the Father.

Collect *From Evening Prayer I*

The Blessing

May Almighty God, the Father of our Lord Jesus Christ grant us to be strengthened with might by the Holy Spirit, that Christ may dwell in our hearts by faith and that we may be filled with all the fullness of God. **Amen.**

The Baptism of Our Lord Noonday Prayer

Hymn Christ, When For Us You Were Baptized *Hymnal 121*

Antiphon The spirit of the Lord God is upon me, because the Lord has anointed me; he has sent me to bring good news. Alleluia.
Psalms from Sunday Week 1 Noonday Prayer page 138

Reading Isaiah 49: 6

It is too light a thing that you should be my servant to raise up the tribes of Jacob and to restore the survivors of Israel; I will give you as a light to the nations, that my salvation may reach to the end of the earth.

Verse and Response
Here is my servant, whom I uphold. Alleluia.
My chosen, in whom my soul delights. Alleluia.

Collect *From Evening Prayer I*

The Baptism of Our Lord Evening Prayer II
Hymn When Jesus Came To Jordan's Stream *Hymnal 139*

Antiphon 1 Jesus cried out, "Let anyone who is thirsty come to me."
Alleluia.
Psalms from Sunday Week 1 Evening Prayer II, page 141
Antiphon 2 The water that I will give will become in them a spring of
water gushing up to eternal life. Alleluia.
Antiphon 3 Out of the believer's heart shall flow rivers of living water.
Alleluia.

Responsory (1 Jn. 5:16, 12)
Jesus Christ came
            — by water and blood.
Whoever has the Son has life
            — by water and blood.
Glory to the Father and to the Son and to the Holy Spirit.
Jesus Christ came
            — by water and blood.

Magnificat Antiphon
Year A A voice from heaven said, "This is my Son, the Beloved, with
whom I am well pleased." Alleluia.
Year B You are my Son, the Beloved; with you I am well pleased.
Alleluia.
Year C A voice came from heaven, "You are my Son, the Beloved; with
you I am well pleased." Alleluia.

Litany
In Baptism you deliver us from the way of sin and death; open our
hearts to your grace and truth.
Lord, have mercy.
In Baptism you fill us with your holy and life-giving Spirit; keep us in
the faith and communion of your holy Church.
Christ, have mercy.
In Baptism you teach us to love others in the power of the Spirit; send
us into the world in witness of your love.
Lord, have mercy.

Invitation to the Lord's Prayer We are buried with Christ in Baptism and raised with Christ in those waters. Reborn in the Holy Spirit, let us pray as beloved daughters and sons.

Collect *From Evening Prayer I*

The Blessing
May we who have entered the household of God confess the faith of Christ crucified, proclaim his resurrection, and share in his eternal priesthood. **Amen.**

The Season after Epiphany

First Sunday after the Epiphany: The Baptism of our Lord
Psalter, Week One

Collect Father in heaven, who at the baptism of Jesus in the River Jordan proclaimed him your beloved Son and anointed him with the Holy Spirit: Grant that all who are baptized into his Name may keep the covenant they have made, and boldly confess him as Lord and Savior; who with you and the Holy Spirit lives and reigns, one God, in glory everlasting. Amen.

Year A
Magnificat Antiphon Jesus came from Galilee to John at the Jordan, to be baptized by him.
Benedictus Antiphon When Jesus had been baptized, just as he came up from the water, suddenly the heavens were opened to him and he saw the Spirit of God descending like a dove and alighting on him.
Magnificat Antiphon A voice from heaven said, "This is my Son, the Beloved, with whom I am well pleased."

Year B
Magnificat Antiphon John the baptizer appeared in the wilderness, proclaiming a baptism of repentance for the forgiveness of sins.
Benedictus Antiphon The one who is more powerful than I is coming after me. I have baptized you with water; but he will baptize you with the Holy Spirit.
Magnificat Antiphon As Jesus was coming up out of the water, he saw the heavens torn apart and the Spirit descending like a dove on him. A voice came from heaven, "You are my Son, the Beloved; with you I am well pleased."

Year C
Magnificat Antiphon I baptize you with water; but one who is more powerful than I is coming. He will baptize you with the Holy Spirit and fire.
Benedictus Antiphon After Jesus had been baptized and was praying, the heaven was opened, and the Holy Spirit descended upon him in bodily form like a dove.
Magnificat Antiphon A voice came from heaven, "You are my Son, the Beloved; with you I am well pleased."

Second Sunday after the Epiphany
Psalter, Week 2

Collect Almighty God, whose Son our Savior Jesus Christ is the light of the world: Grant that your people, illumined by your Word and Sacraments, may shine with the radiance of Christ's glory, that he may be known, worshiped, and obeyed to the ends of the earth; through Jesus Christ our Lord, who with you and the Holy Spirit lives and reigns, one God, now and for ever. Amen.

Year A

Magnificat Antiphon Here is the Lamb of God who takes away the sin of the world.

Benedictus Antiphon They said to Jesus, "Rabbi where are you staying?" He said to them, "Come and see."

Magnificat Antiphon Andrew first found his brother Simon and said to him, "We have found the Messiah." He brought Simon to Jesus.

Year B

Magnificat Antiphon Philip found Nathanael and said to him, "We have found him about whom Moses in the law and also the prophets wrote, Jesus son of Joseph."

Benedictus Antiphon "Here is truly an Israelite in whom there is no deceit!" Nathanael asked him, "Where did you get to know me?" Jesus answered, "I saw you under the fig tree before Philip called you."

Magnificat Antiphon You will see heaven opened and the angels of God ascending and descending upon the Son of Man.

Year C

Magnificat Antiphon Woman, what concern is that to you and to me? My hour has not yet come.

Benedictus Antiphon When the steward tasted the water that had become wine he said to the bridegroom, "You have kept the good wine until now."

Magnificat Antiphon Jesus did this, the first of his signs, in Cana of Galilee, and revealed his glory; and his disciples believed in him.

Third Sunday after the Epiphany

Psalter, Week 3

Collect Give us grace, O Lord, to answer readily the call of our Savior Jesus Christ and proclaim to all people the Good News of his salvation, that we and the whole world may perceive the glory of his marvelous works; who lives and reigns with you and the Holy Spirit, one God, for ever and ever. Amen.

Year A

Magnificat Antiphon When Jesus heard that John had been arrested, he withdrew to Galilee. He began to proclaim, "Repent, for the kingdom of heaven has come near."

Benedictus Antiphon Jesus said to Simon and Andrew his brother, "Follow me, and I will make you fish for people." Immediately they left their nets and followed him.

Magnificat Antiphon Jesus went throughout Galilee, teaching in their synagogues and proclaiming the good news of the kingdom and curing every disease and every sickness among the people.

Year B

Magnificat Antiphon After John was arrested, Jesus came to Galilee, proclaiming: "The time is fulfilled, and the kingdom of God has come near; repent, and believe in the good news."

Benedictus Antiphon Jesus said to Simon and his brother Andrew, "Follow me and I will make you fish for people." And immediately they left their nets and followed him.

Magnificat Antiphon Jesus saw James son of Zebedee and his brother John, who were in their boat mending the nets. Immediately he called them; and they left their father Zebedee in the boat with the hired men, and followed him.

Year C

Magnificat Antiphon Jesus, filled with the power of the Spirit, returned to Galilee. He began to teach in their synagogues and was praised by everyone.

Benedictus Antiphon The Spirit of the Lord is upon me, because he has anointed me to bring good news to the poor.

Magnificat Antiphon Today this scripture has been fulfilled in your hearing.

Fourth Sunday after the Epiphany

Psalter, Week 4

Collect Almighty and everlasting God, you govern all things both in heaven and on earth: Mercifully hear the supplications of your people, and in our time grant us your peace; through Jesus Christ our Lord, who lives and reigns with you and the Holy Spirit, one God, for ever and ever. Amen.

Year A

Magnificat Antiphon Blessed are the poor in spirit, for theirs is the kingdom of heaven. Blessed are those who mourn, for they will be comforted. Blessed are the meek, for they will inherit the earth.

Benedictus Antiphon Blessed are those who hunger and thirst for righteousness, for they will be filled. Blessed are the merciful, for they will receive mercy. Blessed are the pure in heart, for they will see God.

Magnificat Antiphon Blessed are the peacemakers, for they will be called children of God. Blessed are those who are persecuted for righteousness' sake, for theirs is the kingdom of heaven.

Year B

Magnificat Antiphon When the sabbath came, Jesus entered the synagogue and taught. They were astounded at his teaching, for he taught them as one having authority, and not as the scribes.

Benedictus Antiphon They were all amazed, and they kept on asking one another, "What is this? A new teaching—with authority! He commands even the unclean spirits, and they obey him."

Magnificat Antiphon At once Jesus; fame began to spread throughout the surrounding region of Galilee.

Year C

Magnificat Antiphon All spoke well of him and were amazed at the gracious words that came from his mouth.

Benedictus Antiphon No prophet is accepted in the prophet's hometown.

Magnificat Antiphon They led him to the brow of the hill so that they might hurl him off the cliff. But he passed through the midst of them.

Fifth Sunday after the Epiphany

Psalter, Week 1

Collect Set us free, O God, from the bondage of our sins, and give us the liberty of that abundant life which you have made known to us in your Son our Savior Jesus Christ; who lives and reigns with you, in the unity of the Holy Spirit, one God, now and for ever. Amen.

Year A

Magnificat Antiphon You are the salt of the earth. You are the light of the world. A city built on a hill cannot be hid.

Benedictus Antiphon Let your light shine before others, so that they may see your good works and give glory to your Father in heaven.

Magnificat Antiphon Whoever does the least of these commandments and teaches them will be called great in the kingdom of heaven. For unless your righteousness exceeds that of the scribes and Pharisees, you will never enter the kingdom of heaven.

Year B

Magnificat Antiphon Jesus came and took Simon's mother-in-law by the hand and lifted her up. Then the fever left her, and she began to serve them.

Benedictus Antiphon In the morning, while it was still very dark, Jesus got up and went out to a deserted place, and there he prayed.

Magnificat Antiphon Jesus went throughout Galilee, proclaiming the message in their synagogues and casting out demons.

Year C

Magnificat Antiphon While Jesus was standing beside the lake of Gennesaret, the crowd was pressing in on him to hear the word of God.

Benedictus Antiphon "Master, we have caught nothing. Yet if you say so, I will let down the nets." They caught so many fish that their nets were beginning to break.

Magnificat Antiphon "Do not be afraid; from now on you will be catching people." When they had brought their boats to shore, they left everything and followed him.

Sixth Sunday after the Epiphany

Psalter, Week 2

Collect O God, the strength of all who put their trust in you: Mercifully accept our prayers; and because in our weakness we can do nothing good without you, give us the help of your grace, that in keeping your commandments we may please you both in will and deed; through Jesus Christ our Lord, who lives and reigns with you and the Holy Spirit, one God, for ever and ever. Amen.

Year A

Magnificat Antiphon When you are offering your gift at the altar, if you remember that your brother or sister has something against you, leave your gift there before the altar and go; first be reconciled to your brother or sister, and then come and offer your gift.

Benedictus Antiphon Everyone who looks at a woman with lust has already committed adultery with her in his heart.

Magnificat Antiphon Let your word be 'Yes, Yes' or 'No, No'; anything more than this comes from the evil one.

Year B

Magnificat Antiphon Moved with pity, Jesus stretched out his hand and touched the leper, and said to him, 'I do choose. Be made clean!' Immediately the leprosy left him.

Benedictus Antiphon See that you say nothing to anyone; but go, show yourself to the priest, and offer for your cleansing what Moses commanded, as a testimony to them.

Magnificat Antiphon Jesus could no longer go into a town openly, but stayed out in the country; and people came to him from every quarter.

Year C

Magnificat Antiphon The crowd had come to hear Jesus and to be healed of their diseases; and those who were troubled with unclean spirits were cured.

Benedictus Antiphon Blessed are you who are poor, for yours is the kingdom of God.

Magnificat Antiphon Blessed are you when people hate you on account of the Son of Man. Rejoice and leap for joy, for surely your reward is great in heaven.

Seventh Sunday after the Epiphany
Psalter, Week 3

Collect O Lord, you have taught us that without love whatever we do is worth nothing; Send your Holy Spirit and pour into our hearts your greatest gift, which is love, the true bond of peace and of all virtue, without which whoever lives is accounted dead before you. Grant this for the sake of your only Son Jesus Christ, who lives and reigns with you and the Holy Spirit, one God, now and for ever. Amen.

Year A

Magnificat Antiphon Do not resist an evildoer. But if anyone strikes you on the right cheek, turn the other also; and if anyone wants to sue you and take your coat, give your cloak as well.

Benedictus Antiphon Love your enemies and pray for those who persecute you, so that you may be children of your Father in heaven; for he makes his sun rise on the evil and on the good.

Magnificat Antiphon Be perfect as your heavenly Father is perfect.

Year B

Magnificat Antiphon Some people came, bringing to him a paralyzed man, carried by four of them. They removed the roof above him; and they let down the mat on which the paralytic lay.

Benedictus Antiphon When Jesus saw their faith, he said to the paralytic, "Son, your sins are forgiven."

Magnificat Antiphon Jesus said to the paralytic: "Stand up, take your mat and go to your home." He stood up, and immediately took the mat and went out before all of them

Year C

Magnificat Antiphon Love your enemies, do good to those who hate you, bless those who curse you, pray for those who abuse you.

Benedictus Antiphon Do good and you will be children of the Most High who is kind to the ungrateful and the wicked. Be merciful, just as your Father is merciful.

Magnificat Antiphon Forgive, and you will be forgiven; give, and it will be given to you.

Eighth Sunday after the Epiphany

Psalter, Week 4

Collect Most loving Father, whose will it is for us to give thanks for all things, to fear nothing but the loss of you, and to cast all our care on you who care for us: Preserve us from faithless fears and worldly anxieties, that no clouds of this mortal life may hide from us the light of that love which is immortal, and which you have manifested to us in your Son Jesus Christ our Lord; who lives and reigns with you, in the unity of the Holy Spirit, one God, now and for ever. Amen.

Year A

Magnificat Antiphon No one can serve two masters. You cannot serve God and wealth.

Benedictus Antiphon Consider the lilies of the field; they neither toil nor spin, yet I tell you, even Solomon in all his glory was not clothed like one of these. If God so clothes the grass of the field, will he not much more clothe you—you of little faith?

Magnificat Antiphon Seek first for the kingdom of God and his righteousness, and all these things will be given to you as well.

Year B

Magnificat Antiphon Jesus saw Levi sitting at the tax booth, and he said to him, "Follow me." And he got up and followed him. As he sat at dinner in Levi's house, many tax collectors and sinners were also sitting with Jesus and his disciples.

Benedictus Antiphon Those who are well have no need of a physician, but those who are sick; I have come to call not the righteous but sinners.

Magnificat Antiphon The wedding guests cannot fast while the bridegroom is with them, can they? The days will come when the bridegroom is taken away from them, and then they will fast on that day.

Year C

Magnificat Antiphon A disciple is not above the teacher, but everyone who is fully qualified will be like the teacher.

Benedictus Antiphon The good person out of the good treasure of the heart produces good; for it is out of the abundance of the heart that the mouth speaks.

Magnificat Antiphon The person who comes to me, hears my words, and acts on them. is like a one building a house, who dug deeply and laid the foundation on rock.

Last Sunday after the Epiphany
This Proper is always used on the Sunday before Ash Wednesday

Psalter, Week 1

Collect O God, who before the passion of your only-begotten Son revealed his glory upon the holy mountain: Grant to us that we, beholding by faith the light of his countenance, may be strengthened to bear our cross, and be changed into his likeness from glory to glory; through Jesus Christ our Lord, who lives and reigns with you and the Holy Spirit, one God, for ever and ever. Amen.

Year A

Magnificat Antiphon Six days later, Jesus took with him Peter and James and his brother John and led them up a high mountain. He was transfigured before them, and his face shone like the sun, and his clothes became dazzling white.

Benedictus Antiphon A bright cloud overshadowed them, and from the cloud a voice said, "This is my Son, the Beloved; with him I am well pleased; listen to him!"

Magnificat Antiphon When the disciples looked up, they saw no one except Jesus himself alone.

Year B

Magnificat Antiphon Six days later, Jesus took with him Peter and James and John, and led them up a high mountain apart, by themselves. He was transfigured before them, and his clothes became dazzling white, such as no one on earth could bleach them.

Benedictus Antiphon A cloud overshadowed them, and from the cloud there came a voice, "This is my Son, the Beloved; listen to him!"

Magnificat Antiphon As they were coming down the mountain, he ordered them to tell no one about what they had seen, until after the Son of Man had risen from the dead.

Year C

Magnificat Antiphon As Jesus was praying, the appearance of his face changed, and his clothes became dazzling white. They saw Moses and Elijah talking to him of his departure at Jerusalem.

Benedictus Antiphon A cloud came and overshadowed them. From the cloud came a voice that said, "This is my Son, my Chosen; listen to him."

Magnificat Antiphon When the voice had spoken, Jesus was found alone. And they kept silent and in those days told no one any of the things they had seen.

Trinity Sunday
Principal Feast

Trinity Sunday Evening Prayer I

Hymn I bind unto myself today *Hymnal 370*

Antiphon 1 Be ever with us, O most high God, Source of all being, Incarnate Word and Abiding Spirit.
Psalms from Sunday Week 1 Evening Prayer I, page 130
Antiphon 2 Let us worship the one God in Trinity of Persons and in Unity of Substance. Alleluia.
Antiphon 3 O Eternal Trinity of Love, from you all things come forth and to you all things will return. Alleluia.

Responsory
Blessed be the Father and the Son with the Holy Spirit
 — **praise and highly exalt God for ever.**
To the one God be honor and glory
 — **praise and highly exalt God for ever.**
Glory to the Father and to the Son and to the Holy Spirit.
Blessed be the Father and the Son with the Holy Spirit
 — **praise and highly exalt God for ever.**

Magnificat Antiphon Throughout the world the holy Church acclaims you: Father, of majesty unbounded, your true and only Son, worthy of all worship, and the Holy Spirit, advocate and guide. Alleluia.

Litany
Holy Mystery, we will never comprehend your knowledge and love; open our hearts to your forgiving love that we may find our fulfillment in you.
Lord, have mercy.
Incarnate Word, we stand in awe of your humility which accepted our human condition; live in us and through us that we may be permeated by the wonder of your presence.
Christ, have mercy.
Love of God, we sense you presence in the love we experience with one another; increase our freedom and love that we may encounter you in center of our human lives.
Lord, have mercy.

Invitation to the Lord's Prayer In the ecstasy of your Spirit's love, we cry out with the Son to the Father.

Collect Almighty and everlasting God, you have given to us your servants grace, by the confession of a true faith, to acknowledge the glory of the eternal Trinity, and in the power of your divine Majesty to worship the Unity: Keep us steadfast in this faith and worship, and bring us at last to see you in your one and eternal glory, O Father; who with the Son and the Holy Spirit live and reign, one God, for ever and ever. Amen.

The Blessing
May the grace of the Lord Jesus Christ, the love of God, and the communion of the Holy Spirit be with all of us. **Amen.**

Trinity Sunday Morning Prayer
Invitatory Father, Son and Holy Spirit, one God: Come let us adore.

Hymn Holy Father, great Creator *Hymnal 368*

Antiphon 1 God has sent the Spirit of his Son into our hearts, crying, "Abba! Father!"
Psalms from Sunday Week 1 Morning Prayer, page 134
Antiphon 2 The grace of the Lord Jesus Christ, the love of God, and the communion of the Holy Spirit be with all of you.
Antiphon 3 God, who raised Christ from the dead, will give life to your mortal bodies through God's Spirit that dwells in you.

Responsory One
To you be praise, to you be glory
     —O Blessed Trinity.
We give thanks to you for ever and ever
     —O Blessed Trinity.
Glory to the Father and to the Son and to the Holy Spirit.
To you be praise, to you be glory
     —O Blessed Trinity.

Canticle You are God   *Te Deum laudamus page 757*

Responsory Two
O Blessed and Glorious Trinity
     —Father, Son and Holy Spirit.
We praise you and we thank you
     —Father, Son and Holy Spirit.
Glory to the Father and to the Son and to the Holy Spirit.
O Blessed and Glorious Trinity
     —Father, Son and Holy Spirit.

Benedictus Antiphon Alleluia. The Father is love; the Son is grace; the Spirit is their bond of unity. O Blessed Trinity! Alleluia.

Litany
Divine Life, drawing us into your family as adopted children, give us confidence to draw close to you who draws so close to us.
Lord, have mercy.
Incarnate Word, planted in the womb of our soul, open our hearts to the sound of your voice speaking within us.
Christ, have mercy.
Spirit of Life, enlivening us with God's very life, strengthen our hearts to surrender with the Son to the Father that God may be all in all in us.
Lord, have mercy.

Invitation to the Lord's Prayer You continue to disclose to us the mystery of your presence so let us discern your three fold life as we pray.

Collect *From Morning Prayer*

The Blessing
May God grant that you may be strengthened in your inner being with power through his Spirit, and that Christ may dwell in your hearts through faith, as you are being rooted and grounded in love. **Amen.**

Trinity Sunday Noonday Prayer
Hymn Ancient of Days *Hymnal 363*

Antiphon If you love me, you will keep my commandments. And I will ask the Father, and he will give you another Advocate, to be with you forever.
Psalms from Sunday Week One Noonday Prayer page 138

Reading 2 Corinthians 1: 21-22
God establishes us with you in Christ and has anointed us, by putting his seal on us and giving us his Spirit in our hearts as a first installment.

Verse and Response
Go within God's gates giving praise.
Give glory to God, Father, Son and Holy Spirit.

Collect *From Morning Prayer*

Trinity Sunday Evening Prayer II

Hymn Come thou almighty King *Hymnal 365*

Antiphon 1 Go and make disciples of all nations, baptizing them in the name of the Father and of the Son and of the Holy Spirit.
Psalms from Sunday Week 1 Evening Prayer II, page 141
Antiphon 2 You were washed, you were sanctified, you were justified in the name of the Lord Jesus Christ and in the Spirit of our God.
Antiphon 3 May the God of peace sanctify you entirely; and may your spirit and soul and body be kept sound and blameless at the coming of our Lord Jesus Christ.

Responsory
Blessed be the Father and the Son with the Holy Spirit
    −praise and highly exalt God for ever.
To the one God be honor and glory
    −praise and highly exalt God for ever.
Glory to the Father and to the Son and to the Holy Spirit.
Blessed be the Father and the Son with the Holy Spirit
    −praise and highly exalt God for ever.

Magnificat Antiphon Womb of life and Fountain of Being, Incarnate Wisdom and Risen Christ, Life Giving Spirit and Prophetic Voice, praise to you, O God, three in one and one in three. Alleluia.

Litany
Holy Mystery, we will never comprehend your knowledge and love; open our hearts to your forgiving love that we may find our fulfillment in you.
Lord, have mercy.
Incarnate Word, we stand in awe of your humility which accepted our human condition; live in us and through us that we may be permeated by the wonder of your presence.
Christ, have mercy.
Love of God, we sense you presence in the love we experience with one another; increase our freedom and love that we may encounter you in center of our human lives.
Lord, have mercy.

Invitation to the Lord's Prayer In the ecstasy of your Spirit's love, we cry out with the Son to the Father.

Collect *From Morning Prayer*

The Blessing
May the grace of the Lord Jesus Christ, the love of God, and the communion of the Holy Spirit be with all of us. **Amen.**

The Body and Blood of Christ
Thursday after Trinity Sunday
The Body and Blood of Christ Evening Prayer I

Hymn O Food to pilgrims given *Hymnal 308*

Antiphon 1 Christ the Lord, a Priest according to the order of Melchizedek, offered bread and wine, alleluia.
Psalms from Sunday Week One Evening Prayer I page 130
Antiphon 2 I will take the cup of salvation and offer a sacrifice of praise, alleluia.
Antiphon 3 Wisdom has built herself a house, mixed her wine and set her table, alleluia.

Reading Proverbs 9.1-15

Responsory (Jn. 6:31; Ps. 78:25)
God gave them bread from heaven
　　−Alleluia, alleluia.
Mortals ate the bread of angels
　　−Alleluia, alleluia.
Glory to the Father and to the Son and to the Holy Spirit.
God gave them bread from heaven
　　−Alleluia, alleluia.

Magnificat Antiphon How precious is your Spirit, Lord for to show your kindness to your children you feed them with the sweet Bread from heaven. You feed the hungry with good things and send the rich away empty, alleluia.

Litany
Gracious God, you restore all things to yourself through your beloved Son; make us share in the mystery of his dying and rising.
Lord, have mercy.
Christ, Living Bread, you remain with us through the Sacrament of your Body and Blood; draw us deeper into the mystery of your indwelling with us.
Christ, have mercy.

Spirit of holiness, you transform the world as you sanctify bread and wine through the fire of your Love; sanctify us that we may become one body and one spirit, a living sacrifice in Christ.
Lord, have mercy.

Invitation to the Lord's Prayer Father, you dwell in light inaccessible yet your love sent us Christ, the Living Bread, in whom we return to you as we pray.

Collect God our Father, whose Son our Lord Jesus Christ in a wonderful Sacrament has left us a memorial of his passion: Grant us so to venerate the sacred mysteries of his Body and Blood, that we may ever perceive within ourselves the fruit of his redemption; who lives and reigns with you and the Holy Spirit, one God, for ever and ever. *Amen.*

The Blessing
May all who share the Body and Blood of Christ become one body and one spirit, a living sacrifice in Christ, to the praise of God's Name. **Amen.**

The Body and Blood of Christ Morning Prayer
Invitatory Christ is the Bread of Life: Come let us adore.

Hymn Humbly I adore thee *Hymnal 314*

Antiphon 1 Mortals ate the bread of angels; God provided for them food enough, alleluia.
Psalms from Sunday Week 1 Morning Prayer, page 134
Antiphon 2 Your priests offer spiritual sacrifices acceptable to you; and present before you the acceptable offering of a pure, gentle and holy life, alleluia.
Antiphon 3 To everyone who conquers I will give some of the hidden manna, and I will give a white stone on which is written a new name, alleluia.

Reading One Deuteronomy 8:1-11

Responsory One
God gave them bread from heaven
> **−Alleluia, alleluia.**

Mortals ate the bread of angels
> **−Alleluia, alleluia.**

Glory to the Father and to the Son and to the Holy Spirit.
God gave them bread from heaven
> **−Alleluia, alleluia.**

Canticle – Song of the Bread of Life *Ego sum panis vitae*
(John 6: 35-40, 50, 63)

Antiphon Those who eat my flesh and drink my blood abide in me, and I in them, alleluia.

I am the bread of life. *
>   Whoever comes to me will never be hungry,
>   and whoever believes in me will never be thirsty.

I am the bread of life. *
>   Your ancestors ate the manna in the wilderness,
>   and they died.

This is the bread that comes down from heaven, *
>   so that one may eat of it and not die.

I am the living bread that came down from heaven. *
>   Whoever eats of this bread will live forever;

The bread that I will give for the life of the world *
>   is my flesh.

Unless you eat the flesh of the Son of Man and drink his blood, *
>   you have no life in you.

Those who eat my flesh and drink my blood have eternal life, *
>   and I will raise them up on the last day.

For my flesh is true food *
>   and my blood is true drink.

Those who eat my flesh and drink my blood *
>   abide in me, and I in them.

Just as the living Father sent me, and I live because of the Father, *
>   so whoever eats me will live because of me.

Antiphon Those who eat my flesh and drink my blood abide in me, and I in them, alleluia.

Reading Two Luke 9:11-17

Responsory Two (Ps. 104:16, 15)
God gave them bread to strengthen the heart
>   **−Alleluia, alleluia.**
Wine to gladden our hearts
>   **−Alleluia, alleluia.**
Glory to the Father and to the Son and to the Holy Spirit.

God gave them bread to strengthen the heart
    ─Alleluia, alleluia.

Benedictus Antiphon Those who eat my flesh and drink my blood abide in me, and I in them. Just as the living Father sent me, and I live because of the Father, so whoever eats me will live because of me, alleluia.

Litany
As we celebrate the memorial of our redemption, accept the offering of our selves, our souls and bodies to be a reasonable, holy and living sacrifice unto you.
Lord, have mercy.
While we are not worthy to gather up the crumbs under your table, grant us to eat the flesh of your Son and drink his blood that we may evermore dwell in him and he in us.
Christ, have mercy.
Through the most precious Body and Blood of your Son we are very members incorporate in his mystical body, let us do the good works you have prepared for us to walk in.
Lord, have mercy.

Invitation to the Lord's Prayer As we pray that the Body and Blood of Christ preserve us unto everlasting life let us be filled with your grace and heavenly benediction as we pray.

Collect *From Evening Prayer I*

The Blessing
May we, for whom Christ, our Paschal Lamb, has been sacrificed, celebrate the feast, not with the old yeast, the yeast of malice and evil, but with the unleavened bread of sincerity and truth. **Amen.**

The Body and Blood of Christ Noonday Prayer
Hymn O saving Victim *Hymnal 311*

Antiphon Blessed is anyone who will eat bread in the kingdom of God, alleluia.
Psalms from Sunday Week 1 Noonday Prayer page 138

Reading 1 Corinthians 10: 16-17
The cup of blessing that we bless, is it not a sharing in the blood of Christ? The bread that we break, is it not a sharing in the body of Christ? Because there is one bread, we who are many are one body, for we all partake of the one bread.

Verse and Response

I will go to the altar of God.

The God of my joy and gladness.

Collect Be present, be present, O Jesus, our great High Priest, as you were present with your disciples, and be known to us in the breaking of bread; who live and reign with the Father and the Holy Spirit, now and for ever. Amen.

The Body and Blood of Christ Evening Prayer II

Hymn Zion praise thy Savior *Hymnal 320*

Antiphon 1 I shall go to the altar of God, where I shall receive Christ, the God of my joy and gladness, alleluia.

Psalms from Sunday Week One Evening Prayer II page 141

Antiphon 2 My soul has a desire and longing for the courts of the Lord where we receive the living Christ in whom my heart and my flesh rejoice, alleluia.

Antiphon 3 In these holy Mysteries we are made one with Christ, and Christ with us; we are made one body in him, and members one of another, alleluia.

Reading 1 Corinthians 11:23-32

Responsory (Jn. 6:31; Ps. 78:25)

God gave them bread from heaven

−Alleluia, alleluia.

Mortals ate the bread of angels

−Alleluia, alleluia.

Glory to the Father and to the Son and to the Holy Spirit.

God gave them bread from heaven

−Alleluia, alleluia.

Magnificat Antiphon O Sacred Communion in which the memory of Christ's passion is recalled, the mind is filled with grace and a pledge of eternal life given to us, alleluia.

Litany

Gracious God, you restore all things to yourself through your beloved Son; make us share in the mystery of his dying and rising.

Lord, have mercy.

Christ, Living Bread, you remain with us through the Sacrament of your Body and Blood; draw us deeper into the mystery of your indwelling with us.

Christ, have mercy.

Spirit of holiness, you transform the world as you sanctify bread and wine through the fire of your Love; sanctify us that we may become one body and one spirit, a living sacrifice in Christ.
Lord, have mercy.

Invitation to the Lord's Prayer Father, you dwell in light inaccessible yet your love sent us Christ, the Living Bread, in whom we return to you as we pray.

Collect *From Evening Prayer I*

The Blessing
May we who eat the flesh and drink the blood of the Risen One, abide in Christ, and Christ in us. **Amen.**

The Season after Pentecost

Proper 1 *Week of the Sunday closest to May 11*

Psalter, Week 1

Collect Remember, O Lord, what you have wrought in us and not what we deserve; and, as you have called us to your service, make us worthy of our calling; through Jesus Christ our Lord, who lives and reigns with you and the Holy Spirit, one God, now and for ever. Amen.

Year A

Magnificat Antiphon When you are offering your gift at the altar, if you remember that your brother or sister has something against you, leave your gift there before the altar and go; first be reconciled to your brother or sister, and then come and offer your gift.

Benedictus Antiphon Everyone who looks at a woman with lust has already committed adultery with her in his heart.

Magnificat Antiphon Let your word be 'Yes, Yes' or 'No, No'; anything more than this comes from the evil one.

Year B

Magnificat Antiphon Moved with pity, Jesus stretched out his hand and touched the leper, and said to him, 'I do choose. Be made clean!' Immediately the leprosy left him.

Benedictus Antiphon See that you say nothing to anyone; but go, show yourself to the priest, and offer for your cleansing what Moses commanded, as a testimony to them.

Magnificat Antiphon Jesus could no longer go into a town openly, but stayed out in the country; and people came to him from every quarter.

Year C

Magnificat Antiphon The crowd had come to hear him and to be healed of their diseases; and those who were troubled with unclean spirits were cured.

Benedictus Antiphon Blessed are you who are poor, for yours is the kingdom of God.

Magnificat Antiphon Blessed are you when people hate you on account of the Son of Man. Rejoice and leap for joy, for surely your reward is great in heaven.

Proper 2 *Week of the Sunday closest to May 18*

Collect Almighty and merciful God, in your goodness keep us, we pray, from all things that may hurt us, that we, being ready both in mind and body, may accomplish with free hearts those things which belong to your purpose; through Jesus Christ our Lord, who lives and reigns with you and the Holy Spirit, one God, now and for ever. Amen.

Year A

Magnificat Antiphon Do not resist an evildoer. But if anyone strikes you on the right cheek, turn the other also; and if anyone wants to sue you and take your coat, give your cloak as well.
Benedictus Antiphon Love your enemies and pray for those who persecute you, so that you may be children of your Father in heaven; for he makes his sun rise on the evil and on the good.
Magnificat Antiphon Be perfect as your heavenly Father is perfect.

Year B

Magnificat Antiphon Some people came, bringing to him a paralyzed man, carried by four of them. They removed the roof above him; and they let down the mat on which the paralytic lay.
Benedictus Antiphon When Jesus saw their faith, he said to the paralytic, "Son, your sins are forgiven."
Magnificat Antiphon Jesus said to the paralytic— "Stand up, take your mat and go to your home." He stood up, and immediately took the mat and went out before all of them

Year C

Magnificat Antiphon Love your enemies, do good to those who hate you, bless those who curse you, pray for those who abuse you.
Benedictus Antiphon Do good and you will be children of the Most High who is kind to the ungrateful and the wicked. Be merciful, just as your Father is merciful.
Magnificat Antiphon Forgive, and you will be forgiven; give, and it will be given to you.

Proper 3 *The Sunday closest to May 25*

Collect Grant, O Lord, that the course of this world may be peaceably governed by your providence; and that your Church may joyfully serve you in confidence and serenity; through Jesus Christ our Lord, who lives and reigns with you and the Holy Spirit, one God, for ever and ever. Amen.

Year A

Magnificat Antiphon No one can serve two masters. You cannot serve God and wealth.

Benedictus Antiphon Consider the lilies of the field; they neither toil nor spin, yet I tell you, even Solomon in all his glory was not clothed like one of these. If God so clothes the grass of the field, will he not much more clothe you—you of little faith?

Magnificat Antiphon Seek first for the kingdom of God and his righteousness, and all these things will be given to you as well.

Year B

Magnificat Antiphon Jesus saw Levi sitting at the tax booth, and he said to him, "Follow me." And he got up and followed him. As he sat at dinner in Levi's house, many tax collectors and sinners were also sitting with Jesus and his disciples.

Benedictus Antiphon Those who are well have no need of a physician, but those who are sick; I have come to call not the righteous but sinners.

Magnificat Antiphon The wedding guests cannot fast while the bridegroom is with them, can they? The days will come when the bridegroom is taken away from them, and then they will fast on that day.

Year C

Magnificat Antiphon A disciple is not above the teacher, but everyone who is fully qualified will be like the teacher.

Benedictus Antiphon The good person out of the good treasure of the heart produces good; for it is out of the abundance of the heart that the mouth speaks.

Magnificat Antiphon The person who comes to me, hears my words, and acts on them. is like a one building a house, who dug deeply and laid the foundation on rock.

Proper 4 *The Sunday closest to June 1*

Psalter, Week 4

Collect O God, your never-failing providence sets in order all things both in heaven and earth: Put away from us, we entreat you, all hurtful things, and give us those things which are profitable for us; through Jesus Christ our Lord, who lives and reigns with you and the Holy Spirit, one God, for ever and ever. Amen.

Year A

Magnificat Antiphon Not everyone who says to me, 'Lord, Lord,' will enter the kingdom of heaven, but only the one who does the will of my Father in heaven.

Benedictus Antiphon Everyone then who hears these words of mine and acts on them will be like a wise man who built his house on rock. The rain fell, the floods came, and the winds blew and beat on that house, but it did not fall.

Magnificat Antiphon When Jesus had finished saying these things, the crowds were astounded at his teaching, for he taught them as one having authority, and not as their scribes.

Year B

Magnificat Antiphon The sabbath was made for humankind, and not humankind for the sabbath; so the Son of Man is lord even of the sabbath.

Benedictus Antiphon Jesus entered the synagogue, and a man was there who had a withered hand. They watched him to see whether he would cure him on the sabbath, so that they might accuse him.

Magnificat Antiphon Jesus looked around at them with anger; he was grieved at their hardness of heart and said to the man, "Stretch out your hand." He stretched it out, and his hand was restored.

Year C

Magnificat Antiphon Lord, do not trouble yourself, for I am not worthy to have you come under my roof. But only speak the word, and let my servant be healed.

Benedictus Antiphon When Jesus heard this he was amazed at him, and turning to the crowd that followed him, he said, "I tell you, not even in Israel have I found such faith."

Magnificat Antiphon When those who had been sent returned to the house, they found the slave in good health.

Proper 5 *The Sunday closest to June 8*

Collect O God, from whom all good proceeds: Grant that by your inspiration we may think those things that are right, and by your merciful guiding may do them; through Jesus Christ our Lord, who lives and reigns with you and the Holy Spirit, one God, for ever and ever. Amen.

Year A

Magnificat Antiphon Jesus saw a man called Matthew sitting at the tax booth; and he said to him, "Follow me." And he got up and followed him. As he sat at dinner in the house, many tax collectors and sinners came and were sitting with him and his disciples.

Benedictus Antiphon Those who are well have no need of a physician, but those who are sick. Go and learn what this means, 'I desire mercy, not sacrifice.' For I have come to call not the righteous but sinners."

Magnificat Antiphon "Take heart, daughter; your faith has made you well." And instantly the woman was made well.

Year B

Magnificat Antiphon No one can enter a strong man's house and plunder his property without first tying up the strong man; then indeed the house can be plundered.

Benedictus Antiphon People will be forgiven for their sins and whatever blasphemies they utter; but whoever blasphemes against the Holy Spirit can never have forgiveness.

Magnificat Antiphon Here are my mother and my brothers! Whoever does the will of God is my brother and sister and mother.

Year C

Magnificat Antiphon As Jesus approached the gate of the town, a man who had died was being carried out. He was his mother's only son, and she was a widow; and with her was a large crowd from the town.

Benedictus Antiphon When the Lord saw her, he had compassion for her and said to her, "Do not weep." He said, "Young man, I say to you, rise!"

Magnificat Antiphon Fear seized all of them; and they glorified God, saying, "A great prophet has risen among us!" and "God has looked favorably on his people!"

Proper 6 *The Sunday closest to June 15*

Psalter, Week 2

Collect Keep, O Lord, your household the Church in your steadfast faith and love, that through your grace we may proclaim your truth with boldness, and minister your justice with compassion; for the sake of our Savior Jesus Christ, who lives and reigns with you and the Holy Spirit, one God, now and for ever. Amen.

Year A

Magnificat Antiphon When Jesus saw the crowds, he had compassion for them, because they were harassed and helpless, like sheep without a shepherd.

Benedictus Antiphon The harvest is plentiful, but the laborers are few; therefore ask the Lord of the harvest to send out laborers into his harvest.

Magnificat Antiphon Proclaim the good news, cure the sick, raise the dead, cleanse the lepers, cast out demons. You received without payment; give without payment.

Year B

Magnificat Antiphon The kingdom of God is as if someone would scatter seed on the ground, and would sleep and rise night and day, and the seed would sprout and grow, he does not know how.

Benedictus Antiphon The kingdom of God is like a mustard seed, which, when sown upon the ground, is the smallest of all the seeds on earth yet becomes the greatest of all shrubs

Magnificat Antiphon With many such parables he spoke the word to them, as they were able to hear it; he did not speak to them except in parables.

Year C

Magnificat Antiphon A woman in the city, who was a sinner, brought an alabaster jar of ointment. She stood behind him at his feet, weeping, and began to bathe his feet with her tears and to dry them with her hair.

Benedictus Antiphon I tell you, her sins, which were many, have been forgiven; hence she has shown great love. But the one to whom little is forgiven, loves little."

Magnificat Antiphon Jesus said to the woman, "Your faith has saved you; go in peace."

Proper 7 *The Sunday closest to June 22*

Collect O Lord, make us have perpetual love and reverence for your holy Name, for you never fail to help and govern those whom you have set upon the sure foundation of your loving-kindness; through Jesus Christ our Lord, who lives and reigns with you and the Holy Spirit, one God, for ever and ever. Amen.

Year A

Magnificat Antiphon A disciple is not above the teacher, nor a slave above the master; it is enough for the disciple to be like the teacher, and the slave like the master.

Benedictus Antiphon Do not think that I have come to bring peace to the earth; I have not come to bring peace, but a sword.

Magnificat Antiphon Whoever does not take up the cross and follow me is not worthy of me. Those who find their life will lose it, and those who lose their life for my sake will find it.

Year B

Magnificat Antiphon A great windstorm arose, and the waves beat into the boat, so that the boat was already being swamped. But he was in the stern, asleep on the cushion.

Benedictus Antiphon Jesus woke up and rebuked the wind, and said to the sea, "Peace! Be still!"

Magnificat Antiphon They were filled with great awe and said to one another, "Who then is this, that even the wind and the sea obey him?"

Year C

Magnificat Antiphon "What have you to do with me, Jesus, Son of the Most High God? I beg you, do not torment me." Jesus had commanded the unclean spirit to come out of the man.

Benedictus Antiphon People came out to see what had happened, and when they came to Jesus, they found the man from whom the demons had gone sitting at the feet of Jesus, clothed and in his right mind.

Magnificat Antiphon The man from whom the demons had gone begged that he might be with him; but Jesus sent him away, saying, "Return to your home, and declare how much God has done for you."

Proper 8 *The Sunday closest to June 29*

Psalter, Week 4

Collect Almighty God, you have built your Church upon the foundation of the apostles and prophets, Jesus Christ himself being the chief cornerstone: Grant us so to be joined together in unity of spirit by their teaching, that we may be made a holy temple acceptable to you; through Jesus Christ our Lord, who lives and reigns with you and the Holy Spirit, one God, for ever and ever. Amen.

Year A

Magnificat Antiphon Whoever welcomes you welcomes me, and whoever welcomes me welcomes the one who sent me.

Benedictus Antiphon Whoever welcomes a prophet in the name of a prophet will receive a prophet's reward; and whoever welcomes a righteous person in the name of a righteous person will receive the reward of the righteous.

Magnificat Antiphon Whoever gives even a cup of cold water to one of these little ones in the name of a disciple -- truly I tell you, none of these will lose their reward.

Year B

Magnificat Antiphon The woman came in fear and trembling, fell down before Jesus, and told him the whole truth. He said to her, "Daughter, your faith has made you well; go in peace, and be healed of your disease."

Benedictus Antiphon Jesus said to the leader of the synagogue, "Do not fear, only believe."

Magnificat Antiphon Jesus took the little girl by the hand and said to her, "Talitha cum," which means, "Little girl, get up!" And immediately the girl got up and began to walk about.

Year C

Magnificat Antiphon When the days drew near for him to be taken up, Jesus set his face to go to Jerusalem.

Benedictus Antiphon Foxes have holes, and birds of the air have nests; but the Son of Man has nowhere to lay his head.

Magnificat Antiphon Let the dead bury their own dead; but as for you, go and proclaim the kingdom of God.

Proper 9 *The Sunday closest to July 6*

Collect O God, you have taught us to keep all your commandments by loving you and our neighbor: Grant us the grace of your Holy Spirit, that we may be devoted to you with our whole heart, and united to one another with pure affection; through Jesus Christ our Lord, who lives and reigns with you and the Holy Spirit, one God, for ever and ever. Amen.

Year A

Magnificat Antiphon I thank you, Father, Lord of heaven and earth, because you have hidden these things from the wise and the intelligent and have revealed them to infants.

Benedictus Antiphon No one knows the Son except the Father, and no one knows the Father except the Son and anyone to whom the Son chooses to reveal him.

Magnificat Antiphon Come to me, all you that are weary and are carrying heavy burdens, and I will give you rest. Take my yoke upon you, and learn from me; for I am gentle and humble in heart, and you will find rest for your souls.

Year B

Magnificat Antiphon Prophets are not without honor, except in their hometown, and among their own kin, and in their own house.

Benedictus Antiphon Jesus called the twelve and began to send them out two by two, and gave them authority over the unclean spirits.

Magnificat Antiphon The twelve went out and proclaimed that all should repent. They cast out many demons, and anointed with oil many who were sick and cured them.

Year C

Magnificat Antiphon The harvest is plentiful, but the laborers are few; therefore ask the Lord of the harvest to send out laborers into his harvest.

Benedictus Antiphon Whenever you enter a town and its people welcome you, eat what is set before you; cure the sick who are there, and say to them, "The kingdom of God has come near to you."

Magnificat Antiphon Do not rejoice that the spirits submit to you, but rejoice that your names are written in heaven.

Proper 10   *The Sunday closest to July 13*

Psalter, Week 2

Collect O Lord, mercifully receive the prayers of your people who call upon you, and grant that they may know and understand what things they ought to do, and also may have grace and power faithfully to accomplish them; through Jesus Christ our Lord, who lives and reigns with you and the Holy Spirit, one God, now and for ever. Amen.

Year A

Magnificat Antiphon Christ is the sower, the seed is the word of God sown in the hearts of those who believe.

Benedictus Antiphon Jesus got into a boat and sat there, while the whole crowd stood on the beach. He told them many things in parables, saying: "Listen! A sower went out to sow."

Magnificat Antiphon They hear the word and understand it, and bear fruit and yield a hundred or sixty or thirtyfold.

Year B

Magnificat Antiphon Herod had sent men who arrested John, bound him, and put him in prison on account of Herodias, his brother Philip's wife, because Herod had married her.

Benedictus Antiphon The king was deeply grieved; yet out of regard for his oaths and for the guests, he did not want to refuse her.

Magnificat Antiphon The king sent a soldier of the guard with orders to bring John's head. He beheaded him in the prison, brought his head on a platter, and gave it to the girl who gave it to her mother.

Year C

Magnificat Antiphon You shall love the Lord your God with all your heart, and with all your soul, and with all your strength, and with all your mind; and your neighbor as yourself.

Benedictus Antiphon A Samaritan while traveling came near him; and when he saw him, he was moved with pity. He went to him and bandaged his wounds, having poured oil and wine on them.

Magnificat Antiphon "Which of these three, do you think, was a neighbor to the man who fell into the hands of the robbers?" He said, "The one who showed him mercy." Jesus said to him, "Go and do likewise."

Proper 11 *The Sunday closest to July 20*

Collect Almighty God, the fountain of all wisdom, you know our necessities before we ask and our ignorance in asking: Have compassion on our weakness, and mercifully give us those things which for our unworthiness we dare not, and for our blindness we cannot ask; through the worthiness of your Son Jesus Christ our Lord, who lives and reigns with you and the Holy Spirit, one God, now and for ever. Amen.

Year A

Magnificat Antiphon Let both of them grow together; and at harvest time I will tell the reapers, Collect the weeds first and bind them in bundles to be burned, but gather the wheat into my barn.

Benedictus Antiphon The one who sows the good seed is the Son of Man; the field is the world, and the good seed are the children of the kingdom; the weeds are the children of the evil one, and the reapers are angels.

Magnificat Antiphon The righteous will shine like the sun in the kingdom of their Father. Let anyone with ears listen.

Year B

Magnificat Antiphon Come away to a deserted place all by yourselves and rest a while.

Benedictus Antiphon As Jesus went ashore, he saw a great crowd; and he had compassion for them, because they were like sheep without a shepherd; and he began to teach them many things.

Magnificat Antiphon Wherever he went, into villages or cities or farms, they laid the sick in the marketplaces, and begged him that they might touch even the fringe of his cloak; and all who touched it were healed.

Year C

Magnificat Antiphon Jesus entered a certain village, where a woman named Martha welcomed him into her home. She had a sister named Mary, who sat at the Lord's feet and listened to what he was saying.

Benedictus Antiphon Lord, do you not care that my sister has left me to do all the work by myself? Tell her then to help me.

Magnificat Antiphon Martha, Martha, you are worried and distracted by many things; there is need of only one thing. Mary has chosen the better part, which will not be taken away from her.

Proper 12 *The Sunday closest to July 27*

Collect O God, the protector of all who trust in you, without whom nothing is strong, nothing is holy: Increase and multiply upon us your mercy; that, with you as our ruler and guide, we may so pass through things temporal, that we lose not the things eternal; through Jesus Christ our Lord, who lives and reigns with you and the Holy Spirit, one God, for ever and ever. Amen.

Year A

Magnificat Antiphon The kingdom of heaven is like a mustard seed; it is the smallest of all the seeds, but when it has grown it is the greatest of shrubs.

Benedictus Antiphon The kingdom of heaven is like treasure hidden in a field, which someone found and hid; then in his joy he goes and sells all that he has and buys that field.

Magnificat Antiphon The kingdom of heaven is like a merchant in search of fine pearls; on finding one pearl of great value, he went and sold all that he had and bought it.

Year B

Magnificat Antiphon Jesus took the loaves, and when he had given thanks, he distributed them to those who were seated; so also the fish, as much as they wanted.

Benedictus Antiphon When the people saw the sign that he had done, they began to say, "This is indeed the prophet who is to come into the world."

Magnificat Antiphon The disciples saw Jesus walking on the sea and coming near the boat, and they were terrified. But he said to them, "It is I; do not be afraid."

Year C

Magnificat Antiphon Father, hallowed be your name. Your kingdom come. Give us each day our daily bread. And forgive us our sins, for we ourselves forgive everyone indebted to us.

Benedictus Antiphon Ask, and it will be given you; search, and you will find; knock, and the door will be opened for you.

Magnificat Antiphon If you then, who are evil, know how to give good gifts to your children, how much more will the heavenly Father give the Holy Spirit to those who ask him.

Proper 13   *The Sunday closest to August 3*
Psalter, Week 1

Collect Let your continual mercy, O Lord, cleanse and defend your Church; and, because it cannot continue in safety without your help, protect and govern it always by your goodness; through Jesus Christ our Lord, who lives and reigns with you and the Holy Spirit, one God, for ever and ever. Amen.

Year A

Magnificat Antiphon Jesus withdrew from there in a boat to a deserted place by himself. When he went ashore, he saw a great crowd; and he had compassion for them and cured their sick.

Benedictus Antiphon Taking the five loaves and the two fish, he looked up to heaven, and blessed and broke the loaves, and gave them to the disciples, and the disciples gave them to the crowds.

Magnificat Antiphon All ate and were filled; and they took up what was left over of the broken pieces, twelve baskets full. Those who ate were about five thousand men, besides women and children.

Year B

Magnificat Antiphon Do not work for the food that perishes, but for the food that endures for eternal life, which the Son of Man will give you.

Benedictus Antiphon The bread of God is that which comes down from heaven and gives life to the world.

Magnificat Antiphon I am the bread of life. Whoever comes to me will never be hungry, and whoever believes in me will never be thirsty.

Year C

Magnificat Antiphon Be on your guard against all kinds of greed; for one's life does not consist in the abundance of possessions.

Benedictus Antiphon Soul, you have ample goods laid up for many years; relax, eat, drink, be merry. You fool! This very night your life is being demanded of you.

Magnificat Antiphon So it is with those who store up treasures for themselves but are not rich toward God.

Proper 14   *The Sunday closest to August 10*

Collect Grant to us, Lord, we pray, the spirit to think and do always those things that are right, that we, who cannot exist without you, may by you be enabled to live according to your will; through Jesus Christ our Lord, who lives and reigns with you and the Holy Spirit, one God, for ever and ever. Amen.

Year A

Magnificat Antiphon Jesus went up the mountain by himself to pray. When evening came, he was there alone.
Benedictus Antiphon "Lord, if it is you, command me to come to you on the water." Jesus said, "Come." Peter got out of the boat, started walking on the water, and came toward Jesus.
Magnificat Antiphon Jesus immediately reached out his hand and caught Pete, saying to him, "You of little faith, why did you doubt?"

Year B

Magnificat Antiphon I have come down from heaven, not to do my own will, but the will of him who sent me.
Benedictus Antiphon This is indeed the will of my Father, that all who see the Son and believe in him may have eternal life; and I will raise them up on the last day.
Magnificat Antiphon I am the living bread that came down from heaven. Whoever eats of this bread will live forever; and the bread that I will give for the life of the world is my flesh.

Year C

Magnificat Antiphon Do not be afraid, little flock, for it is your Father's good pleasure to give you the kingdom. Sell your possessions, and give alms.
Benedictus Antiphon Blessed are those slaves whom the master finds alert when he comes; truly I tell you, he will fasten his belt and have them sit down to eat, and he will come and serve them.
Magnificat Antiphon From everyone to whom much has been given, much will be required; and from the one to whom much has been entrusted, even more will be demanded.

Proper 15 *The Sunday closest to August 17*

Collect Almighty God, you have given your only Son to be for us a sacrifice for sin, and also an example of godly life: Give us grace to receive thankfully the fruits of this redeeming work, and to follow daily in the blessed steps of his most holy life; through Jesus Christ your Son our Lord, who lives and reigns with you and the Holy Spirit, one God, now and for ever. Amen.

Year A

Magnificat Antiphon What comes out of the mouth proceeds from the heart, and this is what defiles. For out of the heart come evil intentions, murder, adultery, fornication, theft, false witness, slander. These are what defile a person

Benedictus Antiphon Lord, yet even the dogs eat the crumbs that fall from their masters' table.

Magnificat Antiphon "Woman, great is your faith! Let it be done for you as you wish." And her daughter was healed instantly.

Year B

Magnificat Antiphon Unless you eat the flesh of the Son of Man and drink his blood, you have no life in you.

Benedictus Antiphon My flesh is true food and my blood is true drink. Those who eat my flesh and drink my blood abide in me, and I in them.

Magnificat Antiphon Just as the living Father sent me, and I live because of the Father, so whoever eats me will live because of me.

Year C

Magnificat Antiphon I came to bring fire to the earth, and how I wish it were already kindled! I have a baptism with which to be baptized, and what stress I am under until it is completed!

Benedictus Antiphon Do you think that I have come to bring peace to the earth? No, I tell you, but rather division.

Magnificat Antiphon You know how to interpret the appearance of earth and sky, but why do you not know how to interpret the present time?

Proper 16 *The Sunday closest to August 24*

Collect Grant, O merciful God, that your Church, being gathered together in unity by your Holy Spirit, may show forth your power among all peoples, to the glory of your Name; through Jesus Christ our Lord, who lives and reigns with you and the Holy Spirit, one God, for ever and ever. Amen.

Year A

Magnificat Antiphon Who do people say that the Son of Man is? Who do you say that I am?"

Benedictus Antiphon You are the Messiah, the Son of the living God.

Magnificat Antiphon I will give you the keys of the kingdom of heaven, and whatever you bind on earth will be bound in heaven, and whatever you loose on earth will be loosed in heaven.

Year B

Magnificat Antiphon What if you were to see the Son of Man ascending to where he was before?

Benedictus Antiphon It is the spirit that gives life; the flesh is useless. The words that I have spoken to you are spirit and life.

Magnificat Antiphon Lord, to whom can we go? You have the words of eternal life. We have come to believe and know that you are the Holy One of God.

Year C

Magnificat Antiphon "Woman, you are set free from your ailment." When he laid his hands on her, immediately she stood up straight and began praising God.

Benedictus Antiphon Ought not this woman, a daughter of Abraham whom Satan bound for eighteen long years, be set free from this bondage on the sabbath day?

Magnificat Antiphon All his opponents were put to shame; and the entire crowd was rejoicing at all the wonderful things that he was doing.

Proper 17 *The Sunday closest to August 31*

Collect Lord of all power and might, the author and giver of all good things: Graft in our hearts the love of your Name; increase in us true religion; nourish us with all goodness; and bring forth in us the fruit of good works; through Jesus Christ our Lord, who lives and reigns with you and the Holy Spirit, one God, for ever and ever. Amen.

Year A

Magnificat Antiphon Jesus began to show his disciples that he must go to Jerusalem and undergo great suffering at the hands of the elders and chief priests and scribes, and be killed, and on the third day be raised.

Benedictus Antiphon If any want to become my followers, let them deny themselves and take up their cross and follow me.

Magnificat Antiphon For those who want to save their life will lose it, and those who lose their life for my sake will find it.

Year B

Magnificat Antiphon You abandon the commandment of God and hold to human tradition.

Benedictus Antiphon There is nothing outside a person that by going in can defile, but the things that come out are what defile.

Magnificat Antiphon It is from within, from the human heart, that evil intentions come. All these evil things come from within, and they defile a person.

Year C

Magnificat Antiphon "Is it lawful to cure people on the sabbath, or not?" But they were silent. So Jesus took the man with dropsy and healed him, and sent him away.

Benedictus Antiphon All who exalt themselves will be humbled, and those who humble themselves will be exalted.

Magnificat Antiphon When you give a banquet, invite the poor, the crippled, the lame, and the blind. And you will be blessed, because they cannot repay you, for you will be repaid at the resurrection of the righteous.

Proper 18   *The Sunday closest to September 7*

Collect Grant us, O Lord, to trust in you with all our hearts; for, as you always resist the proud who confide in their own strength, so you never forsake those who make their boast of your mercy; through Jesus Christ our Lord, who lives and reigns with you and the Holy Spirit, one God, now and for ever. Amen.

Year A

Magnificat Antiphon If another member of the church sins against you, go and point out the fault when the two of you are alone. If the member listens to you, you have regained that one.

Benedictus Antiphon Whatever you bind on earth will be bound in heaven, and whatever you loose on earth will be loosed in heaven.

Magnificat Antiphon Where two or three are gathered in my name, I am there among them.

Year B

Magnificat Antiphon "It is not fair to take the children's food and throw it to the dogs." "Sir, even the dogs under the table eat the children's crumbs."

Benedictus Antiphon Looking up to heaven, Jesus sighed and said to him, "Ephphatha," that is, "Be opened." And immediately his ears were opened, his tongue was released, and he spoke plainly.

Magnificat Antiphon They were astounded beyond measure, saying, "He has done everything well; he even makes the deaf to hear and the mute to speak."

Year C

Magnificat Antiphon Whoever comes to me and does not hate father and mother, wife and children, brothers and sisters, yes, and even life itself, cannot be my disciple.

Benedictus Antiphon Whoever does not carry the cross and follow me cannot be my disciple.

Magnificat Antiphon None of you can become my disciple if you do not give up all your possessions.

Proper 19 *The Sunday closest to September 14*

Psalter, Week 3

Collect O God, because without you we are not able to please you, mercifully grant that your Holy Spirit may in all things direct and rule our hearts; through Jesus Christ our Lord, who lives and reigns with you and the Holy Spirit, one God, now and for ever. Amen.

Year A

Magnificat Antiphon "Lord, if someone sins against me, how often should I forgive? Seven times?" Jesus said, "Not seven times, but, I tell you, seventy-seven times."

Benedictus Antiphon Out of pity for him, the lord of that slave released him and forgave him the debt.

Magnificat Antiphon I forgave you all that debt because you pleaded with me. Should you not have had mercy on your fellow slave, as I had mercy on you?

Year B

Magnificat Antiphon "Who do you say that I am?" Peter answered him, "You are the Messiah."

Benedictus Antiphon Jesus began to teach them that the Son of Man must undergo great suffering, and be rejected by the elders, the chief priests, and the scribes, and be killed, and after three days rise again.

Magnificat Antiphon If any want to become my followers, let them deny themselves and take up their cross and follow me.

Year C

Magnificat Antiphon Rejoice with me, for I have found my sheep that was lost. Just so, I tell you, there will be more joy in heaven over one sinner who repents than over ninety-nine righteous persons who need no repentance.

Benedictus Antiphon Rejoice with me, for I have found the coin that I had lost. Just so, I tell you, there is joy in the presence of the angels of God over one sinner who repents.

Magnificat Antiphon While he was still far off, his father saw him and was filled with compassion; he ran and put his arms around him and kissed him.

The Wednesday, Friday, and Saturday after September 14 are the traditional autumnal Ember Days. The Ember Day Propers are found on page 699.

Proper 20 *The Sunday closest to September 21*

Psalter, Week 4

Collect Grant us, Lord, not to be anxious about earthly things, but to love things heavenly; and even now, while we are placed among things that are passing away, to hold fast to those that shall endure; through Jesus Christ our Lord, who lives and reigns with you and the Holy Spirit, one God, for ever and ever. Amen.

Year A

Magnificat Antiphon The kingdom of heaven is like a landowner who went out early in the morning to hire laborers for his vineyard.

Benedictus Antiphon I choose to give to this last the same as I give to you. Am I not allowed to do what I choose with what belongs to me? Or are you envious because I am generous?

Magnificat Antiphon The last will be first, and the first will be last.

Year B

Magnificat Antiphon Jesus was teaching his disciples, saying to them, "The Son of Man is to be betrayed into human hands, and they will kill him, and three days after being killed, he will rise again."

Benedictus Antiphon Whoever wants to be first must be last of all and servant of all.

Magnificat Antiphon Whoever welcomes one such child in my name welcomes me, and whoever welcomes me welcomes not me but the one who sent me.

Year C

Magnificat Antiphon Whoever is faithful in a very little is faithful also in much.

Benedictus Antiphon If you have not been faithful with what belongs to another, who will give you what is your own?

Magnificat Antiphon You cannot serve God and wealth.

Proper 21   *The Sunday closest to September 28*

Collect O God, you declare your almighty power chiefly in showing mercy and pity: Grant us the fullness of your grace, that we, running to obtain your promises, may become partakers of your heavenly treasure; through Jesus Christ our Lord, who lives and reigns with you and the Holy Spirit, one God, for ever and ever. Amen.

Year A

Magnificat Antiphon By what authority are you doing these things, and who gave you this authority?

Benedictus Antiphon Truly I tell you, the tax collectors and the prostitutes are going into the kingdom of God ahead of you.

Magnificat Antiphon The tax collectors and the prostitutes believed John the Baptist; and even after you saw it, you did not change your minds and believe him.

Year B

Magnificat Antiphon Whoever is not against us is for us. Whoever gives you a cup of water to drink because you bear the name of Christ will by no means lose the reward.

Benedictus Antiphon If any of you put a stumbling block before one of these little ones who believe in me, it would be better for you if a great millstone were hung around your neck and you were thrown into the sea.

Magnificat Antiphon Everyone will be salted with fire. Salt is good; but if salt has lost its saltiness, how can you season it? Have salt in yourselves, and be at peace with one another.

Year C

Magnificat Antiphon Lazarus, covered with sores, longed to satisfy his hunger with what fell from the rich man's table; even the dogs would come and lick his sores.

Benedictus Antiphon Child, remember that during your lifetime you received your good things, and Lazarus in like manner evil things; but now he is comforted here, and you are in agony.

Magnificat Antiphon If they do not listen to Moses and the prophets, neither will they be convinced even if someone rises from the dead.

Proper 22 *The Sunday closest to October 5*

Collect Almighty and everlasting God, you are always more ready to hear than we to pray, and to give more than we either desire or deserve: Pour upon us the abundance of your mercy, forgiving us those things of which our conscience is afraid, and giving us those good things for which we are not worthy to ask, except through the merits and mediation of Jesus Christ our Savior; who lives and reigns with you and the Holy Spirit, one God, for ever and ever. Amen.

Year A

Magnificat Antiphon They seized him, threw him out of the vineyard, and killed him.

Benedictus Antiphon The kingdom of God will be taken away from you and given to a people that produces the fruits of the kingdom.

Magnificat Antiphon The chief priests and the Pharisees wanted to arrest him, but they feared the crowds, because they regarded him as a prophet.

Year B

Magnificat Antiphon A man shall leave his father and mother and be joined to his wife, and the two shall become one flesh.' What God has joined together, let no one separate.

Benedictus Antiphon Let the little children come to me; do not stop them; for it is to such as these that the kingdom of God belongs.

Magnificat Antiphon "Whoever does not receive the kingdom of God as a little child will never enter it." And he took them up in his arms, laid his hands on them, and blessed them.

Year C

Magnificat Antiphon The apostles said to the Lord, "Increase our faith!"

Benedictus Antiphon If you had faith the size of a mustard seed, you could say to this mulberry tree, 'Be uprooted and planted in the sea,' and it would obey you.

Magnificat Antiphon When you have done all that you were ordered to do, say, "We are worthless slaves; we have done only what we ought to have done!"

Proper 23   *The Sunday closest to October 12*

Collect Lord, we pray that your grace may always precede and follow us, that we may continually be given to good works; through Jesus Christ our Lord, who lives and reigns with you and the Holy Spirit, one God, now and for ever. Amen.

Year A

Magnificat Antiphon The kingdom of heaven may be compared to a king who gave a wedding banquet for his son.

Benedictus Antiphon The wedding is ready, but those invited were not worthy. Go therefore into the main streets, and invite everyone you find to the wedding banquet.

Magnificat Antiphon Many are called, but few are chosen.

Year B

Magnificat Antiphon Jesus, looking at him, loved him and said, "You lack one thing; go, sell what you own, and give the money to the poor, and you will have treasure in heaven; then come, follow me."

Benedictus Antiphon It is easier for a camel to go through the eye of a needle than for someone who is rich to enter the kingdom of God.

Magnificat Antiphon There is no one who has left house or brothers or sisters for my sake and for the sake of the good news, who will not receive a hundredfold now in this age and in the age to come eternal life.

Year C

Magnificat Antiphon Ten lepers approached him. Keeping their distance, they called out, saying, "Jesus, Master, have mercy on us!" He said to them, "Go and show yourselves to the priests."

Benedictus Antiphon One of them, when he saw that he was healed, turned back, praising God with a loud voice. He prostrated himself at Jesus' feet and thanked him. And he was a Samaritan.

Magnificat Antiphon Jesus said to him, "Get up and go on your way; your faith has made you well."

Proper 24   *The Sunday closest to October 19*

Collect Almighty and everlasting God, in Christ you have revealed your glory among the nations: Preserve the works of your mercy, that your Church throughout the world may persevere with steadfast faith in the confession of your Name; through Jesus Christ our Lord, who lives and reigns with you and the Holy Spirit, one God, for ever and ever. Amen.

Year A

Magnificat Antiphon Is it lawful to pay taxes to the emperor, or not?
Benedictus Antiphon Give to the emperor the things that are the emperor's, and to God the things that are God's.
Magnificat Antiphon When they heard this, they were amazed; and they left him and went away.

Year B

Magnificat Antiphon The cup that I drink you will drink; and with the baptism with which I am baptized, you will be baptized.
Benedictus Antiphon Whoever wishes to become great among you must be your servant, and whoever wishes to be first among you must be slave of all.
Magnificat Antiphon The Son of Man came not to be served but to serve, and to give his life a ransom for many.

Year C

Magnificat Antiphon There was a judge who neither feared God nor had respect for people and a widow who kept coming to him and saying, "Grant me justice against my opponent."
Benedictus Antiphon Will not God grant justice to his chosen ones who cry to him day and night? I tell you, he will quickly grant justice to them.
Magnificat Antiphon When Son of Man comes, will he find faith on earth?

Proper 25   *The Sunday closest to October 26*

Psalter, Week 1

Collect Almighty and everlasting God, increase in us the gifts of faith, hope, and charity; and, that we may obtain what you promise, make us love what you command; through Jesus Christ our Lord, who lives and reigns with you and the Holy Spirit, one God, for ever and ever. Amen.

Year A

Magnificat Antiphon You shall love the Lord your God with all your heart, and with all your soul, and with all your mind. You shall love your neighbor as yourself.

Benedictus Antiphon On these two commandments hang all the law and the prophets.

Magnificat Antiphon How is it then that David by the Spirit calls the Messiah Lord? If David thus calls him Lord, how can he be his son?

Year B

Magnificat Antiphon Jesus, Son of David, have mercy on me!

Benedictus Antiphon Jesus stood still and said, "Call him here." And they called the blind man, saying to him, "Take heart; get up, he is calling you."

Magnificat Antiphon Jesus said to him, "Go; your faith has made you well." Immediately he regained his sight and followed him on the way.

Year C

Magnificat Antiphon Jesus told this parable to some who trusted in themselves that they were righteous and regarded others with contempt.

Benedictus Antiphon The tax collector, standing far off, would not even look up to heaven, but was beating his breast and saying, 'God, be merciful to me, a sinner!'

Magnificat Antiphon All who exalt themselves will be humbled, but all who humble themselves will be exalted.

Proper 26   *The Sunday closest to November 2*

Psalter, Week 2

Collect Almighty and merciful God, it is only by your gift that your faithful people offer you true and laudable service: Grant that we may run without stumbling to obtain your heavenly promises; through Jesus Christ our Lord, who lives and reigns with you and the Holy Spirit, one God, now and for ever. Amen.

Year A

Magnificat Antiphon Call no one your father on earth, for you have one Father—the one in heaven.

Benedictus Antiphon The greatest among you will be your servant.

Magnificat Antiphon All who exalt themselves will be humbled, and all who humble themselves will be exalted.

Year B

Magnificat Antiphon Hear, O Israel: the Lord our God, the Lord is one; you shall love the Lord your God with all your heart, all your soul, all your mind, and all your strength.

Benedictus Antiphon You shall love your neighbor as yourself.

Magnificat Antiphon To love him with all the heart, and to love one's neighbor as oneself, —this is much more important than all whole burnt offerings and sacrifices.

Year C

Magnificat Antiphon Zacchaeus was a chief tax collector and was rich. He was trying to see who Jesus was, but he could not, because he was short in stature. So he ran ahead and climbed a sycamore tree to see him.

Benedictus Antiphon "Zacchaeus, hurry and come down; for I must stay at your house today." So he hurried down and joyfully welcomed him.

Magnificat Antiphon Today salvation has come to this house, because he too is a son of Abraham. For the Son of Man came to seek out and to save the lost.

Proper 27 *The Sunday closest to November 9*

Psalter, Week 3

Collect O God, whose blessed Son came into the world that he might destroy the works of the devil and make us children of God and heirs of eternal life: Grant that, having this hope, we may purify ourselves as he is pure; that, when he comes again with power and great glory, we may be made like him in his eternal and glorious kingdom; where he lives and reigns with you and the Holy Spirit, one God, for ever and ever. Amen.

Year A

Magnificat Antiphon Ten bridesmaids took their lamps and went to meet the bridegroom. Five of them were foolish, and five were wise.

Benedictus Antiphon At midnight there was a shout, "Look! Here is the bridegroom! Come out to meet him."

Magnificat Antiphon Keep awake therefore, for you know neither the day nor the hour.

Year B

Magnificat Antiphon Beware of the scribes, who like to walk around in long robes, and to be greeted with respect in the marketplaces, and to have the places of honor at banquets!

Benedictus Antiphon A poor widow came and put in two small copper coins, which are worth a penny.

Magnificat Antiphon All of them have contributed out of their abundance; but she out of her poverty has put in everything she had, all she had to live on.

Year C

Magnificat Antiphon Those who belong to this age marry and are given in marriage; but those who are considered worthy of a place in that age and in the resurrection from the dead neither marry nor are given in marriage.

Benedictus Antiphon They cannot die anymore, because they are like angels and are children of God, being children of the resurrection.

Magnificat Antiphon The God of Abraham, the God of Isaac, and the God of Jacob is God not of the dead, but of the living; for to him all of them are alive.

Proper 28 *The Sunday closest to November 16*

Psalter, Week 4

Collect Blessed Lord, who caused all holy Scriptures to be written for our learning: Grant us so to hear them, read, mark, learn, and inwardly digest them, that we may embrace and ever hold fast the blessed hope of everlasting life, which you have given us in our Savior Jesus Christ; who lives and reigns with you and the Holy Spirit, one God, for ever and ever. Amen.

Year A

Magnificat Antiphon A man, going on a journey, summoned his slaves and entrusted his property to them; to one he gave five talents, to another two, to another one, to each according to his ability.

Benedictus Antiphon Well done, good and trustworthy slave; you have been trustworthy in a few things, I will put you in charge of many things; enter into the joy of your master.

Magnificat Antiphon To all those who have, more will be given, and they will have an abundance; but from those who have nothing, even what they have will be taken away.

Year B

Magnificat Antiphon Do you see these great buildings? Not one stone will be left here upon another; all will be thrown down.

Benedictus Antiphon Beware that no one leads you astray. Many will come in my name and say, 'I am he!' and they will lead many astray.

Magnificat Antiphon Nation will rise against nation, and kingdom against kingdom. This is but the beginning of the birthpangs.

Year C

Magnificat Antiphon When you hear of wars and insurrections, do not be terrified; for these things must take place first, but the end will not follow immediately.

Benedictus Antiphon You will be hated by all because of my name. But not a hair of your head will perish.

Magnificat Antiphon By your endurance you will gain your souls.

Proper 29 *The Sunday closest to November 23*

Psalter, Week 1

Collect Almighty and everlasting God, whose will it is to restore all things in your well-beloved Son, the King of kings and Lord of lords: Mercifully grant that the peoples of the earth, divided and enslaved by sin, may be freed and brought together under his most gracious rule; who lives and reigns with you and the Holy Spirit, one God, now and for ever. Amen.

Year A

Magnificat Antiphon When the Son of Man comes in his glory, and all the angels with him, then he will sit on the throne of his glory. He will separate people one from another as a shepherd separates the sheep from the goats

Benedictus Antiphon Come, you that are blessed by my Father, inherit the kingdom prepared for you from the foundation of the world.

Magnificat Antiphon Truly I tell you, just as you did it to one of the least of these who are members of my family, you did it to me.

Year B

Magnificat Antiphon Pilate entered the headquarters, summoned Jesus, and asked him, "Are you the King of the Jews?

Benedictus Antiphon My kingdom is not from this world. If my kingdom were from this world, my followers would be fighting to keep me from being handed over to the Jews.

Magnificat Antiphon For this I was born, and for this I came into the world, to testify to the truth. Everyone who belongs to the truth listens to my voice.

Year C

Magnificat Antiphon The soldiers mocked him saying, "If you are the King of the Jews, save yourself!" There was also an inscription over him, "This is the King of the Jews."

Benedictus Antiphon Jesus, remember me when you come into your kingdom.

Magnificat Antiphon Truly I tell you, today you will be with me in Paradise.

The Ordinary of The Daily Office

The Ordinary of The Daily Office

Morning Prayer

The Invitation

Officiant   Lord, open our lips.

People   **And our mouth shall proclaim your praise.**

Officiant and People

**Glory to the Father, and to the Son, and to the Holy Spirit:
as it was in the beginning, is now, and will be for ever. Amen.**

Except in Lent, add **Alleluia.**

The Invitatory

The Daily Office begins with the Invitatory. While the Rule of St. Benedict provides for Psalm 95 this set of alternate Invitatory Psalms is taken from the Thesaurus Liturgiae Horarum Monasticae. Each Invitatory Psalm includes a set of antiphons for the four weeks of the Psalter. The antiphon for the seasons or the proper or common of the saints are found in the assigned places. The antiphon is repeated after each section of the Invitatory Psalm.

Sunday Invitatory Psalm
Psalm 95 *Venite, exultemus*

Week 1 God blesses us in Christ with the hope of resurrection: Come let us adore.

Week 2 The Lord creates the world in its diversity: Come let us worship.

Week 3 The Spirit of holiness has raised the Son of God: Come let us adore.

Week 4 The Spirit draws us into the life of God: Come let us worship.

(Antiphon)
1 Come, let us sing to the LORD; *
    let us shout for joy to the Rock of our salvation.
2 Let us come before his presence with thanksgiving *
    and raise a loud shout to him with psalms.
    (Antiphon)
3 For the LORD is a great God, *
    and a great King above all gods.
4 In his hand are the caverns of the earth, *
    and the heights of the hills are his also.
5 The sea is his, for he made it, *
    and his hands have molded the dry land.
    (Antiphon)
6 Come, let us bow down, and bend the knee, *
    and kneel before the LORD our Maker.
7 For he is our God,
    and we are the people of his pasture and the sheep of his hand. *
    Oh, that today you would hearken to his voice!
    (Antiphon)
8 Harden not your hearts,
    as your forebears did in the wilderness,*
    at Meribah, and on that day at Massah,
    when they tempted me.
9 They put me to the test,*
    though they had seen my works.
    (Antiphon)
10 Forty years long I detested that generation and said, *
    "This people are wayward in their hearts;
    they do not know my ways."
11So I swore in my wrath, *
    "They shall not enter into my rest.
    (Antiphon)

Monday Invitatory Psalm
Psalm 29 *Afferte Domino*

Week 1 God, our Creator, is worthy of worship: Come let us adore.

Week 2 Ascribe to the Lord, our Maker, the glory due God's Name: Come let us worship.

Week 3 Let us listen to the splendid voice of our Creator: Come let us adore.

Week 4 The Lord shall give us the blessing of peace: Come let us worship.

(*Antiphon*)

1 Ascribe to the LORD, you gods, *
    ascribe to the LORD glory and strength.
2 Ascribe to the LORD the glory due his Name; *
    worship the LORD in the beauty of holiness.
(*Antiphon*)

3 The voice of the LORD is upon the waters;
  the God of glory thunders; *
    the LORD is upon the mighty waters.
4 The voice of the LORD is a powerful voice; *
    the voice of the LORD is a voice of splendor.
(*Antiphon*)

5 The voice of the LORD breaks the cedar trees; *
    the LORD breaks the cedars of Lebanon;
6 He makes Lebanon skip like a calf, *
    and Mount Hermon like a young wild ox.
(*Antiphon*)

7 The voice of the LORD splits the flames of fire;
  the voice of the LORD shakes the wilderness; *
    the LORD shakes the wilderness of Kadesh.
8 The voice of the LORD makes the oak trees writhe *
    and strips the forests bare.
9 And in the temple of the LORD *
    all are crying, "Glory!"
(*Antiphon*)

10 The LORD sits enthroned above the flood; *
    the LORD sits enthroned as King for evermore.
11 The LORD shall give strength to his people; *
    the LORD shall give his people the blessing of peace.
(*Antiphon*)

Tuesday Invitatory Psalm
Psalm 8 *Domine, Dominus noster*

Week 1 The Lord's Name is exalted in all the world: Come let us adore.
Week 2 The Lord's majesty is praised above the heavens: Come let us worship.
Week 3 Jesus, made lower than the angels, is crowned with glory and honor: Come let us adore Christ the Lord.
Week 4 God has put all things under Christ's feet; Come let us worship Christ the Lord.

(Antiphon)
1 O LORD our Governor, *
    how exalted is your Name in all the world!
2 Out of the mouths of infants and children *
    your majesty is praised above the heavens.
3 You have set up a stronghold against your adversaries, *
    to quell the enemy and the avenger.
    (Antiphon)

4 When I consider your heavens, the work of your fingers, *
    the moon and the stars you have set in their courses,
5 What is man that you should be mindful of him? *
    the son of man that you should seek him out?
    (Antiphon)

6 You have made him but little lower than the angels; *
    you adorn him with glory and honor;
7 You give him mastery over the works of your hands; *
    you put all things under his feet:
    (Antiphon)

8 All sheep and oxen, *
    even the wild beasts of the field,
9 The birds of the air, the fish of the sea, *
    and whatsoever walks in the paths of the sea.
10 O LORD our Governor, *
    how exalted is your Name in all the world!
    (Antiphon)

Wednesday Invitatory Psalm
Psalm 95 *Venite, exultemus*

Week 1 In Abraham, all the families of the earth shall be blessed: Come let us adore.

Week 2 God will bring all things together in Christ: Come let us worship.

Week 3 God's hidden plan of salvation is revealed in Christ: Come let us adore.

Week 4 All nations will be blessed in God's people: Come let us worship.

    (Antiphon)

1 Come, let us sing to the LORD; *
    let us shout for joy to the Rock of our salvation.
2 Let us come before his presence with thanksgiving *
    and raise a loud shout to him with psalms.
    (Antiphon)
3 For the LORD is a great God, *
    and a great King above all gods.
4 In his hand are the caverns of the earth, *
    and the heights of the hills are his also.
5 The sea is his, for he made it, *
    and his hands have molded the dry land.
    (Antiphon)
6 Come, let us bow down, and bend the knee, *
    and kneel before the LORD our Maker.
7 For he is our God,
  and we are the people of his pasture and the sheep of his hand. *
    Oh, that today you would hearken to his voice!
    (Antiphon)
8 Harden not your hearts,
  as your forebears did in the wilderness,*
    at Meribah, and on that day at Massah,
    when they tempted me.
9 They put me to the test,*
    though they had seen my works.
    (Antiphon)
10 Forty years long I detested that generation and said, *
    "This people are wayward in their hearts;
    they do not know my ways."
11 So I swore in my wrath, *
    "They shall not enter into my rest.
    (Antiphon)

Thursday Invitatory Psalm
Psalm 122 *Lætatus sum*

Week 1 Let us go to the house of the LORD: Come let us adore.
Week 2 Let us offer God a sacrifice of praise and thanksgiving: Come let us worship.
Week 3 The Lord feeds us with the Bread of Angels: Come let us adore.
Week 4 The new Jerusalem is the Bride of the Lamb, come let us worship Christ the Lord.

(*Antiphon*)

1 I was glad when they said to me, *
    "Let us go to the house of the LORD."
2 Now our feet are standing *
    within your gates, O Jerusalem.

(*Antiphon*)

3 Jerusalem is built as a city *
    that is at unity with itself;
4 To which the tribes go up,
    the tribes of the LORD, *
        the assembly of Israel,
        to praise the Name of the LORD.
5 For there are the thrones of judgment, *
    the thrones of the house of David.

(*Antiphon*)

6 Pray for the peace of Jerusalem: *
    "May they prosper who love you.
7 Peace be within your walls *
    and quietness within your towers.

(*Antiphon*)

8 For my brethren and companions' sake, *
    I pray for your prosperity.
9 Because of the house of the LORD our God, *
    I will seek to do you good."

(*Antiphon*)

Friday Invitatory Psalm
Psalm 95 *Venite, exultemus*

Week 1 The Lord cleanses us from our sin; Come let us adore.

Week 2 God purges our sin and purifies us: Come let us worship.

Week 3 The Lord delivers us from death: Come let us adore.

Week 4 God accepts a contrite heart: Come let us worship.

(Antiphon)

1 Come, let us sing to the LORD; *
> let us shout for joy to the Rock of our salvation.

2 Let us come before his presence with thanksgiving *
> and raise a loud shout to him with psalms.
> *(Antiphon)*

3 For the LORD is a great God, *
> and a great King above all gods.

4 In his hand are the caverns of the earth, *
> and the heights of the hills are his also.

5 The sea is his, for he made it, *
> and his hands have molded the dry land.
> *(Antiphon)*

6 Come, let us bow down, and bend the knee, *
> and kneel before the LORD our Maker.

7 For he is our God,
> and we are the people of his pasture and the sheep of his hand. *
> Oh, that today you would hearken to his voice!
> *(Antiphon)*

8 Harden not your hearts,
> as your forebears did in the wilderness,*
> at Meribah, and on that day at Massah,
> when they tempted me.

9 They put me to the test,*
> though they had seen my works.
> *(Antiphon)*

10 Forty years long I detested that generation and said, *
> "This people are wayward in their hearts;
> they do not know my ways."

11 So I swore in my wrath, *
> "They shall not enter into my rest.
> *(Antiphon)*

Saturday Invitatory Psalm
Psalm 100 *Jubilate Deo*

Week 1 We are the Lord's people and the sheep of God's pasture: Come use us worship.

Week 2 Serve the LORD with gladness: Come let us adore.

Week 3 The LORD is good; God's mercy is everlasting: Come let us worship.

Week 4 God's faithfulness endures from age to age, come let us adore.

(Antiphon)

1   Be joyful in the LORD, all you lands; *
      serve the LORD with gladness
      and come before his presence with a song.

2   Know this: The LORD himself is God; *
      he himself has made us, and we are his;
      we are his people and the sheep of his pasture.

(Antiphon)

3   Enter his gates with thanksgiving;
    go into his courts with praise; *
      give thanks to him and call upon his Name.

4   For the LORD is good;
    his mercy is everlasting; *
      and his faithfulness endures from age to age.

(Antiphon)

Hymn

The Hymn follows the Invitatory. The Hymn is found in the proper of either the season or of the saints.

Psalmody.

The Psalmody consists of three psalms with antiphons. The Psalms are found in the appropriate week of the Psalter. For major feasts and lesser feasts the antiphons are taken from the Proper of the day or from the Common of the Saints. The antiphons for the season are found in the Psalter.

Reading One

The office is structured so that there will be two readings at Morning Prayer. The readings are used in the order in which they appear in the Daily Office Lectionary. For Principal Feasts, Feasts of our Lord and Major Feasts, the readings are found in the lectionary for Holy Days.

Response to the Word of God

A period of silence appropriately follows the reading. The Responsory follows the period of silence.

The First Canticle

The First Canticle continues the prayer. An appropriate antiphon is included. The antiphons are found with the canticle. For Major and Lesser Feasts, the Canticle is taken from the proper of the saints. On Major Feasts, when a Proper Canticle is not assigned the *Te Deum laudamus* is used.

Canticle You are God   *Te Deum laudamus*

You are God: we praise you;
You are the Lord: we acclaim you;
You are the eternal Father:
All creation worships you.
To you all angels, all the powers of heaven,
Cherubim and Seraphim, sing in endless praise:
    Holy, holy, holy Lord, God of power and might,
    heaven and earth are full of your glory.
The glorious company of apostles praise you.
The noble fellowship of prophets praise you.
The white-robed army of martyrs praise you.

Throughout the world the holy Church acclaims you;
    Father, of majesty unbounded,
     your true and only Son, worthy of all worship,
     and the Holy Spirit, advocate and guide.
You, Christ, are the king of glory,
the eternal Son of the Father.
When you became man to set us free
you did not shun the Virgin's womb.
You overcame the sting of death
and opened the kingdom of heaven to all believers.
You are seated at God's right hand in glory.
We believe that you will come and be our judge.
    Come then, Lord, and help your people,
     bought with the price of your own blood,
     and bring us with your saints
     to glory everlasting.

The Second Reading

Response to the Word of God
A period of silence appropriately follows the reading. The Responsory follows the period of silence.

The Gospel Canticle
The Gospel Canticle, the Song of Zechariah, continues the prayer. An appropriate antiphon is included. For the Seasons of the Church Year, the antiphon is found in the material for that day. For Major and Lesser Feasts, the antiphon is taken from the proper or common of the saints.

The Song of Zechariah *Benedictus Dominus Deus*
Luke 1: 68-79

Blessed be the Lord, the God of Israel; *
    he has come to his people and set them free.
He has raised up for us a mighty savior, *
    born of the house of his servant David.
Through his holy prophets he promised of old,
    that he would save us from our enemies, *
    from the hands of all who hate us.
He promised to show mercy to our fathers *
    and to remember his holy covenant.
This was the oath he swore to our father Abraham, *
    to set us free from the hands of our enemies,

Free to worship him without fear, *
    holy and righteous in his sight
    all the days of our life.
You, my child, shall be called the prophet of the Most High, *
    for you will go before the Lord to prepare his way,
To give his people knowledge of salvation *
    by the forgiveness of their sins.
In the tender compassion of our God *
    the dawn from on high shall break upon us,
To shine on those who dwell in darkness and the
    shadow of death, *
and to guide our feet into the way of peace.

The Litany
Intercessions are offered for the needs of the world, of the church and
of the persons saying the office. Intercessions are found in the office of
the day.

The Lord's Prayer
There is an Invitation to begin the Lord's Prayer.

Our Father in heaven,
    hallowed be your Name,
    your kingdom come,
    your will be done,
        on earth as in heaven.
Give us today our daily bread.
Forgive us our sins
    as we forgive those
        who sin against us.
Save us from the time of trial,
    and deliver us from evil.
For the kingdom, the power,
    and the glory are yours,
        now and for ever. Amen.

The Collect
*After the Lord's Prayer, the concluding collect is said. It is said without an
Invitation. The collect is taken from the Sunday, the season, or from the Major or
Lesser Feast.*

The Blessing
Let us bless the Lord.
Thanks be to God.

The Blessing is taken from the Season, the Sanctoral or the Ferial.

Noonday Prayer

Officiant O God, make speed to save us.
People O Lord, make haste to help us.
Officiant and People
Glory to the Father, and to the Son, and to the Holy Spirit:
as it was in the beginning, is now, and will be for ever. Amen.
Except in Lent, add **Alleluia.**

Hymn

Psalmody

Reading

Verse and Response

The Short Litany
Officiant Let us pray for the needs of the world. *(Petitions are offered.)*
People Lord, have mercy.
Officiant Let us pray for the needs of the church. *(Petitions are offered.)*
People Christ, have mercy.
Officiant Let us pray for those who ask our prayer. *(Petitions are offered.)*
People Lord, have mercy.

Officiant Let us pray to the Father in the words of Christ, our Lord.
People Our Father in heaven,
    hallowed be your Name,
    your kingdom come,
    your will be done,
        on earth as in heaven.
Give us today our daily bread.
Forgive us our sins
    as we forgive those
        who sin against us.
Save us from the time of trial,
    and deliver us from evil.
For the kingdom, the power,
    and the glory are yours,
        now and for ever. Amen.

Concluding Prayer.
The concluding collect is taken from the proper of the season or the major or lesser feast.

The Conclusion
Let us bless the Lord.
Thanks be to God.

Evening Prayer

The Invitation
Officiant O God, make speed to save us.
People O Lord, make haste to help us.
Officiant and People
**Glory to the Father, and to the Son, and to the Holy Spirit:
as it was in the beginning, is now, and will be for ever. Amen.**
Except in Lent, add **Alleluia.**

Hymn
The Hymn is found in the proper of either the season or of the saints.

Psalmody.
The Psalmody consists of three psalms with antiphons. For major feasts and lesser feasts the antiphons are taken from the Proper of the day or from the Common of the Saints. The antiphons for the seasons are found in the Psalter.

Reading
The readings is taken from the Daily Office Lectionary. At Evening Prayer, the reading is taken from the Gospel.

Response to the Word of God
A period of silence follows the reading. The Responsory follows the period of silence.

The Gospel Canticle
The Gospel Canticle, the Song of Mary, continues the prayer. An appropriate antiphon is included. The antiphons are found with the canticle. For Major and Lesser Feasts, the Canticle is taken from the proper of the saints.

The Song of Mary *Magnificat*
Luke 1:46-55

My soul proclaims the greatness of the Lord,
      my spirit rejoices in God my Savior; *
      for he has looked with favor on his lowly servant.
From this day all generations will call me blessed: *
      the Almighty has done great things for me,
      and holy is his Name.
He has mercy on those who fear him *
      in every generation.
He has shown the strength of his arm, *
      he has scattered the proud in their conceit.
He has cast down the mighty from their thrones, *
      and has lifted up the lowly.
He has filled the hungry with good things, *
      and the rich he has sent away empty.
He has come to the help of his servant Israel, *
      for he has remembered his promise of mercy,
The promise he made to our fathers, *
      to Abraham and his children for ever.

Intercessions
The Rule of St. Benedict provides for intercessions after the Gospel Canticle. The intercessions are related to the season or the saint and ask God to look on the diverse needs of the world and the people of God.

The Lord's Prayer
There is an Invitation to begin the Lord's Prayer.

Our Father in heaven,
  hallowed be your Name,
  your kingdom come,
  your will be done,
    on earth as in heaven.
Give us today our daily bread.
Forgive us our sins
  as we forgive those
    who sin against us.
Save us from the time of trial,
  and deliver us from evil.
For the kingdom, the power,
  and the glory are yours,
  now and for ever. Amen.

The Collect

After the Lord's Prayer, the concluding collect is said. It is said without an Invitation. The collect is taken from the Sunday, the season, if available, or from the Major or Lesser Feast.

The Blessing

Let us bless the Lord.
Thanks be to God.

The Blessing is taken from the Season, the Sanctoral or the Ferial.

Compline

The Invitation
Officiant O God, make speed to save us.
People O Lord, make haste to help us.
Glory to the Father, and to the Son, and to the Holy Spirit:
as it was in the beginning, is now, and will be for ever. Amen.
Alleluia.

The Confession and Absolution
The Confession and Absolution follow. If a deacon is present, the deacon bids the
congregation to the confession. If a bishop or priest are present they give the
absolution. If there is no deacon, the bishop or priest bid the confession and give the
absolution. If an ordained person is not present, the officiant bids the confession and
gives the assurance of forgiveness.

Let us confess our sins to God.
A Period of Silence is observed.

Almighty God, our heavenly Father:
We have sinned against you,
through our own fault,
in thought, and word, and deed,
and in what we have left undone.
For the sake of your Son our Lord Jesus Christ,
forgive us all our offenses;
and grant that we may serve you
in newness of life,
to the glory of your Name. Amen.

The Bishop, when present, or the Priest, stands and says
Almighty God have mercy on you, forgive you all your sins through our
Lord Jesus Christ, strengthen you in all goodness, and by the power of
the Holy Spirit keep you in eternal life. Amen.

Or in the absence of a bishop or priest:
Officiant May the Almighty God grant us forgiveness of all our sins, and
the grace and comfort of the Holy Spirit. Amen.

Hymn *All stand*
Week I & III

Before the ending of the day,
  Creator of the world, we pray,
  that with thy wonted favor thou
  wouldst be our guard and keeper now.

From all ill dreams defend our eyes,
  from nightly fears and fantasies;
  tread under foot our ghostly foe,
  that no pollution we may know.

O Father, that we ask be done,
  through Jesus Christ thine only Son,
  who, with the Holy Ghost and thee,
  doth live and reign eternally. Amen.
Author (attributed to): St. Ambrose; Translator: J. M. Neale (1852)

Week II & IV

All praise to You, my God, this night,
  For all the blessings of the light.
  Keep me, O keep me, King of kings,
  Beneath the shelter of Your wings.

Forgive me, Lord, for this I pray,
  The wrong that I have done this day.
  May peace with God and neighbor be,
  Before I sleep restored to me.

Lord, may I be at rest in You
  And sweetly sleep the whole night thro'.
  Refresh my strength, for Your own sake,
  So I may serve You when I wake.

Praise God, from whom all blessings flow;
  Praise Him all creatures here below;
  Praise Him above, ye heav'nly host;
  Praise Father, Son, and Holy Ghost.
Author: Thomas Ken

Psalmody

Psalm 4 *Cum invocarem*

1 Answer me when I call, O God, defender of my cause; *
    you set me free when I am hard-pressed;
    have mercy on me and hear my prayer.

2 "You mortals, how long will you dishonor my glory; *
    how long will you worship dumb idols
    and run after false gods?"

3 Know that the LORD does wonders for the faithful; *
    when I call upon the LORD, he will hear me.

4 Tremble, then, and do not sin; *
    speak to your heart in silence upon your bed.

5 Offer the appointed sacrifices *
    and put your trust in the LORD.

6 Many are saying, "Oh, that we might see better times!" *
    Lift up the light of your countenance upon us, O LORD.

7 You have put gladness in my heart, *
    more than when grain and wine and oil increase.

8 I lie down in peace; at once I fall asleep; *
    for only you, LORD, make me dwell in safety.

Psalm 91 *Qui habitat*

1 He who dwells in the shelter of the Most High, *
    abides under the shadow of the Almighty.

2 He shall say to the LORD,
    "You are my refuge and my stronghold, *
    my God in whom I put my trust."

3 He shall deliver you from the snare of the hunter *
    and from the deadly pestilence.

4 He shall cover you with his pinions,
    and you shall find refuge under his wings; *
    his faithfulness shall be a shield and buckler.

5 You shall not be afraid of any terror by night, *
    nor of the arrow that flies by day;

6 Of the plague that stalks in the darkness, *
    nor of the sickness that lays waste at mid-day.

7   A thousand shall fall at your side
      and ten thousand at your right hand, *
          but it shall not come near you.

8   Your eyes have only to behold *
          to see the reward of the wicked.

9   Because you have made the LORD your refuge, *
          and the Most High your habitation,

10 There shall no evil happen to you, *
          neither shall any plague come near your dwelling.

11 For he shall give his angels charge over you, *
          to keep you in all your ways.

12 They shall bear you in their hands, *
          lest you dash your foot against a stone.

13 You shall tread upon the lion and adder; *
          you shall trample the young lion
          and the serpent under your feet.

14 Because he is bound to me in love,
      therefore will I deliver him; *
          I will protect him, because he knows my Name.

15 He shall call upon me, and I will answer him; *
          I am with him in trouble;
          I will rescue him and bring him to honor.

16 With long life will I satisfy him, *
          and show him my salvation.

Psalm 134   *Ecce nunc*

1   Behold now, bless the LORD, all you servants of the LORD, *
          you that stand by night in the house of the LORD.

2   Lift up your hands in the holy place and bless the LORD; *
          the LORD who made heaven and earth
          bless you out of Zion.

Reading
Saturday
Jeremiah 14:9,22
Lord, you are in the midst of us, and we are called by your Name: Do
not forsake us, O Lord our God.
People   Thanks be to God.

Sunday

Hebrews 13:20-21

May the God of peace, who brought again from the dead our Lord Jesus, and great shepherd of the sheep, by the blood of the eternal covenant, equip you with everything good that you may do his will, working in you that which is pleasing in his sight; through Jesus Christ, to whom be glory for ever and ever.

People   Thanks be to God.

Monday

Matthew 11:28-30

Come to me, all who labor and are heavy-laden, and I will give you rest. Take my yoke upon you, and learn from me; for I am gentle and lowly in heart, and you will find rest for your souls. For my yoke is easy, and my burden is light.

People   Thanks be to God.

Tuesday

1 Thessalonians 5: 9-10

God has destined us not for wrath but for obtaining salvation through our Lord Jesus Christ, who died for us, so that whether we are awake or asleep we may live with him.

People   Thanks be to God.

Wednesday

Ephesians 4: 26-67

Be angry but do not sin; do not let the sun go down on your anger, and do not make room for the devil.

People   Thanks be to God.

Thursday

1 Thessalonians 5: 223-24

May the God of peace himself sanctify you entirely; and may your spirit and soul and body be kept sound[f] and blameless at the coming of our Lord Jesus Christ. The one who calls you is faithful, and he will do this.

People   Thanks be to God.

Friday

1 Peter 5:8-9a

Be sober, be watchful. Your adversary the devil prowls around like a roaring lion, seeking someone to devour. Resist him, firm in your faith.

People   Thanks be to God.

Responsory
Into your hands, O Lord
　　– I commend my spirit.
You have redeemed me, O Lord, O God of truth.
　　– I commend my spirit.
Glory to the Father and to the Son and to the Holy Spirit.
Into your hands, O Lord
　　– I commend my spirit.

Canticle: The Song of Simeon *Nunc Dimittis (Luke 2: 29-31*

The Canticle Nunc Dimittis is said with its proper antiphon.
Antiphon Guide us waking, O Lord, and guard us sleeping; that awake
we may watch with Christ, and asleep we may rest in peace.
Sanctoral Antiphon Shine in us, O God, with your light, and may you
Spirt illumine the darkness of our hearts that we may abide in Christ, the
light of the world.

The Song of Simeon *Nunc Dimittis*
Luke 2:29-32

Lord, you now have set your servant free *
　　to go in peace as you have promised;
For these eyes of mine have seen the Savior, *
　　whom you have prepared for all the world to see:
A Light to enlighten the nations, *
　　and the glory of your people Israel.

Antiphon Guide us waking, O Lord, and guard us sleeping; that awake
we may watch with Christ, and asleep we may rest in peace.
Sanctoral Antiphon Shine in us, O God, with your light, and may you
Spirt illumine the darkness of our hearts that we may abide in Christ, the
light of the world.

The Lord's Prayer

Lord, have mercy.
Christ, have mercy.
Lord, have mercy.

Our Father in heaven, hallowed be your Name,
your kingdom come, your will be done,
on earth as in heaven.
Give us today our daily bread.

Forgive us our sins
as we forgive those who sin against us.
Save us from the time of trial, and deliver us from evil.

Collect

The collect for the day follows the Lord's Prayer.
Let us pray.

Saturday

We give you thanks, O God, for revealing your Son Jesus Christ to us by the light of his resurrection: Grant that as we sing your glory at the close of this day, our joy may abound in the morning as we celebrate the Paschal mystery; through Jesus Christ our Lord. Amen.

Sunday

Be our light in the darkness, O Lord, and in your great mercy defend us from all perils and dangers of this night; for the love of your only Son, our Savior Jesus Christ. Amen.

Monday

Be present, O merciful God, and protect us through the hours of this night, so that we who are wearied by the changes and chances of this life may rest in your eternal changelessness; through Jesus Christ our Lord. Amen.

Tuesday

Look down, O Lord, from your heavenly throne, and illumine this night with your celestial brightness; that by night as by day your people may glorify your holy Name; through Jesus Christ our Lord. Amen.

Wednesday

Visit this place, O Lord, and drive far from it all snares of the enemy; let your holy angels dwell with us to preserve us in peace; and let your blessing be upon us always; through Jesus Christ our Lord. Amen.

Thursday

Keep watch, dear Lord, with those who work, or watch, or weep this night, and give your angels charge over those who sleep. Tend the sick, Lord Christ; give rest to the weary, bless the dying, soothe the suffering, pity the afflicted, shield the joyous; and all for your love's sake. Amen.

Friday

O God, your unfailing providence sustains the world we live in and the life we live: Watch over those, both night and day, who work while others sleep, and grant that we may never forget that our common life depends upon each other's toil; through Jesus Christ our Lord. Amen.

Conclusion and Blessing
Let us bless the Lord.
Thanks be to God.

The Lord grant us a quiet night and a peaceful death.
Amen

Final Antiphon of the Blessed Virgin Mary

Advent through February 2
Alma Redemptoris Mater
Loving Mother of the Redeemer,
Gate of heaven, star of the sea,
Assist your people
who have fallen yet strive to rise again.
To the wonderment of nature you bore your Creator,
yet remained a virgin after as before.
You who received Gabriel's joyful greeting,
have pity on us, poor sinners

February 2 through Good Friday
Ave Regina Caelorum
Hail, Queen of Heaven.
Hail, Queen of the Angels.
Hail, Root of Jesse and Gate of the morning,
From you the world's true light was born.
Rejoice, O Glorious Virgin,
Beautiful beyond all others.
O you who are fair beyond the fairest
Pray for us to Christ.

After Pentecost
Salve Regina
Hail, holy Queen, Mother of mercy;
our life, our sweetness and our hope.
To you do we cry, poor banished children of Eve.
To you do we raise our prayer,
grieving and lamenting in this desolate valley.
Turn then, most gracious intercessor,
your eyes of mercy toward us,
and after this exile

show us the blessed fruit of your womb, Jesus.
O clement, O loving, O sweet Virgin Mary.

Or

Sub Tuum Praesidium

We turn to you for protection, O holy Mother of God.
Hear our prayers and help us in our needs.
Protect us from every danger, O glorious and blessed Virgin.

The Four Week Psalter

Week 1

Sunday Week 1 Evening Prayer I

Officiant: O God, make speed to save us.

People: **O Lord, make haste to help us.**

Officiant and People **Glory to the Father, and to the Son, and to the Holy Spirit:**

as it was in the beginning, is now, and will be for ever. Amen. Alleluia.

Hymn We the Lord's people *Hymnal 51*

Psalm 146 *Lauda, anima mea*

I will put my Spirit upon him, and he will proclaim justice to the Gentiles. Mt. 12:18

Epiphany God gives justice to those who are oppressed, and food to those who hunger, hallelujah.

Pentecost I will praise the Lord as long as I live, hallelujah.

1   Hallelujah!
    Praise the LORD, O my soul! *
        I will praise the LORD as long as I live;
        I will sing praises to my God while I have my being.

2   Put not your trust in rulers, nor in any child of earth, *
        for there is no help in them.

3   When they breathe their last, they return to earth, *
        and in that day their thoughts perish.

4   Blessed are they who have the God of Jacob for their help! *
        whose hope is in the LORD their God;

5   Who made heaven and earth, the seas, and all that is in them; *
        who keeps his promise for ever;

6   Who gives justice to those who are oppressed, *
        and food to those who hunger.

7   The LORD sets the prisoners free;
    the LORD opens the eyes of the blind; *
        the LORD lifts up those who are bowed down;

8   The LORD loves the righteous;
    the LORD cares for the stranger; *
        he sustains the orphan and widow,
        but frustrates the way of the wicked.

9   The LORD shall reign for ever, *
        your God, O Zion, throughout all generations.
        Hallelujah!

Glory to the Father, and to the Son, and to the Holy Spirit:
as it was in the beginning, is now, and will be for ever. Amen.

Epiphany God gives justice to those who are oppressed, and food to those who hunger, hallelujah.
Pentecost I will praise the Lord as long as I live, hallelujah.

All Psalms and Canticles are concluded with the Gloria unless otherwise indicated.
The Antiphon is repeated after the Gloria.

Psalm 147 A *Laudate Dominum*

We give thanks to the Father, who has enabled us to share
in the inheritance of the saints in the light. Col. 1:12

Epiphany God counts the number of the stars and calls them all by their names, hallelujah.
Pentecost How pleasant it is to honor God with praise, hallelujah.

1 Hallelujah!
    How good it is to sing praises to our God! *
        how pleasant it is to honor him with praise!

2 The LORD rebuilds Jerusalem; *
        he gathers the exiles of Israel.

3 He heals the brokenhearted *
        and binds up their wounds.

4 He counts the number of the stars *
        and calls them all by their names.

5 Great is our LORD and mighty in power; *
        there is no limit to his wisdom.

6 The LORD lifts up the lowly, *
        but casts the wicked to the ground.

7 Sing to the LORD with thanksgiving; *
        make music to our God upon the harp.

8 He covers the heavens with clouds *
        and prepares rain for the earth;

9 He makes grass to grow upon the mountains *
        and green plants to serve mankind.

10 He provides food for flocks and herds *
        and for the young ravens when they cry.

11 He is not impressed by the might of a horse; *
    he has no pleasure in the strength of a man;

12 But the LORD has pleasure in those who fear him, *
    in those who await his gracious favor.

Epiphany God counts the number of the stars and calls them all by their names, hallelujah.

Pentecost How pleasant it is to honor God with praise, hallelujah.

Psalm 147 B *Lauda Hierusalem*

Let the peace of Christ rule in your hearts, to which indeed you were called in the one body. Col. 3:15

Epiphany God sends forth his word and melts them; he blows with his wind, and the waters flow, hallelujah.

Pentecost Praise your God, O Zion, for he has established peace on your borders, hallelujah.

13 Worship the LORD, O Jerusalem; *
    praise your God, O Zion;

14 For he has strengthened the bars of your gates; *
    he has blessed your children within you.

15 He has established peace on your borders; *
    he satisfies you with the finest wheat.

16 He sends out his command to the earth, *
    and his word runs very swiftly.

17 He gives snow like wool; *
    he scatters hoarfrost like ashes.

18 He scatters his hail like bread crumbs; *
    who can stand against his cold?

19 He sends forth his word and melts them; *
    he blows with his wind, and the waters flow.

20 He declares his word to Jacob, *
    his statutes and his judgments to Israel.

21 He has not done so to any other nation; *
    to them he has not revealed his judgments.
    Hallelujah!

Epiphany God sends forth his word and melts them; he blows with his wind, and the waters flow, hallelujah.

Pentecost Praise your God, O Zion, for he has established peace on your borders, hallelujah.

Reading
The Proper Reading is taken from the Lectionary.

Responsory (Rm. 6:4)
Christ was raised from the dead
    — by the glory of the Father.
We too walk in newness of life
    — by the glory of the Father.
Glory to the Father and to the Son and to the Holy Spirit.
Christ was raised from the dead
    — by the glory of the Father.

The Gospel Canticle — The Song of Mary
Magnificat Antiphon *From the proper of the day*

Litany
For _____ our Presiding Bishop, and _____ (_____) our Bishop(s), and for all bishops and other ministers; for all who serve God in the Church.
Lord, have mercy.
We thank you, Lord, for all the blessings of this life. We will exalt you, O God our King; and praise your Name for ever and ever.
Christ, have mercy.
We pray for all who have died, that they may have a place in your eternal kingdom. Lord, let your loving-kindness be upon them, who put their trust in you.
Lord, have mercy.

Invitation to the Lord's Prayer Celebrating the holiness of God, we draw near to the Father and call on God's holy Name.

The Collect
The collect is taken from the Sunday, the season, if available, or from the Major or Lesser Feast or
 O God, the source of eternal light: Shed forth your unending day upon us who watch for you, that our lips may praise you, our lives may bless you, and our worship on the morrow give you glory; through Jesus Christ our Lord. Amen.

The Blessing
May Christ dwell in our hearts through faith, as we are being rooted and grounded in love. **Amen**

Sunday Week 1 Morning Prayer

Officiant: Lord, open our lips.

People: **And our mouth shall proclaim your praise.**

Officiant and People **Glory to the Father ... Alleluia.**

The Invitatory Psalm 95

God blesses us in Christ with the hope of resurrection: Come let us adore.

Hymn O splendor of God's glory bright *Hymnal 5*

Psalm 118 A *Confitemini Domino*

The God of our ancestors raised up Jesus...
God exalted him at his right hand as Leader and Savior. Acts 5: 30-31

Epiphany Peace I leave with you; my peace I give to you. Do not let your hearts be troubled or afraid, hallelujah.

Pentecost The LORD is at my side, therefore I will not fear; what can anyone do to me? Hallelujah.

1 Give thanks to the LORD, for he is good; *
>   his mercy endures for ever.

2 Let Israel now proclaim, *
>   "His mercy endures for ever."

3 Let the house of Aaron now proclaim, *
>   "His mercy endures for ever."

4 Let those who fear the LORD now proclaim, *
>   "His mercy endures for ever."

5 I called to the LORD in my distress; *
>   the LORD answered by setting me free.

6 The LORD is at my side, therefore I will not fear; *
>   what can anyone do to me?

7 The LORD is at my side to help me; *
>   I will triumph over those who hate me.

8 It is better to rely on the LORD *
>   than to put any trust in flesh.

9 It is better to rely on the LORD *
>   than to put any trust in rulers.

10 All the ungodly encompass me; *
>   in the name of the LORD I will repel them.

11   They hem me in, they hem me in on every side; *
        in the name of the LORD I will repel them.

12 They swarm about me like bees;
        they blaze like a fire of thorns; *
            in the name of the LORD I will repel them.

13 I was pressed so hard that I almost fell, *
        but the LORD came to my help.

14 The LORD is my strength and my song, *
        and he has become my salvation.

Epiphany Peace I leave with you; my peace I give to you. Do not let
your hearts be troubled or afraid, hallelujah.
Pentecost The LORD is at my side, therefore I will not fear; what can
anyone do to me? Hallelujah.

Psalm 118 B *Vox exsultationis*
Christ entered into heaven itself,
now to appear in the presence of God on our behalf. Heb. 9: 24

Epiphany God is the LORD; he has shined upon us, hallelujah.
Pentecost I shall not die, but live, and declare the works of the LORD,
hallelujah.

15 There is a sound of exultation and victory *
        in the tents of the righteous:

16"The right hand of the LORD has triumphed! *
        the right hand of the LORD is exalted!
        the right hand of the LORD has triumphed!"

17 I shall not die, but live, *
        and declare the works of the LORD.

18 The LORD has punished me sorely, *
        but he did not hand me over to death.

19 Open for me the gates of righteousness; *
        I will enter them;
        I will offer thanks to the LORD.

20 "This is the gate of the LORD; *
        he who is righteous may enter."

21 I will give thanks to you, for you answered me *
        and have become my salvation.

22 The same stone which the builders rejected *
    has become the chief cornerstone.

23 This is the LORD's doing, *
    and it is marvelous in our eyes.

24 On this day the LORD has acted; *
    we will rejoice and be glad in it.

25 Hosannah, LORD, hosannah! *
    LORD, send us now success.

26 Blessed is he who comes in the name of the Lord; *
    we bless you from the house of the LORD.

27 God is the LORD; he has shined upon us; *
    form a procession with branches up to the horns of the altar.

28 "You are my God, and I will thank you; *
    you are my God, and I will exalt you."

29 Give thanks to the LORD, for he is good; *
    his mercy endures for ever.

Epiphany God is the LORD; he has shined upon us, hallelujah.
Pentecost I shall not die, but live, and declare the works of the LORD,
hallelujah.

Psalm 100 *Jubilate Deo*

You are a chosen race, a royal priesthood, a holy nation, God's own people. 1 Pt. 2:9
Epiphany We are God's people and the sheep of the Lord's pasture,
hallelujah.
Pentecost Come before God's presence with a song, hallelujah.

1 Be joyful in the LORD, all you lands; *
    serve the LORD with gladness
    and come before his presence with a song.

2 Know this: The LORD himself is God; *
    he himself has made us, and we are his;
    we are his people and the sheep of his pasture.

3 Enter his gates with thanksgiving;
    go into his courts with praise; *
    give thanks to him and call upon his Name.

4 For the LORD is good;
    his mercy is everlasting; *
    and his faithfulness endures from age to age.

Epiphany We are God's people and the sheep of the Lord's pasture, hallelujah.

Pentecost Come before God's presence with a song, hallelujah.

Reading One

Responsory One (Lk. 18:38)
Christ, Son of the Living God
> **– have mercy on us.**

You sit at the right hand of the Father
> **– have mercy on us.**

Glory to the Father and to the Son and to the Holy Spirit.
Christ, Son of the Living God
> **– have mercy on us.**

The First Canticle – You are God *Te Deum laudamus*

You are God: we praise you;
You are the Lord: we acclaim you;
You are the eternal Father:
All creation worships you.
To you all angels, all the powers of heaven,
Cherubim and Seraphim, sing in endless praise:
  Holy, holy, holy Lord, God of power and might,
  heaven and earth are full of your glory.
The glorious company of apostles praise you.
The noble fellowship of prophets praise you.
The white-robed army of martyrs praise you.
Throughout the world the holy Church acclaims you;
  Father, of majesty unbounded,
  your true and only Son, worthy of all worship,
  and the Holy Spirit, advocate and guide.
You, Christ, are the king of glory,
the eternal Son of the Father.
When you became man to set us free
you did not shun the Virgin's womb.
You overcame the sting of death
and opened the kingdom of heaven to all believers.
You are seated at God's right hand in glory.
We believe that you will come and be our judge.
  Come then, Lord, and help your people,
  bought with the price of your own blood,
  and bring us with your saints
  to glory everlasting.

The Gloria is not said with the Te Deum.

Reading Two

Responsory Two (Ps. 86: 12; Ps. 9:1)
I will thank you, O God
> **– I will call upon your name.**
I will tell of all your marvelous works
> **– I will call upon your name.**
Glory to the Father and to the Son and to the Holy Spirit
I will thank you, O God
> **– I will call upon your name.**

The Gospel Canticle – The Song of Zechariah
Benedictus Antiphon *From the proper of the day*

Litany
Show us your mercy, O Lord; and grant us your salvation.
Lord, have mercy.
Clothe your ministers with righteousness; let your people sing with joy.
Christ, have mercy.
Give peace, O Lord, in all the world; for only in you can we live in safety.
Lord, have mercy.

Invitation to the Lord's Prayer As we celebrate the Lord's Resurrection, let us pray to the Father with joyful hearts.

The Collect *From the Proper of the day or*
 O God, you make us glad with the weekly remembrance of the glorious resurrection of your Son our Lord: Give us this day such blessing through our worship of you, that the week to come may be spent in your favor; through Jesus Christ our Lord. Amen.

The Blessing
May the God of hope fill you with all joy and peace in believing, so that you may abound in hope by the power of the Holy Spirit. **Amen**

Sunday Week 1 Noonday Prayer
Officiant: O God, make speed to save us.
People: **O Lord, make haste to help us.**
Officiant and People **Glory to the Father... Alleluia.**

Hymn The golden sun lights up the sky *Hymnal 12*

Psalm 1 *Beatus vir qui non abiit*

This is the person who comes to me, hears my words, and acts on them. Lk. 6:47

Epiphany The blessed of the Lord are like trees planted by streams of water, everything they do shall prosper.

Pentecost Blessed are they whose delight is in the law of the Lord.

1 Blessed are they who have not walked
   in the counsel of the wicked, *
       nor lingered in the way of sinners,
       nor sat in the seats of the scornful!

2 Their delight is in the law of the LORD, *
       and they meditate on his law day and night.

3 They are like trees planted by streams of water,
   bearing fruit in due season, with leaves that do not wither; *
       everything they do shall prosper.

4 It is not so with the wicked; *
       they are like chaff which the wind blows away.

5 Therefore the wicked shall not stand upright
   when judgment comes, *
       nor the sinner in the council of the righteous.

6 For the LORD knows the way of the righteous, *
       but the way of the wicked is doomed.

Psalm 2 *Quare fremuerunt gentes?*

God put his power to work in Christ when he raised him from the dead and seated him at his right hand. Col. 1: 20

1 Why are the nations in an uproar? *
       Why do the peoples mutter empty threats?

2 Why do the kings of the earth rise up in revolt,
   and the princes plot together, *
       against the LORD and against his Anointed?

3 "Let us break their yoke," they say; *
       "let us cast off their bonds from us."

4 He whose throne is in heaven is laughing; *
       the Lord has them in derision.

5 Then he speaks to them in his wrath, *
       and his rage fills them with terror.

6 "I myself have set my king *
       upon my holy hill of Zion."

7 Let me announce the decree of the LORD: *
    he said to me, "You are my Son;
    this day have I begotten you.

8 Ask of me, and I will give you
    the nations for your inheritance *
    and the ends of the earth for your possession.

9 You shall crush them with an iron rod *
    and shatter them like a piece of pottery."

10 And now, you kings, be wise; *
    be warned, you rulers of the earth.

11 Submit to the LORD with fear, *
    and with trembling bow before him;

12 Lest he be angry and you perish; *
    for his wrath is quickly kindled.

13 Blessed are they all *
    who take refuge in him!

Psalm 20 *Exaudiat te Dominus*

Christ is the head of the body, the church; he is the beginning, the firstborn from the dead. Col. 1: 18

1 May the LORD answer you in the day of trouble, *
    the Name of the God of Jacob defend you;

2 Send you help from his holy place *
    and strengthen you out of Zion;

3 Remember all your offerings *
    and accept your burnt sacrifice;

4 Grant you your heart's desire *
    and prosper all your plans.

5 We will shout for joy at your victory
    and triumph in the Name of our God; *
    may the LORD grant all your requests.

6 Now I know that the LORD gives victory to his anointed; *
    he will answer him out of his holy heaven,
    with the victorious strength of his right hand.

7 Some put their trust in chariots and some in horses, *
    but we will call upon the Name of the LORD our God.

8 They collapse and fall down, *
    but we will arise and stand upright.

9   O LORD, give victory to the king *
  and answer us when we call.

Epiphany The blessed of the Lord are like trees planted by streams of water, everything they do shall prosper.
Pentecost Blessed are they whose delight is in the law of the Lord.

Reading Ephesians 3: 16-19
I pray that, according to the riches of God's glory, he may grant that you may be strengthened in your inner being with power through his Spirit, and that Christ may dwell in your hearts through faith, as you are being rooted and grounded in love. I pray that you may have the power to comprehend, with all the saints, what is the breadth and length and height and depth, and to know the love of Christ that surpasses knowledge, so that you may be filled with all the fullness of God.

Verse and Response
May the Lord direct your hearts to the love of God.
And to the steadfastness of Christ.

The Short Litany and the Lord's Prayer

Collect Almighty God, the Father of our Lord Jesus Christ, from whom every family in heaven and earth is named; grant us to be strengthened with might by your Holy Spirit, that Christ, dwelling in our hearts by faith; we may be filled with all the fullness of God. Amen.

Let us bless the Lord.
Thanks be to God.

Sunday Week 1 Evening Prayer II
Officiant: O God, make speed to save us.
People: **O Lord, make haste to help us.**
Officiant and People **Glory to the Father ... Alleluia.**

Hymn This is the day the Lord hath made *Hymnal 50*

Psalm 110 *Dixit Dominus*
Jesus has entered the inner sanctuary, having become a high priest forever according to the order of Melchizedek. Heb. 6:20

Epiphany Dominion belongs to the Lord, and he rules over the nations, hallelujah.
Pentecost Christ the Lord is a priest for ever after the order of Melchizedek, hallelujah.

1   The LORD said to my Lord, "Sit at my right hand, *
  until I make your enemies your footstool."

2 The LORD will send the scepter of your power out of Zion, *
     saying, "Rule over your enemies round about you.

3 Princely state has been yours from the day of your birth; *
     in the beauty of holiness have I begotten you,
     like dew from the womb of the morning."

4 The LORD has sworn and he will not recant: *
     "You are a priest for ever after the order of Melchizedek."

5 The Lord who is at your right hand
   will smite kings in the day of his wrath; *
     he will rule over the nations.

6 He will heap high the corpses; *
     he will smash heads over the wide earth.

7 He will drink from the brook beside the road; *
     therefore he will lift high his head.

Epiphany Dominion belongs to the Lord, and he rules over the
nations, hallelujah.
Pentecost Christ the Lord is a priest for ever after the order of
Melchizedek, hallelujah.

Psalm 111 *Confitebor tibi*
Christ entered once for all into the Holy Place, with his own blood,
thus obtaining eternal redemption. Heb. 9:12

Epiphany Give thanks to the Father, who has enabled you to share in
the inheritance of the saints in the light, hallelujah.
Pentecost The fear of the LORD is the beginning of wisdom; those who
act accordingly have a good understanding, hallelujah.

1 Hallelujah!
   I will give thanks to the LORD with my whole heart, *
     in the assembly of the upright, in the congregation.

2 Great are the deeds of the LORD! *
     they are studied by all who delight in them.

3 His work is full of majesty and splendor, *
     and his righteousness endures for ever.

4 He makes his marvelous works to be remembered; *
     the LORD is gracious and full of compassion.

5 He gives food to those who fear him; *
     he is ever mindful of his covenant.

6 He has shown his people the power of his works *
>   in giving them the lands of the nations.

7 The works of his hands are faithfulness and justice; *
>   all his commandments are sure.

8 They stand fast for ever and ever, *
>   because they are done in truth and equity.

9 He sent redemption to his people;
>   he commanded his covenant for ever; *
>   holy and awesome is his Name.

10 The fear of the LORD is the beginning of wisdom; *
>   those who act accordingly have a good understanding;
>   his praise endures for ever.

Epiphany Give thanks to the Father, who has enabled you to share in the inheritance of the saints in the light, hallelujah.
Pentecost The fear of the LORD is the beginning of wisdom; those who act accordingly have a good understanding, hallelujah.

Psalm 112 *Beatus vir*
The righteous will shine like the sun in the kingdom of their Father. Mt. 13: 43

Epiphany The light shines in the darkness, and the darkness did not overcome it, hallelujah.
Pentecost The righteous are generous in lending and they manage their affairs with justice, hallelujah.

1 Hallelujah!
>   Blessed are they who fear the Lord *
>   and have great delight in his commandments!

2 Their descendants will be mighty in the land; *
>   the generation of the upright will be blessed.

3 Wealth and riches will be in their house, *
>   and their righteousness will last for ever.

4 Light shines in the darkness for the upright; *
>   the righteous are merciful and full of compassion.

5 It is good for them to be generous in lending *
>   and to manage their affairs with justice.

6 For they will never be shaken; *
>   the righteous will be kept in everlasting remembrance.

7 They will not be afraid of any evil rumors; *
     their heart is right;
     they put their trust in the Lord.

8 Their heart is established and will not shrink, *
     until they see their desire upon their enemies.

9 They have given freely to the poor, *
     and their righteousness stands fast for ever;
     they will hold up their head with honor.

10 The wicked will see it and be angry;
     they will gnash their teeth and pine away; *
     the desires of the wicked will perish.

Epiphany The light shines in the darkness, and the darkness did not overcome it, hallelujah.
Pentecost The righteous are generous in lending and they manage their affairs with justice, hallelujah.

Reading

Responsory (Ps. 104:24)
How manifold are your works, O Lord
       – in wisdom you have made them all.
The earth is full of your creatures
       – in wisdom you have made them all.
Glory to the Father and to the Son and to the Holy Spirit.
How manifold are your works, O Lord
       – in wisdom you have made them all.

The Gospel Canticle – The Song of Mary
Magnificat Antiphon *From the proper of the day*

Litany
That this evening may be holy, good, and peaceful.
Lord, have mercy.
That your holy angels may lead us in paths of peace and goodwill,
Christ, have mercy.
That we may depart this life in your faith and fear, and not be condemned before the great judgment seat of Christ.
Lord, have mercy.

Invitation to the Lord's Prayer Confident of the abiding presence of the Risen Christ, let us pray in the Holy Spirit to the Father.

Collect *From the proper of the day or*

Lord God, whose Son our Savior Jesus Christ triumphed over the powers of death and prepared for us our place in the new Jerusalem: Grant that we, who have this day given thanks for his resurrection, may praise you in that City of which he is the light, and where he lives and reigns for ever and ever. Amen.

The Blessing

May we progress in this way of life and in faith that we may run on the path of God's commandments, our hearts overflowing with the inexpressible delight of love. **Amen**

Monday Week 1 Morning Prayer

Officiant: Lord, open our lips.

People: **And our mouth shall proclaim your praise.**

Officiant and People **Glory to the Father... Alleluia.**

The Invitatory Psalm 29

God, our Creator, is worthy of worship: Come let us adore.

Hymn Father we praise thee *Hymnal 1*

Psalm 5 *Verba mea auribus*

In the morning, while it was still very dark, he got up
and went out to a deserted place, and there he prayed. Mk. 1:35

Epiphany Early in the morning I make my appeal and watch for you.
Pentecost I make my morning prayer to you; for you, O Lord, will hear my voice.

1　Give ear to my words, O LORD; *
　　consider my meditation.

2　Hearken to my cry for help, my King and my God, *
　　for I make my prayer to you.

3　In the morning, LORD, you hear my voice; *
　　early in the morning I make my appeal and watch for you.

4　For you are not a God who takes pleasure in wickedness, *
　　and evil cannot dwell with you.

5　Braggarts cannot stand in your sight; *
　　you hate all those who work wickedness.

6　You destroy those who speak lies; *
　　the bloodthirsty and deceitful, O LORD, you abhor.

7 But as for me, through the greatness of your mercy
I will go into your house; *
    I will bow down toward your holy temple in awe of you.

8 Lead me, O LORD, in your righteousness,
because of those who lie in wait for me; *
    make your way straight before me.

9 For there is no truth in their mouth; *
    there is destruction in their heart;

10 Their throat is an open grave; *
    they flatter with their tongue.

11 Declare them guilty, O God; *
    let them fall, because of their schemes.

12 Because of their many transgressions cast them out, *
    for they have rebelled against you.

13 But all who take refuge in you will be glad; *
    they will sing out their joy for ever.

14 You will shelter them, *
    so that those who love your Name may exult in you.

15 For you, O LORD, will bless the righteous; *
    you will defend them with your favor as with a shield.

Epiphany Early in the morning I make my appeal and watch for you.
Pentecost I make my morning prayer to you; for you, O Lord, will hear
my voice.

Psalm 36 *Dixit injustus*
In him was life, and the life was the light of all people. Jn. 1:4

Epiphany In your light, O God, we see light.
Pentecost How priceless is your love, O God! Your people take refuge
under the shadow of your wings.

1 There is a voice of rebellion deep in the heart of the wicked; *
    there is no fear of God before his eyes.

2 He flatters himself in his own eyes *
    that his hateful sin will not be found out.

3 The words of his mouth are wicked and deceitful; *
    he has left off acting wisely and doing good.

4 He thinks up wickedness upon his bed
   and has set himself in no good way; *
      he does not abhor that which is evil.

5 Your love, O LORD, reaches to the heavens, *
      and your faithfulness to the clouds.

6 Your righteousness is like the strong mountains,
   your justice like the great deep; *
      you save both man and beast, O LORD.

7 How priceless is your love, O God! *
      your people take refuge
      under the shadow of your wings.

8 They feast upon the abundance of your house; *
      you give them drink from the river of your delights.

9 For with you is the well of life, *
      and in your light we see light.

10 Continue your loving-kindness to those who know you, *
      and your favor to those who are true of heart.

11 Let not the foot of the proud come near me, *
      nor the hand of the wicked push me aside.

12 See how they are fallen, those who work wickedness! *
      they are cast down and shall not be able to rise.

Epiphany In your light, O God, we see light.
Pentecost How priceless is your love, O God! Your people take refuge under the shadow of your wings.

Psalm 148 *Laudate Dominum*

At Jesus' name every knee should bend, in heaven and on earth and under the earth. Phil 2:10
Epiphany Let Kings of the earth and all peoples praise the Name of the LORD.
Pentecost Praise the Lord from the heavens, praise the Lord from the earth.

1 Hallelujah!
   Praise the LORD from the heavens; *
      praise him in the heights.

2 Praise him, all you angels of his; *
      praise him, all his host.

3 Praise him, sun and moon; *
   praise him, all you shining stars.

4 Praise him, heaven of heavens, *
   and you waters above the heavens.

5 Let them praise the Name of the LORD; *
   for he commanded, and they were created.

6 He made them stand fast for ever and ever; *
   he gave them a law which shall not pass away.

7 Praise the LORD from the earth, *
   you sea-monsters and all deeps;

8 Fire and hail, snow and fog, *
   tempestuous wind, doing his will;

9 Mountains and all hills, *
   fruit trees and all cedars;

10 Wild beasts and all cattle, *
   creeping things and wingèd birds;

11 Kings of the earth and all peoples, *
   princes and all rulers of the world;

12 Young men and maidens, *
   old and young together.

13 Let them praise the Name of the LORD, *
   for his Name only is exalted,
   his splendor is over earth and heaven.

14 He has raised up strength for his people
   and praise for all his loyal servants, *
   the children of Israel, a people who are near him.
   Hallelujah!

Epiphany Let Kings of the earth and all peoples praise the Name of the LORD.

Pentecost Praise the Lord from the heavens, praise the Lord from the earth.

Reading One

Responsory One (Ps. 41:13; Ps. 136:4)
Blessed be the Lord
   – from age to age.

The Lord does great wonders
> **– from age to age.**

Glory to the Father and to the Son and to the Holy Spirit.

Blessed be the Lord
> **– from age to age.**

The First Canticle – A Song of Creation *Benedicite omnia opera Domini*
(Song of the Three Young Men, 35-65)

One or more sections of this Canticle may be used. Whatever the selection, it begins with the Invocation and concludes with the Doxology. The Doxology replaces the Gloria for the Canticle

Epiphany Sun and moon and stars of the sky, glorify the Lord.
Pentecost Worthy are you, O Lord our God, to receive glory and honor from every creature.

Invocation
Glorify the Lord, all you works of the Lord, *
  praise him and highly exalt him for ever.
In the firmament of his power, glorify the Lord, *
  praise him and highly exalt him for ever.

I   The Cosmic Order
Glorify the Lord, you angels and all powers of the Lord, *
  O heavens and all waters above the heavens.
Sun and moon and stars of the sky, glorify the Lord, *
  praise him and highly exalt him for ever.

Glorify the Lord, every shower of rain and fall of dew, *
  all winds and fire and heat.
Winter and summer, glorify the Lord, *
 praise him and highly exalt him for ever.

Glorify the Lord, O chill and cold, *
  drops of dew and flakes of snow.
Frost and cold, ice and sleet, glorify the Lord, *
  praise him and highly exalt him for ever.

Glorify the Lord, O nights and days, *
  O shining light and enfolding dark.
Storm clouds and thunderbolts, glorify the Lord, *
  praise him and highly exalt him for ever.

II   The Earth and its Creatures
Let the earth glorify the Lord, *
  praise him and highly exalt him for ever.

Glorify the Lord, O mountains and hills,
and all that grows upon the earth, *
  praise him and highly exalt him for ever.

Glorify the Lord, O springs of water, seas, and streams, *
  O whales and all that move in the waters.
All birds of the air, glorify the Lord, *
  praise him and highly exalt him for ever.

Glorify the Lord, O beasts of the wild, *
  and all you flocks and herds.
O men and women everywhere, glorify the Lord, *
  praise him and highly exalt him for ever.

III The People of God
Let the people of God glorify the Lord, *
  praise him and highly exalt him for ever.
Glorify the Lord, O priests and servants of the Lord, *
  praise him and highly exalt him for ever.

Glorify the Lord, O spirits and souls of the righteous, *
  praise him and highly exalt him for ever.
You that are holy and humble of heart, glorify the Lord, *
  praise him and highly exalt him for ever.

Doxology
Let us glorify the Lord: Father, Son, and Holy Spirit; *
  praise him and highly exalt him for ever.
In the firmament of his power, glorify the Lord, *
  praise him and highly exalt him for ever.

Epiphany Sun and moon and stars of the sky, glorify the Lord.
Pentecost Worthy are you, O Lord our God, to receive glory and
honor from every creature.

Reading Two

Responsory Two (Ps. 33:1; Ps. 96:1)
Rejoice in the Lord, you righteous
      – it is good for the just to sing praises.
Sing to the Lord a new song
      – it is good for the just to sing praises.
Glory to the Father and to the Son and to the Holy Spirit.
Rejoice in the Lord, you righteous
      – it is good for the just to sing praises.

The Gospel Canticle – The Song of Zechariah

Epiphany In the tender compassion of our God the dawn from on high shall break upon us.

Pentecost God has raised up for us a mighty savior, born of the house of his servant David.

Litany

For the peace from above, for the loving-kindness of God, and for the salvation of our souls, let us pray to the Lord.

Lord, have mercy.

For the peace of the world, for the welfare of the Holy Church of God, and for the unity of all peoples, let us pray to the Lord.

Christ have mercy.

For the aged and infirm, for the widowed and orphans, and for the sick and the suffering, let us pray to the Lord.

Lord, have mercy.

Invitation to the Lord's Prayer Since we share in God's nature through Baptism, let us raise our hearts to our Father.

Collect *From the proper of the day or*

O God, the King eternal, whose light divides the day from the night and turns the shadow of death into the morning: Drive far from us all wrong desires, incline our hearts to keep your law, and guide our feet into the way of peace; that, having done your will with cheerfulness while it was day, we may, when night comes, rejoice to give you thanks; through Jesus Christ our Lord. Amen.

The Blessing

May we have unity of spirit, sympathy, love for one another, a tender heart, and a humble mind. **Amen**

Monday Week 1 Noonday Prayer

Officiant: O God, make speed to save us.

People: **O Lord, make haste to help us.**

Officiant and People **Glory to the Father... Alleluia.**

Hymn As now the sun shines down at noon *Hymnal 18 (Verse for Monday)*

Psalm 119 Aleph *Beati immaculate*

Blessed are those who hear the word of God and obey it. Lk. 11:28

Epiphany You will seek the Lord your God, and you will find him if you search after him with all your heart and soul.

Pentecost Blessed are they who walk in the law of the Lord.

1 Blessed are they whose way is blameless, *
    who walk in the law of the LORD!

2 Blessed are they who observe his decrees *
    and seek him with all their hearts!

3 Who never do any wrong, *
    but always walk in his ways.

4 You laid down your commandments, *
    that we should fully keep them.

5 Oh, that my ways were made so direct *
    that I might keep your statutes!

6 Then I should not be put to shame, *
    when I regard all your commandments.

7 I will thank you with an unfeigned heart, *
    when I have learned your righteous judgments.

8 I will keep your statutes; *
    do not utterly forsake me.

Psalm 40 A *Expectans, expectavi*
I have come to call not the righteous but sinners. Mt. 9:13

1 I waited patiently upon the LORD; *
    he stooped to me and heard my cry.

2 He lifted me out of the desolate pit, out of the mire and clay; *
    he set my feet upon a high cliff and made my footing sure.

3 He put a new song in my mouth,
    a song of praise to our God; *
        many shall see, and stand in awe,
        and put their trust in the LORD.

4 Blessed are they who trust in the LORD! *
    they do not resort to evil spirits or turn to false gods.

5 Great things are they that you have done, O LORD my God!
    how great your wonders and your plans for us! *
        there is none who can be compared with you.

6 Oh, that I could make them known and tell them! *
    but they are more than I can count.

7 In sacrifice and offering you take no pleasure *
    (you have given me ears to hear you);

8 Burnt-offering and sin-offering you have not required, *
   and so I said, "Behold, I come.

9 In the roll of the book it is written concerning me: *
   'I love to do your will, O my God;
   your law is deep in my heart.'"

10 I proclaimed righteousness in the great congregation; *
   behold, I did not restrain my lips;
   and that, O LORD, you know.

11 Your righteousness have I not hidden in my heart;
   I have spoken of your faithfulness and your deliverance; *
   I have not concealed your love and faithfulness
   from the great congregation.

12 You are the LORD;
   do not withhold your compassion from me; *
   let your love and your faithfulness keep me safe for ever,

13 For innumerable troubles have crowded upon me;
   my sins have overtaken me, and I cannot see; *
   they are more in number than the hairs of my head,
   and my heart fails me.

Psalm 40 B *Complaceat tibi*
*Ask, and it will be given you; search, and you will find;
knock, and the door will be opened for you. Mt. 7:7*

14 Be pleased, O LORD, to deliver me; *
   O LORD, make haste to help me.

15 Let them be ashamed and altogether dismayed
   who seek after my life to destroy it; *
   let them draw back and be disgraced
   who take pleasure in my misfortune.

16 Let those who say "Aha!" and gloat over me be confounded, *
   because they are ashamed.

17 Let all who seek you rejoice in you and be glad; *
   let those who love your salvation continually say,
   "Great is the LORD!"

18 Though I am poor and afflicted, *
   the Lord will have regard for me.

19 You are my helper and my deliverer; *
   do not tarry, O my God.

Epiphany You will seek the Lord your God, and you will find him if you search after him with all your heart and soul.
Pentecost Blessed are they who walk in the law of the Lord.

Reading Matthew 3: 16-17
When Jesus had been baptized, just as he came up from the water, suddenly the heavens were opened to him and he saw the Spirit of God descending like a dove and alighting on him. And a voice from heaven said, "This is my Son, the Beloved, with whom I am well pleased."

Verse and Response
All who received him, who believed in his name.
He gave power to become children of God.

The Short Litany and the Lord's Prayer

The Collect
Heavenly Father, we thank you that by water and the Holy Spirit you have bestowed on us your servants the forgiveness of sin, and have raised us to the new life of grace. Sustain us, O Lord, in your Holy Spirit. Give us inquiring minds and discerning hearts, the courage to will and to persevere, a spirit to know and to love you, and the gift of joy and wonder in all your works. Amen.

Let us bless the Lord.
Thanks be to God.

Monday Week 1 Evening Prayer
Officiant: O God, make speed to save us.
People: **O Lord, make haste to help us.**
Officiant and People **Glory to the Father... Alleluia.**

Hymn O gracious Light *Hymnal 26*

Psalm 139 A *Domine, probasti*
The peace of God, which surpasses all understanding,
will guard your hearts and your minds in Christ Jesus. Phil 4:7

Epiphany Where can I go then from your Spirit? where can I flee from your presence?
Pentecost Darkness is not dark to you; the night is as bright as the day; darkness and light to you are both alike.

1 LORD, you have searched me out and known me; *
    you know my sitting down and my rising up;
    you discern my thoughts from afar.

2 You trace my journeys and my resting-places *
    and are acquainted with all my ways.

3 Indeed, there is not a word on my lips, *
    but you, O LORD, know it altogether.

4 You press upon me behind and before *
    and lay your hand upon me.

5 Such knowledge is too wonderful for me; *
    it is so high that I cannot attain to it.

6 Where can I go then from your Spirit? *
    where can I flee from your presence?

7 If I climb up to heaven, you are there; *
    if I make the grave my bed, you are there also.

8 If I take the wings of the morning *
    and dwell in the uttermost parts of the sea,

9 Even there your hand will lead me *
    and your right hand hold me fast.

10 If I say, "Surely the darkness will cover me, *
    and the light around me turn to night,"

11 Darkness is not dark to you;
    the night is as bright as the day; *
    darkness and light to you are both alike.

Epiphany Where can I go then from your Spirit? where can I flee from your presence?

Pentecost Darkness is not dark to you; the night is as bright as the day; darkness and light to you are both alike.

Psalm 139 B *Quia tu*

If anyone is in Christ, there is a new creation: everything old has passed away;
see, everything has become new. 2 Cor. 5:17

Epiphany Your eyes beheld my limbs, yet unfinished in the womb; all of them were written in your book.

Pentecost Search me out, O God, and know my heart; and lead me in the way that is everlasting.

12 For you yourself created my inmost parts; *
    you knit me together in my mother's womb.

13 I will thank you because I am marvelously made; *
    your works are wonderful, and I know it well.

14 My body was not hidden from you, *
      while I was being made in secret
      and woven in the depths of the earth.

15 Your eyes beheld my limbs, yet unfinished in the womb;
    all of them were written in your book; *
      they were fashioned day by day,
      when as yet there was none of them.

16 How deep I find your thoughts, O God! *
      how great is the sum of them!

17 If I were to count them,
    they would be more in number than the sand; *
      to count them all, my life span
      would need to be like yours.

18 Oh, that you would slay the wicked, O God! *
      You that thirst for blood, depart from me.

19 They speak despitefully against you; *
      your enemies take your Name in vain.

20 Do I not hate those, O LORD, who hate you? *
      and do I not loathe those who rise up against you?

21 I hate them with a perfect hatred; *
      they have become my own enemies.

22 Search me out, O God, and know my heart; *
      try me and know my restless thoughts.

23 Look well whether there be any wickedness in me *
      and lead me in the way that is everlasting.

Epiphany Your eyes beheld my limbs, yet unfinished in the womb; all
of them were written in your book.
Pentecost Search me out, O God, and know my heart; and lead me in
the way that is everlasting.

Psalm 90 *Domine, refugium*
In Christ are hidden all the treasures of wisdom and knowledge. Col. 2:3
Epiphany Satisfy us by your loving-kindness in the morning; so shall
we rejoice and be glad all the days of our life.
Pentecost Teach us, O Lord, to number our days, that we may apply
our hearts to wisdom.

1 Lord, you have been our refuge *
      from one generation to another.

2 Before the mountains were brought forth,
  or the land and the earth were born, *
    from age to age you are God.

3 You turn us back to the dust and say, *
  "Go back, O child of earth."

4 For a thousand years in your sight
  are like yesterday when it is past *
    and like a watch in the night.

5 You sweep us away like a dream; *
  we fade away suddenly like the grass.

6 In the morning it is green and flourishes; *
  in the evening it is dried up and withered.

7 For we consume away in your displeasure; *
  we are afraid because of your wrathful indignation.

8 Our iniquities you have set before you, *
  and our secret sins in the light of your countenance.

9 When you are angry, all our days are gone; *
  we bring our years to an end like a sigh.

10 The span of our life is seventy years,
  perhaps in strength even eighty; *
    yet the sum of them is but labor and sorrow,
    for they pass away quickly and we are gone.

11 Who regards the power of your wrath? *
  who rightly fears your indignation?

12 So teach us to number our days *
  that we may apply our hearts to wisdom.

13 Return, O LORD; how long will you tarry? *
  be gracious to your servants.

14 Satisfy us by your loving-kindness in the morning; *
  so shall we rejoice and be glad all the days of our life.

15 Make us glad by the measure of the days that you afflicted us *
  and the years in which we suffered adversity.

16 Show your servants your works *
  and your splendor to their children.

17 May the graciousness of the LORD our God be upon us; *
    prosper the work of our hands;
    prosper our handiwork.

Epiphany Satisfy us by your loving-kindness in the morning; so shall
we rejoice and be glad all the days of our life.
Pentecost Teach us, O Lord, to number our days, that we may apply
our hearts to wisdom.

Reading

Responsory (Ps. 41:4; Ps. 57:1)
Heal my soul
    – for I have sinned against you.
Lord, be merciful to me
    – for I have sinned against you.
Glory to the Father and to the Son and to the Holy Spirit.
Heal my soul
    – for I have sinned against you.

The Gospel Canticle – The Song of Mary
Epiphany Those who do what is true come to the light, so that it may
be clearly seen that their deeds have been done in God.
Pentecost God has looked with favor on me, a lowly servant. My spirit
rejoices in God, my Savior.

Litany
For those who travel on land, on water, or in the air [or through outer
space], let us pray to the Lord.
Lord, have mercy.
For the poor and the oppressed, for the unemployed and the destitute,
for prisoners and captives, and for all who remember and care for them,
let us pray to the Lord.
Christ, have mercy.
For all who have died in the hope of the resurrection, and for all the
departed, let us pray to the Lord.
Lord, have mercy.

Invitation to the Lord's Prayer Bringing our prayer and praise to a
conclusion let us pray in the words of Christ.

Collect *From the proper of the day or*
Most holy God, the source of all good desires, all right judgements, and
all just works: Give to us, your servants, that peace which the world
cannot give, so that our minds may be fixed on the doing of your will,

and that we, being delivered from the fear of all enemies, may live in peace and quietness; through the mercies of Christ Jesus our Savior. Amen.

The Blessing
May we bear one another's burdens, and so fulfill the law of Christ.
Amen

Tuesday Week 1 Morning Prayer
Officiant: Lord, open our lips.
People: **And our mouth shall proclaim your praise.**
Officiant and People **Glory to the Father... Alleluia.**

The Invitatory Psalm 8
The Lord's Name is exalted in all the world: Come let us adore.

Hymn Awake my soul *Hymnal 11*

Psalm 57 *Miserere mei, Deus*
Do not fear those who kill the body but cannot kill the soul. Mt. 10:28
Epiphany I will confess you among the peoples, O Lord; I will sing praise to you among the nations.
Pentecost Awake, lute and harp, I myself will waken the dawn.

1 Be merciful to me, O God, be merciful,
    for I have taken refuge in you; *
        in the shadow of your wings will I take refuge
        until this time of trouble has gone by.

2 I will call upon the Most High God, *
        the God who maintains my cause.

3 He will send from heaven and save me;
    he will confound those who trample upon me; *
        God will send forth his love and his faithfulness.

4 I lie in the midst of lions that devour the people; *
        their teeth are spears and arrows,
        their tongue a sharp sword.

5 They have laid a net for my feet,
    and I am bowed low; *
        they have dug a pit before me,
        but have fallen into it themselves.

6 Exalt yourself above the heavens, O God, *
        and your glory over all the earth.

7　My heart is firmly fixed, O God, my heart is fixed; *
　　　I will sing and make melody.

8　Wake up, my spirit;
　　awake, lute and harp; *
　　　I myself will waken the dawn.

9　I will confess you among the peoples, O LORD; *
　　　I will sing praise to you among the nations.

10 For your loving-kindness is greater than the heavens, *
　　　and your faithfulness reaches to the clouds.

11 Exalt yourself above the heavens, O God, *
　　　and your glory over all the earth.

Epiphany I will confess you among the peoples, O LORD; I will sing
praise to you among the nations.
Pentecost Awake, lute and harp, I myself will waken the dawn.

Psalm 3 *Domine, quid multiplicati*

You will be betrayed even by parents and brothers, by relatives and friends;
and they will put some of you to death. Lk. 21:16

Epiphany Rise up, O LORD; set me free, O my God.
Pentecost You, O Lord, are a shield about me; you are the one who
lifts up my head.

1　LORD, how many adversaries I have! *
　　　how many there are who rise up against me!

2　How many there are who say of me, *
　　　"There is no help for him in his God."

3　But you, O LORD, are a shield about me; *
　　　you are my glory, the one who lifts up my head.

4　I call aloud upon the LORD, *
　　　and he answers me from his holy hill;

5　I lie down and go to sleep; *
　　　I wake again, because the LORD sustains me.

6　I do not fear the multitudes of people *
　　　who set themselves against me all around.

7　Rise up, O LORD; set me free, O my God; *
　　　surely, you will strike all my enemies across the face,
　　　you will break the teeth of the wicked.

8 Deliverance belongs to the LORD. *
  Your blessing be upon your people!

Epiphany Rise up, O LORD; set me free, O my God.
Pentecost You, O Lord, are a shield about me; you are the one who lifts up my head.

Psalm 98 *Cantate Domino*
*The throne of God and of the Lamb will be in it, and his servants will worship him;
they will see his face. Rev. 22:3-4*

Epiphany In righteousness shall God judge the world and the peoples with equity.
Pentecost Shout with joy before the King, the Lord.

1 Sing to the LORD a new song, *
  for he has done marvelous things.

2 With his right hand and his holy arm *
  has he won for himself the victory.

3 The LORD has made known his victory; *
  his righteousness has he openly shown
  in the sight of the nations.

4 He remembers his mercy and faithfulness
  to the house of Israel, *
  and all the ends of the earth have seen
  the victory of our God.

5 Shout with joy to the LORD, all you lands; *
  lift up your voice, rejoice, and sing.

6 Sing to the LORD with the harp, *
  with the harp and the voice of song.

7 With trumpets and the sound of the horn *
  shout with joy before the King, the LORD.

8 Let the sea make a noise and all that is in it, *
  the lands and those who dwell therein.

9 Let the rivers clap their hands, *
  and let the hills ring out with joy before the LORD,
  when he comes to judge the earth.

10 In righteousness shall he judge the world *
  and the peoples with equity.

Epiphany In righteousness shall God judge the world and the peoples with equity.

Pentecost Shout with joy before the King, the Lord.

Reading One

Responsory One (Ps. 18:1-2)
The Lord is my Rock
> **– I will trust in God.**

The Lord is my stronghold and my haven
> **– I will trust in God.**

Glory to the Father and to the Son and to the Holy Spirit.
The Lord is my Rock
> **– I will trust in God.**

The First Canticle – The Third Song of Isaiah *Surge illuminare*
(Isaiah 60:1-3, 11a, 14c, 18-19)

Epiphany The glory of the Lord has dawned upon you.

Pentecost Nations will stream to your light, and kings to the brightness of your dawning.

Arise, shine, for your light has come, *
> and the glory of the Lord has dawned upon you.

For behold, darkness covers the land; *
> deep gloom enshrouds the peoples.

But over you the Lord will rise, *
> and his glory will appear upon you.

Nations will stream to your light, *
> and kings to the brightness of your dawning.

Your gates will always be open; *
> by day or night they will never be shut.

They will call you, The City of the Lord, *
> The Zion of the Holy One of Israel.

Violence will no more be heard in your land, *
> ruin or destruction within your borders.

You will call your walls, Salvation, *
> and all your portals, Praise.

The sun will no more be your light by day; *
> by night you will not need the brightness of the moon.

The Lord will be your everlasting light, *
  and your God will be your glory.

Epiphany The glory of the Lord has dawned upon you.
Pentecost Nations will stream to your light, and kings to the brightness of your dawning.

Reading Two

Responsory Two (Ps 5:3; Ps. 118:25)
In the morning, Lord,
  – you hear my voice.
Give me life according to your word.
  – you hear my voice.
Glory to the Father and to the Son and to the Holy Spirit.
In the morning, Lord,
  – you hear my voice.

The Gospel Canticle – The Song of Zechariah
Epiphany God will shine on those who dwell in darkness and the shadow of death, and guide our feet into the way of peace.
Pentecost God promised to show mercy to our ancestors and to remember his holy covenant.

Litany
For those who lost limbs and abilities through war, violence, accident and ill health.
Lord, have mercy.
For those enduring domestic violence, spousal abuse and elder abuse.
Christ have mercy.
For nuclear disarmament, for an end to gun violence, for the de-escalation of conflict among gangs, criminal networks and nations.
Lord, have mercy.

Invitation to the Lord's Prayer We celebrate with joy this new day and we praise our Father.

Collect *From the proper of the day or*
O God, the author of peace and lover of concord, to know you is eternal life and to serve you is perfect freedom: Defend us, your humble servants, in all assaults of our enemies; that we, surely trusting in your defense, may not fear the power of any adversaries; through the might of Jesus Christ our Lord. Amen.

The Blessing

May we show respect for one another supporting with the greatest patience one another's weaknesses of body or behavior and earnestly obey one another. **Amen**

Tuesday Week 1 Noonday Prayer

Officiant: O God, make speed to save us.
People: **O Lord, make haste to help us.**
Officiant and People **Glory to the Father... Alleluia.**

Hymn O God creation's secret force *Hymnal 14*

Psalm 119 Beth *In quo corrigit?*

If you wish to be perfect, go, sell your possessions, and give the money to the poor, and you will have treasure in heaven; then come, follow me. Mt. 19:21

Epiphany Let all those whom the LORD has redeemed proclaim that he redeemed them from the hand of the foe.

Pentecost Give thanks to the Lord for his mercy, and the wonders he does for his children.

9 How shall a young man cleanse his way? *
    By keeping to your words.

10 With my whole heart I seek you; *
    let me not stray from your commandments.

11 I treasure your promise in my heart, *
    that I may not sin against you.

12 Blessed are you, O LORD; *
    instruct me in your statutes.

13 With my lips will I recite *
    all the judgments of your mouth.

14 I have taken greater delight in the way of your decrees *
    than in all manner of riches.

15 I will meditate on your commandments *
    and give attention to your ways.

16 My delight is in your statutes; *
    I will not forget your word.

Psalm 107 A *Confitemini Domino*

Many will come from east and west and will eat with Abraham and Isaac and Jacob in the kingdom of heaven. Mt. 8:11

1 Give thanks to the LORD, for he is good, *
    and his mercy endures for ever.

2 Let all those whom the LORD has redeemed proclaim *
    that he redeemed them from the hand of the foe.

3 He gathered them out of the lands; *
    from the east and from the west,
    from the north and from the south.

4 Some wandered in desert wastes; *
    they found no way to a city where they might dwell.

5 They were hungry and thirsty; *
    their spirits languished within them.

6 Then they cried to the LORD in their trouble, *
    and he delivered them from their distress.

7 He put their feet on a straight path *
    to go to a city where they might dwell.

8 Let them give thanks to the LORD for his mercy *
    and the wonders he does for his children.

9 For he satisfies the thirsty *
    and fills the hungry with good things.

Psalm 107 B *Sedentes in tenebris*

The dead man came out, his hands and feet bound with strips of cloth, and his face wrapped in a cloth. Jesus said to them, "Unbind him, and let him go." Jn. 11:44

10 Some sat in darkness and deep gloom, *
    bound fast in misery and iron;

11 Because they rebelled against the words of God *
    and despised the counsel of the Most High.

12 So he humbled their spirits with hard labor; *
    they stumbled, and there was none to help.

13 Then they cried to the LORD in their trouble, *
    and he delivered them from their distress.

14 He led them out of darkness and deep gloom *
    and broke their bonds asunder.

15 Let them give thanks to the LORD for his mercy *
    and the wonders he does for his children.

16 For he shatters the doors of bronze *
    and breaks in two the iron bars.

17 Some were fools and took to rebellious ways; *
    they were afflicted because of their sins.

18 They abhorred all manner of food *
    and drew near to death's door.

19 Then they cried to the LORD in their trouble, *
    and he delivered them from their distress.

20 He sent forth his word and healed them *
    and saved them from the grave.

21 Let them give thanks to the LORD for his mercy *
    and the wonders he does for his children.

22 Let them offer a sacrifice of thanksgiving *
    and tell of his acts with shouts of joy.

Epiphany Let all those whom the LORD has redeemed proclaim that he redeemed them from the hand of the foe.
Pentecost Give thanks to the Lord for his mercy, and the wonders he does for his children.

Reading Ephesians 4: 1-6
I therefore, the prisoner in the Lord, beg you to lead a life worthy of the calling to which you have been called, with all humility and gentleness, with patience, bearing with one another in love, making every effort to maintain the unity of the Spirit in the bond of peace. There is one body and one Spirit, just as you were called to the one hope of your calling, one Lord, one faith, one baptism, one God and Father of all, who is above all and through all and in all.

Verse and Response
Make every effort to maintain the unity of the Spirit.
In the bond of peace.

The Short Litany and the Lord's Prayer

The Collect Grant, Lord God, to all who have been baptized into the death and resurrection of your son Jesus Christ, that, as we have put away the old life of sin, so we may be renewed in the spirit of our minds, and live in righteousness and true holiness; through Jesus Christ our Lord, who lives and reigns with you, in the unity of the Holy Spirit, one God, now and forever. Amen.

Let us bless the Lord.
Thanks be to God.

Tuesday Week 1 Evening Prayer

Officiant: O God, make speed to save us.

People: **O Lord, make haste to help us.**

Officiant and People **Glory to the Father... Alleluia.**

Hymn O blest Creator, source of light *Hymnal 27*

Psalm 131 *Domine, non est*

Whoever does not receive the kingdom of God as a little child will never enter it. Lk. 18:19

Epiphany All who exalt themselves will be humbled, but all who humble themselves will be exalted.

Pentecost Whoever becomes humble like a child is the greatest in the kingdom of heaven.

1   O LORD, I am not proud; *
     I have no haughty looks.

2   I do not occupy myself with great matters, *
     or with things that are too hard for me.

3   But I still my soul and make it quiet,
     like a child upon its mother's breast; *
     my soul is quieted within me.

4   O Israel, wait upon the LORD, *
     from this time forth for evermore.

Epiphany All who exalt themselves will be humbled, but all who humble themselves will be exalted.

Pentecost Whoever becomes humble like a child is the greatest in the kingdom of heaven.

Psalm 132 *Memento, Domine*

He will be called the Son of the Most High, and the Lord God will give to him the throne of his ancestor David. Lk. 1:32

Epiphany I have prepared a lamp for my Anointed and his crown will shine.

Pentecost The Lord has chosen Zion; he has desired her for his habitation.

1   LORD, remember David, *
     and all the hardships he endured;

2   How he swore an oath to the LORD *
     and vowed a vow to the Mighty One of Jacob:

3 "I will not come under the roof of my house, *
    nor climb up into my bed;

4 I will not allow my eyes to sleep, *
    nor let my eyelids slumber;

5 Until I find a place for the LORD, *
    a dwelling for the Mighty One of Jacob."

6 "The ark! We heard it was in Ephratah; *
    we found it in the fields of Jearim.

7 Let us go to God's dwelling place; *
    let us fall upon our knees before his footstool."

8 Arise, O LORD, into your resting-place, *
    you and the ark of your strength.

9 Let your priests be clothed with righteousness; *
    let your faithful people sing with joy.

10 For your servant David's sake, *
    do not turn away the face of your Anointed.

11 The LORD has sworn an oath to David; *
    in truth, he will not break it:

12 "A son, the fruit of your body *
    will I set upon your throne.

13 If your children keep my covenant
    and my testimonies that I shall teach them, *
    their children will sit upon your throne for evermore."

14 For the LORD has chosen Zion; *
    he has desired her for his habitation:

15 "This shall be my resting-place for ever; *
    here will I dwell, for I delight in her.

16 I will surely bless her provisions, *
    and satisfy her poor with bread.

17 I will clothe her priests with salvation, *
    and her faithful people will rejoice and sing.

18 There will I make the horn of David flourish; *
    I have prepared a lamp for my Anointed.

19 As for his enemies, I will clothe them with shame; *
>   but as for him, his crown will shine."

Epiphany I have prepared a lamp for my Anointed and his crown will shine.
Pentecost The Lord has chosen Zion; he has desired her for his habitation.

Psalm 133 *Ecce, quam bonum!*
Lead a life worthy of the calling to which you have been called,
with all humility and gentleness. Eph. 4: 1-2

Epiphany May you be blameless and innocent, children of God without blemish as you shine like stars in the world.
Pentecost Clothe yourselves with compassion, kindness, humility, meekness and patience. Bear with one another.

1 Oh, how good and pleasant it is, *
>   when brethren live together in unity!

2 It is like fine oil upon the head *
>   that runs down upon the beard,

3 Upon the beard of Aaron, *
>   and runs down upon the collar of his robe.

4 It is like the dew of Hermon *
>   that falls upon the hills of Zion.

5 For there the LORD has ordained the blessing: *
>   life for evermore.

Epiphany May you be blameless and innocent, children of God without blemish as you shine like stars in the world.
Pentecost Clothe yourselves with compassion, kindness, humility, meekness and patience. Bear with one another.

Reading

Responsory (Ps. 119:89, 90)
O Lord, your word is everlasting
>   **– it stands firm in the heavens.**
Your faithfulness remains from one generation to another
>   **– it stands firm in the heavens.**
Glory to the Father and to the Son and to the Holy Spirit.
O Lord, your word is everlasting
>   **– it stands firm in the heavens.**

The Gospel Canticle – The Song of Mary

Epiphany I came into the world for judgment so that those who do not see may see, and those who do see may become blind.

Pentecost All generations will call me blessed: the Almighty has done great things for me.

Litany

For an end to the financial exploitation of the poor, for those who seek just working conditions, for a cessation of corporate greed and hording.
Lord, have mercy.

For those who will suffer painful and unanticipated death, for the elderly enduring loneliness, for children who feel alone and forgotten.
Christ, have mercy.

For those living and working in hospice care, for those abandoned as they die, for those seeking a peaceful death.
Lord, have mercy.

Invitation to the Lord's Prayer We conclude our prayer and offer this day's work to God as we pray in the Spirit.

Collect *From the proper of the day or*
Be our light in the darkness, O Lord, and in your great mercy defend us from all perils and dangers of this night; for the love of your only Son, our Savior Jesus Christ. Amen.

The Blessing

May we not grow weary in doing what is right, for we will reap at harvest time, if we do not give up. **Amen.**

Wednesday Week 1 Morning Prayer

Officiant: Lord, open our lips.
People: **And our mouth shall proclaim your praise.**
Officiant and People **Glory to the Father … Alleluia.**

The Invitatory Psalm 95

In Abraham, all the families of the earth shall be blessed: Come let us adore.

Hymn Christ whose glory fills the skies *Hymnal 7*

Psalm 64 *Exaudi, Deus*

*Jesus knew all people and needed no one to bear witness of people;
for he himself knew what was in people. Jn. 2:25*

Epiphany The human mind and heart are a mystery.
Pentecost Let us approach the sanctuary with a true heart in full assurance of faith, with our hearts sprinkled clean.

1 Hear my voice, O God, when I complain; *
   protect my life from fear of the enemy.

2 Hide me from the conspiracy of the wicked, *
   from the mob of evildoers.

3 They sharpen their tongue like a sword, *
   and aim their bitter words like arrows,

4 That they may shoot down the blameless from ambush; *
   they shoot without warning and are not afraid.

5 They hold fast to their evil course; *
   they plan how they may hide their snares.

6 They say, "Who will see us?
 who will find out our crimes? *
   we have thought out a perfect plot."

7 The human mind and heart are a mystery; *
   but God will loose an arrow at them,
   and suddenly they will be wounded.

8 He will make them trip over their tongues, *
   and all who see them will shake their heads.

9 Everyone will stand in awe and declare God's deeds; *
   they will recognize his works.

10 The righteous will rejoice in the LORD and put their trust in him, *
   and all who are true of heart will glory.

Epiphany The human mind and heart are a mystery.
Pentecost Let us approach the sanctuary with a true heart in full assurance of faith, with our hearts sprinkled clean.

Psalm 99 *Dominus regnavit*

I saw no temple in the city, for its temple is the Lord God the Almighty and the Lamb. Rev. 21:22

Epiphany Let all peoples confess his Name, which is great and awesome; he is the Holy One.

Pentecost Proclaim the greatness of the Lord our God and worship him upon his holy hill.

1 The LORD is King;
    let the people tremble; *
        he is enthroned upon the cherubim;
        let the earth shake.

2 The LORD is great in Zion; *
        he is high above all peoples.

3 Let them confess his Name, which is great and awesome; *
        he is the Holy One.

4 "O mighty King, lover of justice,
    you have established equity; *
        you have executed justice and righteousness in Jacob."

5 Proclaim the greatness of the LORD our God
    and fall down before his footstool; *
        he is the Holy One.

6 Moses and Aaron among his priests,
    and Samuel among those who call upon his Name, *
        they called upon the LORD, and he answered them.

7 He spoke to them out of the pillar of cloud; *
        they kept his testimonies and the decree that he gave them.

8 "O LORD our God, you answered them indeed; *
        you were a God who forgave them,
        yet punished them for their evil deeds."

9 Proclaim the greatness of the LORD our God
    and worship him upon his holy hill; *
        for the LORD our God is the Holy One.

Epiphany Let all peoples confess his Name, which is great and awesome; he is the Holy One.
Pentecost Proclaim the greatness of the Lord our God and worship him upon his holy hill.

Psalm 67 *Deus misereatur*
I thank my God through Jesus Christ for all of you, because your faith is proclaimed throughout the world. Rm 1:8

Epiphany Show us the light of your countenance and come to us.
Pentecost May the Lord's face shine upon us, and be gracious to us.

1 May God be merciful to us and bless us, *
     show us the light of his countenance and come to us.

2 Let your ways be known upon earth, *
     your saving health among all nations.

3 Let the peoples praise you, O God; *
     let all the peoples praise you.

4 Let the nations be glad and sing for joy, *
     for you judge the peoples with equity
     and guide all the nations upon earth.

5 Let the peoples praise you, O God; *
     let all the peoples praise you.

6 The earth has brought forth her increase; *
     may God, our own God, give us his blessing.

7 May God give us his blessing, *
     and may all the ends of the earth stand in awe of him.

Epiphany Show us the light of your countenance and come to us.
Pentecost May the Lord's face shine upon us, and be gracious to us.

Reading One

Responsory One (Ps. 119:36; 131:37)
Incline my heart to your word
       – I long for your commandments.
Give me life in your ways
       – I long for your commandments.
Glory to the Father and to the Son and to the Holy Spirit.
Incline my heart to your word
       – I long for your commandments.

The First Canticle – Song of David *Benedictus es Domine*
(1 Chr. 29: 10-13)
Epiphany Riches and honor come from you, and you rule over all.
Pentecost Yours is the kingdom, O Lord; you are exalted as head above all.

Blessed are you, O Lord, *
     the God of our ancestor Israel,
     forever and ever.

Yours, O Lord, are the greatness, the power, *
     the glory, the victory, and the majesty.

For all that is in the heavens and on the earth is yours; *
>> yours is the kingdom, O Lord;
>> you are exalted as head above all.

Riches and honor come from you, *
>> and you rule over all.

In your hand are power and might; *
>> and it is in your hand to make great
>> and to give strength to all.

Now, our God, we give thanks to you *
>> and praise your glorious name.

Epiphany Riches and honor come from you, and you rule over all.
Pentecost Yours is the kingdom, O Lord; you are exalted as head above all.

Reading Two

Responsory Two (Ps. 34:1)
Bless the Lord
>> **– at all times.**
God's praise will always be on my tongue
>> **– at all times.**
Glory to the Father and to the Son and to the Holy Spirit.
Bless the Lord
>> **– at all times.**

The Gospel Canticle – The Song of Zechariah
Epiphany God the only Son, who is close to the Father's heart, has made God known.
Pentecost God set us free to worship him without fear, holy and righteous in his sight.

Litany
Father, we pray for your holy Catholic Church; that we all may be one.
Lord, have mercy.
Grant that every member of the Church may truly and humbly serve you; that your Name may be glorified by all people.
Christ, have mercy.
Give us grace to do your will in all that we undertake; that our works may find favor in your sight.
Lord, have mercy.

Invitation to the Lord's Prayer In our prayer may the Spirit utter in our depths and cry out through us to God.

Collect *From the proper of the day or*
Lord God, almighty and everlasting Father, you have brought us in safety to this new day: Preserve us with your mighty power, that we may not fall into sin, nor be overcome by adversity; and in all we do, direct us to the fulfilling of your purpose; through Jesus Christ our Lord. Amen.

The Blessing
May we work for the good of all, and especially for those of the family of the faith. **Amen**

Wednesday Week 1 Noonday Prayer
Officiant: O God, make speed to save us.
People: **O Lord, make haste to help us.**
Officiant and People **Glory to the Father... Alleluia.**

Hymn From all the dwell below the skies *Hymnal 380*

Psalm 119 Gimel *Retribue servo tuo*
Jesus said to the blind man, "Go; your faith has made you well."
Immediately he regained his sight and followed Jesus on the way. Mk. 10:52
Epiphany They beheld the works of the LORD and his wonders in the deep.
Pentecost Let them exalt him in the congregation of the people and praise him in the council of the elders.

17 Deal bountifully with your servant, *
       that I may live and keep your word.

18 Open my eyes, that I may see *
       the wonders of your law.

19 I am a stranger here on earth; *
       do not hide your commandments from me.

20 My soul is consumed at all times *
       with longing for your judgments.

21 You have rebuked the insolent; *
       cursed are they who stray from your commandments!

22 Turn from me shame and rebuke, *
       for I have kept your decrees.

23 Even though rulers sit and plot against me, *
       I will meditate on your statutes.

24 For your decrees are my delight, *
   and they are my counselors.

Psalm 107 C *Qui descendunt mare*

He woke up and rebuked the wind, and said to the sea, "Peace! Be still!" Mk. 4:39

23 Some went down to the sea in ships *
   and plied their trade in deep waters;

24 They beheld the works of the LORD *
   and his wonders in the deep.

25 Then he spoke, and a stormy wind arose, *
   which tossed high the waves of the sea.

26 They mounted up to the heavens and fell back to the depths; *
   their hearts melted because of their peril.

27 They reeled and staggered like drunkards *
   and were at their wits' end.

28 Then they cried to the LORD in their trouble, *
   and he delivered them from their distress.

29 He stilled the storm to a whisper *
   and quieted the waves of the sea.

30 Then were they glad because of the calm, *
   and he brought them to the harbor they were bound for.

31 Let them give thanks to the LORD for his mercy *
   and the wonders he does for his children.

32 Let them exalt him in the congregation of the people *
   and praise him in the council of the elders.

Psalm 107 D *Posuit flumina*

God has brought down the powerful from their thrones, and lifted up the lowly. Lk. 1:52

33 The LORD changed rivers into deserts, *
   and water-springs into thirsty ground,

34 A fruitful land into salt flats, *
   because of the wickedness of those who dwell there.

35 He changed deserts into pools of water *
   and dry land into water-springs.

36 He settled the hungry there, *
   and they founded a city to dwell in.

37 They sowed fields, and planted vineyards, *
and brought in a fruitful harvest.

38 He blessed them, so that they increased greatly; *
he did not let their herds decrease.

39 Yet when they were diminished and brought low, *
through stress of adversity and sorrow,

40 (He pours contempt on princes *
and makes them wander in trackless wastes)

41 He lifted up the poor out of misery *
and multiplied their families like flocks of sheep.

42 The upright will see this and rejoice, *
but all wickedness will shut its mouth.

43 Whoever is wise will ponder these things, *
and consider well the mercies of the LORD.

Epiphany They beheld the works of the LORD and his wonders in the deep.
Pentecost Let them exalt him in the congregation of the people and praise him in the council of the elders.

Reading 1 Cor. 1: 26-30
Consider your own call, brothers and sisters: not many of you were wise by human standards, not many were powerful, not many were of noble birth. But God chose what is foolish in the world to shame the wise; God chose what is weak in the world to shame the strong; God chose what is low and despised in the world, things that are not, to reduce to nothing things that are, so that no one might boast in the presence of God. He is the source of your life in Christ Jesus, who became for us wisdom from God, and righteousness and sanctification and redemption.

Verse and Response
The message about the cross is foolishness to those who are perishing.
But to us who are being saved it is the power of God.

The Short Litany and the Lord's Prayer

The Collect Almighty Father, whose blessed Son before his passion prayed for his disciples that they might be one, as you and he are one: Grant that your Church, being bound together in love and obedience to you, may be united in one body by the one Spirit; that the world may believe in him who you have sent, your Son Jesus Christ our Lord; who lives and reigns with you, in the unity of the Holy Spirit, one God, now and for ever. Amen.

Let us bless the Lord.
Thanks be to God.

Wednesday Week 1 Evening Prayer
Officiant: O God, make speed to save us.
People: **O Lord, make haste to help us.**
Officiant and People **Glory to the Father... Alleluia.**

Hymn Most holy God, the Lord of heaven *Hymnal 32*

Psalm 135 A *Laudate nomen*
Jesus Christ purified for himself a people of his own who are zealous for good deeds. Titus 2:15
Epiphany The Lord brings up rain clouds from the ends of the earth; he sends out lightning with the rain.
Pentecost Praise the Lord, for the Lord is good; sing praises to his Name for it is lovely.

1 Hallelujah!
  Praise the Name of the LORD; *
    give praise, you servants of the LORD,

2 You who stand in the house of the LORD, *
    in the courts of the house of our God.

3 Praise the LORD, for the LORD is good; *
    sing praises to his Name, for it is lovely.

4 For the LORD has chosen Jacob for himself *
    and Israel for his own possession.

5 For I know that the LORD is great, *
    and that our Lord is above all gods.

6 The LORD does whatever pleases him, in heaven and on earth, *
    in the seas and all the deeps.

7 He brings up rain clouds from the ends of the earth; *
    he sends out lightning with the rain,
    and brings the winds out of his storehouse.

8 It was he who struck down the firstborn of Egypt, *
    the firstborn both of man and beast.

9 He sent signs and wonders into the midst of you, O Egypt, *
    against Pharaoh and all his servants.

10 He overthrew many nations *
 and put mighty kings to death:

11 Sihon, king of the Amorites,
 and Og, the king of Bashan, *
 and all the kingdoms of Canaan.

12 He gave their land to be an inheritance, *
 an inheritance for Israel his people.

Epiphany The Lord brings up rain clouds from the ends of the earth;
he sends out lightning with the rain.
Pentecost Praise the Lord, for the Lord is good; sing praises to his
Name for it is lovely.

Psalm 135 B *Domine nomen tuum*
Will not God grant justice to his chosen ones who cry to him day and night? Lk. 18:7

Epiphany You who fear the LORD, bless the LORD.
Pentecost The Lord gives his people justice and shows compassion to
his servants.

13 O LORD, your Name is everlasting; *
 your renown, O LORD, endures from age to age.

14 For the LORD gives his people justice *
 and shows compassion to his servants.

15 The idols of the heathen are silver and gold, *
 the work of human hands.

16 They have mouths, but they cannot speak; *
 eyes have they, but they cannot see.

17 They have ears, but they cannot hear; *
 neither is there any breath in their mouth.

18 Those who make them are like them, *
 and so are all who put their trust in them.

19 Bless the LORD, O house of Israel; *
 O house of Aaron, bless the LORD.

20 Bless the LORD, O house of Levi; *
 you who fear the LORD, bless the LORD.

21 Blessed be the LORD out of Zion, *
 who dwells in Jerusalem.
 Hallelujah!

Epiphany The Lord brings up rain clouds from the ends of the earth; he sends out lightning with the rain.

Pentecost Praise the Lord, for the Lord is good; sing praises to his Name for it is lovely.

Psalm 138 *Confitebor tibi*

The Lord is faithful; he will strengthen you and guard you from the evil one. 2 Thes. 3:3

Epiphany Though the LORD be high, he cares for the lowly; he perceives the haughty from afar.

Pentecost I will bow down toward your holy temple, and praise your Name, O Lord.

1 I will give thanks to you, O LORD, with my whole heart; *
      before the gods I will sing your praise.

2 I will bow down toward your holy temple
   and praise your Name, *
      because of your love and faithfulness;

3 For you have glorified your Name *
      and your word above all things.

4 When I called, you answered me; *
      you increased my strength within me.

5 All the kings of the earth will praise you, O LORD, *
      when they have heard the words of your mouth.

6 They will sing of the ways of the LORD, *
      that great is the glory of the LORD.

7 Though the LORD be high, he cares for the lowly; *
      he perceives the haughty from afar.

8 Though I walk in the midst of trouble, you keep me safe; *
      you stretch forth your hand against the fury of my enemies;
      your right hand shall save me.

9 The LORD will make good his purpose for me; *
      O LORD, your love endures for ever;
      do not abandon the works of your hands.

Epiphany Though the LORD be high, he cares for the lowly; he perceives the haughty from afar.

Pentecost I will bow down toward your holy temple, and praise your Name, O Lord.

Reading

Responsory (Ps. 26:11, 9)
Redeem me, O Lord
> **– have pity on me.**
Do not sweep me away with sinners
> **– have pity on me.**
Glory to the Father and to the Son and to the Holy Spirit.
Redeem me, O Lord
> **– have pity on me.**

The Gospel Canticle – The Song of Mary
Epiphany Let us open our eyes to the deifying light, let us hear with attentive ears the warning which the divine voice cries daily to us.
Pentecost God has cast the powerful from their thrones and has lifted up the lowly.

Litany
Guide all who govern and hold authority in the nations of the world; that there may be justice and peace on the earth.
Lord, have mercy.
Have compassion on those who suffer from any grief or trouble; that they may be delivered from their distress.
Christ, have mercy.
Give to the departed eternal rest. Let light perpetual shine upon them.
Lord, have mercy.

Invitation to the Lord's Prayer We offer our Father a sacrifice of praise and thanksgiving as we pray with Christ.

The Collect *From the proper of the day or*
O God, the life of all who live, the light of the faithful, the strength of those who labor, and the repose of the dead: We thank you for the blessings of the day that is past, and humbly ask for your protection through the coming night. Bring us in safety to the morning hours; through him who died and rose again for us, your Son our Savior Jesus Christ. Amen.

The Blessing
May the peace of God, which surpasses all understanding, guard our hearts and our minds in Christ Jesus. **Amen**

Thursday Week 1 Morning Prayer

Officiant: Lord, open our lips.

People: **And our mouth shall proclaim your praise.**

Officiant and People **Glory to the Father... Alleluia.**

The Invitatory Psalm 122

Let us go to the house of the LORD: Come let us adore.

Hymn Morning has broken *Hymnal 8*

Psalm 16 *Conserva me, Domine*

This Jesus God raised up, and of that all of us are witnesses. Acts 2:32

Epiphany I will bless the LORD who gives me counsel; my heart teaches me, night after night.

Pentecost I have said to the LORD, "You are my Lord, my good above all other."

1   Protect me, O God, for I take refuge in you; *
        I have said to the LORD, "You are my Lord,
        my good above all other."

2   All my delight is upon the godly that are in the land, *
        upon those who are noble among the people.

3   But those who run after other gods *
        shall have their troubles multiplied.

4   Their libations of blood I will not offer, *
        nor take the names of their gods upon my lips.

5   O LORD, you are my portion and my cup; *
        it is you who uphold my lot.

6   My boundaries enclose a pleasant land; *
        indeed, I have a goodly heritage.

7   I will bless the LORD who gives me counsel; *
        my heart teaches me, night after night.

8   I have set the LORD always before me; *
        because he is at my right hand I shall not fall.

9   My heart, therefore, is glad, and my spirit rejoices; *
        my body also shall rest in hope.

10 For you will not abandon me to the grave, *
        nor let your holy one see the Pit.

11 You will show me the path of life; *
>> in your presence there is fullness of joy,
>> and in your right hand are pleasures for evermore.

Epiphany I will bless the LORD who gives me counsel; my heart teaches me, night after night.
Pentecost I have said to the LORD, "You are my Lord, my good above all other."

Psalm 42 *Quemadmodum*

The water that I will give will become in them a spring of water gushing up to eternal life. Jn. 4:14
Epiphany The LORD grants his loving-kindness in the daytime; in the night season his song is with me.
Pentecost My soul is athirst for God, athirst for the living God.

1 As the deer longs for the water-brooks, *
>> so longs my soul for you, O God.

2 My soul is athirst for God, athirst for the living God; *
>> when shall I come to appear before the presence of God?

3 My tears have been my food day and night, *
>> while all day long they say to me,
>> "Where now is your God?"

4 I pour out my soul when I think on these things: *
>> how I went with the multitude
>> and led them into the house of God,

5 With the voice of praise and thanksgiving, *
>> among those who keep holy-day.

6 Why are you so full of heaviness, O my soul? *
>> and why are you so disquieted within me?

7 Put your trust in God; *
>> for I will yet give thanks to him,
>> who is the help of my countenance, and my God.

8 My soul is heavy within me; *
>> therefore I will remember you from the land of Jordan,
>> and from the peak of Mizar among the heights of Hermon.

9 One deep calls to another in the noise of your cataracts; *
>> all your rapids and floods have gone over me.

10 The LORD grants his loving-kindness in the daytime; *
>> in the night season his song is with me,
>> a prayer to the God of my life.

11 I will say to the God of my strength,
    "Why have you forgotten me? *
        and why do I go so heavily
        while the enemy oppresses me?"

12 While my bones are being broken, *
        my enemies mock me to my face;

13 All day long they mock me *
        and say to me, "Where now is your God?"

14 Why are you so full of heaviness, O my soul? *
        and why are you so disquieted within me?

15 Put your trust in God; *
        for I will yet give thanks to him,
        who is the help of my countenance, and my God.

Epiphany The LORD grants his loving-kindness in the daytime; in the
night season his song is with me.
Pentecost My soul is athirst for God, athirst for the living God.

Psalm 149 *Cantate Domino*

All who see them shall acknowledge that they are a people whom the Lord has blessed. Is. 61: 9

Epiphany The LORD takes pleasure in his people and adorns the poor
with victory.
Pentecost Let the children of Zion be joyful in their King.

1 Hallelujah!
    Sing to the LORD a new song; *
        sing his praise in the congregation of the faithful.

2 Let Israel rejoice in his Maker; *
        let the children of Zion be joyful in their King.

3 Let them praise his Name in the dance; *
        let them sing praise to him with timbrel and harp.

4 For the LORD takes pleasure in his people *
        and adorns the poor with victory.

5 Let the faithful rejoice in triumph; *
        let them be joyful on their beds.

6 Let the praises of God be in their throat *
        and a two-edged sword in their hand;

7 To wreak vengeance on the nations *
        and punishment on the peoples;

8 To bind their kings in chains *
> and their nobles with links of iron;

9 To inflict on them the judgment decreed; *
> this is glory for all his faithful people.
> Hallelujah!

Epiphany The LORD takes pleasure in his people and adorns the poor with victory.

Pentecost Let the children of Zion be joyful in their King.

Reading One

Responsory One (Ps. 119:45; 146)
I call with my whole heart
> **– answer me, O Lord.**

I will keep your decrees
> **– answer me, O Lord.**

Glory to the Father and to the Son and to the Holy Spirit.
I call with my whole heart
> **– answer me, O Lord.**

The First Canticle – Song of the Bread of Angels *Angelorum esca nutrivisti*
(Wisdom 16: 20-21.26; 17:1)

Epiphany One does not live by bread alone, but by every word that comes from the mouth of the Lord.

Pentecost I am the living bread that came down from heaven. Whoever eats of this bread will live forever.

You gave your people food of angels; *
> without their toil you supplied them from heaven with bread.

Your bread provided every pleasure *
> and suited to every taste.

For your sustenance manifested your sweetness
toward your children; *
> and the bread, ministered to the desire of the one who ate it.

It was changed *
> to suit everyone's liking.

So your children, whom you loved, O Lord, might learn *
> that it is not the production of crops that feeds humankind.

Your word sustains *
> those who trust in you.

Epiphany One does not live by bread alone, but by every word that comes from the mouth of the Lord.

Pentecost I am the living bread that came down from heaven. Whoever eats of this bread will live forever.

Reading Two

Responsory Two (Ps. 143:8; Ps. 40:19)
In the morning, O Lord
> – **let me hear of your loving-kindness.**

You are my Helper
> – **let me hear of your loving-kindness.**

Glory to the Father and to the Son and to the Holy Spirit.
In the morning, O Lord
> – **let me hear of your loving-kindness.**

The Gospel Canticle – The Song of Zechariah

Epiphany While you have the light, believe in the light, so that you may become children of light.

Pentecost God will shine on those who dwell in darkness and the shadow of death, and guide our feet into the way of peace.

Litany
For all who produce food for the people of the world, for all who labor in fields, for all who research new foods.
Lord, have mercy.
For all who share the Body and Blood of Christ that the Spirit may infuse in our hearts an understanding of our communion in Christ.
Christ have mercy.
For the hungry, for the thirsty, for all who suffer from eating disorders.
Lord, have mercy.

Invitation to the Lord's Prayer We hunger for Christ, the living bread and ask God to nurture us.

The Collect *From the proper of the day or*
Heavenly Father, in you we live and move and have our being: We humbly pray you so to guide and govern us by your Holy Spirit, that in all the cares and occupations of our life we may not forget you, but may remember that we are ever walking in your sight; through Jesus Christ our Lord. Amen.

The Blessing
May God give us gladness of heart, and may there be peace in our days in Israel, as in the days of old. **Amen**

Thursday Week 1 Noonday Prayer

Officiant: O God, make speed to save us.

People: **O Lord, make haste to help us.**

Officiant and People **Glory to the Father... Alleluia.**

Hymn Now let us sing our praise to God *Hymnal 16*

Psalm 119 Daleth *Adhæsit pavimento*

*We shall run on the path of God's commandments, our hearts overflowing
with the inexpressible delights of love. RB Prol 49*

Epiphany The Lord who made you, who formed you in the womb will
help you.

Pentecost I will run the way of your commandments, for you have set
my heart at liberty.

25 My soul cleaves to the dust; *
　　give me life according to your word.

26 I have confessed my ways, and you answered me; *
　　instruct me in your statutes.

27 Make me understand the way of your commandments, *
　　that I may meditate on your marvelous works.

28 My soul melts away for sorrow; *
　　strengthen me according to your word.

29 Take from me the way of lying; *
　　let me find grace through your law.

30 I have chosen the way of faithfulness; *
　　I have set your judgments before me.

31 I hold fast to your decrees; *
　　O LORD, let me not be put to shame.

32 I will run the way of your commandments, *
　　for you have set my heart at liberty.

Psalm 59 A *Eripe me de inimicis*

The assembly rose as a body and brought Jesus before Pilate. Lk. 23:1

1 Rescue me from my enemies, O God; *
　　protect me from those who rise up against me.

2 Rescue me from evildoers *
　　and save me from those who thirst for my blood.

3 See how they lie in wait for my life,
how the mighty gather together against me; *
    not for any offense or fault of mine, O LORD.

4 Not because of any guilt of mine *
    they run and prepare themselves for battle.

5 Rouse yourself, come to my side, and see; *
    for you, LORD God of hosts, are Israel's God.

6 Awake, and punish all the ungodly; *
    show no mercy to those who are faithless and evil.

7 They go to and fro in the evening; *
    they snarl like dogs and run about the city.

8 Behold, they boast with their mouths,
and taunts are on their lips; *
    "For who." they say, "will hear us?"

9 But you, O LORD, you laugh at them; *
    you laugh all the ungodly to scorn.

10 My eyes are fixed on you, O my Strength; *
    for you, O God, are my stronghold.

11 My merciful God comes to meet me; *
    God will let me look in triumph on my enemies.

Psalm 59 B *Et tu, Domine*

This is your hour, and the power of darkness. Lk. 22:53

12 Slay them, O God, lest my people forget; *
    send them reeling by your might
    and put them down, O Lord our shield.

13 For the sins of their mouths, for the words of their lips,
for the cursing and lies that they utter, *
    let them be caught in their pride.

14 Make an end of them in your wrath; *
    make an end of them, and they shall be no more.

15 Let everyone know that God rules in Jacob, *
    and to the ends of the earth.

16 They go to and fro in the evening; *
    they snarl like dogs and run about the city.

17 They forage for food, *
    and if they are not filled, they howl.

18 For my part, I will sing of your strength; *
    I will celebrate your love in the morning;

19 For you have become my stronghold, *
    a refuge in the day of my trouble.

20 To you, O my Strength, will I sing; *
    for you, O God, are my stronghold and my merciful God.

Epiphany The Lord who made you, who formed you in the womb will help you.
Pentecost I will run the way of your commandments, for you have set my heart at liberty.

Reading John 6: 35-38
Jesus said to them, "I am the bread of life. Whoever comes to me will never be hungry, and whoever believes in me will never be thirsty. But I said to you that you have seen me and yet do not believe. Everything that the Father gives me will come to me, and anyone who comes to me I will never drive away; for I have come down from heaven, not to do my own will, but the will of him who sent me.

Verse and Response
I will abundantly bless your provisions.
I will satisfy your poor with bread.

The Short Litany and the Lord's Prayer

The Collect O God, whose blessed Son made himself known to his disciples in the breaking of bread: Open the eyes of our faith, that we may behold him in all his redeeming work; who lives and reigns with you, in the unity of the Holy Spirit, one God, now and for ever. Amen.

Let us bless the Lord.
Thanks be to God.

Thursday Week 1 Evening Prayer
Officiant: O God, make speed to save us.
People: **O Lord, make haste to help us.**
Officiant and People **Glory to the Father … Alleluia.**

Hymn The day thou gavest, Lord *Hymnal 24*

Psalm 78 Part I A *Attendite, popule*
You faithless generation, how much longer must I be among you? Mk. 9:19
Epiphany The Lord brought streams out of the cliff, and the waters gushed out like rivers.

Pentecost We will recount to generations to come the praiseworthy deeds and the power of the LORD

1 Hear my teaching, O my people; *
    incline your ears to the words of my mouth.

2 I will open my mouth in a parable; *
    I will declare the mysteries of ancient times.

3 That which we have heard and known,
    and what our forefathers have told us, *
    we will not hide from their children.

4 We will recount to generations to come
    the praiseworthy deeds and the power of the LORD, *
    and the wonderful works he has done.

5 He gave his decrees to Jacob
    and established a law for Israel, *
        which he commanded them to teach their children;

6 That the generations to come might know,
    and the children yet unborn; *
        that they in their turn might tell it to their children;

7 So that they might put their trust in God, *
        and not forget the deeds of God,
        but keep his commandments;

8 And not be like their forefathers,
    a stubborn and rebellious generation, *
        a generation whose heart was not steadfast,
        and whose spirit was not faithful to God.

9 The people of Ephraim, armed with the bow, *
        turned back in the day of battle;

10 They did not keep the covenant of God, *
        and refused to walk in his law;

11 They forgot what he had done, *
        and the wonders he had shown them.

12 He worked marvels in the sight of their forefathers, *
        in the land of Egypt, in the field of Zoan.

13 He split open the sea and let them pass through; *
        he made the waters stand up like walls.

14 He led them with a cloud by day, *
    and all the night through with a glow of fire.

15 He split the hard rocks in the wilderness *
    and gave them drink as from the great deep.

16 He brought streams out of the cliff, *
    and the waters gushed out like rivers.

17 But they went on sinning against him, *
    rebelling in the desert against the Most High.

Epiphany The Lord brought streams out of the cliff, and the waters gushed out like rivers.
Pentecost We will recount to generations to come the praiseworthy deeds and the power of the LORD

Psalm 78 Part I B *Et appposuerunt*
When the Son of Man comes, will he find faith on earth? Lk. 18:8

Epiphany Blessed are those who trust in the Lord, whose trust is the Lord.
Pentecost Our ancestors were all under the cloud, and all passed through the sea, and all were baptized into Moses in the cloud and in the sea.

18 They tested God in their hearts, *
    demanding food for their craving.

19 They railed against God and said, *
    "Can God set a table in the wilderness?

20 True, he struck the rock, the waters gushed out,
    and the gullies overflowed; *
        but is he able to give bread
        or to provide meat for his people?"

21 When the LORD heard this, he was full of wrath; *
    a fire was kindled against Jacob,
    and his anger mounted against Israel;

22 For they had no faith in God, *
    nor did they put their trust in his saving power.

23 So he commanded the clouds above *
    and opened the doors of heaven.

24 He rained down manna upon them to eat *
    and gave them grain from heaven.

25 So mortals ate the bread of angels; *
     he provided for them food enough.

26 He caused the east wind to blow in the heavens *
     and led out the south wind by his might.

27 He rained down flesh upon them like dust *
     and wingèd birds like the sand of the sea.

28 He let it fall in the midst of their camp *
     and round about their dwellings.

29 So they ate and were well filled, *
     for he gave them what they craved.

Epiphany Blessed are those who trust in the Lord, whose trust is the
Lord.
Pentecost Our ancestors were all under the cloud, and all passed
through the sea, and all were baptized into Moses in the cloud and in
the sea.

Psalm 78 Part I C *Non sunt fraudati*
*Be steadfast, immovable, always excelling in the work of the Lord, because you know that in the Lord
your labor is not in vain. 1 Cor. 15:58*
Epiphany They shall be like a tree planted by water, sending out its
roots by the stream.
Pentecost The children of Israel ate the manna and drank from the
spiritual rock which followed after them and the rock was Christ.

30 But they did not stop their craving, *
     though the food was still in their mouths.

31 So God's anger mounted against them; *
     he slew their strongest men
     and laid low the youth of Israel.

32 In spite of all this, they went on sinning *
     and had no faith in his wonderful works.

33 So he brought their days to an end like a breath *
     and their years in sudden terror.

34 Whenever he slew them, they would seek him, *
     and repent, and diligently search for God.

35 They would remember that God was their rock, *
     and the Most High God their redeemer.

36 But they flattered him with their mouths *
    and lied to him with their tongues.

37 Their heart was not steadfast toward him, *
    and they were not faithful to his covenant.

38 But he was so merciful that he forgave their sins
    and did not destroy them; *
      many times he held back his anger
      and did not permit his wrath to be roused.

39 For he remembered that they were but flesh, *
    a breath that goes forth and does not return.

Epiphany They shall be like a tree planted by water, sending out its roots by the stream.
Pentecost The children of Israel ate the manna and drank from the spiritual rock which followed after them and the rock was Christ.

Reading

Responsory (Ps. 81:16)
The Lord would feed us
    — **with the finest wheat.**
God will satisfy us with honey
    — **with the finest wheat.**
Glory to the Father and to the Son and to the Holy Spirit.
The Lord would feed us
    — **with the finest wheat.**

The Gospel Canticle -- The Song of Mary
Epiphany I am the light of the world. We must work the works of him who sent me while it is day.
Pentecost God has fed the hungry with good things, and the rich he has sent away empty.

Litany
For the aged, the hospitalized and those who live in institutions.
Lord, have mercy.
For children and adults who suffer from bullies, for those deprived of the right to vote, for those denied their civil rights.
Christ, have mercy.
For those who die suddenly, for those who lost their lives in wars and civil unrest, for those deprived of life by unjust judicial systems.
Lord, have mercy.

Invitation to the Lord's Prayer Since the Father feeds us with the true bread from heaven let us ask God to nourish us.

The Collect *From the proper of the day or*
Lord Jesus, stay with us, for evening is at hand and the day is past; be our companion in the way, kindle our hearts, and awaken hope, that we may know you as you are revealed in Scripture and the breaking of bread. Grant this for the sake of your love. Amen.

The Blessing
May the Lord entrust mercy to us, and may God deliver us in our days.
Amen

Friday Week 1 Morning Prayer

Officiant: Lord, open our lips.
People: **And our mouth shall proclaim your praise.**
Officiant and People **Glory to the Father... Alleluia.**

The Invitatory Psalm 51
The Lord cleanses us from our sin; Come let us adore.

Hymn Not here for high and holy things *Hymnal 9 vv. 1-3*

Psalm 51 *Miserere mei, Deus*

How much more will the blood of Christ, who through the eternal Spirit offered himself without blemish to God, purify our conscience from dead works to worship the living God! Heb. 9: 15

Epiphany Give me the joy of your saving help again and sustain me with your bountiful Spirit.

Pentecost Create in me a clean heart, O God, and renew a right spirit within me.

1 Have mercy on me, O God,
   according to your loving-kindness; *
      in your great compassion blot out my offenses.

2 Wash me through and through from my wickedness *
      and cleanse me from my sin.

3 For I know my transgressions, *
      and my sin is ever before me.

4 Against you only have I sinned *
      and done what is evil in your sight.

5 And so you are justified when you speak *
      and upright in your judgment.

6   Indeed, I have been wicked from my birth, *
       a sinner from my mother's womb.

7   For behold, you look for truth deep within me, *
       and will make me understand wisdom secretly.

8   Purge me from my sin, and I shall be pure; *
       wash me, and I shall be clean indeed.

9   Make me hear of joy and gladness, *
       that the body you have broken may rejoice.

10 Hide your face from my sins *
       and blot out all my iniquities.

11 Create in me a clean heart, O God, *
       and renew a right spirit within me.

12 Cast me not away from your presence *
       and take not your holy Spirit from me.

13 Give me the joy of your saving help again *
       and sustain me with your bountiful Spirit.

14 I shall teach your ways to the wicked, *
       and sinners shall return to you.

15 Deliver me from death, O God, *
       and my tongue shall sing of your righteousness,
       O God of my salvation.

16 Open my lips, O Lord, *
       and my mouth shall proclaim your praise.

17 Had you desired it, I would have offered sacrifice, *
       but you take no delight in burnt-offerings.

18 The sacrifice of God is a troubled spirit; *
       a broken and contrite heart, O God, you will not despise.

19 Be favorable and gracious to Zion, *
       and rebuild the walls of Jerusalem.

20 Then you will be pleased with the appointed sacrifices,
       with burnt-offerings and oblations; *
    then shall they offer young bullocks upon your altar.

Epiphany Give me the joy of your saving help again and sustain me
with your bountiful Spirit.

Pentecost Create in me a clean heart, O God, and renew a right spirit within me.

Psalm 88 A *Domine, Deus*
Joseph of Arimathea, who was a disciple of Jesus,
asked Pilate to let him take away the body of Jesus. Jn. 19:38

Epiphany Out of their gloom and darkness the eyes of the blind shall see.

Pentecost LORD, I have called upon you daily; I have stretched out my hands to you.

1   O LORD, my God, my Savior, *
       by day and night I cry to you.

2   Let my prayer enter into your presence; *
       incline your ear to my lamentation.

3   For I am full of trouble; *
       my life is at the brink of the grave.

4   I am counted among those who go down to the Pit; *
       I have become like one who has no strength;

5   Lost among the dead, *
       like the slain who lie in the grave,

6   Whom you remember no more, *
       for they are cut off from your hand.

7   You have laid me in the depths of the Pit, *
       in dark places, and in the abyss.

8   Your anger weighs upon me heavily, *
       and all your great waves overwhelm me.

9   You have put my friends far from me;
    you have made me to be abhorred by them; *
       I am in prison and cannot get free.

10 My sight has failed me because of trouble; *
       LORD, I have called upon you daily;
       I have stretched out my hands to you.

Epiphany Out of their gloom and darkness the eyes of the blind shall see.

Pentecost LORD, I have called upon you daily; I have stretched out my hands to you.

Psalm 88 B *Numquid mortuis*

In the garden there was a new tomb in which no one had ever been laid.
Because the tomb was nearby, they laid Jesus there. Jn. 19:41-42

Epiphany The meek shall obtain fresh joy in the Lord, and the neediest people shall exult in the Holy One of Israel.

Pentecost O LORD, I cry to you for help; in the morning my prayer
   comes before you.

11 Do you work wonders for the dead? *
   will those who have died stand up and give you thanks?

12 Will your loving-kindness be declared in the grave? *
   your faithfulness in the land of destruction?

13 Will your wonders be known in the dark? *
   or your righteousness in the country
   where all is forgotten?

14 But as for me, O LORD, I cry to you for help; *
   in the morning my prayer comes before you.

15 LORD, why have you rejected me? *
   why have you hidden your face from me?

16 Ever since my youth, I have been wretched
   and at the point of death; *
   I have borne your terrors with a troubled mind.

17 Your blazing anger has swept over me; *
   your terrors have destroyed me;

18 They surround me all day long like a flood; *
   they encompass me on every side.

19 My friend and my neighbor you have put away from me, *
   and darkness is my only companion.

Epiphany The meek shall obtain fresh joy in the Lord, and the neediest people shall exult in the Holy One of Israel.

Pentecost O LORD, I cry to you for help; in the morning my prayer
   comes before you.

Reading One

Responsory One (Ps. 5:3; Ps. 27:13)
Early in the morning
   – I watch for you.

You have been my helper
>   — **I watch for you.**
Glory to the Father and to the Son and to the Holy Spirit.
Early in the morning
>   — **I watch for you.**

The First Canticle — Song of the Suffering Christ *Christus passus est*
(1 Peter 2: 21-24)

Epiphany Christ himself bore our sins in his body on the cross.
Pentecost Christ left you an example, so that you should follow in his steps.

Christ suffered for you, *
>   leaving you an example,
>   so that you should follow in his steps.

He committed no sin; *
>   no deceit was found in his mouth.

When he was abused, *
>   he did not return abuse.

When he suffered, *
>   he did not threaten.

He entrusted himself *
>   to the one who judges justly.

He himself bore our sins *
>   in his body on the cross.

Free from sins, we might live for righteousness. *
>   By his wounds you have been healed.

Epiphany Christ himself bore our sins in his body on the cross.
Pentecost Christ left you an example, so that you should follow in his steps.

Reading Two

Responsory Two (Ps. 57:2. 3)
I will call on the Most High God
>   — **the God who maintains my cause.**
The Lord will send from heaven and save me
>   — **the God who maintains my cause.**
Glory to the Father and to the Son and to the Holy Spirit.

I will call on the Most High God
– the God who maintains my cause.

The Gospel Canticle – The Song of Zechariah

Epiphany The light shines in the darkness and the darkness did not overcome the light.

Pentecost You, O child, will give people knowledge of salvation by the forgiveness of their sins.

Litany

From all evil and mischief; from pride, vanity and hypocrisy; from envy, hatred and malice; and from all evil intent.

Lord, deliver us.

From sloth, worldliness and love of money; from hardness of heart and contempt for your word and your laws.

Christ, deliver us.

From sins of body and mind; from deceits of the world, flesh and the devil.

Lord, deliver us.

Invitation to the Lord's Prayer Let us commit ourselves to mutual forgiveness as we ask the Father's mercy.

The Collect *From the proper of the day or*

Almighty God, whose most dear Son went not up to joy but first he suffered pain, and entered not into glory before he was crucified: Mercifully grant that we, walking in the way of the cross, may find it none other than the way of life and peace; through Jesus Christ our Lord. Amen.

The Blessing

May God fully satisfy our every need according to his riches in glory in Christ Jesus. To our God and Father be glory forever and ever. **Amen**

Friday Week 1 Noonday Prayer

Officiant: O God, make speed to save us.

People: **O Lord, make haste to help us.**

Officiant and People **Glory to the Father... Alleluia.**

Hymn Now let us sing our praise to God *Hymnal 17*

Psalm 119 He *Legem pone*

They hear the word, hold it fast in an honest and good heart,
and bear fruit with patient endurance. Lk. 8:15

Epiphany I will be gracious to whom I will be gracious, and will show mercy on whom I will show mercy.

Pentecost Judgment will be without mercy to anyone who has shown no mercy; mercy triumphs over judgment.

33 Teach me, O LORD, the way of your statutes, *
    and I shall keep it to the end.

34 Give me understanding, and I shall keep your law; *
    I shall keep it with all my heart.

35 Make me go in the path of your commandments, *
    for that is my desire.

36 Incline my heart to your decrees *
    and not to unjust gain.

37 Turn my eyes from watching what is worthless; *
    give me life in your ways.

38 Fulfill your promise to your servant, *
    which you make to those who fear you.

39 Turn away the reproach which I dread, *
    because your judgments are good.

40 Behold, I long for your commandments; *
    in your righteousness preserve my life.

Psalm 109 A *Deus, laudem*

The soldiers began saluting Jesus, "Hail, King of the Jews!" They struck his head with a reed, spat upon him, and knelt down in homage to him. Mk. 16:18-19

1 Hold not your tongue, O God of my praise; *
    for the mouth of the wicked,
    the mouth of the deceitful, is opened against me.

2 They speak to me with a lying tongue; *
    they encompass me with hateful words
    and fight against me without a cause.

3 Despite my love, they accuse me; *
    but as for me, I pray for them.

4 They repay evil for good, *
    and hatred for my love.

5 Set a wicked man against him, *
    and let an accuser stand at his right hand.

6 When he is judged, let him be found guilty, *
    and let his appeal be in vain.

7 Let his days be few, *
    and let another take his office.

8 Let his children be fatherless, *
    and his wife become a widow.

9 Let his children be waifs and beggars; *
    let them be driven from the ruins of their homes.

10 Let the creditor seize everything he has; *
    let strangers plunder his gains.

11 Let there be no one to show him kindness, *
    and none to pity his fatherless children.

12 Let his descendants be destroyed, *
    and his name be blotted out in the next generation.

13 Let the wickedness of his fathers
   be remembered before the LORD, *
    and his mother's sin not be blotted out;

14 Let their sin be always before the LORD; *
    but let him root out their names from the earth;

15 Because he did not remember to show mercy, *
    but persecuted the poor and needy
    and sought to kill the brokenhearted.

16 He loved cursing,
   let it come upon him; *
    he took no delight in blessing,
    let it depart from him.

17 He put on cursing like a garment, *
    let it soak into his body like water
    and into his bones like oil;

18 Let it be to him like the cloak
   which he wraps around himself, *
    and like the belt that he wears continually.

19 Let this be the recompense from the LORD to my accusers, *
    and to those who speak evil against me.

Psalm 109 B *Et tu, Domine*

*They compelled a passer-by, who was coming in from the country, to carry his cross;
it was Simon of Cyrene. Mk 15:21*

20 But you, O Lord my God,
  oh, deal with me according to your Name; *
    for your tender mercy's sake, deliver me.

21 For I am poor and needy, *
  and my heart is wounded within me.

22 I have faded away like a shadow when it lengthens; *
  I am shaken off like a locust.

23 My knees are weak through fasting, *
  and my flesh is wasted and gaunt.

24 I have become a reproach to them; *
  they see and shake their heads.

25 Help me, O LORD my God; *
  save me for your mercy's sake.

26 Let them know that this is your hand, *
  that you, O LORD, have done it.

27 They may curse, but you will bless; *
  let those who rise up against me be put to shame,
    and your servant will rejoice.

28 Let my accusers be clothed with disgrace *
  and wrap themselves in their shame as in a cloak.

29 I will give great thanks to the LORD with my mouth; *
  in the midst of the multitude will I praise him;

30 Because he stands at the right hand of the needy, *
  to save his life from those who would condemn him.

Epiphany I will be gracious to whom I will be gracious, and will show
mercy on whom I will show mercy.
Pentecost Judgment will be without mercy to anyone who has shown
no mercy; mercy triumphs over judgment.

Reading Romans 6:3-5

Do you not know that all of us who have been baptized into Christ
Jesus were baptized into his death? Therefore we have been buried with
him by baptism into death, so that, just as Christ was raised from the
dead by the glory of the Father, so we too might walk in newness of life.

For if we have been united with him in a death like his, we will certainly be united with him in a resurrection like his.

Verse and Response

You were buried with Christ in baptism.
You were also raised with Christ through faith in the power of God.

The Short Litany and the Lord's Prayer

The Collect Lord Jesus Christ, by your death you took away the sting of death: Grant to us your servants so to follow in faith where you have led the way, that we may at length fall asleep peacefully in you and wake up in your likeness; for your tender mercies' sake. Amen.

Let us bless the Lord.
Thanks be to God.

Friday Week 1 Evening Prayer

Officiant: O God, make speed to save us.
People: **O Lord, make haste to help us.**
Officiant and People **Glory to the Father... Alleluia.**

Hymn When I survey the wondrous cross *Hymnal 474*

Psalm 130 *De profundis*
*Jesus offered up prayers and supplications, with loud cries and tears,
to the one who was able to save him from death. Heb 5:7*

Epiphany For there is forgiveness with you; therefore you shall be feared.
Pentecost LORD, hear my voice; let your ears consider well the voice of my supplication.

1 Out of the depths have I called to you, O LORD;
   LORD, hear my voice; *
      let your ears consider well the voice of my supplication.

2 If you, LORD, were to note what is done amiss, *
      O LORD, who could stand?

3 For there is forgiveness with you; *
      therefore you shall be feared.

4 I wait for the LORD; my soul waits for him; *
      in his word is my hope.

5 My soul waits for the LORD,
      more than watchmen for the morning, *
         more than watchmen for the morning.

6 O Israel, wait for the LORD, *
      for with the LORD there is mercy;

7 With him there is plenteous redemption, *
      and he shall redeem Israel from all their sins.

Epiphany For there is forgiveness with you; therefore you shall be feared.
Pentecost LORD, hear my voice; let your ears consider well the voice of my supplication.

Psalm 35 *Judica, Domine*

The people stood by, watching; but the leaders scoffed at him, saying,
"He saved others; let him save himself if he is the Messiah of God. Lk. 23:35

Epiphany Give me justice, O LORD my God, according to your righteousness.
Pentecost Rise up to help me. Say to my soul, "I am your salvation."

1 Fight those who fight me, O LORD; *
      attack those who are attacking me.

2 Take up shield and armor *
      and rise up to help me.

3 Draw the sword and bar the way
   against those who pursue me; *
      say to my soul, "I am your salvation."

4 Let those who seek after my life be shamed and humbled; *
      let those who plot my ruin fall back and be dismayed.

5 Let them be like chaff before the wind, *
      and let the angel of the LORD drive them away.

6 Let their way be dark and slippery, *
      and let the angel of the LORD pursue them.

7 For they have secretly spread a net for me without a cause; *
      without a cause they have dug a pit to take me alive.

8 Let ruin come upon them unawares; *
      let them be caught in the net they hid;
      let them fall into the pit they dug.

9 Then I will be joyful in the LORD; *
      I will glory in his victory.

10 My very bones will say, "LORD, who is like you? *
    You deliver the poor from those who are too strong for them,
    the poor and needy from those who rob them."

11 Malicious witnesses rise up against me; *
    they charge me with matters I know nothing about.

12 They pay me evil in exchange for good; *
    my soul is full of despair.

13 But when they were sick I dressed in sack-cloth *
    and humbled myself by fasting;

14 I prayed with my whole heart,
  as one would for a friend or a brother; *
    I behaved like one who mourns for his mother,
    bowed down and grieving.

15 But when I stumbled, they were glad and gathered together;
  they gathered against me; *
    strangers whom I did not know tore me to pieces
    and would not stop.

16 They put me to the test and mocked me; *
    they gnashed at me with their teeth.

17 O Lord, how long will you look on? *
    rescue me from the roaring beasts,
    and my life from the young lions.

18 I will give you thanks in the great congregation; *
    I will praise you in the mighty throng.

19 Do not let my treacherous foes rejoice over me, *
    nor let those who hate me without a cause
    wink at each other.

20 For they do not plan for peace, *
    but invent deceitful schemes
    against the quiet in the land.

21 They opened their mouths at me and said, *
    "Aha! we saw it with our own eyes."

22 You saw it, O LORD; do not be silent; *
    O Lord, be not far from me.

23 Awake, arise, to my cause! *
    to my defense, my God and my Lord!

24 Give me justice, O LORD my God,
according to your righteousness; *
do not let them triumph over me.

25 Do not let them say in their hearts,
"Aha! just what we want!" *
Do not let them say, "We have swallowed him up."

26 Let all who rejoice at my ruin be ashamed and disgraced; *
let those who boast against me
be clothed with dismay and shame.

27 Let those who favor my cause sing out with joy and be glad; *
let them say always, "Great is the LORD,
who desires the prosperity of his servant."

28 And my tongue shall be talking of your righteousness *
and of your praise all the day long.

Epiphany Give me justice, O LORD my God, according to your
righteousness.
Pentecost Rise up to help me. Say to my soul, "I am your salvation."

Psalm 142 *Voce mea ad Dominum*
Jesus gave a loud cry and breathed his last. Mk. 15:37

Epiphany Jesus was led up by the Spirit into the wilderness to be
tempted by the devil.
Pentecost You are my refuge, O Lord; my portion in the land of the
living.

1 I cry to the LORD with my voice; *
to the LORD I make loud supplication.

2 I pour out my complaint before him *
and tell him all my trouble.

3 When my spirit languishes within me, you know my path; *
in the way wherein I walk they have hidden a trap for me.

4 I look to my right hand and find no one who knows me; *
I have no place to flee to, and no one cares for me.

5 I cry out to you, O LORD; *
I say, "You are my refuge,
my portion in the land of the living."

6 Listen to my cry for help, for I have been brought very low; *
save me from those who pursue me,
for they are too strong for me.

7 Bring me out of prison, that I may give thanks to your Name; *
        when you have dealt bountifully with me,
        the righteous will gather around me.

Epiphany Jesus was led up by the Spirit into the wilderness to be
tempted by the devil.
Pentecost You are my refuge, O Lord; my portion in the land of the
living.

Reading

Responsory (Rev. 1:5)
Christ loves us and freed us from our sins
        – by his blood.
He made us to be a kingdom, priests serving his God
        – by his blood.
Glory to the Father and to the Son and to the Holy Spirit.
Christ loves us and freed us from our sins
        – by his blood.

The Gospel Canticle – The Song of Mary
Epiphany Run while you have the light of life, lest the darkness of
death overtake you.
Pentecost God has come to the help of his servant Israel, ever mindful
of his merciful promise.

Litany
From famine and disaster; from violence, murder, and dying
unprepared.
Lord, have mercy.
From lightning and tempest; from earthquake, fire and flood; from
plague, pestilence and famine.
Christ, have mercy.
Hear us as we remember those who have died and grant us with them a
share in your eternal glory.
Lord, have mercy.

Invitation to the Lord's Prayer Reconciled to God by the blood of
Christ, let us pray with Christ to the Father.

The Collect *From the proper of the day or*
Lord Jesus Christ, by your death you took away the sting of death: Grant
to us your servants so to follow in faith where you have led the way, that
we may at length fall asleep peacefully in you and wake up in your likeness;
for your tender mercies' sake. Amen.

The Blessing

May the God of steadfastness and encouragement grant us to live in harmony with one another, in accordance with Christ Jesus. **Amen**

Saturday Week 1 Morning Prayer

Officiant: Lord, open our lips.
People: **And our mouth shall proclaim your praise.**
Officiant and People **Glory to the Father... Alleluia.**

The Invitatory Psalm 100

We are the Lord's people and the sheep of God's pasture: Come use us worship.

Hymn O splendor of God's glory bright *Hymnal 5*

Psalm 9 *Confitebor tibi*

I was dead, and see, I am alive forever and ever;
and I have the keys of Death and of Hades. Rev. 1:18

Epiphany Those who know your Name will put their trust in you, for you never forsake those who seek you, O LORD

Pentecost You never forsake those who seek you, O LORD.

1   I will give thanks to you, O LORD, with my whole heart; *
     I will tell of all your marvelous works.

2   I will be glad and rejoice in you; *
     I will sing to your Name, O Most High.

3   When my enemies are driven back, *
     they will stumble and perish at your presence.

4   For you have maintained my right and my cause; *
     you sit upon your throne judging right.

5   You have rebuked the ungodly and destroyed the wicked; *
     you have blotted out their name for ever and ever.

6   As for the enemy, they are finished, in perpetual ruin, *
     their cities ploughed under, the memory of them perished;

7   But the LORD is enthroned for ever; *
     he has set up his throne for judgment.

8   It is he who rules the world with righteousness; *
     he judges the peoples with equity.

9   The LORD will be a refuge for the oppressed, *
     a refuge in time of trouble.

10 Those who know your Name will put their trust in you, *
>   for you never forsake those who seek you, O LORD.

11 Sing praise to the LORD who dwells in Zion; *
>   proclaim to the peoples the things he has done.

12 The Avenger of blood will remember them; *
>   he will not forget the cry of the afflicted.

13 Have pity on me, O LORD; *
>   see the misery I suffer from those who hate me,
>   O you who lift me up from the gate of death;

14 So that I may tell of all your praises
>   and rejoice in your salvation *
>   in the gates of the city of Zion.

15 The ungodly have fallen into the pit they dug, *
>   and in the snare they set is their own foot caught.

16 The LORD is known by his acts of justice; *
>   the wicked are trapped in the works of their own hands.

17 The wicked shall be given over to the grave, *
>   and also all the peoples that forget God.

18 For the needy shall not always be forgotten, *
>   and the hope of the poor shall not perish for ever.

19 Rise up, O LORD, let not the ungodly have the upper hand; *
>   let them be judged before you.

20 Put fear upon them, O LORD; *
>   let the ungodly know they are but mortal.

Epiphany Those who know your Name will put their trust in you, for you never forsake those who seek you, O LORD
Pentecost You never forsake those who seek you, O LORD.

Psalm 101 *Misericordiam et judicium*
Everyone who does what is right is righteous, just as he is righteous. 1 Jn. 3:7
Epiphany The path of the righteous is like the light of dawn, which shines brighter and brighter until full day.
Pentecost To you, O Lord, will I sing praises, I will strive to follow a blameless course.

1 I will sing of mercy and justice; *
>   to you, O LORD, will I sing praises.

2   I will strive to follow a blameless course;
    oh, when will you come to me? *
        I will walk with sincerity of heart within my house.

3   I will set no worthless thing before my eyes; *
        I hate the doers of evil deeds;
        they shall not remain with me.

4   A crooked heart shall be far from me; *
        I will not know evil.

5   Those who in secret slander their neighbors I will destroy; *
        those who have a haughty look and a proud heart
        I cannot abide.

6   My eyes are upon the faithful in the land,
    that they may dwell with me, *
        and only those who lead a blameless life
        shall be my servants.

7   Those who act deceitfully shall not dwell in my house, *
        and those who tell lies shall not continue in my sight.

8   I will soon destroy all the wicked in the land, *
        that I may root out all evildoers from the city of the LORD.

Epiphany The path of the righteous is like the light of dawn, which shines brighter and brighter until full day.
Pentecost To you, O Lord, will I sing praises, I will strive to follow a blameless course.

Psalm 150 *Laudate Dominum*
The whole multitude of the disciples began to praise God joyfully with a loud voice. Lk. 19: 37
Epiphany All nations will come and worship before you.
Pentecost Praise the Lord for his excellent greatness.

1   Hallelujah!
    Praise God in his holy temple; *
        praise him in the firmament of his power.

2   Praise him for his mighty acts; *
        praise him for his excellent greatness.

3   Praise him with the blast of the ram's-horn; *
        praise him with lyre and harp.

4   Praise him with timbrel and dance; *
        praise him with strings and pipe.

5 Praise him with resounding cymbals; *
    praise him with loud-clanging cymbals.

6 Let everything that has breath *
    praise the Lord.
    Hallelujah!

Epiphany All nations will come and worship before you.
Pentecost Praise the Lord for his excellent greatness.

Reading One

Responsory One (Ps. 142:5)
I cry out to you, O Lord
        – you are my refuge.
My portion in the land of the living
        – you are my refuge.
Glory to the Father and to the Son and to the Holy Spirit.
I cry out to you, O Lord
        – you are my refuge.

The First Canticle – Song of Deep Wisdom *O altitudo divitiarum sapientiae*
(Rom 11: 33-36)
Epiphany Who has known the mind of the Lord? Or who has been
God's counselor?"
Pentecost May the God of our Lord Jesus Christ, the Father of glory,
give you a spirit of wisdom and revelation as you come to know God.

O the depth of the riches and wisdom and knowledge of God! *
    How unsearchable are his judgments
    and how inscrutable his ways!

For who has known the mind of the Lord? *
    Or who has been his counselor?"

Who has given a gift to God, *
    to receive a gift in return?"

For from him and through him *
    and to him are all things.
    To him be the glory forever. Amen.

Epiphany Who has known the mind of the Lord? Or who has been
God's counselor?"
Pentecost May the God of our Lord Jesus Christ, the Father of glory,
give you a spirit of wisdom and revelation as you come to know God.

Reading Two

Responsory Two (Ps. 71: 23-24)
My lips will sing with joy
> **– when I play to you.**

My tongue will proclaim your righteousness
> **– when I play to you.**

Glory to the Father and to the Son and to the Holy Spirit.
My lips will sing with joy
> **– when I play to you.**

The Gospel Canticle – The Song of Zechariah
Epiphany Wisdom teaches her children and gives help to those who seek her.

Pentecost With all wisdom and insight God has made known to us the mystery of his will, that he set forth in Christ, to gather up all things in Christ.

Litany

For this congregation [for those who are present, and for those who are absent], that we may be delivered from hardness of heart, and show forth your glory in all that we do, we pray to you, O Lord.
Lord, have mercy.

For the poor, the persecuted, the sick, and all who suffer; for refugees, prisoners, and all who are in danger; that they may be relieved and protected, we pray to you, O Lord.
Christ, have mercy.

For ourselves; for the forgiveness of our sins, and for the grace of the Holy Spirit to amend our lives, we pray to you, O Lord.
Lord, have mercy.

Invitation to the Lord's Prayer We join the countless throngs of angels who stand before you and, giving voice to every creature under heaven, we glorify your Name.

The Collect *From the proper of the day or*

Almighty God, who after the creation of the world rested from all your works and sanctified a day of rest for all your creatures: Grant that we, putting away all earthly anxieties, may be duly prepared for the service of your sanctuary, and that our rest here upon earth may be a preparation for the eternal rest promised to your people in heaven; through Jesus Christ our Lord. Amen.

The Blessing

May the grace of the Lord Jesus Christ be with our spirits. **Amen**

Saturday Week 1 Noonday Prayer

Officiant: O God, make speed to save us.

People: **O Lord, make haste to help us.**

Officiant and People **Glory to the Father ... Alleluia.**

Hymn Now Holy Spirit ever One *Hymnal 19*

Psalm 119 Waw *Et veniat super me*

You will know the truth, and the truth will make you free. Jn. 8:32

Epiphany I am bound by the vow I made to you, O God; I will present to you thank-offerings.

Pentecost O Lord my God, I cried out to you, and you restored me to health.

41 Let your loving-kindness come to me, O LORD, *
    and your salvation, according to your promise.

42 Then shall I have a word for those who taunt me, *
    because I trust in your words.

43 Do not take the word of truth out of my mouth, *
    for my hope is in your judgments.

44 I shall continue to keep your law; *
    I shall keep it for ever and ever.

45 I will walk at liberty, *
    because I study your commandments.

46 I will tell of your decrees before kings *
    and will not be ashamed.

47 I delight in your commandments, *
    which I have always loved.

48 I will lift up my hands to your commandments, *
    and I will meditate on your statutes.

Psalm 30 *Exaltabo te, Domine*

Jesus Christ, our Lord, was declared to be Son of God with power according to the spirit of holiness by resurrection from the dead. Rm. 1:4

1 I will exalt you, O LORD,
    because you have lifted me up *
    and have not let my enemies triumph over me.

2 O LORD my God, I cried out to you, *
    and you restored me to health.

3 You brought me up, O LORD, from the dead; *
    you restored my life as I was going down to the grave.

4 Sing to the LORD, you servants of his; *
    give thanks for the remembrance of his holiness.

5 For his wrath endures but the twinkling of an eye, *
    his favor for a lifetime.

6 Weeping may spend the night, *
    but joy comes in the morning.

7 While I felt secure, I said,
  "I shall never be disturbed. *
    You, LORD, with your favor,
    made me as strong as the mountains."

8 Then you hid your face, *
    and I was filled with fear.

9 I cried to you, O LORD; *
    I pleaded with the Lord, saying,

10 "What profit is there in my blood, if I go down to the Pit? *
    will the dust praise you or declare your faithfulness?

11 Hear, O LORD, and have mercy upon me; *
    O LORD, be my helper."

12 You have turned my wailing into dancing; *
    you have put off my sack-cloth and clothed me with joy.

13 Therefore my heart sings to you without ceasing; *
    O LORD my God, I will give you thanks for ever.

Psalm 56 *Miserere mei, Deus*

Do not let your hearts be troubled, and do not let them be afraid. Jn. 14:27

1 Have mercy on me, O God,
  for my enemies are hounding me; *
    all day long they assault and oppress me.

2 They hound me all the day long; *
    truly there are many who fight against me, O Most High.

3 Whenever I am afraid, *
    I will put my trust in you.

4 In God, whose word I praise,
    In God I trust and will not be afraid, *
        for what can flesh do to me?

5 All day long they damage my cause; *
        their only thought is to do me evil.

6 They band together; they lie in wait; *
        they spy upon my footsteps;
        because they seek my life.

7 Shall they escape despite their wickedness? *
        O God, in your anger, cast down the peoples.

8 You have noted my lamentation;
    put my tears into your bottle; *
        are they not recorded in your book?

9 Whenever I call upon you, my enemies will be put to flight; *
        this I know, for God is on my side.

10 In God the LORD, whose word I praise,
    in God I trust and will not be afraid, *
        for what can mortals do to me?

11 I am bound by the vow I made to you, O God; *
        I will present to you thank-offerings;

12 For you have rescued my soul from death
    and my feet from stumbling, *
        that I may walk before God in the light of the living.

Epiphany I am bound by the vow I made to you, O God; I will present to you thank-offerings.
Pentecost O Lord my God, I cried out to you, and you restored me to health.

Reading Genesis 2: 1-3
Thus the heavens and the earth were finished, and all their multitude. And on the seventh day God finished the work that he had done, and he rested on the seventh day from all the work that he had done. So God blessed the seventh day and hallowed it, because on it God rested from all the work that he had done in creation.

Verse and Response
A sabbath rest still remains for the people of God.
All who enter God's rest cease from their labors as God did.

The Short Litany and the Lord's Prayer

The Collect Almighty and most merciful God, grant that by the indwelling of your Holy Spirit we may be enlightened and strengthened for your service; through Jesus Christ our Lord, who lives and reigns with you, in the unity of the Holy Spirit, one God, now and for ever. Amen.

Let us bless the Lord.
Thanks be to God.

Week 2

Sunday Week 2 Evening Prayer I

Officiant: O God, make speed to save us.

People: **O Lord, make haste to help us.**

Officiant and People **Glory to the Father... Alleluia.**

Hymn Christ mighty Savior *Hymnal 34*

Psalm 146 *Lauda, anima mea*
I will put my Spirit upon him, and he will proclaim justice to the Gentiles. Mt. 12:18

Epiphany God gives justice to those who are oppressed, and food to those who hunger, hallelujah.

Pentecost I will praise the Lord as long as I live, hallelujah.

1   Hallelujah!
    Praise the LORD, O my soul! *
        I will praise the LORD as long as I live;
        I will sing praises to my God while I have my being.

2   Put not your trust in rulers, nor in any child of earth, *
        for there is no help in them.

3   When they breathe their last, they return to earth, *
        and in that day their thoughts perish.

4   Blessed are they who have the God of Jacob for their help! *
        whose hope is in the LORD their God;

5   Who made heaven and earth, the seas, and all that is in them; *
        who keeps his promise for ever;

6   Who gives justice to those who are oppressed, *
        and food to those who hunger.

7   The LORD sets the prisoners free;
    the LORD opens the eyes of the blind; *
        the LORD lifts up those who are bowed down;

8   The LORD loves the righteous;
    the LORD cares for the stranger; *
        he sustains the orphan and widow,
        but frustrates the way of the wicked.

9   The LORD shall reign for ever, *
        your God, O Zion, throughout all generations.
        Hallelujah!

Epiphany God gives justice to those who are oppressed, and food to those who hunger, hallelujah.

Pentecost I will praise the Lord as long as I live, hallelujah.

Psalm 147 A *Laudate Dominum*

We give thanks to the Father, who has enabled us to share
in the inheritance of the saints in the light. Col. 1:12

Epiphany God counts the number of the stars and calls them all by their names, hallelujah.

Pentecost How pleasant it is to honor God with praise, hallelujah.

1 Hallelujah!
   How good it is to sing praises to our God! *
      how pleasant it is to honor him with praise!

2 The LORD rebuilds Jerusalem; *
      he gathers the exiles of Israel.

3 He heals the brokenhearted *
      and binds up their wounds.

4 He counts the number of the stars *
      and calls them all by their names.

5 Great is our LORD and mighty in power; *
      there is no limit to his wisdom.

6 The LORD lifts up the lowly, *
      but casts the wicked to the ground.

7 Sing to the LORD with thanksgiving; *
      make music to our God upon the harp.

8 He covers the heavens with clouds *
      and prepares rain for the earth;

9 He makes grass to grow upon the mountains *
      and green plants to serve mankind.

10 He provides food for flocks and herds *
      and for the young ravens when they cry.

11 He is not impressed by the might of a horse; *
      he has no pleasure in the strength of a man;

12 But the LORD has pleasure in those who fear him, *
      in those who await his gracious favor.

Epiphany God counts the number of the stars and calls them all by their names, hallelujah.

Pentecost How pleasant it is to honor God with praise, hallelujah.

Psalm 147 B *Lauda Hierusalem*

Let the peace of Christ rule in your hearts, to which indeed you were called in the one body. Col. 3:15

Epiphany God sends forth his word and melts them; he blows with his wind, and the waters flow, hallelujah.

Pentecost Praise your God, O Zion, for he has established peace on your borders, hallelujah.

13 Worship the LORD, O Jerusalem; *
  praise your God, O Zion;

14 For he has strengthened the bars of your gates; *
  he has blessed your children within you.

15 He has established peace on your borders; *
  he satisfies you with the finest wheat.

16 He sends out his command to the earth, *
  and his word runs very swiftly.

17 He gives snow like wool; *
  he scatters hoarfrost like ashes.

18 He scatters his hail like bread crumbs; *
  who can stand against his cold?

19 He sends forth his word and melts them; *
  he blows with his wind, and the waters flow.

20 He declares his word to Jacob, *
  his statutes and his judgments to Israel.

21 He has not done so to any other nation; *
  to them he has not revealed his judgments.
  Hallelujah!

Epiphany God sends forth his word and melts them; he blows with his wind, and the waters flow, hallelujah.

Pentecost Praise your God, O Zion, for he has established peace on your borders, hallelujah.

Reading

Responsory (Rm. 6:4)
Christ suffered for sins once for all
  – to bring you to God.
Christ was put to death in the flesh, but made alive in the spirit
  – to bring you to God.
Glory to the Father and to the Son and to the Holy Spirit.

Christ suffered for sins once for all
— to bring you to God.

The Gospel Canticle — The Song of Mary

Magnificat Antiphon *From the proper of the day.*

Litany

For all who are in danger, sorrow, or any kind of trouble; for those who minister to the sick, the friendless, and the needy.
Lord, have mercy.
For the peace and unity of the Church of God; for all who proclaim the Gospel, and all who seek the Truth.
Christ, have mercy.
For all who have died, that they may have a place in your eternal kingdom; for all who mourn and all who care for them.
Lord, have mercy.

Invitation to the Lord's Prayer We hope to share in Christ's Resurrection so we pray with Christ to the Father.

The Collect *From the proper of the day or*

O God, the source of eternal light: Shed forth your unending day upon us who watch for you, that our lips may praise you, our lives may bless you, and our worship on the morrow give you glory; through Jesus Christ our Lord. Amen.

The Blessing

May the God of hope fill us with all joy and peace in believing, so that we may abound in hope by the power of the Holy Spirit. **Amen**

Sunday Week 2 Morning Prayer

Officiant: Lord, open our lips.
People: **And our mouth shall proclaim your praise.**
Officiant and People **Glory to the Father... Alleluia.**

The Invitatory Psalm 95

The Lord creates the world in its diversity: Come let us worship.

Hymn O Trinity of blessed light *Hymnal 52*

Psalm 93 *Dominus regnavit*
Jesus Christ is the faithful witness, the firstborn of the dead,
and the ruler of the kings of the earth. Rev. 1:5

Epiphany God sends forth his word and melts them; he blows with his wind, and the waters flow, hallelujah.
Pentecost Mighty is the Lord who dwells on high, hallelujah.

1　The LORD is King;
　　he has put on splendid apparel; *
　　　　the LORD has put on his apparel
　　　　and girded himself with strength.

2　He has made the whole world so sure *
　　　　that it cannot be moved;

3　Ever since the world began, your throne has been established; *
　　　　you are from everlasting.

4　The waters have lifted up, O LORD,
　　the waters have lifted up their voice; *
　　　　the waters have lifted up their pounding waves.

5　Mightier than the sound of many waters,
　　mightier than the breakers of the sea, *
　　　　mightier is the LORD who dwells on high.

6　Your testimonies are very sure, *
　　　　and holiness adorns your house, O LORD,
　　　　for ever and for evermore.

Epiphany God sends forth his word and melts them; he blows with his wind, and the waters flow, hallelujah.
Pentecost Mighty is the Lord who dwells on high, hallelujah.

Psalm 63 *Deus, Deus meus*
Let anyone who is thirsty come to me, and let the one who believes in me drink. Jn. 7: 37-38
Epiphany I have gazed upon you in your holy place, that I might behold your power and your glory, hallelujah.
Pentecost My soul clings to you; your right hand holds me fast, hallelujah.

1　O God, you are my God; eagerly I seek you; *
　　　　my soul thirsts for you, my flesh faints for you,
　　　　as in a barren and dry land where there is no water.

2　Therefore I have gazed upon you in your holy place, *
　　　　that I might behold your power and your glory.

3　For your loving-kindness is better than life itself; *
　　　　my lips shall give you praise.

4　So will I bless you as long as I live *
　　　　and lift up my hands in your Name.

5　My soul is content, as with marrow and fatness, *
　　　　and my mouth praises you with joyful lips,

6   When I remember you upon my bed, *
    and meditate on you in the night watches.

7   For you have been my helper, *
    and under the shadow of your wings I will rejoice.

8   My soul clings to you; *
    your right hand holds me fast.

9   May those who seek my life to destroy it *
    go down into the depths of the earth;

10 Let them fall upon the edge of the sword, *
    and let them be food for jackals.

11 But the king will rejoice in God;
    all those who swear by him will be glad; *
      for the mouth of those who speak lies shall be stopped.

Epiphany I have gazed upon you in your holy place, that I might behold your power and your glory, hallelujah.
Pentecost My soul clings to you; your right hand holds me fast, hallelujah.

Psalm 47 *Omnes gentes, plaudite*
God has made him the head over all things for the church, which is his body,
the fullness of him who fills all in all. Eph. 1:22-23

Epiphany God reigns over the nations; God sits upon his holy throne, hallelujah.
Pentecost Shout to God with a cry of joy, hallelujah .

1   Clap your hands, all you peoples; *
    shout to God with a cry of joy.

2   For the LORD Most High is to be feared; *
    he is the great King over all the earth.

3   He subdues the peoples under us, *
    and the nations under our feet.

4   He chooses our inheritance for us, *
    the pride of Jacob whom he loves.

5   God has gone up with a shout, *
    the LORD with the sound of the ram's-horn.

6   Sing praises to God, sing praises; *
    sing praises to our King, sing praises.

7 For God is King of all the earth; *
  sing praises with all your skill.

8 God reigns over the nations; *
  God sits upon his holy throne.

9 The nobles of the peoples have gathered together *
  with the people of the God of Abraham.

10 The rulers of the earth belong to God, *
  and he is highly exalted.

Epiphany God reigns over the nations; God sits upon his holy throne, hallelujah.

Pentecost Shout to God with a cry of joy, hallelujah .

Reading One

Responsory One (Lk. 18:38)
Christ, Son of the Living God
  – have mercy on us.
You are risen from the dead
  – have mercy on us.
Glory to the Father and to the Son and to the Holy Spirit.
Christ, Son of the Living God
  – have mercy on us.

The First Canticle – You are God *Te Deum laudamus*

You are God: we praise you;
You are the Lord: we acclaim you;
You are the eternal Father:
All creation worships you.
To you all angels, all the powers of heaven,
Cherubim and Seraphim, sing in endless praise:
  Holy, holy, holy Lord, God of power and might,
  heaven and earth are full of your glory.
The glorious company of apostles praise you.
The noble fellowship of prophets praise you.
The white-robed army of martyrs praise you.
Throughout the world the holy Church acclaims you;
  Father, of majesty unbounded,
  your true and only Son, worthy of all worship,
  and the Holy Spirit, advocate and guide.
You, Christ, are the king of glory,
the eternal Son of the Father.

When you became man to set us free
you did not shun the Virgin's womb.
You overcame the sting of death
and opened the kingdom of heaven to all believers.
You are seated at God's right hand in glory.
We believe that you will come and be our judge.
  Come then, Lord, and help your people,
  bought with the price of your own blood,
  and bring us with your saints
  to glory everlasting.
The Gloria is not said with the Te Deum.

Reading Two

Responsory Two (Lam. 3: 22-23)
The steadfast love of the Lord never ceases
  – God's mercies never come to an end.
They are new every morning
  – God's mercies never come to an end.
Glory to the Father and to the Son and to the Holy Spirit.
The steadfast love of the Lord never ceases
  – God's mercies never come to an end.

The Gospel Canticle – The Song of Zechariah
Benedictus Antiphon *From the proper of the day*

Litany
Lord, keep this nation under your care; and guide us in the way of justice and truth.
Lord, have mercy.
Let your way be known upon earth; your saving health among all nations.
Christ, have mercy.
Let not the needy, O Lord, be forgotten; nor the hope of the poor be taken away.
Lord, have mercy.

Invitation to the Lord's Prayer As the sun radiates the world, so the Spirit illumines our hearts and we call upon our God.

The Collect *From the Proper of the day or*
 O God, you make us glad with the weekly remembrance of the glorious resurrection of your Son our Lord: Give us this day such blessing

through our worship of you, that the week to come may be spent in your favor; through Jesus Christ our Lord. Amen.

The Blessing
May we rejoice always, pray without ceasing and give thanks in all circumstances. **Amen**

Sunday Week 2 Noonday Prayer

Officiant: O God, make speed to save us.
People: **O Lord, make haste to help us.**
Officiant and People **Glory to the Father ... Alleluia.**

Hymn Now Holy Spirit ever One *Hymnal 20*

Psalm 72 A Deus, judicium

On entering the house, they saw the child with Mary his mother; and they knelt down and paid him homage. Mt. 2:11

Epiphany The kings of Tarshish and of the isles shall pay tribute, and the kings of Arabia and Saba offer gifts, hallelujah.
Pentecost In his time shall the righteous flourish; there shall be abundance of peace till the moon shall be no more, hallelujah.

1 Give the King your justice, O God, *
     and your righteousness to the King's Son;

2 That he may rule your people righteously *
     and the poor with justice;

3 That the mountains may bring prosperity to the people, *
     and the little hills bring righteousness.

4 He shall defend the needy among the people; *
     he shall rescue the poor and crush the oppressor.

5 He shall live as long as the sun and moon endure, *
     from one generation to another.

6 He shall come down like rain upon the mown field, *
     like showers that water the earth.

7 In his time shall the righteous flourish; *
     there shall be abundance of peace
     till the moon shall be no more.

8 He shall rule from sea to sea, *
     and from the River to the ends of the earth.

9 His foes shall bow down before him, *
     and his enemies lick the dust.

10 The kings of Tarshish and of the isles shall pay tribute, *
    and the kings of Arabia and Saba offer gifts.

11 All kings shall bow down before him, *
    and all the nations do him service.

Psalm 72 B *Quia liberabit*

Jesus saw a great crowd; and he had compassion for them and cured their sick. Mt. 14:14

12 For he shall deliver the poor who cries out in distress, *
    and the oppressed who has no helper.

13 He shall have pity on the lowly and poor; *
    he shall preserve the lives of the needy.

14 He shall redeem their lives from oppression and violence, *
    and dear shall their blood be in his sight.

15 Long may he live!
    and may there be given to him gold from Arabia; *
        may prayer be made for him always,
        and may they bless him all the day long.

16 May there be abundance of grain on the earth,
    growing thick even on the hilltops; *
        may its fruit flourish like Lebanon,
        and its grain like grass upon the earth.

17 May his Name remain for ever
    and be established as long as the sun endures; *
        may all the nations bless themselves in him
        and call him blessed.

18 Blessed be the LORD God, the God of Israel, *
    who alone does wondrous deeds!

19 And blessed be his glorious Name for ever! *
    and may all the earth be filled with his glory.
    Amen. Amen.

Psalm 117 *Laudate Dominum*

Once you were not a people, but now you are God's people. 1 Pt. 2:10

1 Praise the LORD, all you nations; *
    laud him, all you peoples.

2 For his loving-kindness toward us is great, *
    and the faithfulness of the LORD endures for ever.
    Hallelujah!

Epiphany The kings of Tarshish and of the isles shall pay tribute, and the kings of Arabia and Saba offer gifts, hallelujah.

Pentecost In his time shall the righteous flourish; there shall be abundance of peace till the moon shall be no more, hallelujah.

Reading Genesis 12: 1-4

Now the Lord said to Abram, "Go from your country and your kindred and your father's house to the land that I will show you. I will make of you a great nation, and I will bless you, and make your name great, so that you will be a blessing. I will bless those who bless you, and the one who curses you I will curse; and in you all the families of the earth shall be blessed." So Abram went, as the Lord had told him.

Verse and Response

In Christ Jesus the blessing of Abraham has come to the Gentiles.
That we might receive the promise of the Spirit through faith.

The Short Litany and the Lord's Prayer

The Collect God and Father of all believers, for the glory of your Name multiply, by the grace of the Paschal sacrament, the number of your children; that your Church may rejoice to see fulfilled your promise to our father Abraham; through Jesus Christ our Lord. Amen.

Let us bless the Lord.
Thanks be to God.

Sunday Week 2 Evening Prayer II

Officiant: O God, make speed to save us.
People: **O Lord, make haste to help us.**
Officiant and People **Glory to the Father … Alleluia.**

Hymn Lord of all hopefulness *Hymnal 482*

Psalm 113 *Laudate, pueri*

Salvation belongs to our God who is seated on the throne, and to the Lamb! Rev. 7:10

Epiphany Who is like the LORD our God, who sits enthroned on high, but stoops to behold the heavens and the earth? Hallelujah.

Pentecost From the rising of the sun to its going down, let the Name of the Lord be praised, hallelujah.

1 Hallelujah!
    Give praise, you servants of the LORD; *
        praise the Name of the LORD.

2 Let the Name of the LORD be blessed, *
        from this time forth for evermore.

3 From the rising of the sun to its going down *
    let the Name of the LORD be praised.

4 The LORD is high above all nations, *
    and his glory above the heavens.

5 Who is like the LORD our God, who sits enthroned on high, *
    but stoops to behold the heavens and the earth?

6 He takes up the weak out of the dust *
    and lifts up the poor from the ashes.

7 He sets them with the princes, *
    with the princes of his people.

8 He makes the woman of a childless house *
    to be a joyful mother of children.

Epiphany Who is like the LORD our God, who sits enthroned on high, but stoops to behold the heavens and the earth? Hallelujah.
Pentecost From the rising of the sun to its going down, let the Name of the Lord be praised, hallelujah.

Psalm 114 *In exitu Israel*
Now have come the salvation and the power and the kingdom of our God
and the authority of his Messiah. Rev. 12:10

Epiphany The sea beheld it and fled; Jordan turned and went back, hallelujah.
Pentecost Tremble, O earth, at the presence of the Lord, hallelujah.

1 Hallelujah!
    When Israel came out of Egypt, *
        the house of Jacob from a people of strange speech,

2 Judah became God's sanctuary *
    and Israel his dominion.

3 The sea beheld it and fled; *
    Jordan turned and went back.

4 The mountains skipped like rams, *
    and the little hills like young sheep.

5 What ailed you, O sea, that you fled? *
    O Jordan, that you turned back?

6 You mountains, that you skipped like rams? *
    you little hills like young sheep?

7 Tremble, O earth, at the presence of the Lord, *
   at the presence of the God of Jacob,

8 Who turned the hard rock into a pool of water *
   and flint-stone into a flowing spring.

Epiphany The sea beheld it and fled; Jordan turned and went back,
hallelujah.
Pentecost Tremble, O earth, at the presence of the Lord, hallelujah.

Psalm 115 *Non nobis, Domine*

Jesus Christ loves us and freed us from our sins by his blood, and made us to be a kingdom,
Epiphany God will bless those who fear the LORD, both small and
great together, hallelujah.
Pentecost Our God is in heaven; whatever he wills to do he does,
hallelujah.

1 Not to us, O LORD, not to us,
   but to your Name give glory; *
      because of your love and because of your faithfulness.

2 Why should the heathen say, *
   "Where then is their God?"

3 Our God is in heaven; *
   whatever he wills to do he does.

4 Their idols are silver and gold, *
   the work of human hands.

5 They have mouths, but they cannot speak; *
   eyes have they, but they cannot see;

6 They have ears, but they cannot hear; *
   noses, but they cannot smell;

7 They have hands, but they cannot feel;
   feet, but they cannot walk; *
      they make no sound with their throat.

8 Those who make them are like them, *
   and so are all who put their trust in them.

9 O Israel, trust in the LORD; *
   he is their help and their shield.

10 O house of Aaron, trust in the LORD; *
   he is their help and their shield.

11 You who fear the LORD, trust in the LORD; *
 he is their help and their shield.

12 The LORD has been mindful of us, and he will bless us; *
 he will bless the house of Israel;
 he will bless the house of Aaron;

13 He will bless those who fear the LORD, *
 both small and great together.

14 May the LORD increase you more and more, *
 you and your children after you.

15 May you be blessed by the LORD, *
 the maker of heaven and earth.

16 The heaven of heavens is the LORD'S, *
 but he entrusted the earth to its peoples.

17 The dead do not praise the LORD, *
 nor all those who go down into silence;

18 But we will bless the LORD, *
 from this time forth for evermore.
 Hallelujah!

Epiphany God will bless those who fear the LORD, both small and great together, hallelujah.
Pentecost Our God is in heaven; whatever he wills to do he does, hallelujah.

Reading

Responsory (Dan. 3: 56)
Glorify the Lord
  − in the firmament of God's power.
Praise and highly exalt God for ever
  − in the firmament of God's power.
Glory to the Father and to the Son and to the Holy Spirit.
Glorify the Lord
  − in the firmament of God's power.

The Gospel Canticle − The Song of Mary
Magnificat Antiphon *From the proper of the day*

Litany
That there may be peace to your Church and to the whole world.
Lord, have mercy.
That we may be pardoned and forgiven for our sins and offenses.
Christ, have mercy.
That we may be bound together by your Holy Spirit in the communion
of Blessed Mary and all your saints, entrusting one another and all our
life to Christ.
Lord, have mercy.

Invitation to the Lord's Prayer Nourished with the Bread of Life and
Cup of Salvation, we thank our Father for feeding us with Christ, the
Living Bread.

Collect *From the proper of the day or*
Lord God, whose Son our Savior Jesus Christ triumphed over the powers
of death and prepared for us our place in the new Jerusalem: Grant that
we, who have this day given thanks for his resurrection, may praise you
in that City of which he is the light, and where he lives and reigns for ever
and ever. Amen.

The Blessing
May we not quench the Spirit, not despise the words of prophets, but
test everything, hold fast to what is good and abstain from every form
of evil. **Amen**

Monday Week 2 Morning Prayer
Officiant: Lord, open our lips.
People: **And our mouth shall proclaim your praise.**
Officiant and People **Glory to the Father... Alleluia.**

The Invitatory Psalm 29
Ascribe to the Lord, our Maker, the glory due God's Name: Come let us
worship.

Hymn New every morning *Hymnal 10*

Psalm 19 *Cæli enarrant*
For you who revere my name the sun of righteousness shall rise, with healing in its wings. Mal 4:2
Epiphany The sun comes forth like a bridegroom out of his chamber;
it rejoices like a champion to run its course.
Pentecost Let the words of my mouth and the meditation of my heart
be acceptable in your sight.

1   The heavens declare the glory of God, *
    and the firmament shows his handiwork.

2   One day tells its tale to another, *
      and one night imparts knowledge to another.

3   Although they have no words or language, *
      and their voices are not heard,

4   Their sound has gone out into all lands, *
      and their message to the ends of the world.

5   In the deep has he set a pavilion for the sun; *
      it comes forth like a bridegroom out of his chamber;
      it rejoices like a champion to run its course.

6   It goes forth from the uttermost edge of the heavens
    and runs about to the end of it again; *
      nothing is hidden from its burning heat.

7   The law of the LORD is perfect
    and revives the soul; *
      the testimony of the LORD is sure
      and gives wisdom to the innocent.

8   The statutes of the LORD are just
    and rejoice the heart; *
      the commandment of the LORD is clear
      and gives light to the eyes.

9   The fear of the LORD is clean
    and endures for ever; *
      the judgments of the LORD are true
      and righteous altogether.

10 More to be desired are they than gold,
    more than much fine gold, *
      sweeter far than honey,
      than honey in the comb.

11 By them also is your servant enlightened, *
      and in keeping them there is great reward.

12 Who can tell how often he offends? *
      cleanse me from my secret faults.

13 Above all, keep your servant from presumptuous sins;
    let them not get dominion over me; *
      then shall I be whole and sound,
      and innocent of a great offense.

14 Let the words of my mouth and the meditation of my heart
    be acceptable in your sight, *
        O LORD, my strength and my redeemer.

Epiphany The sun comes forth like a bridegroom out of his chamber;
it rejoices like a champion to run its course.
Pentecost Let the words of my mouth and the meditation of my heart
be acceptable in your sight.

Psalm 65 *Te decet hymnus*

Jesus got up and rebuked the winds and the sea; and there was a dead calm. Mt. 8:26

Epiphany O God of our salvation, you are the hope of all the ends of
the earth and of the seas that are far away.
Pentecost Awesome things will you show us in your righteousness, O
God of our salvation.

1 You are to be praised, O God, in Zion; *
       to you shall vows be performed in Jerusalem.

2 To you that hear prayer shall all flesh come, *
       because of their transgressions.

3 Our sins are stronger than we are, *
       but you will blot them out.

4 Blessed are they whom you choose
   and draw to your courts to dwell there! *
       they will be satisfied by the beauty of your house,
       by the holiness of your temple.

5 Awesome things will you show us in your righteousness,
   O God of our salvation, *
       O Hope of all the ends of the earth
       and of the seas that are far away.

6 You make fast the mountains by your power; *
       they are girded about with might.

7 You still the roaring of the seas, *
       the roaring of their waves,
       and the clamor of the peoples.

8 Those who dwell at the ends of the earth
   will tremble at your marvelous signs; *
       you make the dawn and the dusk to sing for joy.

9 You visit the earth and water it abundantly;
      you make it very plenteous; *
            the river of God is full of water.

10 You prepare the grain, *
      for so you provide for the earth.

11 You drench the furrows and smooth out the ridges; *
      with heavy rain you soften the ground and bless its increase.

12 You crown the year with your goodness, *
      and your paths overflow with plenty.

13 May the fields of the wilderness be rich for grazing, *
      and the hills be clothed with joy.

14 May the meadows cover themselves with flocks,
      and the valleys cloak themselves with grain; *
            let them shout for joy and sing.

Epiphany O God of our salvation, you are the hope of all the ends of the earth and of the seas that are far away.
Pentecost Awesome things will you show us in your righteousness, O God of our salvation.

Psalm 148 *Laudate Dominum*

At Jesus' name every knee should bend, in heaven and on earth and under the earth. Phil 2:10
Epiphany Let Kings of the earth and all peoples praise the Name of the LORD.
Pentecost Praise the Lord from the heavens, praise the Lord from the earth.

1 Hallelujah!
   Praise the LORD from the heavens; *
      praise him in the heights.

2 Praise him, all you angels of his; *
      praise him, all his host.

3 Praise him, sun and moon; *
      praise him, all you shining stars.

4 Praise him, heaven of heavens, *
      and you waters above the heavens.

5 Let them praise the Name of the LORD; *
      for he commanded, and they were created.

6 He made them stand fast for ever and ever; *
    he gave them a law which shall not pass away.

7 Praise the LORD from the earth, *
    you sea-monsters and all deeps;

8 Fire and hail, snow and fog, *
    tempestuous wind, doing his will;

9 Mountains and all hills, *
    fruit trees and all cedars;

10 Wild beasts and all cattle, *
    creeping things and wingèd birds;

11 Kings of the earth and all peoples, *
    princes and all rulers of the world;

12 Young men and maidens, *
    old and young together.

13 Let them praise the Name of the LORD, *
    for his Name only is exalted,
    his splendor is over earth and heaven.

14 He has raised up strength for his people
  and praise for all his loyal servants, *
    the children of Israel, a people who are near him.
    Hallelujah!

Epiphany Let Kings of the earth and all peoples praise the Name of the LORD.
Pentecost Praise the Lord from the heavens, praise the Lord from the earth.

Reading One

Responsory One (Ps. 5:3)
In the morning, Lord
    – you hear my voice.
I make my appeal and watch for you
    – you hear my voice.
Glory to the Father and to the Son and to the Holy Spirit.
In the morning, Lord
    – you hear my voice.

The First Canticle – Song of Victory *Incipite Domino in tympanis*
(Judith 16:13-16)

Epiphany You sent your breath and it formed them; no one is able to resist your voice.

Pentecost Let the whole creation serve you, for you spoke and all things came into being.

Begin a song to my God with tambourines, *
 sing to my Lord with cymbals.

Raise to him a new psalm; *
 exalt him, and call upon his name.

I will sing a new song to my God, *
 for you are great and glorious, wonderful in strength, invincible.

Let the whole creation serve you, *
 for you spoke and all things came into being.

You sent your breath and it formed them, *
 no one is able to resist your voice.

Mountains and seas are stirred to their depths, *
 rocks melt like wax at your presence.

But to those who fear you, *
 you continue to show mercy.

No sacrifice, however fragrant, can please you, *
 but whoever fears the Lord shall stand in your sight for ever.

Epiphany You sent your breath and it formed them; no one is able to resist your voice.

Pentecost Let the whole creation serve you, for you spoke and all things came into being.

Reading Two

Responsory Two (Ps. 22:23)
Praise the Lord
 – you who fear God.
Stand in awe of the Lord
 – you who fear God.
Glory to the Father and to the Son and to the Holy Spirit.
Praise the Lord
 – you who fear God.

The Gospel Canticle – The Song of Zechariah

Epiphany In the tender compassion of our God the dawn from on high shall break upon us.

Pentecost God has raised up for us a mighty savior, born of the house of his servant David.

Litany

For N., our Presiding Bishop, N. our Bishop, for all the clergy, for consecrated women and men and for all the people, let us pray to the Lord.

Lord, have mercy.

For N. our President, for the leaders of the nations, and for all in authority, let us pray to the Lord.

Christ, have mercy.

For this city (town, village, _____), for every city and community, and for those who live in them, let us pray to the Lord.

Lord, have mercy.

Invitation to the Lord's Prayer That we might live no longer for ourselves but for Christ, who died and rose for us, we ask the Father to sanctify us by the Holy Spirit.

The Collect *From the proper of the day or*

Almighty and everlasting God, by whose Spirit the whole body of your faithful people is governed and sanctified: Receive our supplications and prayers which we offer before you for all members of your holy Church, that in their vocation and ministry they may truly and devoutly serve you; through our Lord and Savior Jesus Christ. Amen.

The Blessing

May we pursue righteousness, godliness, faith, love, endurance and gentleness. Let us fight the good fight of the faith and take hold of the eternal life, to which we were called. **Amen**

Monday Week 2 Noonday Prayer

Officiant: O God, make speed to save us.

People: **O Lord, make haste to help us.**

Officiant and People **Glory to the Father ... Alleluia.**

Hymn The golden sun lights up the sky *Hymnal 13*

Psalm 119 Zayin *Memor esto verbi tui*

Suffering produces endurance, and endurance produces character, and character produces hope, and hope does not disappoint us. Rm. 5: 3-5

Epiphany The LORD thundered out of heaven; the Most High uttered his voice.

Pentecost The Lord brought me out into an open place; he rescued me because he delighted in me.

49 Remember your word to your servant, *
   because you have given me hope.

50 This is my comfort in my trouble, *
   that your promise gives me life.

51 The proud have derided me cruelly, *
   but I have not turned from your law.

52 When I remember your judgments of old, *
   O LORD, I take great comfort.

53 I am filled with a burning rage , *
   because of the wicked who forsake your law.

54 Your statutes have been like songs to me *
   wherever I have lived as a stranger.

55 I remember your Name in the night, O LORD, *
   and dwell upon your law.

56 This is how it has been with me, *
   because I have kept your commandments.

Psalm 18 Part I A *Diligam te, Domine*

Jesus began to be distressed and agitated. "I am deeply grieved, even to death." Mk. 14:33-35

1 I love you, O LORD my strength, *
   O LORD my stronghold, my crag, and my haven.

2 My God, my rock in whom I put my trust, *
   my shield, the horn of my salvation, and my refuge;
   you are worthy of praise.

3 I will call upon the LORD, *
   and so shall I be saved from my enemies.

4 The breakers of death rolled over me, *
   and the torrents of oblivion made me afraid.

5 The cords of hell entangled me, *
   and the snares of death were set for me.

6 I called upon the LORD in my distress *
    and cried out to my God for help.

7 He heard my voice from his heavenly dwelling; *
    my cry of anguish came to his ears.

Psalm 18 Part I B *Commota est*

Jesus gave a loud cry and breathed his last.
And the curtain of the temple was torn in two, from top to bottom. Mk. 15:37-38

8 The earth reeled and rocked; *
      the roots of the mountains shook;
      they reeled because of his anger.

9 Smoke rose from his nostrils
  and a consuming fire out of his mouth; *
    hot burning coals blazed forth from him.

10 He parted the heavens and came down *
    with a storm cloud under his feet.

11 He mounted on cherubim and flew; *
    he swooped on the wings of the wind.

12 He wrapped darkness about him; *
    he made dark waters and thick clouds his pavilion.

13 From the brightness of his presence, through the clouds, *
    burst hailstones and coals of fire.

14 The LORD thundered out of heaven; *
    the Most High uttered his voice.

15 He loosed his arrows and scattered them; *
    he hurled thunderbolts and routed them.

16 The beds of the seas were uncovered,
  and the foundations of the world laid bare, *
    at your battle cry, O LORD,
    at the blast of the breath of your nostrils.

17 He reached down from on high and grasped me; *
    he drew me out of great waters.

18 He delivered me from my strong enemies
  and from those who hated me; *
    for they were too mighty for me.

19 They confronted me in the day of my disaster; *
    but the LORD was my support.

20 He brought me out into an open place; *
    he rescued me because he delighted in me.

Epiphany The LORD thundered out of heaven; the Most High uttered his voice.

Pentecost The Lord brought me out into an open place; he rescued me because he delighted in me.

Reading Exodus 3: 4-6
When the Lord saw that Moses had turned aside to see, God called to him out of the bush, "Moses, Moses!" And he said, "Here I am." Then he said, "Come no closer! Remove the sandals from your feet, for the place on which you are standing is holy ground." He said further, "I am the God of your father, the God of Abraham, the God of Isaac, and the God of Jacob." And Moses hid his face, for he was afraid to look at God.

Verse and Response
Let your face shine upon your servant.
Save me in your steadfast love.

The Short Litany and the Lord's Prayer

The Collect Heavenly Father, we thank you that by water and the Holy Spirit you have bestowed on us your servants the forgiveness of sin, and have raised us to the new life of grace. Sustain us, O Lord, in your Holy Spirit. Give us inquiring minds and discerning hearts, the courage to will and to persevere, a spirit to know and to love you, and the gift of joy and wonder in all your works. Amen.

Let us bless the Lord.
Thanks be to God.

Monday Week 2 Evening Prayer
Officiant: O God, make speed to save us.
People: **O Lord, make haste to help us.**
Officiant and People **Glory to the Father ... Alleluia.**

Hymn O brightness of the immortal Father's face *Hymnal 37*

Psalm 33 A *Exultate, justi*
All things came into being through the Word, and without him not one thing came into being. Jn. 1:3
Epiphany The Lord gathers up the waters of the ocean as in a water skin and stores up the depths of the sea.
Pentecost By the word of the LORD were the heavens made, by the breath of his mouth all the heavenly hosts.

1 Rejoice in the LORD, you righteous; *
  it is good for the just to sing praises.

2 Praise the LORD with the harp; *
  play to him upon the psaltery and lyre.

3 Sing for him a new song; *
  sound a fanfare with all your skill upon the trumpet.

4 For the word of the LORD is right, *
  and all his works are sure.

5 He loves righteousness and justice; *
  the loving-kindness of the LORD fills the whole earth.

6 By the word of the LORD were the heavens made, *
  by the breath of his mouth all the heavenly hosts.

7 He gathers up the waters of the ocean as in a water-skin *
  and stores up the depths of the sea.

8 Let all the earth fear the LORD; *
  let all who dwell in the world stand in awe of him.

9 For he spoke, and it came to pass; *
  he commanded, and it stood fast.

10 The LORD brings the will of the nations to naught; *
  he thwarts the designs of the peoples.

11 But the LORD'S will stands fast for ever, *
  and the designs of his heart from age to age.

12 Blessed is the nation whose God is the LORD! *
  blessed the people he has chosen to be his own!

Epiphany The Lord gathers up the waters of the ocean as in a water skin and stores up the depths of the sea.
Pentecost By the word of the LORD were the heavens made, by the breath of his mouth all the heavenly hosts.

Psalm 33 B *De caelo respexit*
We are what he has made us, created in Christ Jesus for good works,
which God prepared beforehand to be our way of life. Eph. 2:10
Epiphany The Lord beholds all the people in the world.
Pentecost Let your loving-kindness, O LORD, be upon us, as we have put our trust in you.

13 The LORD looks down from heaven, *
  and beholds all the people in the world.

14 From where he sits enthroned he turns his gaze *
    on all who dwell on the earth.

15 He fashions all the hearts of them *
    and understands all their works.

16 There is no king that can be saved by a mighty army; *
    a strong man is not delivered by his great strength.

17 The horse is a vain hope for deliverance; *
    for all its strength it cannot save.

18 Behold, the eye of the LORD is upon those who fear him, *
    on those who wait upon his love,

19 To pluck their lives from death, *
    and to feed them in time of famine.

20 Our soul waits for the LORD; *
    he is our help and our shield.

21 Indeed, our heart rejoices in him, *
    for in his holy Name we put our trust.

22 Let your loving-kindness, O LORD, be upon us, *
    as we have put our trust in you.

Epiphany The Lord beholds all the people in the world.
Pentecost Let your loving-kindness, O LORD, be upon us, as we have
put our trust in you.

Psalm 94 *Deus ultionum*

*I thank you, Father, Lord of heaven and earth, because you have hidden these things
from the wise and the intelligent and have revealed them to infants. Lk. 10:21*

Epiphany When many cares fill my mind, your consolations cheer my
soul.
Pentecost Blessed are they whom you instruct, O Lord! whom you
teach out of your law.

1 O LORD God of vengeance, *
    O God of vengeance, show yourself.

2 Rise up, O Judge of the world; *
    give the arrogant their just deserts.

3 How long shall the wicked, O LORD, *
    how long shall the wicked triumph?

4 They bluster in their insolence; *
    all evildoers are full of boasting.

5 They crush your people, O LORD, *
  and afflict your chosen nation.

6 They murder the widow and the stranger *
  and put the orphans to death.

7 Yet they say, "The LORD does not see, *
  the God of Jacob takes no notice."

8 Consider well, you dullards among the people; *
  when will you fools understand?

9 He that planted the ear, does he not hear? *
  he that formed the eye, does he not see?

10 He who admonishes the nations, will he not punish? *
  he who teaches all the world, has he no knowledge?

11 The LORD knows our human thoughts; *
  how like a puff of wind they are.

12 Blessed are they whom you instruct, O Lord! *
  whom you teach out of your law;

13 To give them rest in evil days, *
  until a pit is dug for the wicked.

14 For the LORD will not abandon his people, *
  nor will he forsake his own.

15 For judgment will again be just, *
  and all the true of heart will follow it.

16 Who rose up for me against the wicked? *
  who took my part against the evildoers?

17 If the LORD had not come to my help, *
  I should soon have dwelt in the land of silence.

18 As often as I said, "My foot has slipped," *
  your love, O LORD, upheld me.

19 When many cares fill my mind, *
  your consolations cheer my soul.

20 Can a corrupt tribunal have any part with you, *
  one which frames evil into law?

21 They conspire against the life of the just *
  and condemn the innocent to death.

22 But the LORD has become my stronghold, *
  and my God the rock of my trust.

23 He will turn their wickedness back upon them
  and destroy them in their own malice; *
    the LORD our God will destroy them.

Epiphany When many cares fill my mind, your consolations cheer my soul.

Pentecost Blessed are they whom you instruct, O Lord! whom you teach out of your law.

Reading

Responsory (Ps. 141:2; Rev. 8:4)
Let my prayer be set forth as incense
  – the lifting of my hands as the evening sacrifice.
Let the prayers of the saints rise before God
  – the lifting of my hands as the evening sacrifice.
Glory to the Father and to the Son and to the Holy Spirit.
Let my prayer be set forth as incense
  – the lifting of my hands as the evening sacrifice.

The Gospel Canticle – The Song of Mary
Epiphany Those who do what is true come to the light, so that it may be clearly seen that their deeds have been done in God.

Pentecost God has looked with favor on me, a lowly servant. My spirit rejoices in God, my Savior.

Litany
For seasonable weather, and for an abundance of the fruits of the earth, let us pray to the Lord.
Lord, have mercy.
For deliverance from all danger, violence, oppression, and degradation, let us pray to the Lord.
Christ, have mercy.
For all who have died in the hope of the resurrection, and for all the departed, let us pray to the Lord.
Lord, have mercy.

Invitation to the Lord's Prayer Let us offer our daily work to God and seek God's blessing on this night.

The Collect *From the proper of the day or*
O God and Father of all, whom the whole heavens adore: Let the whole earth also worship you, all nations obey you, all tongues confess and bless you, and men and women everywhere love you and serve you in peace; through Jesus Christ our Lord. Amen.

The Blessing
May the Lord rescue us from every evil and save us for his heavenly kingdom. **Amen**

Tuesday Week 2 Morning Prayer
Officiant: Lord, open our lips.
People: **And our mouth shall proclaim your praise.**
Officiant and People **Glory to the Father... Alleluia.**

The Invitatory Psalm 8
The Lord's majesty is praised above the heavens: Come let us worship.

Hymn Father we praise thee *Hymnal 2*

Psalm 27 *Dominus illuminatio*
If you keep my commandments, you will abide in my love, just as I have kept my Father's commandments and abide in his love. Jn. 15:10
Epiphany I shall not fear for you, O Lord, are my saving light.
Pentecost One thing I seek: to behold the fair beauty of the LORD and to seek him in his temple.

1   The LORD is my light and my salvation;
    whom then shall I fear? *
        the LORD is the strength of my life;
        of whom then shall I be afraid?

2   When evildoers came upon me to eat up my flesh, *
        it was they, my foes and my adversaries,
        who stumbled and fell.

3   Though an army should encamp against me, *
        yet my heart shall not be afraid;

4   And though war should rise up against me, *
        yet will I put my trust in him.

5   One thing have I asked of the LORD;
    one thing I seek; *
        that I may dwell in the house of the LORD all the days of my life;

6 To behold the fair beauty of the LORD *
    and to seek him in his temple.

7 For in the day of trouble
    he shall keep me safe in his shelter; *
        he shall hide me in the secrecy of his dwelling
        and set me high upon a rock.

8 Even now he lifts up my head *
    above my enemies round about me.

9 Therefore I will offer in his dwelling an oblation
    with sounds of great gladness; *
        I will sing and make music to the LORD.

10 Hearken to my voice, O LORD, when I call; *
    have mercy on me and answer me.

11 You speak in my heart and say, "Seek my face." *
    Your face, LORD, will I seek.

12 Hide not your face from me, *
    nor turn away your servant in displeasure.

13 You have been my helper;
    cast me not away; *
        do not forsake me, O God of my salvation.

14 Though my father and my mother forsake me, *
    the LORD will sustain me.

15 Show me your way, O LORD; *
    lead me on a level path, because of my enemies.

16 Deliver me not into the hand of my adversaries, *
    for false witnesses have risen up against me,
    and also those who speak malice.

17 What if I had not believed
    that I should see the goodness of the LORD *
        in the land of the living!

18 O tarry and await the LORD'S pleasure;
    be strong, and he shall comfort your heart; *
        wait patiently for the LORD.

Epiphany I shall not fear for you, O Lord, are my saving light.
Pentecost One thing I seek: to behold the fair beauty of the LORD and to seek him in his temple.

Psalm 76 *Notus in Judæa*

In the world you face persecution. But take courage; I have conquered the world. Jn. 16:33

Epiphany God rose up to judgment and to save all the oppressed of the earth.

Pentecost How glorious you are! More splendid than the everlasting mountains!

1   In Judah is God known; *
       his Name is great in Israel.

2   At Salem is his tabernacle, *
       and his dwelling is in Zion.

3   There he broke the flashing arrows, *
       the shield, the sword, and the weapons of battle.

4   How glorious you are! *
       more splendid than the everlasting mountains!

5   The strong of heart have been despoiled;
     they sink into sleep; *
       none of the warriors can lift a hand.

6   At your rebuke, O God of Jacob, *
       both horse and rider lie stunned.

7   What terror you inspire! *
       who can stand before you when you are angry?

8   From heaven you pronounced judgment; *
       the earth was afraid and was still;

9   When God rose up to judgment *
       and to save all the oppressed of the earth.

10 Truly, wrathful Edom will give you thanks, *
       and the remnant of Hamath will keep your feasts.

11 Make a vow to the LORD your God and keep it; *
       let all around him bring gifts to him
       who is worthy to be feared.

12 He breaks the spirit of princes, *
       and strikes terror in the kings of the earth.

Epiphany God rose up to judgment and to save all the oppressed of the earth.

Pentecost How glorious you are! More splendid than the everlasting mountains!

Psalm 98 *Cantate Domino*

The throne of God and of the Lamb will be in it, and his servants will worship him;
they will see his face. Rev. 22:3-4

Epiphany In righteousness shall God judge the world and the peoples with equity.

Pentecost Shout with joy before the King, the Lord.

1 Sing to the LORD a new song, *
  for he has done marvelous things.

2 With his right hand and his holy arm *
  has he won for himself the victory.

3 The LORD has made known his victory; *
  his righteousness has he openly shown
  in the sight of the nations.

4 He remembers his mercy and faithfulness
  to the house of Israel, *
  and all the ends of the earth have seen
  the victory of our God.

5 Shout with joy to the LORD, all you lands; *
  lift up your voice, rejoice, and sing.

6 Sing to the LORD with the harp, *
  with the harp and the voice of song.

7 With trumpets and the sound of the horn *
  shout with joy before the King, the LORD.

8 Let the sea make a noise and all that is in it, *
  the lands and those who dwell therein.

9 Let the rivers clap their hands, *
  and let the hills ring out with joy before the LORD,
  when he comes to judge the earth.

10 In righteousness shall he judge the world *
  and the peoples with equity.

Epiphany In righteousness shall God judge the world and the peoples with equity.

Pentecost Shout with joy before the King, the Lord.

Reading One

Responsory One (Ps. 59: 18-19)
I will sing of your strength
　　− I will celebrate your love in the morning.
You have become my stronghold
　　− I will celebrate your love in the morning.
Glory to the Father and to the Son and to the Holy Spirit.
I will sing of your strength
　　− I will celebrate your love in the morning.

The First Canticle − Song of the Servant of Light *Ego Dominus vocavi*
(Isaiah 42:6-9)

Epiphany I have given you as a covenant to the people, a light to the
nations.
Pentecost See, the former things have come to pass, and new things I
now declare; before they spring forth, I tell you of them.

I am the Lord, I have called you in righteousness, *
　　I have taken you by the hand and kept you.

I have given you as a covenant to the people, *
　　a light to the nations,

To open the eyes that are blind, *
　　to bring out the prisoners from the dungeon,
　　from the prison those who sit in darkness.

I am the Lord, that is my name; *
　　my glory I give to no other, nor my praise to idols.

See, the former things have come to pass,
and new things I now declare; *
　　before they spring forth, I tell you of them.

Epiphany I have given you as a covenant to the people, a light to the
nations.
Pentecost See, the former things have come to pass, and new things I
now declare; before they spring forth, I tell you of them.

Reading Two

Responsory Two (Ps. 86:9)
All nations will come
　　− and worship you, O Lord.
They will glorify your Name
　　− and worship you, O Lord.
Glory to the Father and to the Son and to the Holy Spirit.

All nations will come
  – and worship you, O Lord.

The Gospel Canticle – The Song of Zechariah

Epiphany God will shine on those who dwell in darkness and the shadow of death, and guide our feet into the way of peace.
Pentecost God promised to show mercy to our ancestors and to remember his holy covenant.

Litany

For children threatened by gangs, for parents unable to provide for their children's emotional and financial needs, for community organizers working to deescalate violence.
Lord, have mercy.
For the restoration of peace in neighborhoods torn by violence, for police officers who confront dangerous situations, for firefighters who encounter life-threatening blazes.
Christ, have mercy.
For refugees who cannot find acceptance in new countries, for immigrants struggling to learn new languages, for communities which are discovering ways to embrace strangers and aliens.
Lord, have mercy.

Invitation to the Lord's Prayer As the sun rises upon us let us ask the Father to illumine our hearts.

Collect *From the proper of the day or*
O God, the author of peace and lover of concord, to know you is eternal life and to serve you is perfect freedom: Defend us, your humble servants, in all assaults of our enemies; that we, surely trusting in your defense, may not fear the power of any adversaries; through the might of Jesus Christ our Lord. Amen.

The Blessing

May the Lord rescue us from every evil and save us for his heavenly kingdom. **Amen**

Tuesday Week 2 Noonday Prayer

Officiant: O God, make speed to save us.
People: **O Lord, make haste to help us.**
Officiant and People **Glory to the Father … Alleluia.**

Hymn The golden sun lights up the day *Hymnal 13*

Psalm 119 Heth *Portio mea, Domine*

Be renewed in the spirit of your minds, and put on the new nature,
created after the likeness of God. Eph. 4:33-34

Epiphany You, O LORD, are my lamp; my God, you make my darkness bright.

Pentecost God makes me sure footed like a deer and lets me stand firm on the heights.

57 You only are my portion, O LORD; *
    I have promised to keep your words.

58 I entreat you with all my heart, *
    be merciful to me according to your promise.

59 I have considered my ways *
    and turned my feet toward your decrees.

60 I hasten and do not tarry *
    to keep your commandments.

61 Though the cords of the wicked entangle me, *
    I do not forget your law.

62 At midnight I will rise to give you thanks, *
    because of your righteous judgments.

63 I am a companion of all who fear you *
    and of those who keep your commandments.

64 The earth, O LORD, is full of your love; *
    instruct me in your statutes.

Psalm 18: Part II A *Et retribuet mihi*

The light shines in the darkness, and the darkness has not overcome it. Jn. 1:5

21 The LORD rewarded me because of my righteous dealing; *
    because my hands were clean he rewarded me;

22 For I have kept the ways of the LORD *
    and have not offended against my God;

23 For all his judgments are before my eyes, *
    and his decrees I have not put away from me;

24 For I have been blameless with him *
    and have kept myself from iniquity;

25 Therefore the LORD rewarded me
according to my righteous dealing, *
    because of the cleanness of my hands in his sight.

26 With the faithful you show yourself faithful, O God; *
    with the forthright you show yourself forthright.

27 With the pure you show yourself pure, *
    but with the crooked you are wily.

28 You will save a lowly people, *
    but you will humble the haughty eyes.

29 You, O LORD, are my lamp; *
    my God, you make my darkness bright.

30 With you I will break down an enclosure; *
    with the help of my God I will scale any wall.

31 As for God, his ways are perfect;
    the words of the LORD are tried in the fire; *
    he is a shield to all who trust in him.

Psalm 18: Part II B *Quoniam quis*

Take the whole armor of God, that you may be able to withstand in the evil day, and having done all, to stand. Eph. 6:13

32 For who is God, but the LORD? *
    who is the Rock, except our God?

33 It is God who girds me about with strength *
    and makes my way secure.

34 He makes me sure-footed like a deer *
    and lets me stand firm on the heights.

35 He trains my hands for battle *
    and my arms for bending even a bow of bronze.

36 You have given me your shield of victory; *
    your right hand also sustains me;
    your loving care makes me great.

37 You lengthen my stride beneath me, *
    and my ankles do not give way.

38 I pursue my enemies and overtake them; *
    I will not turn back till I have destroyed them.

39 I strike them down, and they cannot rise; *
    they fall defeated at my feet.

40 You have girded me with strength for the battle; *
    you have cast down my adversaries beneath me;
    you have put my enemies to flight.

41 I destroy those who hate me;
     they cry out, but there is none to help them; *
          they cry to the LORD, but he does not answer.

42 I beat them small like dust before the wind; *
          I trample them like mud in the streets.

43 You deliver me from the strife of the peoples; *
          you put me at the head of the nations.

44 A people I have not known shall serve me;
     no sooner shall they hear than they shall obey me; *
          strangers will cringe before me.

45 The foreign peoples will lose heart; *
          they shall come trembling out of their strongholds.

46 The LORD lives! Blessed is my Rock! *
          Exalted is the God of my salvation!

47 He is the God who gave me victory *
          and cast down the peoples beneath me.

48 You rescued me from the fury of my enemies;
     you exalted me above those who rose against me; *
          you saved me from my deadly foe.

49 Therefore will I extol you among the nations, O LORD, *
          and sing praises to your Name.

50 He multiplies the victories of his king; *
          he shows loving-kindness to his anointed,
          to David and his descendants for ever.

Epiphany You, O LORD, are my lamp; my God, you make my darkness bright.

Pentecost God makes me sure footed like a deer and lets me stand firm on the heights.

Reading Isaiah 6: 6-8
One of the seraphs flew to me, holding a live coal that had been taken from the altar with a pair of tongs. The seraph touched my mouth with it and said: "Now that this has touched your lips, your guilt has departed and your sin is blotted out." Then I heard the voice of the Lord saying, "Whom shall I send, and who will go for us?" And I said, "Here am I; send me!"

Verse and Response
I am sending my messenger to prepare the way before me.
The Lord whom you seek will suddenly come to his temple.

The Short Litany and the Lord's Prayer

The Collect Grant, Lord God, to all who have been baptized into the death and resurrection of your son Jesus Christ, that, as we have put away the old life of sin, so we may be renewed in the spirit of our minds, and live in righteousness and true holiness; through Jesus Christ our Lord, who lives and reigns with you, in the unity of the Holy Spirit, one God, now and forever. Amen.

Let us bless the Lord.
Thanks be to God.

Tuesday Week 2 Evening Prayer
Officiant: O God, make speed to save us.
People: **O Lord, make haste to help us.**
Officiant and People **Glory to the Father...Alleluia.**

Hymn O gracious Light *Hymnal 25*

Psalm 45 A *Eructavit cor meum*
Here is the bridegroom! Come out to meet him. Mt. 25:6
Epiphany I am my beloved's, and his desire is for me.
Pentecost Grace flows from your lips, O king, because God has blessed you for ever.

1 My heart is stirring with a noble song;
   let me recite what I have fashioned for the king; *
      my tongue shall be the pen of a skilled writer.

2 You are the fairest of men; *
      grace flows from your lips,
      because God has blessed you for ever.

3 Strap your sword upon your thigh, O mighty warrior, *
      in your pride and in your majesty.

4 Ride out and conquer in the cause of truth *
      and for the sake of justice.

5 Your right hand will show you marvelous things; *
      your arrows are very sharp, O mighty warrior.

6 The peoples are falling at your feet, *
      and the king's enemies are losing heart.

7 Your throne, O God, endures for ever and ever, *
    a scepter of righteousness is the scepter of your kingdom;
    you love righteousness and hate iniquity.

8 Therefore God, your God, has anointed you *
    with the oil of gladness above your fellows.

9 All your garments are fragrant with myrrh, aloes, and cassia, *
    and the music of strings from ivory palaces makes you glad.

10 Kings' daughters stand among the ladies of the court; *
    on your right hand is the queen,
    adorned with the gold of Ophir.

Epiphany I am my beloved's, and his desire is for me.
Pentecost Grace flows from your lips, O king, because God has blessed you for ever.

Psalm 45 B *Audi filia et vide*
Come, I will show you the bride, the wife of the Lamb. Rev. 21:9

Epiphany I am my beloved's and my beloved is mine; he pastures his flock among the lilies.
Pentecost The king will have pleasure in your beauty; he is your master; therefore do him honor.

11 "Hear, O daughter; consider and listen closely; *
    forget your people and your father's house.

12 The king will have pleasure in your beauty; *
    he is your master; therefore do him honor.

13 The people of Tyre are here with a gift; *
    the rich among the people seek your favor."

14 All glorious is the princess as she enters; *
    her gown is cloth-of-gold.

15 In embroidered apparel she is brought to the king; *
    after her the bridesmaids follow in procession.

16 With joy and gladness they are brought, *
    and enter into the palace of the king.

17 "In place of fathers, O king, you shall have sons; *
    you shall make them princes over all the earth.

18 I will make your name to be remembered
    from one generation to another; *
    therefore nations will praise you for ever and ever."

Epiphany I am my beloved's and my beloved is mine; he pastures his flock among the lilies.

Pentecost The king will have pleasure in your beauty; he is your master; therefore do him honor.

Psalm 46 *Deus noster refugium*
I am with you always, to the close of the age. Mt. 28:20

Epiphany I will be exalted among the nations; I will be exalted in the earth.

Pentecost The Lord of hosts is with us; the God of Jacob is our stronghold.

1 God is our refuge and strength, *
      a very present help in trouble.

2 Therefore we will not fear, though the earth be moved, *
      and though the mountains be toppled
      into the depths of the sea;

3 Though its waters rage and foam, *
      and though the mountains tremble at its tumult.

4 The LORD of hosts is with us; *
      the God of Jacob is our stronghold.

5 There is a river whose streams make glad the city of God, *
      the holy habitation of the Most High.

6 God is in the midst of her;
   she shall not be overthrown; *
      God shall help her at the break of day.

7 The nations make much ado, and the kingdoms are shaken; *
      God has spoken, and the earth shall melt away.

8 The LORD of hosts is with us; *
      the God of Jacob is our stronghold.

9 Come now and look upon the works of the LORD, *
      what awesome things he has done on earth.

10 It is he who makes war to cease in all the world; *
      he breaks the bow, and shatters the spear,
      and burns the shields with fire.

11 "Be still, then, and know that I am God; *
      I will be exalted among the nations;
      I will be exalted in the earth."

12 The LORD of hosts is with us; *
   the God of Jacob is our stronghold.

Epiphany I will be exalted among the nations; I will be exalted in the earth.
Pentecost The Lord of hosts is with us; the God of Jacob is our stronghold.

Reading

Responsory (Ps. 16:11)
In your presence
      – there is fullness of joy.
In your right hand are pleasures for evermore
      – there is fullness of joy.
Glory to the Father and to the Son and to the Holy Spirit.
In your presence
      – there is fullness of joy.

The Gospel Canticle – The Song of Mary
Epiphany I came into the world for judgment so that those who do not see may see, and those who do see may become blind.
Pentecost All generations will call me blessed: the Almighty has done great things for me.

Litany
For those struggling with addiction, for those who have no way to go, for those for whom God is searching.
Lord, have mercy.
For disheartened prophets, for writers who are stuck, for artists searching for inspiration.
Christ, have mercy.
For the dead who are forgotten, for whose who care for the dead and their families, for all who work in cemeteries.
Lord, have mercy.

Invitation to the Lord's Prayer We join the Son in unceasing prayer and praise and, at the end of the day, we return to the Father.

Collect *From the proper of the day or*
Be our light in the darkness, O Lord, and in your great mercy defend us from all perils and dangers of this night; for the love of your only Son, our Savior Jesus Christ. Amen.

The Blessing

May our mutual love continue. Let us not neglect to show hospitality to strangers, for by doing that some have entertained angels without knowing it. **Amen**

Wednesday Week 2 Morning Prayer

Officiant: Lord, open our lips.
People: **And our mouth shall proclaim your praise.**
Officiant and People **Glory to the Father... Alleluia.**

The Invitatory Psalm 95

God will bring all things together in Christ: Come let us worship.

Hymn Give praise and glory unto God *Hymnal 375*

Psalm 28 *Ad te, Domine*

When he has found the lost sheep, he lays it on his shoulders, rejoicing. Lk. 15:5

Epiphany The LORD is my strength and my shield; my heart trusts in him, and I have been helped.
Pentecost My heart trusts in the Lord, and I have been helped.

1 O LORD, I call to you;
    my Rock, do not be deaf to my cry; *
      lest, if you do not hear me,
      I become like those who go down to the Pit.

2 Hear the voice of my prayer when I cry out to you, *
      when I lift up my hands to your holy of holies.

3 Do not snatch me away with the wicked
    or with the evildoers, *
      who speak peaceably with their neighbors,
      while strife is in their hearts.

4 Repay them according to their deeds, *
      and according to the wickedness of their actions.

5 According to the work of their hands repay them, *
      and give them their just deserts.

6 They have no understanding of the LORD'S doings,
    nor of the works of his hands; *
      therefore he will break them down
      and not build them up.

7 Blessed is the LORD! *
      for he has heard the voice of my prayer.

8 The LORD is my strength and my shield; *
    my heart trusts in him, and I have been helped;

9 Therefore my heart dances for joy, *
    and in my song will I praise him.

10 The LORD is the strength of his people, *
    a safe refuge for his anointed.

11 Save your people and bless your inheritance; *
    shepherd them and carry them for ever.

Epiphany The LORD is my strength and my shield; my heart trusts in
him, and I have been helped.
Pentecost My heart trusts in the Lord, and I have been helped.

Psalm 96 *Cantate Domino*

For us there is one God, the Father, from whom are all things and for whom we exist, and one Lord,
Jesus Christ, through whom are all things and through whom we exist. 1 Cor. 8:6

Epiphany Declare God's glory among the nations and his wonders
among all peoples.
Pentecost Sing to the Lord and bless God's name.

1 Sing to the LORD a new song; *
    sing to the LORD, all the whole earth.

2 Sing to the LORD and bless his Name; *
    proclaim the good news of his salvation from day to day.

3 Declare his glory among the nations *
    and his wonders among all peoples.

4 For great is the LORD and greatly to be praised; *
    he is more to be feared than all gods.

5 As for all the gods of the nations, they are but idols; *
    but it is the LORD who made the heavens.

6 Oh, the majesty and magnificence of his presence! *
    Oh, the power and the splendor of his sanctuary!

7 Ascribe to the LORD, you families of the peoples; *
    ascribe to the LORD honor and power.

8 Ascribe to the LORD the honor due his Name; *
    bring offerings and come into his courts.

9 Worship the LORD in the beauty of holiness; *
    let the whole earth tremble before him.

10 Tell it out among the nations: "The LORD is King! *
    he has made the world so firm that it cannot be moved;
    he will judge the peoples with equity."

11 Let the heavens rejoice, and let the earth be glad;
    let the sea thunder and all that is in it; *
    let the field be joyful and all that is therein.

12 Then shall all the trees of the wood shout for joy
    before the LORD when he comes, *
    when he comes to judge the earth.

13 He will judge the world with righteousness *
    and the peoples with his truth.

Epiphany Declare God's glory among the nations and his wonders among all peoples.
Pentecost Sing to the Lord and bless God's name.

Psalm 67   *Deus misereatur*

I thank my God through Jesus Christ for all of you, because your faith is proclaimed throughout the world. Rm 1:8

Epiphany Show us the light of your countenance and come to us.
Pentecost May the Lord's face shine upon us, and be gracious to us.

1   May God be merciful to us and bless us, *
    show us the light of his countenance and come to us.

2   Let your ways be known upon earth, *
    your saving health among all nations.

3   Let the peoples praise you, O God; *
    let all the peoples praise you.

4   Let the nations be glad and sing for joy, *
    for you judge the peoples with equity
    and guide all the nations upon earth.

5   Let the peoples praise you, O God; *
    let all the peoples praise you.

6   The earth has brought forth her increase; *
    may God, our own God, give us his blessing.

7   May God give us his blessing, *
    and may all the ends of the earth stand in awe of him.

Epiphany Show us the light of your countenance and come to us.
Pentecost May the Lord's face shine upon us, and be gracious to us.

Reading One

Responsory One (Ps. 88: 14, 10)
I cry to you for help
> − **in the morning my prayer comes before you.**

I have called upon you daily
> − **in the morning my prayer comes before you.**

Glory to the Father and to the Son and to the Holy Spirit.
I cry to you for help
> − **in the morning my prayer comes before you.**

The First Canticle − Song of the New Heart *Tollam quippe vos*
(Ezekiel 36:24-28)

Epiphany I will help you walk in my laws and cherish my commandments and do them.
Pentecost You shall be my people, and I will be your God.

I will take you from among all nations; *
> and gather you from all lands to bring you home.

I will sprinkle clean water upon you; *
> and purify you from false gods and uncleanness.

A new heart I will give you *
> and a new spirit put within you.

I will take the stone heart from your chest *
> and give you a heart of flesh.

I will help you walk in my laws *
> and cherish my commandments and do them.

You shall be my people, *
> and I will be your God.

Epiphany I will help you walk in my laws and cherish my commandments and do them.
Pentecost You shall be my people, and I will be your God.

Reading Two

Responsory Two (Ps. 86:12)
I will thank you, O Lord, my God
> − **with all my heart.**

I will glorify your Name
> − **with all my heart.**

Glory to the Father and to the Son and to the Holy Spirit.

I will thank you, O Lord, my God
 − with all my heart.

The Gospel Canticle − The Song of Zechariah

Epiphany God the only Son, who is close to the Father's heart, has made God known.

Pentecost God set us free to worship him without fear, holy and righteous in his sight.

Litany

Grant, Almighty God, that all who confess your Name may be united in your truth, live together in your love, and reveal your glory in the world.
Lord, have mercy.

Guide the people of this land, and of all the nations, in the ways of justice and peace; that we may honor one another and serve the common good.
Christ, have mercy.

Give us all a reverence for the earth as your own creation, that we may use its resources rightly in the service of others and to your honor and glory.
Lord, have mercy.

Invitation to the Lord's Prayer As children of God in Christ, the Spirit prays through us to the Father.

The Collect *From the proper of the day or*

O God, you have made of one blood all the peoples of the earth, and sent your blessed Son to preach peace to those who are far off and to those who are near: Grant that people everywhere may seek after you and find you; bring the nations into your fold; pour out your Spirit upon all flesh; and hasten the coming of your kingdom; through Jesus Christ our Lord. Amen.

The Blessing

May our mutual love continue. Let us not neglect to show hospitality to strangers, for by doing that some have entertained angels without knowing it. **Amen**

Wednesday Week 2 Noonday Prayer

Officiant: O God, make speed to save us.
People: **O Lord, make haste to help us.**
Officiant and People **Glory to the Father… Alleluia.**

Hymn The fleeting day is nearly gone *Hymnal 23*

Psalm 119 Teth *Bonitatem fecisti*

If you continue in my word, you are truly my disciples. Jn. 8: 31

Epiphany The Lord has saved us according to his mercy, according to the abundance of his steadfast love.

Pentecost Our eyes look to the Lord our God, until he shows us his mercy.

65 O LORD, you have dealt graciously with your servant, *
  according to your word.

66 Teach me discernment and knowledge, *
  for I have believed in your commandments.

67 Before I was afflicted I went astray, *
  but now I keep your word.

68 You are good and you bring forth good; *
  instruct me in your statutes.

69 The proud have smeared me with lies, *
  but I will keep your commandments with my whole heart.

70 Their heart is gross and fat, *
  but my delight is in your law.

71 It is good for me that I have been afflicted, *
  that I might learn your statutes.

72 The law of your mouth is dearer to me *
  than thousands in gold and silver.

Psalm 123 *Ad te levavi oculos meos*

*With the eyes of your heart enlightened, you may know what is the hope
to which he has called you. Eph. 1: 18*

1 To you I lift up my eyes, *
  to you enthroned in the heavens.

2 As the eyes of servants look to the hand of their masters, *
  and the eyes of a maid to the hand of her mistress,

3 So our eyes look to the LORD our God, *
  until he show us his mercy.

4 Have mercy upon us, O LORD, have mercy, *
  for we have had more than enough of contempt,

5 Too much of the scorn of the indolent rich, *
  and of the derision of the proud.

Psalm 124 *Nisi quia Dominus*
Do not fear those who kill the body but cannot kill the soul. Mt. 10: 28

1 If the LORD had not been on our side, *
     let Israel now say;

2 If the LORD had not been on our side, *
     when enemies rose up against us;

3 Then would they have swallowed us up alive *
     in their fierce anger toward us;

4 Then would the waters have overwhelmed us *
     and the torrent gone over us;

5 Then would the raging waters *
     have gone right over us.

6 Blessed be the LORD! *
     he has not given us over to be a prey for their teeth.

7 We have escaped like a bird from the snare of the fowler; *
     the snare is broken, and we have escaped.

8 Our help is in the Name of the LORD, *
     the maker of heaven and earth.

Epiphany The Lord has saved us according to his mercy, according to the abundance of his steadfast love.
Pentecost Our eyes look to the Lord our God, until he shows us his mercy.

Reading Jeremiah 1: 4-8
Now the word of the Lord came to me saying, "Before I formed you in the womb I knew you, and before you were born I consecrated you; I appointed you a prophet to the nations." Then I said, "Ah, Lord God! Truly I do not know how to speak, for I am only a boy." But the Lord said to me, "Do not say, 'I am only a boy'; for you shall go to all to whom I send you, and you shall speak whatever I command you. Do not be afraid of them, for I am with you to deliver you, says the Lord."

Verse and Response
Do not let your hearts be troubled.
Do not let them be afraid.

The Short Litany and the Lord's Prayer

The Collect Almighty Father, whose blessed Son before his passion prayed for his disciples that they might be one, as you and he are one:

Grant that your Church, being bound together in love and obedience to you, may be united in one body by the one Spirit; that the world may believe in him who you have sent, your Son Jesus Christ our Lord; who lives and reigns with you, in the unity of the Holy Spirit, one God, now and for ever. Amen.

Let us bless the Lord.
Thanks be to God.

Wednesday Week 2 Evening Prayer

Officiant: O God, make speed to save us.
People: **O Lord, make haste to help us.**
Officiant and People **Glory to the Father ... Alleluia.**

Hymn King of glory, King of peace *Hymnal 382*

Psalm 105 A *Confitemini Domino*
God had provided something better so that our ancestors would not,
apart from us, be made perfect. Heb 11: 40

Epiphany Make known the Lord's deeds among the peoples. Sing to God, sing praises.
Pentecost Glory in God's holy Name; let the hearts of those who seek the LORD rejoice.

1   Give thanks to the LORD and call upon his Name; *
      make known his deeds among the peoples.

2   Sing to him, sing praises to him, *
      and speak of all his marvelous works.

3   Glory in his holy Name; *
      let the hearts of those who seek the LORD rejoice.

4   Search for the LORD and his strength; *
      continually seek his face.

5   Remember the marvels he has done, *
      his wonders and the judgments of his mouth,

6   O offspring of Abraham his servant, *
      O children of Jacob his chosen.

7   He is the LORD our God; *
      his judgments prevail in all the world.

8   He has always been mindful of his covenant, *
      the promise he made for a thousand generations:

9 The covenant he made with Abraham, *
>   the oath that he swore to Isaac,

10 Which he established as a statute for Jacob, *
>   an everlasting covenant for Israel,

11 Saying, "To you will I give the land of Canaan *
>   to be your allotted inheritance."

12 When they were few in number, *
>   of little account, and sojourners in the land,

13 Wandering from nation to nation *
>   and from one kingdom to another,

14 He let no one oppress them *
>   and rebuked kings for their sake,

15 Saying, "Do not touch my anointed *
>   and do my prophets no harm."

16 Then the LORD called for a famine in the land *
>   and destroyed the supply of bread.

17 He sent a man before them, *
>   Joseph, who was sold as a slave.

18 They bruised his feet in fetters; *
>   his neck they put in an iron collar.

19 Until his prediction came to pass, *
>   the word of the LORD tested him.

20 The king sent and released him; *
>   the ruler of the peoples set him free.

21 He set him as a master over his household, *
>   as a ruler over all his possessions,

22 To instruct his princes according to his will *
>   and to teach his elders wisdom.

Epiphany Make known the Lord's deeds among the peoples. Sing to God, sing praises.
Pentecost Glory in God's holy Name; let the hearts of those who seek the LORD rejoice.

Psalm 105 B *Et intravit Israel*

*By faith Moses left Egypt, unafraid of the king's anger; for he persevered
as though he saw him who is invisible. Heb. 11: 27*

Epiphany No power of fire was able to give light, nor did the brilliant
flames of the stars avail to illumine that hateful night.

Pentecost Faith is the assurance of things hoped for. By faith our
ancestors received approval.

23 Israel came into Egypt, *
    and Jacob became a sojourner in the land of Ham.

24 The LORD made his people exceedingly fruitful; *
    he made them stronger than their enemies;

25 Whose heart he turned, so that they hated his people, *
    and dealt unjustly with his servants.

26 He sent Moses his servant, *
    and Aaron whom he had chosen.

27 They worked his signs among them, *
    and portents in the land of Ham.

28 He sent darkness, and it grew dark; *
    but the Egyptians rebelled against his words.

29 He turned their waters into blood *
    and caused their fish to die.

30 Their land was overrun by frogs, *
    in the very chambers of their kings.

31 He spoke, and there came swarms of insects *
    and gnats within all their borders.

32 He gave them hailstones instead of rain, *
    and flames of fire throughout their land.

33 He blasted their vines and their fig trees *
    and shattered every tree in their country.

34 He spoke, and the locust came, *
    and young locusts without number,

35 Which ate up all the green plants in their land *
    and devoured the fruit of their soil.

36 He struck down the firstborn of their land, *
    the firstfruits of all their strength.

Epiphany No power of fire was able to give light, nor did the brilliant flames of the stars avail to illumine that hateful night.

Pentecost Faith is the assurance of things hoped for. By faith our ancestors received approval.

Psalm 105 C *Et eduxit eos*

By faith the people passed through the Red Sea as if it were dry land. Heb. 11: 29

Epiphany The Lord spread out a cloud for a covering and a fire to give light in the night season.

Pentecost Though our ancestors were commended for their faith, they did not receive what was promised, since God had provided something better so that they would not, apart from us, be made perfect.

37 The LORD led out his people with silver and gold; *
    in all their tribes there was not one that stumbled.

38 Egypt was glad of their going, *
    because they were afraid of them.

39 He spread out a cloud for a covering *
    and a fire to give light in the night season.

40 They asked, and quails appeared, *
    and he satisfied them with bread from heaven.

41 He opened the rock, and water flowed, *
    so the river ran in the dry places.

42 For God remembered his holy word *
    and Abraham his servant.

43 So he led forth his people with gladness, *
    his chosen with shouts of joy.

44 He gave his people the lands of the nations, *
    and they took the fruit of others' toil,

45 That they might keep his statutes *
    and observe his laws.
    Hallelujah!

Epiphany The Lord spread out a cloud for a covering and a fire to give light in the night season.

Pentecost Though our ancestors were commended for their faith, they did not receive what was promised, since God had provided something better so that they would not, apart from us, be made perfect.

Reading

Responsory (Ps. 26: 2, 1)

Your love is before my eyes
  – I have walked faithfully with you.
I have trusted in the Lord and have not faltered
  – I have walked faithfully with you.
Glory to the Father and to the Son and to the Holy Spirit.
Your love is before my eyes
  – I have walked faithfully with you.

The Gospel Canticle – The Song of Mary

Epiphany Let us open our eyes to the deifying light, let us hear with attentive ears the warning which the divine voice cries daily to us.
Pentecost God has cast the powerful from their thrones and has lifted up the lowly.

Litany

Bless all whose lives are closely linked with ours, and grant that we may serve Christ in them, and love one another as he loves us.
Lord, have mercy.
Comfort and heal all those who suffer in body, mind, or spirit; give them courage and hope in their troubles, and bring them the joy of your salvation.
Christ, have mercy.
We commend to your mercy all who have died, that your will for them may be fulfilled; and we pray that we may share with all your saints in your eternal kingdom.
Lord, have mercy.

Invitation to the Lord's Prayer The Spirit prays to the Father through us and so we open our hearts in prayer.

The Collect *From the proper of the day or*

Keep watch, dear Lord, with those who work, or watch, or weep this night, and give your angels charge over those who sleep. Tend the sick, Lord Christ; give rest to the weary, bless the dying, soothe the suffering, pity the afflicted, shield the joyous; and all for your love's sake. Amen.

The Blessing

May we do good and share what we have, for such sacrifices are pleasing to God. **Amen**

Thursday Week 2 Morning Prayer

Officiant: Lord, open our lips.
People: **And our mouth shall proclaim your praise.**
Officiant and People **Glory to the Father... Alleluia.**

The Invitatory Psalm 122

Let us offer God a sacrifice of praise and thanksgiving: Come let us worship.

Hymn Christ whose glory fills the skies *Hymnal 6*

Psalm 34 *Benedicam Dominum*

All of us, with unveiled faces, seeing the glory of the Lord,
are being transformed into the same image. 2 Cor. 3:18

Epiphany The eyes of the LORD are upon the righteous, and his ears are open to their cry.

Pentecost Those who seek the Lord lack nothing that is good.

1 I will bless the LORD at all times; *
    his praise shall ever be in my mouth.

2 I will glory in the LORD; *
    let the humble hear and rejoice.

3 Proclaim with me the greatness of the LORD; *
    let us exalt his Name together.

4 I sought the LORD, and he answered me *
    and delivered me out of all my terror.

5 Look upon him and be radiant, *
    and let not your faces be ashamed.

6 I called in my affliction and the LORD heard me *
    and saved me from all my troubles.

7 The angel of the LORD encompasses those who fear him, *
    and he will deliver them.

8 Taste and see that the LORD is good; *
    blessed are they who trust in him!

9 Fear the LORD, you that are his saints, *
    for those who fear him lack nothing.

10 The young lions lack and suffer hunger, *
    but those who seek the LORD lack nothing that is good.

11 Come, children, and listen to me; *
    I will teach you the fear of the LORD.

12 Who among you loves life *
    and desires long life to enjoy prosperity?

13 Keep your tongue from evil-speaking *
　and your lips from lying words.

14 Turn from evil and do good; *
　seek peace and pursue it.

15 The eyes of the LORD are upon the righteous, *
　and his ears are open to their cry.

16 The face of the LORD is against those who do evil, *
　to root out the remembrance of them from the earth.

17 The righteous cry, and the LORD hears them *
　and delivers them from all their troubles.

18 The LORD is near to the brokenhearted *
　and will save those whose spirits are crushed.

19 Many are the troubles of the righteous, *
　but the LORD will deliver him out of them all.

20 He will keep safe all his bones; *
　not one of them shall be broken.

21 Evil shall slay the wicked, *
　and those who hate the righteous will be punished.

22 The LORD ransoms the life of his servants, *
　and none will be punished who trust in him.

Epiphany The eyes of the LORD are upon the righteous, and his ears are open to their cry.
Pentecost Those who seek the Lord lack nothing that is good.

Psalm 27 *Dominus illuminatio*
God rewards those who seek him. Heb. 11: 16

Epiphany I shall not fear for you, O Lord, are my saving light.
Pentecost You speak in my heart and say, "Seek my face." Your face, LORD, will I seek.

1 The LORD is my light and my salvation;
　whom then shall I fear? *
　　the LORD is the strength of my life;
　　of whom then shall I be afraid?

2 When evildoers came upon me to eat up my flesh, *
　it was they, my foes and my adversaries,
　who stumbled and fell.

3　Though an army should encamp against me, *
　　　yet my heart shall not be afraid;

4　And though war should rise up against me, *
　　　yet will I put my trust in him.

5　One thing have I asked of the LORD;
　　one thing I seek; *
　　　that I may dwell in the house of the LORD
　　　all the days of my life;

6　To behold the fair beauty of the LORD *
　　　and to seek him in his temple.

7　For in the day of trouble
　　he shall keep me safe in his shelter; *
　　　he shall hide me in the secrecy of his dwelling
　　　and set me high upon a rock.

8　Even now he lifts up my head *
　　　above my enemies round about me.

9　Therefore I will offer in his dwelling an oblation
　　with sounds of great gladness; *
　　　I will sing and make music to the LORD.

10 Hearken to my voice, O LORD, when I call; *
　　　have mercy on me and answer me.

11 You speak in my heart and say, "Seek my face." *
　　　Your face, LORD, will I seek.

12 Hide not your face from me, *
　　　nor turn away your servant in displeasure.

13 You have been my helper;
　　cast me not away; *
　　　do not forsake me, O God of my salvation.

14 Though my father and my mother forsake me, *
　　　the LORD will sustain me.

15 Show me your way, O LORD; *
　　　lead me on a level path, because of my enemies.

16 Deliver me not into the hand of my adversaries, *
　　　for false witnesses have risen up against me,
　　　and also those who speak malice.

17 What if I had not believed
    that I should see the goodness of the LORD *
        in the land of the living!

18 O tarry and await the LORD'S pleasure;
    be strong, and he shall comfort your heart; *
        wait patiently for the LORD.

Epiphany I shall not fear for you, O Lord, are my saving light.
Pentecost You speak in my heart and say, "Seek my face." Your face,
LORD, will I seek.

Psalm 149 *Cantate Domino*
All who see them shall acknowledge that they are a people whom the Lord has blessed. Is. 61: 9
Epiphany The LORD takes pleasure in his people and adorns the poor
with victory.
Pentecost Let the children of Zion be joyful in their King.

1 Hallelujah!
   Sing to the LORD a new song; *
       sing his praise in the congregation of the faithful.

2 Let Israel rejoice in his Maker; *
       let the children of Zion be joyful in their King.

3 Let them praise his Name in the dance; *
       let them sing praise to him with timbrel and harp.

4 For the LORD takes pleasure in his people *
       and adorns the poor with victory.

5 Let the faithful rejoice in triumph; *
       let them be joyful on their beds.

6 Let the praises of God be in their throat *
       and a two-edged sword in their hand;

7 To wreak vengeance on the nations *
       and punishment on the peoples;

8 To bind their kings in chains *
       and their nobles with links of iron;

9 To inflict on them the judgment decreed; *
       this is glory for all his faithful people.
       Hallelujah!

Epiphany The LORD takes pleasure in his people and adorns the poor
with victory.

Pentecost Let the children of Zion be joyful in their King.

Reading One

Responsory One (Is. 33: 2)
O Lord, be gracious to us
  – we wait for you.
Be our arm every morning
  – we wait for you.
Glory to the Father and to the Son and to the Holy Spirit.
O Lord, be gracious to us
  – we wait for you.

The First Canticle – Song of Confident Love *Non relinquam vos orfanos*
(John 14: 18-21, 23-24)

Epiphany Those who love me will keep my word, and my Father will love them and we will come to them and make our home with them.
Pentecost I am in my Father, and you in me, and I in you.

I will not leave you orphaned; *
  I am coming to you.

In a little while the world will no longer see me,
but you will see me. *
  Because I live, you also will live.

On that day you will know that I am in my Father, *
  and you in me, and I in you.

They who have my commandments and keep them *
  are those who love me.

Those who love me will be loved by my Father, *
  and I will love them and reveal myself to them.

Those who love me will keep my word, *
  and my Father will love them.

We will come to them *
  and make our home with them.

Whoever does not love me does not keep my words; *
  and the word that you hear is not mine,
  but is from the Father who sent me.

Epiphany Those who love me will keep my word, and my Father will love them and we will come to them and make our home with them.
Pentecost I am in my Father, and you in me, and I in you.

Reading Two

Responsory Two (Ps. 86:11)
Teach me your way, O Lord
  – I will walk in your truth.
Knit my heart to you
  – I will walk in your truth.
Glory to the Father and to the Son and to the Holy Spirit.
Teach me your way, O Lord
  – I will walk in your truth.

The Gospel Canticle – The Song of Zechariah

Epiphany While you have the light, believe in the light, so that you may become children of light.
Pentecost God will shine on those who dwell in darkness and the shadow of death, and guide our feet into the way of peace.

Litany

For people who struggle with justice systems, for those unjustly imprisoned, for those suffering torture.
Lord, have mercy.
For families who live with difficult children, for children who endure abuse from parents, for spouses struggling to understand one another.
Christ, have mercy.
For deeper compassion among the religions of the world, for growth among communities of faith, for the support of struggling believers.
Lord, have mercy.

Invitation to the Lord's Prayer Our hearts hunger for God who satisfies our hunger as we pray.

The Collect *From the proper of the day or*

Heavenly Father, in you we live and move and have our being: We humbly pray you so to guide and govern us by your Holy Spirit, that in all the cares and occupations of our life we may not forget you, but may remember that we are ever walking in your sight; through Jesus Christ our Lord. Amen.

The Blessing

May the God of all grace, who has called us to eternal glory in Christ, restore, support, strengthen, and establish us. **Amen**

Thursday Week 2 Noonday Prayer

Officiant: O God, make speed to save us.

People: **O Lord, make haste to help us.**

Officiant and People **Glory to the Father... Alleluia.**

Hymn Praise our great and gracious Lord *Hymnal 393*

Psalm 119 Yodh *Manus tuæ fecerunt me*

I tell you, anyone who hears my word and believes him who sent me has eternal life. Jn. 5: 24

Epiphany God led them to safety, and they were not afraid.

Pentecost He shepherded them with a faithful and true heart and guided them with the skillfulness of his hands.

73 Your hands have made me and fashioned me; *
>give me understanding,
>that I may learn your commandments.

74 Those who fear you will be glad when they see me, *
>because I trust in your word.

75 I know, O LORD, that your judgments are right *
>and that in faithfulness you have afflicted me.

76 Let your loving-kindness be my comfort, *
>as you have promised to your servant.

77 Let your compassion come to me, that I may live, *
>for your law is my delight.

78 Let the arrogant be put to shame,
>for they wrong me with lies; *
>but I will meditate on your commandments.

79 Let those who fear you turn to me, *
>and also those who know your decrees.

80 Let my heart be sound in your statutes, *
>that I may not be put to shame.

Psalm 78 C *Quotiens exacerbaverunt*

You faithless generation, how much longer must I be among you? Mk. 9: 19

40 How often the people disobeyed God in the wilderness *
>and offended him in the desert!

41 Again and again they tempted God *
>and provoked the Holy One of Israel.

42 They did not remember his power *
>in the day when he ransomed them from the enemy;

43 How he wrought his signs in Egypt *
    and his omens in the field of Zoan.

44 He turned their rivers into blood, *
    so that they could not drink of their streams.

45 He sent swarms of flies among them, which ate them up, *
    and frogs, which destroyed them.

46 He gave their crops to the caterpillar, *
    the fruit of their toil to the locust.

47 He killed their vines with hail *
    and their sycamores with frost.

48 He delivered their cattle to hailstones *
    and their livestock to hot thunderbolts.

49 He poured out upon them his blazing anger: *
    fury, indignation, and distress,
    a troop of destroying angels.

50 He gave full rein to his anger;
   did not spare their souls from death; *
    but delivered their lives to the plague.

51 He struck down all the firstborn of Egypt, *
    the flower of manhood in the dwellings of Ham.

52 He led out his people like sheep *
    and guided them in the wilderness like a flock.

53 He led them to safety, and they were not afraid; *
    but the sea overwhelmed their enemies.

54 He brought them to his holy land, *
    the mountain his right hand had won.

55 He drove out the Canaanites before them
   apportioned an inheritance to them by lot; *
    he made the tribes of Israel to dwell in their tents.

Psalm 78 D *Et tentaverunt*

I am the good shepherd. I know my own and my own know me. Jn. 10:14

56 But they tested the Most High God, and defied him, *
    and did not keep his commandments.

57 They turned away and were disloyal like their fathers; *
    they were undependable like a warped bow.

58 They grieved him with their hill-altars *
    and provoked his displeasure with their idols.

59 When God heard this, he was angry *
    and utterly rejected Israel.

60 He forsook the shrine at Shiloh, *
    the tabernacle where he had lived among his people.

61 He delivered the ark into captivity, *
    his glory into the adversary's hand.

62 He gave his people to the sword *
    and was angered against his inheritance.

63 The fire consumed their young men; *
    there were no wedding songs for their maidens.

64 Their priests fell by the sword, *
    and their widows made no lamentation.

65 Then the LORD woke as though from sleep, *
    like a warrior refreshed with wine.

66 He struck his enemies on the backside *
    and put them to perpetual shame.

67 He rejected the tent of Joseph *
    and did not choose the tribe of Ephraim;

68 He chose instead the tribe of Judah *
    and Mount Zion, which he loved.

69 He built his sanctuary like the heights of heaven, *
    like the earth which he founded for ever.

70 He chose David his servant, *
    and took him away from the sheepfolds.

71 He brought him from following the ewes, *
    to be a shepherd over Jacob his people
    and over Israel his inheritance.

72 So he shepherded them with a faithful and true heart *
    and guided them with the skillfulness of his hands.

Epiphany God led them to safety, and they were not afraid.
Pentecost He shepherded them with a faithful and true heart and guided them with the skillfulness of his hands.

Reading Proverbs 9: 1-6
Wisdom has built her house; she has hewn her seven pillars. She has
slaughtered her animals, she has mixed her wine, she has also set her
table. She has sent out her servant-girls, she calls from the highest places
in the town, "You that are simple, turn in here!" To those without
sense she says, "Come, eat of my bread and drink of the wine I have
mixed. Lay aside immaturity, and live, and walk in the way of insight."

Verse and Response
Mortals ate of the bread of angels.
God sent them food in abundance.

The Short Litany and the Lord's Prayer

The Collect God our Father, whose Son our Lord Jesus Christ in a
wonderful Sacrament has left us a memorial of his passion: Grant us so
to venerate the sacred mysteries of his Body and Blood, that we may
ever perceive within ourselves the fruit of his redemption; who lives and
reigns with you and the Holy Spirit, one God, for ever and ever. Amen.

Let us bless the Lord.
Thanks be to God.

Thursday Week 2 Evening Prayer
Officiant: O God, make speed to save us.
People: **O Lord, make haste to help us.**
Officiant and People **Glory to the Father... Alleluia.**

Hymn Most holy God, the Lord of heaven *Hymnal 31*

Psalm 116 *Dilexi, quoniam*
This cup that is poured out for you is the new covenant in my blood. Lk. 22: 20
Epiphany I formed you, you are my servant; O Israel, you will not be
forgotten by me.
Pentecost I will lift up the cup of salvation, and call upon the Name of
the Lord.

1 I love the LORD, because he has heard
  the voice of my supplication, *
     because he has inclined his ear to me
     whenever I called upon him.

2 The cords of death entangled me;
  the grip of the grave took hold of me; *
     I came to grief and sorrow.

3 Then I called upon the Name of the LORD: *
   "O LORD, I pray you, save my life."

4 Gracious is the LORD and righteous; *
   our God is full of compassion.

5 The LORD watches over the innocent; *
   I was brought very low, and he helped me.

6 Turn again to your rest, O my soul, *
   for the LORD has treated you well.

7 For you have rescued my life from death, *
   my eyes from tears, and my feet from stumbling.

8 I will walk in the presence of the LORD *
   in the land of the living.

9 I believed, even when I said,
   "I have been brought very low." *
   In my distress I said, "No one can be trusted."

10 How shall I repay the LORD *
   for all the good things he has done for me?

11 I will lift up the cup of salvation *
   and call upon the Name of the LORD.

12 I will fulfill my vows to the LORD *
   in the presence of all his people.

13 Precious in the sight of the LORD *
   is the death of his servants.

14 O LORD, I am your servant; *
   I am your servant and the child of your handmaid;
   you have freed me from my bonds.

15 I will offer you the sacrifice of thanksgiving *
   and call upon the Name of the LORD.

16 I will fulfill my vows to the LORD *
   in the presence of all his people,

17 In the courts of the LORD'S house, *
   in the midst of you, O Jerusalem.

Epiphany I formed you, you are my servant; O Israel, you will not be forgotten by me.

Pentecost I will lift up the cup of salvation, and call upon the Name of the Lord.

Psalm 144 *Benedictus Dominus*

Do not worry about your life, what you will eat or what you will drink,
or about your body, what you will wear. Mt. 6: 25

Epiphany Blessed are the people whose God is the LORD!
Pentecost God is my help and fortress, my shield in whom I trust.

1 Blessed be the LORD my rock! *
 who trains my hands to fight and my fingers to battle;

2 My help and my fortress, my stronghold and my deliverer, *
 my shield in whom I trust,
 who subdues the peoples under me.

3 O LORD, what are we that you should care for us? *
 mere mortals that you should think of us?

4 We are like a puff of wind; *
 our days are like a passing shadow.

5 Bow your heavens, O LORD, and come down; *
 touch the mountains, and they shall smoke.

6 Hurl the lightning and scatter them; *
 shoot out your arrows and rout them.

7 Stretch out your hand from on high; *
 rescue me and deliver me from the great waters,
 from the hand of foreign peoples,

8 Whose mouths speak deceitfully *
 and whose right hand is raised in falsehood.

9 O God, I will sing to you a new song; *
 I will play to you on a ten-stringed lyre.

10 You give victory to kings *
 and have rescued David your servant.

11 Rescue me from the hurtful sword *
 and deliver me from the hand of foreign peoples,

12 Whose mouths speak deceitfully *
 and whose right hand is raised in falsehood.

13 May our sons be like plants well nurtured from their youth, *
 and our daughters like sculptured corners of a palace.

14 May our barns be filled to overflowing
   with all manner of crops; *
       may the flocks in our pastures increase
       by thousands and tens of thousands;
       may our cattle be fat and sleek.

15 May there be no breaching of the walls, no going into exile, *
   no wailing in the public squares.

16 Blessed are the people of whom this is so! *
   blessed are the people whose God is the LORD!

Epiphany Blessed are the people whose God is the LORD!
Pentecost God is my help and fortress, my shield in whom I trust.

Psalm 84 *Quam dilecta!*

*Though you do not see him now, you believe in him
and rejoice with an indescribable and glorious joy. 1 Pt. 1: 8*

Epiphany The LORD God is both sun and shield; he will give grace and glory.
Pentecost My soul has a desire and longing for the courts of the LORD.

1 How dear to me is your dwelling, O LORD of hosts! *
       My soul has a desire and longing
       for the courts of the LORD;
       my heart and my flesh rejoice in the living God.

2 The sparrow has found her a house
   and the swallow a nest where she may lay her young; *
       by the side of your altars, O LORD of hosts,
       my King and my God.

3 Blessed are they who dwell in your house! *
       they will always be praising you.

4 Blessed are the people whose strength is in you! *
       whose hearts are set on the pilgrims' way.

5 Those who go through the desolate valley
   will find it a place of springs, *
       for the early rains have covered it with pools of water.

6 They will climb from height to height, *
       and the God of gods will reveal himself in Zion.

7 LORD God of hosts, hear my prayer; *
       hearken, O God of Jacob.

8 Behold our defender, O God; *
     and look upon the face of your Anointed.

9 For one day in your courts is better
     than a thousand in my own room, *
         and to stand at the threshold of the house of my God
         than to dwell in the tents of the wicked.

10 For the LORD God is both sun and shield; *
     he will give grace and glory;

11 No good thing will the LORD withhold *
     from those who walk with integrity.

12 O LORD of hosts, *
     blessed are they who put their trust in you!

Epiphany The LORD God is both sun and shield; he will give grace and glory.
Pentecost My soul has a desire and longing for the courts of the LORD.

Reading

Responsory (Ps. 81: 1,2)
Sing with joy to God our strength
     – raise a loud shout to the God of Jacob.
Raise a song and sound the timbrel
     – raise a loud shout to the God of Jacob.
Glory to the Father and to the Son and to the Holy Spirit.
Sing with joy to God our strength
     – raise a loud shout to the God of Jacob.

The Gospel Canticle – The Song of Mary
Epiphany I am the light of the world. We must work the works of him who sent me while it is day.
Pentecost God has fed the hungry with good things, and the rich he has sent away empty.

Litany
For those who prepare wine for the feast, for those who bake bread for the Eucharist, for those who grow flowers to adorn houses of worship.
Lord, have mercy.
For artists who adorn liturgy with beauty, for candle makers and metal workers, for carpenters and painters who adorn sanctuaries for God.
Christ, have mercy.

For an awareness of the communion of the living and dead, for the comfort of those who mourn, for all who died away from home.
Lord, have mercy.

Invitation to the Lord's Prayer Nourished with Christ, the Bread of Life, we return to the Father.

The Collect *From the proper of the day or*
Lord Jesus, stay with us, for evening is at hand and the day is past; be our companion in the way, kindle our hearts, and awaken hope, that we may know you as you are revealed in Scripture and the breaking of bread. Grant this for the sake of your love. Amen.

The Blessing
May we imitate what is good for whoever does good is from God.
Amen

Friday Week 2 Morning Prayer

Officiant: Lord, open our lips.
People: **And our mouth shall proclaim your praise.**
Officiant and People **Glory to the Father... Alleluia.**

The Invitatory Psalm 95
God purges our sin and purifies us: Come let us worship.

Hymn The Christ who died *Hymnal 447*

Psalm 38 *Domine, ne in furore*
Many women were also there, looking on from a distance;
they had followed Jesus from Galilee and had provided for him. Mt. 27: 55

Epiphany In you, O LORD, have I fixed my hope; you will answer me, O Lord my God.
Pentecost O Lord, you know all my desires, and my sighing is not hidden from you.

1 O LORD, do not rebuke me in your anger; *
     do not punish me in your wrath.

2 For your arrows have already pierced me, *
     and your hand presses hard upon me.

3 There is no health in my flesh,
   because of your indignation; *
     there is no soundness in my body, because of my sin.

4 For my iniquities overwhelm me; *
     like a heavy burden they are too much for me to bear.

5   My wounds stink and fester *
      by reason of my foolishness.

6   I am utterly bowed down and prostrate; *
      I go about in mourning all the day long.

7   My loins are filled with searing pain; *
      there is no health in my body.

8   I am utterly numb and crushed; *
      I wail, because of the groaning of my heart.

9   O Lord, you know all my desires, *
      and my sighing is not hidden from you.

10 My heart is pounding, my strength has failed me, *
      and the brightness of my eyes is gone from me.

11 My friends and companions draw back from my affliction; *
      my neighbors stand afar off.

12 Those who seek after my life lay snares for me; *
      those who strive to hurt me speak of my ruin
      and plot treachery all the day long.

13 But I am like the deaf who do not hear, *
      like those who are mute and do not open their mouth.

14 I have become like one who does not hear *
      and from whose mouth comes no defense.

15 For in you, O LORD, have I fixed my hope; *
      you will answer me, O Lord my God.

16 For I said, "Do not let them rejoice at my expense, *
      those who gloat over me when my foot slips."

17 Truly, I am on the verge of falling, *
      and my pain is always with me.

18 I will confess my iniquity *
      and be sorry for my sin.

19 Those who are my enemies without cause are mighty, *
      and many in number are those who wrongfully hate me.

20 Those who repay evil for good slander me, *
      because I follow the course that is right.

21 O LORD, do not forsake me; *
  be not far from me, O my God.

22 Make haste to help me, *
  O Lord of my salvation.

Epiphany In you, O LORD, have I fixed my hope; you will answer me, O Lord my God.
Pentecost O Lord, you know all my desires, and my sighing is not hidden from you.

Psalm 140 *Eripe me, Domine*
The Pharisees went and plotted to entrap him in what he said. Mt. 22: 15

Epiphany I have said to the LORD, "You are my God; listen, O LORD, to my supplication."
Pentecost Keep me, O Lord, from the hands of the wicked; for you are the strength of my salvation.

1 Deliver me, O LORD, from evildoers; *
  protect me from the violent,

2 Who devise evil in their hearts *
  and stir up strife all day long.

3 They have sharpened their tongues like a serpent; *
  adder's poison is under their lips.

4 Keep me, O LORD, from the hands of the wicked; *
  protect me from the violent,
  who are determined to trip me up.

5 The proud have hidden a snare for me
  and stretched out a net of cords; *
  they have set traps for me along the path.

6 I have said to the LORD, "You are my God; *
  listen, O LORD, to my supplication.

7 O LORD God, the strength of my salvation, *
  you have covered my head in the day of battle.

8 Do not grant the desires of the wicked, O LORD, *
  nor let their evil plans prosper.

9 Let not those who surround me lift up their heads; *
  let the evil of their lips overwhelm them.

10 Let hot burning coals fall upon them; *
    let them be cast into the mire, never to rise up again."

11 A slanderer shall not be established on the earth, *
    and evil shall hunt down the lawless.

12 I know that the LORD will maintain the cause of the poor *
    and render justice to the needy.

13 Surely, the righteous will give thanks to your Name, *
    and the upright shall continue in your sight.

Epiphany I have said to the LORD, "You are my God; listen, O LORD, to my supplication."
Pentecost Keep me, O Lord, from the hands of the wicked; for you are the strength of my salvation.

Psalm 41 *Beatus qui intelligit*

Blessed are those slaves whom the master finds alert when he comes; truly I tell you, he will fasten his belt and have them sit down to eat, and he will come and serve them. Lk. 12:37

Epiphany The LORD sustains them on their sickbed and ministers to them in their illness.
Pentecost LORD, be merciful to me; heal me, for I have sinned against you.

1 Blessed are they who consider the poor and needy! *
    the LORD will deliver them in the time of trouble.

2 The LORD preserves them and keeps them alive,
    so that they may be blessed in the land; *
      he does not hand them over to the will of their enemies.

3 The LORD sustains them on their sickbed *
    and ministers to them in their illness.

4 I said, "LORD, be merciful to me; *
    heal me, for I have sinned against you."

5 My enemies are saying wicked things about me: *
    "When will he die, and his name perish?"

6 Even if they come to see me, they speak empty words; *
    their heart collects false rumors;
    they go outside and spread them.

7 All my enemies whisper together about me *
    and devise evil against me.

8 "A deadly thing," they say, "has fastened on him; *
    he has taken to his bed and will never get up again."

9 Even my best friend, whom I trusted,
  who broke bread with me, *
    has lifted up his heel and turned against me.

10 But you, O LORD, be merciful to me and raise me up, *
    and I shall repay them.

11 By this I know you are pleased with me, *
    that my enemy does not triumph over me.

12 In my integrity you hold me fast, *
    and shall set me before your face for ever.

13 Blessed be the LORD God of Israel, *
    from age to age. Amen. Amen.

Epiphany The LORD sustains them on their sickbed and ministers to them in their illness.
Pentecost LORD, be merciful to me; heal me, for I have sinned against you.

Reading One

Responsory One (2 Pt. 1:19)
You will do well to be attentive to the word
    – as a lamp shining in a dark place.
The morning star rises in your hearts
    – as a lamp shining in a dark place.
Glory to the Father and to the Son and to the Holy Spirit.
You will do well to be attentive to the word
    – as a lamp shining in a dark place.

The First Canticle – Song of Restoration *In tribulatione*
(Hosea 6:1-6)

Epiphany God's justice will come to us like a shower, like spring rains that water the earth.
Pentecost God's justice dawns like morning light, its dawning as sure as the sunrise.

Come, let us return to the Lord; *
    for it is he who has torn, and he will heal us;
    he has struck down, and he will bind us up.

After two days he will revive us; *
    on the third day he will raise us up,
    that we may live before him.

Let us know, let us press on to know the Lord; *
    his appearing is as sure as the dawn.

He will come to us like the showers, *
    like the spring rains that water the earth."

What shall I do with you, O Ephraim? *
    What shall I do with you, O Judah?

Your love is like a morning cloud, *
    like the dew that goes away early.

Therefore I have hewn them by the prophets, *
    I have killed them by the words of my mouth,
    and my judgment goes forth as the light.

For I desire steadfast love and not sacrifice, *
    the knowledge of God rather than burnt offerings.

Epiphany God's justice will come to us like a shower, like spring rains that water the earth.
Pentecost God's justice dawns like morning light, its dawning as sure as the sunrise.

Reading Two

Responsory Two (Ps. 9:13)
Have pity on me, O Lord
        — see the misery I suffer.
You lift me up from the gate of death
        — see the misery I suffer.
Glory to the Father and to the Son and to the Holy Spirit.
Have pity on me, O Lord
        — see the misery I suffer.

The Gospel Canticle – The Song of Zechariah
Epiphany The light shines in the darkness and the darkness did not overcome the light.
Pentecost You, O child, will give people knowledge of salvation by the forgiveness of their sins.

Litany

Govern and direct your holy Church; fill it with love and truth; and grant it that unity which is your will.
Lord, have mercy.
Give us boldness to preach the gospel in all the world, and to make disciples of all the nations.
Christ, have mercy.
Enlighten your bishops, priests and deacons with knowledge and understanding, that by their teaching and their lives they may proclaim your word.
Lord, have mercy.

Invitation to the Lord's Prayer Reconciled to God and with one another, we pray to the Father.

The Collect *From the proper of the day or*
Lord Jesus Christ, you stretched out your arms of love on the hard wood of the cross that everyone might come within the reach of your saving embrace: So clothe us in your Spirit that we, reaching forth our hands in love, may bring those who do not know you to the knowledge and love of you; for the honor of your Name. Amen.

The Blessing

May we pray that all may go well with us and that we may be in good health, just as it is well with our souls. **Amen**

Friday Week 2 Noonday Prayer

Officiant: O God, make speed to save us.
People: **O Lord, make haste to help us.**
Officiant and People **Glory to the Father... Alleluia.**

Hymn Glory be to Jesus *Hymnal 479*

Psalm 119 Kaph *Defecit in salutare*
Joseph bought a linen cloth, and taking down the body, wrapped it in the linen cloth, and laid it in a tomb that had been hewn out of the rock. Mk. 15:46

Epiphany Yours is the day, yours also the night; you established the moon and the sun.
Pentecost Do not hand over the life of your dove to wild beasts; never forget the lives of your poor.

81 My soul has longed for your salvation; *
　　I have put my hope in your word.

82 My eyes have failed from watching for your promise, *
　　and I say, "When will you comfort me?"

83 I have become like a leather flask in the smoke, *
     but I have not forgotten your statutes.

84 How much longer must I wait? *
     when will you give judgment
     against those who persecute me?

85 The proud have dug pits for me; *
     they do not keep your law.

86 All your commandments are true; *
     help me, for they persecute me with lies.

87 They had almost made an end of me on earth, *
     but I have not forsaken your commandments.

88 In your loving-kindness, revive me, *
     that I may keep the decrees of your mouth.

Psalm 129 *Sæpe expugnaverunt*
After they have flogged him, they will kill him, and on the third day he will rise again. Lk. 18: 33

1 "Greatly have they oppressed me since my youth," *
     let Israel now say;

2 "Greatly have they oppressed me since my youth, *
     but they have not prevailed against me."

3 The plowmen plowed upon my back *
     and made their furrows long.

4 The LORD, the Righteous One, *
     has cut the cords of the wicked.

5 Let them be put to shame and thrown back, *
     all those who are enemies of Zion.

6 Let them be like grass upon the housetops, *
     which withers before it can be plucked;

7 Which does not fill the hand of the reaper, *
     nor the bosom of him who binds the sheaves;

8 So that those who go by say not so much as,
     "The LORD prosper you. *
     We wish you well in the Name of the LORD."

Psalm 74 *Ut quid, Deus?*
Destroy this temple, and in three days I will raise it up. Jn. 2: 19

1 O God, why have you utterly cast us off? *
     why is your wrath so hot against the sheep of your pasture?

2 Remember your congregation that you purchased long ago, *
    the tribe you redeemed to be your inheritance,
    and Mount Zion where you dwell.

3 Turn your steps toward the endless ruins; *
    the enemy has laid waste everything in your sanctuary.

4 Your adversaries roared in your holy place; *
    they set up their banners as tokens of victory.

5 They were like men coming up with axes to a grove of trees; *
    they broke down all your carved work
    with hatchets and hammers.

6 They set fire to your holy place; *
    they defiled the dwelling-place of your Name
    and razed it to the ground.

7 They said to themselves, "Let us destroy them altogether." *
    They burned down
    all the meeting-places of God in the land.

8 There are no signs for us to see;
    there is no prophet left; *
    there is not one among us who knows how long.

9 How long, O God, will the adversary scoff? *
    will the enemy blaspheme your Name for ever?

10 Why do you draw back your hand? *
    why is your right hand hidden in your bosom?

11 Yet God is my King from ancient times, *
    victorious in the midst of the earth.

12 You divided the sea by your might *
    and shattered the heads of the dragons upon the waters;

13 You crushed the heads of Leviathan *
    and gave him to the people of the desert for food.

14 You split open spring and torrent; *
    you dried up ever-flowing rivers.

15 Yours is the day, yours also the night; *
    you established the moon and the sun.

16 You fixed all the boundaries of the earth; *
    you made both summer and winter.

17 Remember, O Lord, how the enemy scoffed, *
    how a foolish people despised your Name.

18 Do not hand over the life of your dove to wild beasts; *
    never forget the lives of your poor.

19 Look upon your covenant; *
    the dark places of the earth are haunts of violence.

20 Let not the oppressed turn away ashamed; *
    let the poor and needy praise your Name.

21 Arise, O God, maintain your cause; *
    remember how fools revile you all day long.

22 Forget not the clamor of your adversaries, *
    the unending tumult of those who rise up against you.

Epiphany Yours is the day, yours also the night; you established the moon and the sun.
Pentecost Do not hand over the life of your dove to wild beasts; never forget the lives of your poor.

Reading Isaiah 52: 13-15
See, my servant shall prosper; he shall be exalted and lifted up, and shall be very high. Just as there were many who were astonished at him —so marred was his appearance, beyond human semblance, and his form beyond that of mortals— so he shall startle many nations; kings shall shut their mouths because of him; for that which had not been told them they shall see, and that which they had not heard they shall contemplate.

Verse and Response
I, when I am lifted up from the earth.
I will draw all people to myself.

The Short Litany and the Lord's Prayer

The Collect O God, by the passion of your blessed Son you made an instrument of shameful death to be for us the means of life: Grant us so to glory in the cross of Christ, that we may gladly suffer shame and loss for the sake of your Son our Savior Jesus Christ; who lives and reigns with you and the Holy Spirit, one God, for ever and ever. Amen.

Let us bless the Lord.
Thanks be to God.

Friday Week 2 Evening Prayer

Officiant: O God, make speed to save us.

People: **O Lord, make haste to help us.**

Officiant and People **Glory to the Father... Alleluia.**

Hymn What wondrous love is this *Hymnal 439*

Psalm 79 *Deus, venerunt*

This fellow said, "I am able to destroy the temple of God and to build it in three days." Mt. 26: 51

Epiphany The curtain of the temple was torn in two, from top to bottom. The earth shook, and the rocks were split.

Pentecost Help us, O God our savior, and forgive us our sins.

1 O God, the heathen have come into your inheritance;
    they have profaned your holy temple; *
        they have made Jerusalem a heap of rubble.

2 They have given the bodies of your servants
    as food for the birds of the air, *
        and the flesh of your faithful ones
        to the beasts of the field.

3 They have shed their blood like water
    on every side of Jerusalem, *
        and there was no one to bury them.

4 We have become a reproach to our neighbors, *
        an object of scorn and derision to those around us.

5 How long will you be angry, O LORD? *
        will your fury blaze like fire for ever?

6 Pour out your wrath upon the heathen
    who have not known you *
        and upon the kingdoms
        that have not called upon your Name.

7 For they have devoured Jacob *
        and made his dwelling a ruin.

8 Remember not our past sins;
    let your compassion be swift to meet us; *
        for we have been brought very low.

9 Help us, O God our Savior, for the glory of your Name; *
        deliver us and forgive us our sins, for your Name's sake.

10 Why should the heathen say, "Where is their God?" *
>   Let it be known among the heathen and in our sight
>   that you avenge the shedding of your servants' blood.

11 Let the sorrowful sighing of the prisoners come before you, *
>   and by your great might
>   spare those who are condemned to die.

12 May the revilings with which they reviled you, O Lord, *
>   return seven-fold into their bosoms.

13 For we are your people and the sheep of your pasture; *
>   we will give you thanks for ever
>   and show forth your praise from age to age.

Epiphany The curtain of the temple was torn in two, from top to bottom. The earth shook, and the rocks were split.
Pentecost Help us, O God our savior, and forgive us our sins.

Psalm 6 *Domine, ne in furore*
I am deeply grieved, even to death; remain here, and stay awake with me. Mt. 26: 38

Epiphany You led them by night with a pillar of fire, to give them light on the way in which they should go.
Pentecost Turn, O LORD, and deliver me; save me for your mercy's sake.

1 LORD, do not rebuke me in your anger; *
>   do not punish me in your wrath.

2 Have pity on me, LORD, for I am weak; *
>   heal me, LORD, for my bones are racked.

3 My spirit shakes with terror; *
>   how long, O LORD, how long?

4 Turn, O LORD, and deliver me; *
>   save me for your mercy's sake.

5 For in death no one remembers you; *
>   and who will give you thanks in the grave?

6 I grow weary because of my groaning; *
>   every night I drench my bed
>   and flood my couch with tears.

7 My eyes are wasted with grief *
>   and worn away because of all my enemies.

8 Depart from me, all evildoers, *
    for the LORD has heard the sound of my weeping.

9 The LORD has heard my supplication; *
    the LORD accepts my prayer.

10 All my enemies shall be confounded and quake with fear; *
    they shall turn back and suddenly be put to shame.

Epiphany You led them by night with a pillar of fire, to give them light
on the way in which they should go.
Pentecost Turn, O LORD, and deliver me; save me for your mercy's
sake.

Psalm 77 *Voce mea ad Dominum*

My Father, if this cannot pass unless I drink it, your will be done. Mt. 26: 42

Epiphany When Joseph heard that Archelaus was ruling over Judea in
place of his father Herod, he was afraid to go there.
Pentecost I commune with my heart in the night; I ponder and search
my mind.

1 I will cry aloud to God; *
    I will cry aloud, and he will hear me.

2 In the day of my trouble I sought the Lord; *
    my hands were stretched out by night and did not tire;
    I refused to be comforted.

3 I think of God, I am restless, *
    I ponder, and my spirit faints.

4 You will not let my eyelids close; *
    I am troubled and I cannot speak.

5 I consider the days of old; *
    I remember the years long past;

6 I commune with my heart in the night; *
    I ponder and search my mind.

7 Will the Lord cast me off for ever? *
    will he no more show his favor?

8 Has his loving-kindness come to an end for ever? *
    has his promise failed for evermore?

9 Has God forgotten to be gracious? *
    has he, in his anger, withheld his compassion?

10 And I said, "My grief is this: *
　　the right hand of the Most High has lost its power."

11 I will remember the works of the LORD, *
　　and call to mind your wonders of old time.

12 I will meditate on all your acts *
　　and ponder your mighty deeds.

13 Your way, O God, is holy; *
　　who is so great a god as our God?

14 You are the God who works wonders *
　　and have declared your power among the peoples.

15 By your strength you have redeemed your people, *
　　the children of Jacob and Joseph.

16 The waters saw you, O God;
　　the waters saw you and trembled; *
　　　the very depths were shaken.

17 The clouds poured out water;
　　the skies thundered; *
　　　your arrows flashed to and fro;

18 The sound of your thunder was in the whirlwind;
　　your lightnings lit up the world; *
　　　the earth trembled and shook.

19 Your way was in the sea,
　　and your paths in the great waters, *
　　　yet your footsteps were not seen.

20 You led your people like a flock *
　　by the hand of Moses and Aaron.

Epiphany When Joseph heard that Archelaus was ruling over Judea in place of his father Herod, he was afraid to go there.
Pentecost I commune with my heart in the night; I ponder and search my mind.

Reading

Responsory (Ps. 23: 1,2)
The Lord is my shepherd
　　　– I shall not be in want.
God makes me lie down in green pastures
　　　– I shall not be in want.

Glory to the Father and to the Son and to the Holy Spirit.
The Lord is my shepherd
> **– I shall not be in want.**

The Gospel Canticle – The Song of Mary

Epiphany Run while you have the light of life, lest the darkness of death overtake you.

Pentecost God has come to the help of his servant Israel, ever mindful of his merciful promise.

Litany

Give your people grace to witness to your word and bring forth the fruit of your Spirit.
Lord, have mercy.
Bring into the way of truth all who have erred and are deceived.
Christ, have mercy.
Strengthen those who stand; comfort and help the fainthearted; raise up the fallen; and finally beat down Satan under our feet.
Lord, have mercy.

Invitation to the Lord's Prayer Forgiven by the Father we pray with grateful hearts.

The Collect *From the proper of the day or*
O God, you manifest in your servants the signs of your presence: Send forth upon us the spirit of love, that in companionship with one another your abounding grace may increase among us; through Jesus Christ our Lord. Amen.

The Blessing

May we know what is the hope to which God has called us, what are the riches of his glorious inheritance among the saints, and what is the immeasurable greatness of his power for us who believe. **Amen**

Saturday Week 2 Morning Prayer

Officiant: Lord, open our lips.
People: **And our mouth shall proclaim your praise.**
Officiant and People **Glory to the Father... Alleluia.**

The Invitatory Psalm 100

Serve the LORD with gladness: Come let us adore.

Hymn Joyful, joyful we adore thee *Hymnal 376*

Psalm 49 A *Audite hæc, omnes*

Those who want to save their life will lose it, and those who lose their life
for my sake will find it. Mt. 16:25

Epiphany Wisdom is radiant and unfading, and she is easily discerned by those who love her.

Pentecost Lay up for your selves treasures in heaven.

1 Hear this, all you peoples;
    hearken, all you who dwell in the world, *
        you of high degree and low, rich and poor together.

2 My mouth shall speak of wisdom, *
        and my heart shall meditate on understanding.

3 I will incline my ear to a proverb *
        and set forth my riddle upon the harp.

4 Why should I be afraid in evil days, *
        when the wickedness of those at my heels surrounds me,

5 The wickedness of those who put their trust in their goods, *
        and boast of their great riches?

6 We can never ransom ourselves, *
        or deliver to God the price of our life;

7 For the ransom of our life is so great, *
        that we should never have enough to pay it,

8 In order to live for ever and ever, *
        and never see the grave.

Epiphany Wisdom is radiant and unfading, and she is easily discerned by those who love her.

Pentecost Lay up for your selves treasures in heaven.

Psalm 49 B *Cum viderit*

For what will it profit them if they gain the whole world but forfeit their life? Mt. 16:26

Epiphany Wisdom hastens to make herself known to those who desire her.

Pentecost Such is the way of those who foolishly trust in themselves, and the end of those who delight in their own words.

9 For we see that the wise die also;
    like the dull and stupid they perish *
        and leave their wealth to those who come after them.

10 Their graves shall be their homes for ever,
 their dwelling places from generation to generation, *
  though they call the lands after their own names.

11 Even though honored, they cannot live for ever; *
 they are like the beasts that perish.

12 Such is the way of those who foolishly trust in themselves, *
 and the end of those who delight in their own words.

13 Like a flock of sheep they are destined to die;
 Death is their shepherd; *
  they go down straightway to the grave.

14 Their form shall waste away, *
 and the land of the dead shall be their home.

15 But God will ransom my life; *
 he will snatch me from the grasp of death.

16 Do not be envious when some become rich, *
 or when the grandeur of their house increases;

17 For they will carry nothing away at their death, *
 nor will their grandeur follow them.

18 Though they thought highly of themselves while they lived, *
 and were praised for their success,

19 They shall join the company of their forebears, *
 who will never see the light again.

20 Those who are honored, but have no understanding, *
 are like the beasts that perish.

Epiphany Wisdom hastens to make herself known to those who desire her.
Pentecost Such is the way of those who foolishly trust in themselves, and the end of those who delight in their own words.

Psalm 150 *Laudate Dominum*
The whole multitude of the disciples began to praise God joyfully with a loud voice. Lk. 19: 37
Epiphany All nations will come and worship before you.
Pentecost Praise the Lord for his excellent greatness.

1 Hallelujah!
 Praise God in his holy temple; *
  praise him in the firmament of his power.

2 Praise him for his mighty acts; *
      praise him for his excellent greatness.

3 Praise him with the blast of the ram's-horn; *
      praise him with lyre and harp.

4 Praise him with timbrel and dance; *
      praise him with strings and pipe.

5 Praise him with resounding cymbals; *
      praise him with loud-clanging cymbals.

6 Let everything that has breath *
      praise the Lord.
      Hallelujah!

Epiphany All nations will come and worship before you.
Pentecost Praise the Lord for his excellent greatness.

Reading One

Responsory One (Ps. 119:25, 32)
My soul cleaves to the dust
      – revive me by your word.
You have set my heart at liberty
      – revive me by your word.
Glory to the Father and to the Son and to the Holy Spirit.
My soul cleaves to the dust
      – revive me by your word.

The First Canticle – Canticle of Mother Jerusalem
Laetamini cum Hierusalem
(Isaiah 66:10-14)

Epiphany I will extend peace to her like a river, the wealth of nations like an overflowing stream.
Pentecost The Lord will make a river of peace flow through Jerusalem.

Rejoice with Jerusalem and be glad for her *
      all you who love her,

Rejoice, rejoice with her, *
      all you who mourn over her,

That you may drink deeply with delight *
      from her comforting breast.

For thus says our God, *
> "I will extend peace to her like a river,
> the wealth of nations like an overflowing stream.

"You shall nurse and be carried on her arm, *
> and you shall nestle in her lap.

"As a mother comforts her child, so will I comfort you; *
> you shall be comforted in Jerusalem.

"You shall see, and your heart shall rejoice, *
> you shall flourish like the grass of the fields."

Epiphany I will extend peace to her like a river, the wealth of nations like an overflowing stream.
Pentecost The Lord will make a river of peace flow through Jerusalem.

Reading Two

Responsory Two (Ps. 9:11, 7)
Sing praise to the Lord
> **– who dwells in Zion.**

The Lord is enthroned for ever
> **– who dwells in Zion.**

Glory to the Father and to the Son and to the Holy Spirit.
Sing praise to the Lord
> **– who dwells in Zion.**

The Gospel Canticle – The Song of Zechariah
Epiphany I loved wisdom and sought her from my youth; I desired to take her for my bride, and became enamored of her beauty.
Pentecost Let the word of Christ dwell in you richly; teach and admonish one another in all wisdom.

Litany
For all people in their daily life and work;
For our families, friends, and neighbors, and for those who are alone.
Lord, have mercy.
For this community, the nation, and the world;
For all who work for justice, freedom, and peace.
Christ, have mercy.
For the just and proper use of your creation;
For the victims of hunger, fear, injustice, and oppression.
Lord, have mercy.

Invitation to the Lord's Prayer Confident that Christ raises up the lowly, let us approach the Father with humble hearts.

The Collect *From the proper of the day or*
Almighty God, who after the creation of the world rested from all your works and sanctified a day of rest for all your creatures: Grant that we, putting away all earthly anxieties, may be duly prepared for the service of your sanctuary, and that our rest here upon earth may be a preparation for the eternal rest promised to your people in heaven; through Jesus Christ our Lord. Amen.

The Blessing
May the God of our Lord Jesus Christ, the Father of glory, give us a spirit of wisdom and revelation as we come to know him. **Amen**

Saturday Week 2 Noonday Prayer
Officiant: O God, make speed to save us.
People: **O Lord, make haste to help us.**
Officiant and People **Glory to the Father... Alleluia.**

Hymn Spirit of mercy *Hymnal 229*

Psalm 119 Lamedh *In æternum, Domine*
The words that I have spoken to you are spirit and life. Jn. 6: 63
Epiphany You, O LORD, are gracious and full of compassion, slow to anger, and full of kindness and truth.
Pentecost Gladden the soul of your servant, for to you, O LORD, I lift up my soul.

89 O LORD, your word is everlasting; *
   it stands firm in the heavens.

90 Your faithfulness remains from one generation to another; *
   you established the earth, and it abides.

91 By your decree these continue to this day, *
   for all things are your servants.

92 If my delight had not been in your law, *
   I should have perished in my affliction.

93 I will never forget your commandments, *
   because by them you give me life.

94 I am yours; oh, that you would save me! *
   for I study your commandments.

95 Though the wicked lie in wait for me to destroy me, *
 I will apply my mind to your decrees.

96 I see that all things come to an end, *
 but your commandment has no bounds.

Psalm 86 A *Inclina, Domine*

Jesus told them a parable about their need to pray always and not to lose heart. Lk. 18:1

1 Bow down your ear, O LORD, and answer me, *
 for I am poor and in misery.

2 Keep watch over my life, for I am faithful; *
 save your servant who puts his trust in you.

3 Be merciful to me, O LORD, for you are my God; *
 I call upon you all the day long.

4 Gladden the soul of your servant, *
 for to you, O LORD, I lift up my soul.

5 For you, O LORD, are good and forgiving, *
 and great is your love toward all who call upon you.

6 Give ear, O LORD, to my prayer, *
 and attend to the voice of my supplications.

7 In the time of my trouble I will call upon you, *
 for you will answer me.

8 Among the gods there is none like you, O LORD, *
 nor anything like your works.

Psalm 86 B *Omnes gentes*

All nations will come and worship before you, for your judgments have been revealed. Rev. 15:4

9 All nations you have made will come
 and worship you, O LORD, *
 and glorify your Name.

10 For you are great;
 you do wondrous things; *
 and you alone are God.

11 Teach me your way, O LORD,
 and I will walk in your truth; *
 knit my heart to you that I may fear your Name.

12 I will thank you, O LORD my God, with all my heart, *
 and glorify your Name for evermore.

13 For great is your love toward me; *
    you have delivered me from the nethermost Pit.

14 The arrogant rise up against me, O God,
   and a band of violent men seeks my life; *
    they have not set you before their eyes.

15 But you, O LORD, are gracious and full of compassion, *
    slow to anger, and full of kindness and truth.

16 Turn to me and have mercy upon me; *
    give your strength to your servant;
    and save the child of your handmaid.

17 Show me a sign of your favor,
   so that those who hate me may see it and be ashamed; *
    because you, O LORD, have helped me and comforted me.

Epiphany You, O LORD, are gracious and full of compassion, slow to anger, and full of kindness and truth.
Pentecost Gladden the soul of your servant, for to you, O LORD, I lift up my soul.

Reading Luke 1: 26-31
In the sixth month the angel Gabriel was sent by God to a town in Galilee called Nazareth, to a virgin engaged to a man whose name was Joseph, of the house of David. The virgin's name was Mary. And he came to her and said, "Greetings, favored one! The Lord is with you." But she was much perplexed by his words and pondered what sort of greeting this might be. The angel said to her, "Do not be afraid, Mary, for you have found favor with God. And now, you will conceive in your womb and bear a son, and you will name him Jesus."

Verse and Response
Sing and rejoice, O daughter Zion!
For lo, I will come and dwell in your midst.

The Short Litany and the Lord's Prayer

The Collect Father in heaven, by your grace the virgin mother of your incarnate Son was blessed in bearing him, but still more blessed in keeping your word: Grant us who honor the exaltation of her lowliness to follow the example of her devotion to your will; through Jesus Christ our Lord, who lives and reigns with you and the Holy Spirit, one God, for ever and ever. Amen.

Let us bless the Lord.
Thanks be to God.

Week 3

Sunday Week 3 Evening Prayer I

Officiant: O God, make speed to save us.
People: **O Lord, make haste to help us.**
Officiant and People **Glory to the Father... Alleluia.**

Hymn Christ Mighty Savior *Hymnal 34*

Psalm 21 *Domine, in virtute tua*
*God has put all things under Christ's feet and has made him
the head over all things for the church. Eph. 1: 28*

Epiphany The king puts his trust in the LORD; because of the
loving-kindness of the Most High, he will not fall, hallelujah.
Pentecost Be exalted, O Lord, in your might, we will sing and praise
your power, hallelujah.

1 The king rejoices in your strength, O LORD; *
　　how greatly he exults in your victory!

2 You have given him his heart's desire; *
　　you have not denied him the request of his lips.

3 For you meet him with blessings of prosperity, *
　　and set a crown of fine gold upon his head.

4 He asked you for life, and you gave it to him: *
　　length of days, for ever and ever.

5 His honor is great, because of your victory; *
　　splendor and majesty have you bestowed upon him.

6 For you will give him everlasting felicity *
　　and will make him glad with the joy of your presence.

7 For the king puts his trust in the LORD; *
　　because of the loving-kindness of the Most High,
　　he will not fall.

8 Your hand will lay hold upon all your enemies; *
　　your right hand will seize all those who hate you.

9 You will make them like a fiery furnace *
　　at the time of your appearing, O LORD;

10 You will swallow them up in your wrath, *
　　and fire shall consume them.

11 You will destroy their offspring from the land *
　　and their descendants from among the peoples of the earth.

12 Though they intend evil against you
    and devise wicked schemes, *
        yet they shall not prevail.

13 For you will put them to flight *
        and aim your arrows at them.

14 Be exalted, O LORD, in your might; *
        we will sing and praise your power.

Epiphany The king puts his trust in the LORD; because of the
loving-kindness of the Most High, he will not fall, hallelujah.
Pentecost Be exalted, O Lord, in your might, we will sing and praise
your power, hallelujah.

Psalm 136 A *Confitemini*

*God has confirmed the promises given to the patriarchs, in order that the Gentiles
might glorify God for his mercy. Rm. 15: 8-9*

Epiphany The Lord created great lights: the sun to rule the day and the
moon and the stars to govern the night, hallelujah.
Pentecost Worthy is the Lamb that was slain to receive power and
wealth and wisdom and might, hallelujah.

1 Give thanks to the LORD, for he is good, *
        for his mercy endures for ever.

2 Give thanks to the God of gods, *
        for his mercy endures for ever.

3 Give thanks to the Lord of lords, *
        for his mercy endures for ever.

4 Who only does great wonders, *
        for his mercy endures for ever;

5 Who by wisdom made the heavens, *
        for his mercy endures for ever;

6 Who spread out the earth upon the waters, *
        for his mercy endures for ever;

7 Who created great lights, *
        for his mercy endures for ever;

8 The sun to rule the day, *
        for his mercy endures for ever;

9 The moon and the stars to govern the night, *
        for his mercy endures for ever.

Epiphany The Lord created great lights: the sun to rule the day and the moon and the stars to govern the night, hallelujah.

Pentecost Worthy is the Lamb that was slain to receive power and wealth and wisdom and might, hallelujah.

Psalm 136 B *Qui percussit*

God, who is rich in mercy, out of the great love with which he loved us,
made us alive together with Christ Eph. 2:4-5

Epiphany The Lord divided the Red Sea in two, and made Israel to pass through the midst of it, hallelujah.

Pentecost To the one seated on the throne and to the Lamb be blessing and honor and glory and might, hallelujah.

10 Who struck down the firstborn of Egypt, *
    for his mercy endures for ever;

11 And brought out Israel from among them, *
    for his mercy endures for ever;

12 With a mighty hand and a stretched-out arm, *
    for his mercy endures for ever;

13 Who divided the Red Sea in two, *
    for his mercy endures for ever;

14 And made Israel to pass through the midst of it, *
    for his mercy endures for ever;

15 But swept Pharaoh and his army into the Red Sea, *
    for his mercy endures for ever;

16 Who led his people through the wilderness, *
    for his mercy endures for ever.

17 Who struck down great kings, *
    for his mercy endures for ever;

18 And slew mighty kings, *
    for his mercy endures for ever;

19 Sihon, king of the Amorites, *
    for his mercy endures for ever;

20 And Og, the king of Bashan, *
    for his mercy endures for ever;

21 And gave away their lands for an inheritance, *
    for his mercy endures for ever;

22 An inheritance for Israel his servant, *
   for his mercy endures for ever.

23 Who remembered us in our low estate, *
   for his mercy endures for ever;

24 And delivered us from our enemies, *
   for his mercy endures for ever;

25 Who gives food to all creatures, *
   for his mercy endures for ever.

26 Give thanks to the God of heaven, *
   for his mercy endures for ever.

Epiphany The Lord divided the Red Sea in two, and made Israel to pass through the midst of it, hallelujah.
Pentecost To the one seated on the throne and to the Lamb be blessing and honor and glory and might, hallelujah.

Reading

Responsory (Phil 2:9, 10)
God gave Jesus the name
   – the name that is above every name.
Every knee should bend at Jesus' name
   – the name that is above every name.
Glory to the Father and to the Son and to the Holy Spirit.
God gave Jesus the name
   – the name that is above every name.

The Gospel Canticle – The Song of Mary
Magnificat Antiphon *From the proper of the day*

Litany
Bless physicians, nurses, and all others who minister to the suffering and grant them wisdom and skill, sympathy and patience.
Lord, have mercy.
Restore to wholeness whatever is broken by human sin, and restore wholeness to our lives, our nation, and the world.
Christ, have mercy.
Grant to the dying peace and a holy death, and uphold by the grace and consolation of your Holy Spirit those who are bereaved.
Lord, have mercy.

Invitation to the Lord's Prayer As our sacrifice of praise rises like incense to God, let us ask God's loving kindness to descend upon us.

The Collect *From the proper of the day*
O God, the source of eternal light: Shed forth your unending day upon us who watch for you, that our lips may praise you, our lives may bless you, and our worship on the morrow give you glory; through Jesus Christ our Lord. Amen.

The Blessing
May Christ dwell in our hearts through faith, as we are being rooted and grounded in love. **Amen**

Sunday Week 3 Morning Prayer

Officiant: Lord, open our lips.
People: **And our mouth shall proclaim your praise.**
Officiant and People **Glory to the Father... Alleluia.**

The Invitatory Psalm 95
The Spirit of holiness has raised the Son of God: Come let us adore.

Hymn On this day the first of days *Hymnal 47*

Psalm 118 A *Confitemini Domino*
The God of our ancestors raised up Jesus...
God exalted him at his right hand as Leader and Savior. Acts 5: 30-31

Epiphany Peace I leave with you; my peace I give to you. Do not let your hearts be troubled or afraid, hallelujah.
Pentecost The LORD is at my side, therefore I will not fear; what can anyone do to me? Hallelujah.

1 Give thanks to the LORD, for he is good; *
    his mercy endures for ever.

2 Let Israel now proclaim, *
    "His mercy endures for ever."

3 Let the house of Aaron now proclaim, *
    "His mercy endures for ever."

4 Let those who fear the LORD now proclaim, *
    "His mercy endures for ever."

5 I called to the LORD in my distress; *
    the LORD answered by setting me free.

6 The LORD is at my side, therefore I will not fear; *
    what can anyone do to me?

7 The LORD is at my side to help me; *
    I will triumph over those who hate me.

8 It is better to rely on the LORD *
    than to put any trust in flesh.

9 It is better to rely on the LORD *
    than to put any trust in rulers.

10 All the ungodly encompass me; *
    in the name of the LORD I will repel them.

11 They hem me in, they hem me in on every side; *
    in the name of the LORD I will repel them.

12 They swarm about me like bees;
    they blaze like a fire of thorns; *
      in the name of the LORD I will repel them.

13 I was pressed so hard that I almost fell, *
    but the LORD came to my help.

14 The LORD is my strength and my song, *
    and he has become my salvation.

Epiphany Peace I leave with you; my peace I give to you. Do not let your hearts be troubled or afraid, hallelujah.
Pentecost The LORD is at my side, therefore I will not fear; what can anyone do to me? Hallelujah.

Psalm 118 B *Vox exsultationis*
Christ entered into heaven itself,
now to appear in the presence of God on our behalf. Heb. 9: 24

Epiphany God is the LORD; he has shined upon us, hallelujah.
Pentecost I shall not die, but live, and declare the works of the LORD, hallelujah .

15 There is a sound of exultation and victory *
    in the tents of the righteous:

16 "The right hand of the LORD has triumphed! *
    the right hand of the LORD is exalted!
    the right hand of the LORD has triumphed!"

17 I shall not die, but live, *
    and declare the works of the LORD.

18 The LORD has punished me sorely, *
    but he did not hand me over to death.

19 Open for me the gates of righteousness; *
  I will enter them;
  I will offer thanks to the LORD.

20 "This is the gate of the LORD; *
  he who is righteous may enter."

21 I will give thanks to you, for you answered me *
  and have become my salvation.

22 The same stone which the builders rejected *
  has become the chief cornerstone.

23 This is the LORD'S doing, *
  and it is marvelous in our eyes.

24 On this day the LORD has acted; *
  we will rejoice and be glad in it.

25 Hosannah, LORD, hosannah! *
  LORD, send us now success.

26 Blessed is he who comes in the name of the Lord; *
  we bless you from the house of the LORD.

27 God is the LORD; he has shined upon us; *
  form a procession with branches up to the horns of the altar.

28 "You are my God, and I will thank you; *
  you are my God, and I will exalt you."

29 Give thanks to the LORD, for he is good; *
  his mercy endures for ever.

Epiphany God is the LORD; he has shined upon us, hallelujah.
Pentecost I shall not die, but live, and declare the works of the LORD,
hallelujah .

Psalm 100 *Jubilate Deo*
You are a chosen race, a royal priesthood, a holy nation, God's own people. 1 Pt. 2:9
Epiphany We are God's people and the sheep of the Lord's pasture,
hallelujah.
Pentecost Come before God's presence with a song, hallelujah.

1 Be joyful in the LORD, all you lands; *
  serve the LORD with gladness
  and come before his presence with a song.

2 Know this: The LORD himself is God; *
> he himself has made us, and we are his;
>> we are his people and the sheep of his pasture.

3 Enter his gates with thanksgiving;
> go into his courts with praise; *
>> give thanks to him and call upon his Name.

4 For the LORD is good;
> his mercy is everlasting; *
>> and his faithfulness endures from age to age.

Epiphany We are God's people and the sheep of the Lord's pasture, hallelujah.

Pentecost Come before God's presence with a song, hallelujah.

Reading One

Responsory One (Lk. 18:38)
Christ, Son of the Living God
> **– have mercy on us.**

You sit at the right hand of the Father
> **– have mercy on us.**

Glory to the Father and to the Son and to the Holy Spirit.
Christ, Son of the Living God
> **– have mercy on us.**

The First Canticle – You are God   *Te Deum laudamus*

You are God: we praise you;
You are the Lord: we acclaim you;
You are the eternal Father:
All creation worships you.
To you all angels, all the powers of heaven,
Cherubim and Seraphim, sing in endless praise:
> Holy, holy, holy Lord, God of power and might,
> heaven and earth are full of your glory.

The glorious company of apostles praise you.
The noble fellowship of prophets praise you.
The white-robed army of martyrs praise you.
Throughout the world the holy Church acclaims you;
> Father, of majesty unbounded,
> your true and only Son, worthy of all worship,
> and the Holy Spirit, advocate and guide.

You, Christ, are the king of glory,
the eternal Son of the Father.

When you became man to set us free
you did not shun the Virgin's womb.
You overcame the sting of death
and opened the kingdom of heaven to all believers.
You are seated at God's right hand in glory.
We believe that you will come and be our judge.
  Come then, Lord, and help your people,
  bought with the price of your own blood,
  and bring us with your saints
  to glory everlasting.

The Gloria is not said with the Te Deum.

Reading Two

Responsory Two (Ps. 11:4, 5)
The Lord is in his holy temple
   – the Lord's throne is in heaven.
God's eyes behold the inhabited world
   – the Lord's throne is in heaven.
Glory to the Father and to the Son and to the Holy Spirit.
The Lord is in his holy temple
   – the Lord's throne is in heaven.

The Gospel Canticle – The Song of Zechariah

Benedictus Antiphon *From the proper of the day*

Litany
Save your people, Lord, and bless your inheritance; govern them and
uphold them, now and always.
Lord, have mercy.
Day by day we bless you; we praise your name for ever.
Christ, have mercy.
Lord, show us your love and mercy; for we put our trust in you.
Lord, have mercy.

Invitation to the Lord's Prayer Since the Father wills to raise us up to
new life, let us ask the Father to accomplish the work of new life in us.

The Collect *From the Proper of the day or*
 O God, you make us glad with the weekly remembrance of the glorious
resurrection of your Son our Lord: Give us this day such blessing
through our worship of you, that the week to come may be spent in
your favor; through Jesus Christ our Lord. Amen.

The Blessing
May we rejoice always, pray without ceasing, and give thanks in all circumstances; for this is the will of God in Christ Jesus for us. **Amen**

Sunday Week 3 Noonday Prayer
Officiant: O God, make speed to save us.
People: **O Lord, make haste to help us.**
Officiant and People **Glory to the Father… Alleluia.**

Hymn O God, creation's secret force *Hymnal 15*

Psalm 1 *Beatus vir qui non abiit*
This is the person who comes to me, hears my words, and acts on them. Lk. 6:47
Epiphany I know that the LORD gives victory to his anointed; he will answer him out of his holy heaven, hallelujah.
Pentecost Blessed are they whose delight is in the law of the Lord, hallelujah.

1 Blessed are they who have not walked
   in the counsel of the wicked, *
       nor lingered in the way of sinners,
       nor sat in the seats of the scornful!

2 Their delight is in the law of the LORD, *
       and they meditate on his law day and night.

3 They are like trees planted by streams of water,
   bearing fruit in due season, with leaves that do not wither; *
       everything they do shall prosper.

4 It is not so with the wicked; *
       they are like chaff which the wind blows away.

5 Therefore the wicked shall not stand upright
   when judgment comes, *
       nor the sinner in the council of the righteous.

6 For the LORD knows the way of the righteous, *
       but the way of the wicked is doomed.

Psalm 2 *Quare fremuerunt gentes?*
God put his power to work in Christ when he raised him from the dead and seated him at his right hand. Col. 1: 20
1 Why are the nations in an uproar? *
       Why do the peoples mutter empty threats?

2 Why do the kings of the earth rise up in revolt,
    and the princes plot together, *
      against the LORD and against his Anointed?

3 "Let us break their yoke," they say; *
      "let us cast off their bonds from us."

4 He whose throne is in heaven is laughing; *
      the Lord has them in derision.

5 Then he speaks to them in his wrath, *
      and his rage fills them with terror.

6 "I myself have set my king *
      upon my holy hill of Zion."

7 Let me announce the decree of the LORD: *
      he said to me, "You are my Son;
      this day have I begotten you.

8 Ask of me, and I will give you
    the nations for your inheritance *
      and the ends of the earth for your possession.

9 You shall crush them with an iron rod *
      and shatter them like a piece of pottery."

10 And now, you kings, be wise; *
      be warned, you rulers of the earth.

11 Submit to the LORD with fear, *
      and with trembling bow before him;

12 Lest he be angry and you perish; *
      for his wrath is quickly kindled.

13 Blessed are they all *
      who take refuge in him!

Psalm 20 *Exaudiat te Dominus*

Christ is the head of the body, the church; he is the beginning, the firstborn from the dead. Col. 1: 18

1 May the LORD answer you in the day of trouble, *
      the Name of the God of Jacob defend you;

2 Send you help from his holy place *
      and strengthen you out of Zion;

3 Remember all your offerings *
      and accept your burnt sacrifice;

4 Grant you your heart's desire *
   and prosper all your plans.

5 We will shout for joy at your victory
   and triumph in the Name of our God; *
     may the LORD grant all your requests.

6 Now I know that the LORD gives victory to his anointed; *
     he will answer him out of his holy heaven,
     with the victorious strength of his right hand.

7 Some put their trust in chariots and some in horses, *
     but we will call upon the Name of the LORD our God.

8 They collapse and fall down, *
     but we will arise and stand upright.

9 O LORD, give victory to the king *
     and answer us when we call.

Epiphany I know that the LORD gives victory to his anointed; he will answer him out of his holy heaven, hallelujah.
Pentecost Blessed are they whose delight is in the law of the Lord, hallelujah.

Reading Genesis 1: 1-5
In the beginning when God created the heavens and the earth, the earth was a formless void and darkness covered the face of the deep, while a wind from God swept over the face of the waters. Then God said, "Let there be light"; and there was light. And God saw that the light was good; and God separated the light from the darkness. God called the light Day, and the darkness he called Night. And there was evening and there was morning, the first day.

Verse and Response
All things came into being through the Word.
Without the Word not one thing came into being.

The Short Litany and the Lord's Prayer

The Collect O God, who wonderfully created, and yet more wonderfully restored, the dignity of human nature: Grant that we may share the divine life of him who humbled himself to share our humanity, your Son Jesus Christ our Lord. Amen.

Let us bless the Lord.
Thanks be to God.

Sunday Week 3 Evening Prayer II

Officiant: O God, make speed to save us.

People: **O Lord, make haste to help us.**

Officiant and People **Glory to the Father... Alleluia.**

Hymn O Trinity of blessed light *Hymnal 29*

Psalm 110 *Dixit Dominus*

*Jesus has entered the inner sanctuary, having become a high priest forever
according to the order of Melchizedek. Heb. 6:20*

Epiphany Dominion belongs to the Lord, and he rules over the
nations, hallelujah.

Pentecost Christ the Lord is a priest for ever after the order of
Melchizedek, hallelujah.

1   The LORD said to my Lord, "Sit at my right hand, *
        until I make your enemies your footstool."

2   The LORD will send the scepter of your power out of Zion, *
        saying, "Rule over your enemies round about you.

3   Princely state has been yours from the day of your birth; *
        in the beauty of holiness have I begotten you,
        like dew from the womb of the morning."

4   The LORD has sworn and he will not recant: *
        "You are a priest for ever after the order of Melchizedek."

5   The Lord who is at your right hand
    will smite kings in the day of his wrath; *
        he will rule over the nations.

6   He will heap high the corpses; *
        he will smash heads over the wide earth.

7   He will drink from the brook beside the road; *
        therefore he will lift high his head.

Epiphany Dominion belongs to the Lord, and he rules over the
nations, hallelujah.

Pentecost Christ the Lord is a priest for ever after the order of
Melchizedek, hallelujah.

Psalm 111 *Confitebor tibi*

*Christ entered once for all into the Holy Place, with his own blood,
thus obtaining eternal redemption. Heb. 9:12*

Epiphany Give thanks to the Father, who has enabled you to share in
the inheritance of the saints in the light, hallelujah.

Pentecost The fear of the LORD is the beginning of wisdom; those who act accordingly have a good understanding, hallelujah.

1 Hallelujah!
   I will give thanks to the LORD with my whole heart, *
      in the assembly of the upright, in the congregation.

2 Great are the deeds of the LORD! *
      they are studied by all who delight in them.

3 His work is full of majesty and splendor, *
      and his righteousness endures for ever.

4 He makes his marvelous works to be remembered; *
      the LORD is gracious and full of compassion.

5 He gives food to those who fear him; *
      he is ever mindful of his covenant.

6 He has shown his people the power of his works *
      in giving them the lands of the nations.

7 The works of his hands are faithfulness and justice; *
      all his commandments are sure.

8 They stand fast for ever and ever, *
      because they are done in truth and equity.

9 He sent redemption to his people;
   he commanded his covenant for ever; *
      holy and awesome is his Name.

10 The fear of the LORD is the beginning of wisdom; *
      those who act accordingly have a good understanding;
      his praise endures for ever.

Epiphany Give thanks to the Father, who has enabled you to share in the inheritance of the saints in the light, hallelujah.
Pentecost The fear of the LORD is the beginning of wisdom; those who act accordingly have a good understanding, hallelujah.

Psalm 112 *Beatus vir*
The righteous will shine like the sun in the kingdom of their Father. Mt. 13: 43

Epiphany The light shines in the darkness, and the darkness did not overcome it, hallelujah.
Pentecost The righteous are generous in lending and they manage their affairs with justice, hallelujah.

1 Hallelujah!
   Blessed are they who fear the Lord *
      and have great delight in his commandments!

2 Their descendants will be mighty in the land; *
      the generation of the upright will be blessed.

3 Wealth and riches will be in their house, *
      and their righteousness will last for ever.

4 Light shines in the darkness for the upright; *
      the righteous are merciful and full of compassion.

5 It is good for them to be generous in lending *
      and to manage their affairs with justice.

6 For they will never be shaken; *
      the righteous will be kept in everlasting remembrance.

7 They will not be afraid of any evil rumors; *
      their heart is right;
      they put their trust in the Lord.

8 Their heart is established and will not shrink, *
      until they see their desire upon their enemies.

9 They have given freely to the poor, *
      and their righteousness stands fast for ever;
      they will hold up their head with honor.

10 The wicked will see it and be angry;
      they will gnash their teeth and pine away; *
      the desires of the wicked will perish.

Epiphany The light shines in the darkness, and the darkness did not overcome it, hallelujah.
Pentecost The righteous are generous in lending and they manage their affairs with justice, hallelujah.

Reading

Responsory (Ps. 113: 3, 4)
From the rising of the sun to its going down
      – let the name of the Lord be praised.
God's glory is above the heavens
      – let the name of the Lord be praised.
Glory to the Father and to the Son and to the Holy Spirit.

From the rising of the sun to its going down
 — let the name of the Lord be praised.

The Gospel Canticle – The Song of Mary
Magnificat Antiphon *From the proper of the day*

Litany
Show us your mercy, O Lord; and grant us your salvation.
Lord, have mercy.
Clothe your ministers with righteousness; let your people sing with joy.
Christ, have mercy.
Give peace, O Lord, in all the world; for only in you can we live in safety.
Lord, have mercy.

Invitation to the Lord's Prayer The Father draws us to the Son through the Spirit so we ask the Father to draw us deeper into the divine life.

Collect *From the proper of the day or*
Lord God, whose Son our Savior Jesus Christ triumphed over the powers of death and prepared for us our place in the new Jerusalem: Grant that we, who have this day given thanks for his resurrection, may praise you in that City of which he is the light, and where he lives and reigns for ever and ever. Amen.

The Blessing
May we progress in this way of life and in faith that we may run on the path of God's commandments, our hearts overflowing with the inexpressible delight of love. **Amen**

Monday Week 3 Morning Prayer
Officiant: Lord, open our lips.
People: **And our mouth shall proclaim your praise.**
Officiant and People **Glory to the Father ... Alleluia.**

The Invitatory Psalm 29
Let us listen to the splendid voice of our Creator: Come let us adore.

Hymn Holy, holy, holy *Hymnal 362*

Psalm 17 *Exaudi, Domine*
Seeing the glory of the Lord, we are being transformed into the same image from one degree of glory to another. 2 Cor. 3:18
Epiphany Let your eyes be fixed on justice.

Pentecost Keep me, O Lord, as the apple of you eye; hide me under the shadow of your wings.

1 Hear my plea of innocence, O LORD;
     give heed to my cry; *
         listen to my prayer, which does not come from lying lips.

2 Let my vindication come forth from your presence; *
         let your eyes be fixed on justice.

3 Weigh my heart, summon me by night, *
         melt me down; you will find no impurity in me.

4 I give no offense with my mouth as others do; *
         I have heeded the words of your lips.

5 My footsteps hold fast to the ways of your law; *
         in your paths my feet shall not stumble.

6 I call upon you, O God, for you will answer me; *
         incline your ear to me and hear my words.

7 Show me your marvelous loving-kindness, *
         O Savior of those who take refuge at your right hand
         from those who rise up against them.

8 Keep me as the apple of your eye; *
         hide me under the shadow of your wings,

9 From the wicked who assault me, *
         from my deadly enemies who surround me.

10 They have closed their heart to pity, *
         and their mouth speaks proud things.

11 They press me hard,
     now they surround me, *
         watching how they may cast me to the ground,

12 Like a lion, greedy for its prey, *
         and like a young lion lurking in secret places.

13 Arise, O LORD; confront them and bring them down; *
         deliver me from the wicked by your sword.

14 Deliver me, O LORD, by your hand *
         from those whose portion in life is this world;

15 Whose bellies you fill with your treasure, *
    who are well supplied with children
    and leave their wealth to their little ones.

16 But at my vindication I shall see your face; *
    when I awake, I shall be satisfied,
    beholding your likeness.

Epiphany Let your eyes be fixed on justice.
Pentecost Keep me, O Lord, as the apple of you eye; hide me under the shadow of your wings.

Psalm 108 *Paratum cor meum*
The nations will walk by its light,
and the kings of the earth will bring their glory into it. Rev. 21: 24

Epiphany I will sing praises to you among the nations.
Pentecost I will confess you among the peoples, O Lord.

1 My heart is firmly fixed, O God, my heart is fixed; *
    I will sing and make melody.

2 Wake up, my spirit;
awake, lute and harp; *
    I myself will waken the dawn.

3 I will confess you among the peoples, O LORD; *
    I will sing praises to you among the nations.

4 For your loving-kindness is greater than the heavens, *
    and your faithfulness reaches to the clouds.

5 Exalt yourself above the heavens, O God, *
    and your glory over all the earth.

6 So that those who are dear to you may be delivered, *
    save with your right hand and answer me.

7 God spoke from his holy place and said, *
    "I will exult and parcel out Shechem;
    I will divide the valley of Succoth.

8 Gilead is mine and Manasseh is mine; *
    Ephraim is my helmet and Judah my scepter.

9 Moab is my washbasin,
on Edom I throw down my sandal to claim it, *
    and over Philistia will I shout in triumph."

10 Who will lead me into the strong city? *
    who will bring me into Edom?

11 Have you not cast us off, O God? *
    you no longer go out, O God, with our armies.

12 Grant us your help against the enemy, *
    for vain is the help of man.

13 With God we will do valiant deeds, *
    and he shall tread our enemies under foot.

Epiphany I will sing praises to you among the nations.
Pentecost I will confess you among the peoples, O Lord.

Psalm 148 *Laudate Dominum*
*At Jesus' name every knee should bend, in heaven and on earth
and under the earth. Phil 2:10*

Epiphany Let Kings of the earth and all peoples praise the Name of the LORD.
Pentecost Praise the Lord from the heavens, praise the Lord from the earth.

1 Hallelujah!
   Praise the LORD from the heavens; *
       praise him in the heights.

2 Praise him, all you angels of his; *
       praise him, all his host.

3 Praise him, sun and moon; *
       praise him, all you shining stars.

4 Praise him, heaven of heavens, *
       and you waters above the heavens.

5 Let them praise the Name of the LORD; *
       for he commanded, and they were created.

6 He made them stand fast for ever and ever; *
       he gave them a law which shall not pass away.

7 Praise the LORD from the earth, *
       you sea-monsters and all deeps;

8 Fire and hail, snow and fog, *
       tempestuous wind, doing his will;

9 Mountains and all hills, *
       fruit trees and all cedars;

10 Wild beasts and all cattle, *
> creeping things and wingèd birds;

11 Kings of the earth and all peoples, *
> princes and all rulers of the world;

12 Young men and maidens, *
> old and young together.

13 Let them praise the Name of the LORD, *
> for his Name only is exalted,
> his splendor is over earth and heaven.

14 He has raised up strength for his people
> and praise for all his loyal servants, *
>> the children of Israel, a people who are near him.
>> Hallelujah!

Epiphany Let Kings of the earth and all peoples praise the Name of the LORD.

Pentecost Praise the Lord from the heavens, praise the Lord from the earth.

Reading One

Responsory One (Ps. 90:14)
In the morning satisfy us
> **– in your loving-kindness.**

We shall rejoice and be glad
> **– in your loving-kindness.**

Glory to the Father and to the Son and to the Holy Spirit.
In the morning satisfy us
> **– in your loving-kindness.**

The First Canticle – Praise of the Creator *Ecce formans montes*
(Amos 4: 13; 5:8; 9: 5-6)

Epiphany The Lord calls for the waters of the sea, and pours them out upon the surface of the earth

Pentecost The Lord made the Pleiades and Orion, and turns deep darkness into the morning.

Behold, the one who forms the mountains, creates the wind, *
> reveals his thoughts to mortals.

The Lord makes the morning darkness, *
> and treads on the heights of the earth—
> the Lord, the God of hosts, is his name!

The Lord made the Pleiades and Orion, *
>   and turns deep darkness into the morning,
>   and darkens the day into night,

The Lord calls for the waters of the sea, *
>   and pours them out on the surface of the earth,
>   the Lord is his name,

The LORD, God of hosts, touches the earth and it melts, *
>   and all who live in it mourn.

All of it rises like the Nile, *
>   and sinks again, like the Nile of Egypt.

The Lord builds his upper chambers in the heavens, *
>   and founds his vault upon the earth;

The Lord calls for the waters of the sea, *
>   and pours them out upon the surface of the earth—
>   the LORD is his name.

Epiphany The Lord calls for the waters of the sea, and pours them out upon the surface of the earth

Pentecost The Lord made the Pleiades and Orion, and turns deep darkness into the morning.

Reading Two

Responsory One (Ps. 30:4)
Sing to the Lord
>   **− you servants of God.**

Give thanks for the remembrance of God's holiness
>   **− you servants of God.**

Glory to the Father and to the Son and to the Holy Spirit.
Sing to the Lord
>   **− you servants of God.**

The Gospel Canticle − The Song of Zechariah
Epiphany In the tender compassion of our God the dawn from on high shall break upon us.

Pentecost God has raised up for us a mighty savior, born of the house of his servant David.

Litany
For the good earth which God has given us, and for the wisdom and will to conserve it, let us pray to the Lord.
Lord, have mercy.

For deliverance from all danger, violence, oppression, and degradation, let us pray to the Lord.
Christ, have mercy.
For the absolution and remission of our sins and offenses, let us pray to the Lord.
Lord, have mercy.

Invitation to the Lord's Prayer United with monastics throughout the world, let us draw close to the Father in prayer.

Collect *From the proper of the day or*
O God, the King eternal, whose light divides the day from the night and turns the shadow of death into the morning: Drive far from us all wrong desires, incline our hearts to keep your law, and guide our feet into the way of peace; that, having done your will with cheerfulness while it was day, we may, when night comes, rejoice to give you thanks; through Jesus Christ our Lord. Amen.

The Blessing
May we have unity of spirit, sympathy, love for one another, a tender heart, and a humble mind. **Amen**

Monday Week 3 Noonday Prayer
Officiant: O God, make speed to save us.
People: **O Lord, make haste to help us.**
Officiant and People **Glory to the Father… Alleluia.**

Hymn O God of truth, O Lord of might *Hymnal 21*

Psalm 119 Mem *Quomodo dilexi!*
They found him in the temple, sitting among the teachers,
listening to them and asking them questions. Lk. 2:46
Epiphany Learn where there is wisdom there is light for the eyes, and peace.
Pentecost You are my hiding-place; you preserve me from trouble; you surround me with shouts of deliverance.

97 Oh, how I love your law! *
    all the day long it is in my mind.

98 Your commandment has made me wiser than my enemies, *
    and it is always with me.

99 I have more understanding than all my teachers, *
    for your decrees are my study.

100 I am wiser than the elders, *
    because I observe your commandments.

101 I restrain my feet from every evil way, *
    that I may keep your word.

102 I do not shrink from your judgments, *
    because you yourself have taught me.

103 How sweet are your words to my taste! *
    they are sweeter than honey to my mouth.

104 Through your commandments I gain understanding; *
    therefore I hate every lying way.

Psalm 120 *Ad Dominum*

If you, even you, had only recognized on this day the things that make for peace! Lk: 19:42

1 When I was in trouble, I called to the LORD; *
    I called to the LORD, and he answered me.

2 Deliver me, O LORD, from lying lips *
    and from the deceitful tongue.

3 What shall be done to you, and what more besides, *
    O you deceitful tongue?

4 The sharpened arrows of a warrior, *
    along with hot glowing coals.

5 How hateful it is that I must lodge in Meshech *
    and dwell among the tents of Kedar!

6 Too long have I had to live *
    among the enemies of peace.

7 I am on the side of peace, *
    but when I speak of it, they are for war.

Psalm 121 *Levavi oculos*

Holy Father, protect them in your name that you have given me,
so that they may be one, as we are one. Jn. 17:11

1 I lift up my eyes to the hills; *
    from where is my help to come?

2 My help comes from the LORD, *
    the maker of heaven and earth.

3 He will not let your foot be moved *
    and he who watches over you will not fall asleep.

4   Behold, he who keeps watch over Israel *
        shall neither slumber nor sleep;

5   The LORD himself watches over you; *
        the LORD is your shade at your right hand,

6   So that the sun shall not strike you by day, *
        nor the moon by night.

7   The LORD shall preserve you from all evil; *
        it is he who shall keep you safe.

8   The LORD shall watch over your going out
    and your coming in, *
        from this time forth for evermore.

Epiphany Learn where there is wisdom there is light for the eyes, and peace.

Pentecost You are my hiding-place; you preserve me from trouble; you surround me with shouts of deliverance.

Reading Genesis 2: 4-7

In the day that the Lord God made the earth and the heavens, when no plant of the field was yet in the earth and no herb of the field had yet sprung up—for the Lord God had not caused it to rain upon the earth, and there was no one to till the ground; but a stream would rise from the earth, and water the whole face of the ground— then the Lord God formed man from the dust of the ground, and breathed into his nostrils the breath of life; and the man became a living being.

Verse and Response
The first man, Adam, became a living being.
The last Adam became a life-giving spirit.

The Short Litany and the Lord's Prayer

The Collect Heavenly Father, we thank you that by water and the Holy Spirit you have bestowed on us your servants the forgiveness of sin, and have raised us to the new life of grace. Sustain us, O Lord, in your Holy Spirit. Give us an inquiring mind and discerning heart, the courage to will and to persevere, a spirit to know and to love you, and the gift of joy and wonder in all your works. Amen.

Let us bless the Lord.
Thanks be to God.

Monday Week 3 Evening Prayer

Officiant: O God, make speed to save us.

People: **O Lord, make haste to help us.**

Officiant and People **Glory to the Father... Alleluia.**

Hymn I sing the almighty power of God *Hymnal 398*

Psalm 8 *Domine, Dominus noster*
We do see Jesus, who for a little while was made lower than the angels,
now crowned with glory and honor. Heb. 2:9

Epiphany Christ had to become like his brothers and sisters, so that he might be a merciful and faithful high priest in the service of God.
Pentecost How exalted is your Name, O Lord, in all the world.

1   O LORD our Governor, *
    how exalted is your Name in all the world!

2   Out of the mouths of infants and children *
    your majesty is praised above the heavens.

3   You have set up a stronghold against your adversaries, *
    to quell the enemy and the avenger.

4   When I consider your heavens, the work of your fingers, *
    the moon and the stars you have set in their courses,

5   What is man that you should be mindful of him? *
    the son of man that you should seek him out?

6   You have made him but little lower than the angels; *
    you adorn him with glory and honor;

7   You give him mastery over the works of your hands; *
    you put all things under his feet:

8   All sheep and oxen, *
    even the wild beasts of the field,

9   The birds of the air, the fish of the sea, *
    and whatsoever walks in the paths of the sea.

10 O LORD our Governor, *
   how exalted is your Name in all the world!

Epiphany Christ had to become like his brothers and sisters, so that he might be a merciful and faithful high priest in the service of God.
Pentecost How exalted is your Name, O Lord, in all the world.

Psalm 52 *Quid gloriaris?*

I know the one in whom I have put my trust. 1 Tim. !:12

Epiphany Christ had to become like his brothers and sisters, so that he might be a merciful and faithful high priest in the service of God.
Pentecost I am like a green olive tree in the house of God; I trust in the mercy of God for ever and ever.

1 You tyrant, why do you boast of wickedness *
    against the godly all day long?

2 You plot ruin;
    your tongue is like a sharpened razor, *
      O worker of deception.

3 You love evil more than good *
    and lying more than speaking the truth.

4 You love all words that hurt, *
    O you deceitful tongue.

5 Oh, that God would demolish you utterly, *
    topple you, and snatch you from your dwelling,
    and root you out of the land of the living!

6 The righteous shall see and tremble, *
    and they shall laugh at him, saying,

7 "This is the one who did not take God for a refuge, *
    but trusted in great wealth
    and relied upon wickedness."

8 But I am like a green olive tree in the house of God; *
    I trust in the mercy of God for ever and ever.

9 I will give you thanks for what you have done *
    and declare the goodness of your Name
    in the presence of the godly.

Epiphany Christ had to become like his brothers and sisters, so that he might be a merciful and faithful high priest in the service of God.
Pentecost I am like a green olive tree in the house of God; I trust in the mercy of God for ever and ever.

Psalm 128 *Beati omnes*

*Living in the fear of the Lord and in the comfort of the Holy Spirit,
the church increased in numbers. Acts 9:31*

Epiphany Who among you walks in darkness and has no light, yet trusts in the name of the Lord and relies upon his God?

Pentecost The Lord bless you from Zion all the days of your life.

1 Blessed are they all who fear the LORD, *
      and who follow in his ways!

2 You shall eat the fruit of your labor; *
      happiness and prosperity shall be yours.

3 Your wife shall be like a fruitful vine within your house, *
      your children like olive shoots round about your table.

4 The man who fears the LORD *
      shall thus indeed be blessed.

5 The LORD bless you from Zion, *
      and may you see the prosperity of Jerusalem
      all the days of your life.

6 May you live to see your children's children; *
      may peace be upon Israel.

Epiphany Who among you walks in darkness and has no light, yet trusts in the name of the Lord and relies upon his God?
Pentecost The Lord bless you from Zion all the days of your life.

Reading

Responsory (Ps. 141:1)
O Lord, I call to you
      – come to me quickly.
Hear my voice when I cry to you
      – come to me quickly.
Glory to the Father and to the Son and to the Holy Spirit.
O Lord, I call to you
      – come to me quickly.

The Gospel Canticle – The Song of Mary
Epiphany Those who do what is true come to the light, so that it may be clearly seen that their deeds have been done in God.
Pentecost God has looked with favor on me, a lowly servant. My spirit rejoices in God, my Savior.

Litany
That we may end our lives in faith and hope, without suffering and without reproach, let us pray to the Lord.
Lord, have mercy.

That we be defended and delivered and protected by God's gracious compassion, let us pray to the Lord.
Christ, have mercy.
For all who have died in the hope of the resurrection, and for all the departed, let us pray to the Lord.
Lord, have mercy.

Invitation to the Lord's Prayer As beloved children of God, we return at the end of the day to rest in the Father's love.

Collect *From the proper of the day or*
Most holy God, the source of all good desires, all right judgements, and all just works: Give to us, your servants, that peace which the world cannot give, so that our minds may be fixed on the doing of your will, and that we, being delivered from the fear of all enemies, may live in peace and quietness; through the mercies of Christ Jesus our Savior. Amen.

The Blessing
May we bear one another's burdens, and so fulfill the law of Christ.
Amen

Tuesday Week 3 Morning Prayer
Officiant: Lord, open our lips.
People: **And our mouth shall proclaim your praise.**
Officiant and People **Glory to the Father... Alleluia.**

The Invitatory Psalm 8
Jesus, made lower than the angels, is crowned with glory and honor: Come let us adore Christ the Lord.

Hymn Praise to the living God *Hymnal 372*

Psalm 87 *Fundamenta ejus*
Sarah corresponds to the Jerusalem above; she is free, and she is our mother. Gal. 4:26
Epiphany Of Zion it shall be said, "Everyone was born in her, and the Most High himself shall sustain her."
Pentecost Glorious things are spoken of you, O city of our God.

1 On the holy mountain stands the city he has founded; *
    the LORD loves the gates of Zion
    more than all the dwellings of Jacob.

2 Glorious things are spoken of you, *
    O city of our God.

3   I count Egypt and Babylon among those who know me; *
  behold Philistia, Tyre, and Ethiopia:
  in Zion were they born.

4   Of Zion it shall be said, "Everyone was born in her, *
  and the Most High himself shall sustain her."

5   The LORD will record as he enrolls the peoples, *
  "These also were born there."

6   The singers and the dancers will say, *
  "All my fresh springs are in you."

Epiphany Of Zion it shall be said, "Everyone was born in her, and the
Most High himself shall sustain her."
Pentecost Glorious things are spoken of you, O city of our God.

Psalm 48 *Magnus Dominus*

*I saw the holy city, the new Jerusalem, coming down out of heaven from God,
prepared as a bride adorned for her husband. Rev. 21:2*

Epiphany Your praise, like your Name, O God, reaches to the world's
end.
Pentecost Beautiful and lofty, the joy of all the earth, is the hill of Zion.

1   Great is the LORD, and highly to be praised; *
  in the city of our God is his holy hill.

2   Beautiful and lofty, the joy of all the earth,
 is the hill of Zion, *
  the very center of the world and the city of the great King.

3   God is in her citadels; *
  he is known to be her sure refuge.

4   Behold, the kings of the earth assembled *
  and marched forward together.

5   They looked and were astounded; *
  they retreated and fled in terror.

6   Trembling seized them there; *
  they writhed like a woman in childbirth,
  like ships of the sea when the east wind shatters them.

7   As we have heard, so have we seen,
 in the city of the LORD of hosts, in the city of our God; *
  God has established her for ever.

8 We have waited in silence on your loving-kindness, O God, *
    in the midst of your temple.

9 Your praise, like your Name, O God,
  reaches to the world's end; *
    your right hand is full of justice.

10 Let Mount Zion be glad
  and the cities of Judah rejoice, *
    because of your judgments.

11 Make the circuit of Zion;
  walk round about her; *
    count the number of her towers.

12 Consider well her bulwarks;
  examine her strongholds; *
    that you may tell those who come after.

13 This God is our God for ever and ever; *
    he shall be our guide for evermore.

Epiphany Your praise, like your Name, O God, reaches to the world's end.

Pentecost Beautiful and lofty, the joy of all the earth, is the hill of Zion.

Psalm 98 *Cantate Domino*

The throne of God and of the Lamb will be in it, and his servants will worship him;
they will see his face. Rev. 22:3-4

Epiphany In righteousness shall God judge the world and the peoples with equity.

Pentecost Shout with joy before the King, the Lord.

1 Sing to the LORD a new song, *
    for he has done marvelous things.

2 With his right hand and his holy arm *
    has he won for himself the victory.

3 The LORD has made known his victory; *
    his righteousness has he openly shown
    in the sight of the nations.

4 He remembers his mercy and faithfulness
  to the house of Israel, *
    and all the ends of the earth have seen
    the victory of our God.

5 Shout with joy to the LORD, all you lands; *
    lift up your voice, rejoice, and sing.

6 Sing to the LORD with the harp, *
    with the harp and the voice of song.

7 With trumpets and the sound of the horn *
    shout with joy before the King, the LORD.

8 Let the sea make a noise and all that is in it, *
    the lands and those who dwell therein.

9 Let the rivers clap their hands, *
    and let the hills ring out with joy before the LORD,
    when he comes to judge the earth.

10 In righteousness shall he judge the world *
    and the peoples with equity.

Epiphany In righteousness shall God judge the world and the peoples
with equity.
Pentecost Shout with joy before the King, the Lord.

Reading One

Responsory One (Ps. 130:5, 6)
My soul waits for the Lord
        − more than watchmen for the morning.
O Israel, wait for the Lord
        − more than watchmen for the morning.
Glory to the Father and to the Son and to the Holy Spirit.
My soul waits for the Lord
        − more than watchmen for the morning.

The First Canticle − The First Song of Isaiah *Ecce Deus*
(Isaiah 12:2-6)
Epiphany Make God's deeds known among the peoples; see that they
remember that his Name is exalted.
Pentecost Sing praises of the Lord, for he has done great things.

Surely, it is God who saves me; *
    I will trust in him and not be afraid.

For the Lord is my stronghold and my sure defense, *
    and he will be my Savior.

Therefore you shall draw water with rejoicing *
    from the springs of salvation.

And on that day you shall say, *
>Give thanks to the Lord and call upon his Name;

Make his deeds known among the peoples; *
>see that they remember that his Name is exalted.

Sing the praises of the Lord, for he has done great things, *
>and this is known in all the world.

Cry aloud, inhabitants of Zion, ring out your joy, *
>for the great one in the midst of you is the Holy One of Israel.

Epiphany Make God's deeds known among the peoples; see that they remember that his Name is exalted.
Pentecost Sing praises of the Lord, for he has done great things.

Reading Two

Responsory Two (Ps. 33:1, 2)
Rejoice in the Lord you righteous
>**– it is good for the just to sing praises.**
Praise the Lord with the harp
>**– it is good for the just to sing praises.**
Glory to the Father and to the Son and to the Holy Spirit.
Rejoice in the Lord you righteous
>**– it is good for the just to sing praises.**

The Gospel Canticle – The Song of Zechariah
Epiphany God will shine on those who dwell in darkness and the shadow of death, and guide our feet into the way of peace.
Pentecost God promised to show mercy to our ancestors and to remember his holy covenant.

Litany
For singers and entertainers, for dancers and stage workers, for all employed in the entertainment industries.
Lord, have mercy.
For those who haul trash and recycle waste, for children working in trash heaps, for all working to recycle products.
Christ, have mercy.
For secretaries, and administrators, for flight control officers and people involved in travel, for those who cook, serve and clean.
Lord, have mercy.

Invitation to the Lord's Prayer As peacemaking children of God, we draw near to the Father, the source of peace.

Collect *From the proper of the day or*
O God, the author of peace and lover of concord, to know you is eternal life and to serve you is perfect freedom: Defend us, your humble servants, in all assaults of our enemies; that we, surely trusting in your defense, may not fear the power of any adversaries; through the might of Jesus Christ our Lord. Amen.

The Blessing
May we show respect for one another supporting with the greatest patience one another's weaknesses of body or behavior and earnestly obey one another. **Amen**

Tuesday Week 3 Noonday Prayer
Officiant: O God, make speed to save us.
People: **O Lord, make haste to help us.**
Officiant and People **Glory to the Father... Alleluia.**

Hymn Praise the Lord, ye heavens adore him *Hymnal 373*

Psalm 119   Nun *Lucerna pedibus meis*
I have no greater joy than this, to hear that my children are walking in the truth. 3 Jn. 1:4
Epiphany God makes his angels spirits, and his servants flames of fire.
Pentecost Bless the LORD, all you works of his, in all places of his dominion; bless the LORD, O my soul.

105 Your word is a lantern to my feet *
    and a light upon my path.

106 I have sworn and am determined *
    to keep your righteous judgments.

107 I am deeply troubled; *
    preserve my life, O LORD, according to your word.

108 Accept, O LORD, the willing tribute of my lips, *
    and teach me your judgments.

109 My life is always in my hand, *
    yet I do not forget your law.

110 The wicked have set a trap for me, *
    but I have not strayed from your commandments.

111 Your decrees are my inheritance for ever; *
    truly, they are the joy of my heart.

112 I have applied my heart to fulfill your statutes *
    for ever and to the end.

Psalm 103 A *Benedic, anima mea*

Together may you with one voice glorify the God and Father of our Lord Jesus Christ. Rm 15:6

1 Bless the LORD, O my soul, *
   and all that is within me, bless his holy Name.

2 Bless the LORD, O my soul, *
   and forget not all his benefits.

3 He forgives all your sins *
   and heals all your infirmities;

4 He redeems your life from the grave *
   and crowns you with mercy and loving-kindness;

5 He satisfies you with good things, *
   and your youth is renewed like an eagle's.

6 The LORD executes righteousness *
   and judgment for all who are oppressed.

7 He made his ways known to Moses *
   and his works to the children of Israel.

8 The LORD is full of compassion and mercy, *
   slow to anger and of great kindness.

9 He will not always accuse us, *
   nor will he keep his anger for ever.

10 He has not dealt with us according to our sins, *
   nor rewarded us according to our wickedness.

11 For as the heavens are high above the earth, *
   so is his mercy great upon those who fear him.

12 As far as the east is from the west, *
   so far has he removed our sins from us.

13 As a father cares for his children, *
   so does the LORD care for those who fear him.

14 For he himself knows whereof we are made; *
   he remembers that we are but dust.

Psalm 103 B *Homo, sicut*

You have been born anew, not of perishable but of imperishable seed, through the living and enduring word of God. 1 Pt. 1:23

15 Our days are like the grass; *
   we flourish like a flower of the field;

16 When the wind goes over it, it is gone, *
    and its place shall know it no more.

17 But the merciful goodness of the LORD endures for ever
   on those who fear him, *
    and his righteousness on children's children;

18 On those who keep his covenant *
    and remember his commandments and do them.

19 The LORD has set his throne in heaven, *
    and his kingship has dominion over all.

20 Bless the LORD, you angels of his,
   you mighty ones who do his bidding, *
    and hearken to the voice of his word.

21 Bless the LORD, all you his hosts, *
    you ministers of his who do his will.

22 Bless the LORD, all you works of his,
   in all places of his dominion; *
    bless the LORD, O my soul.

Epiphany God makes his angels spirits, and his servants flames of fire.
Pentecost Bless the LORD, all you works of his, in all places of his
dominion; bless the LORD, O my soul.

Reading Isaiah 42: 5-7
Thus says God, the Lord, who created the heavens and stretched them
out, who spread out the earth and what comes from it, who gives breath
to the people upon it and spirit to those who walk in it: I am the Lord, I
have called you in righteousness, I have taken you by the hand and kept
you; I have given you as a covenant to the people, a light to the nations,
to open the eyes that are blind, to bring out the prisoners from the
dungeon, from the prison those who sit in darkness.

Verse and Response
Be glad and rejoice forever in what I am creating.
**I am about to create Jerusalem as a joy, and its people as a
delight.**

The Short Litany and the Lord's Prayer

The Collect Grant, Lord God, to all who have been baptized into the
death and resurrection of your son Jesus Christ, that, as we have put away
the old life of sin, so we may be renewed in the spirit of our minds, and
live in righteousness and true holiness; through Jesus Christ our Lord,

who lives and reigns with you, in the unity of the Holy Spirit, one God, now and forever. Amen.

Let us bless the Lord.
Thanks be to God.

Tuesday Week 3 Evening Prayer

Officiant: O God, make speed to save us.
People: **O Lord, make haste to help us.**
Officiant and People **Glory to the Father... Alleluia.**

Hymn O worship the King *Hymnal 388*

Psalm 85 *Benedixisti, Domine*

Glory to God in the highest heaven, and on earth peace among those whom he favors! Lk. 2:14

Epiphany Truth shall spring up from the earth, and righteousness shall look down from heaven.

Pentecost Righteousness shall go before him, and peace shall be a pathway for his feet.

1 You have been gracious to your land, O LORD, *
    you have restored the good fortune of Jacob.

2 You have forgiven the iniquity of your people *
    and blotted out all their sins.

3 You have withdrawn all your fury *
    and turned yourself from your wrathful indignation.

4 Restore us then, O God our Savior; *
    let your anger depart from us.

5 Will you be displeased with us for ever? *
    will you prolong your anger from age to age?

6 Will you not give us life again, *
    that your people may rejoice in you?

7 Show us your mercy, O LORD, *
    and grant us your salvation.

8 I will listen to what the LORD God is saying, *
    for he is speaking peace to his faithful people
    and to those who turn their hearts to him.

9 Truly, his salvation is very near to those who fear him, *
    that his glory may dwell in our land.

10 Mercy and truth have met together; *
    righteousness and peace have kissed each other.

11 Truth shall spring up from the earth, *
    and righteousness shall look down from heaven.

12 The LORD will indeed grant prosperity, *
    and our land will yield its increase.

13 Righteousness shall go before him, *
    and peace shall be a pathway for his feet.

Epiphany Truth shall spring up from the earth, and righteousness shall look down from heaven.

Pentecost Righteousness shall go before him, and peace shall be a pathway for his feet.

Psalm 62 *Nonne Deo?*

To one who without works trusts him who justifies the ungodly,
such faith is reckoned as righteousness. Rm. 4:5

Epiphany God alone is my rock and my salvation, my stronghold, so that I shall not be shaken.

Pentecost In God is my safety and my honor; God is my strong rock and my refuge.

1 For God alone my soul in silence waits; *
    from him comes my salvation.

2 He alone is my rock and my salvation, *
    my stronghold, so that I shall not be greatly shaken.

3 How long will you assail me to crush me,
all of you together, *
    as if you were a leaning fence, a toppling wall?

4 They seek only to bring me down from my place of honor; *
    lies are their chief delight.

5 They bless with their lips, *
    but in their hearts they curse.

6 For God alone my soul in silence waits; *
    truly, my hope is in him.

7 He alone is my rock and my salvation, *
    my stronghold, so that I shall not be shaken.

8 In God is my safety and my honor; *
    God is my strong rock and my refuge.

9 Put your trust in him always, O people, *
    pour out your hearts before him, for God is our refuge.

10 Those of high degree are but a fleeting breath, *
  even those of low estate cannot be trusted.

11 On the scales they are lighter than a breath, *
  all of them together.

12 Put no trust in extortion;
  in robbery take no empty pride; *
  though wealth increase, set not your heart upon it.

13 God has spoken once, twice have I heard it, *
  that power belongs to God.

14 Steadfast love is yours, O Lord, *
  for you repay everyone according to his deeds.

Epiphany God alone is my rock and my salvation, my stronghold, so that I shall not be shaken.
Pentecost In God is my safety and my honor; God is my strong rock and my refuge.

Psalm 125 *Qui confidunt*

*For those who will follow this rule—peace be upon them, and mercy,
and upon the Israel of God. Gal. 6:16*

Epiphany Peace be upon you, and mercy, and upon the Israel of God.
Pentecost You have come to mount Zion and the city of the living God, the heavenly Jerusalem.

1 Those who trust in the LORD are like Mount Zion, *
  which cannot be moved, but stands fast for ever.

2 The hills stand about Jerusalem; *
  so does the LORD stand round about his people,
  from this time forth for evermore.

3 The scepter of the wicked shall not hold sway
  over the land allotted to the just, *
  so that the just shall not put their hands to evil.

4 Show your goodness, O LORD, to those who are good *
  and to those who are true of heart.

5 As for those who turn aside to crooked ways,
  the LORD will lead them away with the evildoers; *
  but peace be upon Israel.

Epiphany Peace be upon you, and mercy, and upon the Israel of God.
Pentecost You have come to mount Zion and the city of the living God, the heavenly Jerusalem.

Reading

Responsory (Ps. 16:7, 8)
I will bless the Lord who gives me counsel
　　– my heart teaches me, night by night.
You are my portion and my cup
　　– my heart teaches me, night by night.
Glory to the Father and to the Son and to the Holy Spirit.
I will bless the Lord who gives me counsel
　　– my heart teaches me, night by night.

The Gospel Canticle – The Song of Mary
Epiphany I came into the world for judgment so that those who do not see may see, and those who do see may become blind.
Pentecost All generations will call me blessed: the Almighty has done great things for me.

Litany
For people who work while others sleep, for people who work in solitude and difficult circumstances, for people who work to restore the broken.
Lord, have mercy.
For all involved in education and instruction, for those who work in museums and entertainment venues, for those whose job will never return.
Christ, have mercy.
For those who will die today, for those who are preparing for their death, for those overcome by grief.
Lord, have mercy.

Invitation to the Lord's Prayer We join the saints of countless generations and pray to the Father.

Collect *From the proper of the day or*
Be our light in the darkness, O Lord, and in your great mercy defend us from all perils and dangers of this night; for the love of your only Son, our Savior Jesus Christ. Amen.

The Blessing
May we not grow weary in doing what is right, for we will reap at harvest time, if we do not give up. **Amen**

Wednesday Week 3 Morning Prayer

Officiant: Lord, open our lips.
People: **And our mouth shall proclaim your praise.**
Officiant and People **Glory to the Father... Alleluia.**

The Invitatory Psalm 95

God's hidden plan of salvation is revealed in Christ: Come let us adore.

Hymn Now that the daylight fills the sky *Hymnal 3*

Psalm 90 *Domine, refugium*

With the Lord one day is like a thousand years, and a thousand years are like one day. 2 Pt. 3:8

Epiphany Satisfy us by your loving-kindness in the morning; so shall we rejoice and be glad all the days of our life.
Pentecost Teach us, O Lord, to number our days, that we may apply our hearts to wisdom.

1 Lord, you have been our refuge *
        from one generation to another.

2 Before the mountains were brought forth,
     or the land and the earth were born, *
        from age to age you are God.

3 You turn us back to the dust and say, *
        "Go back, O child of earth."

4 For a thousand years in your sight
     are like yesterday when it is past *
        and like a watch in the night.

5 You sweep us away like a dream; *
        we fade away suddenly like the grass.

6 In the morning it is green and flourishes; *
        in the evening it is dried up and withered.

7 For we consume away in your displeasure; *
        we are afraid because of your wrathful indignation.

8 Our iniquities you have set before you, *
        and our secret sins in the light of your countenance.

9 When you are angry, all our days are gone; *
        we bring our years to an end like a sigh.

10 The span of our life is seventy years,
　　perhaps in strength even eighty; *
　　　　yet the sum of them is but labor and sorrow,
　　　　for they pass away quickly and we are gone.

11 Who regards the power of your wrath? *
　　who rightly fears your indignation?

12 So teach us to number our days *
　　that we may apply our hearts to wisdom.

13 Return, O LORD; how long will you tarry? *
　　be gracious to your servants.

14 Satisfy us by your loving-kindness in the morning; *
　　so shall we rejoice and be glad all the days of our life.

15 Make us glad by the measure of the days that you afflicted us *
　　and the years in which we suffered adversity.

16 Show your servants your works *
　　and your splendor to their children.

17 May the graciousness of the LORD our God be upon us; *
　　prosper the work of our hands;
　　prosper our handiwork.

Epiphany Satisfy us by your loving-kindness in the morning; so shall
we rejoice and be glad all the days of our life.
Pentecost Teach us, O Lord, to number our days, that we may apply
our hearts to wisdom.

Psalm 75 *Confitebimur tibi*

God, through Jesus Christ, will judge the secret thoughts of all. Rm. 2:16

Epiphany My judgment goes forth as the light.
Pentecost God does not judge by what the eyes see, but in truth and
equity.

1　We give you thanks, O God, we give you thanks, *
　　calling upon your Name
　　and declaring all your wonderful deeds.

2　"I will appoint a time," says God; *
　　"I will judge with equity.

3　Though the earth and all its inhabitants are quaking, *
　　I will make its pillars fast.

4   I will say to the boasters, 'Boast no more,' *
    and to the wicked, 'Do not toss your horns;

5   Do not toss your horns so high, *
    nor speak with a proud neck.'"

6   For judgment is neither from the east nor from the west, *
    nor yet from the wilderness or the mountains.

7   It is God who judges; *
    he puts down one and lifts up another.

8   For in the LORD'S hand there is a cup,
    full of spiced and foaming wine, which he pours out, *
      and all the wicked of the earth
      shall drink and drain the dregs.

9   But I will rejoice for ever; *
    I will sing praises to the God of Jacob.

10 He shall break off all the horns of the wicked; *
    but the horns of the righteous shall be exalted.

Epiphany My judgment goes forth as the light.
Pentecost God does not judge by what the eyes see, but in truth and equity.

Psalm 67 *Deus misereatur*

I thank my God through Jesus Christ for all of you,
because your faith is proclaimed throughout the world. Rm 1:8

Epiphany Show us the light of your countenance and come to us.
Pentecost May the Lord's face shine upon us, and be gracious to us.

1   May God be merciful to us and bless us, *
    show us the light of his countenance and come to us.

2   Let your ways be known upon earth, *
    your saving health among all nations.

3   Let the peoples praise you, O God; *
    let all the peoples praise you.

4   Let the nations be glad and sing for joy, *
    for you judge the peoples with equity
    and guide all the nations upon earth.

5   Let the peoples praise you, O God; *
    let all the peoples praise you.

6 The earth has brought forth her increase; *
    may God, our own God, give us his blessing.

7 May God give us his blessing, *
    and may all the ends of the earth stand in awe of him.

Epiphany Show us the light of your countenance and come to us.
Pentecost May the Lord's face shine upon us, and be gracious to us.

Reading One

Responsory One (Ps. 34: 2, 3)
I will glory in the Lord
    – let the humble hear and rejoice.
Let us exalt God's Name together
    – let the humble hear and rejoice.
Glory to the Father and to the Son and to the Holy Spirit.
I will glory in the Lord
    – let the humble hear and rejoice.

The First Canticle – Canticle of the Mystery of Christ *In mysterio Christi*
(Ephesians 3: 5-10)
Epiphany The mystery of Christ lay hidden for ages in God who created all things.
Pentecost The Gentiles have become members of the same body, and sharers in the promise in Christ Jesus through the gospel.

The mystery of Christ was not made known to humankind *
    in former generations.

It has now been revealed *
    to his holy apostles and prophets by the Spirit.

The Gentiles have become fellow-heirs,
members of the same body, *
    and sharers in the promise in Christ Jesus through the gospel.

Of this gospel I have become a servant *
    according to the gift of God's grace.

The Gospel was given to me *
    by the working of God's power.

Although I am the very least of all the saints, *
    this grace was given to me:

To bring to the Gentiles
the news of the boundless riches of Christ, *
    and to make everyone see what is the plan of the mystery.

That mystery of Christ lay hidden for ages in God *
    who created all things;

So that through the church *
    the wisdom of God in its rich variety

Might now be made known *
    to the rulers and authorities in the heavenly places.

Epiphany The mystery of Christ lay hidden for ages in God who created all things.
Pentecost The Gentiles have become members of the same body, and sharers in the promise in Christ Jesus through the gospel.

Reading Two

Responsory Two (Ps. 34:17, 18)
The righteous cry
    – the Lord hears them.
The Lord is near to the brokenhearted
    – the Lord hears them.
Glory to the Father and to the Son and to the Holy Spirit.
The righteous cry
    – the Lord hears them.

The Gospel Canticle – The Song of Zechariah
Epiphany God the only Son, who is close to the Father's heart, has made God known.
Pentecost God set us free to worship without fear, holy and righteous in God's sight.

Litany
For _____ our Presiding Bishop, for _____ (_____) our own Bishop(s), for all bishops and other ministers, and for all the holy people of God, we pray to you, O Lord.
Lord, have mercy.
For the peace of the world, that a spirit of respect and forbearance may grow among nations and peoples, we pray to you, O Lord.
Christ, have mercy.
For our enemies and those who wish us harm, and for all whom we have injured or offended, we pray to you, O Lord.
Lord, have mercy.

Invitation to the Lord's Prayer Yearning for the dawning of God's reign among us let us pray to the Father.

Collect *From the proper of the day or*
Lord God, almighty and everlasting Father, you have brought us in safety to this new day: Preserve us with your mighty power, that we may not fall into sin, nor be overcome by adversity; and in all we do, direct us to the fulfilling of your purpose; through Jesus Christ our Lord. Amen.

The Blessing
May we work for the good of all, and especially for those of the family of faith. **Amen**

Wednesday Week 3 Noonday Prayer
Officiant: O God, make speed to save us.
People: **O Lord, make haste to help us.**
Officiant and People **Glory to the Father... Alleluia.**

Hymn As the sun shines down at noon *Hymnal 18 Verse for Wednesday*

Psalm 119 Samekh *Iniquos odio habui*
The monastic who is to be received comes before the community in the oratory and promises stability, fidelity to monastic life and obedience. RB 58:17

Epiphany Whatever you do, in word or deed, do everything in the name of the Lord Jesus.
Pentecost Sustain me, O Lord, according to you promise, that I may live.

113 I hate those who have a divided heart, *
    but your law do I love.

114 You are my refuge and shield; *
    my hope is in your word.

115 Away from me, you wicked! *
    I will keep the commandments of my God.

116 Sustain me according to your promise, that I may live, *
    and let me not be disappointed in my hope.

117 Hold me up, and I shall be safe, *
    and my delight shall be ever in your statutes.

118 You spurn all who stray from your statutes; *
    their deceitfulness is in vain.

119 In your sight all the wicked of the earth are but dross; *
    therefore I love your decrees.

120 My flesh trembles with dread of you; *
    I am afraid of your judgments.

Psalm 12 *Salvum me fac*
All of them deserted Jesus and fled. Mk. 14:50

1 Help me, LORD, for there is no godly one left; *
    the faithful have vanished from among us.

2 Everyone speaks falsely with his neighbor; *
    with a smooth tongue they speak from a double heart.

3 Oh, that the LORD would cut off all smooth tongues, *
    and close the lips that utter proud boasts!

4 Those who say, "With our tongue will we prevail; *
    our lips are our own; who is lord over us?"

5 "Because the needy are oppressed,
    and the poor cry out in misery, *
        I will rise up," says the LORD,
        "and give them the help they long for."

6 The words of the LORD are pure words, *
    like silver refined from ore
    and purified seven times in the fire.

7 O LORD, watch over us *
    and save us from this generation for ever.

8 The wicked prowl on every side, *
    and that which is worthless is highly prized by everyone.

Psalm 83 *Deus, quis similis?*
You will be hated by all because of my name.
But the one who endures to the end will be saved. Mk. 13:13

1 O God, do not be silent; *
    do not keep still nor hold your peace, O God;

2 For your enemies are in tumult, *
    and those who hate you have lifted up their heads.

3 They take secret counsel against your people *
    and plot against those whom you protect.

4 They have said, "Come, let us wipe them out
    from among the nations; *
        let the name of Israel be remembered no more."

5 They have conspired together; *
    they have made an alliance against you:

6 The tents of Edom and the Ishmaelites; *
    the Moabites and the Hagarenes;

7 Gebal, and Ammon, and Amalek; *
    the Philistines and those who dwell in Tyre.

8 The Assyrians also have joined them, *
    and have come to help the people of Lot.

9 Do to them as you did to Midian, *
    to Sisera, and to Jabin at the river of Kishon:

10 They were destroyed at Endor; *
    they became like dung upon the ground.

11 Make their leaders like Oreb and Zeëb, *
    and all their commanders like Zebah and Zalmunna,

12 Who said, "Let us take for ourselves *
    the fields of God as our possession."

13 O my God, make them like whirling dust *
    and like chaff before the wind;

14 Like fire that burns down a forest, *
    like the flame that sets mountains ablaze.

15 Drive them with your tempest *
    and terrify them with your storm;

16 Cover their faces with shame, O LORD, *
    that they may seek your Name.

17 Let them be disgraced and terrified for ever; *
    let them be put to confusion and perish.

18 Let them know that you, whose Name is YAHWEH, *
    you alone are the Most High over all the earth.

Epiphany Whatever you do, in word or deed, do everything in the name of the Lord Jesus.
Pentecost Sustain me, O Lord, according to you promise, that I may live.

Reading Ephesians 4: 21-24
You have heard about Christ and were taught in him, as truth is in Jesus. You were taught to put away your former way of life, your old self,

corrupt and deluded by its lusts, and to be renewed in the spirit of your minds, and to clothe yourselves with the new self, created according to the likeness of God in true righteousness and holiness.

Verse and Response
Forgive one another.
As God in Christ has forgiven you.

The Short Litany and the Lord's Prayer

The Collect Almighty Father, whose blessed Son before his passion prayed for his disciples that they might be one, as you and he are one: Grant that your Church, being bound together in love and obedience to you, may be united in one body by the one Spirit; that the world may believe in him who you have sent, your Son Jesus Christ our Lord; who lives and reigns with you, in the unity of the Holy Spirit, one God, now and for ever. Amen.

Let us bless the Lord.
Thanks be to God.

Wednesday Week 3 Evening Prayer

Officiant: O God, make speed to save us.
People: **O Lord, make haste to help us.**
Officiant and People **Glory to the Father... Alleluia.**

Hymn O blest Creator, source of light *Hymnal 28*

Psalm 106 A *Confitemini Domino*

Our ancestors were unwilling to obey Moses; instead, they pushed him aside, and in their hearts they turned back to Egypt. Acts 7:39

Epiphany Give glory to the Lord your God before he brings darkness, and before your feet stumble on the mountains at twilight.

Pentecost Remember me, O LORD, with the favor you have for your people, and visit me with your saving help.

1 Hallelujah!
   Give thanks to the LORD, for he is good, *
      for his mercy endures for ever.

2 Who can declare the mighty acts of the LORD *
      or show forth all his praise?

3 Blessed are those who act with justice *
      and always do what is right!

4 Remember me, O LORD,
   with the favor you have for your people, *
     and visit me with your saving help;

5 That I may see the prosperity of your elect
   and be glad with the gladness of your people, *
     that I may glory with your inheritance.

6 We have sinned as our forebears did; *
   we have done wrong and dealt wickedly.

7 In Egypt they did not consider your marvelous works,
   nor remember the abundance of your love; *
     they defied the Most High at the Red Sea.

8 But he saved them for his Name's sake, *
   to make his power known.

9 He rebuked the Red Sea, and it dried up, *
   and he led them through the deep as through a desert.

10 He saved them from the hand of those who hated them *
   and redeemed them from the hand of the enemy.

11 The waters covered their oppressors; *
   not one of them was left.

12 Then they believed his words *
   and sang him songs of praise.

13 But they soon forgot his deeds *
   and did not wait for his counsel.

14 A craving seized them in the wilderness, *
   and they put God to the test in the desert.

15 He gave them what they asked, *
   but sent leanness into their soul.

16 They envied Moses in the camp, *
   and Aaron, the holy one of the LORD.

17 The earth opened and swallowed Dathan *
   and covered the company of Abiram.

18 Fire blazed up against their company, *
   and flames devoured the wicked.

Epiphany Give glory to the Lord your God before he brings darkness, and before your feet stumble on the mountains at twilight.

Pentecost Remember me, O LORD, with the favor you have for your people, and visit me with your saving help.

Psalm 106 B *Et fecerunt*

God turned away from them and handed them over to worship the host of heaven. Acts 7:42

Epiphany My eyes will weep bitterly and run down with tears, because the Lord's flock has been taken captive.

Pentecost Moses, his chosen, stood before him in the breach, to turn away his wrath from consuming them.

19 Israel made a bull-calf at Horeb *
    and worshiped a molten image;

20 And so they exchanged their Glory *
    for the image of an ox that feeds on grass.

21 They forgot God their Savior, *
    who had done great things in Egypt,

22 Wonderful deeds in the land of Ham, *
    and fearful things at the Red Sea.

23 So he would have destroyed them,
    had not Moses his chosen stood before him in the breach, *
        to turn away his wrath from consuming them.

26 So God lifted his hand against them, *
    to overthrow them in the wilderness,

27 To cast out their seed among the nations, *
    and to scatter them throughout the lands.

28 They joined themselves to Baal-Peor *
    and ate sacrifices offered to the dead.

29 They provoked him to anger with their actions, *
    and a plague broke out among them.

30 Then Phinehas stood up and interceded, *
    and the plague came to an end.

31 This was reckoned to him as righteousness *
    throughout all generations for ever.

32 Again they provoked his anger at the waters of Meribah, *
    so that he punished Moses because of them;

33 For they so embittered his spirit *
    that he spoke rash words with his lips.

Epiphany My eyes will weep bitterly and run down with tears, because the Lord's flock has been taken captive.

Pentecost Moses, his chosen, stood before him in the breach, to turn away his wrath from consuming them.

Psalm 106 C *Non disperdiderunt*

You stiff-necked people, uncircumcised in heart and ears, you are forever opposing the Holy Spirit, just as your ancestors used to do. Acts 7:51

Epiphany God will bring me out to the light; I shall see his vindication.

Pentecost Save us, O LORD our God, and gather us from among the nations

34 They did not destroy the peoples *
   as the LORD had commanded them.

35 They intermingled with the heathen *
   and learned their pagan ways,

36 So that they worshiped their idols, *
   which became a snare to them.

37 They sacrificed their sons *
   and their daughters to evil spirits.

38 They shed innocent blood,
   the blood of their sons and daughters, *
   which they offered to the idols of Canaan,
   and the land was defiled with blood.

39 Thus they were polluted by their actions *
   and went whoring in their evil deeds.

40 Therefore the wrath of the LORD was kindled against his people *
   and he abhorred his inheritance.

41 He gave them over to the hand of the heathen, *
   and those who hated them ruled over them.

42 Their enemies oppressed them, *
   and they were humbled under their hand.

43 Many a time did he deliver them,
   but they rebelled through their own devices, *
   and were brought down in their iniquity.

44 Nevertheless, God saw their distress, *
   when he heard their lamentation.

45 He remembered his covenant with them *
   and relented in accordance with his great mercy.

46 He caused them to be pitied *
>> by those who held them captive.

47 Save us, O LORD our God,
>> and gather us from among the nations, *
>>> that we may give thanks to your holy Name
>>> and glory in your praise.

48 Blessed be the LORD, the God of Israel,
>> from everlasting and to everlasting; *
>>> and let all the people say, "Amen!"
>>> Hallelujah!

Epiphany God will bring me out to the light; I shall see his vindication.
Pentecost Save us, O LORD our God, and gather us from among the nations

Reading

Responsory (Ps. 26: 8, 12)
I love the house where you dwell
>> **– the place where your glory abides.**
My foot stands on level ground,
>> **– the place where your glory abides.**
Glory to the Father and to the Son and to the Holy Spirit.
I love the house where you dwell,
>> **– the place where your glory abides.**

The Gospel Canticle – The Song of Mary
Epiphany Let us open our eyes to the deifying light, let us hear with attentive ears the warning which the divine voice cries daily to us.
Pentecost God has cast the powerful from their thrones and has lifted up the lowly.

Litany
For all who fear God and believe in you, Lord Christ, that our divisions may cease, and that all may be one as you and the Father are one, we pray to you, O Lord.
Lord, have mercy.
For those in positions of public trust [especially _____], that they may serve justice, and promote the dignity and freedom of every person, we pray to you, O Lord.
Christ, have mercy.

For all who have died in the communion of your Church, and those whose faith is known to you alone, that, with all the saints, they may have rest in that place where there is no pain or grief, but life eternal, we pray to you, O Lord.
Lord, have mercy.

Invitation to the Lord's Prayer Having labored for God's kingdom during the day, let us ask God to give growth to the kingdom among us.

The Collect *From the proper of the day or*
O God, the life of all who live, the light of the faithful, the strength of those who labor, and the repose of the dead: We thank you for the blessings of the day that is past, and humbly ask for your protection through the coming night. Bring us in safety to the morning hours; through him who died and rose again for us, your Son our Savior Jesus Christ. Amen.

The Blessing
May the peace of God, which surpasses all understanding, guard our hearts and our minds in Christ Jesus. **Amen**

Thursday Week 3 Morning Prayer
Officiant: Lord, open our lips.
People: **And our mouth shall proclaim your praise.**
Officiant and People **Glory to the Father... Alleluia.**

The Invitatory Psalm 122
The Lord feeds us with the Bread of Angels: Come let us adore.

Hymn We sing of God the mighty source *Hymnal 386*

Psalm 23 *Dominus regit me*
The good shepherd lays down his life for the sheep. Jn. 10:11
Epiphany You have anointed my head with oil, and my cup is running over.
Pentecost You spread a table before me in the presence of those who trouble me.

1 The LORD is my shepherd; *
    I shall not be in want.

2 He makes me lie down in green pastures *
    and leads me beside still waters.

3 He revives my soul *
    and guides me along right pathways for his Name's sake.

4   Though I walk through the valley of the shadow of death,
      I shall fear no evil; *
          for you are with me;
          your rod and your staff, they comfort me.

5   You spread a table before me
      in the presence of those who trouble me; *
          you have anointed my head with oil,
          and my cup is running over.

6   Surely your goodness and mercy shall follow me
      all the days of my life, *
          and I will dwell in the house of the LORD for ever.

Epiphany You have anointed my head with oil, and my cup is running
over.
Pentecost You spread a table before me in the presence of those who
trouble me.

Psalm 81 *Exultate Deo*

Those who eat my flesh and drink my blood abide in me, and I in them. Jn. 6:56

Epiphany Mercy has come to us from you, O Lord, to uncover a light
for us in the house of the Lord our God, and to give us food in the time
of our servitude.
Pentecost Israel would I feed with the finest wheat and satisfy him with
honey from the rock.

1   Sing with joy to God our strength *
      and raise a loud shout to the God of Jacob.

2   Raise a song and sound the timbrel, *
      the merry harp, and the lyre.

3   Blow the ram's-horn at the new moon, *
      and at the full moon, the day of our feast.

4   For this is a statute for Israel, *
      a law of the God of Jacob.

5   He laid it as a solemn charge upon Joseph, *
      when he came out of the land of Egypt.

6   I heard an unfamiliar voice saying, *
      "I eased his shoulder from the burden;
      his hands were set free from bearing the load."

7 You called on me in trouble, and I saved you; *
      I answered you from the secret place of thunder
      and tested you at the waters of Meribah.

8 Hear, O my people, and I will admonish you: *
      O Israel, if you would but listen to me!

9 There shall be no strange god among you; *
      you shall not worship a foreign god.

10 I am the LORD your God,
      who brought you out of the land of Egypt and said, *
      "Open your mouth wide, and I will fill it."

11 And yet my people did not hear my voice, *
      and Israel would not obey me.

12 So I gave them over to the stubbornness of their hearts, *
      to follow their own devices.

13 Oh, that my people would listen to me! *
      that Israel would walk in my ways!

14 I should soon subdue their enemies *
      and turn my hand against their foes.

15 Those who hate the LORD would cringe before him, *
      and their punishment would last for ever.

16 But Israel would I feed with the finest wheat *
      and satisfy him with honey from the rock.

Epiphany Mercy has come to us from you, O Lord, to uncover a light
for us in the house of the Lord our God, and to give us food in the time
of our servitude.
Pentecost Israel would I feed with the finest wheat and satisfy him with
honey from the rock.

Psalm 149 *Cantate Domino*
All who see them shall acknowledge that they are a people whom the Lord has blessed. Is. 61: 9
Epiphany The LORD takes pleasure in his people and adorns the poor
with victory.
Pentecost Let the children of Zion be joyful in their King.

1 Hallelujah!
      Sing to the LORD a new song; *
      sing his praise in the congregation of the faithful.

2 Let Israel rejoice in his Maker; *
    let the children of Zion be joyful in their King.

3 Let them praise his Name in the dance; *
    let them sing praise to him with timbrel and harp.

4 For the LORD takes pleasure in his people *
    and adorns the poor with victory.

5 Let the faithful rejoice in triumph; *
    let them be joyful on their beds.

6 Let the praises of God be in their throat *
    and a two-edged sword in their hand;

7 To wreak vengeance on the nations *
    and punishment on the peoples;

8 To bind their kings in chains *
    and their nobles with links of iron;

9 To inflict on them the judgment decreed; *
    this is glory for all his faithful people.
    Hallelujah!

Epiphany The LORD takes pleasure in his people and adorns the poor with victory.
Pentecost Let the children of Zion be joyful in their King.

Reading One

Responsory One (Wis. 8:2)
I loved wisdom
    – I sought her from my youth.
I desired to take her for my bride
    – I sought her from my youth.
Glory to the Father and to the Son and to the Holy Spirit.
I loved wisdom
    – I sought her from my youth.

The First Canticle – Song of Ransomed Jacob *Audite verbum Domini gentes*
(Jeremiah 31: 10-14)
Epiphany The young women shall rejoice in the dance, and the young men and the old shall be merry.
Pentecost They shall be radiant over the goodness of the Lord. They shall rejoice over the grain, the wine, and the oil.

Hear the word of the Lord, O nations, *
>> and declare it in the coastlands far away:

"He who scattered Israel will gather him, *
>> and will keep him as a shepherd a flock."

For the Lord has ransomed Jacob, *
>> and has redeemed him from hands too strong for him.

They shall come and sing aloud on the height of Zion, *
>> and they shall be radiant over the goodness of the Lord.

They shall rejoice over the grain, the wine, and the oil, *
>> and over the young of the flock and the herd.

Their life shall become like a watered garden, *
>> and they shall never languish again.

Then shall the young women rejoice in the dance, *
>> and the young men and the old shall be merry.

I will turn their mourning into joy, *
>> I will comfort them, and give them gladness for sorrow.

I will give the priests their fill of choice portions, *
>> and my people shall be satisfied with my bounty.

Epiphany The young women shall rejoice in the dance, and the young men and the old shall be merry.
Pentecost They shall be radiant over the goodness of the Lord. They shall rejoice over the grain, the wine, and the oil.

Reading Two

Responsory Two (Ps. 34:8; Ps. 40:4)
Taste and see
>> **– the Lord is good.**
Blessed are they who trust in God
>> **– the Lord is good.**
Glory to the Father and to the Son and to the Holy Spirit.
Taste and see
>> **– the Lord is good.**

The Gospel Canticle – The Song of Zechariah
Epiphany While you have the light, believe in the light, so that you may become children of light.
Pentecost God will shine on those who dwell in darkness and the shadow of death, and guide our feet into the way of peace.

Litany

For all living with autism, for pregnant women, for families enduring infertility.

Lord, have mercy.

For all who endure sexual exploitation, for victims of human trafficking, for families of abducted children.

Christ, have mercy.

For those caught in patterns of prejudice and ignorance, for all overwhelmed by debt, for those who work in dangerous situations.

Lord, have mercy.

Invitation to the Lord's Prayer In solidarity with the hungry throughout the world, we yearn for God who feeds our hungry hearts.

The Collect *From the proper of the day or*

Heavenly Father, in you we live and move and have our being: We humbly pray you so to guide and govern us by your Holy Spirit, that in all the cares and occupations of our life we may not forget you, but may remember that we are ever walking in your sight; through Jesus Christ our Lord. Amen.

The Blessing

May God give us gladness of heart, and may there be peace in our days in Israel, as in the days of old. **Amen**

Thursday Week 3 Noonday Prayer

Officiant: O God, make speed to save us.

People: **O Lord, make haste to help us.**

Officiant and People **Glory to the Father... Alleluia.**

Hymn A mighty sound from heaven *Hymnal 230*

Psalm 119 Ayin *Feci judicium*

Blessed is that slave whom his master will find at work when he arrives. Lk. 12:43

Epiphany I have prepared a lamp for my Anointed.

Pentecost I am your servant; grant me understanding, that I may know your decrees.

121 I have done what is just and right; *
    do not deliver me to my oppressors.

122 Be surety for your servant's good; *
    let not the proud oppress me.

123 My eyes have failed from watching for your salvation *
    and for your righteous promise.

124 Deal with your servant according to your loving-kindness *
  and teach me your statutes.

125 I am your servant; grant me understanding, *
  that I may know your decrees.

126 It is time for you to act, O LORD, *
  for they have broken your law.

127 Truly, I love your commandments *
  more than gold and precious stones.

128 I hold all your commandments to be right for me; *
  all paths of falsehood I abhor.

Psalm 132 A *Memento, Domine*
*Joseph, son of David, do not be afraid to take Mary as your wife,
for the child conceived in her is from the Holy Spirit. Mt. 1:20*

1 LORD, remember David, *
  and all the hardships he endured;

2 How he swore an oath to the LORD *
  and vowed a vow to the Mighty One of Jacob:

3 "I will not come under the roof of my house, *
  nor climb up into my bed;

4 I will not allow my eyes to sleep, *
  nor let my eyelids slumber;

5 Until I find a place for the LORD, *
  a dwelling for the Mighty One of Jacob."

6 "The ark! We heard it was in Ephratah; *
  we found it in the fields of Jearim.

7 Let us go to God's dwelling place; *
  let us fall upon our knees before his footstool."

8 Arise, O LORD, into your resting-place, *
  you and the ark of your strength.

9 Let your priests be clothed with righteousness; *
  let your faithful people sing with joy.

10 For your servant David's sake, *
  do not turn away the face of your Anointed.

Psalm 132 B *Juravit Dominus*

He will be called the Son of the Most High, and the Lord God will give to him
the throne of his ancestor David. Lk. 1:32

11 The LORD has sworn an oath to David; *
    in truth, he will not break it:

12 "A son, the fruit of your body *
    will I set upon your throne.

13 If your children keep my covenant
    and my testimonies that I shall teach them, *
        their children will sit upon your throne for evermore."

14 For the LORD has chosen Zion; *
    he has desired her for his habitation:

15 "This shall be my resting-place for ever; *
    here will I dwell, for I delight in her.

16 I will surely bless her provisions, *
    and satisfy her poor with bread.

17 I will clothe her priests with salvation, *
    and her faithful people will rejoice and sing.

18 There will I make the horn of David flourish; *
    I have prepared a lamp for my Anointed.

19 As for his enemies, I will clothe them with shame; *
    but as for him, his crown will shine."

Epiphany I have prepared a lamp for my Anointed.
Pentecost I am your servant; grant me understanding, that I may know
your decrees.

Reading Matthew 9: 10-13
As Jesus sat at dinner in the house, many tax collectors and sinners
came and were sitting with him and his disciples. When the Pharisees
saw this, they said to his disciples, "Why does your teacher eat with tax
collectors and sinners?" But when he heard this, he said, "Those who
are well have no need of a physician, but those who are sick. Go and
learn what this means, 'I desire mercy, not sacrifice.' For I have come to
call not the righteous but sinners."

Verse and Response
The Son of Man came eating and drinking.
They say, 'Look, a glutton and a drunkard, a friend of tax
collectors and sinners!'

The Short Litany and the Lord's Prayer

The Collect O God, whose blessed Son made himself known to his disciples in the breaking of bread: Open the eyes of our faith, that we may behold him in all his redeeming work; who lives and reigns with you, in the unity of the Holy Spirit, one God, now and for ever. Amen.

Let us bless the Lord.
Thanks be to God.

Thursday Week 3 Evening Prayer

Officiant: O God, make speed to save us.
People: **O Lord, make haste to help us.**
Officiant and People **Glory to the Father... Alleluia.**

Hymn Come we that love the Lord *Hymnal 392*

Psalm 104 A *Benedic, anima mea*

Consider the lilies, how they grow: they neither toil nor spin; yet I tell you,
even Solomon in all his glory was not clothed like one of these. Lk. 12:27

Epiphany You wrap yourself with light as with a cloak and spread out the heavens like a curtain.
Pentecost O Lord my God, you are clothed with majesty and splendor; you wrap yourself with light as with a cloak.

1　Bless the LORD, O my soul; *
　　O LORD my God, how excellent is your greatness!
　　you are clothed with majesty and splendor.

2　You wrap yourself with light as with a cloak *
　　and spread out the heavens like a curtain.

3　You lay the beams of your chambers in the waters above; *
　　you make the clouds your chariot;
　　you ride on the wings of the wind.

4　You make the winds your messengers *
　　and flames of fire your servants.

5　You have set the earth upon its foundations, *
　　so that it never shall move at any time.

6　You covered it with the Deep as with a mantle; *
　　the waters stood higher than the mountains.

7　At your rebuke they fled; *
　　at the voice of your thunder they hastened away.

8   They went up into the hills and down to the valleys beneath, *
    to the places you had appointed for them.

9   You set the limits that they should not pass; *
    they shall not again cover the earth.

10 You send the springs into the valleys; *
    they flow between the mountains.

11 All the beasts of the field drink their fill from them, *
    and the wild asses quench their thirst.

12 Beside them the birds of the air make their nests *
    and sing among the branches.

13 You water the mountains from your dwelling on high; *
    the earth is fully satisfied by the fruit of your works.

14 You make grass grow for flocks and herds *
    and plants to serve mankind;

15 That they may bring forth food from the earth, *
    and wine to gladden our hearts,

16 Oil to make a cheerful countenance, *
    and bread to strengthen the heart.

17 The trees of the LORD are full of sap, *
    the cedars of Lebanon which he planted,

18 In which the birds build their nests, *
    and in whose tops the stork makes his dwelling.

19 The high hills are a refuge for the mountain goats, *
    and the stony cliffs for the rock badgers.

20 You appointed the moon to mark the seasons, *
    and the sun knows the time of its setting.

21 You make darkness that it may be night, *
    in which all the beasts of the forest prowl.

22 The lions roar after their prey *
    and seek their food from God.

23 The sun rises, and they slip away *
    and lay themselves down in their dens.

24 Man goes forth to his work *
    and to his labor until the evening.

Epiphany You wrap yourself with light as with a cloak and spread out the heavens like a curtain.

Pentecost O Lord my God, you are clothed with majesty and splendor; you wrap yourself with light as with a cloak.

Psalm 104 B *Quam magnificata sunt*
The heavenly Father will give the Holy Spirit to those who ask him. Lk. 11:13

Epiphany The sun looks down on everything with its light, and the work of the Lord is full of his glory.

Pentecost All creatures look to you to give them their food in due season.

25 O LORD, how manifold are your works! *
    in wisdom you have made them all;
    the earth is full of your creatures.

26 Yonder is the great and wide sea
    with its living things too many to number, *
    creatures both small and great.

27 There move the ships,
  and there is that Leviathan, *
    which you have made for the sport of it.

28 All of them look to you *
    to give them their food in due season.

29 You give it to them; they gather it; *
    you open your hand, and they are filled with good things.

30 You hide your face, and they are terrified; *
    you take away their breath,
    and they die and return to their dust.

31 You send forth your Spirit, and they are created; *
    and so you renew the face of the earth.

Epiphany The sun looks down on everything with its light, and the work of the Lord is full of his glory.

Pentecost All creatures look to you to give them their food in due season.

Psalm 104 C *Sit gloria Domini*
People will faint from fear and foreboding of what is coming upon the world,
for the powers of the heavens will be shaken. Lk. 21:26

Epiphany God saw everything that he had made, and indeed, it was very good.

Pentecost May the LORD rejoice in all his works.

32 May the glory of the LORD endure for ever; *
　　may the LORD rejoice in all his works.

33 He looks at the earth and it trembles; *
　　he touches the mountains and they smoke.

34 I will sing to the LORD as long as I live; *
　　I will praise my God while I have my being.

35 May these words of mine please him; *
　　I will rejoice in the LORD.

36 Let sinners be consumed out of the earth, *
　　and the wicked be no more.

37 Bless the LORD,
　　O my soul. *
　　　Hallelujah!

Epiphany God saw everything that he had made, and indeed, it was very good.
Pentecost May the LORD rejoice in all his works.

Reading

Responsory (Ps. 81:8, 10)
Hear, O my people, and I will admonish you
　　　− O Israel, if you would but listen to me.
I am the Lord, your God
　　　− O Israel, if you would but listen to me.
Glory to the Father and to the Son and to the Holy Spirit.
Hear, O my people, and I will admonish you
　　　− O Israel, if you would but listen to me.

The Gospel Canticle − The Song of Mary
Epiphany I am the light of the world. We must work the works of him who sent me while it is day.
Pentecost God has fed the hungry with good things, and the rich he has sent away empty.

Litany
For prisoners condemned to death, for those whose lives are threatened, for those living with fatal diseases.
Lord, have mercy.
For those who deceive and those who enlighten, for those who subvert and those who build up, for those who steal and those who work.
Christ, have mercy.

For the comfort of the dying, the enlightenment of the dead and the consolation of the mourning.
Lord, have mercy.

Invitation to the Lord's Prayer Since we hunger and thirst for holiness, let us receive the Bread of Life from the Father.

The Collect *From the proper of the day or*
Lord Jesus, stay with us, for evening is at hand and the day is past; be our companion in the way, kindle our hearts, and awaken hope, that we may know you as you are revealed in Scripture and the breaking of bread. Grant this for the sake of your love. Amen.

The Blessing
May God entrust to us his mercy, and may he deliver us in our days.
Amen

Friday Week 3 Morning Prayer
Officiant: Lord, open our lips.
People: **And our mouth shall proclaim your praise.**
Officiant and People **Glory to the Father... Alleluia.**

The Invitatory Psalm 95
The Lord delivers us from death: Come let us adore.

Hymn In the cross of Christ *Hymnal 441*

Psalm 143 *Domine, exaudi*
The Son of Man must undergo great suffering, and be killed, and on the third day be raised. Lk. 9:22

Epiphany Help me, O Lord my God; save me for your mercy's sake.
Pentecost Let me hear of your loving-kindness in the morning, for I put my trust in you.

1 LORD, hear my prayer,
  and in your faithfulness heed my supplications; *
    answer me in your righteousness.

2 Enter not into judgment with your servant, *
    for in your sight shall no one living be justified.

3 For my enemy has sought my life;
  he has crushed me to the ground; *
    he has made me live in dark places
    like those who are long dead.

4 My spirit faints within me; *
    my heart within me is desolate.

5 I remember the time past;
  I muse upon all your deeds; *
    I consider the works of your hands.

6 I spread out my hands to you; *
    my soul gasps to you like a thirsty land.

7 O LORD, make haste to answer me; my spirit fails me; *
    do not hide your face from me
    or I shall be like those who go down to the Pit.

8 Let me hear of your loving-kindness in the morning,
  for I put my trust in you; *
    show me the road that I must walk,
    for I lift up my soul to you.

9 Deliver me from my enemies, O LORD, *
    for I flee to you for refuge.

10 Teach me to do what pleases you, for you are my God; *
    let your good Spirit lead me on level ground.

11 Revive me, O LORD, for your Name's sake; *
    for your righteousness' sake, bring me out of trouble.

Epiphany Help me, O Lord my God; save me for your mercy's sake.
Pentecost Let me hear of your loving-kindness in the morning, for I
put my trust in you.

Psalm 39 *Dixi, custodiam*
Jesus gave Pilate no answer. Jn. 19:9

Epiphany I am but a sojourner with you, a wayfarer, as all my forebears
were.
Pentecost Hear my prayer, O LORD, and give ear to my cry; hold not
your peace at my tears.

1 I said, "I will keep watch upon my ways, *
    so that I do not offend with my tongue.

2 I will put a muzzle on my mouth *
    while the wicked are in my presence."

3 So I held my tongue and said nothing; *
    I refrained from rash words;
    but my pain became unbearable.

4 My heart was hot within me;
      while I pondered, the fire burst into flame; *
         I spoke out with my tongue:

5 LORD, let me know my end and the number of my days, *
         so that I may know how short my life is.

6 You have given me a mere handful of days,
      and my lifetime is as nothing in your sight; *
         truly, even those who stand erect are but a puff of wind.

7 We walk about like a shadow,
      and in vain we are in turmoil; *
         we heap up riches and cannot tell who will gather them.

8 And now, what is my hope? *
         O Lord, my hope is in you.

9 Deliver me from all my transgressions *
         and do not make me the taunt of the fool.

10 I fell silent and did not open my mouth, *
         for surely it was you that did it.

11 Take your affliction from me; *
         I am worn down by the blows of your hand.

12 With rebukes for sin you punish us;
      like a moth you eat away all that is dear to us; *
         truly, everyone is but a puff of wind.

13 Hear my prayer, O LORD,
      and give ear to my cry; *
         hold not your peace at my tears.

14 For I am but a sojourner with you, *
         a wayfarer, as all my forebears were.

15 Turn your gaze from me, that I may be glad again, *
         before I go my way and am no more.

Epiphany I am but a sojourner with you, a wayfarer, as all my forebears
were.
Pentecost Hear my prayer, O LORD, and give ear to my cry; hold not
your peace at my tears.

Psalm 32 *Beati quorum*

There will be more joy in heaven over one sinner who repents
than over ninety-nine righteous persons who need no repentance. Lk. 15:7

Epiphany All the faithful will make their prayers to you in time of trouble; when the great waters overflow, they shall not reach them.

Pentecost You are my hiding-place; you preserve me from trouble; you surround me with shouts of deliverance.

1 Blessed are they whose transgressions are forgiven, *
     and whose sin is put away!

2 Blessed are they to whom the LORD imputes no guilt, *
     and in whose spirit there is no guile!

3 While I held my tongue, my bones withered away, *
     because of my groaning all day long.

4 For your hand was heavy upon me day and night; *
     my moisture was dried up as in the heat of summer.

5 Then I acknowledged my sin to you, *
     and did not conceal my guilt.

6 I said, "I will confess my transgressions to the LORD." *
     Then you forgave me the guilt of my sin.

7 Therefore all the faithful will make their prayers to you
   in time of trouble; *
     when the great waters overflow, they shall not reach them.

8 You are my hiding-place;
   you preserve me from trouble; *
     you surround me with shouts of deliverance.

9 "I will instruct you and teach you
   in the way that you should go; *
     I will guide you with my eye.

10 Do not be like horse or mule, which have no understanding; *
     who must be fitted with bit and bridle,
     or else they will not stay near you."

11 Great are the tribulations of the wicked; *
     but mercy embraces those who trust in the LORD.

12 Be glad, you righteous, and rejoice in the LORD; *
     shout for joy, all who are true of heart.

Epiphany All the faithful will make their prayers to you in time of trouble; when the great waters overflow, they shall not reach them.
Pentecost You are my hiding-place; you preserve me from trouble; you surround me with shouts of deliverance.

Reading One

Responsory One (Wis. 9:4)
Give me the wisdom that sits by your throne
          – do not reject me from among your servants.
I am your servant
          – do not reject me from among your servants.
Glory to the Father and to the Son and to the Holy Spirit.
Give me the wisdom that sits by your throne
          – do not reject me from among your servants.

The First Canticle – Song of the Suffering Servant V
Oblatus est quia ipse voluit (Isaiah 53: 7-12)

Epiphany Out of his anguish he shall see light; he shall find satisfaction through his knowledge.
Pentecost The righteous one, my servant, shall make many righteous, and he shall bear their iniquities.

He was oppressed, and he was afflicted, *
      yet he did not open his mouth.

Like a lamb that is led to the slaughter,
and like a sheep that before its shearers is silent, *
      so he did not open his mouth.

By a perversion of justice he was taken away. *
      Who could have imagined his future?

For he was cut off from the land of the living, *
      stricken for the transgression of my people.

They made his grave with the wicked *
      and his tomb with the rich.

He had done no violence, *
      and there was no deceit in his mouth
      yet it was the will of the Lord to crush him with pain.

When you make his life an offering for sin, *
      he shall see his offspring, and shall prolong his days;
      through him the will of the Lord shall prosper.

Out of his anguish he shall see light; *
    he shall find satisfaction through his knowledge.

The righteous one, my servant, shall make many righteous, *
    and he shall bear their iniquities.

Therefore I will allot him a portion with the great, *
    and he shall divide the spoil with the strong.

He poured out himself to death, *
    and was numbered with the transgressors.

Yet he bore the sin of many, *
    and made intercession for the transgressors.

Epiphany Out of his anguish he shall see light; he shall find satisfaction through his knowledge.
Pentecost The righteous one, my servant, shall make many righteous, and he shall bear their iniquities.

Reading Two

Responsory Two (Ps. 34:14)
Turn from evil
    − and do good.
Seek peace and pursue it
    − and do good.
Glory to the Father and to the Son and to the Holy Spirit.
Turn from evil
    − and do good.

The Gospel Canticle − The Song of Zechariah
Epiphany The light shines in the darkness and the darkness did not overcome the light.
Pentecost You, O child, will give people knowledge of salvation by the forgiveness of their sins.

Litany
Give your wisdom and strength to _____, the President of the United States, _____ the Governor of this state, (and _____, the Mayor of this city) that in all things they may do your will, for your glory and the common good.
Lord, have mercy.
Give to the Congress of the United States, the members of the President's Cabinet, those who serve in our state legislature, and all others in authority the grace to walk always in the ways of truth.
Christ, have mercy.

Bless the justices of the Supreme Court and all those who administer the law, that they may act with integrity and do justice for all your people. **Lord, have mercy.**

Invitation to the Lord's Prayer Seeking greater purity of heart, we ask the Spirit to set our hearts on God alone.

The Collect *From the proper of the day or*
Almighty God, whose most dear Son went not up to joy but first he suffered pain, and entered not into glory before he was crucified: Mercifully grant that we, walking in the way of the cross, may find it none other than the way of life and peace; through Jesus Christ our Lord. Amen.

The Blessing
May God fully satisfy every need of yours according to his riches in glory in Christ Jesus. To our God and Father be glory forever and ever. **Amen**

Friday Week 3 Noonday Prayer
Officiant: O God, make speed to save us.
People: **O Lord, make haste to help us.**
Officiant and People **Glory to the Father...Alleluia.**

Hymn From God Christ's deity came forth *Hymnal 443*

Psalm 119 Pe *Mirabilia*
While you have the light, believe in the light, so that you may become children of light. Jn. 12:36
Epiphany I have set you to be a light for the Gentiles, so that you may bring salvation to the ends of the earth.
Pentecost The afflicted shall see and be glad; you who seek God, your heart shall live.

129 Your decrees are wonderful; *
therefore I obey them with all my heart.

130 When your word goes forth it gives light; *
it gives understanding to the simple.

131 I open my mouth and pant; *
I long for your commandments.

132 Turn to me in mercy, *
as you always do to those who love your Name.

133 Steady my footsteps in your word; *
let no iniquity have dominion over me.

134 Rescue me from those who oppress me, *
    and I will keep your commandments.

135 Let your countenance shine upon your servant *
    and teach me your statutes.

136 My eyes shed streams of tears, *
    because people do not keep your law.

Psalm 69 A *Salvum me fac*

*When Jesus knew that all was now finished, he said (in order to fulfill the scripture),
"I am thirsty." Jn. 19:29*

1 Save me, O God, *
    for the waters have risen up to my neck.

2 I am sinking in deep mire, *
    and there is no firm ground for my feet.

3 I have come into deep waters, *
    and the torrent washes over me.

4 I have grown weary with my crying;
    my throat is inflamed; *
        my eyes have failed from looking for my God.

5 Those who hate me without a cause
    are more than the hairs of my head;
    my lying foes who would destroy me are mighty. *
        Must I then give back what I never stole?

6 O God, you know my foolishness, *
    and my faults are not hidden from you.

7 Let not those who hope in you be put to shame through me,
    LORD God of hosts; *
        let not those who seek you be disgraced because of me,
        O God of Israel.

8 Surely, for your sake have I suffered reproach, *
    and shame has covered my face.

9 I have become a stranger to my own kindred, *
    an alien to my mother's children.

10 Zeal for your house has eaten me up; *
    the scorn of those who scorn you has fallen upon me.

11 I humbled myself with fasting, *
    but that was turned to my reproach.

12 I put on sack-cloth also, *
    and became a byword among them.

13 Those who sit at the gate murmur against me, *
    and the drunkards make songs about me.

Psalm 69 B *Ego vero*

They offered Jesus wine to drink, mixed with gall; but when he tasted it,
he would not drink it. Mt. 27:34

14 But as for me, this is my prayer to you, *
    at the time you have set, O LORD:

15 "In your great mercy, O God, *
    answer me with your unfailing help.

16 Save me from the mire; do not let me sink; *
    let me be rescued from those who hate me
    and out of the deep waters.

17 Let not the torrent of waters wash over me,
   neither let the deep swallow me up; *
    do not let the Pit shut its mouth upon me.

18 Answer me, O LORD, for your love is kind; *
    in your great compassion, turn to me."

19 "Hide not your face from your servant; *
    be swift and answer me, for I am in distress.

20 Draw near to me and redeem me; *
    because of my enemies deliver me.

21 You know my reproach, my shame, and my dishonor; *
    my adversaries are all in your sight."

22 Reproach has broken my heart, and it cannot be healed; *
    I looked for sympathy, but there was none,
    for comforters, but I could find no one.

23 They gave me gall to eat, *
    and when I was thirsty, they gave me vinegar to drink.

24 Let the table before them be a trap *
    and their sacred feasts a snare.

25 Let their eyes be darkened, that they may not see, *
    and give them continual trembling in their loins.

26 Pour out your indignation upon them, *
    and let the fierceness of your anger overtake them.

27 Let their camp be desolate, *
    and let there be none to dwell in their tents.

28 For they persecute him whom you have stricken *
    and add to the pain of those whom you have pierced.

29 Lay to their charge guilt upon guilt, *
    and let them not receive your vindication.

30 Let them be wiped out of the book of the living *
    and not be written among the righteous.

31 As for me, I am afflicted and in pain; *
    your help, O God, will lift me up on high.

32 I will praise the Name of God in song; *
    I will proclaim his greatness with thanksgiving.

33 This will please the LORD more than an offering of oxen, *
    more than bullocks with horns and hoofs.

34 The afflicted shall see and be glad; *
    you who seek God, your heart shall live.

35 For the LORD listens to the needy, *
    and his prisoners he does not despise.

36 Let the heavens and the earth praise him, *
    the seas and all that moves in them;

37 For God will save Zion and rebuild the cities of Judah; *
    they shall live there and have it in possession.

38 The children of his servants will inherit it, *
    and those who love his Name will dwell therein.

Epiphany I have set you to be a light for the Gentiles, so that you may bring salvation to the ends of the earth.
Pentecost The afflicted shall see and be glad; you who seek God, your heart shall live.

Reading Ephesians 2: 14-17
For Christ is our peace; in his flesh he has made both groups into one and has broken down the dividing wall, that is, the hostility between us. He has abolished the law with its commandments and ordinances, that he might create in himself one new humanity in place of the two, thus making peace, and might reconcile both groups to God in one body through the cross, thus putting to death that hostility through it. So he

came and proclaimed peace to you who were far off and peace to those who were near.

Verse and Response

Peace I leave with you; my peace I give to you.
I do not give to you as the world gives.

The Short Litany and the Lord's Prayer

The Collect Almighty God, whose most dear Son went not up to joy but first he suffered pain, and entered not into glory before he was crucified: Mercifully grant that we, walking in the way of the cross, may find it none other than the way of life and peace; through Jesus Christ our Lord. Amen.

Let us bless the Lord.
Thanks be to God.

Friday Week 3 Evening Prayer

Officiant: O God, make speed to save us.
People: **O Lord, make haste to help us.**
Officiant and People **Glory to the Father... Alleluia.**

Hymn O love how deep *Hymnal 449*

Psalm 31 *In te, Domine, speravi*
Jesus gave a loud cry and breathed his last. Mk. 15:37

Epiphany I will rejoice and be glad because of your mercy.
Pentecost Incline your ear to me, O Lord; make haste to deliver me.

1 In you, O LORD, have I taken refuge;
   let me never be put to shame; *
      deliver me in your righteousness.

2 Incline your ear to me; *
      make haste to deliver me.

3 Be my strong rock, a castle to keep me safe,
   for you are my crag and my stronghold; *
      for the sake of your Name, lead me and guide me.

4 Take me out of the net that they have secretly set for me, *
      for you are my tower of strength.

5 Into your hands I commend my spirit, *
      for you have redeemed me,
         O LORD, O God of truth.

6 I hate those who cling to worthless idols, *
      and I put my trust in the LORD.

7 I will rejoice and be glad because of your mercy; *
      for you have seen my affliction;
      you know my distress.

8 You have not shut me up in the power of the enemy; *
      you have set my feet in an open place.

9 Have mercy on me, O LORD, for I am in trouble; *
      my eye is consumed with sorrow,
      and also my throat and my belly.

10 For my life is wasted with grief,
   and my years with sighing; *
      my strength fails me because of affliction,
      and my bones are consumed.

11 I have become a reproach to all my enemies
   and even to my neighbors,
   a dismay to those of my acquaintance; *
      when they see me in the street they avoid me.

12 I am forgotten like a dead man, out of mind; *
      I am as useless as a broken pot.

13 For I have heard the whispering of the crowd;
   fear is all around; *
      they put their heads together against me;
      they plot to take my life.

14 But as for me, I have trusted in you, O LORD. *
      I have said, "You are my God.

15 My times are in your hand; *
      rescue me from the hand of my enemies,
      and from those who persecute me.

16 Make your face to shine upon your servant, *
      and in your loving-kindness save me."

17 LORD, let me not be ashamed for having called upon you; *
      rather, let the wicked be put to shame;
      let them be silent in the grave.

18 Let the lying lips be silenced
   which speak against the righteous, *
      haughtily, disdainfully, and with contempt.

19 How great is your goodness, O LORD!
   which you have laid up for those who fear you; *
      which you have done in the sight of all
      for those who put their trust in you.

20 You hide them in the covert of your presence
   from those who slander them; *
      you keep them in your shelter from the strife of tongues.

21 Blessed be the LORD! *
      for he has shown me the wonders of his love
      in a besieged city.

22 Yet I said in my alarm,
   "I have been cut off from the sight of your eyes." *
      Nevertheless, you heard the sound of my entreaty
      when I cried out to you.

23 Love the LORD, all you who worship him; *
      the LORD protects the faithful,
      but repays to the full those who act haughtily.

24 Be strong and let your heart take courage, *
      all you who wait for the LORD.

Epiphany I will rejoice and be glad because of your mercy.
Pentecost Incline your ear to me, O Lord; make haste to deliver me.

Psalm 13 *Usquequo, Domine?*
"Now my soul is troubled. And what should I say—'Father, save me from this hour'?
Father, glorify your name." Jn. 12:27-28
Epiphany Give light to my eyes, lest I sleep in death.
Pentecost My heart is joyful because of your saving help.

1 How long, O LORD?
   will you forget me for ever? *
      how long will you hide your face from me?

2 How long shall I have perplexity in my mind,
   and grief in my heart, day after day? *
      how long shall my enemy triumph over me?

3 Look upon me and answer me, O LORD my God; *
      give light to my eyes, lest I sleep in death;

4 Lest my enemy say, "I have prevailed over him," *
      and my foes rejoice that I have fallen.

5 But I put my trust in your mercy; *
    my heart is joyful because of your saving help.

6 I will sing to the LORD, for he has dealt with me richly; *
    I will praise the Name of the Lord Most High.

Epiphany Give light to my eyes, lest I sleep in death.
Pentecost My heart is joyful because of your saving help.

Psalm 71 *In te, Domine, speravi*
Those who passed by derided Jesus, shaking their heads. Mk. 15:29

Epiphany Let my mouth be full of your praise and your glory all the day long.
Pentecost You strengthen me more and more; you enfold and comfort me.

1 In you, O LORD, have I taken refuge; *
    let me never be ashamed.

2 In your righteousness, deliver me and set me free; *
    incline your ear to me and save me.

3 Be my strong rock, a castle to keep me safe; *
    you are my crag and my stronghold.

4 Deliver me, my God, from the hand of the wicked, *
    from the clutches of the evildoer and the oppressor.

5 For you are my hope, O LORD God, *
    my confidence since I was young.

6 I have been sustained by you ever since I was born;
    from my mother's womb you have been my strength; *
        my praise shall be always of you.

7 I have become a portent to many; *
    but you are my refuge and my strength.

8 Let my mouth be full of your praise *
    and your glory all the day long.

9 Do not cast me off in my old age; *
    forsake me not when my strength fails.

10 For my enemies are talking against me, *
    and those who lie in wait for my life take counsel together.

11 They say, "God has forsaken him;
   go after him and seize him; *
      because there is none who will save."

12 O God, be not far from me; *
  come quickly to help me, O my God.

13 Let those who set themselves against me
 be put to shame and be disgraced; *
  let those who seek to do me evil
  be covered with scorn and reproach.

14 But I shall always wait in patience, *
  and shall praise you more and more.

15 My mouth shall recount your mighty acts
 and saving deeds all day long; *
  though I cannot know the number of them.

16 I will begin with the mighty works of the LORD God; *
  I will recall your righteousness, yours alone.

17 O God, you have taught me since I was young, *
  and to this day I tell of your wonderful works.

18 And now that I am old and gray-headed,
 O God, do not forsake me, *
  till I make known your strength to this generation
  and your power to all who are to come.

19 Your righteousness, O God, reaches to the heavens; *
  you have done great things;
  who is like you, O God?

20 You have showed me great troubles and adversities, *
  but you will restore my life
  and bring me up again from the deep places of the earth.

21 You strengthen me more and more; *
  you enfold and comfort me,

22 Therefore I will praise you upon the lyre
 for your faithfulness, O my God; *
  I will sing to you with the harp, O Holy One of Israel.

23 My lips will sing with joy when I play to you, *
  and so will my soul, which you have redeemed.

24 My tongue will proclaim your righteousness all day long, *
  for they are ashamed and disgraced
  who sought to do me harm.

Epiphany Let my mouth be full of your praise and your glory all the day long.

Pentecost You strengthen me more and more; you enfold and comfort me.

Reading

Responsory (1 Pt. 1:19, 21)
You were ransomed
> **– with the precious blood of Christ.**

You have come to trust in God
> **– with the precious blood of Christ.**

Glory to the Father and to the Son and to the Holy Spirit.
You were ransomed
> **– with the precious blood of Christ.**

The Gospel Canticle – The Song of Mary
Epiphany Run while you have the light of life, lest the darkness of death overtake you.

Pentecost God has come to the help of his servant Israel, ever mindful of his merciful promise.

Litany
As the sun sets and the stars shine, open our hearts to your unending illumination.
Lord, have mercy.
As we enter into the peace of the night, give our bodies rest and comfort our souls.
Christ, have mercy.
As the end of day reminds us of the end of life, shine on those who dwell in the shadow of death.
Lord, have mercy.

Invitation to the Lord's Prayer We return to the Father seeking purification for the sins of the day.

The Collect *From the proper of the day or*
Lord Jesus Christ, by your death you took away the sting of death: Grant to us your servants so to follow in faith where you have led the way, that we may at length fall asleep peacefully in you and wake up in your likeness; for your tender mercies' sake. Amen.

The Blessing
May the God of steadfastness and encouragement grant you to live in harmony with one another, in accordance with Christ Jesus. **Amen**

Saturday Week 3 Morning Prayer

Officiant: Lord, open our lips.

People: **And our mouth shall proclaim your praise.**

Officiant and People **Glory to the Father... Alleluia.**

The Invitatory Psalm 100

The LORD is good; God's mercy is everlasting: Come let us worship.

Hymn Before the Lord's eternal throne *Hymnal 391*

Psalm 73 A *Quam bonus Israel!*

So it is with those who store up treasures for themselves but are not rich toward God. Lk. 12:21

Epiphany Strive for the kingdom of your Father and all things will be given to you.

Pentecost Store up for yourselves treasures in heaven.

1 Truly, God is good to Israel, *
    to those who are pure in heart.

2 But as for me, my feet had nearly slipped; *
    I had almost tripped and fallen;

3 Because I envied the proud *
    and saw the prosperity of the wicked:

4 For they suffer no pain, *
    and their bodies are sleek and sound;

5 In the misfortunes of others they have no share; *
    they are not afflicted as others are;

6 Therefore they wear their pride like a necklace *
    and wrap their violence about them like a cloak.

7 Their iniquity comes from gross minds, *
    and their hearts overflow with wicked thoughts.

8 They scoff and speak maliciously; *
    out of their haughtiness they plan oppression.

9 They set their mouths against the heavens, *
    and their evil speech runs through the world.

10 And so the people turn to them *
    and find in them no fault.

11 They say, "How should God know? *
    is there knowledge in the Most High?"

12 So then, these are the wicked; *
    always at ease, they increase their wealth.

13 In vain have I kept my heart clean, *
    and washed my hands in innocence.

14 I have been afflicted all day long, *
    and punished every morning.

Epiphany Strive for the kingdom of your Father and all things will be given to you.

Pentecost Store up for yourselves treasures in heaven.

Psalm 73 B *Si dicebam*

If then you have not been faithful with the dishonest wealth,
who will entrust to you the true riches? Lk. 16:11

Epiphany It is good for me to be near God; I have made the LORD God my refuge.

Pentecost You will guide me by your counsel, and afterwards receive me with glory.

15 Had I gone on speaking this way, *
    I should have betrayed the generation of your children.

16 When I tried to understand these things, *
    it was too hard for me;

17 Until I entered the sanctuary of God *
    and discerned the end of the wicked.

18 Surely, you set them in slippery places; *
    you cast them down in ruin.

19 Oh, how suddenly do they come to destruction, *
    come to an end, and perish from terror!

20 Like a dream when one awakens, O Lord, *
    when you arise you will make their image vanish.

21 When my mind became embittered, *
    I was sorely wounded in my heart.

22 I was stupid and had no understanding; *
    I was like a brute beast in your presence.

23 Yet I am always with you; *
    you hold me by my right hand.

24 You will guide me by your counsel, *
    and afterwards receive me with glory.

25 Whom have I in heaven but you? *
    and having you I desire nothing upon earth.

26 Though my flesh and my heart should waste away, *
    God is the strength of my heart and my portion for ever.

27 Truly, those who forsake you will perish; *
    you destroy all who are unfaithful.

28 But it is good for me to be near God; *
    I have made the LORD God my refuge.

29 I will speak of all your works *
    in the gates of the city of Zion.

Epiphany It is good for me to be near God; I have made the LORD God my refuge.
Pentecost You will guide me by your counsel, and afterwards receive me with glory.

Psalm 150 *Laudate Dominum*
The whole multitude of the disciples began to praise God joyfully with a loud voice. Lk. 19: 37
Epiphany All nations will come and worship before you.
Pentecost Praise the Lord for his excellent greatness.

1 Hallelujah!
Praise God in his holy temple; *
    praise him in the firmament of his power.

2 Praise him for his mighty acts; *
    praise him for his excellent greatness.

3 Praise him with the blast of the ram's-horn; *
    praise him with lyre and harp.

4 Praise him with timbrel and dance; *
    praise him with strings and pipe.

5 Praise him with resounding cymbals; *
    praise him with loud-clanging cymbals.

6 Let everything that has breath *
    praise the Lord. Hallelujah!

Epiphany All nations will come and worship before you.
Pentecost Praise the Lord for his excellent greatness.

Reading One

Responsory One (Ps. 143:11)
Revive me, O Lord
> **– for your Name's sake.**

Bring me out of trouble
> **– for your Name's sake.**

Glory to the Father and to the Son and to the Holy Spirit.
Revive me, O Lord
> **– for your Name's sake.**

The First Canticle – Song of Solomon *Deus patrum meorum*
(Wisdom 9: 1-6.9-11)

Epiphany Wisdom understands what is pleasing in your sight and what is right according to your commandments.

Pentecost Send forth Wisdom from the holy heavens that I may learn what is pleasing to you.

O God of my ancestors and Lord of mercy, *
> who have made all things by your word,

And by your wisdom have formed humankind *
> to have dominion over the creatures you have made,

And rule the world in holiness and righteousness, *
> and pronounce judgment in uprightness of soul,

Give me the wisdom that sits by your throne, *
> and do not reject me from among your servants.

For I am your servant the son of your handmaid, *
> a man who is weak and short-lived,
> with little understanding of judgment and laws;

With you is wisdom, she who knows your works *
> and was present when you made the world;

She understands what is pleasing in your sight *
> and what is right according to your commandments.

Send her forth from the holy heavens, *
> and from the throne of your glory send her,

That she may labor at my side, *
> and that I may learn what is pleasing to you.

For she knows and understands all things, *
> and she will guide me wisely in my actions
> and guard me with her glory.

Epiphany Wisdom understands what is pleasing in your sight and what is right according to your commandments.

Pentecost Send forth Wisdom from the holy heavens that I may learn what is pleasing to you.

Reading Two

Responsory Two (Ps. 36:5,7)
Your love, O Lord, reaches to the heavens
   – your faithfulness rises to the clouds.
How priceless is your love, O God
   – your faithfulness rises to the clouds.
Glory to the Father and to the Son and to the Holy Spirit.
Your love, O Lord, reaches to the heavens
   – your faithfulness rises to the clouds.

The Gospel Canticle – The Song of Zechariah

Epiphany Wisdom will come into your heart, and knowledge will be pleasant to your soul; prudence will watch over you; and understanding will guard you.

Pentecost God is the source of your life in Christ Jesus, who became for us wisdom from God, and righteousness and sanctification and redemption.

Litany

Grant your healing grace to all who are sick, injured, or disabled, that they may be made whole.
Lord, have mercy.
Grant to all who seek your guidance, and to all who are lonely, anxious, or despondent, a knowledge of your will and an awareness of your presence.
Christ, have mercy.
Mend broken relationships, and restore those in emotional distress to soundness of mind and serenity of spirit.
Lord, have mercy.

Invitation to the Lord's Prayer Buried with Christ in our Baptism, we ask the Father to raise us up to newness of life.

The Collect *From the proper of the day or*
Almighty God, who after the creation of the world rested from all your works and sanctified a day of rest for all your creatures: Grant that we, putting away all earthly anxieties, may be duly prepared for the service of your sanctuary, and that our rest here upon earth may be a preparation

for the eternal rest promised to your people in heaven; through Jesus Christ our Lord. Amen.

The Blessing
May the grace of the Lord Jesus Christ be with our spirits. **Amen**

Saturday Week 3 Noonday Prayer
Officiant: O God, make speed to save us.
People: **O Lord, make haste to help us.**
Officiant and People **Glory to the Father... Alleluia.**

Hymn Holy Spirit, font of life *Hymnal 228*

Psalm 119 Sadhe *Justus es, Domine*
Let the word of Christ dwell in you richly. Col. 3:16
Epiphany Whatever you do, in word or deed, do everything in the name of the Lord Jesus.
Pentecost God is my shield and defense; God is the savior of the true in heart.

137 You are righteous, O LORD, *
    and upright are your judgments.

138 You have issued your decrees *
    with justice and in perfect faithfulness.

139 My indignation has consumed me, *
    because my enemies forget your words.

140 Your word has been tested to the uttermost, *
    and your servant holds it dear.

141 I am small and of little account, *
    yet I do not forget your commandments.

142 Your justice is an everlasting justice *
    and your law is the truth.

143 Trouble and distress have come upon me, *
    yet your commandments are my delight.

144 The righteousness of your decrees is everlasting; *
    grant me understanding, that I may live.

Psalm 83 *Deus, quis similis?*
See, I am sending you out like sheep into the midst of wolves;
so be wise as serpents and innocent as doves. Mt. 10:16
1 O God, do not be silent; *
    do not keep still nor hold your peace, O God;

2 For your enemies are in tumult, *
    and those who hate you have lifted up their heads.

3 They take secret counsel against your people *
    and plot against those whom you protect.

4 They have said, "Come, let us wipe them out
    from among the nations; *
      let the name of Israel be remembered no more."

5 They have conspired together; *
    they have made an alliance against you:

6 The tents of Edom and the Ishmaelites; *
    the Moabites and the Hagarenes;

7 Gebal, and Ammon, and Amalek; *
    the Philistines and those who dwell in Tyre.

8 The Assyrians also have joined them, *
    and have come to help the people of Lot.

9 Do to them as you did to Midian, *
    to Sisera, and to Jabin at the river of Kishon:

10 They were destroyed at Endor; *
    they became like dung upon the ground.

11 Make their leaders like Oreb and Zeëb, *
    and all their commanders like Zebah and Zalmunna,

12 Who said, "Let us take for ourselves *
    the fields of God as our possession."

13 O my God, make them like whirling dust *
    and like chaff before the wind;

14 Like fire that burns down a forest, *
    like the flame that sets mountains ablaze.

15 Drive them with your tempest *
    and terrify them with your storm;

16 Cover their faces with shame, O LORD, *
    that they may seek your Name.

17 Let them be disgraced and terrified for ever; *
    let them be put to confusion and perish.

18 Let them know that you, whose Name is YAHWEH, *
    you alone are the Most High over all the earth.

Psalm 7 *Domine, Deus meus*

You also must be ready, for the Son of Man is coming at an unexpected hour. Mt. 24:44

1 O LORD my God, I take refuge in you; *
　　save and deliver me from all who pursue me;

2 Lest like a lion they tear me in pieces *
　　and snatch me away with none to deliver me.

3 O LORD my God, if I have done these things: *
　　if there is any wickedness in my hands,

4 If I have repaid my friend with evil, *
　　or plundered him who without cause is my enemy;

5 Then let my enemy pursue and overtake me, *
　　trample my life into the ground,
　　and lay my honor in the dust.

6 Stand up, O LORD, in your wrath; *
　　rise up against the fury of my enemies.

7 Awake, O my God, decree justice; *
　　let the assembly of the peoples gather round you.

8 Be seated on your lofty throne, O Most High; *
　　O LORD, judge the nations.

9 Give judgment for me according to my
　　righteousness, O LORD, *
　　and according to my innocence, O Most High.

10 Let the malice of the wicked come to an end,
　　but establish the righteous; *
　　for you test the mind and heart, O righteous God.

11 God is my shield and defense; *
　　he is the savior of the true in heart.

12 God is a righteous judge; *
　　God sits in judgment every day.

13 If they will not repent, God will whet his sword; *
　　he will bend his bow and make it ready.

14 He has prepared his weapons of death; *
　　he makes his arrows shafts of fire.

15 Look at those who are in labor with wickedness, *
　　who conceive evil, and give birth to a lie.

16 They dig a pit and make it deep *
     and fall into the hole that they have made.

17 Their malice turns back upon their own head; *
     their violence falls on their own scalp.

18 I will bear witness that the LORD is righteous; *
     I will praise the Name of the LORD Most High.

Epiphany Whatever you do, in word or deed, do everything in the name of the Lord Jesus.
Pentecost God is my shield and defense; God is the savior of the true in heart.

Reading Revelation 21: 1-5
Then I saw a new heaven and a new earth; for the first heaven and the first earth had passed away, and the sea was no more. And I saw the holy city, the new Jerusalem, coming down out of heaven from God, prepared as a bride adorned for her husband. And I heard a loud voice from the throne saying, See, the home of God is among mortals. He will dwell with them; they will be his people, and God himself will be with them; he will wipe every tear from their eyes. Death will be no more; mourning and crying and pain will be no more, for the first things have passed away." And the one who was seated on the throne said, "See, I am making all things new."

Verse and Response
From this time forward I make you hear new things.
Hidden things that you have not known.

The Short Litany and the Lord's Prayer

The Collect Almighty and most merciful God, grant that by the indwelling of your Holy Spirit we may be enlightened and strengthened for your service; through Jesus Christ our Lord, who lives and reigns with you, in the unity of the Holy Spirit, one God, now and for ever. Amen.

Let us bless the Lord.
Thanks be to God.

Week 4

Sunday Week 4 Evening Prayer I

Officiant: O God, make speed to save us.

People: **O Lord, make haste to help us.**

Officiant and People **Glory to the Father ... Alleluia.**

Hymn O day of radiant gladness *Hymnal 48*

Psalm 141 *Domine, clamavi*

The smoke of the incense, with the prayers of the saints,
rose before God from the hand of the angel. Rev. 8:4

Epiphany God who establishes us with you in Christ has anointed us, by giving us his Spirit in our hearts, hallelujah.

Pentecost Let my prayer be set forth in your sight as incense, the lifting up of my hands as the evening sacrifice, hallelujah.

1 O LORD, I call to you; come to me quickly; *
     hear my voice when I cry to you.

2 Let my prayer be set forth in your sight as incense, *
     the lifting up of my hands as the evening sacrifice.

3 Set a watch before my mouth, O LORD,
     and guard the door of my lips; *
     let not my heart incline to any evil thing.

4 Let me not be occupied in wickedness with evildoers, *
     nor eat of their choice foods.

5 Let the righteous smite me in friendly rebuke;
     let not the oil of the unrighteous anoint my head; *
     for my prayer is continually against their wicked deeds.

6 Let their rulers be overthrown in stony places, *
     that they may know my words are true.

7 As when a plowman turns over the earth in furrows, *
     let their bones be scattered at the mouth of the grave.

8 But my eyes are turned to you, LORD God; *
     in you I take refuge;
     do not strip me of my life.

9 Protect me from the snare which they have laid for me *
     and from the traps of the evildoers.

10 Let the wicked fall into their own nets, *
     while I myself escape.

Epiphany God who establishes us with you in Christ has anointed us, by giving us his Spirit in our hearts, hallelujah.

Pentecost Let my prayer be set forth in your sight as incense, the lifting up of my hands as the evening sacrifice, hallelujah.

Psalm 145 A *Exaltabo te, Deus*
Many will come from east and west and will eat with Abraham and Isaac and Jacob in the kingdom of heaven. Mt. 8:11

Epiphany I will ponder the glorious splendor of your majesty and all your marvelous works, hallelujah.

Pentecost Great is the LORD and greatly to be praised; there is no end to his greatness, hallelujah.

1 I will exalt you, O God my King, *
 and bless your Name for ever and ever.

2 Every day will I bless you *
 and praise your Name for ever and ever.

3 Great is the LORD and greatly to be praised; *
 there is no end to his greatness.

4 One generation shall praise your works to another *
 and shall declare your power.

5 I will ponder the glorious splendor of your majesty *
 and all your marvelous works.

6 They shall speak of the might of your wondrous acts, *
 and I will tell of your greatness.

7 They shall publish the remembrance of your great goodness; *
 they shall sing of your righteous deeds.

8 The LORD is gracious and full of compassion, *
 slow to anger and of great kindness.

9 The LORD is loving to everyone *
 and his compassion is over all his works.

Epiphany I will ponder the glorious splendor of your majesty and all your marvelous works, hallelujah.

Pentecost Great is the LORD and greatly to be praised; there is no end to his greatness, hallelujah.

Psalm 145 B *Confiteantur tibi*
The kingdom of God has come near to you. Lk. 10:9

Epiphany My mouth shall speak the praise of the LORD; let all flesh bless his holy Name for ever and ever, hallelujah.
Pentecost Your kingdom, O Lord, is an everlasting kingdom, hallelujah.

10 All your works praise you, O LORD, *
　　and your faithful servants bless you.

11 They make known the glory of your kingdom *
　　and speak of your power;

12 That the peoples may know of your power *
　　and the glorious splendor of your kingdom.

13 Your kingdom is an everlasting kingdom; *
　　your dominion endures throughout all ages.

14 The LORD is faithful in all his words *
　　and merciful in all his deeds.

15 The LORD upholds all those who fall; *
　　he lifts up those who are bowed down.

16 The eyes of all wait upon you, O LORD, *
　　and you give them their food in due season.

17 You open wide your hand *
　　and satisfy the needs of every living creature.

18 The LORD is righteous in all his ways *
　　and loving in all his works.

19 The LORD is near to those who call upon him, *
　　to all who call upon him faithfully.

20 He fulfills the desire of those who fear him; *
　　he hears their cry and helps them.

21 The LORD preserves all those who love him, *
　　but he destroys all the wicked.

22 My mouth shall speak the praise of the LORD; *
　　let all flesh bless his holy Name for ever and ever.

Epiphany My mouth shall speak the praise of the LORD; let all flesh bless his holy Name for ever and ever, hallelujah.
Pentecost Your kingdom, O Lord, is an everlasting kingdom, hallelujah.

Reading

Responsory (Phil. 2:11)
Every tongue should confess
   – Jesus Christ is Lord.
We proclaim to the glory of God the Father
   – Jesus Christ is Lord.
Glory to the Father and to the Son and to the Holy Spirit.
Every tongue should confess
   – Jesus Christ is Lord.

The Gospel Canticle – The Song of Mary
Magnificat Antiphon *From the proper of the day*

Litany
Give your wisdom and compassion to health care workers, that they may minister to the sick and dying with knowledge, skill, and kindness.
Lord, have mercy.
Comfort, relieve, and heal all sick children; surround them with compassionate caregivers.
Christ, have mercy.
Help us to prepare for death with confident expectation and hope of Easter joy and lead all the departed to see your face.
Lord, have mercy.

Invitation to the Lord's Prayer Risen with Christ in Baptism, our hope is in the Spirit who will raise us up to life with God.

The Collect *From the proper of the day or*
O God, the source of eternal light: Shed forth your unending day upon us who watch for you, that our lips may praise you, our lives may bless you, and our worship on the morrow give you glory; through Jesus Christ our Lord. Amen.

The Blessing
May the God of hope fill us with all joy and peace in believing, so that we may abound in hope by the power of the Holy Spirit. **Amen**

Sunday Week 4 Morning Prayer
Officiant: Lord, open our lips.
People: **And our mouth shall proclaim your praise.**
Officiant and People **Glory to the Father... Alleluia.**

The Invitatory Psalm 95
The Spirit draws us into the life of God: Come let us worship.

Hymn Come, let us with our Lord arise *Hymnal 49*

Psalm 93 *Dominus regnavit*

Jesus Christ is the faithful witness, the firstborn of the dead,
and the ruler of the kings of the earth. Rev. 1:5

Epiphany God sends forth his word and melts them; he blows with his wind, and the waters flow, hallelujah.

Pentecost Holiness adorns your house, O LORD, for ever and for evermore, hallelujah.

1 The LORD is King;
    he has put on splendid apparel; *
        the LORD has put on his apparel
        and girded himself with strength.

2 He has made the whole world so sure *
        that it cannot be moved;

3 Ever since the world began, your throne has been established; *
        you are from everlasting.

4 The waters have lifted up, O LORD,
    the waters have lifted up their voice; *
        the waters have lifted up their pounding waves.

5 Mightier than the sound of many waters,
    mightier than the breakers of the sea, *
        mightier is the LORD who dwells on high.

6 Your testimonies are very sure, *
        and holiness adorns your house, O LORD,
        for ever and for evermore.

Epiphany God sends forth his word and melts them; he blows with his wind, and the waters flow, hallelujah.

Pentecost Holiness adorns your house, O LORD, for ever and for evermore, hallelujah.

Psalm 63 *Deus, Deus meus*

Let anyone who is thirsty come to me, and let the one who believes in me drink. Jn. 7: 37-38

Epiphany I have gazed upon you in your holy place, that I might behold your power and your glory, hallelujah.

Pentecost My soul clings to you; your right hand holds me fast, hallelujah.

1 O God, you are my God; eagerly I seek you; *
        my soul thirsts for you, my flesh faints for you,
        as in a barren and dry land where there is no water.

2 Therefore I have gazed upon you in your holy place, *
    that I might behold your power and your glory.

3 For your loving-kindness is better than life itself; *
    my lips shall give you praise.

4 So will I bless you as long as I live *
    and lift up my hands in your Name.

5 My soul is content, as with marrow and fatness, *
    and my mouth praises you with joyful lips,

6 When I remember you upon my bed, *
    and meditate on you in the night watches.

7 For you have been my helper, *
    and under the shadow of your wings I will rejoice.

8 My soul clings to you; *
    your right hand holds me fast.

9 May those who seek my life to destroy it *
    go down into the depths of the earth;

10 Let them fall upon the edge of the sword, *
    and let them be food for jackals.

11 But the king will rejoice in God;
    all those who swear by him will be glad; *
    for the mouth of those who speak lies shall be stopped.

Epiphany I have gazed upon you in your holy place, that I might behold your power and your glory, hallelujah.
Pentecost My soul clings to you; your right hand holds me fast, hallelujah.

Psalm 47 *Omnes gentes, plaudite*
God has made him the head over all things for the church, which is his body,
the fullness of him who fills all in all. Eph. 1:22-23

Epiphany God reigns over the nations; God sits upon his holy throne, hallelujah.
Pentecost Shout to God with a cry of joy for we are God's people, hallelujah.

1 Clap your hands, all you peoples; *
    shout to God with a cry of joy.

2 For the LORD Most High is to be feared; *
    he is the great King over all the earth.

3 He subdues the peoples under us, *
    and the nations under our feet.

4 He chooses our inheritance for us, *
    the pride of Jacob whom he loves.

5 God has gone up with a shout, *
    the LORD with the sound of the ram's-horn.

6 Sing praises to God, sing praises; *
    sing praises to our King, sing praises.

7 For God is King of all the earth; *
    sing praises with all your skill.

8 God reigns over the nations; *
    God sits upon his holy throne.

9 The nobles of the peoples have gathered together *
    with the people of the God of Abraham.

10 The rulers of the earth belong to God, *
    and he is highly exalted.

Epiphany God reigns over the nations; God sits upon his holy throne,
hallelujah.
Pentecost Shout to God with a cry of joy for we are God's people,
hallelujah.

Reading One

Responsory One (Lk. 18:38)
Christ, Son of the Living God
        – have mercy on us.
You are risen from the dead
        – have mercy on us.
Glory to the Father and to the Son and to the Holy Spirit.
Christ, Son of the Living God
        – have mercy on us.

The First Canticle – You are God *Te Deum laudamus*

You are God: we praise you;
You are the Lord: we acclaim you;
You are the eternal Father:
All creation worships you.
To you all angels, all the powers of heaven,
Cherubim and Seraphim, sing in endless praise:

Holy, holy, holy Lord, God of power and might,
heaven and earth are full of your glory.
The glorious company of apostles praise you.
The noble fellowship of prophets praise you.
The white-robed army of martyrs praise you.
Throughout the world the holy Church acclaims you;
Father, of majesty unbounded,
your true and only Son, worthy of all worship,
and the Holy Spirit, advocate and guide.
You, Christ, are the king of glory,
the eternal Son of the Father.
When you became man to set us free
you did not shun the Virgin's womb.
You overcame the sting of death
and opened the kingdom of heaven to all believers.
You are seated at God's right hand in glory.
We believe that you will come and be our judge.
Come then, Lord, and help your people,
bought with the price of your own blood,
and bring us with your saints
to glory everlasting.

The Gloria is not said with the Te Deum.

Reading Two

Responsory Two (Ps. 86: 12; Ps. 9:1)
The steadfast love of the Lord never ceases
– God's mercies never come to an end.
They are new every morning
– God's mercies never come to an end.
Glory to the Father and to the Son and to the Holy Spirit.
The steadfast love of the Lord never ceases
– God's mercies never come to an end.

The Gospel Canticle – The Song of Zechariah
Benedictus Antiphon *From the proper of the day*

Litany
Drive far from us all wrong desires, incline our hearts to keep your law,
and guide our feet into the way of peace.
Lord, have mercy.
Let us do your will with cheerfulness while it is day, that we may, when
night comes, rejoice to give you thanks.
Christ, have mercy.

Give us this day such blessing through our worship of you, that the week to come may be spent in your favor.
Lord, have mercy.

Invitation to the Lord's Prayer With Christians throughout the world, let us celebrate the Father's love in the Resurrection of Christ.

The Collect *From the Proper of the day or*
 O God, you make us glad with the weekly remembrance of the glorious resurrection of your Son our Lord: Give us this day such blessing through our worship of you, that the week to come may be spent in your favor; through Jesus Christ our Lord. Amen.

The Blessing
May we rejoice always, pray without ceasing and give thanks in all circumstances. **Amen**

Sunday Week 4 Noonday Prayer

Officiant: O God, make speed to save us.
People: **O Lord, make haste to help us.**
Officiant and People **Glory to the Father... Alleluia.**

Hymn Come thou Holy Spirit bright *Hymnal 227*

Psalm 72 A *Deus, judicium*

On entering the house, they saw the child with Mary his mother;
and they knelt down and paid him homage. Mt. 2:11

Epiphany The kings of Tarshish and of the isles shall pay tribute, and the kings of Arabia and Saba offer gifts, hallelujah.
Pentecost In his time shall the righteous flourish; there shall be abundance of peace till the moon shall be no more, hallelujah.

1   Give the King your justice, O God, *
    and your righteousness to the King's Son;

2   That he may rule your people righteously *
    and the poor with justice;

3   That the mountains may bring prosperity to the people, *
    and the little hills bring righteousness.

4   He shall defend the needy among the people; *
    he shall rescue the poor and crush the oppressor.

5   He shall live as long as the sun and moon endure, *
    from one generation to another.

6 He shall come down like rain upon the mown field, *
      like showers that water the earth.

7 In his time shall the righteous flourish; *
      there shall be abundance of peace
      till the moon shall be no more.

8 He shall rule from sea to sea, *
      and from the River to the ends of the earth.

9 His foes shall bow down before him, *
      and his enemies lick the dust.

10 The kings of Tarshish and of the isles shall pay tribute, *
      and the kings of Arabia and Saba offer gifts.

11 All kings shall bow down before him, *
      and all the nations do him service.

Psalm 72 B *Quia liberabit*

Jesus saw a great crowd; and he had compassion for them and cured their sick. Mt. 14:14

12 For he shall deliver the poor who cries out in distress, *
      and the oppressed who has no helper.

13 He shall have pity on the lowly and poor; *
      he shall preserve the lives of the needy.

14 He shall redeem their lives from oppression and violence, *
      and dear shall their blood be in his sight.

15 Long may he live!
   and may there be given to him gold from Arabia; *
      may prayer be made for him always,
      and may they bless him all the day long.

16 May there be abundance of grain on the earth,
   growing thick even on the hilltops; *
      may its fruit flourish like Lebanon,
      and its grain like grass upon the earth.

17 May his Name remain for ever
   and be established as long as the sun endures; *
      may all the nations bless themselves in him
      and call him blessed.

18 Blessed be the LORD God, the God of Israel, *
      who alone does wondrous deeds!

19 And blessed be his glorious Name for ever! *
   and may all the earth be filled with his glory.
   Amen. Amen.

Psalm 117 *Laudate Dominum*
Once you were not a people, but now you are God's people. 1 Pt. 2:10

1 Praise the LORD, all you nations; *
    laud him, all you peoples.

2 For his loving-kindness toward us is great, *
    and the faithfulness of the LORD endures for ever.
    Hallelujah!

Epiphany The kings of Tarshish and of the isles shall pay tribute, and
the kings of Arabia and Saba offer gifts, hallelujah.
Pentecost In his time shall the righteous flourish; there shall be
abundance of peace till the moon shall be no more, hallelujah.

Reading Exodus 33:18-20
Moses said, "Show me your glory, I pray." And he said, "I will make all
my goodness pass before you, and will proclaim before you the name,
'The Lord'; and I will be gracious to whom I will be gracious, and will
show mercy on whom I will show mercy. But," he said, "you cannot
see my face; for no one shall see me and live."

Verse and Response
Let your face shine upon your servant.
Save me in your steadfast love.

The Short Litany and the Lord's Prayer

The Collect Direct us, O Lord, in all our doings with your most gracious
favor, and further us with your continual help; that in all our works
begun, continued, and ended in you, we may glorify your holy Name, and
finally, by your mercy, obtain everlasting life; through Jesus Christ our
Lord. Amen.

Let us bless the Lord.
Thanks be to God.

Sunday Week 4 Evening Prayer II
Officiant: O God, make speed to save us.
People: **O Lord, make haste to help us.**
Officiant and People **Glory to the Father... Alleluia.**

Hymn God my King, thy might confessing *Hymnal 414*

Psalm 113 *Laudate, pueri*

Salvation belongs to our God who is seated on the throne, and to the Lamb! Rev. 7:10

Epiphany Who is like the LORD our God, who sits enthroned on high, but stoops to behold the heavens and the earth? Hallelujah.

Pentecost From the rising of the sun to its going down, let the Name of the Lord be praised, hallelujah.

1 Hallelujah!
    Give praise, you servants of the LORD; *
        praise the Name of the LORD.

2 Let the Name of the LORD be blessed, *
        from this time forth for evermore.

3 From the rising of the sun to its going down *
        let the Name of the LORD be praised.

4 The LORD is high above all nations, *
        and his glory above the heavens.

5 Who is like the LORD our God, who sits enthroned on high, *
        but stoops to behold the heavens and the earth?

6 He takes up the weak out of the dust *
        and lifts up the poor from the ashes.

7 He sets them with the princes, *
        with the princes of his people.

8 He makes the woman of a childless house *
        to be a joyful mother of children.

Epiphany Who is like the LORD our God, who sits enthroned on high, but stoops to behold the heavens and the earth? Hallelujah.

Pentecost From the rising of the sun to its going down, let the Name of the Lord be praised, hallelujah.

Psalm 114 *In exitu Israel*

Now have come the salvation and the power and the kingdom of our God and the authority of his Messiah. Rev. 12:10

Epiphany The sea beheld it and fled; Jordan turned and went back, hallelujah.

Pentecost Tremble, O earth, at the presence of the Lord, hallelujah.

1 Hallelujah!
    When Israel came out of Egypt, *
        the house of Jacob from a people of strange speech,

2 Judah became God's sanctuary *
    and Israel his dominion.

3 The sea beheld it and fled; *
    Jordan turned and went back.

4 The mountains skipped like rams, *
    and the little hills like young sheep.

5 What ailed you, O sea, that you fled? *
    O Jordan, that you turned back?

6 You mountains, that you skipped like rams? *
    you little hills like young sheep?

7 Tremble, O earth, at the presence of the Lord, *
    at the presence of the God of Jacob,

8 Who turned the hard rock into a pool of water *
    and flint-stone into a flowing spring.

Epiphany The sea beheld it and fled; Jordan turned and went back, hallelujah.

Pentecost Tremble, O earth, at the presence of the Lord, hallelujah.

Psalm 115 *Non nobis, Domine*
Jesus Christ loves us and freed us from our sins by his blood, and made us to be a kingdom, priests serving his God and Father.
Rev. 1:5-6

Epiphany God will bless those who fear the LORD, both small and great together, hallelujah.

Pentecost Our God is in heaven; whatever he wills to do he does, hallelujah.

1 Not to us, O LORD, not to us,
    but to your Name give glory; *
        because of your love and because of your faithfulness.

2 Why should the heathen say, *
    "Where then is their God?"

3 Our God is in heaven; *
    whatever he wills to do he does.

4 Their idols are silver and gold, *
    the work of human hands.

5 They have mouths, but they cannot speak; *
    eyes have they, but they cannot see;

6 They have ears, but they cannot hear; *
    noses, but they cannot smell;

7 They have hands, but they cannot feel;
feet, but they cannot walk; *
    they make no sound with their throat.

8 Those who make them are like them, *
    and so are all who put their trust in them.

9 O Israel, trust in the LORD; *
    he is their help and their shield.

10 O house of Aaron, trust in the LORD; *
    he is their help and their shield.

11 You who fear the LORD, trust in the LORD; *
    he is their help and their shield.

12 The LORD has been mindful of us, and he will bless us; *
    he will bless the house of Israel;
    he will bless the house of Aaron;

13 He will bless those who fear the LORD, *
    both small and great together.

14 May the LORD increase you more and more, *
    you and your children after you.

15 May you be blessed by the LORD, *
    the maker of heaven and earth.

16 The heaven of heavens is the LORD'S, *
    but he entrusted the earth to its peoples.

17 The dead do not praise the LORD, *
    nor all those who go down into silence;

18 But we will bless the LORD, *
    from this time forth for evermore.
    Hallelujah!

Epiphany God will bless those who fear the LORD, both small and great together, hallelujah.
Pentecost Our God is in heaven; whatever he wills to do he does, hallelujah.

Reading

Responsory (Ps. 147:5)
Great is our Lord
> **– mighty is God's power.**

There is no limit to God's wisdom
> **– mighty is God's power.**

Glory to the Father and to the Son and to the Holy Spirit.
Great is our Lord
> **– mighty is God's power.**

The Gospel Canticle – The Song of Mary
Magnificat Antiphon *From the proper of the day*

Litany
Let the whole earth worship you, all nations obey you, all tongues confess and bless you.
Lord, have mercy.
Let men and women everywhere love you and serve you in peace.
Christ, have mercy.
Give rest to the weary, bless the dying, soothe the suffering, pity the afflicted, shield the joyous.
Lord, have mercy.

Invitation to the Lord's Prayer Having celebrated the Resurrection of Christ, let us praise the Father's love.

Collect *From the proper of the day or*
Lord God, whose Son our Savior Jesus Christ triumphed over the powers of death and prepared for us our place in the new Jerusalem: Grant that we, who have this day given thanks for his resurrection, may praise you in that City of which he is the light, and where he lives and reigns for ever and ever. Amen.

The Blessing
May we know what is the hope to which our Lord has called us, what are the riches of God's glorious inheritance among the saints, and what is the immeasurable greatness of God's power for us who believe. **Amen**

Monday Week 4 Morning Prayer
Officiant: Lord, open our lips.
People: **And our mouth shall proclaim your praise.**
Officiant and People **Glory to the Father... Alleluia.**

The Invitatory Psalm 29
The Lord shall give us the blessing of peace: Come let us worship.

Hymn Awake, awake to love and work *Hymnal 9, Verses 4-6*

Psalm 97 *Dominus regnavit*

You will see the Son of Man seated at the right hand of Power
and coming on the clouds of heaven. Mt. 26:64

Epiphany The heavens declare the Lord's righteousness, and all the peoples see his glory.
Pentecost You are the LORD, most high over all the earth.

1 The LORD is King;
   let the earth rejoice; *
      let the multitude of the isles be glad.

2 Clouds and darkness are round about him, *
      righteousness and justice are the foundations of his throne.

3 A fire goes before him *
      and burns up his enemies on every side.

4 His lightnings light up the world; *
      the earth sees it and is afraid.

5 The mountains melt like wax at the presence of the LORD, *
      at the presence of the Lord of the whole earth.

6 The heavens declare his righteousness, *
      and all the peoples see his glory.

7 Confounded be all who worship carved images
   and delight in false gods! *
      Bow down before him, all you gods.

8 Zion hears and is glad, and the cities of Judah rejoice, *
      because of your judgments, O LORD.

9 For you are the LORD,
   most high over all the earth; *
      you are exalted far above all gods.

10 The LORD loves those who hate evil; *
      he preserves the lives of his saints
      and delivers them from the hand of the wicked.

11 Light has sprung up for the righteous, *
      and joyful gladness for those who are truehearted.

12 Rejoice in the LORD, you righteous, *
      and give thanks to his holy Name.

Epiphany The heavens declare the Lord's righteousness, and all the peoples see his glory.

Pentecost You are the LORD, most high over all the earth.

Psalm 24 *Domini est terra*

The aim of instruction is love that comes from a pure heart, a good conscience,
and sincere faith. 1 Tim. 1:5

Epiphany The LORD of hosts, he is the King of glory.
Pentecost The Lord founded the earth upon the seas and made it firm upon the rivers of the deep.

1 The earth is the LORD'S and all that is in it, *
    the world and all who dwell therein.

2 For it is he who founded it upon the seas *
    and made it firm upon the rivers of the deep.

3 "Who can ascend the hill of the LORD? *
    and who can stand in his holy place?"

4 "Those who have clean hands and a pure heart, *
    who have not pledged themselves to falsehood,
    nor sworn by what is a fraud.

5 They shall receive a blessing from the Lord *
    and a just reward from the God of their salvation."

6 Such is the generation of those who seek him, *
    of those who seek your face, O God of Jacob.

7 Lift up your heads, O gates;
lift them high, O everlasting doors; *
    and the King of glory shall come in.

8 "Who is this King of glory?" *
    "The LORD, strong and mighty,
    the LORD, mighty in battle."

9 Lift up your heads, O gates;
lift them high, O everlasting doors; *
    and the King of glory shall come in.

10 "Who is he, this King of glory?" *
    "The LORD of hosts,
    he is the King of glory."

Epiphany The LORD of hosts, he is the King of glory.
Pentecost The Lord founded the earth upon the seas and made it firm upon the rivers of the deep.

Psalm 148 *Laudate Dominum*

*At Jesus' name every knee should bend, in heaven and on earth
and under the earth. Phil 2:10*

Epiphany Let Kings of the earth and all peoples praise the Name of
the LORD.

Pentecost Praise the Lord from the heavens, praise the Lord from the
earth.

1 Hallelujah!
   Praise the LORD from the heavens; *
       praise him in the heights.

2 Praise him, all you angels of his; *
       praise him, all his host.

3 Praise him, sun and moon; *
       praise him, all you shining stars.

4 Praise him, heaven of heavens, *
       and you waters above the heavens.

5 Let them praise the Name of the LORD; *
       for he commanded, and they were created.

6 He made them stand fast for ever and ever; *
       he gave them a law which shall not pass away.

7 Praise the LORD from the earth, *
       you sea-monsters and all deeps;

8 Fire and hail, snow and fog, *
       tempestuous wind, doing his will;

9 Mountains and all hills, *
       fruit trees and all cedars;

10 Wild beasts and all cattle, *
       creeping things and wingèd birds;

11 Kings of the earth and all peoples, *
       princes and all rulers of the world;

12 Young men and maidens, *
       old and young together.

13 Let them praise the Name of the LORD, *
       for his Name only is exalted,
       his splendor is over earth and heaven.

14 He has raised up strength for his people
> and praise for all his loyal servants, *
>> the children of Israel, a people who are near him.
>> Hallelujah!

Epiphany Let Kings of the earth and all peoples praise the Name of the LORD.

Pentecost Praise the Lord from the heavens, praise the Lord from the earth.

Reading One

Responsory One (Ps. 40:3; Ps. 71:22)

God put a new song in my mouth
> **— a song of praise to our God.**

Sing to God with the harp
> **— a song of praise to our God.**

Glory to the Father and to the Son and to the Holy Spirit.

God put a new song in my mouth
> **— a song of praise to our God.**

The First Canticle – Song of the Anointed Prophet *Spiritus Domini*
(Isaiah 61.1-3, 11)

Epiphany Here is my servant, whom I uphold, my chosen, in whom my soul delights.

Pentecost The Lord has anointed me and sent me to bring good news to the oppressed.

The Spirit of the Lord is upon me *
> because he has anointed me.

He has sent me to bring good news to the oppressed, *
> to bind up the broken-hearted,

To proclaim liberty to the captives, *
> and the opening of the prison to those who are bound;

To proclaim the year of the Lord's favor, *
> to comfort all who mourn,

To give them a garland instead of ashes, *
> the oil of gladness instead of mourning,
> the mantle of praise instead of a faint spirit,

That they may be called oaks of righteousness, *
> the planting of the Lord, that he may be glorified.

For as the earth puts forth her blossom, *
    and as seeds in the garden spring up,

So shall the Lord God make righteousness and praise *
    blossom before all the nations.

Epiphany Here is my servant, whom I uphold, my chosen, in whom my soul delights.
Pentecost The Lord has anointed me and sent me to bring good news to the oppressed.

Reading Two

Responsory Two (Ps. 47:1)
Clap your hands
        – all you people.
Shout to God with a cry of joy
        – all you people.
Glory to the Father and to the Son and to the Holy Spirit.
Clap your hands
        – all you people.

The Gospel Canticle – The Song of Zechariah
Epiphany In the tender compassion of our God the dawn from on high shall break upon us.
Pentecost God has raised up for us a mighty savior, born of the house of his servant David.

Litany
For God's people throughout the world; for N., our Presiding Bishop, , N. our Bishop(s); for this gathering; and for all ministers and people. Pray for the Church.
Lord, have mercy.
For peace; for goodwill among nations; and for the well-being of all people. Pray for justice and peace.
Christ, have mercy.
For the poor, the sick, the hungry, the oppressed, and those in prison. Pray for those in any need or trouble.
Lord, have mercy.

Invitation to the Lord's Prayer Abandoning our willfulness, let us ask the Father to do his will among us.

The Collect *From the proper of the day or*
Almighty and everlasting God, by whose Spirit the whole body of your faithful people is governed and sanctified: Receive our supplications and

prayers which we offer before you for all members of your holy Church, that in their vocation and ministry they may truly and devoutly serve you; through our Lord and Savior Jesus Christ. Amen.

The Blessing

May we pursue righteousness, godliness, faith, love, endurance, gentleness. Let us fight the good fight of the faith and take hold of the eternal life, to which we are called. **Amen**

Monday Week 4 Noonday Prayer

Officiant: O God, make speed to save us.
People: **O Lord, make haste to help us.**
Officiant and People **Glory to the Father... Alleluia.**

Hymn Come Holy Spirit, heavenly Dove *Hymnal 510*

Psalm 119 Qoph *Clamavi in toto corde meo*
Have pity on us and help us. Mk. 9:22

Epiphany You led them by night with a pillar of fire, to give them light on the way in which they should go.
Pentecost Whoever speaks the truth from the heart shall dwell in the tabernacle of the Lord.

145 I call with my whole heart; *
    answer me, O LORD, that I may keep your statutes.

146 I call to you;
    oh, that you would save me! *
      I will keep your decrees.

147 Early in the morning I cry out to you, *
    for in your word is my trust.

148 My eyes are open in the night watches, *
    that I may meditate upon your promise.

149 Hear my voice, O LORD, according to your loving-kindness; *
    according to your judgments, give me life.

150 They draw near who in malice persecute me; *
    they are very far from your law.

151 You, O LORD, are near at hand, *
    and all your commandments are true.

152 Long have I known from your decrees *
    that you have established them for ever.

Psalm 14 *Dixit insipiens*
God is righteous and justifies the one who has faith in Jesus. Rm. 3:26

1 The fool has said in his heart, "There is no God." *
    All are corrupt and commit abominable acts;
    there is none who does any good.

2 The LORD looks down from heaven upon us all, *
    to see if there is any who is wise,
    if there is one who seeks after God.

3 Every one has proved faithless;
all alike have turned bad; *
    there is none who does good; no, not one.

4 Have they no knowledge, all those evildoers *
    who eat up my people like bread
    and do not call upon the LORD?

5 See how they tremble with fear, *
    because God is in the company of the righteous.

6 Their aim is to confound the plans of the afflicted, *
    but the LORD is their refuge.

7 Oh, that Israel's deliverance would come out of Zion! *
    when the LORD restores the fortunes of his people,
    Jacob will rejoice and Israel be glad.

Psalm 15 *Domine, quis habitabit?*
Blessed are the pure in heart, for they will see God. Mt. 5:8

1 LORD, who may dwell in your tabernacle? *
    who may abide upon your holy hill?

2 Whoever leads a blameless life and does what is right, *
    who speaks the truth from his heart.

3 There is no guile upon his tongue;
he does no evil to his friend; *
    he does not heap contempt upon his neighbor.

4 In his sight the wicked is rejected, *
    but he honors those who fear the LORD.

5 He has sworn to do no wrong *
    and does not take back his word.

6 He does not give his money in hope of gain, *
    nor does he take a bribe against the innocent.

7   Whoever does these things *
        shall never be overthrown.

Epiphany You led them by night with a pillar of fire, to give them light on the way in which they should go.
Pentecost Whoever speaks the truth from the heart shall dwell in the tabernacle of the Lord.

Reading Exodus 22: 21-27
You shall not wrong or oppress a resident alien, for you were aliens in the land of Egypt. You shall not abuse any widow or orphan. If you do abuse them, when they cry out to me, I will surely heed their cry; my wrath will burn, and I will kill you with the sword, and your wives shall become widows and your children orphans. If you lend money to my people, to the poor among you, you shall not deal with them as a creditor; you shall not exact interest from them. If you take your neighbor's cloak in pawn, you shall restore it before the sun goes down; for it may be your neighbor's only clothing to use as cover; in what else shall that person sleep? And if your neighbor cries out to me, I will listen, for I am compassionate.

Verse and Response
As a father has compassion for his children.
So the Lord has compassion for those who fear him.

The Short Litany and the Lord's Prayer

The Collect Heavenly Father, we thank you that by water and the Holy Spirit you have bestowed on us your servants the forgiveness of sin, and have raised us to the new life of grace. Sustain us, O Lord, in your Holy Spirit. Give us inquiring minds and discerning hearts, the courage to will and to persevere, a spirit to know and to love you, and the gift of joy and wonder in all your works. Amen.

Let us bless the Lord.
Thanks be to God.

Monday Week 4 Evening Prayer
Officiant: O God, make speed to save us.
People: **O Lord, make haste to help us.**
Officiant and People **Glory to the Father... Alleluia.**

Hymn O gladsome Light *Hymnal 36*

Psalm 68 A *Exsurgat Deus*

Blessed are you who are poor, for yours is the kingdom of God. Lk. 6:20

Epiphany God gives the solitary a home and brings forth prisoners into freedom.

Pentecost Come, father of the poor, giver of gifts, and light of the heart.

1 Let God arise, and let his enemies be scattered; *
    let those who hate him flee before him.

2 Let them vanish like smoke when the wind drives it away; *
    as the wax melts at the fire, so let the wicked perish
        at the presence of God.

3 But let the righteous be glad and rejoice before God; *
    let them also be merry and joyful.

4 Sing to God, sing praises to his Name;
    exalt him who rides upon the heavens; *
        YAHWEH is his Name, rejoice before him!

5 Father of orphans, defender of widows, *
    God in his holy habitation!

6 God gives the solitary a home
    and brings forth prisoners into freedom; *
        but the rebels shall live in dry places.

7 O God, when you went forth before your people, *
    when you marched through the wilderness,

8 The earth shook, and the skies poured down rain,
    at the presence of God, the God of Sinai, *
        at the presence of God, the God of Israel.

9 You sent a gracious rain, O God, upon your inheritance; *
    you refreshed the land when it was weary.

10 Your people found their home in it; *
    in your goodness, O God,
    you have made provision for the poor.

Epiphany God gives the solitary a home and brings forth prisoners into freedom.

Pentecost Come, father of the poor, giver of gifts, and light of the heart.

Psalm 68 B *Dominus dabit*

Our Savior Christ Jesus, abolished death and brought life and immortality to light
through the gospel. 2 Tim. 1:10

Epiphany I will bring them back from Bashan; I will bring them back from the depths of the sea.

Pentecost Blessed be the Lord day by day, the God of our salvation, who bears our burdens.

11 The Lord gave the word; *
    great was the company of women who bore the tidings:

12 "Kings with their armies are fleeing away; *
    the women at home are dividing the spoils."

13 Though you lingered among the sheepfolds, *
    you shall be like a dove whose wings are covered with silver,
    whose feathers are like green gold.

14 When the Almighty scattered kings, *
    it was like snow falling in Zalmon.

15 O mighty mountain, O hill of Bashan! *
    O rugged mountain, O hill of Bashan!

16 Why do you look with envy, O rugged mountain,
    at the hill which God chose for his resting place? *
    truly, the LORD will dwell there for ever.

17 The chariots of God are twenty thousand,
    even thousands of thousands; *
    the Lord comes in holiness from Sinai.

18 You have gone up on high and led captivity captive;
    you have received gifts even from your enemies, *
    that the LORD God might dwell among them.

19 Blessed be the Lord day by day, *
    the God of our salvation, who bears our burdens.

20 He is our God, the God of our salvation; *
    God is the LORD, by whom we escape death.

21 God shall crush the heads of his enemies, *
    and the hairy scalp of those
    who go on still in their wickedness.

22 The Lord has said, "I will bring them back from Bashan; *
    I will bring them back from the depths of the sea;

23 That your foot may be dipped in blood, *
   the tongues of your dogs in the blood of your enemies."

Epiphany I will bring them back from Bashan; I will bring them back from the depths of the sea.
Pentecost Blessed be the Lord day by day, the God of our salvation, who bears our burdens.

Psalm 68 C *Viderunt ingressus tui*
Look! He is coming with the clouds; every eye will see him,
even those who pierced him. Rev. 1:7

Epiphany Kings shall bring gifts to you, for your temple's sake at Jerusalem..
Pentecost Sing to the Lord, O kingdoms of the earth; sing praises to the Lord.

24 They see your procession, O God, *
   your procession into the sanctuary, my God and my King.

25 The singers go before, musicians follow after, *
   in the midst of maidens playing upon the hand-drums.

26 Bless God in the congregation; *
   bless the LORD, you that are of the fountain of Israel.

27 There is Benjamin, least of the tribes, at the head;
   the princes of Judah in a company; *
   and the princes of Zebulon and Naphtali.

28 Send forth your strength, O God; *
   establish, O God, what you have wrought for us.

29 Kings shall bring gifts to you, *
   for your temple's sake at Jerusalem.

30 Rebuke the wild beast of the reeds, *
   and the peoples, a herd of wild bulls with its calves.

31 Trample down those who lust after silver; *
   scatter the peoples that delight in war.

32 Let tribute be brought out of Egypt; *
   let Ethiopia stretch out her hands to God.

33 Sing to God, O kingdoms of the earth; *
   sing praises to the Lord.

34 He rides in the heavens, the ancient heavens; *
   he sends forth his voice, his mighty voice.

35 Ascribe power to God; *
>> his majesty is over Israel;
>> his strength is in the skies.

36 How wonderful is God in his holy places! *
>> the God of Israel giving strength and power to his people!
>> Blessed be God!

Epiphany Kings shall bring gifts to you, for your temple's sake at Jerusalem..

Pentecost Sing to the Lord, O kingdoms of the earth; sing praises to the Lord.

Reading

Responsory (Mal. 1:11)
From the rising of the sun to its setting
>> **− my name is great among the nations.**

In every place incense is offered to my name
>> **− my name is great among the nations.**

Glory to the Father and to the Son and to the Holy Spirit.
From the rising of the sun to its setting
>> **− my name is great among the nations.**

The Gospel Canticle – The Song of Mary
Epiphany Those who do what is true come to the light, so that it may be clearly seen that their deeds have been done in God.

Pentecost God has looked with favor on me, a lowly servant. My spirit rejoices in God, my Savior.

Litany
For all who seek our Lord, or a deeper knowledge of God; we pray that they may find and be found by God.
Lord, have mercy.

For those who are sick and those recommended to our prayer; we pray that God grant them healing and the assurance of eternal life.
Christ, have mercy.

For those departed in the faith of the Church and all the dead whose faith is known to God alone; we pray for those who have died and those who mourn.
Lord, have mercy.

Invitation to the Lord's Prayer Our Father beckons us to return to his embrace so at the end of the day we come back to the Father's home.

The Collect *From the proper of the day or*

O God and Father of all, whom the whole heavens adore: Let the whole earth also worship you, all nations obey you, all tongues confess and bless you, and men and women everywhere love you and serve you in peace; through Jesus Christ our Lord. Amen.

The Blessing

May the Lord rescue us from every evil and save us for God's heavenly kingdom. **Amen**

Tuesday Week 4 Morning Prayer

Officiant: Lord, open our lips.

People: **And our mouth shall proclaim your praise.**

Officiant and People **Glory to the Father... Alleluia.**

The Invitatory Psalm 8

God has put all things under Christ's feet; Come let us worship Christ the Lord.

Hymn God is Love *Hymnal 379*

Psalm 89 Part I A *Misericordias Domini*

Jacob was the father of Joseph the husband of Mary, of whom Jesus was born, who is called the Messiah. Mt. 1:16

Epiphany From age to age my mouth will proclaim your faithfulness.
Pentecost I am the root and the descendant of David, the bright morning star.

1 Your love, O LORD, for ever will I sing; *
    from age to age my mouth will proclaim your faithfulness.

2 For I am persuaded that your love is established for ever; *
    you have set your faithfulness firmly in the heavens.

3 "I have made a covenant with my chosen one; *
    I have sworn an oath to David my servant:

4 'I will establish your line for ever, *
    and preserve your throne for all generations.'"

Epiphany From age to age my mouth will proclaim your faithfulness.
Pentecost I am the root and the descendant of David, the bright morning star.

Psalm 89 Part I B *Confitebuntur caeli*

*Jesus woke up and rebuked the wind and the raging waves; they ceased,
and there was a calm. Lk. 8:24*

Epiphany Blessed are the people who know the festal shout! they walk,
O LORD, in the light of your presence.
Pentecost Righteousness and justice, O God, are the foundations of
your throne.

5 The heavens bear witness to your wonders, O LORD, *
      and to your faithfulness in the assembly of the holy ones;

6 For who in the skies can be compared to the LORD? *
      who is like the LORD among the gods?

7 God is much to be feared in the council of the holy ones, *
      great and terrible to all those round about him.

8 Who is like you, LORD God of hosts? *
      O mighty LORD, your faithfulness is all around you.

9 You rule the raging of the sea *
      and still the surging of its waves.

10 You have crushed Rahab of the deep with a deadly wound; *
      you have scattered your enemies with your mighty arm.

11 Yours are the heavens; the earth also is yours; *
      you laid the foundations of the world and all that is in it.

12 You have made the north and the south; *
      Tabor and Hermon rejoice in your Name.

13 You have a mighty arm; *
      strong is your hand and high is your right hand.

14 Righteousness and justice are the foundations of your throne; *
      love and truth go before your face.

15 Blessed are the people who know the festal shout! *
      they walk, O LORD, in the light of your presence.

16 They rejoice daily in your Name; *
      they are jubilant in your righteousness.

17 For you are the glory of their strength, *
      and by your favor our might is exalted.

18 Truly, the LORD is our ruler; *
      the Holy One of Israel is our King.

Epiphany Blessed are the people who know the festal shout! they walk, O LORD, in the light of your presence.

Pentecost Righteousness and justice, O God, are the foundations of your throne.

Psalm 98 *Cantate Domino*

The throne of God and of the Lamb will be in it, and his servants will worship him; they will see his face. Rev. 22:3-4

Epiphany In righteousness shall God judge the world and the peoples with equity.

Pentecost Shout with joy before the King, the Lord.

1 Sing to the LORD a new song, *
>   for he has done marvelous things.

2 With his right hand and his holy arm *
>   has he won for himself the victory.

3 The LORD has made known his victory; *
>   his righteousness has he openly shown
>   in the sight of the nations.

4 He remembers his mercy and faithfulness
> to the house of Israel, *
>   and all the ends of the earth have seen
>   the victory of our God.

5 Shout with joy to the LORD, all you lands; *
>   lift up your voice, rejoice, and sing.

6 Sing to the LORD with the harp, *
>   with the harp and the voice of song.

7 With trumpets and the sound of the horn *
>   shout with joy before the King, the LORD.

8 Let the sea make a noise and all that is in it, *
>   the lands and those who dwell therein.

9 Let the rivers clap their hands, *
>   and let the hills ring out with joy before the LORD,
>   when he comes to judge the earth.

10 In righteousness shall he judge the world *
>   and the peoples with equity.

Epiphany In righteousness shall God judge the world and the peoples with equity.

Pentecost Shout with joy before the King, the Lord.

Reading One

Responsory One (Ps. 18:49)
I will confess you, O Lord
> **– among the people.**
I will sing praise to you
> **– among the people.**
Glory to the Father and to the Son and to the Holy Spirit.
I will confess you, O Lord
> **– among the people.**

The First Canticle – Song of Transformation *Laetabitur deserta*
(Isaiah 35:1-7,10)
Epiphany They shall see the glory of the Lord, the majesty of our God.
Pentecost The ransomed of God shall return with singing, with
everlasting joy upon their heads.

The wilderness and the dry land shall be glad, *
> the desert shall rejoice and blossom;

It shall blossom abundantly, *
> and rejoice with joy and singing.

They shall see the glory of the Lord, *
> the majesty of our God.

Strengthen the weary hands, *
> and make firm the feeble knees.

Say to the anxious, "Be strong, do not fear! *
> Here is your God, coming with judgment to save you."

Then shall the eyes of the blind be opened, *
> and the ears of the deaf be unstopped.

Then shall the lame leap like a deer, *
> and the tongue of the speechless sing for joy.

For waters shall break forth in the wilderness *
> and streams in the desert;

The burning sand shall become a pool *
> and the thirsty ground, springs of water.

The ransomed of God shall return with singing, *
> with everlasting joy upon their heads.

Joy and gladness shall be theirs, *
> and sorrow and sighing shall flee away.

Epiphany They shall see the glory of the Lord, the majesty of our God.
Pentecost The ransomed of God shall return with singing, with everlasting joy upon their heads.

Reading Two

Responsory Two (Ps. 61:3, 4)
You, O Lord, have been my refuge
    – I will dwell in your house for ever.
I will take refuge under your wings
    – I will dwell in your house for ever.
Glory to the Father and to the Son and to the Holy Spirit.
You, O Lord, have been my refuge
    – I will dwell in your house for ever.

The Gospel Canticle – The Song of Zechariah
Epiphany God will shine on those who dwell in darkness and the shadow of death, and guide our feet into the way of peace.
Pentecost God promised to show mercy to our ancestors and to remember his holy covenant.

Litany
For families destroyed by addiction, for social workers and guidance counsellors, for spiritual directors and those discerning vocational calls.
Lord, have mercy.
For the blind and the deaf, for the crippled and deformed, for the abused and neglected.
Christ, have mercy.
For prisoners of war, for soldiers engaged in military combat, for peacemakers and justice seekers.
Lord, have mercy.

Invitation to the Lord's Prayer Rooted in the Father's steadfast love, we ask the Father to deepen our stability in God.

Collect *From the proper of the day or*
O God, the author of peace and lover of concord, to know you is eternal life and to serve you is perfect freedom: Defend us, your humble servants, in all assaults of our enemies; that we, surely trusting in your defense, may not fear the power of any adversaries; through the might of Jesus Christ our Lord. Amen.

The Blessing
May we be obedient, be ready for every good work, speak evil of no one, avoid quarreling, be gentle, and show every courtesy to everyone. **Amen**

Tuesday Week 4 Noonday Prayer

Officiant: O God, make speed to save us.

People: **O Lord, make haste to help us.**

Officiant and People **Glory to the Father... Alleluia.**

Hymn O God of truth *Hymnal 22*

Psalm 119 Resh *Vide humilitatem*

Sanctify them in the truth; your word is truth. Jn. 17:17

Epiphany Let all who seek you, O God, rejoice and be glad in you.

Pentecost See how I love your commandments! O LORD, in your mercy, preserve me.

153 Behold my affliction and deliver me, *
    for I do not forget your law.

154 Plead my cause and redeem me; *
    according to your promise, give me life.

155 Deliverance is far from the wicked, *
    for they do not study your statutes.

156 Great is your compassion, O LORD; *
    preserve my life, according to your judgments.

157 There are many who persecute and oppress me, *
    yet I have not swerved from your decrees.

158 I look with loathing at the faithless, *
    for they have not kept your word.

159 See how I love your commandments! *
    O LORD, in your mercy, preserve me.

160 The heart of your word is truth; *
    all your righteous judgments endure for evermore.

Psalm 54 *Deus, in nomine*

Do not be afraid, little flock, for it is your Father's good pleasure to give you the kingdom. Lk. 12:32

1 Save me, O God, by your Name; *
    in your might, defend my cause.

2 Hear my prayer, O God; *
    give ear to the words of my mouth.

3 For the arrogant have risen up against me,
    and the ruthless have sought my life, *
        those who have no regard for God.

4 Behold, God is my helper; *
      it is the Lord who sustains my life.

5 Render evil to those who spy on me; *
      in your faithfulness, destroy them.

6 I will offer you a freewill sacrifice *
      and praise your Name, O LORD, for it is good.

7 For you have rescued me from every trouble, *
      and my eye has seen the ruin of my foes.

Psalm 70 *Deus, in adjutorium*

Will not God grant justice to his chosen ones who cry to him day and night? Lk. 18:7

1 Be pleased, O God, to deliver me; *
      O LORD, make haste to help me.

2 Let those who seek my life be ashamed
   and altogether dismayed; *
      let those who take pleasure in my misfortune
      draw back and be disgraced.

3 Let those who say to me "Aha!" and gloat over me turn back, *
      because they are ashamed.

4 Let all who seek you rejoice and be glad in you; *
      let those who love your salvation say for ever,
      "Great is the LORD!"

5 But as for me, I am poor and needy; *
      come to me speedily, O God.

6 You are my helper and my deliverer; *
      O LORD, do not tarry.

Epiphany Let all who seek you, O God, rejoice and be glad in you.
Pentecost See how I love your commandments! O LORD, in your
mercy, preserve me.

Reading Proverbs 3: 15-17
Wisdom is more precious than jewels, and nothing you desire can
compare with her. Long life is in her right hand; in her left hand are
riches and honor. Her ways are ways of pleasantness, and all her paths
are peace.

Verse and Response
Put your neck under the yoke of wisdom.
Let your souls receive instruction.

The Short Litany and the Lord's Prayer

The Collect Grant, Lord God, to all who have been baptized into the death and resurrection of your son Jesus Christ, that, as we have put away the old life of sin, so we may be renewed in the spirit of our minds, and live in righteousness and true holiness; through Jesus Christ our Lord, who lives and reigns with you, in the unity of the Holy Spirit, one God, now and forever. Amen.

Let us bless the Lord.
Thanks be to God.

Tuesday Week 4 Evening Prayer

Officiant: O God, make speed to save us.
People: **O Lord, make haste to help us.**
Officiant and People **Glory to the Father... Alleluia.**

Hymn Christ mighty Savior *Hymnal 33*

Psalm 89 Part II A *Tunc locutus es*
The Holy Spirit descended upon him in bodily form like a dove. Lk. 3:22

Epiphany With my holy oil have I anointed him; my faithfulness and love shall be with him.
Pentecost I have sworn an oath to David my servant, I will establish his line forever.

19 You spoke once in a vision and said to your faithful people: *
    "I have set the crown upon a warrior
    and have exalted one chosen out of the people.

20 I have found David my servant; *
    with my holy oil have I anointed him.

21 My hand will hold him fast *
    and my arm will make him strong.

22 No enemy shall deceive him, *
    nor any wicked man bring him down.

23 I will crush his foes before him *
    and strike down those who hate him.

24 My faithfulness and love shall be with him, *
    and he shall be victorious through my Name.

25 I shall make his dominion extend *
    from the Great Sea to the River.

26 He will say to me, 'You are my Father, *
    my God, and the rock of my salvation.'

27 I will make him my firstborn *
    and higher than the kings of the earth.

28 I will keep my love for him for ever, *
    and my covenant will stand firm for him.

29 I will establish his line for ever *
    and his throne as the days of heaven."

Epiphany With my holy oil have I anointed him; my faithfulness and love shall be with him.

Pentecost I have sworn an oath to David my servant, I will establish his line forever.

Psalm 89 Part II B *Si autem*

They will not leave within you one stone upon another;
because you did not recognize the time of your visitation from God. Lk. 19:44

Epiphany David's line shall endure for ever and his throne as the sun before me.

Pentecost Blessed is the coming kingdom of our ancestor David! Hosanna in the highest heaven!

30 "If his children forsake my law *
    and do not walk according to my judgments;

31 If they break my statutes *
    and do not keep my commandments;

32 I will punish their transgressions with a rod *
    and their iniquities with the lash;

33 But I will not take my love from him, *
    nor let my faithfulness prove false.

34 I will not break my covenant, *
    nor change what has gone out of my lips.

35 Once for all I have sworn by my holiness: *
    'I will not lie to David.

36 His line shall endure for ever *
    and his throne as the sun before me;

37 It shall stand fast for evermore like the moon, *
    the abiding witness in the sky.'"

38 But you have cast off and rejected your anointed; *
    you have become enraged at him.

39 You have broken your covenant with your servant, *
    defiled his crown, and hurled it to the ground.

40 You have breached all his walls *
    and laid his strongholds in ruins.

41 All who pass by despoil him; *
    he has become the scorn of his neighbors.

42 You have exalted the right hand of his foes *
    and made all his enemies rejoice.

43 You have turned back the edge of his sword *
    and have not sustained him in battle.

44 You have put an end to his splendor *
    and cast his throne to the ground.

45 You have cut short the days of his youth *
    and have covered him with shame.

Epiphany David's line shall endure for ever and his throne as the sun before me.
Pentecost Blessed is the coming kingdom of our ancestor David! Hosanna in the highest heaven!

Psalm 89 Part II C *Usquequo, Domine*
The Son of Man will be handed over to the Gentiles;
and he will be mocked and insulted and spat upon. Lk. 18:32

Epiphany I will cause a righteous Branch to spring up for David; and he shall execute justice and righteousness in the land.
Pentecost A fountain shall be opened for the house of David and the inhabitants of Jerusalem, to cleanse them from sin and impurity.

46 How long will you hide yourself, O LORD?
    will you hide yourself for ever? *
      how long will your anger burn like fire?

47 Remember, LORD, how short life is, *
      how frail you have made all flesh.

48 Who can live and not see death? *
      who can save himself from the power of the grave?

49 Where, Lord, are your loving-kindnesses of old, *
      which you promised David in your faithfulness?

50 Remember, Lord, how your servant is mocked, *
    how I carry in my bosom the taunts of many peoples,

51 The taunts your enemies have hurled, O LORD, *
    which they hurled at the heels of your anointed.

52 Blessed be the LORD for evermore! *
    Amen, I say, Amen.

Epiphany I will cause a righteous Branch to spring up for David; and he shall execute justice and righteousness in the land.
Pentecost A fountain shall be opened for the house of David and the inhabitants of Jerusalem, to cleanse them from sin and impurity.

Reading

Responsory (Ps. 16:9)
My heart is glad
        – and my spirit rejoices.
My body shall rest in hope
        – and my spirit rejoices.
Glory to the Father and to the Son and to the Holy Spirit.
My heart is glad
        – and my spirit rejoices.

The Gospel Canticle – The Song of Mary
Epiphany I came into the world for judgment so that those who do not see may see, and those who do see may become blind.
Pentecost All generations will call me blessed: the Almighty has done great things for me.

Litany
For persons contemplating suicide, for all who have lost hope, for those living on the margins.
Lord, have mercy.
For persons tempted to compromise their values, for victims of senseless crimes, for all living with unresolved issues.
Christ, have mercy.
For children who have died, for survivors of unexpected deaths, for parents who bury their children.
Lord, have mercy.

Invitation to the Lord's Prayer With Christ who humbled himself by becoming a servant, let us offer ourselves to the Father in humble prayer.

Collect *From the proper of the day or*

Be our light in the darkness, O Lord, and in your great mercy defend us from all perils and dangers of this night; for the love of your only Son, our Savior Jesus Christ. Amen.

The Blessing

May our mutual love continue. Let us not neglect to show hospitality to strangers, for by doing that some have entertained angels without knowing it. **Amen**

Wednesday Week 4 Morning Prayer

Officiant: Lord, open our lips.

People: **And our mouth shall proclaim your praise.**

Officiant and People **Glory to the Father... Alleluia.**

The Invitatory Psalm 95

All nations will be blessed in God's people: Come let us worship.

Hymn Thy strong word *Hymnal 381*

Psalm 66 *Jubilate Deo*

You have given him authority over all people,
to give eternal life to all whom you have given him. Jn. 17:2

Epiphany Come now and see the works of God, how wonderful he is in his doing toward all people.

Pentecost Come and listen, all you who fear God, and I will tell you what he has done for me.

1   Be joyful in God, all you lands; *
      sing the glory of his Name;
      sing the glory of his praise.

2   Say to God, "How awesome are your deeds! *
      because of your great strength
      your enemies cringe before you.

3   All the earth bows down before you, *
      sings to you, sings out your Name."

4   Come now and see the works of God, *
      how wonderful he is in his doing toward all people.

5   He turned the sea into dry land,
      so that they went through the water on foot, *
      and there we rejoiced in him.

6 In his might he rules for ever;
   his eyes keep watch over the nations; *
      let no rebel rise up against him.

7 Bless our God, you peoples; *
      make the voice of his praise to be heard;

8 Who holds our souls in life, *
      and will not allow our feet to slip.

9 For you, O God, have proved us; *
      you have tried us just as silver is tried.

10 You brought us into the snare; *
      you laid heavy burdens upon our backs.

11 You let enemies ride over our heads;
   we went through fire and water; *
      but you brought us out into a place of refreshment.

12 I will enter your house with burnt-offerings
   and will pay you my vows, *
      which I promised with my lips
      and spoke with my mouth when I was in trouble.

13 I will offer you sacrifices of fat beasts
   with the smoke of rams; *
      I will give you oxen and goats.

14 Come and listen, all you who fear God, *
      and I will tell you what he has done for me.

15 I called out to him with my mouth, *
      and his praise was on my tongue.

16 If I had found evil in my heart, *
      the Lord would not have heard me;

17 But in truth God has heard me; *
      he has attended to the voice of my prayer.

18 Blessed be God, who has not rejected my prayer, *
      nor withheld his love from me.

Epiphany Come now and see the works of God, how wonderful he is in his doing toward all people.
Pentecost Come and listen, all you who fear God, and I will tell you what he has done for me.

Psalm 50 *Deus deorum*

You, then, that teach others, will you not teach yourself? Rm. 2:21

Epiphany I will make myself known among you, when I judge you.
Pentecost I desire mercy more than sacrifice, and the knowledge of
God more than burnt offerings.

1 The LORD, the God of gods, has spoken; *
    he has called the earth
    from the rising of the sun to its setting.

2 Out of Zion, perfect in its beauty, *
    God reveals himself in glory.

3 Our God will come and will not keep silence; *
    before him there is a consuming flame,
    and round about him a raging storm.

4 He calls the heavens and the earth from above *
    to witness the judgment of his people.

5 "Gather before me my loyal followers, *
    those who have made a covenant with me
    and sealed it with sacrifice."

6 Let the heavens declare the rightness of his cause; *
    for God himself is judge.

7 Hear, O my people, and I will speak:
    "O Israel, I will bear witness against you; *
    for I am God, your God.

8 I do not accuse you because of your sacrifices; *
    your offerings are always before me.

9 I will take no bull-calf from your stalls, *
    nor he-goats out of your pens;

10 For all the beasts of the forest are mine, *
    the herds in their thousands upon the hills.

11 I know every bird in the sky, *
    and the creatures of the fields are in my sight.

12 If I were hungry, I would not tell you, *
    for the whole world is mine and all that is in it.

13 Do you think I eat the flesh of bulls, *
    or drink the blood of goats?

14 Offer to God a sacrifice of thanksgiving *
　　and make good your vows to the Most High.

15 Call upon me in the day of trouble; *
　　I will deliver you, and you shall honor me."

16 But to the wicked God says: *
　　"Why do you recite my statutes,
　　and take my covenant upon your lips;

17 Since you refuse discipline, *
　　and toss my words behind your back?

18 When you see a thief, you make him your friend, *
　　and you cast in your lot with adulterers.

19 You have loosed your lips for evil, *
　　and harnessed your tongue to a lie.

20 You are always speaking evil of your brother *
　　and slandering your own mother's son.

21 These things you have done, and I kept still, *
　　and you thought that I am like you."

22 I have made my accusation; *
　　I have put my case in order before your eyes.

23 Consider this well, you who forget God, *
　　lest I rend you and there be none to deliver you.

24 Whoever offers me the sacrifice of thanksgiving
　　honors me; *
　　　　but to those who keep in my way
　　　　will I show the salvation of God."

Epiphany I will make myself known among you, when I judge you.
Pentecost I desire mercy more than sacrifice, and the knowledge of
God more than burnt offerings.

Psalm 67 *Deus misereatur*
I thank my God through Jesus Christ for all of you,
because your faith is proclaimed throughout the world. Rm 1:8
Epiphany Show us the light of your countenance and come to us.
Pentecost May the Lord's face shine upon us, and be gracious to us.

1　May God be merciful to us and bless us, *
　　show us the light of his countenance and come to us.

2 Let your ways be known upon earth, *
   your saving health among all nations.

3 Let the peoples praise you, O God; *
   let all the peoples praise you.

4 Let the nations be glad and sing for joy, *
   for you judge the peoples with equity
   and guide all the nations upon earth.

5 Let the peoples praise you, O God; *
   let all the peoples praise you.

6 The earth has brought forth her increase; *
   may God, our own God, give us his blessing.

7 May God give us his blessing, *
   and may all the ends of the earth stand in awe of him.

Epiphany Show us the light of your countenance and come to us.
Pentecost May the Lord's face shine upon us, and be gracious to us.

Reading One

Responsory One (Ps. 61:8)
Day by day
   – I will fulfill my vows.
I will sing the praise of your Name
   – I will fulfill my vows.
Glory to the Father and to the Son and to the Holy Spirit.
Day by day
   – I will fulfill my vows.

The First Canticle – A Song of Praise *Benedictus es Domine*
(Song of the Three Young Men, 29-34)
Epiphany Nations shall come to your light, and kings to the brightness of your dawn.
Pentecost Ascribe to the LORD the glory due his Name; worship the LORD in the beauty of holiness.

Glory to you, Lord God of our fathers; *
   you are worthy of praise; glory to you.

Glory to you for the radiance of your holy Name; *
   we will praise you and highly exalt you for ever.

Glory to you in the splendor of your temple; *
   on the throne of your majesty, glory to you.

Glory to you, seated between the Cherubim; *
    we will praise you and highly exalt you for ever.

Glory to you, beholding the depths; *
    in the high vault of heaven, glory to you.

Glory to you, Father, Son, and Holy Spirit; *
    we will praise you and highly exalt you for ever.
(The Gloria is not said with this canticle.)

Epiphany Nations shall come to your light, and kings to the brightness of your dawn.
Pentecost Ascribe to the LORD the glory due his Name; worship the LORD in the beauty of holiness.

Reading Two

Responsory Two (Ps. 63:1)
O God, you are my God
    – eagerly I seek you.
My soul thirsts for you
    – eagerly I seek you.
Glory to the Father and to the Son and to the Holy Spirit.
O God, you are my God
    – eagerly I seek you.

The Gospel Canticle – The Song of Zechariah
Epiphany God the only Son, who is close to the Father's heart, has made God known.
Pentecost God set us free to worship him without fear, holy and righteous in his sight.

Litany
For the mission of the Church, that in faithful witness it may preach the Gospel to the ends of the earth, we pray to you, O Lord.
Lord, have mercy.
For all who live and work in this community [especially _____], we pray to you, O Lord.
Christ, have mercy.
For all who have commended themselves to our prayers; for our families, friends, and neighbors; that being freed from anxiety, they may live in joy, peace, and health, we pray to you, O Lord.
Lord, have mercy.

Invitation to the Lord's Prayer Obedient with the obedient Christ, we seek to do the Father's will.

The Collect *From the proper of the day or*

O God, you have made of one blood all the peoples of the earth, and sent your blessed Son to preach peace to those who are far off and to those who are near: Grant that people everywhere may seek after you and find you; bring the nations into your fold; pour out your Spirit upon all flesh; and hasten the coming of your kingdom; through Jesus Christ our Lord. Amen.

The Blessing

May we continually offer a sacrifice of praise to God, that is, the fruit of lips that confess his name. **Amen**

Wednesday Week 4 Noonday Prayer

Officiant: O God, make speed to save us.
People: **O Lord, make haste to help us.**
Officiant and People **Glory to the Father... Alleluia.**

Hymn Holy Ghost, dispel our sadness *Hymnal 515*

Psalm 119 Shin *Principes persecuti sunt*
I have said this to you, so that in me you may have peace. Jn. 16:33

Epiphany I always sing the praise of your Name, and day by day I will fulfill my vows.

Pentecost You, O Lord, have been our refuge, a strong tower against the enemy.

161 Rulers have persecuted me without a cause, *
    but my heart stands in awe of your word.

162 I am as glad because of your promise *
    as one who finds great spoils.

163 As for lies, I hate and abhor them, *
    but your law is my love.

164 Seven times a day do I praise you, *
    because of your righteous judgments.

165 Great peace have they who love your law; *
    for them there is no stumbling block.

166 I have hoped for your salvation, O LORD, *
    and have fulfilled your commandments.

167 I have kept your decrees *
    and I have loved them deeply.

168 I have kept your commandments and decrees, *
    for all my ways are before you.

Psalm 61 *Exaudi, Deus*

*How often have I desired to gather your children together
as a hen gathers her brood under her wings. Lk. 13:34*

1 Hear my cry, O God, *
    and listen to my prayer.

2 I call upon you from the ends of the earth
with heaviness in my heart; *
    set me upon the rock that is higher than I.

3 For you have been my refuge, *
    a strong tower against the enemy.

4 I will dwell in your house for ever; *
    I will take refuge under the cover of your wings.

5 For you, O God, have heard my vows; *
    you have granted me the heritage
    of those who fear your Name.

6 Add length of days to the king's life; *
    let his years extend over many generations.

7 Let him sit enthroned before God for ever; *
    bid love and faithfulness watch over him.

8 So will I always sing the praise of your Name, *
    and day by day I will fulfill my vows.

Psalm 53 *Dixit insipiens*

*Since all have sinned and fall short of the glory of God;
they are now justified by his grace as a gift. Rm. 3:23*

1 The fool has said in his heart, "There is no God." *
    All are corrupt and commit abominable acts;
    there is none who does any good.

2 God looks down from heaven upon us all, *
    to see if there is any who is wise,
    if there is one who seeks after God.

3 Every one has proved faithless;
all alike have turned bad; *
    there is none who does good; no, not one.

4 Have they no knowledge, those evildoers *
    who eat up my people like bread
    and do not call upon God?

5 See how greatly they tremble,
    such trembling as never was; *
        for God has scattered the bones of the enemy;
        they are put to shame, because God has rejected them.

6 Oh, that Israel's deliverance would come out of Zion! *
    when God restores the fortunes of his people
    Jacob will rejoice and Israel be glad.

Epiphany I always sing the praise of your Name, and day by day I will fulfill my vows.
Pentecost You, O Lord, have been our refuge, a strong tower against the enemy.

Reading Isaiah 14: 1-3
The Lord will have compassion on Jacob and will again choose Israel, and will set them in their own land; and aliens will join them and attach themselves to the house of Jacob. And the nations will take them and bring them to their place, and the house of Israel will possess the nations as male and female slaves in the Lord's land; they will take captive those who were their captors, and rule over those who oppressed them.

Verse and Response
The Lord will vindicate his people.
And have compassion on his servants.

The Short Litany and the Lord's Prayer

The Collect Almighty Father, whose blessed Son before his passion prayed for his disciples that they might be one, as you and he are one: Grant that your Church, being bound together in love and obedience to you, may be united in one body by the one Spirit; that the world may believe in him who you have sent, your Son Jesus Christ our Lord; who lives and reigns with you, in the unity of the Holy Spirit, one God, now and for ever. Amen.

Let us bless the Lord.
Thanks be to God.

Wednesday Week 4 Evening Prayer

Officiant: O God, make speed to save us.

People: **O Lord, make haste to help us.**

Officiant and People **Glory to the Father... Alleluia.**

Hymn Fairest Lord Jesus *Hymnal 383*

Psalm 25 A *Ad te, Domine, levavi*

All who exalt themselves will be humbled, and all who humble themselves will be exalted. Mt. 23:12

Epiphany The Lord guides the humble in doing right and teaches his way to the lowly.

Pentecost Show me your ways, O LORD, and teach me your paths.

1 To you, O LORD, I lift up my soul;
   my God, I put my trust in you; *
      let me not be humiliated,
      nor let my enemies triumph over me.

2 Let none who look to you be put to shame; *
      let the treacherous be disappointed in their schemes.

3 Show me your ways, O LORD, *
      and teach me your paths.

4 Lead me in your truth and teach me, *
      for you are the God of my salvation;
      in you have I trusted all the day long.

5 Remember, O LORD, your compassion and love, *
      for they are from everlasting.

6 Remember not the sins of my youth and my transgressions; *
      remember me according to your love
      and for the sake of your goodness, O LORD.

7 Gracious and upright is the LORD; *
      therefore he teaches sinners in his way.

8 He guides the humble in doing right *
      and teaches his way to the lowly.

Epiphany The Lord guides the humble in doing right and teaches his way to the lowly.

Pentecost Show me your ways, O LORD, and teach me your paths.

Psalm 25 B *Universae viae Domini*
Blessed are the meek, for they will inherit the earth. Mt. 5:5

Epiphany My eyes are ever looking to the LORD.
Pentecost The LORD is a friend to those who fear him.

9   All the paths of the LORD are love and faithfulness *
    to those who keep his covenant and his testimonies.

10 For your Name's sake, O LORD, *
    forgive my sin, for it is great.

11 Who are they who fear the LORD? *
    he will teach them the way that they should choose.

12 They shall dwell in prosperity, *
    and their offspring shall inherit the land.

13 The LORD is a friend to those who fear him *
    and will show them his covenant.

14 My eyes are ever looking to the LORD, *
    for he shall pluck my feet out of the net.

15 Turn to me and have pity on me, *
    for I am left alone and in misery.

16 The sorrows of my heart have increased; *
    bring me out of my troubles.

17 Look upon my adversity and misery *
    and forgive me all my sin.

18 Look upon my enemies, for they are many, *
    and they bear a violent hatred against me.

19 Protect my life and deliver me; *
    let me not be put to shame, for I have trusted in you.

20 Let integrity and uprightness preserve me, *
    for my hope has been in you.

21 Deliver Israel, O God, *
    out of all his troubles.

Epiphany My eyes are ever looking to the LORD.
Pentecost The LORD is a friend to those who fear him.

Psalm 27 *Dominus illuminatio*

Do not be afraid, for I have overcome the world Jn. 16:33

Epiphany I shall not fear for you, O Lord, are my saving light.

Pentecost One thing I seek: to behold the fair beauty of the LORD and to seek him in his temple

1 The LORD is my light and my salvation;
   whom then shall I fear? *
       the LORD is the strength of my life;
       of whom then shall I be afraid?

2 When evildoers came upon me to eat up my flesh, *
       it was they, my foes and my adversaries,
       who stumbled and fell.

3 Though an army should encamp against me, *
       yet my heart shall not be afraid;

4 And though war should rise up against me, *
       yet will I put my trust in him.

5 One thing have I asked of the LORD;
   one thing I seek; *
       that I may dwell in the house of the LORD
       all the days of my life;

6 To behold the fair beauty of the LORD *
       and to seek him in his temple.

7 For in the day of trouble he shall keep me safe
   in his shelter; *
       he shall hide me in the secrecy of his dwelling
       and set me high upon a rock.

8 Even now he lifts up my head *
       above my enemies round about me.

9 Therefore I will offer in his dwelling an oblation
   with sounds of great gladness; *
       I will sing and make music to the LORD.

10 Hearken to my voice, O LORD, when I call; *
       have mercy on me and answer me.

11 You speak in my heart and say, "Seek my face." *
       Your face, LORD, will I seek.

12 Hide not your face from me, *
       nor turn away your servant in displeasure.

13 You have been my helper;
    cast me not away; *
      do not forsake me, O God of my salvation.

14 Though my father and my mother forsake me, *
    the LORD will sustain me.

15 Show me your way, O LORD; *
    lead me on a level path, because of my enemies.

16 Deliver me not into the hand of my adversaries, *
    for false witnesses have risen up against me,
    and also those who speak malice.

17 What if I had not believed
    that I should see the goodness of the LORD *
    in the land of the living!

18 O tarry and await the LORD'S pleasure;
    be strong, and he shall comfort your heart; *
    wait patiently for the LORD.

Epiphany I shall not fear for you, O Lord, are my saving light.
Pentecost One thing I seek: to behold the fair beauty of the LORD and to seek him in his temple

Reading

Responsory (Ps. 9:1; Ps. 26:6)
I will sing a song of thanksgiving
    — I will recount all your wonderful deeds.
I will go in procession around your altar
    — I will recount all your wonderful deeds.
Glory to the Father and to the Son and to the Holy Spirit.
I will sing a song of thanksgiving
    — I will recount all your wonderful deeds.

The Gospel Canticle – The Song of Mary
Epiphany Let us open our eyes to the deifying light, let us hear with attentive ears the warning which the divine voice cries daily to us.
Pentecost God has cast the powerful from their thrones and has lifted up the lowly.

Litany

For those who do not yet believe, and for those who have lost their faith, we that they may receive the light of the Gospel, we pray to you, O Lord.
Lord, have mercy.
For a blessing upon all human labor, and for the right use of the riches of creation, that the world may be freed from poverty, famine, and disaster, we pray to you, O Lord.
Christ, have mercy.
For all who have died in the communion of your Church, and those whose faith is known to you alone, that, with all the saints, they may have rest in that place where there is no pain or grief, but life eternal, we pray to you, O Lord.
Lord, have mercy.

Invitation to the Lord's Prayer Exercising our baptismal anointing as priests, we sanctify the Father's name.

The Collect *From the proper of the day or*
Keep watch, dear Lord, with those who work, or watch, or weep this night, and give your angels charge over those who sleep. Tend the sick, Lord Christ; give rest to the weary, bless the dying, soothe the suffering, pity the afflicted, shield the joyous; and all for your love's sake. Amen.

The Blessing

May we do good and share what we have, for such sacrifices are pleasing to God. **Amen**

Thursday Week 4 Morning Prayer

Officiant: Lord, open our lips.
People: **And our mouth shall proclaim your praise.**
Officiant and People **Glory to the Father... Alleluia.**

The Invitatory Psalm 122

The new Jerusalem is the Bride of the Lamb: Come let us worship Christ the Lord.

Hymn Now that the daylight fills the sky *Hymnal 4*

Psalm 43 *Judica me, Deus*
We are going up to Jerusalem, and everything that is written about the Son of Man by the prophets will be accomplished. Lk. 18:31

Epiphany The path of the righteous is like the light of dawn, which shines brighter and brighter until full day.
Pentecost Send out your light and your truth, O Lord, that they may lead me.

1 Give judgment for me, O God,
   and defend my cause against an ungodly people; *
       deliver me from the deceitful and the wicked.

2 For you are the God of my strength;
   why have you put me from you? *
       and why do I go so heavily
       while the enemy oppresses me?

3 Send out your light and your truth, that they may lead me, *
       and bring me to your holy hill
       and to your dwelling;

4 That I may go to the altar of God,
   to the God of my joy and gladness; *
       and on the harp I will give thanks to you, O God my God.

5 Why are you so full of heaviness, O my soul? *
       and why are you so disquieted within me?

6 Put your trust in God; *
       for I will yet give thanks to him,
       who is the help of my countenance, and my God.

Epiphany The path of the righteous is like the light of dawn, which
shines brighter and brighter until full day.
Pentecost Send out your light and your truth, O Lord, that they may
lead me.

Psalm 26 *Judica me, Domine*

The blood of Christ will purify our conscience from dead works to worship the living God. Heb. 9:14
Epiphany I will wash my hands in innocence, O LORD, that I may go
in procession round your altar.
Pentecost I have trusted in the Lord and have not faltered.

1 Give judgment for me, O LORD,
   for I have lived with integrity; *
       I have trusted in the Lord and have not faltered.

2 Test me, O LORD, and try me; *
       examine my heart and my mind.

3 For your love is before my eyes; *
       I have walked faithfully with you.

4 I have not sat with the worthless, *
       nor do I consort with the deceitful.

5 I have hated the company of evildoers; *
     I will not sit down with the wicked.

6 I will wash my hands in innocence, O LORD, *
     that I may go in procession round your altar,

7 Singing aloud a song of thanksgiving *
     and recounting all your wonderful deeds.

8 LORD, I love the house in which you dwell *
     and the place where your glory abides.

9 Do not sweep me away with sinners, *
     nor my life with those who thirst for blood,

10 Whose hands are full of evil plots, *
     and their right hand full of bribes.

11 As for me, I will live with integrity; *
     redeem me, O LORD, and have pity on me.

12 My foot stands on level ground; *
     in the full assembly I will bless the LORD.

Epiphany I will wash my hands in innocence, O LORD, that I may go
in procession round your altar.
Pentecost I have trusted in the Lord and have not faltered.

Psalm 149 *Cantate Domino*
All who see them shall acknowledge that they are a people whom the Lord has blessed. Is. 61: 9
Epiphany The LORD takes pleasure in his people and adorns the poor
with victory.
Pentecost Let the children of Zion be joyful in their King.

1 Hallelujah!
   Sing to the LORD a new song; *
     sing his praise in the congregation of the faithful.

2 Let Israel rejoice in his Maker; *
     let the children of Zion be joyful in their King.

3 Let them praise his Name in the dance; *
     let them sing praise to him with timbrel and harp.

4 For the LORD takes pleasure in his people *
     and adorns the poor with victory.

5 Let the faithful rejoice in triumph; *
     let them be joyful on their beds.

6 Let the praises of God be in their throat *
      and a two-edged sword in their hand;

7 To wreak vengeance on the nations *
      and punishment on the peoples;

8 To bind their kings in chains *
      and their nobles with links of iron;

9 To inflict on them the judgment decreed; *
      this is glory for all his faithful people.
      Hallelujah!

Epiphany The LORD takes pleasure in his people and adorns the poor
with victory.
Pentecost Let the children of Zion be joyful in their King.

Reading One

Responsory One (Ps. 145:16)
You open your hand
      − we are filled with good things.
You give us our food in due season
      − we are filled with good things.
Glory to the Father and to the Son and to the Holy Spirit.
You open your hand
      − we are filled with good things.

The First Canticle − Song of Divine Charity *Carissimi diligamus invicem*
(1 John 4:7-11)
Epiphany Whoever loves a brother or sister lives in the light, and in
such a person there is no cause for stumbling.
Pentecost In this is love, not that we loved God but that God loved us
and sent his Son that sins might be forgiven.

Beloved, let us love one another, *
      for love is of God.

Whoever does not love does not know God, *
      for God is Love.

In this the love of God was revealed among us, *
      that God sent his only Son into the world,
      so that we might live through Jesus Christ.

In this is love, not that we loved God but that God loved us *
      and sent his Son that sins might be forgiven.

Beloved, since God loved us so much, *
> we ought also to love one another.

For if we love one another, God abides in us, *
> and God's love will be perfected in us.

Epiphany Whoever loves a brother or sister lives in the light, and in such a person there is no cause for stumbling.
Pentecost In this is love, not that we loved God but that God loved us and sent his Son that sins might be forgiven.

Reading Two

Responsory Two (Ps. 104:34)
I will sing to the Lord
> **– as long as I live.**

I will praise my God
> **– as long as I live.**

Glory to the Father and to the Son and to the Holy Spirit.
I will sing to the Lord
> **– as long as I live.**

The Gospel Canticle – The Song of Zechariah
Epiphany While you have the light, believe in the light, so that you may become children of light.
Pentecost God will shine on those who dwell in darkness and the shadow of death, and guide our feet into the way of peace.

Litany
For animals, those who are loved and those who are abused, for wildlife living in threatened habitats, for fish and water mammals endangered by human activity.
Lord, have mercy.
For forests and jungles threatened by human intrusion, for waters and air polluted by industry, for lands polluted by chemical waste.
Christ, have mercy.
For birds and insects whose migratory paths are compromised, for animals confined in zoos and displays, for endangered species.
Lord, have mercy.

Invitation to the Lord's Prayer O Holy Father, trusting not in our merit but obedient to the command of your Son, our Lord Jesus Christ, we dare to say.

The Collect *From the proper of the day or*
Heavenly Father, in you we live and move and have our being: We humbly pray you so to guide and govern us by your Holy Spirit, that in all the cares and occupations of our life we may not forget you, but may remember that we are ever walking in your sight; through Jesus Christ our Lord. Amen.

The Blessing
May the God of all grace, who has called us to his eternal glory in Christ, restore, support, strengthen, and establish us. **Amen**

Thursday Week 4 Noonday Prayer

Officiant: O God, make speed to save us.
People: **O Lord, make haste to help us.**
Officiant and People **Glory to the Father... Alleluia.**

Hymn As now the sun shines down at noon *Hymnal 18 Thursday Verse*

Psalm 119 Taw *Appropinquet deprecatio*
Rejoice with me, for I have found my sheep that was lost. Lk. 15:6
Epiphany The light of the righteous rejoices, but the lamp of the wicked goes out.
Pentecost The LORD is King for ever and ever.

169 Let my cry come before you, O LORD; *
    give me understanding, according to your word.

170 Let my supplication come before you; *
    deliver me, according to your promise.

171 My lips shall pour forth your praise, *
    when you teach me your statutes.

172 My tongue shall sing of your promise, *
    for all your commandments are righteous.

173 Let your hand be ready to help me, *
    for I have chosen your commandments.

174 I long for your salvation, O LORD, *
    and your law is my delight.

175 Let me live, and I will praise you, *
    and let your judgments help me.

176 I have gone astray like a sheep that is lost; *
    search for your servant,
    for I do not forget your commandments.

Psalm 10 A *Ut quid, Domine?*

When they hand you over, do not worry about how you are to speak or what you are to say;
for what you are to say will be given to you at that time. Mt. 10:19

1 Why do you stand so far off, O LORD, *
and hide yourself in time of trouble?

2 The wicked arrogantly persecute the poor, *
but they are trapped in the schemes they have devised.

3 The wicked boast of their heart's desire; *
the covetous curse and revile the LORD.

4 The wicked are so proud that they care not for God; *
their only thought is, "God does not matter."

5 Their ways are devious at all times;
your judgments are far above out of their sight; *
they defy all their enemies.

6 They say in their heart, "I shall not be shaken; *
no harm shall happen to me ever."

7 Their mouth is full of cursing, deceit, and oppression; *
under their tongue are mischief and wrong.

8 They lurk in ambush in public squares
and in secret places they murder the innocent; *
they spy out the helpless.

9 They lie in wait, like a lion in a covert;
they lie in wait to seize upon the lowly; *
they seize the lowly and drag them away in their net.

10 The innocent are broken and humbled before them; *
the helpless fall before their power.

11 They say in their heart, "God has forgotten; *
he hides his face; he will never notice."

Psalm 10 B *Exsurge Domine Deus*

You will be hated by all because of my name.
But the one who endures to the end will be saved. Mt. 10:22

12 Rise up, O LORD;
lift up your hand, O God; *
do not forget the afflicted.

13 Why should the wicked revile God? *
why should they say in their heart, "You do not care"?

14 Surely, you behold trouble and misery; *
    you see it and take it into your own hand.

15 The helpless commit themselves to you, *
    for you are the helper of orphans.

16 Break the power of the wicked and evil; *
    search out their wickedness until you find none.

17 The LORD is King for ever and ever; *
    the ungodly shall perish from his land.

18 The LORD will hear the desire of the humble; *
    you will strengthen their heart and your ears shall hear;

19 To give justice to the orphan and oppressed, *
    so that mere mortals may strike terror no more.

Epiphany The light of the righteous rejoices, but the lamp of the wicked goes out.
Pentecost The LORD is King for ever and ever.

Reading John 6: 53-56
Jesus said to them, "Very truly, I tell you, unless you eat the flesh of the Son of Man and drink his blood, you have no life in you. Those who eat my flesh and drink my blood have eternal life, and I will raise them up on the last day; for my flesh is true food and my blood is true drink. Those who eat my flesh and drink my blood abide in me, and I in them."

Verse and Response
As the Father has loved me, so I have loved you.
Abide in my love.

The Short Litany and the Lord's Prayer

The Collect God our Father, whose Son our Lord Jesus Christ in a wonderful Sacrament has left us a memorial of his passion: Grant us so to venerate the sacred mysteries of his Body and Blood, that we may ever perceive within ourselves the fruit of his redemption; who lives and reigns with you and the Holy Spirit, one God, for ever and ever. Amen.

Let us bless the Lord.
Thanks be to God.

Thursday Week 4 Evening Prayer

Officiant: O God, make speed to save us.

People: **O Lord, make haste to help us.**

Officiant and People **Glory to the Father... Alleluia.**

Hymn Creating God, your fingers trace *Hymnal 394*

Psalm 80 A *Qui regis Israel*

Just as the branch cannot bear fruit by itself unless it abides in the vine,
neither can you unless you abide in me. Jn. 15:4

Epiphany Shine forth, you that are enthroned upon the cherubim.
Pentecost Restore us, O God of hosts; show the light of your
countenance, and we shall be saved.

1   Hear, O Shepherd of Israel, leading Joseph like a flock; *
    shine forth, you that are enthroned upon the cherubim.

2   In the presence of Ephraim, Benjamin, and Manasseh, *
    stir up your strength and come to help us.

3   Restore us, O God of hosts; *
    show the light of your countenance, and we shall be saved.

4   O LORD God of hosts, *
    how long will you be angered
    despite the prayers of your people?

5   You have fed them with the bread of tears; *
    you have given them bowls of tears to drink.

6   You have made us the derision of our neighbors, *
    and our enemies laugh us to scorn.

7   Restore us, O God of hosts; *
    show the light of your countenance, and we shall be saved.

Epiphany Shine forth, you that are enthroned upon the cherubim.
Pentecost Restore us, O God of hosts; show the light of your
countenance, and we shall be saved.

Psalm 80 B *Vineam de Aegypto*

Those who abide in me and I in them bear much fruit,
because apart from me you can do nothing. Jn. 15:5

Epiphany Give us life, that we may call upon your Name.
Pentecost O God of hosts, preserve what your right hand has planted.

8   You have brought a vine out of Egypt; *
    you cast out the nations and planted it.

9 You prepared the ground for it; *
    it took root and filled the land.

10 The mountains were covered by its shadow *
    and the towering cedar trees by its boughs.

11 You stretched out its tendrils to the Sea *
    and its branches to the River.

12 Why have you broken down its wall, *
    so that all who pass by pluck off its grapes?

13 The wild boar of the forest has ravaged it, *
    and the beasts of the field have grazed upon it.

14 Turn now, O God of hosts, look down from heaven;
    behold and tend this vine; *
    preserve what your right hand has planted.

15 They burn it with fire like rubbish; *
    at the rebuke of your countenance let them perish.

16 Let your hand be upon the man of your right hand, *
    the son of man you have made so strong for yourself.

17 And so will we never turn away from you; *
    give us life, that we may call upon your Name.

18 Restore us, O LORD God of hosts; *
    show the light of your countenance, and we shall be saved.

Epiphany Give us life, that we may call upon your Name.
Pentecost O God of hosts, preserve what your right hand has planted.

Psalm 126 *In convertendo*

*I consider that the sufferings of this present time are not worth comparing
with the glory about to be revealed to us. Rm. 8:18*

Epiphany They said among the nations, "The LORD has done great things for them."
Pentecost Those who sowed with tears will reap with songs of joy.

1 When the LORD restored the fortunes of Zion, *
    then were we like those who dream.

2 Then was our mouth filled with laughter, *
    and our tongue with shouts of joy.

3 Then they said among the nations, *
    "The LORD has done great things for them."

4 The LORD has done great things for us, *
     and we are glad indeed.

5 Restore our fortunes, O LORD, *
     like the watercourses of the Negev.

6 Those who sowed with tears *
     will reap with songs of joy.

7 Those who go out weeping, carrying the seed, *
     will come again with joy, shouldering their sheaves.

Epiphany They said among the nations, "The LORD has done great
things for them."
Pentecost Those who sowed with tears will reap with songs of joy.

Reading

Responsory (Ps. 81:10, 16)
Israel I would feed
        – with the finest wheat.
Open your mouth wide and I will fill it
        – with the finest wheat.
Glory to the Father and to the Son and to the Holy Spirit.
Israel I would feed
        – with the finest wheat.

The Gospel Canticle – The Song of Mary
Epiphany I am the light of the world. We must work the works of him
who sent me while it is day.
Pentecost God has fed the hungry with good things, and the rich he
has sent away empty.

Litany
For those who pray and those who struggle with prayer, for those who
read and those who cannot read, for those who work and those who
cannot find work.
Lord, have mercy.
For those who serve God as religious and clergy, for those who support
worship as printers and writers, for those who lead worship and
communities without worship leaders.
Christ, have mercy.
For those who die alone and forgotten, for those who mourn without
comfort, for those who lost faith because of death.
Lord, have mercy.

Invitation to the Lord's Prayer Having offered God the sacrifice of our day, we ask the Father to make us holy.

The Collect *From the proper of the day or*
Lord Jesus, stay with us, for evening is at hand and the day is past; be our companion in the way, kindle our hearts, and awaken hope, that we may know you as you are revealed in Scripture and the breaking of bread. Grant this for the sake of your love. Amen.

The Blessing
May we not imitate what is evil but imitate what is good for whoever does good is from God.
Amen

Friday Week 4 Morning Prayer

Officiant: Lord, open our lips.
People: **And our mouth shall proclaim your praise.**
Officiant and People **Glory to the Father... Alleluia.**

The Invitatory Psalm 95
God accepts a contrite heart: Come let us worship.

Hymn We sing the praise of him who died *Hymnal 471*

Psalm 44 A *Deus, auribus*
He humbled himself and became obedient to the point of death—
even death on a cross. Phil 2:8

Epiphany I will turn the darkness before them into light.
Pentecost My humiliation is daily before me, and shame has covered my face.

1 We have heard with our ears, O God,
   our forefathers have told us, *
       the deeds you did in their days,
       in the days of old.

2 How with your hand you drove the peoples out
   and planted our forefathers in the land; *
       how you destroyed nations and made your people flourish.

3 For they did not take the land by their sword,
   nor did their arm win the victory for them; *
       but your right hand, your arm,
       and the light of your countenance,
       because you favored them.

4 You are my King and my God; *
   you command victories for Jacob.

5 Through you we pushed back our adversaries; *
   through your Name we trampled
   on those who rose up against us.

6 For I do not rely on my bow, *
   and my sword does not give me the victory.

7 Surely, you gave us victory over our adversaries *
   and put those who hate us to shame.

8 Every day we gloried in God, *
   and we will praise your Name for ever.

9 Nevertheless, you have rejected and humbled us *
   and do not go forth with our armies.

10 You have made us fall back before our adversary, *
   and our enemies have plundered us.

11 You have made us like sheep to be eaten *
   and have scattered us among the nations.

12 You are selling your people for a trifle *
   and are making no profit on the sale of them.

13 You have made us the scorn of our neighbors, *
   a mockery and derision to those around us.

14 You have made us a byword among the nations, *
   a laughing-stock among the peoples.

15 My humiliation is daily before me, *
   and shame has covered my face;

16 Because of the taunts of the mockers and blasphemers, *
   because of the enemy and avenger.

Epiphany I will turn the darkness before them into light.
Pentecost My humiliation is daily before me, and shame has covered
my face.

Psalm 44 B *Haec omnia venerunt*
Jesus threw himself on the ground and prayed that,
if it were possible, the hour might pass from him. Mk. 14:35

Epiphany Your light shall rise in the darkness and your gloom be like
the noonday.

Pentecost Awake, O Lord! why are you sleeping? Arise! do not reject us for ever.

17 All this has come upon us; *
> yet we have not forgotten you,
> nor have we betrayed your covenant.

18 Our heart never turned back, *
> nor did our footsteps stray from your path;

19 Though you thrust us down into a place of misery, *
> and covered us over with deep darkness.

20 If we have forgotten the Name of our God, *
> or stretched out our hands to some strange god,

21 Will not God find it out? *
> for he knows the secrets of the heart.

22 Indeed, for your sake we are killed all the day long; *
> we are accounted as sheep for the slaughter.

23 Awake, O Lord! why are you sleeping? *
> Arise! do not reject us for ever.

24 Why have you hidden your face *
> and forgotten our affliction and oppression?

25 We sink down into the dust; *
> our body cleaves to the ground.

26 Rise up, and help us, *
> and save us, for the sake of your steadfast love.

Epiphany Your light shall rise in the darkness and your gloom be like the noonday.
Pentecost Awake, O Lord! why are you sleeping? Arise! do not reject us for ever.

Psalm 137 *Super flumina*

The women who had come with Jesus from Galilee followed,
and they saw the tomb and how his body was laid. Lk. 23:5

Epiphany I form light and create darkness, I make weal and create woe; I the Lord do all these things.
Pentecost If I forget you, O Jerusalem, let my right hand forget its skill.

1 By the waters of Babylon we sat down and wept, *
> when we remembered you, O Zion.

2 As for our harps, we hung them up *
    on the trees in the midst of that land.

3 For those who led us away captive asked us for a song,
    and our oppressors called for mirth: *
      "Sing us one of the songs of Zion."

4 How shall we sing the LORD'S song *
    upon an alien soil?

5 If I forget you, O Jerusalem, *
    let my right hand forget its skill.

6 Let my tongue cleave to the roof of my mouth
    if I do not remember you, *
      if I do not set Jerusalem above my highest joy.

7 Remember the day of Jerusalem, O LORD,
    against the people of Edom, *
      who said, "Down with it! down with it!
      even to the ground!"

8 O Daughter of Babylon, doomed to destruction, *
      blessed the one who pays you back
      for what you have done to us!

9 Blessed shall he be who takes your little ones, *
    and dashes them against the rock!

Epiphany I form light and create darkness, I make weal and create woe;
I the Lord do all these things.
Pentecost If I forget you, O Jerusalem, let my right hand forget its skill.

Reading One

Responsory One (Ps. 5:3; Ps. 42:8; Ps. 63:7)
Early in the morning
      – I will remember you.
You have been my helper
      – I will remember you.
Glory to the Father and to the Son and to the Holy Spirit.
Early in the morning
      – I will remember you.

The First Canticle – Song of the Lord, our Rock *Audite caeli*
(Deuteronomy 32: 1-6)

Epiphany May my teaching drop like the rain, my speech condense like the dew.

Pentecost You shielded us, cared for us, and guarded us as the apple of your eye.

Give ear, O heavens, and I will speak; *
    let the earth hear the words of my mouth.

May my teaching drop like the rain, *
    my speech condense like the dew;

Like gentle rain on grass, *
    like showers on new growth.

For I will proclaim the name of the LORD; *
    ascribe greatness to our God!

The Rock, his work is perfect, *
    and all his ways are just.

A faithful God, without deceit, *
    just and upright is he.

His degenerate children have dealt falsely with him, *
    a perverse and crooked generation.

Do you thus repay the Lord, *
    O foolish and senseless people?

Is not he your father, who created you, *
    who made you and established you?

Remember the days of old, *
    consider the years long past.

Ask your father, and he will inform you; *
    your elders, and they will tell you.

When the Most High apportioned the nations, *
    when he divided humankind,

He fixed the boundaries of the peoples *
    according to the number of the gods;

The Lord's own portion was his people, *
    Jacob his allotted share.

He sustained him in a desert land, *
    in a howling wilderness waste.

He shielded him, cared for him, *
    guarded him as the apple of his eye.

As an eagle stirs up its nest, *
    and hovers over its young;

As it spreads its wings, takes them up, *
    and bears them aloft on its pinions,

The Lord alone guided him; *
    no foreign god was with him.

Epiphany May my teaching drop like the rain, my speech condense like the dew.

Pentecost You shielded us, cared for us, and guarded us as the apple of your eye.

Reading Two

Responsory Two (Ps. 59:19, 20)
You have become my stronghold
    − a refuge in the day of my trouble.
I will sing to you, my Strength
    − a refuge in the day of my trouble.
Glory to the Father and to the Son and to the Holy Spirit.
You have become my stronghold
    − a refuge in the day of my trouble.

The Gospel Canticle − The Song of Zechariah
Epiphany The light shines in the darkness and the darkness did not overcome the light.

Pentecost You, O child, will give people knowledge of salvation by the forgiveness of their sins.

Litany
Comfort and liberate the lonely, the bereaved and the oppressed.
Lord, have mercy.
Keep in safety those who travel and all who are in peril.
Christ, have mercy.
Heal the sick in body, mind or spirit and provide for the homeless, the hungry and the destitute.
Lord, have mercy.

Invitation to the Lord's Prayer As agents of reconciliation, we ask the Father's forgiveness that we may forgive others.

The Collect *From the proper of the day or*
Lord Jesus Christ, you stretched out your arms of love on the hard wood of the cross that everyone might come within the reach of your saving embrace: So clothe us in your Spirit that we, reaching forth our hands in love, may bring those who do not know you to the knowledge and love of you; for the honor of your Name. Amen.

The Blessing
May we pray that all may go well with us and that we may be in good health, just as it is well with our souls. **Amen**

Friday Week 4 Noonday Prayer

Officiant: O God, make speed to save us.
People: **O Lord, make haste to help us.**
Officiant and People **Glory to the Father... Alleluia.**

Hymn Jesus our mighty Lord *Hymnal 478*

Psalm 60 *Deus, repulisti nos*
At that moment the curtain of the temple was torn in two, from top to bottom.
The earth shook, and the rocks were split. Mt. 2&;51

Epiphany All the nations of the earth shall gain blessing for themselves through your offspring.
Pentecost Save us by your right hand, O God, that those who are dear to you may be delivered.

1 O God, you have cast us off and broken us; *
    you have been angry;
    oh, take us back to you again.

2 You have shaken the earth and split it open; *
    repair the cracks in it, for it totters.

3 You have made your people know hardship; *
    you have given us wine that makes us stagger.

4 You have set up a banner for those who fear you, *
    to be a refuge from the power of the bow.

5 Save us by your right hand and answer us, *
    that those who are dear to you may be delivered.

6 God spoke from his holy place and said: *
    "I will exult and parcel out Shechem;
    I will divide the valley of Succoth.

7 Gilead is mine and Manasseh is mine; *
   Ephraim is my helmet and Judah my scepter.

8 Moab is my wash-basin,
   on Edom I throw down my sandal to claim it, *
   and over Philistia will I shout in triumph."

9 Who will lead me into the strong city? *
   who will bring me into Edom?

10 Have you not cast us off, O God? *
   you no longer go out, O God, with our armies.

11 Grant us your help against the enemy, *
   for vain is the help of man.

12 With God we will do valiant deeds, *
   and he shall tread our enemies under foot.

Psalm 55 A *Exaudi, Deus*

*In his anguish Jesus prayed more earnestly, and his sweat became like great drops of blood
falling down on the ground. Lk. 22:44*

1 Hear my prayer, O God; *
   do not hide yourself from my petition.

2 Listen to me and answer me; *
   I have no peace, because of my cares.

3 I am shaken by the noise of the enemy *
   and by the pressure of the wicked;

4 For they have cast an evil spell upon me *
   and are set against me in fury.

5 My heart quakes within me, *
   and the terrors of death have fallen upon me.

6 Fear and trembling have come over me, *
   and horror overwhelms me.

7 And I said, "Oh, that I had wings like a dove! *
   I would fly away and be at rest.

8 I would flee to a far-off place *
   and make my lodging in the wilderness.

9 I would hasten to escape *
   from the stormy wind and tempest."

10 Swallow them up, O Lord;
   confound their speech; *
      for I have seen violence and strife in the city.

11 Day and night the watchmen
   make their rounds   upon her walls, *
      but trouble and misery are in the midst of her.

Psalm 55 B *Insidiae in vitalibus*

They asked Peter, "You are not also one of his disciples, are you?"
He denied it and said, "I am not." Jn. 18: 25

12 There is corruption at her heart; *
   her streets are never free of oppression and deceit.

13 For had it been an adversary who taunted me,
   then I could have borne it; *
      or had it been an enemy who vaunted himself against me,
      then I could have hidden from him.

14 But it was you, a man after my own heart, *
   my companion, my own familiar friend.

15 We took sweet counsel together, *
   and walked with the throng in the house of God.

16 Let death come upon them suddenly;
   let them go down alive into the grave; *
      for wickedness is in their dwellings, in their very midst.

17 But I will call upon God, *
   and the LORD will deliver me.

18 In the evening, in the morning, and at noonday,
   I will complain and lament, *
      and he will hear my voice.

19 He will bring me safely back
   from the battle waged against me; *
      for there are many who fight me.

20 God, who is enthroned of old, will hear me
   and bring them down; *
      they never change; they do not fear God.

21 My companion stretched forth his hand against his comrade; *
   he has broken his covenant.

22 His speech is softer than butter, *
   but war is in his heart.

23 His words are smoother than oil, *
    but they are drawn swords.

24 Cast your burden upon the LORD,
  and he will sustain you; *
    he will never let the righteous stumble.

25 For you will bring the bloodthirsty and deceitful *
    down to the pit of destruction, O God.

26 They shall not live out half their days, *
    but I will put my trust in you.

Epiphany All the nations of the earth shall gain blessing for themselves through your offspring.
Pentecost Save us by your right hand, O God, that those who are dear to you may be delivered.

Reading John 19: 31-34
Since it was the day of Preparation, the Jews did not want the bodies left on the cross during the sabbath, especially because that sabbath was a day of great solemnity. So they asked Pilate to have the legs of the crucified men broken and the bodies removed. Then the soldiers came and broke the legs of the first and of the other who had been crucified with him. But when they came to Jesus and saw that he was already dead, they did not break his legs. Instead, one of the soldiers pierced his side with a spear, and at once blood and water came out.

Verse and Response
Out of the believer's heart.
Shall flow rivers of living water.

The Short Litany and the Lord's Prayer

The Collect Lord God, whose blessed Son our Savior gave his body to be whipped and his face to be spit upon: Give us grace to accept joyfully the sufferings of the present time, confident of the glory that shall be revealed; through Jesus Christ your Son our Lord, who lives and reigns with you and the Holy Spirit, one God, for ever and ever. Amen.

Let us bless the Lord.
Thanks be to God.

Friday Week 4 Evening Prayer

Officiant: O God, make speed to save us.

People: **O Lord, make haste to help us.**

Officiant and People **Glory to the Father... Alleluia.**

Hymn O Love of God, how strong and true *Hymnal 456*

Psalm 22 A *Deus, Deus meus*

At three o'clock Jesus cried out with a loud voice,
"My God, my God, why have you forsaken me?" Mk 15:34

Epiphany Out of his anguish he shall see light; he shall find satisfaction through his knowledge.

Pentecost We beheld him despised and rejected, a man of sorrows, and acquainted with grief.

1 My God, my God, why have you forsaken me? *
  and are so far from my cry
  and from the words of my distress?

2 O my God, I cry in the daytime, but you do not answer; *
  by night as well, but I find no rest.

3 Yet you are the Holy One, *
  enthroned upon the praises of Israel.

4 Our forefathers put their trust in you; *
  they trusted, and you delivered them.

5 They cried out to you and were delivered; *
  they trusted in you and were not put to shame.

6 But as for me, I am a worm and no man, *
  scorned by all and despised by the people.

7 All who see me laugh me to scorn; *
  they curl their lips and wag their heads, saying,

8 "He trusted in the LORD; let him deliver him; *
  let him rescue him, if he delights in him."

9 Yet you are he who took me out of the womb, *
  and kept me safe upon my mother's breast.

10 I have been entrusted to you ever since I was born; *
  You were my God
  when I was still in my mother's womb.

11 Be not far from me, for trouble is near, *
  and there is none to help.

12 Many young bulls encircle me; *
   strong bulls of Bashan surround me.

13 They open wide their jaws at me, *
   like a ravening and a roaring lion.

14 I am poured out like water;
   all my bones are out of joint; *
      my heart within my breast is melting wax.

15 My mouth is dried out like a pot-sherd;
   my tongue sticks to the roof of my mouth; *
      and you have laid me in the dust of the grave.

16 Packs of dogs close me in,
   and gangs of evildoers circle around me; *
      they pierce my hands and my feet;
      I can count all my bones.

17 They stare and gloat over me; *
   they divide my garments among them;
      they cast lots for my clothing.

18 Be not far away, O LORD; *
   you are my strength; hasten to help me.

19 Save me from the sword, *
   my life from the power of the dog.

20 Save me from the lion's mouth, *
   my wretched body from the horns of wild bulls.

Epiphany Out of his anguish he shall see light; he shall find satisfaction through his knowledge.
Pentecost We beheld him despised and rejected, a man of sorrows, and acquainted with grief.

Psalm 22 B *Narrabo nomen tuum*

Jesus said to the women, "Do not be afraid; go and tell my brothers to go to Galilee; there they will see me." Mt. 28:10

Epiphany Kingship belongs to the LORD; he rules over the nations.
Pentecost Surely he has borne our infirmities and carried our diseases.

21 I will declare your Name to my brethren; *
   in the midst of the congregation I will praise you.

22 Praise the LORD, you that fear him; *
   stand in awe of him, O offspring of Israel;
      all you of Jacob's line, give glory.

23 For he does not despise nor abhor the poor in their poverty;
  neither does he hide his face from them; *
    but when they cry to him he hears them.

24 My praise is of him in the great assembly; *
    I will perform my vows
    in the presence of those who worship him.

25 The poor shall eat and be satisfied,
  and those who seek the LORD shall praise him: *
    "May your heart live for ever!"

26 All the ends of the earth shall remember
  and turn to the LORD, *
    and all the families of the nations shall bow before him.

27 For kingship belongs to the LORD; *
    he rules over the nations.

28 To him alone all who sleep in the earth
  bow down in worship; *
    all who go down to the dust fall before him.

29 My soul shall live for him;
  my descendants shall serve him; *
    they shall be known as the LORD'S for ever.

30 They shall come and make known to a people yet unborn *
    the saving deeds that he has done.

Epiphany Kingship belongs to the LORD; he rules over the nations.
Pentecost Surely he has borne our infirmities and carried our diseases.

Psalm 102 *Domine, exaudi*
Just as the sufferings of Christ are abundant for us,
so also our consolation is abundant through Christ. 2 Cor. 1:5

Epiphany They will declare in Zion the Name of the LORD when the peoples are gathered together to serve the LORD.
Pentecost You, O Lord, are always the same, and your years will never end.

1 LORD, hear my prayer, and let my cry come before you; *
    hide not your face from me in the day of my trouble.

2 Incline your ear to me; *
    when I call, make haste to answer me,

3 For my days drift away like smoke, *
    and my bones are hot as burning coals.

4 My heart is smitten like grass and withered, *
    so that I forget to eat my bread.

5 Because of the voice of my groaning *
    I am but skin and bones.

6 I have become like a vulture in the wilderness, *
    like an owl among the ruins.

7 I lie awake and groan; *
    I am like a sparrow, lonely on a house-top.

8 My enemies revile me all day long, *
    and those who scoff at me have taken an oath against me.

9 For I have eaten ashes for bread *
    and mingled my drink with weeping.

10 Because of your indignation and wrath *
    you have lifted me up and thrown me away.

11 My days pass away like a shadow, *
    and I wither like the grass.

12 But you, O LORD, endure for ever, *
    and your Name from age to age.

13 You will arise and have compassion on Zion,
    for it is time to have mercy upon her; *
    indeed, the appointed time has come.

14 For your servants love her very rubble, *
    and are moved to pity even for her dust.

15 The nations shall fear your Name, O LORD, *
    and all the kings of the earth your glory.

16 For the LORD will build up Zion, *
    and his glory will appear.

17 He will look with favor on the prayer of the homeless; *
    he will not despise their plea.

18 Let this be written for a future generation, *
    so that a people yet unborn may praise the LORD.

19 For the LORD looked down from his holy place on high; *
    from the heavens he beheld the earth;

20 That he might hear the groan of the captive *
    and set free those condemned to die;

21 That they may declare in Zion the Name of the LORD, *
    and his praise in Jerusalem;

22 When the peoples are gathered together, *
    and the kingdoms also, to serve the LORD.

23 He has brought down my strength before my time; *
    he has shortened the number of my days;

24 And I said, "O my God,
    do not take me away in the midst of my days; *
      your years endure throughout all generations.

25 In the beginning, O LORD,
    you laid the foundations of the earth, *
      and the heavens are the work of your hands;

26 They shall perish, but you will endure;
    they all shall wear out like a garment; *
      as clothing you will change them,
      and they shall be changed;

27 But you are always the same, *
    and your years will never end.

28 The children of your servants shall continue, *
    and their offspring shall stand fast in your sight."

Epiphany They will declare in Zion the Name of the LORD when the peoples are gathered together to serve the LORD.
Pentecost You, O Lord, are always the same, and your years will never end.

Reading

Responsory (Rm. 5:8, 9)
God proves his love for us
    – while we were sinners Christ died for us.
We have been justified by his blood
    – while we were sinners Christ died for us.
Glory to the Father and to the Son and to the Holy Spirit.
God proves his love for us
    – while we were sinners Christ died for us.

The Gospel Canticle – The Song of Mary
Epiphany Run while you have the light of life, lest the darkness of death overtake you.

Pentecost God has come to the help of his servant Israel, ever mindful of his merciful promise.

Litany
Guard and protect all children who are in danger.
Lord, have mercy.
Forgive our enemies, persecutors and slanderers, and turn their hearts.
Christ, have mercy.
Hear us as we remember those who have died (especially _____) and grant us with them a share in your eternal glory.
Lord, have mercy.

Invitation to the Lord's Prayer Seeking a deeper conversion of heart, we return to the Father seeking mercy.

The Collect *From the proper of the day or*
O God, you manifest in your servants the signs of your presence: Send forth upon us the spirit of love, that in companionship with one another your abounding grace may increase among us; through Jesus Christ our Lord. Amen.

The Blessing
May we not quench the Spirit, not despise the words of prophets, but test everything, hold fast to what is good and abstain from every form of evil. **Amen**

Saturday Week 4 Morning Prayer
Officiant: Lord, open our lips.
People: **And our mouth shall proclaim your praise.**
Officiant and People **Glory to the Father... Alleluia.**

The Invitatory Psalm 100
God's faithfulness endures from age to age: Come let us adore.

Hymn Sing my soul, his wondrous love *Hymnal 467*

Psalm 30 *Exaltabo te, Domine*
Jesus was put to death in the flesh, but made alive in the spirit,
in which also he went and made a proclamation to the spirits in prison. 1 Pt. 3:18-19
Epiphany O LORD my God, I will give you thanks for ever.
Pentecost O Lord my God, I cried out to you, and you restored me to health.

1 I will exalt you, O LORD,
    because you have lifted me up *
        and have not let my enemies triumph over me.

2 O LORD my God, I cried out to you, *
    and you restored me to health.

3 You brought me up, O LORD, from the dead; *
    you restored my life as I was going down to the grave.

4 Sing to the LORD, you servants of his; *
    give thanks for the remembrance of his holiness.

5 For his wrath endures but the twinkling of an eye, *
    his favor for a lifetime.

6 Weeping may spend the night, *
    but joy comes in the morning.

7 While I felt secure, I said,
    "I shall never be disturbed. *
    You, LORD, with your favor,
    made me as strong as the mountains."

8 Then you hid your face, *
    and I was filled with fear.

9 I cried to you, O LORD; *
    I pleaded with the Lord, saying,

10 "What profit is there in my blood, if I go down to the Pit? *
    will the dust praise you or declare your faithfulness?

11 Hear, O LORD, and have mercy upon me; *
    O LORD, be my helper."

12 You have turned my wailing into dancing; *
    you have put off my sack-cloth and clothed me with joy.

13 Therefore my heart sings to you without ceasing; *
    O LORD my God, I will give you thanks for ever.

Epiphany O LORD my God, I will give you thanks for ever.
Pentecost O Lord my God, I cried out to you, and you restored me to health.

Psalm 92 *Bonum est confiteri*
With gratitude in your hearts sing psalms, hymns, and spiritual songs to God. Eph. 3:16
Epiphany God anointed Jesus of Nazareth with the Holy Spirit and with power.
Pentecost We will tell of your loving kindness early in the morning, O Lord, and of your faithfulness in the night season.

1 It is a good thing to give thanks to the LORD, *
      and to sing praises to your Name, O Most High;

2 To tell of your loving-kindness early in the morning *
      and of your faithfulness in the night season;

3 On the psaltery, and on the lyre, *
      and to the melody of the harp.

4 For you have made me glad by your acts, O LORD; *
      and I shout for joy because of the works of your hands.

5 LORD, how great are your works! *
      your thoughts are very deep.

6 The dullard does not know,
   nor does the fool understand, *
      that though the wicked grow like weeds,
      and all the workers of iniquity flourish,

7 They flourish only to be destroyed for ever; *
      but you, O LORD, are exalted for evermore.

8 For lo, your enemies, O LORD,
   lo, your enemies shall perish, *
      and all the workers of iniquity shall be scattered.

9 But my horn you have exalted like the horns of wild bulls; *
      I am anointed with fresh oil.

10 My eyes also gloat over my enemies, *
      and my ears rejoice to hear the doom of the wicked
      who rise up against me.

11 The righteous shall flourish like a palm tree, *
      and shall spread abroad like a cedar of Lebanon.

12 Those who are planted in the house of the LORD *
      shall flourish in the courts of our God;

13 They shall still bear fruit in old age; *
      they shall be green and succulent;

14 That they may show how upright the LORD is, *
      my Rock, in whom there is no fault.

Epiphany God anointed Jesus of Nazareth with the Holy Spirit and
with power.
Pentecost We will tell of your loving kindness early in the morning, O
Lord, and of your faithfulness in the night season.

Psalm 143 *Domine, exaudi*

The Son of Man must undergo great suffering, and be killed,
and on the third day be raised. Lk. 9:22

Epiphany Help me, O Lord my God; save me for your mercy's sake.
Pentecost Let me hear of your loving-kindness in the morning, for I
put my trust in you.

1 LORD, hear my prayer,
and in your faithfulness heed my supplications; *
   answer me in your righteousness.

2 Enter not into judgment with your servant, *
   for in your sight shall no one living be justified.

3 For my enemy has sought my life;
he has crushed me to the ground; *
   he has made me live in dark places
   like those who are long dead.

4 My spirit faints within me; *
   my heart within me is desolate.

5 I remember the time past;
I muse upon all your deeds; *
   I consider the works of your hands.

6 I spread out my hands to you; *
   my soul gasps to you like a thirsty land.

7 O LORD, make haste to answer me; my spirit fails me; *
   do not hide your face from me
   or I shall be like those who go down to the Pit.

8 Let me hear of your loving-kindness in the morning,
for I put my trust in you; *
   show me the road that I must walk,
   for I lift up my soul to you.

9 Deliver me from my enemies, O LORD, *
   for I flee to you for refuge.

10 Teach me to do what pleases you, for you are my God; *
   let your good Spirit lead me on level ground.

11 Revive me, O LORD, for your Name's sake; *
   for your righteousness' sake, bring me out of trouble.

Epiphany Help me, O Lord my God; save me for your mercy's sake.

Pentecost Let me hear of your loving-kindness in the morning, for I put my trust in you.

Reading One

Responsory One (Ps. 30:3; Ps. 71:19)
You will restore my life
> **— you will bring me up from the deep places of the earth.**

You have done great things
> **— you will bring me up from the deep places of the earth.**

Glory to the Father and to the Son and to the Holy Spirit.
You will restore my life
> **— you will bring me up from the deep places of the earth.**

The First Canticle – Song of Jerusalem Betrothed *Propter Sion non tacebo*
(Isaiah 62:1-5)

Epiphany Jerusalem's vindication will shine out like the dawn, and her salvation like a burning torch.

Pentecost You shall be a crown of beauty in the hand of the Lord, and a royal diadem in the hand of your God.

For Zion's sake I will not keep silent, *
> and for Jerusalem's sake I will not rest,

Until her vindication shines out like the dawn, *
> and her salvation like a burning torch.

The nations shall see your vindication, *
> and all the kings your glory.

You shall be called by a new name *
> spoken by the mouth of the Lord.

You shall be a crown of beauty in the hand of the Lord, *
> and a royal diadem in the hand of your God.

You shall no more be termed "Forsaken," *
> and your land shall no more be termed "Desolate;"

You shall be called "My Delight," *
> and your land "Espoused".

For the Lord delights in you, *
> and your land shall be married.

For as a young man marries a young woman, *
> so shall your builder marry you,

And as the bridegroom rejoices over the bride, *
 so shall your God rejoice over you.

Epiphany Jerusalem's vindication will shine out like the dawn, and her salvation like a burning torch.
Pentecost You shall be a crown of beauty in the hand of the Lord, and a royal diadem in the hand of your God.

Reading Two

Responsory Two (Ps. 40:1, 2)
I waited patiently upon the Lord
 – God stooped to me.
The Lord lifted me out of the desolate pit
 – God stooped to me.
Glory to the Father and to the Son and to the Holy Spirit.
I waited patiently upon the Lord
 – God stooped to me.

The Gospel Canticle — The Song of Zechariah
Epiphany Wisdom is radiant and unfading, and she is easily discerned by those who love her, and is found by those who seek her.
Pentecost May you have all the riches of assured understanding and have the knowledge of God's mystery, that is, Christ himself, in whom are hidden all the treasures of wisdom and knowledge.

Litany
Give courage and faith to all who are disabled through injury or illness.
Lord, have mercy.
Befriend all who are anxious, lonely, despondent, or afraid.
Christ, have mercy.
Restore those with mental illness to clarity of mind and hopefulness of heart.
Lord, have mercy.

Invitation to the Lord's Prayer Magnifying the mercy of God, we offer thanks with all holy people.

The Collect *From the proper of the day or*
Almighty God, who after the creation of the world rested from all your works and sanctified a day of rest for all your creatures: Grant that we, putting away all earthly anxieties, may be duly prepared for the service of your sanctuary, and that our rest here upon earth may be a preparation for the eternal rest promised to your people in heaven; through Jesus Christ our Lord. Amen.

The Blessing

May the God of our Lord Jesus Christ, the Father of glory, give us a spirit of wisdom and revelation as we come to know God. **Amen**

Saturday Week 4 Noonday Prayer

Officiant: O God, make speed to save us.

People: **O Lord, make haste to help us.**

Officiant and People **Glory to the Father... Alleluia.**

Hymn Creator Spirit, by whose aid *Hymnal 500*

Psalm 37 A *Noli æmulari*
Blessed are the meek, for they will inherit the earth. Mt. 5:5

Epiphany The LORD loves justice; he does not forsake his faithful ones.

Pentecost The mouth of the righteous utters wisdom, and their tongue speaks what is right.

1 Do not fret yourself because of evildoers; *
>   do not be jealous of those who do wrong.

2 For they shall soon wither like the grass, *
>   and like the green grass fade away.

3 Put your trust in the LORD and do good; *
>   dwell in the land and feed on its riches.

4 Take delight in the LORD, *
>   and he shall give you your heart's desire.

5 Commit your way to the LORD and put your trust in him, *
>   and he will bring it to pass.

6 He will make your righteousness as clear as the light *
>   and your just dealing as the noonday.

7 Be still before the LORD *
>   and wait patiently for him.

8 Do not fret yourself over the one who prospers, *
>   the one who succeeds in evil schemes.

9 Refrain from anger, leave rage alone; *
>   do not fret yourself; it leads only to evil.

10 For evildoers shall be cut off, *
>   but those who wait upon the LORD shall possess the land.

11 In a little while the wicked shall be no more; *
    you shall search out their place, but they will not be there.

12 But the lowly shall possess the land; *
    they will delight in abundance of peace.

13 The wicked plot against the righteous *
    and gnash at them with their teeth.

14 The Lord laughs at the wicked, *
    because he sees that their day will come.

15 The wicked draw their sword and bend their bow
    to strike down the poor and needy, *
    to slaughter those who are upright in their ways.

16 Their sword shall go through their own heart, *
    and their bow shall be broken.

17 The little that the righteous has *
    is better than great riches of the wicked.

18 For the power of the wicked shall be broken, *
    but the LORD upholds the righteous.

Psalm 37 B *Novit Dominus*
May you be filled with the knowledge of God's will
in all spiritual wisdom and understanding. Col. 1:9

19 The LORD cares for the lives of the godly, *
    and their inheritance shall last for ever.

20 They shall not be ashamed in bad times, *
    and in days of famine they shall have enough.

21 As for the wicked, they shall perish, *
    and the enemies of the LORD,
    like the glory of the meadows, shall vanish;
    they shall vanish like smoke.

22 The wicked borrow and do not repay, *
    but the righteous are generous in giving.

23 Those who are blessed by God shall possess the land, *
    but those who are cursed by him shall be destroyed.

24 Our steps are directed by the LORD; *
    he strengthens those in whose way he delights.

25 If they stumble, they shall not fall headlong, *
    for the LORD holds them by the hand.

26 I have been young and now I am old, *
  but never have I seen the righteous forsaken,
  or their children begging bread.

27 The righteous are always generous in their lending, *
  and their children shall be a blessing.

28 Turn from evil, and do good, *
  and dwell in the land for ever.

29 For the LORD loves justice; *
  he does not forsake his faithful ones.

30 They shall be kept safe for ever, *
  but the offspring of the wicked shall be destroyed.

31 The righteous shall possess the land *
  and dwell in it for ever.

32 The mouth of the righteous utters wisdom, *
  and their tongue speaks what is right.

33 The law of their God is in their heart, *
  and their footsteps shall not falter.

Psalm 37 C *Considerat peccator*
Show how by your good life that your works are done with gentleness born of wisdom. Jm. 3:13

34 The wicked spy on the righteous *
  and seek occasion to kill them.

35 The LORD will not abandon them to their hand, *
  nor let them be found guilty when brought to trial.

36 Wait upon the LORD and keep his way; *
  he will raise you up to possess the land,
  and when the wicked are cut off, you will see it.

37 I have seen the wicked in their arrogance, *
  flourishing like a tree in full leaf.

38 I went by, and behold, they were not there; *
  I searched for them, but they could not be found.

39 Mark those who are honest;
  observe the upright; *
  for there is a future for the peaceable.

40 Transgressors shall be destroyed, one and all; *
  the future of the wicked is cut off.

41 But the deliverance of the righteous comes from the LORD; *
 he is their stronghold in time of trouble.

42 The LORD will help them and rescue them; *
 he will rescue them from the wicked and deliver them,
 because they seek refuge in him.

Epiphany The LORD loves justice; he does not forsake his faithful ones.

Pentecost The mouth of the righteous utters wisdom, and their tongue speaks what is right.

Reading Luke 2: 33-35

The child's father and mother were amazed at what was being said about him. Then Simeon blessed them and said to his mother Mary, "This child is destined for the falling and the rising of many in Israel, and to be a sign that will be opposed   so that the inner thoughts of many will be revealed—and a sword will pierce your own soul too."

Verse and Response
I will give you as a light to the nations.
That my salvation may reach to the end of the earth.

The Short Litany and the Lord's Prayer

The Collect Almighty God, who after the creation of the world rested from all your works and sanctified a day of rest for all your creatures: Grant that we, putting away all earthly anxieties, may be duly prepared for the service of your sanctuary, and that our rest here upon earth may be a preparation for the eternal rest promised to your people in heaven; through Jesus Christ our Lord. Amen.

Let us bless the Lord.
Thanks be to God.

The Proper of the Saints

January

January 12

Aelred

Cistercian Monk, Abbot of Rievaulx, 1167
Lesser Feast

From the Common of Monastics, page 687, with the following proper antiphons

Benedictus Antiphon God is friendship and all who abide in friendship abide in God and God in them.

Magnificat Antiphon You know, sweet Lord, how much I love them, how my heart goes out to them and melts for them. You know that I choose to serve with love.

Collect Almighty God, you endowed the abbot Aelred with the gift of Christian friendship and the wisdom to lead others in the way of holiness: Grant to your people that same spirit of mutual affection, that, in loving one another, we may know the love of Christ and rejoice in the gift of your eternal goodness; through the same Jesus Christ our Savior, who lives and reigns with you and the Holy Spirit, one God, now and for ever. Amen.

January 13

Hilary

Bishop of Poitiers and Teacher of the Faith, 367
Lesser Feast

From the Common of Teacher of the Faith, page 676

Collect Eternal Father, whose servant Hilary steadfastly confessed your Son Jesus Christ to be true God and true man: We beseech you to keep us firmly grounded in this faith; that we may rejoice to behold his face in heaven who humbled himself to bear our form upon earth, even the same your Son Jesus Christ our Lord, who lives and reigns with you and the Holy Spirit, one God, now and for ever. Amen.

January 15

Maur and Placid

Disciples of St. Benedict
Lesser Feast

From the Common of Monastics, page 687, with the following proper antiphons

Benedictus Antiphon Brother Maur, run as fast as you can, for Placid, who went to the lake to fetch water, has fallen in, and is carried off by the current.

Magnificat Antiphon Those who wait for the Lord shall renew their strength, they shall mount up with wings like eagles, they shall run and not be weary, they shall walk and not faint.

Collect O God, you have filled us with wonder by the example of monastic observance in the lives of your blessed confessors Maur and Placid. As we celebrate their memory and follow in their footsteps, may we come to share in their reward. Through Jesus Christ our Lord, who lives and reigns with you and Holy Spirit, one God, for ever and ever. Amen.

January 16
Richard Meux Benson
Professed Religious, Priest, Founder of the Society of St. John the Evangelist, 1915
Charles Gore
Founder of the Community of the Resurrection, Bishop of Worcester, of Birmingham, and of Oxford,1932
Lesser Feast

From the Common of Professed Religious, page 691

Collect Gracious God, you have inspired a rich variety of ministries in your Church: We give you thanks for Richard Meux Benson and Charles Gore, instruments in the revival of Anglican monasticism. Grant that we, following their example, may call for perennial renewal in your Church through conscious union with Christ, witnessing to the social justice that is a mark of the reign of our Savior Jesus, who is the light of the world; and who lives and reigns with you and the Holy Spirit, one God, for ever and ever. Amen.

January 17
Antony
Abbot in Egypt, 356
Lesser Feast

From the Common of Monastics, page 687, with the following proper antiphons

Benedictus Antiphon Antony maintained utter equilibrium, like one guided by reason; he urged everyone to prefer nothing in the world about the love of Christ.

Magnificat Antiphon When the monks heard of his approaching death, they wept and embraced and kissed the old man. But he, like one sailing from a foreign city to his own, exhorted them to live as though dying daily.

Collect O God, by your Holy Spirit you enabled your servant Antony to withstand the temptations of the world, the flesh, and the devil: Give us grace, with pure hearts and minds, to follow you, the only God; through Jesus Christ our Lord, who lives and reigns with you and the Holy Spirit, one God, for ever and ever. Amen.

January 18
The Confession of Saint Peter the Apostle
Major Feast
Morning Prayer

From the Common of the Apostles, page 648, with the following proper parts.
Invitatory Come let us worship Christ, the cornerstone of the Church.

Hymn You are the Christ, O Lord *Hymnal 254*

Antiphon 1 You are the Messiah, the Son of the living God.
Psalms from Sunday Week 1 Morning Prayer, page 130
Antiphon 2 You are Peter, and on this rock I will build my church.
Antiphon 3 I will give you the keys of the kingdom of heaven.

Reading One Ezekiel 3:4-11

Responsory One (Ez. 3:10; Mt. 16:17)
All my words that I shall speak to you
    – receive the word in your heart and hear it with your ears.
My Father in heaven has revealed his word to you
    – receive the word in your heart and hear it with your ears.
Glory to the Father and to the Son and to the Holy Spirit.
All my words that I shall speak to you
    – receive the word in your heart and hear it with your ears.

Reading Two Acts 10:34-44

Responsory Two (Acts 10:39, 35)
We are witnesses to all that Jesus did
    – He commanded us to preach the Gospel to the people.
Anyone who fears God and does what is right is acceptable to him
    – He commanded us to preach the Gospel to the people.
Glory to the Father and to the Son and to the Holy Spirit.
We are witnesses to all that Jesus did
    – He commanded us to preach the Gospel to the people.
    –

Benedictus Antiphon You are the Messiah, the Son of the living God. Blessed are you, Simon, son of Jonah! For flesh and blood has not revealed this to you, but my Father in heaven.

Collect Almighty Father, who inspired Simon Peter, first among the apostles, to confess Jesus as Messiah and Son of the living God: Keep your Church steadfast upon the rock of this faith, so that in unity and peace we may proclaim the one truth and follow the one Lord, our Savior Jesus Christ; who lives and reigns with you and the Holy Spirit, one God, now and for ever. Amen.

The Confession of Saint Peter the Apostle
Noonday Prayer

From the Common of the Apostles, page 650, with the following proper parts.

Reading 1 Peter 5: 1-3
Now as an elder myself and a witness of the sufferings of Christ, as well as one who shares in the glory to be revealed, I exhort the elders among you to tend the flock of God that is in your charge, exercising the oversight, not under compulsion but willingly, as God would have you do it—not for sordid gain but eagerly. Do not lord it over those in your charge, but be examples to the flock.

Verse and Response
I will give you shepherds after my own heart.
They will feed you with knowledge and understanding.

Collect *From Morning Prayer*

The Confession of Saint Peter the Apostle
Evening Prayer

From the Common of the Apostles, page 651, with the following proper parts.

Hymn You Are The Christ, O Lord *Hymnal 254*

Antiphon 1 Simon, son of John, do you love me more than these?
Psalms from the Common of Apostles Evening Prayer page 645
Antiphon 2 Lord, you know everything; you know that I love you.
Antiphon 3 You will stretch out your hands, and someone else will fasten a belt around you and take you where you do not wish to go.

Reading Ezekiel 34:11-16 or John 21:15-22

Responsory
If any want to become my followers
        − let them take up their cross and follow me.
You will stretch out your hands, and someone will take you where you do not wish to go.
        − let them take up their cross and follow me.

Glory to the Father and to the Son and to the Holy Spirit.
If any want to become my followers,
    – let them take up their cross and follow me.

Magnificat Antiphon "Lord, you know everything; you know that I love you." Jesus said to him, "Feed my sheep."

Collect *From Morning Prayer*

January 19
Wulfstan
Bishop of Worcester, 1095
Lesser Feast
From the Common of Pastors, page 669
Collect Almighty God, your only-begotten Son led captivity captive and gave gifts to your people: Multiply among us faithful pastors, who, like your holy bishop Wulfstan, will give courage to those who are oppressed and held in bondage; and bring us all, we pray, into the true freedom of your kingdom; through Jesus Christ our Lord, who lives and reigns with you and the Holy Spirit, one God, for ever and ever. Amen.

January 20
Fabian,
Bishop and Martyr of Rome, 250
From the Common of Martyrs, page 665
Collect O God, in your providence you singled out the holy martyr Fabian as worthy to be chief pastor of your people, and guided him so to strengthen your Church that it stood fast in the day of persecution: Grant that those whom you call to any ministry in the Church may be obedient to your call in all humility, and be enabled to carry out their tasks with diligence and faithfulness; through Jesus Christ our Lord, who lives and reigns with you and the Holy Spirit, one God, now and for ever. Amen.

January 21
Agnes
Martyr at Rome, 304
Lesser Feast
From the Common of Martyrs, page 665, with the following proper antiphons
Benedictus Antiphon Christ whom I desired is the one whom I see; Christ for whom I hoped I now possess; I am united in heaven with Christ whom on earth I loved with pure devotion.

Magnificat Antiphon As Agnes stood in the fire, she stretched out her hands and prayed to God: Almighty Lord, you are worthy to receive all adoration, fear and worship. I bless your holy name and I glorify you for ever and always.

Collect Almighty and everlasting God, you choose those whom the world deems powerless to put the powerful to shame: Grant us so to cherish the memory of your youthful martyr Agnes, that we may share her pure and steadfast faith in you; through Jesus Christ our Lord, who lives and reigns with you and the Holy Spirit, one God, for ever and ever. Amen.

January 22

Vincent
Deacon of Saragossa, and Martyr, 304
Lesser Feast
From the Common of Martyrs, page 665
Collect Almighty God, your deacon Vincent, upheld by you, was not terrified by threats nor overcome by torments: Strengthen us to endure all adversity with invincible and steadfast faith; through Jesus Christ our Lord, who lives and reigns with you and the Holy Spirit, one God, for ever and ever. Amen.

January 23

Phillips Brooks
Bishop of Massachusetts, 1893
Lesser Feast
From the Common of Pastors, page 669
Collect O everlasting God, you revealed truth to your servant Phillips Brooks, and so formed and molded his mind and heart that he was able to mediate that truth with grace and power: Grant, we pray, that all whom you call to preach the Gospel may steep themselves in your Word, and conform their lives to your will; through Jesus Christ our Lord, who lives and reigns with you and the Holy Spirit, one God, for ever and ever. Amen.

January 24

Florence Li Tim-Oi
First Woman Priest in the Anglican Communion, 1944
Lesser Feast
From the Common of Pastors, page 669, with the following proper antiphons
Benedictus Antiphon I am just an earthen vessel with God's treasure inside me.

Magnificat Antiphon No one can take away the peace that comes from completing one's responsibilities to history and fulfilling God's will.

Collect Gracious God, we thank you for calling Florence Li Tim-Oi, much-beloved daughter, to be the first woman to exercise the office of a priest in our Communion: By the grace of your Spirit inspire us to follow her example, serving your people with patience and happiness all our days, and witnessing in every circumstance to our Savior Jesus Christ, who lives and reigns with you and the same Spirit, one God, for ever and ever. Amen.

January 25
The Conversion of Saint Paul the Apostle
Major Feast
Morning Prayer
From the Common of the Apostles, page 648, with the following proper parts
Invitatory Come let us worship our God as we celebrate the conversion of the Teacher of the Gentiles.

Hymn We Sing The Glorious Conquest *Hymnal 255*

Antiphon 1 As Saul was going along and approaching Damascus, suddenly a light from heaven flashed around him.
Psalms from Sunday Week One Morning Prayer page 134
Antiphon 2 He fell to the ground and heard a voice saying to him, "Saul, Saul, why do you persecute me?"
Antiphon 3 I am Jesus, whom you are persecuting. Get up and enter the city, and you will be told what you are to do.

Reading One Isaiah 45:18-25

Responsory One (Is. 49:1; Is. 50:4)
The Lord called me before I was born
    – while I was in my mother's womb he named me.
The Lord God has given me the tongue of a teacher
    – while I was in my mother's womb he named me.
Glory to the Father and to the Son and to the Holy Spirit.
The Lord called me before I was born
    – while I was in my mother's womb he named me.

Canticle of the Mystery of Christ *In mysterio Christi*
(Ephesians 3: 5-10)
Antiphon I have become a servant of the Gospel according to the gift of God's grace.

The mystery of Christ was not made known to humankind *
    in former generations.

It has now been revealed *
    to his holy apostles and prophets by the Spirit.

The Gentiles have become fellow-heirs,
members of the same body, *
    and sharers in the promise in Christ Jesus through the gospel.

Of this gospel I have become a servant *
    according to the gift of God's grace.

The Gospel was given to me *
    by the working of God's power.

Although I am the very least of all the saints, *
    this grace was given to me:

To bring to the Gentiles
the news of the boundless riches of Christ, *
    and to make everyone see what is the plan of the mystery.

That mystery of Christ lay hidden for ages in God *
    who created all things;

So that through the church *
    the wisdom of God in its rich variety

Might now be made known *
    to the rulers and authorities in the heavenly places.

Antiphon I have become a servant of the Gospel according to the gift of God's grace.

Reading Two Philippians 3:4b-11

Responsory Two (Gal. 1:15, 16)
God had set me apart before I was born
        – and called me through his grace.
God was pleased to reveal his Son to me
        – and called me through his grace.
Glory to the Father and to the Son and to the Holy Spirit.
God had set me apart before I was born
        – and called me through his grace.

Benedictus Antiphon Go, Ananias, and look for Saul. Tell him that he is an instrument whom I have chosen to bring my name before Gentiles.

Collect O God, by the preaching of your apostle Paul you have caused the light of the Gospel to shine throughout the world: Grant, we pray, that we, having his wonderful conversion in remembrance, may show ourselves thankful to you by following his holy teaching; through Jesus Christ our Lord, who lives and reigns with you, in the unity of the Holy Spirit, one God, now and for ever. Amen.

The Conversion of Saint Paul the Apostle
Noonday Prayer

From the Common of the Apostles, page 650, with the following proper parts.
Antiphon Saul began to proclaim Jesus in the synagogues, saying, "He is the Son of God."
Psalms from Sunday Week 1 Noonday Prayer page 138

Reading 1 Timothy 1: 12-14
I am grateful to Christ Jesus our Lord, who has strengthened me, because he judged me faithful and appointed me to his service, even though I was formerly a blasphemer, a persecutor, and a man of violence. But I received mercy because I had acted ignorantly in unbelief, and the grace of our Lord overflowed for me with the faith and love that are in Christ Jesus.

Verse and Response
I did not receive the Gospel from a human source.
I received it through a revelation of Jesus Christ.

Collect *From Morning Prayer*

The Conversion of Saint Paul the Apostle
Evening Prayer

From the Common of the Apostles, page 651, with the following proper parts

Hymn We Sing The Glorious Conquest *Hymnal 255*

Antiphon 1 Last of all, as to one untimely born, Christ appeared also to me.
Psalms from the Common of Apostles Evening Prayer II page 645
Antiphon 2 God, who had set me apart before I was born and called me through his grace, was pleased to reveal his Son to me, so that I might proclaim him among the Gentiles.
Antiphon 3 The one who formerly was persecuting us is now proclaiming the faith he once tried to destroy. And they glorified God because of me.

Reading Ecclesiasticus 39:1-10 or Acts 9:1-22

Responsory (Acts 9:15; Is. 49:6)
He is an instrument whom I have chosen
– to bring my name before Gentiles.
I have given you as a light to the nations
– to bring my name before Gentiles.
Glory to the Father and to the Son and to the Holy Spirit.
He is an instrument whom I have chosen
– to bring my name before Gentiles.

Magnificat Antiphon Brother Saul, the Lord Jesus, who appeared to you on your way here, has sent me so that you may regain your sight and be filled with the Holy Spirit.

Collect O God, by the preaching of your apostle Paul you have caused the light of the Gospel to shine throughout the world: Grant, we pray, that we, having his wonderful conversion in remembrance, may show ourselves thankful to you by following his holy teaching; through Jesus Christ our Lord, who lives and reigns with you, in the unity of the Holy Spirit, one God, now and for ever. Amen.

January 26
Timothy and Titus
Companions of Saint Paul
Lesser Feast
From the Common of Apostles, page 648
Collect Almighty God, you called Timothy and Titus to be evangelists and teachers, and made them strong to endure hardship: Strengthen us to stand fast in adversity, and to live godly and righteous lives in this present time, that with sure confidence we may look for our blessed hope, the glorious appearing of our great God and Savior Jesus Christ; who lives and reigns with you and the Holy Spirit, one God, now and for ever. Amen.

January 26
Robert of Molesme, Alberic and Stephen Harding
Abbots, Founders of the Cistercian Order
Lesser Feast
From the Common of Monastics, page 687, with the following antiphons
Benedictus Antiphon May we all live together in the bond of charity under one rule, and in the practice of the same observances.

Magnificat Antiphon Having spurned the world's riches, the new soldiers of Christ were poor with the poor Christ.

Collect All powerful and ever-living God, you yourself are the very great reward of those who leave all things for the sake of Christ your Son. By the prayer and example of the holy founders of Citeaux, Robert, Alberic and Stephen, may we, like them, hasten with all fervor and zeal to the fullness of eternal life. We ask this through our Lord, Jesus Christ, your Son, who lives and reigns with you and the Holy Spirit, one God, for ever and ever. Amen.

January 27

John Chrysostom
Bishop of Constantinople, Teacher of the Faith, 407
Lesser Feast
From the Common of Teacher of the Faith, page 676

Collect O God, you gave your servant John Chrysostom grace eloquently to proclaim your righteousness in the great congregation, and fearlessly to bear reproach for the honor of your Name: Mercifully grant to all bishops and pastors such excellence in preaching, and faithfulness in ministering your Word, that your people may be partakers with them of the glory that shall be revealed; through Jesus Christ our Lord, who lives and reigns with you and the Holy Spirit, one God, for ever and ever. Amen.

January 28

Thomas Aquinas
Friar, Priest and Teacher of the Faith, 1274
Lesser Feast
From the Common of Teacher of the Faith, page 676

Collect Almighty God, you have enriched your Church with the singular learning and holiness of your servant Thomas Aquinas: Enlighten us more and more, we pray, by the disciplined thinking and teaching of Christian scholars, and deepen our devotion by the example of saintly lives; through Jesus Christ our Lord, who lives and reigns with you and the Holy Spirit, one God, for ever and ever. Amen.

January 31

Marcella of Rome
Monastic and Scholar, 410
Lesser Feast
From the Common of Monastics, page 687

Collect O God, who satisfies the longing soul and fills the hungry with good things: Grant that we, like your servant Marcella, may hunger and thirst after you more than the vain pomp and glory of the world and delight in your word more than all manner of riches. Through Jesus Christ our Lord, who lives and resigns with you and the Holy Spirit, one God, now and forever. Amen.

February

February 1

Brigid (Bride)
Abbess, 523
Lesser Feast

From the Common of Monastics, page 687

Collect Everliving God, we rejoice today in the fellowship of your blessed servant Brigid, and we give you thanks for her life of devoted service. Inspire us with life and light, and give us perseverance to serve you all our days; through Jesus Christ our Lord, who with you and the Holy Spirit lives and reigns, one God, for ever and ever. Amen.

February 2

The Presentation of Our Lord Jesus Christ in the Temple
Feast of our Lord
Evening Prayer I

Hymn O Zion, open wide thy gates *Hymnal 257*

Antiphon 1 When the time came for their purification according to the law of Moses, they brought him up to Jerusalem to present him to the Lord.

Psalms taken from Sunday Week 1 Evening Prayer I

Antiphon 2 Simeon was a righteous and devout man, looking forward to the consolation of Israel, and the Holy Spirit rested on him. The Holy Spirit revealed to him that he would not see death before he had seen the Lord's Messiah.

Antiphon 3 The widow Anna, the daughter of Phanuel, of the tribe of Asher, was a prophet. She never left the temple but worshiped there with fasting and prayer night and day.

Reading 1 Samuel 1:20-28a or Romans 8:14-21

Responsory (Ps. 65:4; Rm. 8:15)
Blessed are they whom you choose
 —and draw to your courts to dwell there.
Blessed are they to whom you give a spirit of adoption
 —and draw to your courts to dwell there.
Glory to the Father and to the Son and to the Holy Spirit.
Blessed are they whom you choose
 —and draw to your courts to dwell there.

Magnificat Antiphon Simeon blessed the child's parents and said to his mother Mary, "This child is destined for the falling and the rising of many in Israel, and to be a sign that will be opposed so that the inner thoughts of many will be revealed—and a sword will pierce your own soul too."

Litany
As you drew Mary and Joseph into the temple, so draw us and all who seek you into the inner temple where you will manifest yourself to us.
Lord, have mercy.
As the aged Anna faithfully sought you in fasting and prayer, so come to all contemplatives whose spiritual practices open them to your Spirit.
Christ, have mercy.
As the elderly Simeon rejoiced in your presence at the end of his days, so draw all the departed to the vision of your face.
Lord, have mercy.

Invitation to the Lord's Prayer
Joining the worship of saints, sages and prophets sanctified under the covenant with Abraham and Sarah, we enter into the spiritual temple and pray with Christ to the Father.

Collect Almighty and everliving God, we humbly pray that, as your only-begotten Son was this day presented in the temple, so we may be presented to you with pure and clean hearts by Jesus Christ our Lord; who lives and reigns with you and the Holy Spirit, one God, now and for ever. Amen.

The Blessing
We are all children of light and children of the day; we are not of the night or of darkness. So then let us not fall asleep as others do, but let us keep awake and be sober.
Amen.

The Presentation Morning Prayer
Invitatory The Lord whom we seek has come to his temple: Rejoice and worship Christ, the Incarnate Word.

Hymn Hail to the Lord who comes *Hymnal 259*

Antiphon 1 The child's parents offered a sacrifice according to what is stated in the law of the Lord, a pair of turtledoves or two young pigeons.
Psalms taken from Sunday Week 1 Morning Prayer

Antiphon 2 Guided by the Spirit, Simeon came into the temple; and when the parents brought in the child Jesus, to do for him what was customary under the law, Simeon took him in his arms and praised God.
Antiphon 3 At that moment Anna came, and began to praise God and to speak about the child to all who were looking for the redemption of Jerusalem.

Reading One 1 Samuel 2:1-10

Responsory One (Song 1:4)
Draw me after you, let us make haste
      —the king has brought me into his chambers.
We will exult and rejoice in you
      —the king has brought me into his chambers.
Glory to the Father and to the Son and to the Holy Spirit.
Draw me after you, let us make haste
      —the king has brought me into his chambers.

Canticle You are God   *Te Deum laudamus*
From the Ordinary of the Daily Office

Reading Two John 8:31-36

Responsory Two (Gal. 5:1, 25;Gal 4: 6)
For freedom Christ has set us free
      —let us be guided by the Spirit.
God has sent the Spirit of his Son into our hearts
      —let us be guided by the Spirit.
Glory to the Father and to the Son and to the Holy Spirit.
For freedom Christ has set us free
      —let us be guided by the Spirit.

Benedictus Antiphon Adorn your bridal chamber, O Zion, to receive Christ the King. Embrace the Messiah and receive his mother who carries the King of Glory, the Sun of new light.

Litany
Christ is the light who illumines the world; let us walk this day in Christ's radiance.
Lord, have mercy.
Christ is the light from the Father; let us invite others to share in Christ's light.
Christ, have mercy.

Christ is the light who shines in the darkness; let us bring Christ's light to the confused and befuddled.
Lord, have mercy.

Invitation to the Lord's Prayer
As our eyes rejoice in the light of this new day, so may our spirits rejoice with Christ, who illumines us, as we pray.

Collect *From Evening Prayer I*

The Blessing
May we be glad for the Lord will be our everlasting light.
Amen.

The Presentation Noonday Prayer

Hymn Sing of Mary, pure and lowly *Hymnal 277*

Antiphon I will bring the foreigners to my holy mountain, and make them joyful in my house of prayer.
Psalms taken from Sunday Week 1 Midday Prayer

Reading (Isaiah 12: 5-6)
Sing praises to the Lord, for he has done gloriously; let this be known in all the earth. Shout aloud and sing for joy, O royal Zion, for great in your midst is the Holy One of Israel

Verse and Response
The Lord has proclaimed to the end of the earth.
Say to daughter Zion, "See, your salvation comes."

Collect *From Evening Prayer I*

The Presentation Evening Prayer II
Hymn Virgin born we bow before thee *Hymnal 258*

Antiphon 1 The child's father and mother were amazed at what was being said about him and Simeon blessed them.
Psalms taken from Sunday Week 1 Evening Prayer II
Antiphon 2 This child is destined for the falling and the rising of many in Israel, and to be a sign that will be opposed so that the inner thoughts of many will be revealed—and a sword will pierce your own soul.
Antiphon 3 They returned to Galilee, to their own town of Nazareth. The child grew and became strong, filled with wisdom; and the favor of God was upon him.

Reading Haggai 2:1-9 or 1 John 3:1-8

Responsory (Ps. 27:5,6)
I desire to behold the fair beauty of the Lord
    —and to seek him in his temple.
I yearn to dwell in the house of the Lord all the days of my life
    —and to seek him in his temple.
Glory to the Father and to the Son and to the Holy Spirit.
I desire to behold the fair beauty of the Lord
    —and to seek him in his temple.

Magnificat Antiphon The old man carried the young boy but the young boy rules over the old man. The child born of a Virgin is worshipped and adored by the Virgin.

Litany
As you drew Mary and Joseph into the temple, so draw us and all who seek you into the inner temple where you will manifest yourself to us.
Lord, have mercy.
As the aged Anna faithfully sought you in fasting and prayer, so come to all contemplatives whose spiritual practices open them to your Spirit.
Christ, have mercy.
As the elderly Simeon rejoiced in your presence at the end of his days, so draw all the departed to the vision of your face.
Lord, have mercy.

Invitation to the Lord's Prayer
Joining the worship of saints, sages and prophets sanctified under the covenant with Abraham, Sarah and Hagar, we enter into the spiritual temple and pray with Christ to the Father.

Collect *From Evening Prayer I*

The Blessing
We are all children of light and children of the day; we are not of the night or of darkness. So then let us not fall asleep as others do, but let us keep awake and be sober. **Amen.**

February 3

Anskar

Archbishop of Hamburg, Missionary to Denmark and Sweden, 865
Lesser Feast

From the Common of Missionaries, page 680

Collect Almighty and everlasting God, you sent your servant Anskar as an apostle to the people of Scandinavia, and enabled him to lay a firm foundation for their conversion, though he did not see the results of his labors: Keep your Church from discouragement in the day of small things, knowing that when you have begun a good work you will bring it to a fruitful conclusion; through Jesus Christ our Lord, who lives and reigns with you and the Holy Spirit, one God, for ever and ever. Amen.

February 4

Cornelius the Centurion

Lesser Feast

From the Common of Holy Persons, page 695, with the following proper antiphons

Benedictus Antiphon In Caesarea there was a man named Cornelius, a centurion. He was a devout man who feared God with all his household; he gave alms generously to the people and prayed constantly to God.

Magnificat Antiphon Peter said, "Can anyone withhold the water for baptizing these people who have received the Holy Spirit just as we have?" So he ordered them to be baptized in the name of Jesus Christ.

Collect O God, by your Spirit you called Cornelius the Centurion to be the first Christian among the Gentiles: Grant to your Church such a ready will to go where you send and to do what you command, that under your guidance it may welcome all who turn to you in love and faith, and proclaim the Gospel to all nations; through Jesus Christ our Lord, who lives and reigns with you and the Holy Spirit, one God, for ever and ever. Amen.

February 5

Agatha of Sicily

Martyr c. 251
Lesser Feast

From the Common of Martyrs, page 665, with the following proper antiphons

Benedictus Antiphon As a bride going to her wedding chamber, Agatha went rejoicing to prison and offered herself as an oblation to God.

Magnificat Antiphon Lord Jesus Christ, my Good Master, I thank you for you have sustained me in my torments. Draw me, my Lord, into your glory which never fades.

Collect Almighty and everlasting God, who strengthened your martyr Agatha with constancy and courage: Grant us for the love of you to make no peace with oppression, to fear no adversity, and to have no tolerance for those who would use their power to abuse or exploit; Through Jesus Christ our Lord, to whom with you and the Holy Spirit be all honor and glory, now and for ever. Amen.

February 6

The Martyrs of Japan
1597
Lesser Feast
From the Common of Martyrs, page 665, with the following proper antiphons
Benedictus Antiphon When you walk through fire you shall not be burned, and the flame shall not consume you.

Magnificat Antiphon May I never boast of anything except the cross of our Lord Jesus Christ, by which the world has been crucified to me, and I to the world.

Collect O God our Father, source of strength to all your saints, you brought the holy martyrs of Japan through the suffering of the cross to the joys of eternal life: Grant that we, encouraged by their example, may hold fast the faith we profess, even to death itself; through Jesus Christ our Lord, who lives and reigns with you and the Holy Spirit, one God, now and for ever. Amen.

February 9

Anne Ayers
Professed Religious and Founder of the Sisterhood of the Holy Communion, 1896
Lesser Feast
From the Common of Professed Religious, page 691
Collect O God, whose blessed Son became poor that we through his poverty might be rich: Deliver us from an inordinate love of this world, that we, inspired by the devotion of your servant Anne Ayers, may serve you with singleness of heart, and attain to the riches of the age to come; through Jesus Christ our Lord, who lives and reigns with you, in the unity of the Holy Spirit, one God, now and for ever.
Amen.

February 10

Scholastica
Nun and Foundress
Principal Feast
From the Common of Monastics, page 687, with the following proper parts
Evening Prayer I
Hymn Blessed City Heavenly Salem *Hymnal 519*

Antiphon 1 The holy Nun Scholastica entreated her brother Benedict to stay with her all night that they might speak of the joys of heaven.
Psalms from Sunday Week 1 Evening Prayer I, page 130
Antiphon 2 In answer to her prayer, such a storm arose that Benedict could not put his head out of doors.
Antiphon 3 Scholastica said to her brother, "I desired you to stay, and you would not hear me; I have desired it of our good Lord, and he has granted my petition."

Reading I John 4: 7-16

Responsory (Jn. 15:7,4)
If you abide in me, and my words abide in you
—ask for whatever you wish, and it will be done for you.
Abide in me as I abide in you
—ask for whatever you wish, and it will be done for you.
Glory to the Father and to the Son and to the Holy Spirit.
If you abide in me, and my words abide in you
—ask for whatever you wish, and it will be done for you.

Magnificat Antiphon Now this wise virgin has gone to Christ. Among the choirs of virgins, she is radiant as the sun in the heavens. Come, spouse of Christ, receive the crown the Lord has prepared for you.

Collect Almighty and ever-living God, who in your only-begotten Son opened for us a door of hope in this valley of tears, grant that we, like the virgin Saint Scholastica, may sing to you as in the days of our youth with purity of heart recovered and holy innocence restored, so that, having preferred nothing to the love of the Bridegroom Christ, it may be given us to sing your praise forever at the wedding feast of the Lamb through the same Christ our Lord. Amen.

The Blessing
May we run in the path of God's commandments, our hearts overflowing with the inexpressible delight of love. **Amen.**

Scholastica Morning Prayer

Invitatory Let us all rejoice in the Lord, celebrating the feast in honor of St. Scholastica, in whose blessed solemnity the angels rejoice and praise the Son of God.

Hymn Come Down of Love Divine *Hymnal 516*

Antiphon 1 I desired you to stay, and you would not hear me; I have desired it of our good Lord, and he has granted my petition.
Psalms from Sunday Week 1 Morning Prayer, page 134
Antiphon 2 Brother, if you can now depart, in God's name return to your monastery, and leave me here alone.
Antiphon 3 She who loved more, did more.

Reading One Song of Songs 8:1-7

Responsory One (Song 6:9)
The maidens saw her
        —they called her blessed.
My dove, my perfect one, is the only one.
        —they called her blessed.
Glory to the Father and to the Son and to the Holy Spirit.
The maidens saw her
        —they called her blessed.

Canticle You are God   *Te Deum laudamus, page 757*

Canticle During Lent
Canticle of Jerusalem Betrothed *Propter Sion non tacebo*
(Isaiah 62:1-5)
Antiphon You shall be a crown of beauty in the hand of the Lord, and a royal diadem in the hand of your God.

For Zion's sake I will not keep silent, *
        and for Jerusalem's sake I will not rest,

Until her vindication shines out like the dawn, *
        and her salvation like a burning torch.

The nations shall see your vindication, *
        and all the kings your glory.

You shall be called by a new name *
        spoken by the mouth of the Lord.

You shall be a crown of beauty in the hand of the Lord, *
        and a royal diadem in the hand of your God.

You shall no more be termed "Forsaken," *
     and your land shall no more be termed "Desolate;"

You shall be called "My Delight," *
     and your land "Espoused."

For the Lord delights in you, *
     and your land shall be married.

For as a young man marries a young woman, *
     so shall your builder marry you,

And as the bridegroom rejoices over the bride, *
     so shall your God rejoice over you.

Antiphon You shall be a crown of beauty in the hand of the Lord, and a royal diadem in the hand of your God.

Reading Two Luke 10: 38-42

Responsory (Ps. 133:1,5)
Oh, how good and pleasant it is
          —when brethren live together in unity.
There the Lord has ordained the blessing
          —when brethren live together in unity.
Glory to the Father and to the Son and to the Holy Spirit.
Oh, how good and pleasant it is
          —when brethren live together in unity.

Benedictus Antiphon Arise my love, my fair one, my dove, who dwell in the cleft of the rock. Come and receive the crown which Christ has prepared for you.

Collect O Lord, who made Saint Scholastica resplendent with the brightness of an incomparable purity, grant that we may please you by the transparency of our daily lives and, by faithfulness in the school of your service, be found worthy of praising you in heaven with all the angels and saints. We make our prayer through our Lord Jesus Christ, your Son, who lives and reigns with you in the unity of the Holy Spirit, God forever and ever. Amen.

The Blessing
May we prefer nothing whatever to Christ, and may he bring us all together to everlasting life. **Amen.**

Scholastica Noonday Prayer
Hymn Like The Murmur Of The Dove's Song *Hymnal 513*

Antiphon At midnight there was a shout, "Look! Here is the bridegroom! Come out to meet him."
Psalms from Sunday Week 1 Noonday Prayer, page 138

Reading
2 Cor. 11: 2b
I promised you in marriage to one husband, to present you as a chaste virgin to Christ.

Verse and Response
You speak in my heart.
Your face, Lord, will I seek.

Collect O Lord, who made Saint Scholastica resplendent with the brightness of an incomparable purity, grant that we may please you by the transparency of our daily lives and, by faithfulness in the school of your service, be found worthy of praising you in heaven with all the angels and saints. We make our prayer through our Lord Jesus Christ, your Son, who lives and reigns with you in the unity of the Holy Spirit, God forever and ever. Amen.

Scholastica Evening Prayer II
Hymn Jerusalem The Golden *Hymnal 624*

Antiphon 1 You are beautiful, my love; you are beautiful; your eyes are doves.
Psalms from Sunday Week 1 Evening Prayer II, page 141
Antiphon 2 I slept, but my heart was awake. Listen! my beloved is knocking. "Open to me, my sister, my love, my dove, my perfect one."
Antiphon 3 Oh, that I had wings like a dove. I would fly away and be at rest.

Reading I John 3: 1-3, 21-23

Responsory (Lk 10:41)
She received more than her brother did from the Lord of her heart
    −because she loved him so much.
She has chosen the better part
    −because she loved him so much.
Glory to the Father and to the Son and to the Holy Spirit.
She received more than her brother did from the Lord of her heart
    −because she loved him so much.

Magnificat Antiphon Standing in his cell, and lifting up his eyes to heaven, Benedict beheld the soul of his sister Scholastica ascend into heaven in the likeness of a dove.

Collect God of love, to show us the beauty of holiness, you caused the soul of St. Scholastica to go up into heaven in the form of a dove. Grant that by her example, we may live in such peace and purity of heart as to enjoy everlasting happiness with her. Grant this through our Lord Jesus Christ, your Son, who lives and reigns with you in the unity of the Holy Spirit, God, for ever and ever. Amen.

The Blessing
May we run in the path of God's commandments, our hearts overflowing with the inexpressible delight of love. **Amen.**

February 13

Absalom Jones
Priest, 1818
Lesser Feast

From the Common of Pastors, page 669, with the following proper antiphons
Benedictus Antiphon We desire to walk in the liberty wherewith Christ has made us free that following peace with all, we may have our fruit unto holiness, and in the end, everlasting life.

Magnificat Antiphon We have gone forward to erect a house for the glory of God, and our mutual advantage to meet in for clarification and social religious worship and more particularly to keep an open door for those of our race.

Collect Set us free, heavenly Father, from every bond of prejudice and fear; that, honoring the steadfast courage of your servant Absalom Jones, we may show forth in our lives the reconciling love and true freedom of the children of God, which you have given us in your Son our Savior Jesus Christ; who lives and reigns with you and the Holy Spirit, one God, now and for ever. Amen.

February 14

Cyril, Monk, and Methodius, Bishop
Missionaries to the Slavs, 869, 885
Lesser Feast

From the Common of Missionaries, page 680
Collect Almighty and everlasting God, by the power of the Holy Spirit you moved your servant Cyril and his brother Methodius to bring the light of the Gospel to a hostile and divided people: Overcome all bitterness

and strife among us by the love of Christ, and make us one united family under the banner of the Prince of Peace; who lives and reigns with you and the Holy Spirit, one God, now and for ever. Amen.

February 15

Thomas Bray
Priest and Missionary, 1730
Lesser Feast

From the Common of Missionaries, page 680

Collect O God of compassion, you opened the eyes of your servant Thomas Bray to see the needs of the Church in the New World, and led him to found societies to meet those needs: Make the Church in this land diligent at all times to propagate the Gospel among those who have not received it, and to promote the spread of Christian knowledge; through Jesus Christ our Lord, who lives and reigns with you and the Holy Spirit, one God, for ever and ever. Amen.

February 17

Janani Luwum
Archbishop of Uganda, and Martyr, 1977
Lesser Feast

From the Common of Martyrs, page 665

Collect O God, whose Son the Good Shepherd laid down his life for the sheep: We give you thanks for your faithful shepherd Janani Luwum, who after his Savior's example, gave up his life for the people of Uganda. Grant us to be so inspired by his witness that we make no peace with oppression, but live as those who are sealed with the cross of Christ, who died and rose again, and now lives and reigns with you and the Holy Spirit, one God, for ever and ever. Amen.

February 18

Martin Luther
Reformer, 1546
Lesser Feast

From the Common of Theologians and Teachers, page 672

Collect O God, our refuge and our strength: You raised up your servant Martin Luther to reform and renew your Church in the light of your word. Defend and purify the Church in our own day and grant that, through faith, we may boldly proclaim the riches of your grace which you have made known in Jesus Christ our Savior, who with you and the Holy Spirit, lives and reigns, one God, now and for ever. Amen.

February 22

Margaret of Cortona
Franciscan Tertiary, 1297
Lesser Feast

From the Common of Holy Persons, page 695

Collect O God, as your servant Margaret of Cortona found a home where her repentance led to a life of prayer, service, and leadership, Grant that we may always seek to dwell where estrangement yields to reconciliation, through Jesus Christ, who is himself the goal of all our seeking and the answer to our desires, unto whom, with you and the Holy Spirit, be honor and glory, now and forever. Amen.

February 23

Polycarp
Bishop and Martyr of Smyrna, 156
Lesser Feast

From the Common of Martyrs, page 665, with the following proper antiphons

Benedictus Antiphon Eighty-six years have I have served him and he has done me no wrong. How can I blaspheme my King and my Savior?"

Magnificat Antiphon O Lord God Almighty I give you thanks that you count me worthy to be numbered among your martyrs, sharing the cup of Christ and the resurrection to eternal life, both of soul and body, through the immortality of the Holy Spirit.

Collect O God, the maker of heaven and earth, you gave your venerable servant, the holy and gentle Polycarp, boldness to confess Jesus Christ as King and Savior, and steadfastness to die for his faith: Give us grace, following his example, to share the cup of Christ and rise to eternal life; through Jesus Christ our Lord, who lives and reigns with you and the Holy Spirit, one God, now and for ever. Amen.

February 24

Saint Matthias the Apostle
Major Feast

From the Common of Apostles, page 648, with the following proper antiphons

Benedictus Antiphon So one of the men who have accompanied us during all the time that the Lord Jesus went in and out among us, one of these must become a witness with us to his resurrection.

Magnificat Antiphon Lord, you know everyone's heart. They cast lots for them, and the lot fell on Matthias; and he was added to the eleven apostles.

Collect Almighty God, who in the place of Judas chose your faithful servant Matthias to be numbered among the Twelve: Grant that your Church, being delivered from false apostles, may always be guided and governed by faithful and true pastors; through Jesus Christ our Lord, who lives and reigns with you, in the unity of the Holy Spirit, one God, now and for ever. Amen.

February 25

Walburga
Benedictine Abbess of Double Monastery of Heidenheim and Missionary, c 777
Lesser Feast

From the Common of Monastics, page 687, with the following proper antiphons

Benedictus Antiphon Walburga, a model of monastic life, gathered together nuns consecrated to Christ and fulfilled the Lord's command with all zeal and eagerness.

Magnificat Antiphon You, Lord, to whom I have been dedicated from my earliest youth, have made me worthy, I who am unworthy, to receive of your divine light to lead me home.

Collect Almighty and merciful God, by your grace blessed Walburga left all things to follow the poor and humble Christ. Perfect the work of conversion which you have begun in us; through Jesus Christ our Lord, who lives and reigns with you and the Holy Spirit, one God, for ever and ever. Amen.

February 26

Photini, The Samaritan Woman
Equal to the Apostles
Lesser Feast

Morning Prayer
From the Common of the Apostles, page 648, with the following proper parts.

Invitatory Christ is the Living Water; come let us drink from the well of salvation.

Hymn The eternal gifts of Christ the King *Hymnal 233*

Antiphon 1 Jesus came to a Samaritan city called Sychar. Jacob's well was there, and Jesus, tired out by his journey, was sitting by the well.
Psalms from the current day of the week.

Antiphon 2 A Samaritan woman came to draw water, and Jesus said to her, "Give me a drink." The Samaritan woman said to him, "How is it that you, a Jew, ask a drink of me, a woman of Samaria?"

Antiphon 3 If you knew the gift of God, and who it is that is saying to you, 'Give me a drink,' you would have asked him, and he would have given you living water.

Reading One 2 Kings 17:28-41

Responsory One (Jn. 4;23; Jn. 9:31)
The true worshipers will worship the Father
        — in spirit and truth.
God listens to one who worships him and obeys his will
        — in spirit and truth.
Glory to the Father and to the Son and to the Holy Spirit.
The true worshipers will worship the Father
        — in spirit and truth.

Canticle — Song of the Mystery of Christ *In mysterio Christi*
(Ephesians 3: 5-10)
Antiphon With joy you will draw water from the wells of salvation.

The mystery of Christ was not made known to humankind *
    in former generations.

It has now been revealed *
    to his holy apostles and prophets by the Spirit.

The Gentiles have become fellow-heirs,
members of the same body, *
    and sharers in the promise in Christ Jesus through the gospel.

Of this gospel I have become a servant *
    according to the gift of God's grace.

The Gospel was given to me *
    by the working of God's power.

Although I am the very least of all the saints, *
    this grace was given to me:

To bring to the Gentiles
the news of the boundless riches of Christ, *
    and to make everyone see what is the plan of the mystery.

That mystery of Christ lay hidden for ages in God *
    who created all things;

So that through the church *
    the wisdom of God in its rich variety

Might now be made known *
> to the rulers and authorities in the heavenly places.

Antiphon With joy you will draw water from the wells of salvation.

Reading Two John 4:1–26

Responsory Two (Song 4:15: Gen. 24: 13)
You are a garden fountain, a well of living water
> **– and flowing streams from Lebanon.**

I am standing here by the spring of water
> **– and flowing streams from Lebanon.**

Glory to the Father and to the Son and to the Holy Spirit.
You are a garden fountain, a well of living water
> **– and flowing streams from Lebanon.**

Benedictus Antiphon The hour is coming, and is now here, when the true worshipers will worship the Father in spirit and truth, for the Father seeks such as these to worship him. God is spirit, and those who worship him must worship in spirit and truth."

Collect O Almighty God, whose most blessed Son revealed to the Samaritan woman that He is indeed the Christ, the Savior of the World; grant us to drink of the well that springs up to everlasting life that we may worship you in spirit and in truth through your Son, Jesus Christ our Lord. Amen.

Photini, The Samaritan Woman Noonday Prayer
From the Common of the Apostles, page 650, with the following proper parts.
Antiphon Illuminated by the Holy Spirit, Photini, equal to the apostles, drank the water of salvation from Christ the Savior. With an open hand she gave it to those who thirst.
Psalms from the current day of the week.

Reading Isaiah 55: 1-3
Ho, everyone who thirsts, come to the waters; and you that have no money, come, buy and eat! Come, buy wine and milk without money and without price. Why do you spend your money for that which is not bread, and your labor for that which does not satisfy? Listen carefully to me, and eat what is good, and delight yourselves in rich food. Incline your ear, and come to me; listen, so that you may live.

Verse and Response
My food is to do the will of him who sent me.
And to complete my Father's work.

Collect *From Morning Prayer*

Photini, The Samaritan Woman Evening Prayer
From the Common of the Apostles, page 651, with the following proper parts
Hymn Jesus Lover of my soul *Hymnal 699*

Antiphon 1 Those who drink of the water that I will give them will never be thirsty. The water that I will give will become in them a spring of water gushing up to eternal life.
Psalms from the current day of the week.
Antiphon 2 The hour is coming when you will worship the Father neither on this mountain nor in Jerusalem. The true worshipers will worship the Father in spirit and truth
Antiphon 3 The woman left her water jar and went back to the city. She said to the people, "Come and see a man who told me everything I have ever done! He cannot be the Messiah, can he?"

Reading Isaiah 55: 1-5

Responsory (Jn. 7:37-38; Is. 12:4)
Let anyone who is thirsty come to me
　　　– let the one who believes in me drink.
With joy you will draw water from the wells of salvation
　　　– let the one who believes in me drink.
Glory to the Father and to the Son and to the Holy Spirit.
Let anyone who is thirsty come to me
　　　– let the one who believes in me drink.

Magnificat Antiphon The woman said to him, "I know that Messiah is coming. When he comes, he will proclaim all things to us." Jesus said to her, "I am he, the one who is speaking to you."

Collect *From Morning Prayer*

February 27
George Herbert
Priest, 1633
Lesser Feast
From the Common of Theologians and Teachers, page 672, with the following antiphons
Benedictus Antiphon Come, my Light, my Feast, my Strength : such a Light, as shows a feast; such a Feast, as mends in length : such a Strength, as makes his guest.

Magnificat Antiphon My God, thou art all love. And in this love, more than in bed, I rest.

Collect Our God and King, you called your servant George Herbert from the pursuit of worldly honors to be a pastor of souls, a poet, and a priest in your temple: Give us grace, we pray, joyfully to perform the tasks you give us to do, knowing that nothing is menial or common that is done for your sake; through Jesus Christ our Lord, who lives and reigns with you and the Holy Spirit, one God, for ever and ever. Amen.

February 28

Anna Julia Haywood Cooper

Educator, 1964

Lesser Feast

From the Common of Holy Persons, page 695

Collect Almighty God, you inspired your servant Anna Julia Haywood Cooper with the love of learning and the skill of teaching: Enlighten us more and more through the discipline of learning, and deepen our commitment to the education of all your children; through Jesus Christ our Lord, who lives and reigns with you and the Holy Spirit, one God, for ever and ever. Amen.

March

March 1

David

Bishop of Menevia, Wales, c. 544

Lesser Feast

From the Common of Pastors, page 669

Collect Almighty God, you called your servant David to be a faithful and wise steward of your mysteries for the people of Wales: Mercifully grant that, following his purity of life and zeal for the Gospel of Christ, we may with him receive our heavenly reward; through Jesus Christ our Lord, who lives and reigns with you and the Holy Spirit, one God, for ever and ever. Amen.

March 2

Chad

Bishop of Lichfield, 672

Lesser Feast

From the Common of Pastors, page 669

Collect Almighty God, for the peace of the Church your servant Chad relinquished cheerfully the honors that had been thrust upon him, only to be rewarded with equal responsibility: Keep us, we pray, from thinking of ourselves more highly than we ought to think, and ready at all times to step aside for others, that the cause of Christ may be advanced; through him who lives and reigns with you and the Holy Spirit, one God, now and for ever. Amen.

March 3

John and Charles Wesley
Priests, 1791, 1788
Lesser Feast

From the Common of Pastors, page 669

Collect Lord God, you inspired your servants John and Charles Wesley with burning zeal for the sanctification of souls, and endowed them with eloquence in speech and song: Kindle in your Church, we entreat you, such fervor, that those whose faith has cooled may be warmed, and those who have not known Christ may turn to him and be saved; who lives and reigns with you and the Holy Spirit, one God, now and for ever. Amen.

March 7

Perpetua, Felicitas and their Companions
Martyrs at Carthage, 202
Lesser Feast

From the Common of Martyrs, page 665, with the following proper antiphons

Benedictus Antiphon The day of the martyrs' victory dawned. They marched from their cells into the amphitheater, as if into heaven. If they trembled it was for joy and not for fear.

Magnificat Antiphon I began to walk in triumph towards the Gate of Life. I knew that I would win the victory.

Collect O God the King of saints, you strengthened your servants Perpetua and Felicitas and their companions to make a good confession, staunchly resisting, for the cause of Christ, the claims of human affection, and encouraging one another in their time of trial: Grant that we who cherish their blessed memory may share their pure and steadfast faith, and win with them the palm of victory; through Jesus Christ our Lord, who lives and reigns with you and the Holy Spirit, one God, for ever and ever. Amen.

March 9

Gregory
Bishop of Nyssa, c. 394
Lesser Feast

From the Common of Theologians and Teachers, page 672

Collect Almighty God, you have revealed to your Church your eternal Being of glorious majesty and perfect love as one God in Trinity of Persons: Give us grace that, like your bishop Gregory of Nyssa, we may continue steadfast in the confession of this faith, and constant in our worship of you, Father, Son, and Holy Spirit; for you live and reign for ever and ever. Amen.

March 9

Frances of Rome
Married Woman, Religious Founder, Benedictine Oblate, 1440
Lesser Feast
From the Common of Monastics, page 687

Collect Father of mercy, you called Frances of Rome to serve you in marriage and as a Benedictine oblate. Give us grace to balance our life commitments and focus our hearts on you; through Jesus Christ our Lord, who lives and reigns with you and the Holy Spirit, one God, for ever and ever. Amen.

May

May 13

Bede Griffiths
Benedictine Monk, Yogi, Priest 1993
From the Common of Theologians and Teachers, page 672

Collect Holy Wisdom, dwelling in all creation, you manifested yourself to Bede through the mystery of your presence in the sacred writings of Hinduism; continue to shine in the wonder of your diverse manifestations but chiefly through Jesus Christ our Savior, who with you and the Holy Spirit, lives and reigns, one God, now and for ever. Amen.

May 15

Pachomius
Abbot, 348
Lesser Feast
From the Common of Monastics, page 687

Collect Lord our God, you raised the blessed abbot Pachomius to the heights of virtue and doctrine. Through his example may we seek before all else the bread of your word which enlightens our minds and brings peace to our hearts. We ask this through our Lord Jesus Christ, your Son, who lives and reigns with you and the Holy Spirit, one God, for ever and ever. Amen.

May 16

The Martyrs of the Sudan

1983-2011

Lesser Feast

From the Common of Martyrs, page 665

Collect O God, steadfast in the midst of persecution, by your providence the blood of the martyrs is the seed of the Church: As the martyrs of the Sudan refused to abandon Christ even in the face of torture and death, and so by their sacrifice brought forth a plentiful harvest, may we, too, be steadfast in our faith in Jesus Christ; who with you and the Holy Spirit lives and reigns, one God, for ever and ever. Amen.

May 19

Dunstan

Monk, Abbot, Restorer of the Monastic Life and Archbishop of Canterbury, 988

Lesser Feast

From the Common of Pastors, page 669

Collect O God of truth and beauty, you richly endowed your bishop Dunstan with skill in music and the working of metals, and with gifts of administration and reforming zeal: Teach us, we pray, to see in you the source of all our talents, and move us to offer them for the adornment of worship and the advancement of true religion; through Jesus Christ our Lord, who lives and reigns with you and the Holy Spirit, one God, now and for ever. Amen.

May 20

Alcuin

Deacon and Abbot of Tours, 804

Lesser Feast

From the Common of Monastics, page 687

Collect Almighty God, in a rude and barbarous age you raised up your deacon Alcuin to rekindle the light of learning: Illumine our minds, we pray, that amid the uncertainties and confusions of our own time we may show forth your eternal truth; through Jesus Christ our Lord, who lives and reigns with you and the Holy Spirit, one God, for ever and ever. Amen.

May 22

Lydia of Thyatira,

Coworker of the Apostle Paul
Lesser Feast

From the Common of the Apostles, page 648, with the following proper antiphons

Benedictus Antiphon Lydia was a worshiper of God and a dealer in purple cloth. The Lord opened her heart to listen eagerly to what was said by Paul.

Magnificat Antiphon When Lydia and her household were baptized, she urged Paul, Silas and Timothy, saying, "If you have judged me to be faithful to the Lord, come and stay at my home."

Collect Eternal God, who gives good gifts to all people, and who teaches us to have the same spirit of generosity: Give us, we pray you, hearts that are always open to hear your word, that following the example of your servant Lydia, we may show hospitality to all who are in any need or trouble, through Jesus Christ our Lord who lives and reigns with you and the Holy Spirit, one God, now and for ever. Amen.

May 24

Jackson Kemper

First Missionary Bishop in the United States, 1870
Lesser Feast

From the Common of Missionaries, page 680

Collect Lord God, in your providence Jackson Kemper was chosen first missionary bishop in this land, and by his arduous labor and travel congregations were established in scattered settlements of the West: Grant that the Church may always be faithful to its mission, and have the vision, courage, and perseverance to make known to all people the Good News of Jesus Christ; who with you and the Holy Spirit lives and reigns, one God, for ever and ever. Amen.

May 25

Bede, the Venerable

Monk of Jarrow, Priest and Teacher of the Faith, 735
Lesser Feast

From the Common of Teacher of the Faith, page 676, with the following proper antiphons

Benedictus Antiphon Christ is the Morning Star who, when the night of this world is past, brings to his saints the promise of the light of life and opens everlasting day.

Magnificat Antiphon I pray you, loving Jesus, that as you have graciously given me to drink in with delight the words of your knowledge, so you would mercifully grant me to attain one day to you, the fountain of all wisdom and to appear forever before your face.

Collect Heavenly Father, you called your servant Bede, while still a child, to devote his life to your service in the disciplines of religion and scholarship: Grant that as he labored in the Spirit to bring the riches of your truth to his generation, so we, in our various vocations, may strive to make you known in all the world; through Jesus Christ our Lord, who lives and reigns with you and the Holy Spirit, one God, for ever and ever. Amen.

May 26

Augustine

Monk, First Archbishop of Canterbury, 605
Lesser Feast

From the Common of Pastors, page 669

Collect O Lord our God, by your Son Jesus Christ you called your apostles and sent them forth to preach the Gospel to the nations: We bless your holy Name for your servant Augustine, first Archbishop of Canterbury, whose labors in propagating your Church among the English people we commemorate today; and we pray that all whom you call and send may do your will, and bide your time, and see your glory; through Jesus Christ our Lord, who lives and reigns with you and the Holy Spirit, one God, for ever and ever. Amen.

May 28

Mechthild of Magdeburg,

Mystic, Beguine, Benedictine Nun c.1282
Lesser Feast

From the Common of Monastics, page 687

Collect Draw near to the souls of your people, O God, that like your servant Mechthild we may yearn to know you ever more, just as we are known intimately by you, who knows each one of us better than we can know ourselves. All this we ask through Jesus Christ our Lord, who lives and reigns with you and the Holy Spirit, one God now and for ever. Amen.

May 31
The Visitation of the Blessed Virgin Mary
Feast of our Lord
Evening Prayer I

From the Common of the Blessed Virgin Mary, page 636, with the following proper parts

Hymn Ye who claim the faith of Jesus *Hymnal 268*

Antiphon 1 Mary set out and went in haste to a Judean town in the hill country, where she entered the house of Zechariah and greeted Elizabeth.

Psalms from the Common of the Blessed Virgin Mary Evening Prayer I, page 636

Antiphon 2 When Elizabeth heard Mary's greeting, the child leaped in her womb and Elizabeth was filled with the Holy Spirit.

Antiphon 3 Blessed are you among women and blessed is the fruit of your womb.

Reading Isaiah 11:1-10 or Hebrews 2:11-18

Responsory (Is. 11:1, 10)
A shoot shall come out from the stock of Jesse,
– and a branch shall grow out of his roots.
His dwelling shall be glorious
– and a branch shall grow out of his roots.
Glory to the Father and to the Son and to the Holy Spirit.
A shoot shall come out from the stock of Jesse,
– and a branch shall grow out of his roots.

Magnificat Antiphon Blessed are you, O Mary, for you believed that there would be a fulfillment of what was spoken to you by the Lord.

Litany
You called Mary to be the Mother of your Incarnate Word; give insight and strength to all families who are raising children.
Lord, have mercy.
You taught Mary to see Jesus not only as her son but also as her Lord; deepen our discipleship of Christ, our Teacher.
Christ, have mercy.
You deepened Mary's faith by revealing to the Church the risen Christ; bring all the dead to share in Christ's risen life.
Lord, have mercy.

Invitation to the Lord's Prayer
As you called Mary to serve you as the Mother of Christ, may we answer your invitation to a more faithful following of Christ as we pray.

Collect Father in heaven, by your grace the virgin mother of your incarnate Son was blessed in bearing him, but still more blessed in keeping your word: Grant us who honor the exaltation of her lowliness to follow the example of her devotion to your will; through Jesus Christ our Lord, who lives and reigns with you and the Holy Spirit, one God, for ever and ever. Amen.

The Blessing
May we be glad and rejoice forever in what God is creating; for God is creating Jerusalem as a joy, and its people as a delight. **Amen.**

The Visitation of the Blessed Virgin Mary
Morning Prayer

Invitatory Let us celebrate the Visitation of St. Mary. Come let us worship Christ, the Incarnate Word.

Hymn Praise we the Lord this day *Hymnal 267*

Antiphon 1 Elizabeth exclaimed, "Why has this happened that the mother of my Lord comes to me?"
Psalms from Sunday Week 1 Morning Prayer, page 134
Antiphon 2 As soon as I heard the sound of your greeting, the child in my womb leaped for joy.
Antiphon 3 Mary remained with her about three months and then returned to her home.

Reading One 1 Samuel 1: 1-20

Responsory One (Zech. 2:10; Is. 12:6)
Sing and rejoice, O daughter Zion!
    −I will come and dwell in your midst.
Sing and rejoice, O daughter Zion!
    − I will come and dwell in your midst.
Great in your midst is the Holy One of Israel
    − I will come and dwell in your midst.
Glory to the Father and to the Son and to the Holy Spirit.
Sing and rejoice, O daughter Zion!
    − I will come and dwell in your midst.

Canticle of the Annunciation *Ave gratia plena*
(Luke 1: 28, 30-33, 35, 38, 42, 45)

Antiphon Blessed is she who believed that there would be a fulfilment of what was spoken to her by the Lord.

Greetings, favored one! *
>   The Lord is with you.'
>   for you have found favor with God.

You will conceive in your womb and bear a son, *
>   and you will name him Jesus.

He will be great, and will be called the Son of the Most High, *
>   and the Lord God will give to him
>   the throne of his ancestor David.

The Holy Spirit will come upon you, *
>   and the power of the Most High will overshadow you;

Therefore the child to be born will be holy; *
>   he will be called Son of God.

Here am I, the servant of the Lord; *
>   let it be with me according to your word.

Blessed are you among women, *
>   and blessed is the fruit of your womb.

Blessed is she who believed *
>   that there would be a fulfilment
>   of what was spoken to her by the Lord.

Antiphon Blessed is she who believed that there would be a fulfilment of what was spoken to her by the Lord.

Reading Two Hebrews 3: 1-6

Responsory Two (Lk. 11:27; Lk. 1:45)
Blessed is the womb that bore you
>   **—Blessed are those who hear the word of God and obey it.**
Blessed is she who believed
>   **—Blessed are those who hear the word of God and obey it.**
Glory to the Father and to the Son and to the Holy Spirit.
Blessed is the womb that bore you
>   **—Blessed are those who hear the word of God and obey it.**

Benedictus Antiphon When Elizabeth heard the sound of Mary's greeting, the child leaped in her womb for joy. Blessed is she who believed that there would be a fulfillment of what was spoken to her by the Lord.

Litany
Mary endured the estrangement of her unconventional motherhood; comfort all who are victims of sexual violence.
Lord, have mercy.
Mary followed your Son even in his agony; support all who endure the inequalities of our justice system.
Christ, have mercy.
Mary joined the disciples in prayer for the Spirit; deepen the prayer of all committed to contemplation.
Lord, have mercy.

Invitation to the Lord's Prayer
As your Word took flesh from Blessed Mary, may you send us your Spirit to us that we may discern the Mystical Body of your Son as we pray.

Collect *From Evening Prayer I*

The Blessing
May we sing aloud, rejoice and exult with all our hearts for the king of Israel, the Lord, is in our midst. **Amen.**

The Visitation of the Blessed Virgin Mary
Noonday Prayer
Hymn Virgin-born, we bow before thee *Hymnal 258*

Antiphon Hark! My lover – here he comes springing over the mountains, leaping over the hills.
Psalms from Sunday Week 1 Noonday Prayer, page 138

Reading Sirach 24: 8-12
Then the Creator of all things gave me a command, and my Creator chose the place for my tent. He said, 'Make your dwelling in Jacob, and in Israel receive your inheritance.' Before the ages, in the beginning, he created me, and for all the ages I shall not cease to be. In the holy tent I ministered before him, and so I was established in Zion. Thus in the beloved city he gave me a resting place, and in Jerusalem was my domain. I took root in an honored people, in the portion of the Lord, his heritage.

Verse and Response
Blessed are you among women.
And blessed is the fruit of your womb.

Collect *From Evening Prayer I*

The Visitation of the Blessed Virgin Mary
Evening Prayer II

Hymn Ye who claim the faith of Jesus *Hymnal 269*

Antiphon 1 Mary set out and went in haste to a Judean town in the hill country, where she entered the house of Zechariah and greeted Elizabeth.

Psalms from Evening Prayer II of the Common of the Blessed Virgin Mary, page 641

Antiphon 2 When Elizabeth heard Mary's greeting, the child leaped in her womb and Elizabeth was filled with the Holy Spirit.

Antiphon 3 Blessed are you among women and blessed is the fruit of your womb.

Reading Zechariah 2:10-13 or John 3:25-30

Responsory (Luke 1: 42; Luke 11: 28)
Blessed are you among women;
 −blessed is the fruit of your womb.
Blessed are they who hear the word of God and keep it.
 −blessed is the fruit of your womb.
Glory to the Father, and to the Son and to the Holy Spirit.
Blessed are you among women;
 −blessed is the fruit of your womb

Magnificat Antiphon All generations shall call me blessed for the Mighty One has done great things for me and holy is his name.

Litany
You called Mary to be the Mother of your Incarnate Word; give insight and strength to all families who are raising children.
Lord, have mercy.
You taught Mary to see Jesus not only as her son but also as her Lord; deepen our discipleship of Christ, our Teacher.
Christ, have mercy.
You deepened Mary's faith by revealing to the Church the risen Christ; bring all the dead to share in Christ's risen life.
Lord, have mercy.

Collect *From Evening Prayer I*

The Blessing
May we be glad and rejoice forever in what God is creating; for God is creating Jerusalem as a joy, and its people as a delight. **Amen.**

The First Book of Common Prayer
1549
This Commemoration is appropriately observed on a weekday
following the Day of Pentecost.
Lesser Feast

Benedictus Antiphon Christ's Gospel is not a ceremonial law, but it is a religion to serve God, not in bondage of the figure or shadow: but in the freedom of spirit.

Magnificat Antiphon Let us worship in the freedom of spirit, being content only with those ceremonies which serve to a decent order and godly discipline.

Collect Almighty and everliving God, whose servant Thomas Cranmer, with others, restored the language of the people in the prayers of your Church: Make us always thankful for this heritage; and help us so to pray in the Spirit and with the understanding, that we may worthily magnify your holy Name; through Jesus Christ our Lord, who lives and reigns with you and the Holy Spirit, one God, for ever and ever. Amen.

June

June 1

Justin
Martyr at Rome, c. 167
Lesser Feast

From the Common of Martyrs, page 659

Collect Almighty and everlasting God, you found your martyr Justin wandering from teacher to teacher, seeking the true God, and you revealed to him the sublime wisdom of your eternal Word: Grant that all who seek you, or a deeper knowledge of you, may find and be found by you; through Jesus Christ our Lord, who lives and reigns with you and the Holy Spirit, one God, for ever and ever. Amen.

June 2

Blandina and her Companions
Martyrs of Lyons, 177
Lesser Feast

From the Common of Martyrs, page 659

Collect Grant, O Lord, that we who keep the feast of the holy martyrs Blandina and her companions may be rooted and grounded in love of you, and may endure the sufferings of this life for the glory that shall be revealed in us; through Jesus Christ our Lord, who lives and reigns with you and the Holy Spirit, one God, now and for ever. Amen.

June 3

The Martyrs of Uganda
1886
Lesser Feast

From the Common of Martyrs, page 659

Collect O God, by your providence the blood of the martyrs is the seed of the Church: Grant that we who remember before you the blessed martyrs of Uganda, may, like them, be steadfast in our faith in Jesus Christ, to whom they gave obedience, even to death, and by their sacrifice brought forth a plentiful harvest; through Jesus Christ our Lord, who lives and reigns with you and the Holy Spirit, one God, for ever and ever. Amen.

June 5

Boniface
Monk, Archbishop of Mainz, Missionary to Germany, and Martyr, 754
Lesser Feast

From the Common of Martyrs, page 659

Collect Almighty God, you called your faithful servant Boniface to be a witness and martyr in Germany, and by his labor and suffering you raised up a people for your own possession: Pour out your Holy Spirit upon your Church in every land, that by the service and sacrifice of many your holy Name may be glorified and your kingdom enlarged; through Jesus Christ our Lord, who lives and reigns with you and the Holy Spirit, one God, for ever and ever. Amen.

June 6

Ini Kopuria
Founder of the Melanesian Brotherhood, 1945
Lesser Feast

From the Common of Professed Religious, page 685

Collect Loving God, we bless your Name for the witness of Ini Kopuria, police officer and founder of the Melanesian Brotherhood, whose members saved many American pilots in a time of war, and who continue to minister courageously to the islanders of Melanesia. Open our eyes that we, with these Anglican brothers, may establish peace and hope in service to others, for the sake of Jesus Christ; who with you and the Holy Spirit lives and reigns, one God, for ever and ever. Amen.

June 8

Melania the Elder

Monastic, 410

Lesser Feast

From the Common of Monastics, page 687

Collect Most High and Merciful God, who called your servant Melania to forsake earthly comforts in order to devote herself to studying the scriptures and to welcoming the poor; instruct us in the ways of poverty and the grace of hospitality, that we might comfort those who have no place to rest and teach the way of your love; through Jesus Christ our Lord. Amen.

June 9

Columba

Abbot of Iona, 597

Lesser Feast

From the Common of Monastics, page 687, with the following proper antiphons

Benedictus Antiphon By some divine intuition, and through a wonderful expansion of his inner soul, he beheld the whole universe drawn together and laid open to his sight, as in one ray of the sun.

Magnificat Antiphon If you thus follow the example of the holy fathers, God, the Comforter of the good, will be your Helper and I, abiding with Him, will intercede for you.

Collect O God, by the preaching of your blessed servant Columba you caused the light of the Gospel to shine in Scotland: Grant, we pray, that, having his life and labors in remembrance, we may show our thankfulness to you by following the example of his zeal and patience; through Jesus Christ our Lord, who lives and reigns with you and the Holy Spirit, one God, for ever and ever. Amen.

June 10

Ephrem of Edessa Syria

Deacon and Teacher of the Faith, 373

Lesser Feast

From the Common of Teacher of the Faith, page 676

Collect Pour out on us, O Lord, that same Spirit by which your deacon Ephrem rejoiced to proclaim in sacred song the mysteries of faith; and so gladden our hearts that we, like him, may be devoted to you alone;

through Jesus Christ our Lord, who lives and reigns with you and the Holy Spirit, one God, now and for ever. Amen.

June 11

Saint Barnabas the Apostle
Major Feast

From the Common of Apostles, page 648, with the following proper antiphons
Benedictus Antiphon There was a Levite, Joseph, to whom the apostles gave the name Barnabas (which means "son of encouragement"). He sold his field and brought the money to the apostles.

Magnificat Antiphon The whole assembly kept silence, and listened to Barnabas and Paul as they told of all the signs and wonders that God had done through them among the Gentiles.

Collect Grant, O God, that we may follow the example of your faithful servant Barnabas, who, seeking not his own renown but the wellbeing of your Church, gave generously of his life and substance for the relief of the poor and the spread of the Gospel; through Jesus Christ our Lord, who lives and reigns with you and the Holy Spirit, one God, for ever and ever. Amen.

June 12

Enmegahbowh
Priest and Missionary, 1902
Lesser Feast

From the Common of Missionaries, page 680
Collect Almighty God, you led your pilgrim people of old with fire and cloud: Grant that the ministers of your Church, following the example of blessed Enmegahbowh, may stand before your holy people, leading them with fiery zeal and gentle humility. This we ask through Jesus, the Christ, who lives and reigns with you in the unity of the Holy Spirit, one God now and for ever. Amen.

June 12

Alice of Schaerbeek
Cistercian Nun and Leper, 1250
Lesser Feast

From the Common of Monastics, page 687, with the following proper antiphons
Canticle Antiphon Jesus, my heart's portion, has returned to the Father, and the remaining portion of my heart has deserted me too and has gone off with him, leaving me deprived of me.

Benedictus Antiphon God longed that his bride be free, be at leisure for him alone, that she linger with him in the bridal change of her mind and there be soothingly inebriated with a fragrance all his own.

Magnificat Antiphon Alice's soul seemed clothed with God, ever caught up in the divine embrace; she hastened toward death as God's virgin bride toward her wedding.

Collect Father, you gave the holy nun Alice the grace of bearing patiently, for the love of Christ, grievous sickness and disease. With the help of her prayer, may all who suffer pain recognize that they are among the chosen ones whom the Lord calls blessed, and know that they are joined to Christ in his suffering for the salvation of the world, for he lives and reigns with you and the Holy Spirit, one God, for ever and ever. Amen.

June 14

Basil the Great
Monk, Author of a Monastic Rule, Bishop of Caesarea, Teacher of the Faith, 379
Lesser Feast
From the Common of Teacher of the Faith, page 676
Collect Almighty God, you have revealed to your Church your eternal Being of glorious majesty and perfect love as one God in Trinity of Persons: Give us grace that, like your bishop Basil of Caesarea, we may continue steadfast in the confession of this faith, and constant in our worship of you, Father, Son, and Holy Spirit; for you live and reign for ever and ever. Amen.

June 15

Evelyn Underhill
Mystic and Theologian, 1941
Lesser Feast
From the Common of Theologians and Teachers, page 672
Collect O God, Origin, Sustainer, and End of all your creatures: Grant that your Church, taught by your servant Evelyn Underhill, guarded evermore by your power, and guided by your Spirit into the light of truth, may continually offer to you all glory and thanksgiving and attain with your saints to the blessed hope of everlasting life, which you have promised by our Savior Jesus Christ; who with you and the Holy Spirit, lives and reigns, one God, now and for ever. Amen.

June 16

Joseph Butler
Bishop of Durham, 1752
Lesser Feast

From the Common of Theologians and Teachers, page 672

Collect O God, by your Holy Spirit you give to some the word of wisdom, to others the word of knowledge, and to others the word of faith: We praise your Name for the gifts of grace manifested in your servant Joseph Butler, and we pray that your Church may never be destitute of such gifts; through Jesus Christ our Lord, who with you and the Holy Spirit lives and reigns, one God, for ever and ever. Amen.

June 16

Lutgard
Cistercian Nun 1246
Lesser Feast

From the Common of Monastics, page 687, with the following proper antiphons

Benedictus Antiphon Lutgard drank so deeply from the torrent of delight that Christ found the vessel of her heart made that much more magnificent and even more widely open because of her desire.

Magnificat Antiphon Like one beloved, she ate the bread of penance with toil; like one more beloved she drank the abundance of his grace and finally, like one most beloved, she became drunk and was filled with exceeding and ineffable joy.

Collect God our Father, you called the nun, Lutgard, to seek your kingdom in this world by striving to live in perfect charity. With her prayers to give us courage., help us to move forward with joyful hearts in the way of love. Grant this through our Lord Jesus Christ, your Son, Who lives and reigns with you and the Holy Spirit, One God, for ever and ever. Amen.

June 18

Bernard Mizeki
Catechist and Martyr in Rhodesia, 1896
Lesser Feast

From the Common of Martyrs, page 665

Collect Almighty and everlasting God, who kindled the flame of your love in the heart of your holy martyr Bernard Mizeki: Grant to us, your humble servants, a like faith and power of love, that we who rejoice in his triumph may profit by his example; through Jesus Christ our Lord, who lives and reigns with you and the Holy Spirit, one God, for ever and ever. Amen.

June 18

Elisabeth of Schönau
Benedictine Abbess and Mystic, 1164
Lesser Feast

From the Common of Monastics, page 687, with the following proper antiphons.

Benedictus Antiphon In the middle of the sun was the likeness of a virgin whose appearance was beautiful. She wore a crown of gold and held a golden cup in her right hand. The virgin is the sacred humanity of the Lord Jesus.

Magnificat Antiphon Rejoice with me, my Lady Hildegard. You are the organ of the Holy Spirit because your words enkindle me like a flame touching my heart and I burst forth in these words.

Collect O God, by whose grace your servant Elisabeth, kindled with the flame of your love, became a burning and a shining light in your Church: Grant that we also may be aflame with the spirit of love and discipline, and walk before you as children of light; through Jesus Christ our Lord, who lives and reigns with you, in the unity of the Holy Spirit, one God, now and for ever. Amen.

June 19

Romuald
Abbot and Founder of the Camaldolese Order , 1027
Lesser Feast

From the Common of Monastics, page 687

Collect Lord God, through your abbot Romuald you brought the eremital life to a new flowering in the Church. Grant that my denying ourselves and following Christ we may reach the happiness of your heavenly kingdom; through Jesus Christ our Lord, who lives and reigns with you and the Holy Spirit, one God, for ever and ever. Amen.

June22

Alban
First Martyr of Britain, c. 304
Lesser Feast

From the Common of Martyrs, page 665

Collect Almighty God, by whose grace and power your holy martyr Alban triumphed over suffering and was faithful even to death: Grant us, who now remember him in thanksgiving, to be so faithful in our witness to you in this world, that we may receive with him the crown of life;

through Jesus Christ our Lord, who lives and reigns with you and the Holy Spirit, one God, for ever and ever. Amen.

June23

Ethelreda
Benedictine Abbess of Double Monastery at Ely, 697
Lesser Feast
From the Common of Monastics, page 687

Collect Eternal God, who bestowed such grace upon your servant Etheldreda that she gave herself wholly to the life of prayer and to the service of your true religion: grant that we, like her, may so live our lives on earth seeking your kingdom that by your guiding we may be joined to the glorious fellowship of your saints; through Jesus Christ our Lord. Amen.

June 24

The Nativity of Saint John the Baptist
Feast of our Lord
Evening Prayer I

Hymn Comfort, comfort ye my people *Hymnal 67*

Antiphon 1 In the spirit and power of Elijah he will go before him to make ready a people prepared for the Lord
Psalms from Sunday Week 1 Evening Prayer I, page 130
Antiphon 2 Elizabeth will bear you a son, and you will name him John. Many will rejoice at his birth
Antiphon 3 He will be great in the sight of the Lord. Even before his birth he will be filled with the Holy Spirit.

Reading Ecclesiasticus 48:1-11 or Luke 1:5-23

Responsory(Sirach 48: 1; Luke 3: 2)
Elijah arose, a prophet like fire
        – and his word burned like a torch.
The word of God came to John in the wilderness.
        – and his word burned like a torch.
Glory to the Father and to the Son and to the Holy Spirit.
Elijah arose, a prophet like fire
        – and his word burned like a torch.

Magnificat Antiphon Zechariah entered the sanctuary of the Lord to offer incense. An angel of the Lord appeared to him standing at the right side of the altar of incense.

Litany

John preached a baptism of repentance; keep us faithful to our
Baptismal Covenant.
Lord, have mercy.
John lived an austere life in the wilderness; help us embrace a disciplined
Christian life.
Christ, have mercy.
John suffered martyrdom for the sake of the truth; strengthen all
Christians who suffer persecution for the sake of the Gospel.
Lord, have mercy.

Invitation to the Lord's Prayer

In union with Christ, the Lamb of God, let us offer our evening
sacrifice of prayer to the Father.

Collect Almighty God, by whose providence your servant John the
Baptist was wonderfully born, and sent to prepare the way of your Son
our Savior by preaching repentance: Make us so to follow his teaching
and holy life, that we may truly repent according to his preaching; and,
following his example, constantly speak the truth, boldly rebuke vice, and
patiently suffer for the truth's sake; through Jesus Christ your Son our
Lord, who lives and reigns with you and the Holy Spirit, one God, for
ever and ever. Amen.

The Blessing

May we be glad and rejoice forever in what God is creating; for God is
creating Jerusalem as a joy, and its people as a delight. **Amen.**

The Nativity of Saint John the Baptist
Morning Prayer

Invitatory Let us celebrate the Nativity of St. John the Baptist. Come
let us worship Christ, the Lamb of God.

Hymn The great forerunner of the morn *Hymnal 271*

Antiphon 1 The time came for Elizabeth to give birth, and she bore a
son.
Psalms from Sunday Week 1 Morning Prayer, page 134
Antiphon 2 His mother said, "He is to be called John."
Antiphon 3 Zechariah's mouth was opened and his tongue freed, and
he began to speak, praising God.

Reading One Malachi 3:1-5

Responsory (Sirach 48: 10-11)
At the appointed time you are destined
> **– to turn the hearts of parents to their children.**

He proclaimed a baptism of repentance for the forgiveness of sins
> **– to turn the hearts of parents to their children.**

Glory to the Father and to the Son and to the Holy Spirit.
At the appointed time you are destined
> **– to turn the hearts of parents to their children.**

Canticle You are God   *Te Deum laudamus page 757*

Reading Two John 3:22-30

Responsory Two (Mt. 11: 11; Mt. 17: 12)
Among those born of women
> **– no one has arisen greater than John the Baptist.**

Elijah has already come, and they did not recognize him
> **– no one has arisen greater than John the Baptist.**

Glory to the Father and to the Son and to the Holy Spirit.
Among those born of women
> **– no one has arisen greater than John the Baptist.**

Benedictus Antiphon His father Zechariah was filled with the Holy Spirit and spoke this prophecy: "Blessed be the Lord God of Israel."

Litany
Zechariah and Elizabeth rejoiced in the birth of their son; bring joy to the elderly and those without hope.
Lord, have mercy.
You surprised Elizabeth with her pregnancy and took away her shame; support all pregnant women, women who cannot give birth and women with difficult pregnancies.
Christ, have mercy.
You blessed Zechariah and Elizabeth with a child; fill all families with the joy of your love.
Lord, have mercy.

Invitation to the Lord's Prayer
As the birth of John was the dawn of the messianic time, so let peace dawn in our hearts as we pray.

Collect *From Evening Prayer I*

The Blessing
May we sing aloud, rejoice and exult with all our hearts for the king of Israel, the Lord, is in our midst. **Amen.**

The Nativity of Saint John the Baptist
Noonday Prayer

Hymn What is the crying at the Jordan? *Hymnal 69*

Antiphon He will be great in the sight of the Lord. Even before his birth he will be filled with the Holy Spirit.
Psalms from Sunday Week 1 Noonday Prayer page 138

Reading Isaiah 49: 5-6
Now the Lord says, who formed me in the womb to be his servant, to bring Jacob back to him, and that Israel might be gathered to him, for I am honored in the sight of the Lord, and my God has become my strength— he says, "It is too light a thing that you should be my servant to raise up the tribes of Jacob and to restore the survivors of Israel; I will give you as a light to the nations, that my salvation may reach to the end of the earth.

Verse and Response
He on whom you see the Spirit descend and remain.
Is the one who baptizes with the Holy Spirit.

Collect *From Evening Prayer I*

The Nativity of Saint John the Baptist
Evening Prayer II

Hymn On Jordan's bank the Baptist's cry *Hymnal 76*

Antiphon 1 There was a man sent from God, whose name was John.
Psalms from Sunday Week 1 Evening Prayer II, page 141
Antiphon 2 John came as a witness to testify to the light, so that all might believe through him.
Antiphon 3 John came to testify to the light. The true light, which enlightens everyone, was coming into the world.

Reading Malachi 4:1-6 or Matthew 11:2-19

Responsory(Sirach 48: 1; Luke 3: 2)
Elijah arose, a prophet like fire
       – and his word burned like a torch.
The word of God came to John in the wilderness
       – and his word burned like a torch.

Glory to the Father and to the Son and to the Holy Spirit.
Elijah arose, a prophet like fire
– and his word burned like a torch.

Magnificat Antiphon Born for us is a boy, greater than any prophet. Of him the Lord said: Among those born of women no one has arisen greater than John the Baptist.

Litany
John preached a baptism of repentance; keep us faithful to our Baptismal Covenant.
Lord, have mercy.
John lived an austere life in the wilderness; help us embrace a disciplined Christian life.
Christ, have mercy.
John suffered martyrdom for the sake of the truth; strengthen all Christians who suffer persecution for the sake of the Gospel.
Lord, have mercy.

Invitation to the Lord's Prayer
In union with Christ, the Lamb of God, let us offer our evening sacrifice of prayer to the Father.

Collect *From Evening Prayer I*

The Blessing
May we be glad and rejoice forever in what God is creating; for God is creating Jerusalem as a joy, and its people as a delight. **Amen.**

June 28
Irenaeus
Bishop of Lyons, c. 202
Lesser Feast
From the Common of Teacher of the Faith, page 676
Collect Almighty God, you upheld your servant Irenaeus with strength to maintain the truth against every blast of vain doctrine: Keep us, we pray, steadfast in your true religion, that in constancy and peace we may walk in the way that leads to eternal life; through Jesus Christ our Lord, who lives and reigns with you and the Holy Spirit, one God, now and for ever. Amen.

June 29

Saint Peter and Saint Paul
Apostles
Major Feast
From the Common of Apostles, page 648, with the following proper parts
Morning Prayer

Invitatory Christ is the foundation of the Church: Come let us worship the Lord of the Apostles.

Hymn Two stalwart trees both rooted *Hymnal 273*

Antiphon 1 I myself am an elder and a witness of the sufferings of Christ, as well as one who shares in the glory to be revealed.
Psalms from Sunday Week 1 Morning Prayer, page 134
Antiphon 2 Paul, a servant of Jesus Christ, called to be an apostle, set apart for the gospel of God.
Antiphon 3 Christ appeared to Cephas, then to the twelve. Last of all, as to one untimely born, he appeared also to me.

Reading One Ezekiel 2: 1-7

Responsory One (Mt. 10: 18; Acts 9: 16)
You will be dragged before kings because of me
     — as a testimony to them and the Gentiles.
I myself will show him how much he must suffer
     — as a testimony to them and the Gentiles.
Glory to the Father and to the Son and to the Holy Spirit.
You will be dragged before kings because of me
     — as a testimony to them and the Gentiles.

Reading Two Acts 11:1-18

Responsory Two (Acts 15: 8 ; Gen. 12: 3)
God, who knows the human heart
     — gave them the Holy Spirit.
God, who blessed all the nations in Abraham
     — gave them the Holy Spirit.
Glory to the Father and to the Son and to the Holy Spirit.
God, who knows the human heart
     — gave them the Holy Spirit.

Benedictus Antiphon While we live, we are always being given up to death for Jesus' sake, so that the life of Jesus may be made visible in our mortal flesh. Alleluia.

Litany
You called Peter to be a shepherd of your flock; call faithful shepherds to teach your word and celebrate your sacraments.
Lord, have mercy.
You called Paul as a teacher to the nations; call creative teachers to proclaim the Good News of your resurrection.
Christ, have mercy.
You called both Peter and Paul to serve you in ways they never imagined; open our minds and hearts to creative patterns of ministry.
Lord, have mercy.

Collect Almighty God, whose blessed apostles Peter and Paul glorified you by their martyrdom: Grant that your Church, instructed by their teaching and example, and knit together in unity by your Spirit, may ever stand firm upon the one foundation, which is Jesus Christ our Lord; who lives and reigns with you, in the unity of the Holy Spirit, one God, now and for ever. Amen.

Saint Peter and Saint Paul Noonday Prayer
Hymn By all your saints still striving *Hymnal 232*

Antiphon I truly understand that God shows no partiality, but in every nation anyone who fears him and does what is right is acceptable to him.
Psalms from Sunday Week 1 Noonday Prayer page 138

Reading Galatians 1: 15-18
But when God, who had set me apart before I was born and called me through his grace, was pleased to reveal his Son to me, so that I might proclaim him among the Gentiles, I did not confer with any human being, nor did I go up to Jerusalem to those who were already apostles before me, but I went away at once into Arabia, and afterwards I returned to Damascus. Then after three years I did go up to Jerusalem to visit Cephas and stayed with him fifteen days.

Verse and Response
Let them confess the Lord's Name.
The Lord is great and awesome.

Collect *From Morning Prayer*

Saint Peter and Saint Paul Evening Prayer
Hymn The eternal gifts of Christ the King *Hymnal 233*

Antiphon 1 When you grow old, you will stretch out your hands, and someone else will fasten a belt around you and take you where you do not wish to go.

Psalms from Common of the Apostles Evening Prayer II, page 651

Antiphon 2 I have been crucified with Christ; and it is no longer I who live, but it is Christ who lives in me.

Antiphon 3 These are the two olive trees and the two lampstands that stand before the Lord of the earth.

Reading Isaiah 49:1-6 or Galatians 2:1-9

Responsory (Romans 15: 15-16)
I am a minister of Christ Jesus to the Gentiles
– in the priestly service of the gospel of God.
God sanctified the offering of the Gentiles by the Holy Spirit
– in the priestly service of the gospel of God.
Glory to the Father and to the Son and to the Holy Spirit.
I am a minister of Christ Jesus to the Gentiles
– in the priestly service of the gospel of God.

Magnificat Antiphon Today Simon Peter ascended the wood of the cross. Alleluia. Today, he who holds the keys of the kingdom, died with joy to be with Christ. Alleluia. Today the Apostle Paul, the light of the whole world, lowered his head, and for Christ's name's sake received the crown of martyrdom. Alleluia.

Litany
Christ Jesus called the apostles to leave all to follow him; teach us to value Christ above all earthly possessions.
Lord, have mercy.
Christ Jesus appeared to the apostles after the Resurrection; make us witnesses with them of your rising to new live.
Christ, have mercy.
Christ Jesus brought them through martyrdom to new life; strengthen all Christians who suffer death for their faith.
Lord, have mercy.

Collect *From Morning Prayer*

July

July 4

Independence Day
Major Feast

From the Common of National Holidays, page 701, with the following proper antiphons

Benedictus Antiphon Love your enemies and pray for those who persecute you, so that you may be children of your Father in heaven; for he makes his sun rise on the evil and on the good.

Magnificat Antiphon Be perfect as your heavenly Father is perfect.

Collect Lord God Almighty, in whose Name the founders of this country won liberty for themselves and for us, and lit the torch of freedom for nations then unborn: Grant that we and all the people of this land may have grace to maintain our liberties in righteousness and peace; through Jesus Christ our Lord, who lives and reigns with you and the Holy Spirit, one God, for ever and ever. Amen.

July 6

Eva Lee Matthews
Professed Religious, Founder of the Sisters of the Transfiguration, 1928
Lesser Feast

From the Common of Professed Religious, page 691

Collect Gracious God, who called Eva Lee Matthews and her companions to dedicate their lives to you: Grant that we, after their example, may ever surrender ourselves to the revelation of your holy will; through our Lord and Savior Jesus Christ, who lives and reigns with you and the Holy Spirit, one God, for ever and ever. Amen.

July 8

Priscilla and Aquila
Coworkers of the Apostle Paul
Lesser Feast

From the Common of Apostles, page 648, with the following proper antiphons

Benedictus Antiphon Paul found a Jew named Aquila, who had recently come from Italy with his wife Priscilla. Paul went to see them, and, because they were tentmakers, he stayed with them, and they worked together.

Magnificat Antiphon Aquila and Prisca, together with the church in their house, greet you warmly in the Lord.

Collect God of grace and might, we praise you for your servants Aquila and Priscilla, to whom you gave gifts to make the good news known. Raise up, we pray, in every country, heralds and evangelists of your kingdom, so that the world may know the immeasurable riches of our Savior Jesus Christ, who lives and reigns with you and the Holy Spirit, one God, now and for ever. Amen.

July 11

Our Holy Father Saint Benedict of Nursia
Abbot of Monte Cassino, c. 540
Principal Feast
Evening Prayer I

Hymn Jerusalem My Happy Home *Hymnal 620*

Antiphon 1 Benedict, blessed in name and grace, abandoned his family and heritage, took the habit of a monk and lived in the presence of the all seeing God.

Psalms from Sunday Week 1 Evening Prayer I, page 130

Antiphon 2 Living here on earth, he despised the world with all its glory when he could have freely enjoyed it.

Antiphon 3 Desiring to please God alone, he abandoned the world knowingly unacquainted with its ways and wisely unlearned in its wisdom.

Reading 1 Kings 17: 1-16

Responsory (Lk. 1:17; RB Pro. 3)
With the spirit and power of Elijah he will go before the Lord
     −and turn the disobedient to the wisdom of the righteous.
Armed with the weapons of obedience let us do battle for the true King.
     −and turn the disobedient to the wisdom of the righteous.
Glory to the Father and to the Son and to the Holy Spirit.
With the spirit and power of Elijah he will go before the Lord
     −and turn the disobedient to the wisdom of the righteous.

Magnificat Antiphon Let all the church exult in the glory of our gracious Father Benedict. Let the company of monks, nuns and oblates joyfully celebrate his solemnity on earth. Let the communion of saints rejoice in heaven. Alleluia.

Litany

You taught St. Benedict the hidden wisdom of the Cross; teach all monks, nuns and oblates to follow that same hidden way laid out in the Holy Rule.
Lord have mercy.
You called many to follow you in the pattern of the monastic life; continue to call faithful disciples to the Benedictine family.
Christ have mercy.
You led St. Benedict, standing in prayer with hands raised to heaven, on the way to you; bring all the departed into the light of your glory.
Lord have mercy.

Invitation to the Lord's Prayer

Teach us to forgive one another as you have forgiven us and teach us to pray.

Collect Almighty and everlasting God, your precepts are the wisdom of a loving Father: Give us grace, following the teaching and example of your servant Benedict, to walk with loving and willing hearts in the school of the Lord's service; let your ears be open to our prayers; and prosper with your blessing the work of our hands; through Jesus Christ our Lord, who lives and reigns with you and the Holy Spirit, one God, for ever and ever. Amen.

The Blessing

May the word of Christ dwell in us richly as we teach and admonish one another in all wisdom. **Amen.**

Our Holy Father Saint Benedict of Nursia
Morning Prayer

Invitatory: Alleluia. Let us all rejoice in the Lord, celebrating the feast in honor of Benedict, in whose blessed solemnity the angels rejoice and praise the Son of God. Alleluia.

Hymn Blessed City Heavenly Salem *Hymnal 519*

Antiphon 1 Benedict, diligent in prayer, rose before the night office and stood at the window, making his prayer to Almighty God.
Psalms from Sunday Week 1 Morning Prayer, page 134
Antiphon 2 Suddenly looking forth, he saw a light glancing from above, so bright and resplendent that it not only dispersed the darkness of the night but shined more clearly than the day.
Antiphon 3 He saw the whole world compacted as it were together represented to his eyes in one ray of light.

Reading One Proverbs 2: 1-9

Responsory One (Wis. 6:17; Wis. 7:7)
The beginning of wisdom is the desire for instruction
    —and concern for instruction is love of her.
I called on God, and the spirit of wisdom came to me.
    —and concern for instruction is love of her.
Glory to the Father and to the Son and to the Holy Spirit.
The beginning of wisdom is the desire for instruction
    —and concern for instruction is love of her.

       Canticle You are God   *Te Deum laudamus page 757*

Reading Two   Luke 14: 26-33

Responsory Two (1 Cor. 1:18; Gal. 6:14)
The message about the cross is foolishness to the perishing,
    —to us it is the power and the wisdom of God.
May I never boast of anything except the cross of our Lord Jesus Christ.
    —to us it is the power and the wisdom of God.
Glory to the Father and to the Son and to the Holy Spirit.
The message about the cross is foolishness to the perishing,
    —to us it is the power and the wisdom of God.

Benedictus Antiphon   O Blessed Benedict, Father and Guide of monks, nuns and oblates, most holy Confessor of the Lord, intercede for us all and for our salvation.

Litany
Open the ear of our hearts to listen carefully and put into practice the teaching of the Rule that we may run in the path of God's commandments our hearts overflowing with the inexpressible delight of love, we pray.
Lord, have mercy.
Quicken our steps on the way of humility and that we may quickly arrive at the perfect love of God, we pray.
Christ, have mercy.
Full us with that good zeal with separates from evil and leads to you and everlasting life that preferring nothing to Christ he may bring us all together to everlasting life, we pray.
Lord, have mercy.

Invitation to the Lord's Prayer
As the morning star rises in our hearts, hear the prayer of your children as we say.

Collect Lord our God, by your grace Saint Benedict became a great teacher in the school of your service. Grant that we may put nothing before our love of you, and may with open hearts run the path of your commandments. We ask this through our Lord Jesus Christ, your Son, who lives and reigns with you and the Holy Spirit, one God, for ever and ever. Amen.

The Blessing
May we prefer nothing whatever to Christ, and may he bring us all together to everlasting life. **Amen.**

Our Holy Father Saint Benedict of Nursia
Noonday Prayer

Hymn Blest Are The Pure Of Heart *Hymnal 656*

Antiphon Let them prefer absolutely nothing to Christ and may he lead us all together to everlasting life.
Psalms from Sunday Week 1 Noonday Prayer page 138

Reading Acts 2:44-47
All who believed were together and had all things in common; they would sell their possessions and goods and distribute the proceeds to all, as any had need. Day by day, as they spent much time together in the temple, they broke bread at home and ate their food with glad and generous hearts, praising God and having the goodwill of all the people. And day by day the Lord added to their number those who were being saved.

Verse and Response
The law of his God is in his heart.
His footsteps shall not falter.

Collect Inspire, O Lord, within your Church the Spirit which the holy abbot Benedict obeyed, so that we, too, Spirit-filled, may be zealous to love what he loved and to put into practice what he taught through Jesus Christ our Lord, who lives and reigns with you and the Holy Spirit, one God, for ever and ever. Amen.

Our Holy Father Saint Benedict of Nursia
Evening Prayer II

Hymn Jerusalem The Golden *Hymnal 624*

Antiphon 1 Benedict was chosen by the Lord to be an example for the monastic life and the author of the Holy Rule.
Psalms from Sunday Week 1 Evening Prayer II, page 141

Antiphon 2 Blessed is that servant who, when the master comes and knocks, the servant is found keeping vigil.

Antiphon 3 Ardently consumed with love of God, he passed from the house of prayer into the heavenly temple to behold the fair beauty of the Lord.

Reading 2 Kings 2: 1-12

Responsory (RB Prol. 50)
Let us never swerve from the Lord's instructions
    −Let us faithfully observe his teaching until death.
As we share in the suffering of Christ so we shall share in his kingdom.
    −Let us faithfully observe his teaching until death.
Glory to the Father and to the Son and to the Holy Spirit.
Let us never swerve from the Lord's instructions
    −Let us faithfully observe his teaching until death.

Magnificat Antiphon O Blessed Benedict, pattern of heavenly life, our Teacher and Leader, your spirit now rejoices with Christ in heaven. O Kind Shepherd, preserve your flock and strengthen them by your holy prayer. Let them enter into heaven on the way you, their Guide, have shown them in your holy Rule.

Litany
You taught St. Benedict the hidden wisdom of the Cross; teach your people to follow that same hidden way laid out in the Holy Rule.
Lord, have mercy.
You called many to follow you in the pattern of the monastic life; continue to call faithful disciples to the Benedictine family.
Christ, have mercy.
You lead St. Benedict, standing in prayer with hands raised to heaven, on the way to you; bring all the departed into the light of your glory.
Lord, have mercy.

Invitation to the Lord's Prayer
Inspire us to forgive one another as you have forgiven us and teach us to pray.

Collect Lord, by your grace Saint Benedict became a great teacher in the school of your service. Grant that we may put nothing before our love of you, and may we walk eagerly in the path of your commandments through Jesus Christ our Lord, who lives and reigns with you and the Holy Spirit, one God, for ever and ever. Amen.

The Blessing

May Christ help us to set out for the loftier summits of spiritual teaching and virtues and under God's protection may we reach them. **Amen.**

July 12

John Gualbert

Abbot, Founder of the Vallumbrosan Order, 1073

Lesser Feast

From the Common of Monastics, page 687

Collect Ever living God, source of true peace and lover of concord, to know you is true life and to serve you is perfect freedom. So fix us in your love that by the example of your abbot John, we may return good for evil and blessings for curses that we may find in you pardon and peace through Jesus Christ our Lord, who lives and reigns with you and the Holy Spirit, one God, now and for ever. Amen.

July 13

Henry

Emperor, Patron of Benedictine Oblates, 1024

Lesser Feast

From the Common of Holy Persons, page 695

Collect O God, you granted gifts upon Henry and turned him from an earthly kingdom to the kingdom of God. Grant that amid the changes and chances of this earthly life we may keep our hearts centered on your kingdom that we may serve you with pure hearts through Jesus Christ our Lord, who lives and reigns with you and the Holy Spirit, one God, now and for ever. Amen.

July 17

William White

Bishop of Pennsylvania, 1836

Lesser Feast

From the Common of Pastors, page 669

Collect O Lord, in a time of turmoil and confusion you raised up your servant William White, and endowed him with wisdom, patience, and a reconciling temper, that he might lead your Church into ways of stability and peace: Hear our prayer, and give us wise and faithful leaders, that through their ministry your people may be blessed and your will be done; through Jesus Christ our Lord, who lives and reigns with you and the Holy Spirit, one God, for ever and ever. Amen.

July 19

Macrina,

Monastic and Teacher, 379

Lesser Feast

From the Common of Theologians and Teachers, page 672

Collect Merciful God, you called your servant Macrina to reveal in her life and her teaching the riches of your grace and truth: May we, following her example, seek after your wisdom and live according to her way; through Jesus Christ our Savior, who lives and reigns with you and the Holy Spirit, one God, for ever and ever. Amen.

July 20

Elizabeth Cady Stanton, Amelia Bloomer, Sojourner Truth, and Harriet Ross Tubman

Liberators and Prophets

Lesser Feast

From the Common of Prophetic Witnesses, page 684

Collect O God, whose Spirit guides us into all truth and makes us free: Strengthen and sustain us as you did your servants Elizabeth, Amelia, Sojourner, and Harriet. Give us vision and courage to stand against oppression and injustice and all that works against the glorious liberty to which you call all your children; through Jesus Christ our Savior, who lives and reigns with you and the Holy Spirit, one God, for ever and ever. Amen.

July 21

Maria Skobtsoba

Monastic and Martyr, 1945

Lesser Feast

From the Common of Martyrs, page 665

Collect O Creator and Giver of Life, you have crowned your martyr Maria Skobtsova with glory and given her as an example of loving service to the suffering and poor, even to the point of death; teach us to love Christ with all our being, to love one another in truth and action, and to strive against injustice and evil in the world that we may shine with the light of the Resurrection; through Jesus Christ our Lord. Amen.

July 22

Saint Mary Magdalene
Apostle to the Apostles
Major Feast
Evening Prayer I

Hymn Christians, to the Paschal Victim *Hymnal 183*

Antiphon 1 There were also women looking on Jesus on the cross from a distance; among them were Mary Magdalene, and Mary the mother of James the younger and of Joses, and Salome.
Psalms from Sunday Week 1 Evening Prayer I, page 130
Antiphon 2 Mary Magdalene and Mary the mother of Joses saw where Jesus' body was laid.
Antiphon 3 Mary stood weeping outside the tomb. As she wept, she bent over to look into the tomb; and she saw two angels in white, sitting where the body of Jesus had been lying.

Reading Revelation 21:1-4, 21:9-14

Responsory (1 Cor. 16: 20, 24, Phil. 4: 3)
Greet one another with a holy kiss.
    – My love be with all of you in Christ Jesus.
These women struggled beside me in the work of the gospel.
    – My love be with all of you in Christ Jesus.
Glory to the Father and to the Son and to the Holy Spirit.
Greet one another with a holy kiss.
    – My love be with all of you in Christ Jesus.

Magnificat Antiphon Do not weep and do not grieve, for Christ's grace will be entirely with you and will protect you. Let us praise his greatness, for he has prepared us and made us courageous. Alleluia.

Litany
Mary Magdalene remained faithful to Jesus even unto his death on the cross; increase our faith in times of crisis.
Lord, have mercy.
Mary Magdalene supported Jesus and the disciples from their resources; make us generous in supporting your church and the poor.
Christ, have mercy.
Mary Magdalene cared for your body in death; transform all the dead by your risen life.
Lord, have mercy.

Invitation to the Lord's Prayer
Jesus invites us to pray to his Father who is our Father so we raise our voice with Jesus in prayer.

Collect Almighty God, whose blessed Son restored Mary Magdalene to health of body and of mind, and called her to be a witness of his resurrection: Mercifully grant that by your grace we may be healed from all our infirmities and know you in the power of his unending life; who with you and the Holy Spirit lives and reigns, one God, now and for ever. Amen.

The Blessing
Let us pray for one another that the word of the Lord may spread rapidly and be glorified everywhere, just as it is among us. **Amen.**

Saint Mary Magdalene Morning Prayer

Invitatory The Risen Christ appeared to Mary Magdalene: Come let us worship the Lord.

Hymn Christ the Lord is risen again! *Hymnal 184*

Antiphon 1 On the first day of the week, when the sun had risen, Mary Magdalene, and Mary the mother of James, and Salome went to the tomb with spices, so that they might anoint the body of Jesus.
Psalms from Sunday Week 1 Evening Prayer I, page 134
Antiphon 2 The angel said to the women, "Do not be afraid; I know that you are looking for Jesus who was crucified. He is not here; for he has been raised, as he said."
Antiphon 3 Mary Magdalene, Joanna, Mary the mother of James, and the other women with them told all this to the eleven and to all the rest.

Reading One Zephaniah 3:14-20

Responsory One (Song of Solomon 2: 10, 16)
My beloved speaks and says to me:
– **Arise, my love, my fair one, and come away.**
My beloved is mine and I am his
– **Arise, my love, my fair one, and come away.**
Glory to the Father and to the Son and to the Holy Spirit.
My beloved speaks and says to me:
– **Arise, my love, my fair one, and come away.**

Canticle of the Apostles *Vos sacerdotes Domini*
(Isaiah 61: 6-9)

Antiphon. Love enflames my heart. I will seek him whom my soul loves.
I do not know where they have hidden him. Alleluia.

You shall be called priests of the Lord, *
    you shall be named ministers of our God;

You shall enjoy the wealth of the nations, *
    and in their riches you shall glory.

Because their shame was double, *
    and dishonor was proclaimed as their lot,

Therefore they shall possess a double portion; *
    everlasting joy shall be theirs.

For I the Lord love justice, *
    I hate robbery and wrongdoing;

I will faithfully give them their recompense, *
    and I will make an everlasting covenant with them.

Their descendants shall be known among the nations, *
    and their offspring among the peoples;

All who see them shall acknowledge *
    that they are a people whom the Lord has blessed.

Antiphon. Love enflames my heart. I will seek him whom my soul loves.
I do not know where they have hidden him. Alleluia.

Reading Two Mark 15:47-16

Responsory Two (Mt. 10: 18; Acts 9: 16)
Mary, do not weep.
    − The Lord has risen from the tomb.
Go and tell the world.
    − The Lord has risen from the tomb.
Glory to the Father and to the Son and to the Holy Spirit.
Mary, do not weep.
    − The Lord has risen from the tomb.

Benedictus Antiphon O lamp of the world, and bright-shining pearl, by announcing the Resurrection of Christ you became the Apostle of the Apostles! Mary Magdalene, in your kindness, intercede for us with Christ, the Risen Lord. Alleluia.

Litany

You chose Mary Magdalene as the first witness to your resurrection. Empower us to proclaim by word and example the Good News of God in Christ.

Lord have mercy.

At your word, Mary Magdalene went as an apostle to the apostles, proclaiming your resurrection. Send us into the world in witness to your love.

Christ have mercy.

Mary Magdalene proclaimed your resurrection to people who refused to believe her. Open the hearts of all people to your grace and truth.

Lord have mercy.

Invitation to the Lord's Prayer

Jesus invites us to pray to his God who is our God so we raise our voice with Jesus and pray.

Collect *From Evening Prayer I*

The Blessing

May we who have been raised with Christ, seek the things that are above, where Christ is, seated at the right hand of God. **Amen.**

Saint Mary Magdalene Noonday Prayer

Hymn Lift your voice rejoicing, Mary *Hymnal 190*

Antiphon Along with Jesus were some women who had been cured of evil spirits and infirmities: Mary, called Magdalene, from whom seven demons had gone out.

Psalms from Sunday Week 1 Noonday Prayer page 138

Reading: Romans 12:1-2

Brothers and sisters, I beg you through the mercy of God to offer your bodies as a living sacrifice holy and acceptable to God, your spiritual worship. Do not conform yourselves to this age but be transformed by the renewal of your mind, so that you may judge what is God's will, what is good, pleasing and perfect.

Verse and Response

Think of the Lord in goodness.

Seek God with sincerity of heart.

Collect *From Evening Prayer I*

Saint Mary Magdalene Evening Prayer II

Hymn Fairest Lord Jesus *Hymnal 384*

Antiphon 1 Jesus said to her, "Woman, why are you weeping? Whom are you looking for?"

Psalms from the Common of the Apostles Evening Prayer II, page 651

Antiphon 2 Jesus said to her, "Mary!" She turned and said to him "Rabbouni!," which means Teacher.

Antiphon 3 "Go to my brothers and say to them, 'I am ascending to my Father and your Father, to my God and your God.'" Mary Magdalene went and announced to the disciples, "I have seen the Lord."

Reading Exodus 15:19-21 or 2 Corinthians 1:3-7

Responsory (Lk. 24: 10, 7,8)
Mary Magdalene and the other women told the apostles
    – that Christ must be crucified, and rise again.
They remembered the words of Jesus
    – that Christ must be crucified, and rise again.
Glory to the Father and to the Son and to the Holy Spirit.
Mary Magdalene and the other women told the apostles
    – that Christ must be crucified, and rise again.

Magnificat Antiphon My heart is burning within me. I desire to see my Lord. I called him, but he gave no answer. Then he said to me, "Mary." Alleluia.

Litany
You healed Mary Magdalene and sent her as an apostle to the apostles and to the world. Send us out as heralds of your good news.
Lord have mercy.
Mary Magdalene provided for you and the disciples. Help us share our resources for the needs of your church.
Christ have mercy.
Mary Magdalene cared for your body after your death. Bring all the dead into the vision of your glory.
Lord have mercy.

Invitation to the Lord's Prayer
Jesus invites us to pray to his Father who is our Father so we raise our voice with Jesus and say. Our Father.

Collect *From Evening Prayer I*

The Blessing
Let us pray for one another that the word of the Lord may spread rapidly and be glorified everywhere, just as it is among us. **Amen.**

July 23

John Cassian
Abbot at Marseilles, 433
Lesser Feast

From the Common of Monastics, page 687

Collect Holy One, whose beloved Son Jesus Christ blessed the pure in heart: Grant that we, together with your servant John Cassian and in union with his prayers, may ever seek the purity with which to behold you as you are; one God now and for ever. Amen.

July 24

Thomas a Kempis
Canon Regular, Priest, 1471
Lesser Feast

From the Common of Monastics, page 687

Collect Holy Father, you have nourished and strengthened your Church by the inspired writings of your servant Thomas a Kempis: Grant that we may learn from him to know what is necessary to be known, to love what is to be loved, to praise what highly pleases you, and always to seek to know and follow your will; through Jesus Christ our Lord, who lives and reigns with you and the Holy Spirit, one God, for ever and ever. Amen.

July 25

St. James the Apostle
Major Feast

From the Common of the Apostles, page 648, with the following proper antiphons

Benedictus Antiphon Jesus saw James, son of Zebedee, and his brother John. He called them; and they left their father Zebedee in the boat with the hired men, and followed him.

Magnificat Antiphon King Herod laid violent hands upon some who belonged to the church. During the festival of Unleavened Bread, he had James, the brother of John, killed with the sword.

Collect O gracious God, we remember before you today your servant and apostle James, first among the Twelve to suffer martyrdom for the Name of Jesus Christ; and we pray that you will pour out upon the leaders of your Church that spirit of selfdenying service by which alone they may have true authority among your people; through Jesus Christ our Lord, who lives and reigns with you and the Holy Spirit, one God, now and for ever. Amen.

July 26

Joachim and Anne
The Parents of the Blessed Virgin Mary
Lesser Feast

From the Common of Holy Persons, page 695, with the following proper antiphons
Benedictus Antiphon I am the God of your ancestors. I have observed the misery of my people and I have come down to deliver them.

Magnificat Antiphon A shoot shall come out from the stump of Jesse, and a branch shall grow out of his roots. The spirit of the Lord shall rest on him.

Collect Almighty God, heavenly Father, who set the solitary in Families: We thankfully remember before you this day the parents of the Blessed Virgin Mary, and we humbly entrust to your never-failing care the homes in which your people dwell; that we may be made true members of the heavenly family of your Son Jesus Christ, who lives and reigns with you and the Holy Spirit, one God, now and ever. Amen.

July 27

William Reed Huntington
Priest, 1909
Lesser Feast

From the Common of Pastors, page 669
Collect O Lord our God, we thank you for instilling in the heart of your servant William Reed Huntington a fervent love for your Church and its mission in the world; and we pray that, with unflagging faith in your promises, we may make known to all people your blessed gift of eternal life; through Jesus Christ our Lord, who lives and reigns with you and the Holy Spirit, one God, for ever and ever. Amen.

July 29

Mary, Martha and Lazarus of Bethany
Hosts and Friends of our Lord
Lesser Feast

From the Common of Holy Persons, page 695, with the following proper antiphons.
Benedictus Antiphon Martha said to Jesus, 'Yes, Lord, I believe that you are the Messiah, the Son of God." When Jesus saw Mary weeping, he was greatly disturbed in spirit. Jesus cried with a loud voice, 'Lazarus, come out!' The dead man came out of the tomb.

Magnificat Antiphon Martha gave a dinner for Jesus. Lazarus was one of those at the table with him. Mary took a pound of pure nard and anointed Jesus' feet.

Collect Generous God, whose Son Jesus Christ enjoyed the friendship and hospitality of Mary, Martha and Lazarus of Bethany: Open our hearts to love you, our ears to hear you, and our hands to welcome and serve you in others, through Jesus Christ our risen Lord; who with you and the Holy Spirit lives and reigns, one God, for ever and ever. Amen.

July 30

William Wilberforce
Politician and Liberator, 1833
Lesser Feast
From the Common of Prophetic Witnesses, page 684

Collect Let your continual mercy, O Lord, kindle in your Church the never-failing gift of love, that, following the example of your servant William Wilberforce, we may have grace to defend the poor, and maintain the cause of those who have no helper; for the sake of him who gave his life for us, your Son our Savior Jesus Christ, who lives and reigns with you and the Holy Spirit, one God, now and for ever. Amen.

July 31

Ignatius of Loyola
Professed Religious, Priest and Founder of the Society of Jesus, 1556
Lesser Feast
From the Common of Professed Religious, page 691

Collect Almighty God, from whom all good things come: You called Ignatius of Loyola to the service of your Divine Majesty and to find you in all things. Inspired by his example and strengthened by his companionship, may we labor without counting the cost and seek no reward other than knowing that we do your will; through Jesus Christ our Savior, who lives and reigns with you and the Holy Spirit, now and for ever. Amen.

August

August 1

Joseph of Arimathaea
Disciple of our Lord
Lesser Feast
From the Common of Holy Persons, page 695, with the following proper antiphons

Benedictus Antiphon Joseph of Arimathea, who was a disciple of Jesus, though a secret one because of his fear of the Jews, asked Pilate to let him take away the body of Jesus.

Magnificat Antiphon Joseph took the body of Jesus down from the Cross. The Lord's body is clothed in glory as with a robe; but seeing him lifeless, naked and unburied, Joseph began to weep and lament, saying: 'Great is my sorrow, O sweet Jesus!'

Collect Merciful God, whose servant Joseph of Arimathaea with reverence and godly fear prepared the body of our Lord and Savior for burial, and laid it in his own tomb: Grant to us, your faithful people, grace and courage to love and serve Jesus with sincere devotion all the days of our life; through Jesus Christ our Lord, who lives and reigns with you and the Holy Spirit, one God, for ever and ever. Amen.

August 3

Joanna, Mary, and Salome
Myrrh-bearing Women
Lesser Feast

From the Common of Apostles, page 648, with the following proper antiphons

Benedictus Antiphon And very early on the first day of the week, when the sun had risen, Mary Magdalene, and Mary the mother of James, and Salome bought spices, so that they might go and anoint him.

Magnificat Antiphon Mary Magdalene, Joanna, Mary the mother of James, and the other women with them remembered Jesus' words, and returning from the tomb, they told all this to the eleven and to all the rest.

Collect Almighty God, who revealed the resurrection of your Son to Joanna, Mary and Salome, as they faithfully came bearing myrrh to his tomb: Grant that we too may perceive the presence of the risen Lord in the midst of pain and fear, that we may go forth proclaiming the resurrection of Jesus Christ, who lives and reigns with you and the Holy Spirit, one God now and forever. Amen.

August 6

The Transfiguration of Our Lord Jesus Christ
Feast of our Lord
Evening Prayer I

Hymn O wondrous type! O vison fair *Hymnal 136*

Antiphon 1 Six days later, Jesus took with him Peter and James and his brother John and led them up a high mountain, by themselves.

Psalms from Sunday Week 1 Evening Prayer I, page 130

Antiphon 2 He was transfigured before them, and his face shone like the sun, and his clothes became dazzling white.

Antiphon 3 Suddenly a bright cloud overshadowed them, and from the cloud a voice said, 'This is my Son, the Beloved; with him I am well pleased; listen to him!'

Reading 1 Kings 19:1-12 or 2 Corinthians 3:1-9,18

Responsory (2 Corinthians 3:18; Romans 12: 2)
All of us, with unveiled faces, see the glory of the Lord
    – we are being transformed from glory to glory.
Be transformed by the renewing of your minds.
    – we are being transformed from glory to glory.
Glory to the Father, and to the Son and to the Holy Spirit.
All of us, with unveiled faces, see the glory of the Lord,
    – we are being transformed from glory to glory.

Magnificat O Radiant Lord Christ, splendor of the Father, perfect icon of God's being, you sustain the universe with your powerful word and purify us from our sins. Today is the day your glory transfigured your very body on the holy mountain. Alleluia.

Litany
O Christ, Light of the world, illumine all who seek you with the vision of your truth.
Lord, have mercy.
O Christ, Light of the world, shine on all who dwell in the darkness of hopelessness and depression.
Christ, have mercy.
O Christ, Light of the world, transform the dead with the radiance of your resurrection.
Lord, have mercy.

Invitation to the Lord's Prayer
With minds illuminated by faith and hearts warmed by love, let us, the beloved children of God, pray to the Father.

Collect O God, who on the holy mount revealed to chosen witnesses your well-beloved Son, wonderfully transfigured, in raiment white and glistening: Mercifully grant that we, being delivered from the disquietude of this world, may by faith behold the King in his beauty; who with you, O Father, and you, O Holy Spirit, lives and reigns, one God, for ever and ever. Amen.

The Blessing

We are all children of light and children of the day; we are not of the night or of darkness. So then let us not fall asleep as others do, but let us keep awake and be sober. **Amen.**

The Transfiguration of Our Lord Jesus Christ
Morning Prayer

Invitatory Christ is the King of glory: Come let us worship

Psalm 24 *Domini est terra*

1 The earth is the LORD'S and all that is in it, *
>   the world and all who dwell therein.
2 For it is he who founded it upon the seas *
>   and made it firm upon the rivers of the deep.

Christ is the King of glory, come let us worship.

3 "Who can ascend the hill of the LORD? *
>   and who can stand in his holy place?"
4 "Those who have clean hands and a pure heart, *
>   who have not pledged themselves to falsehood,
>   nor sworn by what is a fraud.

Christ is the King of glory, come let us worship.

5 They shall receive a blessing from the Lord *
>   and a just reward from the God of their salvation."
6 Such is the generation of those who seek him, *
>   of those who seek your face, O God of Jacob.

Christ is the King of glory, come let us worship.

7 Lift up your heads, O gates;
>   lift them high, O everlasting doors; *
>   and the King of glory shall come in.
8 "Who is this King of glory?" *
>   "The LORD, strong and mighty,
>   the LORD, mighty in battle."

Christ is the King of glory, come let us worship.

9 Lift up your heads, O gates;
>   lift them high, O everlasting doors; *
>   and the King of glory shall come in.

10 "Who is he, this King of glory?" *
>> "The LORD of hosts,
>> he is the King of glory."

Christ is the King of glory, come let us worship.

Glory to the Father, and to the Son, and to the Holy Spirit:
>> as it was in the beginning, is now, and will be for ever. Amen.

Christ is the King of glory, come let us worship.

Hymn Christ upon the mountain peak *Hymnal 129*

Psalm 96 *Cantate Domino*
Antiphon While Jesus was praying, the appearance of his face changed, and his clothes became dazzling white.

1 Sing to the LORD a new song; *
>> sing to the LORD, all the whole earth.

2 Sing to the LORD and bless his Name; *
>> proclaim the good news of his salvation from day to day.

3 Declare his glory among the nations *
>> and his wonders among all peoples.

4 For great is the LORD and greatly to be praised; *
>> he is more to be feared than all gods.

5 As for all the gods of the nations, they are but idols; *
>> but it is the LORD who made the heavens.

6 Oh, the majesty and magnificence of his presence! *
>> Oh, the power and the splendor of his sanctuary!

7 Ascribe to the LORD, you families of the peoples; *
>> ascribe to the LORD honor and power.

8 Ascribe to the LORD the honor due his Name; *
>> bring offerings and come into his courts.

9 Worship the LORD in the beauty of holiness; *
>> let the whole earth tremble before him.

10 Tell it out among the nations: "The LORD is King! *
>> he has made the world so firm that it cannot be moved;
>> he will judge the peoples with equity."

11 Let the heavens rejoice, and let the earth be glad;
   let the sea thunder and all that is in it; *
      let the field be joyful and all that is therein.

12 Then shall all the trees of the wood shout for joy
   before the LORD when he comes, *
      when he comes to judge the earth.

13 He will judge the world with righteousness *
   and the peoples with his truth.

Antiphon While Jesus was praying, the appearance of his face changed, and his clothes became dazzling white.

Psalm 84 *Quam dilecta!*

Antiphon Suddenly they saw two men, Moses and Elijah, talking to him. They appeared in glory and were speaking of his departure, which he was about to accomplish at Jerusalem.

1 How dear to me is your dwelling, O LORD of hosts! *
      My soul has a desire and longing
      for the courts of the LORD;
         my heart and my flesh rejoice in the living God.

2 The sparrow has found her a house
   and the swallow a nest where she may lay her young; *
      by the side of your altars, O LORD of hosts,
      my King and my God.

3 Blessed are they who dwell in your house! *
      they will always be praising you.

4 Blessed are the people whose strength is in you! *
      whose hearts are set on the pilgrims' way.

5 Those who go through the desolate valley
   will find it a place of springs, *
      for the early rains have covered it with pools of water.

6 They will climb from height to height, *
      and the God of gods will reveal himself in Zion.

7 LORD God of hosts, hear my prayer; *
      hearken, O God of Jacob.

8 Behold our defender, O God; *
      and look upon the face of your Anointed.

9 For one day in your courts is better
   than a thousand in my own room, *
      and to stand at the threshold of the house of my God
      than to dwell in the tents of the wicked.

10 For the LORD God is both sun and shield; *
      he will give grace and glory;

11 No good thing will the LORD withhold *
      from those who walk with integrity.

12 O LORD of hosts, *
      blessed are they who put their trust in you!

Antiphon Suddenly they saw two men, Moses and Elijah, talking to him. They appeared in glory and were speaking of his departure, which he was about to accomplish at Jerusalem.

Psalm 29   *Afferte Domino*

Antiphon A cloud came and overshadowed them; and they were terrified as they entered the cloud. Then from the cloud came a voice that said, 'This is my Son, my Chosen; listen to him!'

1 Ascribe to the LORD, you gods, *
      ascribe to the LORD glory and strength.

2 Ascribe to the LORD the glory due his Name; *
      worship the LORD in the beauty of holiness.

3 The voice of the LORD is upon the waters;
   the God of glory thunders; *
      the LORD is upon the mighty waters.

4 The voice of the LORD is a powerful voice; *
      the voice of the LORD is a voice of splendor.

5 The voice of the LORD breaks the cedar trees; *
      the LORD breaks the cedars of Lebanon;

6 He makes Lebanon skip like a calf, *
      and Mount Hermon like a young wild ox.

7 The voice of the LORD splits the flames of fire;
   the voice of the LORD shakes the wilderness; *
      the LORD shakes the wilderness of Kadesh.

8 The voice of the LORD makes the oak trees writhe *
      and strips the forests bare.

9 And in the temple of the LORD *
    all are crying, "Glory!"

10 The LORD sits enthroned above the flood; *
    the LORD sits enthroned as King for evermore.

11 The LORD shall give strength to his people; *
    the LORD shall give his people the blessing of peace.

Antiphon A cloud came and overshadowed them; and they were terrified as they entered the cloud. Then from the cloud came a voice that said, 'This is my Son, my Chosen; listen to him!'

Reading One Exodus 24:12-18

Responsory (Ps. 8:6, 7)
You adorn him with glory and honor
    −Alleluia, alleluia.
You put all things under his feet.
    −Alleluia, alleluia.
Glory to the Father, and to the Son and to the Holy Spirit.
You adorn him with glory and honor;
    −Alleluia, alleluia.

Canticle You are God   *Te Deum laudamus page 757*

Reading Two 2 Corinthians 4:1-6

Responsory Two (Is. 60:19; Mt. 13:43)
The sun shall no longer be your light by day
    − the Lord will be your everlasting light.
The righteous shall shine as the sun in their Father's Kingdom.
    − the Lord will be your everlasting light.
Glory to the Father, and to the Son and to the Holy Spirit.
The sun shall no longer be your light by day,
    − the Lord will be your everlasting light.

Benedictus Antiphon God who said, "Let light shine out of darkness," has shone in our hearts to give the light of the knowledge of the glory of God in the face of Jesus Christ.

Litany
Father, you illumine our hearts with knowledge in beholding by faith the face of your Beloved Son. Let us be faithful in our contemplation.
Lord, have mercy.

Lord Christ, you are the light who illumines the hearts of all people. Open the hearts of the world's leaders to champion the cause of justice for the poor and the oppressed.
Christ, have mercy.
Blest Spirit, you shine in our hearts and fill us with God's love. Open our hearts to forgive those who offend us and those who are aligned with the power of evil.
Lord, have mercy.

Invitation to the Lord's Prayer As the morning star illumines our world, may Christ, the world's light shine in our hearts and inspire us to pray.

Collect *From Evening Prayer I*

The Blessing
May we greatly rejoice in the Lord. May our whole being shall exult in our God who has clothed us with the garments of salvation, and has covered us with the robe of righteousness. **Amen.**

The Transfiguration of Our Lord Jesus Christ
Noonday Prayer
Hymn O Light of Light, Love given birth *Hymnal 134*

Antiphon You are the fairest of men; grace flows from your lips, because God has blessed you for ever.
Psalms from Sunday Week 2 Noonday Prayer page 138

Reading 2 Peter 1: 16-18
For we did not follow cleverly devised myths when we made known to you the power and coming of our Lord Jesus Christ, but we had been eyewitnesses of his majesty. For he received honor and glory from God the Father when that voice was conveyed to him by the Majestic Glory, saying, "This is my Son, my Beloved, with whom I am well pleased." We ourselves heard this voice come from heaven, while we were with him on the holy mountain.

Verse and Response
We have seen the light of the gospel of the glory of Christ.
We proclaim Jesus Christ as Lord and ourselves as your slaves.

Collect *From Vesper I*

The Transfiguration of Our Lord Jesus Christ
Evening Prayer II

Hymn I want to walk as a child of the light *Hymnal 490*

Antiphon 1 Six days later, Jesus took with him Peter and James and his brother John and led them up a high mountain, by themselves.

Psalms from Sunday Week 1 Evening Prayer II, page 141

Antiphon 2 He was transfigured before them, and his face shone like the sun, and his clothes became dazzling white.

Antiphon 3 Suddenly a bright cloud overshadowed them, and from the cloud a voice said, 'This is my Son, the Beloved; with him I am well pleased; listen to him!'

Reading Daniel 7:9-10,13-14 or John 12:27-36a

Responsory (John 8: 12; John 12: 36)
I am the light of the world
> **– whoever follows me will have the light of life.**

Believe in the light that you may become children of light
> **– whoever follows me will have the light of life.**

Glory to the Father, and to the Son and to the Holy Spirit.
I am the light of the world
> **– whoever follows me will have the light of life.**

Magnificat When the voice had spoken, the disciples fell to the ground and were overcome by fear. Jesus came and touched them, saying, "Get up and do not be afraid." Alleluia.

Litany
O Christ, Light of the world, illumine all who seek you with the vision of your truth.
Lord, have mercy.
O Christ, Light of the world, shine on all who dwell in the darkness of hopelessness and depression.
Christ, have mercy.
O Christ, Light of the world, transform the dead with the radiance of your resurrection.
Lord, have mercy.

Invitation to the Lord's Prayer
Today, Christ illumines our hearts with the light of faith so we turn with Christ to the Father and pray.

Collect *From Evening Prayer I*

The Blessing

We are all children of light and children of the day; we are not of the night or of darkness. So then let us not fall asleep as others do, but let us keep awake and be sober. **Amen.**

August 7

John Mason Neale

Priest, 1866

Lesser Feast

From the Common of Pastors, page 669

Collect Grant, O God, that in all time of our testing we may know your presence and obey your will; that, following the example of your servant John Mason Neale, we may with integrity and courage accomplish what you give us to do, and endure what you give us to bear; through Jesus Christ our Lord, who lives and reigns with you and the Holy Spirit, one God, for ever and ever. Amen.

August 8

Dominic

Friar, Priest, and Founder of the Order of Preachers, 1221

Lesser Feast

From the Common of Monastics, page 687, with the following proper antiphons

Benedictus Antiphon In purity of body and a martyrdom of the soul your eloquent speech filled the world. O Poor One of Christ, God gave you the reward of life at the end of the contest.

Magnificat Antiphon Light of the Church, Teacher of truth, Rose of patience, Ivory of chastity, You freely offered the waters of wisdom. Preacher of grace, bring us together with the blessed.

Collect O God of the prophets, you opened the eyes of your servant Dominic to perceive a famine of hearing the word of the Lord, and moved him, and those he drew about him, to satisfy that hunger with sound preaching and fervent devotion: Make your Church, dear Lord, in this and every age, attentive to the hungers of the world, and quick to respond in love to those who are perishing; through Jesus Christ our Lord, who lives and reigns with you and the Holy Spirit one God, for ever and ever. Amen.

August 9

Teresa Benedicta of the Cross

Scholar, Discalced Carmelite Nun and Martyr 1942

Lesser Feast

From the Common of Martyrs, page 665, with the following proper antiphons

Benedictus Antiphon The world is in flames; the fire can spread even to our house, but above all the flames the cross stands on high and it cannot be burned.

Magnificat Antiphon Through the power of the cross, you can be present wherever there is pain, carried there by your compassionate heart, by that very charity that you draw from the divine heart.

Collect Lord, God of our ancestors, your brought Teresa Benedicta to the fullness of the science of the cross in the hour of her martyrdom. Fill us with that same knowledge and allow us always to seek after you, the supreme truth, and to remain faithful until death to the covenant of love ratified in the blood of your Son for the salvation of all men and women. Grant this through our Lord Jesus Christ, your Son, who lives and reigns with you and the Holy Spirit, one God, forever and ever. Amen.

August 10

Laurence
Deacon, and Martyr at Rome, 258
Lesser Feast
From the Common of Martyrs, page 665, with the following proper parts
Morning Prayer
Antiphon 1 Laurence has joined the martyrs who acknowledge the name of our Lord Jesus Christ.
Psalms from current day of the week.
Antiphon 2 The Lord sent his angel to rescue me from the flames and I was not burned.
Antiphon 3 My soul clings to you because my flesh has been burned for you, my God.

Benedictus Antiphon The Blessed Deacon Lawrence prayed: "For me the night is not dark for all things shine as in the light of the midday sun."

Collect Almighty God, you called your deacon Laurence to serve you with deeds of love, and gave him the crown of martyrdom: Grant that we, following his example, may fulfill your commandments by defending and supporting the poor, and by loving you with all our hearts; through Jesus Christ our Lord, who lives and reigns with you and the Holy Spirit, one God, for ever and ever. Amen.

Laurence Evening Prayer
Antiphon 1 Blessed Laurence prayed aloud, " I give you thanks, O Lord, for you have opened for me the gates of heaven.

Psalms from current day of the week.

Antiphon 2 Unless a grain of wheat falls into the earth and dies, it remains just a single grain; but if it dies, it bears much fruit.

Antiphon 3 You prove my heart and summon me by night. You tried me with fire and you found no impurity in me.

Magnificat Antiphon Fear not, for I have redeemed you; I have called you by name, you are mine. When you walk through fire you shall not be burned, and the flame shall not consume you.

Collect *From Morning Prayer*

August 11

Clare

Abbess at Assisi and Foundress of the Poor Clares, 1253
Lesser Feast

From the Common of Monastics, page 687, with the following proper antiphons

Benedictus Antiphon It is your Father's good pleasure to give you the kingdom of heaven.

Magnificat Antiphon You have left all things and followed me; you will be repaid a hundred times over and gain eternal life.

Collect Grant, O God, whose blessed Son became poor that we through his poverty might be rich: Deliver us from an inordinate love of this world, that we, inspired by the devotion of your servant Clare, may serve you with singleness of heart, and attain to the riches of the age to come; through Jesus Christ our Lord, who lives and reigns with you and the Holy Spirit, one God, for ever and ever. Amen.

August 12

Florence Nightingale

Nurse, Social Reformer, 1910
Lesser Feast

From the Common of Prophetic Witnesses, page 684

Collect Life-giving God, you alone have power over life and death, over health and sickness: Give power, wisdom, and gentleness to those who follow the lead of Florence Nightingale, that they, bearing with them your presence, may not only heal but bless, and shine as lanterns of hope in the darkest hours of pain and fear; through Jesus Christ, the healer of body and soul, who lives and reigns with you and the Holy Spirit, one God, now and for ever. Amen.

August 13

Jeremy Taylor

Bishop of Down, Connor, and Dromore, 1667
Lesser Feast

From the Common of Theologians and Teachers, page 672

Collect O God, whose days are without end, and whose mercies cannot be numbered: Make us, like your servant Jeremy Taylor, deeply aware of the shortness and uncertainty of human life; and let your Holy Spirit lead us in holiness and righteousness all our days; through Jesus Christ our Lord, who lives and reigns with you and the Holy Spirit, one God, now and for ever. Amen.

August 14

Jonathan Myrick Daniels

Seminarian, Witness for Civil Rights and Martyr, 1965
Lesser Feast

From the Common of Martyrs, page 665, with the following proper antiphon

Benedictus Antiphon I knew that I had been truly baptized into the Lord's death and resurrection with them, the black men and white men, with all life; in God we are indelibly and unspeakably one.

Collect O God of justice and compassion, who put down the proud and the mighty from their place, and lift up the poor and afflicted: We give you thanks for your faithful witness Jonathan Myrick Daniels, who, in the midst of injustice and violence, risked and gave his life for another; and we pray that we, following his example, may make no peace with oppression; through Jesus Christ the just one: who lives and reigns with you and the Holy Spirit, one God, for ever and ever. Amen.

August 15

Saint Mary the Virgin, Mother of Our Lord Jesus Christ

Major Feast

Evening Prayer I

Hymn Sing of Mary, pure and lowly *Hymnal 277*

Antiphon 1 How beautiful you are, my love, how very beautiful! Your lips distill nectar, my bride; honey and milk are under your tongue; the fragrance of your garments is like the perfume of Lebanon. Arise, my beloved, and come. Come and you shall be crowned.

Psalms from the Common of the Blessed Virgin Mary Evening Prayer I, page 636

Antiphon 2 Why is your beloved better than any other beloved, O fairest among women? My beloved is all radiant and ruddy, distinguished among ten thousand. His left hand is under my head. His right hand embraces me.

Antiphon 3 This is my beloved and this is my friend, O Daughters of Jerusalem.

Reading John 19:23-27 or Acts 1:6-14

Responsory (Ps. 132:13; Ps. 27:4)
The Lord has chosen her
      – **his loved one from the beginning.**
The Lord has taken her to dwell with him.
      – **his loved one from the beginning.**
Glory to the Father, and to the Son and to the Holy Spirit.
The Lord has chosen her
      – **his loved one from the beginning.**

Magnificat Antiphon Christ has ascended above the heavens and has prepared for his Mother an immortal dwelling place. Today is that most celebrated festival above the festivals of all the saints of which the holy church is ever mindful. Today is the day when the glorious and blessed Mary arrived at the heavenly bridal chamber.

Litany
The Father has chosen Mary to be the mother of his Son; let us rejoice with Christ in being called beloved children of God.
Lord have mercy.
Mary proclaimed that God would feed the hungry and lift the downtrodden; may we open our hands and our hearts to serve Christ in the hungry and oppressed.
Christ have mercy.
Mary has entered into the dwelling place prepared for her by Christ; may all the dead enter their heavenly home.
Lord have mercy.

Invitation to the Lord's Prayer
Rejoicing in our hope of sharing the glory of God, let us long for the kingdom of God in the words of Christ.

Collect O God, you have taken to yourself the blessed Virgin Mary, mother of your incarnate Son: Grant that we, who have been redeemed by his blood, may share with her the glory of your eternal kingdom;

through Jesus Christ our Lord, who lives and reigns with you, in the unity of the Holy Spirit, one God, now and for ever. Amen.

The Blessing
May we who celebrate Mary whose womb bore Christ and whose breasts nursed Christ be blessed in hearing the word of God and obeying it. **Amen.**

Saint Mary the Virgin, Mother of Our Lord Jesus Christ
Morning Prayer

Invitatory Let us all rejoice in the Lord, celebrating the feast in honor of the Blessed Virgin Mary at whose festival the angels rejoice and praise the Son of God.

Hymn Sing we of the Blessed Mother *Hymnal 278*

Antiphon 1 Mary is taken into heaven. The Angels rejoice and bless the Lord.
Psalms from Sunday Week 1 Morning Prayer, page 134
Antiphon 2 The Virgin Mary is brought into the heavenly bridal chamber where the King of kings is seated on a throne of stars.
Antiphon 3 You, O Daughter, are blessed by our Lord for by you we have shared the fruit of life.

Reading One 1 Samuel 2:1-10

Responsory One
I saw the fair one like a dove rising above the streams of water
    − her attractive fragrance lingered in her garments.
She was circled about by roses and the lily of the valley
    − her attractive fragrance lingered in her garments.
Glory to the Father, and to the Son and to the Holy Spirit.
I saw the fair one like a dove rising above the streams of water,
    − her attractive fragrance lingered in her garments.

Canticle − Song of the Annunciation page 640

Reading Two John 2:1-12

Responsory Two (Luke 1: 42; Luke 11: 28)
Blessed are you among women
    − blessed is the fruit of your womb.
Blessed are they who hear the word of God and keep it.
    − blessed is the fruit of your womb.
Glory to the Father, and to the Son and to the Holy Spirit.

Blessed are you among women;
– blessed is the fruit of your womb.

Benedictus Antiphon Who is she that comes forth glorious as the morning rising, fair as the moon and bright as the sun?

Litany
You illumined the world when you called Mary to become the mother of your son; illumine our hearts by the light of your Spirit.
Lord have mercy.
Mary went to the aid of her cousin Elizabeth; make us strong in serving those in need.
Christ have mercy.
Mary was faithful in prayer with the disciples; summon us to pray constantly in the Spirit.
Lord have mercy.

Invitation to the Lord's Prayer
Mary has entered into the light of the risen Christ who illumines the world, so with Christ we pray to share the glory of the Father.

Collect *From Evening Prayer I*

The Blessing
May we who believe that God sent his Son, born of a woman, born under the law, be blessed in our redemption and our adoption as children of God. **Amen.**

Saint Mary the Virgin, Mother of Our Lord Jesus Christ
Noonday Prayer
Hymn Virgin born we bow before thee *Hymnal 258*

Antiphon O Daughter of Zion, you are wholly beautiful and sweet, fair as the moon, bright as the sun.
Psalms from Sunday Week 1 Noonday Prayer page 138

Reading Revelation 12: 1
A great portent appeared in heaven: a woman clothed with the sun, with the moon under her feet, and on her head a crown of twelve stars.

Verse and Response
The Virgin Mary is taken into heaven.
The angels rejoice; the archangels shout for joy.

Collect *From Evening Prayer I*

Saint Mary the Virgin, Mother of Our Lord Jesus Christ
Evening Prayer II

Hymn Ye who claim the faith of Jesus *Hymnal 269*

Antiphon 1 My beloved has gone down to his garden to the beds of spices to pasture his flock in the gardens and to gather lilies.
Psalms from the Common of the Blessed Virgin Mary Evening Prayer II, page 641
Antiphon 2 My dove, my perfect one, is the only one. The maidens saw her and called her blessed.
Antiphon 3 I am my beloved's and my beloved is mine. He pastures his flock among the lilies.

Reading Jeremiah 31:1-14 or Zechariah 2:10-13

Responsory (Ps. 132:13; Ps. 27:4)
The Lord has chosen her
  – his loved one from the beginning.
The Lord has taken her to dwell with him.
  – his loved one from the beginning.
Glory to the Father, and to the Son and to the Holy Spirit.
The Lord has chosen her,
  – his loved one from the beginning.

Magnificat Antiphon Today the Virgin Mary entered the reign of heaven; rejoice, for she dwells with Christ forever. Alleluia.

Litany
The Father has chosen Mary to be the mother of his Son; let us rejoice with Christ in being called beloved children of God.
Lord have mercy.
Mary proclaimed that God would feed the hungry and lift the downtrodden; may we open our hands and our hearts to serve Christ in the hungry and oppressed.
Christ have mercy.
Mary has entered into the dwelling place prepared for her by Christ; may all the dead enter their heavenly home.
Lord have mercy.

Invitation to the Lord's Prayer
Rejoicing in our hope of sharing the glory of God, let us long for the kingdom of God in the words of Christ.

Collect *From Evening Prayer I*

The Blessing
May we who celebrate Mary whose womb bore Christ and whose breasts nursed Christ be blessed in hearing the word of God and obeying it. **Amen.**

August 16

Roger Schutz
Monk and Founder of Taizé, 2005
Lesser Feast
From the Common of Monastics, page 687
Collect O gentle God, you called your servant Roger to witness to the unity of the Church and to found an ecumenical religious community at Taizé. Grant to your church that vision to see itself as a single flock under the one shepherd, Jesus Christ, our Lord, and to work with one another in common ministry through Jesus Christ, our Shepherd, who lives and reigns with you and the Holy Spirit, one God for ever and ever. Amen.

August 19

Artemisia Bowden
Educator, 1969
Lesser Feast
From the Common of Prophetic Witness, page 684
Collect O God, by your Holy Spirit, you give gifts to your people so that they might faithfully serve your Church and the world: We give you praise for the gifts of perseverance, teaching and wisdom made manifest in your servant, Artemisia Bowden, whom you called far from home for the sake of educating the daughters and granddaughters of former slaves in Texas. We thank you for blessing and prospering her life's work, and pray that, following her example, we may be ever mindful of the call to serve where you send us; through Jesus Christ our Lord, who with you and the Spirit, lives and reigns, one God, for ever and ever. Amen.

August 20

Bernard
Abbot of Clairvaux and Teacher of the Faith, 1153
Lesser Feast
From the Common of Teacher of the Faith, page 676, with the following proper antiphons
Benedictus Antiphon Holy Bernard, your heart, flooded by the light of the divine Word, illumines the church with your teaching.

Magnificat Antiphon Blessed Bernard, honey tongued teacher of the Faith, friend of the Bridegroom, herald of the Virgin Mother's glory, you became a shepherd to your flock at Clairvaux.

Collect O God, by whose grace your servant Bernard of Clairvaux, kindled with the flame of your love, became a burning and a shining light in your Church: Grant that we also may be aflame with the spirit of love and discipline, and walk before you as children of light; through Jesus Christ our Lord, who lives and reigns with you, in the unity of the Holy Spirit, one God, now and for ever. Amen.

August 24
Saint Bartholomew the Apostle
Major Feast
From the Common of Apostles, page 648, with the following proper antiphons
Benedictus Antiphon "Rabbi, you are the Son of God! You are the King of Israel!" Jesus answered, "You will see heaven opened and the angels of God ascending and descending upon the Son of Man."

Magnificat Antiphon Gathered there together were Simon Peter, Thomas called the Twin, Nathanael of Cana in Galilee, the sons of Zebedee, and two others of his disciples. Jesus came and took the bread and gave it to them, and did the same with the fish.

Collect Almighty and everlasting God, who gave to your apostle Bartholomew grace truly to believe and to preach your Word: Grant that your Church may love what he believed and preach what he taught; through Jesus Christ our Lord, who lives and reigns with you and the Holy Spirit, one God, for ever and ever. Amen.

August 25
Louis
King of France, 1270
Lesser Feast
From the Common of Holy Persons, page 695
Collect O God, you called your servant Louis of France to an earthly throne that he might advance your heavenly kingdom, and gave him zeal for your Church and love for your people: Mercifully grant that we who commemorate him this day may be fruitful in good works, and attain to the glorious crown of your saints; through Jesus Christ our Lord, who lives and reigns with you and the Holy Spirit, one God, for ever and ever. Amen.

August 26
Raimon Panikkar
Priest and Theologian of the New Monasticism, 2010
Lesser Feast

From the Common of Theologians and Teachers, page 672

Collect O God of mystery deep, you taught your theologian Raimon to contemplate the depths of your unknown wonders and to open a way for new monastics by walking the path of blessed simplicity. Open our minds to such daring contemplation and our hearts to bold compassion that we may walk the path you open up to us in union with Jesus Christ, our Lord, who lives and reigns with you and the Holy Spirit, one God forever and ever. Amen.

August 27
Thomas Gallaudet, 1902
Henry Winter Syle, 1890
Priests, Ministers to the Deaf
Lesser Feast

From the Common of Prophetic Witnesses, page 684

Collect O Loving God, whose will it is that everyone should come to you and be saved: We bless your holy Name for your servants Thomas Gallaudet and Henry Winter Syle whose labors with and for those who are deaf we commemorate today, and we pray that you will continually move your Church to respond in love to the needs of all people; through Jesus Christ, who opened the ears of the deaf, and who lives and reigns with you and the Holy Spirit, one God, now and for ever. Amen.

August 28
Augustine
Bishop of Hippo and Teacher of the Faith, 430
Lesser Feast

From the Common of Teacher of the Faith, page 676, with the following proper antiphons

Benedictus Antiphon You have made us for yourself and our hearts are restless until they find their rest in you.

Magnificat Antiphon Late have I loved you, O Beauty, every ancient yet new, late have I loved you. You called, you cried, you shattered my deafness.

Collect Lord God, the light of the minds that know you, the life of the souls that love you, and the strength of the hearts that serve you: Help us, following the example of your servant Augustine of Hippo, so to know you that we may truly love you, and so to love you that we may fully serve you, whom to serve is perfect freedom; through Jesus Christ our Lord, who lives and reigns with you and the Holy Spirit, one God, now and for ever. Amen.

August 31

<h1 style="text-align:center">Aidan</h1>

Monk and Bishop of Lindisfarne, 651

Lesser Feast

From the Common of Pastors, page 669

Collect O loving God, you called your servant Aidan from the peace of a cloister to re-establish the Christian mission in northern England, and endowed him with gentleness, simplicity, and strength: Grant that we, following his example, may use what you have given us for the relief of human need, and may persevere in commending the saving Gospel of our Redeemer Jesus Christ; who lives and reigns with you and the Holy Spirit, one God, for ever and ever. Amen.

September

September 1

<h1 style="text-align:center">David Pendleton Oakerhater</h1>

Deacon and Missionary, 1931

Lesser Feast

From the Common of Missionaries, page 680

Collect O God of unsearchable wisdom and infinite mercy, you chose a captive warrior, David Oakerhater, to be your servant, and sent him to be a missionary to his own people, and to exercise the office of a deacon among them: Liberate us, who commemorate him today, from bondage to self, and empower us for service to you and to the neighbors you have given us; through Jesus Christ, the captain of our salvation; who lives and reigns with you and the Holy Spirit, one God, for ever and ever. Amen.

September 2

<h1 style="text-align:center">The Martyrs of New Guinea</h1>

1942

Lesser Feast

From the Common of Martyrs, page 665

Collect Almighty God, we remember before you this day the blessed martyrs of New Guinea, who, following the example of their Savior, laid down their lives for their friends; and we pray that we who honor their memory may imitate their loyalty and faith; through Jesus Christ our Lord, who lives and reigns with you and the Holy Spirit, one God, for ever and ever. Amen.

September 3

Phoebe

Deacon

Lesser Feast

From the Common of the Apostles, page 648, with the following proper antiphons

Benedictus Antiphon I commend to you our sister Phoebe, a deacon of the church at Cenchreae, so that you may welcome her in the Lord as is fitting for the saints

Magnificat Antiphon Help Phoebe in whatever she may require from you, for she has been a benefactor of many and of myself as well.

Collect Eternal God, who raised up your servant Phoebe as a deacon in your church and benefactor of your Gospel, such that she took the message of your Apostle Paul into the very heart of a hostile empire; may we too, assisted by her prayers and example, be given the same grace to take the Gospel to the ends of the earth. Through Jesus Christ your Son our Lord; who lives and reigns with you, in the unity of the Holy Spirit, one God, for ever and ever. Amen.

September 4

Paul Jones

Bishop and Prophetic Witness for Peace, 1941

Lesser Feast

From the Common of Prophetic Witnesses, page 684, with the following proper antiphons

Benedictus Antiphon I believe that the methods of modern international war are quite incompatible with the Christian principles of reconciliation and brotherhood.

Magnificat Antiphon Christians are not justified in treating the Sermon on the Mount as a scrap of paper.

Collect Merciful God, you sent your beloved Son to preach peace to those who are far off and to those who are near: Raise up in this and every land witnesses who, after the example of your servant Paul Jones, will stand firm in proclaiming the Gospel of the Prince of Peace, our Savior Jesus Christ, who lives and reigns with you and the Holy Spirit, one God, now and for ever. Amen.

September 9
Constance, Thecla, Ruth and Frances
Professed Religious, 1878
Charles Parsons and Louis Schuyler
Priests, 1878
Commonly called "The Martyrs of Memphis," 1878
Lesser Feast
From the Common of Martyrs, page 665, with the following proper antiphons
Benedictus Antiphon Alleluia. Hosanna. I am my beloved's, and my beloved is mine: he feeds among the lilies.

Magnificat Antiphon Greater love has no one than this, that someone lay down his life for his friends.

Collect We give you thanks and praise, O God of compassion, for the heroic witness of Constance and her companions, who, in a time of plague and pestilence, were steadfast in their care for the sick and dying, and loved not their own lives, even unto death: Inspire in us a like love and commitment to those in need, following the example of our Savior Jesus Christ; who with you and the Holy Spirit lives and reigns, one God, now and forever. Amen.

September 10
Alexander Crummell
Priest, Missionary, and Educator, 1898
Lesser Feast
From the Common of Missionaries, page 680
Collect Almighty and everlasting God, we thank you for your servant Alexander Crummell, whom you called to preach the Gospel to those who were far off and to those who were near. Raise up in this and every land evangelists and heralds of your kingdom, that your Church may proclaim the unsearchable riches of our Savior Jesus Christ, who lives and reigns with you and the Holy Spirit, one God, now and for ever. Amen.

September 12
John Henry Hobart
Bishop of New York, 1830
Lesser Feast
From the Common of Pastors, page 669
Collect Revive your Church, Lord God of hosts, whenever it falls into complacency and sloth, by raising up devoted leaders, like your servant John Henry Hobart whom we remember today; and grant that their faith and vigor of mind may awaken your people to your message and their

mission; through Jesus Christ our Lord, who lives and reigns with you and the Holy Spirit, one God, for ever and ever. Amen.

September 13

Cyprian
Bishop and Martyr of Carthage, 258
Lesser Feast
From the Common of Martyrs, page 665, with the following proper antiphons
Benedictus Antiphon We are standing firm in faith and ready to endure suffering, in expectation of winning the crown of eternal life.

Magnificat Antiphon Commit yourselves to the Lord in complete faith and unflinching courage knowing that in this contest the soldiers of God and Christ are not slain but rather win their crowns.

Collect Almighty God, who gave to your servant Cyprian boldness to confess the Name of our Savior Jesus Christ before the rulers of this world, and courage to die for this faith: Grant that we may always be ready to give a reason for the hope that is in us, and to suffer gladly for the sake of our Lord Jesus Christ; who lives and reigns with you and the Holy Spirit, one God, for ever and ever. Amen.

September 14

Holy Cross Day
Feast of our Lord
Evening Prayer I
Hymn The Royal Banners Forward Go *Hymnal 162*

Antiphon 1 The king has been lifted up. Through the holy cross, you draw all things to yourself.
Psalms from Sunday Week 1 Evening Prayer I, page 130
Antiphon 2 O great act of mercy! Death itself died when Christ, our life, died on the cross.
Antiphon 3 Savior of the world, save us. By your cross and blood you redeemed us. Help us, we pray you, O Christ, our God.
Reading 1 Kings 8:22-30 or Ephesians 2:11-22

Responsory (Eph. 2:15; Col. 1:15; Eph. 2:14)
Christ created in himself one new humanity
      – making peace through the blood of the cross.
Christ is our peace; in his flesh he has united all humanity
      – making peace through the blood of the cross.
Glory to the Father, and to the Son, and to the Holy Spirit.

Christ created in himself one new humanity
– making peace through the blood of the cross.

Magnificat Antiphon O Holy Cross, surpassing the stars in splendor, you held on high the price of our redemption. Sweet the nails and sweet the wood but sweetest the Christ who hung on you. Alleluia.

Litany
Christ Jesus, you humbled himself to death on a cross, invite us into the way of humble service.
Lord, have mercy.
Christ Jesus, you opened the way of eternal life, bring the fullness of life to the homeless, the hungry and the abandoned.
Christ, have mercy.
Christ Jesus, you preached the good news to the dead, lead all the dead to the vision of glory.
Lord, have mercy.

Invitation to the Lord's Prayer Let us pray to the Father who raised up the Son who endured death on the cross.

Collect Almighty God, whose Son our Savior Jesus Christ was lifted high upon the cross that he might draw the whole world to himself: Mercifully grant that we, who glory in the mystery of our redemption, may have grace to take up our cross and follow him; who lives and reigns with you and the Holy Spirit, one God, in glory everlasting. Amen.

The Blessing
May we never boast of anything except the cross of our Lord Jesus Christ, by which the world has been crucified to us, and we to the world. **Amen.**

Holy Cross Day Morning Prayer
Invitatory Christ the King is reigning on the cross for us: Come let us adore.

Hymn Lift High the Cross *Hymnal 473*

Antiphon 1 The tree of life grows in the middle of the Holy City, Jerusalem, and its leaves offer healing for the nations, alleluia.
Psalms from Sunday Week 1 Morning Prayer, page 134
Antiphon 2 By the power of your cross, save us, O Christ our Savior. By dying, you destroyed our death and by rising, you restored our life.
Antiphon 3 Shine as the stars with splendor, O Beloved Cross. Christ restored salvation to the world through you, alleluia.

Reading One Numbers 21:4-9

Responsory One (Jn. 3:14; Jn. 3:16)
As Moses lifted up the serpent in the wilderness
    – the Son of Man must be lifted up.
Whoever believes in me will have eternal life
    – the Son of Man must be lifted up.
Glory to the Father, and to the Son, and to the Holy Spirit.
As Moses lifted up the serpent in the wilderness
    – the Son of Man must be lifted up.

Canticle of the Servant Song IV *Quis credidit auditui*
(Isaiah 53: 1-11)

Antiphon O glorious cross, O precious wood, O admirable sign. On you, Christ triumphed over evil and redeemed the world by his blood, alleluia.

Who has believed what we have heard? *
    And to whom has the arm of the Lord been revealed?

For he grew up before him like a young plant, *
    and like a root out of dry ground.

He had no form or majesty that we should look at him, *
    nothing in his appearance that we should desire him.

He was despised and rejected by others; *
    a man of suffering and acquainted with infirmity.

He was as one from whom others hide their faces *
    he was despised, and we held him of no account.

Surely he has borne our infirmities and carried our diseases; *
    yet we accounted him stricken,
    struck down by God, and afflicted.

But he was wounded for our transgressions, *
    crushed for our iniquities.

Upon him was the punishment that made us whole, *
    and by his bruises we are healed.

Antiphon O glorious cross, O precious wood, O admirable sign. On you, Christ triumphed over evil and redeemed the world by his blood, alleluia.

Reading Two John 3:11-17

Responsory Two
We adore you, O Christ
> **— and we bless you.**

By your holy cross, you have redeemed the world.
> **— and we bless you.**

Glory to the Father, and to the Son, and to the Holy Spirit.
We adore you, O Christ
> **— and we bless you.**

Benedictus Antiphon We adore your cross, O Christ, and we praise and glorify your resurrection. By the wood of the cross, you brought joy to the entire world, alleluia.

Litany
Father, you restore us to yourself through the cross; lead us to see your hand at work lifting us up from suffering.
Lord, have mercy.

Christ, you accepted the way of the cross as the way of life and salvation; open our eyes to behold you at work in restoring the brokenness of our world.
Christ, have mercy.

Spirit, you raised Christ who suffered the agony of the cross; lift up all who are experiencing loss and emptiness.
Lord, have mercy.

Invitation to the Lord's Prayer Mindful of the presence of Christ lifting us from our suffering into glory, let us pray with Christ that we may enter into the Father's presence.

Collect *From Evening Prayer I*

The Blessing
May we set minds on things that are above, not on things that are on earth, for we have died, and our life is hidden with Christ in God. **Amen.**

Holy Cross Day Noonday Prayer
Hymn Sunset to Sunrise Changes Now *Hymnal 163*

Antiphon Save us, O Christ. Your mighty sacrifice was offered on the altar of the cross. Help us, O Christ, our God.
Psalms from Sunday Week 1 Noonday Prayer page 138

Reading Ephesians 1: 7-8
In Christ we have redemption through his blood, the forgiveness of our trespasses, according to the riches of his grace that he lavished on us.

Verse and Response
Let all the world adore you and sing to you.
Let them sing psalms to your name, O Lord.

Collect *From Evening Prayer I*

Holy Cross Day Evening Prayer II

Hymn Sing My Tongue *Hymnal 166*

Antiphon 1 The message about the cross is foolishness to those who are perishing, but to us who are being saved it is the power of God.
Psalms from Sunday Week 1 Evening Prayer II, page 141
Antiphon 2 Through the sign of the cross, free us from all danger, O Christ.
Antiphon 3 Christ carried the Holy Cross and broke the power of hell; girded with power, he rose again on the third day. Alleluia

Reading Genesis 3:1-15 or 1 Peter 3:17-22

Responsory
O glorious cross
        – the King of angels triumphed on you.
With his blood, he healed our wounds;
        – the King of angels triumphed on you.
Glory to the Father, and to the Son, and to the Holy Spirit.
O glorious cross,
        – the King of angels triumphed on you.

Magnificat Antiphon O victorious Cross, O Admirable Sign, you brought us triumphant into the court of heaven. Alleluia.

Litany
You restored the broken body of you Son with a glorious body; heal the wounds of all who suffer.
Lord, have mercy.
You opened the eyes of your disciples to see the way of the cross as the path of victory; sustain all who have lost their way in the midst of trials.
Christ, have mercy.
You give hope to the dying and to those who mourn; sustain all who endure the loss of loved ones through death.
Lord, have mercy.

Invitation to the Lord's Prayer
Make us one with you, O Crucified Christ, as we pray in the words you taught us.

Collect *From Evening Prayer I*

The Blessing
May we never boast of anything except the cross of our Lord Jesus Christ, by which the world has been crucified to us, and we to the world. **Amen.**

The Ember Days, traditionally observed on the Wednesday, Friday, and Saturday after Holy Cross Day. On those days use the daily office of the day with proper parts taken from the Common of Ember Days, page 699.

September 16

Ninian

Bishop in Galloway, c. 430
Lesser Feast

From the Common of Pastors, page 669
Collect O God, by the preaching of your blessed servant and bishop Ninian you caused the light of the Gospel to shine in the land of Britain: Grant, we pray, that having his life and labors in remembrance we may show our thankfulness by following the example of his zeal and patience; through Jesus Christ our Lord, who lives and reigns with you and the Holy Spirit, one God, for ever and ever. Amen.

September 17

Hildegard

Abbess and Teacher of the Faith, 1179
Lesser Feast

From the Common of Teacher of the Faith, page 676, with the following proper antiphons
Benedictus Antiphon All living creatures are sparks from the radiation of God's brilliance, and these sparks emerge from God like the rays of the sun.

Magnificat Antiphon I, the fiery life of divine essence, am a flame beyond the beauty of the meadows. I gleam in the waters. I burn in the sun, moon, and stars. With every breeze, as with invisible life that contains everything, I awaken everything to life.

Collect God of all times and seasons: Give us grace that we, after the example of your servant Hildegard, may both know and make known the joy and jubilation of being part of your creation, and show forth your glory not only with our lips but in our lives; through Jesus Christ our Savior, who lives and reigns with you and the Holy Spirit, one God, for ever and ever. Amen.

September 18

Edward Bouverie Pusey

Priest, 1882

Lesser Feast

From the Common of Theologians and Teachers, page 672

Collect Grant, O God, that in all time of our testing we may know your presence and obey your will; that, following the example of your servant Edward Bouverie Pusey, we may with integrity and courage accomplish what you give us to do, and endure what you give us to bear; through Jesus Christ our Lord, who lives and reigns with you and the Holy Spirit, one God, for ever and ever. Amen.

September 19

Theodore of Tarsus

Monk, Archbishop of Canterbury, 690

Lesser Feast

From the Common of Pastors, page 669

Collect Almighty God, you called your servant Theodore of Tarsus from Rome to the see of Canterbury, and gave him gifts of grace and wisdom to establish unity where there had been division, and order where there had been chaos: Create in your Church, by the operation of the Holy Spirit, such godly union and concord that it may proclaim, both by word and example, the Gospel of the Prince of Peace; who lives and reigns with you and the Holy Spirit, one God, for ever and ever. Amen.

September 20

John Coleridge Patteson

Bishop of Melanesia, and his Companions, Martyrs, 1871

Lesser Feast

From the Common of Martyrs, page 665

Collect Almighty God, you called your faithful servant John Coleridge Patteson and his companions to be witnesses and martyrs in the islands of Melanesia, and by their labors and sufferings raised up a people for your own possession: Pour out your Holy Spirit upon your Church in every land, that by the service and sacrifice of many, your holy Name may be glorified and your kingdom enlarged; through Jesus Christ our Lord, who lives and reigns with you and the Holy Spirit, one God, for ever and ever. Amen.

September 21

Saint Matthew

Apostle and Evangelist

Major Feast

From the Common of Evangelists, page 659, with the following proper antiphons

Benedictus Antiphon Every scribe who has been trained for the kingdom of heaven is like a master of a house, who brings out of his treasure both new and old.

Magnificat Antiphon Whoever does the least of these commandments and teaches them will be called great in the kingdom of heaven.

Collect We thank you, heavenly Father, for the witness of your apostle and evangelist Matthew to the Gospel of your Son our Savior; and we pray that, after his example, we may with ready wills and hearts obey the calling of our Lord to follow him; through Jesus Christ our Lord, who lives and reigns with you and the Holy Spirit, one God, now and for ever. Amen.

September 22

Philander Chase

Bishop of Ohio, and of Illinois, 1852

Lesser Feast

From the Common of Missionaries, page 680

Collect Almighty God, whose Son Jesus Christ is the pioneer and perfecter of our faith: We give you heartfelt thanks for the pioneering spirit of your servant Philander Chase, and for his zeal in opening new frontiers for the ministry of your Church. Grant us grace to minister in Christ's name in every place, led by bold witnesses to the Gospel of the Prince of Peace, Jesus Christ our Lord, who lives and reigns with you and the Holy Spirit, one God, for ever and ever. Amen.

September 25

Sergius

Abbot of Holy Trinity, Moscow, 1392

Lesser Feast

From the Common of Monastics, page 687

Collect God, whose blessed Son became poor that we through his poverty might be rich: Deliver us from an inordinate love of this world, that we, inspired by the devotion of your servant Sergius of Moscow, may serve you with singleness of heart, and attain to the riches of the age to come; through Jesus Christ our Lord, who lives and reigns with you and the Holy Spirit, one God, for ever and ever. Amen.

September 26

Lancelot Andrewes

Bishop of Winchester, 1626

Lesser Feast

From the Common of Theologians and Teachers, page 672

Collect Lord and Father, our King and God, by your grace the Church was enriched by the great learning and eloquent preaching of your servant Lancelot Andrewes, but even more by his example of biblical and liturgical prayer: Conform our lives, like his, to the image of Christ, that our hearts may love you, our minds serve you, and our lips proclaim the greatness of your mercy; through Jesus Christ our Lord, who lives and reigns with you and the Holy Spirit, one God, now and for ever. Amen.

September 28

Richard Rolle, 1349, Walter Hilton, 1396, and Margery Kempe, c. 1440

Mystics

Lesser Feast

From the Common of Holy Persons, page 695

Collect Almighty God, who enlightened your Church by the teaching of your servants Richard Rolle, Walter Hilton and Margery Kempe, enrich it evermore with your heavenly grace and raise up faithful witnesses who, by their life and teaching, may proclaim the truth of your salvation, through Jesus Christ, your Son, our Lord, who lives and reigns with you and the Holy Spirit, one God, forever and ever. Amen.

September 28

Lioba

Benedictine Abbess of Bischofsheim and Companion of St Boniface, 782

Lesser Feast

From the Common of Monastics, page 687, with the following proper antiphons

Benedictus Antiphon The blessed Lioba had no desire to gain earthly possessions but only those of heaven, and she spent all her energies on fulfilling her vows.

Magnificat Antiphon She put off this earthly garment and gave back her soul joyfully to her Creator, clean and undefiled as she had received it from God.

Collect O God, by whose grace your abbess Lioba, imitated Christ in his poverty and with a humble heart followed him to the end: Grant that we also may so follow Christ and not look back nor wander from the way but, running in the way of your commandments may attain the crown of eternal life through Jesus Christ our Lord, who lives and reigns with you, in the unity of the Holy Spirit, one God, now and for ever. Amen.

September 29
Saint Michael and All Angels
Major Feast
Evening Prayer I

Hymn As Jacob with travel was weary one day *Hymnal 453*

Antiphon 1 There is no one with me who contends against these princes except Michael, your prince.
Psalms from Sunday Week 1 Evening Prayer I, page 130
Antiphon 2 Now at the time of the incense offering, there appeared to Zechariah an angel of the Lord, standing at the right side of the altar of incense.
Antiphon 3 Tobias found the angel Raphael standing in front of him; but he did not perceive that he was an angel of God.

Reading Mark 13:21-27 or Revelation 5:1-14

Responsory (Heb. 12:22, 24)
We have come to Mount Zion and to the city of the living God
     – and to innumerable angels in festal gathering.
We have come to Jesus, the mediator of a new covenant.
     – and to innumerable angels in festal gathering.
Glory to the Father, and to the Son and to the Holy Spirit.
We have come to Mount Zion and to the city of the living God
     – and to innumerable angels in festal gathering.

Magnificat Antiphon Jesus said, "Very truly, I tell you, you will see heaven opened and the angels of God ascending and descending upon the Son of Man."

Litany
That our prayer may ascend like incense in your sight in the company of the angels.
Lord, have mercy.
That the angels may lead us and all people in paths of peace and good will.
Christ, have mercy.
At the end of our days, may the angels lead us and all the departed into paradise.
Lord, have mercy.

Invitation to the Lord's Prayer Our prayer is one with the Church in all times and places and with the angels we pray with Christ to the Father.

Collect Everlasting God, you have ordained and constituted in a wonderful order the ministries of angels and mortals: Mercifully grant that, as your holy angels always serve and worship you in heaven, so by your appointment they may help and defend us here on earth; through Jesus Christ our Lord, who lives and reigns with you and the Holy Spirit, one God, for ever and ever. Amen.

The Blessing
May God send angels in front of us, to guard us on the way and to bring us to the places that God has prepared for us. **Amen.**

Saint Michael and All Angels Morning Prayer

Invitatory Come, let us sing to the Lord, joining our voices with Angels and Archangels and with all the company of heaven.

Hymn Christ the fair glory of the holy angels *Hymnal 282*

Antiphon 1 War broke out in heaven; Michael and his angels fought against the dragon. The dragon and his angels fought back, but they were defeated.
Psalms from Sunday Week 1 Morning Prayer, page 134
Antiphon 2 The angel Gabriel was sent by God to a town in Galilee called Nazareth, to a virgin engaged to a man whose name was Joseph, of the house of David. The virgin's name was Mary.
Antiphon 3 Raphael said, "I will go with Tobias; so do not fear. We shall leave in good health and return to you in good health, because the way is safe."

Reading One Job 38:1-7

Responsory One (Rev. 8:3)
Another angel with a golden censer came and stood at the altar
        – he was given a great quantity of incense to offer.
The smoke of the incense rose before God from the hand of the angel
        – he was given a great quantity of incense to offer.
Glory to the Father, and to the Son and to the Holy Spirit.
Another angel with a golden censer came and stood at the altar
        – he was given a great quantity of incense to offer.

Canticle You are God   *Te Deum laudamus page 757*

Reading Two Hebrews 1:1-14

Responsory Two (Rev. 7:2, 11, 10)
I saw another angel ascending from the rising of the sun
   – and all the angels worshiped God.
Salvation belongs to our God and to the Lamb!
   – and all the angels worshiped God.
Glory to the Father, and to the Son and to the Holy Spirit.
I saw another angel ascending from the rising of the sun.
   – and all the angels worshiped God.

Benedictus Antiphon Bless the Lord, you angels of his, you mighty ones who do his bidding, and hearken to the voice of his word. Bless the Lord, all you his hosts, you ministers of his who do his will.

Litany
May your angels accompany us this day and lead us in paths of peace.
Lord, have mercy.
May your angels pray and bring healing to those who suffer chronic pain.
Christ, have mercy.
May your angels strengthen all who proclaim you good news by word and deed.
Lord, have mercy.

Invitation to the Lord's Prayer In the company of the holy angels and saints, we make our prayer to the Father.

Collect *From Evening Prayer I*

The Blessing
May God give the angels charge over us to keep us in all our ways.
Amen.

Saint Michael and All Angels Noonday Prayer
Hymn Praise the Lord! Ye heavens adore him *Hymnal 373*

Antiphon The angel who had been sent to me, whose name was Uriel, replied: "Your mind has utterly failed with regard to this world, and do you think you can understand the way of the Most High?"
Psalms from Sunday Week 1 Noonday Prayer page 138

Reading Hebrews 13: 1-2

Let mutual love continue. Do not neglect to show hospitality to strangers, for by doing that some have entertained angels without knowing it.

Verse and Response

Bless the Lord, you angels of his.

You mighty ones hearken to the voice of his word.

Collect *From Evening Prayer I*

Saint Michael and All Angels
Evening Prayer II

Hymn Ye Holy Angels Bright *Hymnal 625*

Antiphon 1 An angel of the Lord appeared to him in a dream and said, "Joseph, son of David, do not be afraid to take Mary as your wife, for the child conceived in her is from the Holy Spirit."

Psalms from Sunday Week 1 Evening Prayer II, page 141

Antiphon 2 An angel from heaven appeared to Jesus and gave him strength. In his anguish he prayed more earnestly, and his sweat became like great drops of blood falling down on the ground.

Antiphon 3 Mary Magdalene and the other Mary went to see the tomb. An angel of the Lord rolled back the stone and sat on it. His appearance was like lightning, and his clothing white as snow.

Reading Daniel 12:1-3 or 2 Kings 6:8-17

Responsory (Heb. 12:22, 24)

We have come to Mount Zion and to the city of the living God
 – and to innumerable angels in festal gathering.

We have come to Jesus, the mediator of a new covenant.
 – and to innumerable angels in festal gathering.

Glory to the Father, and to the Son and to the Holy Spirit.

We have come to Mount Zion and to the city of the living God,
 – and to innumerable angels in festal gathering.

Magnificat Antiphon The angel Gabriel said to her, "Do not be afraid, Mary, for you have found favor with God. And now, you will conceive in your womb and bear a son, and you will name him Jesus." Alleluia.

Litany

That our prayer may ascend in your sight like incense in the company of the angels.

Lord, have mercy.

That the angels may lead us and all people in paths of peace and good will.

Christ, have mercy.

At the end of our days, may the angels lead us and all the departed into paradise.

Lord, have mercy.

Invitation to the Lord's Prayer Our prayer is one with the Church in all times and places and with the angels we pray with Christ to the Father.

Collect *From Evening Prayer I*

The Blessing

May God send angels in front of us, to guard us on the way and to bring us to the places that God has prepared for us. **Amen.**

September 30

Jerome

Monk of Bethlehem, Priest and Teacher of the Faith, 420
Lesser Feast

From the Common of Teacher of the Faith, page 676

Collect O Lord, O God of truth, your Word is a lantern to our feet and a light upon our path: We give you thanks for your servant Jerome, and those who, following in his steps, have labored to render the Holy Scriptures in the language of the people; and we pray that your Holy Spirit will overshadow us as we read the written Word, and that Christ, the living Word, will transform us according to your righteous will; through Jesus Christ our Lord, who lives and reigns with you and the Holy Spirit, one God, now and for ever. Amen.

October

October 1

Remigius

Bishop of Rheims, c. 530
Lesser Feast

From the Common of Pastors, page 669

Collect O God, by the teaching of your faithful servant and bishop Remigius you turned the nation of the Franks from vain idolatry to the worship of you, the true and living God, in the fullness of the catholic faith: Grant that we who glory in the name of Christian may show forth our faith in worthy deeds; through Jesus Christ our Lord, who lives and reigns with you and the Holy Spirit, one God, for ever and ever. Amen.

October 1
Therese of the Child Jesus and the Holy Face
Discalced Carmelite Nun, Teacher of the Faith 1897
Lesser Feast

From the Common of Teacher of the Faith, page 676
Gracious Father, who called your servant Therese to a life of fervent prayer, give to us the spirit of prayer and zeal for the ministry of the Gospel, that the love of Christ may be known throughout all the world; through the same Jesus Christ, our Lord. Amen.

October 4
Francis of Assisi
Friar, Deacon and Founder of the Friars Minor, 1226
Lesser Feast

From the Common of Monastics, page 687, with the following proper antiphons
Benedictus Antiphon O most high, almighty, good Lord God, to you belong praise, glory, honor, and all blessing! Praised be my Lord with all his creatures, especially Brother Sun; he signifies you to us!

Magnificat Antiphon I bear on my body the brand-marks of Jesus.

Collect Most high, omnipotent, good Lord, grant your people grace to renounce gladly the vanities of this world; that, following the way of blessed Francis, we may for love of you delight in your whole creation with perfectness of joy; through Jesus Christ our Lord, who lives and reigns with you and the Holy Spirit, one God, for ever and ever. Amen.

October 6
Bruno
Hermit, Priest, Founder of the Carthusian Order, 1101
Lesser Feast

From the Common of Monastics, page 687
Collect All powerful, eternal God, you prepare dwelling places in heaven for those who renounce the world; through the prayers of St. Bruno, may we fulfill the vows of our profession and safely attain those things you have promised to all who persevere in your friendship' through Jesus Christ our Lord, who lives and reigns with you and the Holy Spirit, one God, for ever and ever. Amen. (Carthusian Diurnal)

October 7

William Tyndale

Translator of the Scripture, Priest and Martyr 1536
Lesser Feast

From the Common of Martyrs, page 665

Collect Almighty God, you planted in the heart of your servant William Tyndale a consuming passion to bring the Scriptures to people in their native tongue, and endowed him with the gift of powerful and graceful expression and with strength to persevere against all obstacles: Reveal to us your saving Word, as we read and study the Scriptures, and hear them calling us to repentance and life; through Jesus Christ our Lord, who lives and reigns with you and the Holy Spirit, one God, for ever and ever. Amen.

October 9

Robert Grosseteste

Bishop of Lincoln, 1253
Lesser Feast

From the Common of Pastors, page 669

Collect O God, our heavenly Father, who raised up your faithful servant Robert Grosseteste to be a bishop and pastor in your Church and to feed your flock: Give abundantly to all pastors the gifts of your Holy Spirit, that they may minister in your household as true servants of Christ and stewards of your divine mysteries; through Jesus Christ our Lord, who lives and reigns with you and the Holy Spirit, one God, for ever and ever. Amen.

October 10

Vida Dutton Scudder

Educator and Witness for Peace, 1954
Lesser Feast

From the Common of Prophetic Witnesses, page 684

Collect Most gracious God, you sent your beloved Son to preach peace to those who are far off and to those who are near: Raise up in your Church witnesses who, after the example of your servant Vida Dutton Scudder, stand firm in proclaiming the power of the Gospel of Jesus Christ, who lives and reigns with you and the Holy Spirit, one God, now and for ever. Amen.

October 11

Philip
Deacon and Evangelist
Lesser Feast
From the Common of Apostles, page 648, with the following proper antiphons
Benedictus Antiphon Philip went down to the city of Samaria and proclaimed the Messiah to them.

Magnificat Antiphon Philip and the eunuch, went down into the water, and Philip baptized him.

Collect O God, who has made of one blood all the peoples of the earth and sent your Son to preach peace to those who are far off and to those who are near: Grant that we, following the example of your servant Philip, may bring your Word to those who seek you, for the glory of your Name; through Jesus Christ our Lord, who lives and reigns with you in the unity of the Holy Spirit, one God, now and for ever. Amen.

October 11

Ethelburga
Benedictine Abbess of double monastery at Barking, 675
Lesser Feast
From the Common of Monastics, page 687, with the following proper antiphons
Benedictus Antiphon The Handmaid of Christ lived a holy life and constantly and piously cared for those under her rule.

Magnificat Antiphon The beloved of God, Ethelburga, mother of that community, was delivered out of the prison of the flesh; and an entrance into the heavenly country was open to her.

Collect O God, by whose grace your Abbess Etherburga, kindled with the flame of your love, became a burning and shining light in your Church: Grant that we also may be aflame with the spirit of love and discipline, and walk before you as children of light; through Jesus Christ our Lord, who lives and reigns with you, in the unity of the Holy Spirit, one God, now and for ever. Amen.

October 14

Samuel Isaac Joseph Schereschewsky
Bishop of Shanghai, 1906
Lesser Feast
From the Common of Missionaries, page 680
Collect O God, in your providence you called Joseph Schereschewsky from his home in Eastern Europe to the ministry of this Church, and sent

him as a missionary to China, upholding him in his infirmity, that he might translate the Holy Scriptures into languages of that land. Lead us, we pray, to commit our lives and talents to you, in the confidence that when you give your servants any work to do, you also supply the strength to do it; through Jesus Christ, our Lord, who lives and reigns with you and the Holy Spirit, one God, for ever and ever. Amen.

October 15

Teresa of Jesus

Discalced Carmelite Nun, Founder of the Discalced Carmelites, Mystic and Teacher of the Faith, 1582
Lesser Feast

From the Common of Teacher of the Faith, page 676, with the following proper antiphons

Benedictus Antiphon In my Father's house there are many mansions. If I go and prepare a place for you, I will come again and will take you to myself, so that where I am, there you may be also.

Magnificat Antiphon Holy Teresa, Light of the Church, teach us the way of perfection and lead us to the eternal mansions where Christ has his home.

Collect God, by your Holy Spirit you moved Teresa of Avila to manifest to your Church the way of perfection: Grant us, we pray, to be nourished by her excellent teaching, and enkindle within us a keen and unquenchable longing for true holiness; through Jesus Christ, the joy of loving hearts, who with you and the Holy Spirit lives and reigns, one God, for ever and ever. Amen.

October 16

Hugh Latimer and Nicholas Ridley

Bishops and Martyrs, 1555

Thomas Cranmer

Archbishop of Canterbury and Martyr, 1556
Lesser Feast

From the Common of Martyrs, page 665, with the following proper antiphons.

Benedictus Antiphon The light shines in the darkness, and the darkness did not overcome it.

Magnificat Antiphon I see four men loose, walking in the midst of the fire; and they are not hurt, and the form of the fourth is like the Son of God.

Collect Keep us, O Lord, constant in faith and zealous in witness, that, like your servants Hugh Latimer, Nicholas Ridley, and Thomas Cranmer, we may live in your fear, die in your favor, and rest in your peace; for the sake of Jesus Christ your Son our Lord, who lives and reigns with you and the Holy Spirit, one God, now and for ever. Amen.

October 17

Ignatius
Bishop of Antioch, and Martyr, c. 115
Lesser Feast

From the Common of Martyrs, page 665, with the following proper antiphons.

Benedictus Antiphon He who died in place of us is the one object of my quest. He who rose for our sakes is my one desire. Let me attain pure light. Only on my arrival there can I be fully a human being.

Magnificat Antiphon I am God's wheat, and I am to be ground by the teeth of wild beasts, so that I may become the pure bread of Christ.

Collect Almighty God, we praise your Name for your bishop and martyr Ignatius of Antioch, who offered himself as grain to be ground by the teeth of wild beasts that he might present to you the pure bread of sacrifice. Accept, we pray, the willing tribute of our lives and give us a share in the pure and spotless offering of your Son Jesus Christ; who lives and reigns with you and the Holy Spirit, one God, for ever and ever. Amen.

October 18

Saint Luke the Evangelist
Major Feast

From the Common of Evangelists, page 659, with the following proper antiphons

Benedictus Antiphon We rejoice in the feast of St. Luke and celebrate the tender compassion of Christ who dawns on us like the light from on high. Alleluia.

Magnificat Antiphon Stay with us, because it is almost evening and the day is now nearly over. So he went in to stay with them. Alleluia.

Collect Almighty God, who inspired your servant Luke the physician to set forth in the Gospel the love and healing power of your Son: Graciously continue in your Church this love and power to heal, to the praise and glory of your Name; through Jesus Christ our Lord, who lives and reigns with you, in the unity of the Holy Spirit, one God, now and for ever. Amen.

October 19

Henry Martyn

Priest and Missionary to India and Persia, 1812
Lesser Feast

From the Common of Missionaries, page 680

Collect O God of the nations, you gave your faithful servant Henry Martyn a brilliant mind, a loving heart, and a gift for languages, that he might translate the Scriptures and other holy writings for the peoples of India and Persia: Inspire in us a love like his, eager to commit both life and talents to you who gave them; through Jesus Christ our Lord, who lives and reigns with you and the Holy Spirit, one God, for ever and ever. Amen.

October 23

Saint James of Jerusalem

Brother of Our Lord Jesus Christ, and Martyr, c. 62
Major Feast

From the Common of Apostles, page 648, with the following proper antiphons

Benedictus Antiphon Christ was raised on the third day in accordance with the Scriptures, and he appeared to Cephas, then to the twelve. Then he appeared to James.

Magnificat Antiphon Is not this the carpenter's son? Is not his mother called Mary? And are not his brothers James and Joseph and Simon and Judas?

Collect Grant, O God, that, following the example of your servant James the Just, brother of our Lord, your Church may give itself continually to prayer and to the reconciliation of all who are at variance and enmity; through Jesus Christ our Lord, who lives and reigns with you and the Holy Spirit, one God, now and for ever. Amen.

October 25

Tabitha (Dorcas) of Joppa

Lesser Feast

From the Common of Holy Persons, page 695, with the following proper antiphons

Benedictus Antiphon Now in Joppa there was a disciple whose name was Tabitha. She was devoted to good works and acts of charity.

Magnificat Antiphon Peter knelt down and prayed. He turned to the body and said, "Tabitha, get up." Then she opened her eyes, and seeing Peter, she sat up. He gave her his hand and helped her up.

Collect Most Holy God, whose servant Tabitha you raised from the dead to display your power and confirm your message that your Son is Lord; grant unto us your grace, that aided by her prayers and example, we may be given a new life in your Spirit to do works pleasing in your sight; Through Jesus Christ your Son our Lord; who lives and reigns with you, in the unity of the Holy Spirit, one God, for ever and ever. Amen.

October 26

Alfred the Great

King of the West Saxons, 899
Lesser Feast

From the Common of Holy Persons, page 695

Collect O Sovereign Lord, you brought your servant Alfred to a troubled throne that he might establish peace in a ravaged land and revive learning and the arts among the people: Awake in us also a keen desire to increase our understanding while we are in this world, and an eager longing to reach that endless life where all will be made clear; through Jesus Christ our Lord, who lives and reigns with you and the Holy Spirit, one God, for ever and ever. Amen.

October 28

Saint Simon and Saint Jude

Apostles
Major Feast

From the Common of Apostles, page 648

Collect O God, we thank you for the glorious company of the apostles, and especially on this day for Simon and Jude; and we pray that, as they were faithful and zealous in their mission, so we may with ardent devotion make known the love and mercy of our Lord and Savior Jesus Christ; who lives and reigns with you and the Holy Spirit, one God, for ever and ever. Amen.

October 29

James Hannington

Bishop of Eastern Equatorial Africa, and his Companions, Martyrs, 1885
Lesser Feast

From the Common of Martyrs, page 665

Collect Precious in your sight, O Lord, is the death of your saints, whose faithful witness, by your providence, has its great reward: We give you thanks for your martyrs James Hannington and his companions, who purchased with their blood a road into Uganda for the proclamation of the Gospel; and we pray that with them we also may obtain the crown of righteousness which is laid up for all who love the appearing of our Savior

Jesus Christ; who lives and reigns with you and the Holy Spirit, one God, for ever and ever. Amen.

October 29

Maryam of Qidun
Monastic, 4th century
Lesser Feast
From the Common of Monastics, page 687, with the following proper antiphons
Benedictus Antiphon It is no new thing to fall in the mire, but it is an evil thing to lie there fallen. Bravely return again to your monastery for your enemy shall know you stronger in your rising.

Magnificat Antiphon I marvel at myself how I daily sin and daily do I repent. Be mindful of me, Lover of souls, and lead me out of the prison-house of my sins.

Collect O God, whose glory it is always to have mercy: Be gracious to all who have gone astray from your ways, and restore them again like your servant Maryam of Qidun with penitent hearts and steadfast faith to embrace and hold fast the unchangeable truth of your Word, Jesus Christ; who with you and the Holy Spirit lives and reigns, one God, for ever and ever. Amen.

November
November 1

All Saints
Principal Feast
Evening Prayer I
Hymn Who are these like stars appearing? *Hymnal 286*

Antiphon 1 O how glorious is the kingdom where all the saints rejoice in Christ; dressed in white garments, they follow the Lamb wherever he goes. Alleluia.
Psalms from Sunday Week 1 Evening Prayer I, page 130
Antiphon 2 Holy and wonderful is the true light illuminating those who endured the heat of battle. From Christ they inherit a mansion of unfading splendor. Alleluia.
Antiphon 3 They will shine forth, and will run like sparks through the stubble. They will govern nations and rule over peoples, and the Lord will reign over them forever. Alleluia.

Reading Wisdom 3:1-9 or Revelation 19:1,4-10

Responsory (1 Pt. 2:9)
You are a chosen race, a royal priesthood, a holy nation
  – to proclaim the mighty acts of God.
God called you out of darkness into his marvelous light.
  – to proclaim the mighty acts of God.
Glory to the Father, and to the Son and to the Holy Spirit.
You are a chosen race, a royal priesthood, a holy nation
  – to proclaim the mighty acts of God.

Magnificat Antiphon O Angels and Archangels, Thrones and Dominions, Principalities and Powers. O Virtues, Cherubim and Seraphim. O Patriarchs and Prophets, Holy Teachers of the Law, and Apostles. O Martyrs of Christ, Holy Confessors, Virgins of the Lord, holy Hermits and all saints, pray for us to God. Alleluia.

Litany
O God, the King of saints, we praise and glorify your holy Name for all your servants who have finished their course in your faith and fear.
Lord, have mercy.
For the blessed Virgin Mary; for the holy patriarchs, prophets, apostles, and martyrs; and for all your other righteous servants, known to us and unknown, we offer you thanks.
Christ, have mercy.
We pray that, encouraged by their examples, aided by their prayers, and strengthened by their fellowship, we also may be partakers of the inheritance of the saints in light.
Lord, have mercy.

Invitation to the Lord's Prayer Joining the prayer of the saints in heaven, the saints on earth and generations of saints yet unborn, let us pray to the Father as members of Christ's Mystical Body.

Collect Almighty God, you have knit together your elect in one communion and fellowship in the mystical body of your Son Christ our Lord: Give us grace so to follow your blessed saints in all virtuous and godly living, that we may come to those ineffable joys that you have prepared for those who truly love you; through Jesus Christ our Lord, who with you and the Holy Spirit lives and reigns, one God, in glory everlasting. Amen.

The Blessing
May we receive the power to comprehend, with all the saints, what is the breadth and length and height and depth, and to know the love of Christ

that surpasses knowledge, so that we may be filled with all the fullness of God.. **Amen.**

All Saints Morning Prayer

Invitatory Alleluia. Let us all rejoice in the Lord, celebrating this festival in honor of all the saints. Alleluia.

Hymn Ye watchers and ye hold ones *Hymnal 618*

Antiphon 1 I beheld a great multitude whom no one could count, of every nation, standing before the throne.
Psalms from Sunday Week 1 Morning Prayer, page 134
Antiphon 2 All the angels stood around the throne and fell before the throne on their faces and worshipped God.
Antiphon 3 You have redeemed us, O Lord, our God, for you were slain and by your blood you ransomed for God saints from every tribe and language and people and nation.

Reading One 2 Esdras 2:42-47

Responsory One (Ps. 32:12)
Be glad, you righteous
     − and rejoice in the Lord.
Shout for joy, all who are true of heart.
     − and rejoice in the Lord.
Glory to the Father, and to the Son and to the Holy Spirit.
Be glad, you righteous,
     − and rejoice in the Lord.

Canticle You are God   *Te Deum laudamus page 757*

Reading Two Hebrews 11:32-12:2

Responsory Two (Wis. 3:1)
The souls of the just
     − are in the hand of God.
No torment shall touch them.
     − are in the hand of God.
Glory to the Father, and to the Son and to the Holy Spirit.
The souls of the just
     − are in the hand of God.

Benedictus Antiphon The glorious company of apostles praise you. The noble fellowship of prophets praise you. The white-robed army of martyrs praise you. Throughout the world the holy Church acclaims you,

Father, Son and Holy Spirit. Alleluia.

Litany
Almighty God, the spirits of those who die in the Lord live with you,
and with you the souls of the faithful are in joy and felicity.
Lord, have mercy.
We give you heartfelt thanks for all your servants, who, having finished
their course in faith, now find rest and refreshment.
Christ, have mercy.
May we, with all who have died in the true faith of your holy Name,
have perfect fulfillment and bliss in your eternal and everlasting glory.
Lord, have mercy.

Invitation to the Lord's Prayer Joining our prayer with the prayer of
saints of every time and place, let us pray with them as beloved daughters
and sons in Christ. .

Collect Almighty God, with whom still live the spirits of those who die
in the Lord, and with whom the souls of the faithful are in joy and felicity:
We give you heartfelt thanks for the good examples of all your servants,
who, having finished their course in faith, now find rest and refreshment.
May we, with all who have died in the true faith of your holy Name, have
perfect fulfillment and bliss in your eternal and everlasting glory; through
Jesus Christ our Lord. Amen.

The Blessing
May we rejoice that we are no longer strangers and aliens, but that we are
citizens with the saints and members of the household of God, built upon
the foundation of the apostles and prophets, with Christ Jesus himself as
the cornerstone. **Amen.**

All Saints Noonday Prayer
Hymn O what their joy and their glory must be *Hymnal 623*

Antiphon The church celebrates the wisdom of the saints and the
congregation proclaims their praise.
Psalms from Sunday Week 1 Noonday Prayer page 138

Reading 1 Peter 2: 9-10
You are a chosen race, a royal priesthood, a holy nation, God's own
people, in order that you may proclaim the mighty acts of him who called
you out of darkness into his marvelous light. Once you were not a people,
but now you are God's people; once you had not received mercy, but now
you have received mercy.

Verse and Response
You are wonderful in your saints.
And glorious in your majesty.

Collect *From Evening Prayer I*

All Saints Evening Prayer II
Hymn For all the saints *Hymnal 287*

Antiphon 1 Be glad, you righteous, and rejoice in the Lord; shout for joy, all who are true of heart.
Psalms from Sunday Week 1 Evening Prayer II, page 141
Antiphon 2 You are no longer strangers and aliens, but you are citizens with the saints and also members of the household of God.
Antiphon 3 Rejoice in the Lord, you righteous, and give thanks to his holy Name.

Reading Luke 24:13-35 or John 20:19-23

Responsory (1 Pt. 2:9)
You are a chosen race, a royal priesthood, a holy nation
   – to proclaim the mighty acts of God.
God called you out of darkness into his marvelous light.
   – to proclaim the mighty acts of God.
Glory to the Father, and to the Son and to the Holy Spirit.
You are a chosen race, a royal priesthood, a holy nation
   – to proclaim the mighty acts of God.

Magnificat Antiphon O Savior of the world, save us, and let your holy Virgin Mother pray for us with your holy Apostles, Martyrs, Confessors and Virgins that we may be delivered from all evil and counted worthy, now and forever, to be filled with all good things. Alleluia.

Litany
O God, the King of saints, we praise and glorify your holy Name for all your servants who have finished their course in your faith and fear.
Lord, have mercy.
For the blessed Virgin Mary; for the holy patriarchs, prophets, apostles, and martyrs; and for all your other righteous servants, known to us and unknown, we offer you thanks.
Christ, have mercy.

We pray that, encouraged by their examples, aided by their prayers, and strengthened by their fellowship, we also may be partakers of the inheritance of the saints in light.
Lord, have mercy.

Invitation to the Lord's Prayer Joining the prayer of the saints in heaven, the saints on earth and generations of saints yet unborn, let us pray to the Father as members of Christ's Mystical Body.

Collect

O God, the King of saints, we praise and glorify your holy Name for all your servants who have finished their course in your faith and fear: for the blessed Virgin Mary; for the holy patriarchs, prophets, apostles, and martyrs; and for all your other righteous servants, known to us and unknown; and we pray that, encouraged by their examples, aided by their prayers, and strengthened by their fellowship, we also may be partakers of the inheritance of the saints in light; through the merits of your Son Jesus Christ our Lord. Amen.

The Blessing

May we have the power to comprehend, with all the saints, what is the breadth and length and height and depth, and to know the love of Christ that surpasses knowledge, so that we may be filled with all the fullness of God. **Amen.**

November 2

Commemoration of All Faithful Departed

From the Common of the Faithful Departed, page 711

November 3

Richard Hooker

Priest, 1600

Lesser Feast

From the Common of Teacher of the Faith, page 666

Collect God of truth and peace, you raised up your servant Richard Hooker in a day of bitter controversy to defend with sound reasoning and great charity the catholic and reformed religion: Grant that we may maintain that middle way, not as a compromise for the sake of peace, but as a comprehension for the sake of truth; through Jesus Christ our Lord, who lives and reigns with you and the Holy Spirit, one God, for ever and ever. Amen.

November 6

William Temple
Archbishop of Canterbury, 1944
Lesser Feast

From the Common of Pastors, page 669

Collect O God of light and love, you illumined your Church through the witness of your servant William Temple: Inspire us, we pray, by his teaching and example, that we may rejoice with courage, confidence, and faith in the Word made flesh, and may be led to establish that city which has justice for its foundation and love for its law; through Jesus Christ, the light of the world, who lives and reigns with you and the Holy Spirit, one God, now and for ever. Amen.

November 7

Willibrord
Monk, Archbishop of Utrecht, Missionary to Frisia, 739
Lesser Feast

From the Common of Missionaries, page 680

Collect O Lord our God, you call whom you will and send them where you choose: We thank you for sending your servant Willibrord to be an apostle to the Low Countries, to turn them from the worship of idols to serve you, the living God; and we entreat you to preserve us from the temptation to exchange the perfect freedom of your service for servitude to false gods and to idols of our own devising; through Jesus Christ our Lord, who lives and reigns with you and the Holy Spirit, one God, for ever and ever. Amen.

November 10

Leo the Great
Bishop of Rome and Teacher of the Faith, 461
Lesser Feast

From the Common of Teacher of the Faith, page 676

Collect O Lord our God, grant that your Church, following the teaching of your servant Leo of Rome, may hold fast the great mystery of our redemption, and adore the one Christ, true God and true Man, neither divided from our human nature nor separate from your divine Being; through Jesus Christ our Lord, who lives and reigns with you and the Holy Spirit, one God, now and for ever. Amen.

November 11

Martin
Monk and Bishop of Tours, 397
Lesser Feast

From the Common of Pastors, page 669, with the following proper antiphons

Benedictus Antiphon O Blessed Martin, when you entered heaven the angels rejoiced, the Archangels triumphed and the choirs of saints sang: Stay with us forever.

Magnificat Antiphon O Holy Martin, with all your heart you loved Christ the King and did not fear earthly rulers. While you did not endure a martyr's death you received the martyr's reward.

Collect Lord God of hosts, you clothed your servant Martin the soldier with the spirit of sacrifice, and set him as a bishop in your Church to be a defender of the catholic faith: Give us grace to follow in his holy steps, that at the last we may be found clothed with righteousness in the dwellings of peace; through Jesus Christ our Lord, who lives and reigns with you and the Holy Spirit, one God, for ever and ever. Amen.

November 12
Charles Simeon
Priest, 1836
Lesser Feast
From the Common of Pastors, page 669
Collect O loving God, we know that all things are ordered by your unerring wisdom and unbounded love: Grant us in all things to see your hand; that, following the example and teaching of your servant Charles Simeon, we may walk with Christ in all simplicity, and serve you with a quiet and contented mind; through Jesus Christ our Lord, who lives and reigns with you and the Holy Spirit, one God, for ever and ever. Amen.

November 13
All Saints of the Benedictine Order
Major Feast
From the November 1 Office of All Saints with the following proper parts
Invitatory Let us all rejoice in the Lord, celebrating the feast in honor of all the saints of the Benedictine Order at whose festival the angels rejoice and praise the Son of God.

Benedictus Antiphon You have left everything and followed me. You will receive a hundredfold, and will inherit eternal life.

Magnificat Antiphon Let the faithful exult in the glory of our Father Benedict and of the monks, nuns and oblates who followed in his footsteps. Let the monastic choirs rejoice with the choirs of heaven as they celebrate this feast of the Benedictine saints. Alleluia.

Collect God our Father, you promise to those who leave all to follow Christ a hundredfold now in this time, and in the age to come eternal life. Through the intercession of our holy father Saint Benedict, and of all the holy nuns, monks and oblates who have lived according to his rule, keep our hearts free from worldly desires, and open to us the riches of your charity. We ask this through our Lord Jesus Christ, your Son, who lives and reigns with you and the Holy Spirit, one God, for ever and ever. Amen.

November 14
All the Faithful Departed of the Benedictine Order
From the Common of the Faithful Departed, page 711, with the proper collect
Collect O God, creator and redeemer of all the faithful, grant the souls of your departed servants of our Order forgiveness of all their sins. May our devout prayers obtain for them the pardon that they have always desired; through Jesus Christ our Lord, who lives and reigns with you and the Holy Spirit, one God, now and for ever. Amen.

November 14
Consecration of Samuel Seabury
First American Bishop, 1784
Lesser Feast
From the Common of Pastors, page 669
Collect We give you thanks, O Lord our God, for your goodness in bestowing upon this Church the gift of the episcopate, which we celebrate in this remembrance of the consecration of Samuel Seabury; and we pray that, joined together in unity with our bishops, and nourished by your holy Sacraments, we may proclaim the Gospel of redemption with apostolic zeal; through Jesus Christ our Lord, who lives and reigns with you and the Holy Spirit, one God, now and for ever. Amen.

November 16
Gertrude the Great
Benedictine Nun of Helfta, Mystic and Theologian, 1302
Lesser Feast
From the Common of Monastics, page 687, with the following proper parts
Morning Prayer
Antiphon 1 Sing and rejoice, O daughter Zion! For lo, I will come and dwell in your midst, says the Lord.
Psalms from current day of the week.
Antiphon 2 O blessed soul who merited to be the seat of wisdom and who delighted to be among the human family.

Antiphon 3 Gertrude, faithful and chosen spouse, entered into the heart and joy of her Lord whose love desired her.

Responsory One (Lam. 3: 25, 24)
The Lord is my portion
        — therefore I will hope in him.
The Lord is good to those who wait for him
        — therefore I will hope in him.
Glory to the Father, and to the Son and to the Holy Spirit.
The Lord is my portion
        — therefore I will hope in him.

Canticle of Jerusalem Betrothed *Propter Sion non tacebo*
(Isaiah 62:1-5)

Antiphon As the bridegroom rejoices over the bride, so shall your God rejoice over you.

For Zion's sake I will not keep silent, *
        and for Jerusalem's sake I will not rest,

Until her vindication shines out like the dawn, *
        and her salvation like a burning torch.

The nations shall see your vindication, *
        and all the kings your glory.

You shall be called by a new name *
        spoken by the mouth of the Lord.

You shall be a crown of beauty in the hand of the Lord, *
        and a royal diadem in the hand of your God.

You shall no more be termed "Forsaken," *
        and your land shall no more be termed "Desolate;"

You shall be called "My Delight," *
        and your land "Espoused".

For the Lord delights in you, *
        and your land shall be married.

For as a young man marries a young woman, *
        so shall your builder marry you,

And as the bridegroom rejoices over the bride, *
        so shall your God rejoice over you.

Antiphon As the bridegroom rejoices over the bride, so shall your God rejoice over you.

Responsory Two (Mt. 25:6, 10)
Here is the bridegroom
　　　　− **come out to meet him.**
She went with him into the wedding banquet
　　　　− **come out to meet him.**
Glory to the Father, and to the Son and to the Holy Spirit.
Here is the bridegroom
　　　　− **come out to meet him.**

Benedictus Antiphon O glorious spouse of Christ, illuminated with the light of prophecy, enflamed with apostolic zeal, crowned with the laurel of virginity, your heart was enflamed with the fire of divine love.

Collect O Lord, you loved to dwell in the pure heart of your virgin Gertrude. Aided by her prayer, purify our hearts so that we, too, may become a dwelling place for your divine majesty. Through Jesus Christ our Lord, who lives and reigns with you and the Holy Spirit, one God, now and for ever. Amen.

Gertrude the Great Noonday Prayer
Antiphon As a dove builds its nest in the hollow of the rock so the chaste Gertrude found herself in the hallow of Christ's side and she drew sweet honey from that rock.
Psalms from current day of the week.

Reading Song of Songs 3:4
I found him whom my soul loves. I held him, and would not let him go until I brought him into my mother's house, and into the chamber of her that conceived me.

Verse and Response
She is a wise virgin.
Whom the Lord found keeping vigil.

Collect *From Morning Prayer*

Gertrude the Great Evening Prayer
Antiphon 1 In Gertrude's heart you will discover me, says the Lord, for I desire to dwell in her soul.
Psalms from current day of the week.
Antiphon 2 Christ received the beloved soul of Gertrude, stretched out his arms in embrace and opened his heart to her.

Antiphon 3 Christ spoke to his beloved Gertrude face to face as a person speaks to a friend.

Responsory (Ps. 68:3)
Let the righteous be glad
– and rejoice before God.
Let them be merry and joyful
– and rejoice before God.
Glory to the Father and to the Son and to the Holy Spirit.
Let the righteous be glad
– and rejoice before God.

Magnificat Antiphon Angels descended from heaven and called Gertrude to the joys of paradise saying, "Come, O Beloved, for the delights of heaven are waiting for you." Alleluia.

Collect *From Morning Prayer*

November 16

Margaret
Queen of Scotland, 1093
Lesser Feast
From the Common of Holy Persons, page 695
O God, you called your servant Margaret to an earthly throne that she might advance your heavenly kingdom, and gave her zeal for your Church and love for your people: Mercifully grant that we who commemorate her this day may be fruitful in good works, and attain to the glorious crown of your saints; through Jesus Christ our Lord, who lives and reigns with you and the Holy Spirit, one God, for ever and ever. Amen.

November 17

Hugh
Carthusian Monk and Bishop of Lincoln, 1200
Lesser Feast
From the Common of Pastors, page 669
Collect O holy God, you endowed your servant and bishop Hugh of Lincoln with wise and cheerful boldness, and taught him to commend the discipline of holy life to kings and princes: Grant that we also, rejoicing in the Good News of your mercy, and fearing nothing but the loss of you, may be bold to speak the truth in love, in the name of Jesus Christ our Redeemer; who lives and reigns with you and the Holy Spirit, one God, for ever and ever. Amen.

November 18

Hilda

Abbess of Whitby, 680

Lesser Feast

From the Common of Monastics, page 687, with the following proper antiphons

Benedictus Antiphon Blessed Hilda, most precious jewel, you shone with a light that spread throughout all Britain: your life is a bright example to all who desire to live well.

Magnificat Antiphon The Abbess Hilda, mother of them all, departed this life, and ascended to eternal bliss, to the company of the inhabitants of heaven, with a great light, and with angels conducting her.

Collect O God of peace, by whose grace the abbess Hilda was endowed with gifts of justice, prudence, and strength to rule as a wise mother over the nuns and monks of her household, and to become a trusted and reconciling friend to leaders of the Church: Give us the grace to recognize and accept the varied gifts you bestow on men and women, that our common life may be enriched and your gracious will be done; through Jesus Christ our Lord, who lives and reigns with you and the Holy Spirit, one God, now and for ever. Amen.

November 19

Mechtilde of Hackenburg

Benedictine Nun of Helfta, 1298

Lesser Feast

From the Common of Monastics, page 687

Collect Lord our God, through your loving favor you revealed to blessed Mechtilde, your virgin, the hidden secrets of your providence. May we who know you now through faith rejoice hereafter to see you face to face. Grant this through our Lord Jesus Christ, your Son, who lives and reigns with you and the Holy Spirit, one God, for ever and ever. Amen.

November 19

Elizabeth

Princess of Hungary, 1231

Lesser Feast

From the Common of Holy Persons, page 695

O God, you called your servants Margaret and Elizabeth to an earthly throne that they might advance your heavenly kingdom, and gave them zeal for your Church and love for your people: Mercifully grant that we who commemorate them this day may be fruitful in good works, and attain to the glorious crown of your saints; through Jesus Christ our Lord, who lives and reigns with you and the Holy Spirit, one God, for ever and ever. Amen.

November 20

Edmund

King of East Anglia and Martyr, 870
Lesser Feast

From the Common of Martyrs, page 665

Collect O God of ineffable mercy, you gave grace and fortitude to blessed Edmund the king to triumph over the enemy of his people by nobly dying for your Name: Bestow on us your servants the shield of faith with which we can withstand the assaults of our ancient enemy; through Jesus Christ our Redeemer, who lives and reigns with you and the Holy Spirit, one God, now and for ever. Amen.

November 22

Cecelia

Martyr at Rome, c. 280
Lesser Feast

From the Common of Martyrs, page 665, with the following proper antiphons

Benedictus Antiphon When dawn was breaking Cecelia cried out: Come, soldiers of Christ! Put off the works of darkness and clothe yourselves with the armor of light.

Magnificat Antiphon Blessed Cecelia cherished the Gospel of Christ in her heart. She prayed without ceasing by night and day.

Collect Most gracious God, whose blessed martyr Cecilia sang in her heart to strengthen her witness to you: We give you thanks for the makers of music whom you have gifted with Pentecostal fire; and we pray that we may join with them in creation's song of praise until at the last, with Cecelia and all your saints, we come to share in the song of those redeemed by our Savior Jesus Christ; who with you and the Holy Spirit lives and reigns, one God, in glory everlasting. Amen.

November 22

Clive Staples Lewis

Apologist and Spiritual Writer, 1963
Lesser Feast

From the Common of Theologians and Teachers, page 672

Collect O God of searing truth and surpassing beauty, we give you thanks for Clive Staples Lewis, whose sanctified imagination lights fires of faith in young and old alike; Surprise us also with your joy and draw us into that new and abundant life which is ours in Christ Jesus, who lives and reigns with you and the Holy Spirit, one God, now and for ever. Amen.

November 23

Clement
Bishop of Rome, c. 100
Lesser Feast

From the Common of Martyrs, page 665

Collect Almighty God, you chose your servant Clement of Rome to recall the Church in Corinth to obedience and stability: Grant that your Church may be grounded and settled in your truth by the indwelling of the Holy Spirit; reveal to it what is not yet known; fill up what is lacking; confirm what has already been revealed; and keep it blameless in your service; through Jesus Christ our Lord, who lives and reigns with you and the Holy Spirit, one God, for ever and ever. Amen.

Fourth Thursday in November

Thanksgiving Day
Major Feast

From the Common of National Holidays, page 707

Collect Almighty and gracious Father, we give you thanks for the fruits of the earth in their season and for the labors of those who harvest them. Make us, we pray, faithful stewards of your great bounty, for the provision of our necessities and the relief of all who are in need, to the glory of your Name; through Jesus Christ our Lord, who lives and reigns with you and the Holy Spirit, one God, now and for ever. Amen.

November 25

James Otis Sargent Huntington,
Monk, Priest and Founder of the Order of the Holy Cross, 1935
Lesser Feast

From the Common of Monastics, page 687, with the following proper antiphons

Benedictus Antiphon We cannot help others by giving them what is our own; we must impart to them the strength of Christ's Body, the fruits of the Spirit.

Magnificat Antiphon The ladder of the Cross is planted firmly within our house, and angels pass up and down that stairway.

Collect O loving God, by your grace your servant James Huntington gathered a community dedicated to love and discipline and devotion to the holy Cross of our Savior Jesus Christ: Send your blessing on all who proclaim Christ crucified, and move the hearts of many to look upon him and be saved; who with you and the Holy spirit lives and reigns, one God, for ever and ever. Amen.

November 28
Kamehameha and Emma
King and Queen of Hawaii, 1864, 1885
Lesser Feast

From the Common of Holy Persons, page 695

Collect O Sovereign God, who raised up (King) Kamehameha (IV) and (Queen) Emma to be rulers in Hawaii, and inspired and enabled them to be diligent in good works for the welfare of their people and the good of your Church: Receive our thanks for their witness to the Gospel; and grant that we, with them, may attain to the crown of glory that never fades away; through Jesus Christ our Savior and Redeemer, who with you and the Holy Spirit lives and reigns, one God, for ever and ever. Amen.

November 29
Dorothy Day
Founder of Catholic Worker, Benedictine Oblate and Prophetic Witness 1980
Lesser Feast

From the Common of Prophetic Witnesses, page 684, with the following proper antiphons

Benedictus Antiphon I do not know how to love God except by loving the poor. I do not know how to serve God except by serving the poor.

Magnificat Antiphon When you love people, you see all the good in them, all the Christ in them. God sees Christ, His Son, in us and loves us. And so we should see Christ in others, and nothing else, and love them.

Collect Merciful God, you called your servant Dorothy Day to show us the face of Jesus in the poor and forsaken. By constant practice of the works of mercy, she embraced poverty and witnessed steadfastly to justice and peace. Count her among your saints and lead us all to become friends of the poor ones of the earth, and to recognize you in them. We ask this through your Son Jesus Christ, bringer of good news to the poor. Amen.

November 30
Saint Andrew the Apostle
Major Feast

From the Common of Apostles, page 648, with the following proper antiphons

Benedictus Antiphon Jesus said to the two disciples, "Come and see." One of the two who heard John speak and followed him was Andrew, Simon Peter's brother.

Magnificat Antiphon Unless a grain of wheat falls into the earth and dies, it remains just a single grain; but if it dies, it bears much fruit.

Collect Almighty God, who gave such grace to your apostle Andrew that he readily obeyed the call of your Son Jesus Christ, and brought his brother with him: Give us, who are called by your Holy Word, grace to follow him without delay, and to bring those near to us into his gracious presence; who lives and reigns with you and the Holy Spirit, one God, now and for ever. Amen.

Common of the Saints

Common of the Dedication of a Church

Evening Prayer I

Hymn Blessed city, heavenly Salem *Hymnal 519*

Psalm 147 A *Laudate Dominum*
Antiphon I will go to the altar of God and adore in your holy temple.

1. Hallelujah!
   How good it is to sing praises to our God! *
      how pleasant it is to honor him with praise!

2 The LORD rebuilds Jerusalem; *
      he gathers the exiles of Israel.

3 He heals the brokenhearted *
      and binds up their wounds.

4 He counts the number of the stars *
      and calls them all by their names.

5 Great is our LORD and mighty in power; *
      there is no limit to his wisdom.

6 The LORD lifts up the lowly, *
      but casts the wicked to the ground.

7 Sing to the LORD with thanksgiving; *
      make music to our God upon the harp.

8 He covers the heavens with clouds *
      and prepares rain for the earth;

9 He makes grass to grow upon the mountains *
      and green plants to serve mankind.

10 He provides food for flocks and herds *
      and for the young ravens when they cry.

11 He is not impressed by the might of a horse; *
      he has no pleasure in the strength of a man;

12 But the LORD has pleasure in those who fear him, *
      in those who await his gracious favor.

Antiphon I will go to the altar of God and adore in your holy temple.

Psalm 147 B *Lauda Hierusalem*

Antiphon The Lord is in his holy temple, the Lord, whose throne is in heaven.

13 Worship the LORD, O Jerusalem; *
    praise your God, O Zion;

14 For he has strengthened the bars of your gates; *
    he has blessed your children within you.

15 He has established peace on your borders; *
    he satisfies you with the finest wheat.

16 He sends out his command to the earth, *
    and his word runs very swiftly.

17 He gives snow like wool; *
    he scatters hoarfrost like ashes.

18 He scatters his hail like bread crumbs; *
    who can stand against his cold?

19 He sends forth his word and melts them; *
    he blows with his wind, and the waters flow.

20 He declares his word to Jacob, *
    his statutes and his judgments to Israel.

21 He has not done so to any other nation; *
    to them he has not revealed his judgments.
    Hallelujah!

Antiphon The Lord is in his holy temple, the Lord, whose throne is in heaven.

Psalm 65 *Te decet hymnus*

Antiphon Open wide the doors and gates for Christ the Lord.

1   You are to be praised, O God, in Zion; *
    to you shall vows be performed in Jerusalem.

2   To you that hear prayer shall all flesh come, *
    because of their transgressions.

3   Our sins are stronger than we are, *
    but you will blot them out.

4 Blessed are they whom you choose
and draw to your courts to dwell there! *
   they will be satisfied by the beauty of your house,
   by the holiness of your temple.

5 Awesome things will you show us in your righteousness,
O God of our salvation, *
   O Hope of all the ends of the earth
   and of the seas that are far away.

6 You make fast the mountains by your power; *
   they are girded about with might.

7 You still the roaring of the seas, *
   the roaring of their waves,
   and the clamor of the peoples.

8 Those who dwell at the ends of the earth
will tremble at your marvelous signs; *
   you make the dawn and the dusk to sing for joy.

9 You visit the earth and water it abundantly;
you make it very plenteous; *
   the river of God is full of water.

10 You prepare the grain, *
   for so you provide for the earth.

11 You drench the furrows and smooth out the ridges; *
   with heavy rain you soften the ground and bless its increase.

12 You crown the year with your goodness, *
   and your paths overflow with plenty.

13 May the fields of the wilderness be rich for grazing, *
   and the hills be clothed with joy.

14 May the meadows cover themselves with flocks,
and the valleys cloak themselves with grain; *
   let them shout for joy and sing.

Antiphon Open wide the doors and gates for Christ the Lord.

Reading

Responsory (Ps. 5:7,8)
I will go into your house
   – I will bow down toward your holy temple.

Lead me, O Lord, in your righteousness
> **– I will bow down toward your holy temple.**

Glory to the Father and to the Son and to the Holy Spirit.
I will go into your house
> **– I will bow down toward your holy temple.**

Magnificat Antiphon Rejoice with Jerusalem, and be glad for her, all you who love her; rejoice with her in joy.

Litany

For the Church universal, of which these visible buildings are the symbol, we thank you, Lord.
Lord, have mercy.

For your presence whenever two or three have gathered together in your Name, we thank you, Lord.
Christ, have mercy.

For the faith of those who have gone before us and for our encouragement by their perseverance, we thank you, Lord.
Lord, have mercy.

Invitation to the Lord's Prayer

As living stones built into Christ's temple, let us offer our sacrifice of praise to the Father.

Collect Almighty God, to whose glory we celebrate the dedication of this house of prayer: We give you thanks for the fellowship of those who have worshiped in this place, and we pray that all who seek you here may find you, and be filled with your joy and peace; through Jesus Christ our Lord, who lives and reigns with you, in the unity of the Holy Spirit, one God, now and for ever. Amen.

The Blessing

May we, who celebrate the mystery of the Church, the Bride of Christ, know ourselves to be loved and sanctified by Christ, our Bridegroom. **Amen.**

Common of the Dedication of a Church
Morning Prayer

Invitatory Christ loves the church: Come let us worship.

Hymn Glorious things of thee are spoken *Hymnal 522*

Antiphon 1 My house shall be called a house of prayer for all peoples.
Psalms from Sunday Week 1 Morning Prayer, page 134

Antiphon 2 This is none other than the house of God, and this is the gate of heaven.

Antiphon 3 Like living stones, let yourselves be built into a spiritual house, to be a holy priesthood, to offer spiritual sacrifices

Reading One

Responsory (Ps. 48:1; Ps. 61:4)

Great is the Lord, and highly to be praised
  – in the city of our God is his holy hill.
I will dwell in your house for ever
  – in the city of our God is his holy hill.
Glory to the Father and to the Son and to the Holy Spirit.
Great is the Lord, and highly to be praised
  – in the city of our God is his holy hill.

Canticle of Zion *Erit in novissimis*
(Isaiah 2: 2-5)

Antiphon Come, let us go up to the mountain of the Lord, to the house of the God of Jacob.

In days to come the mountain of the Lord's house *
  shall be established as the highest of the mountains.

It shall be raised above the hills; *
  all the nations shall stream to it.

Many peoples shall come and say, *
  "Come, let us go up to the mountain of the Lord,
  to the house of the God of Jacob.

The Lord will teach us his ways *
  that we may walk in his paths."

For out of Zion shall go forth instruction, *
  and the word of the Lord from Jerusalem.

He shall judge between the nations, *
  and shall arbitrate for many peoples.

They shall beat their swords into plowshares, *
  and their spears into pruning hooks.

Nation shall not lift up sword against nation, *
  neither shall they learn war any more.

Antiphon Come, let us go up to the mountain of the Lord, to the house of the God of Jacob.

Reading Two

Responsory Two (Ps 65:4; Ps. 48:10)
Your people will be satisfied by the beauty of your house
 — by the holiness of your temple.
Let Mount Zion be glad
 — by the holiness of your temple.
Glory to the Father and to the Son and to the Holy Spirit.
Your people will be satisfied by the beauty of your house
 — by the holiness of your temple.

Benedictus Antiphon Zacchaeus, hurry and come down; for I must stay at your house today. So he hurried down and joyfully welcome Christ for salvation came to his house that day.

Litany
Father, we thank you that through the waters of Baptism we die to sin and are made new in Christ. Grant through your Spirit that those baptized at the Font may enjoy the liberty of the children of God.
Lord, have mercy.
Eternal Word, you speak to us through the words of Holy Scripture. Give us ears to hear and hearts to obey.
Christ, have mercy.
Lord God, you sanctified the Holy Table dedicated to you. Accept here the continual recalling of the sacrifice of your Son.
Lord, have mercy.

Invitation to the Lord's Prayer
Christ illumines the Church with the Holy Spirit and draws us into the light of the Father. Let us rejoice in the Father's light.

Collect *From Evening Prayer I*

The Blessing
May all who eat and drink at Table of Christ be fed and refreshed by his flesh and blood, be forgiven for their sins, united with one another, and strengthened for holy service. **Amen.**

Common of the Dedication of a Church
Noonday Prayer

Hymn Singing songs of expectation *Hymnal 527*

Antiphon You are God's temple and God's Spirit dwells in you.
Psalms from Sunday Week 1 Noonday Prayer, page 138

Reading 2 Cor. 6: 16
We are the temple of the living God; as God said, "I will live in them and walk among them, and I will be their God, and they shall be my people.

Verse and Response
Blessed are they whom you choose.
And draw to your courts to dwell there.

Collect *From Evening Prayer I*

Common of the Dedication of a Church
Evening Prayer II

Hymn Christ is made the sure foundation *Hymnal 518*

Psalm 46 *Deus noster refugium*

Antiphon I will dwell in your house for ever; I will take refuge under the cover of your wings.

1   God is our refuge and strength, *
        a very present help in trouble.

2   Therefore we will not fear, though the earth be moved, *
        and though the mountains be toppled
        into the depths of the sea;

3   Though its waters rage and foam, *
        and though the mountains tremble at its tumult.

4   The LORD of hosts is with us; *
        the God of Jacob is our stronghold.

5   There is a river whose streams make glad the city of God, *
        the holy habitation of the Most High.

6   God is in the midst of her;
    she shall not be overthrown; *
        God shall help her at the break of day.

7   The nations make much ado, and the kingdoms are shaken; *
        God has spoken, and the earth shall melt away.

8 The LORD of hosts is with us; *
    the God of Jacob is our stronghold.

9 Come now and look upon the works of the LORD, *
    what awesome things he has done on earth.

10 It is he who makes war to cease in all the world; *
    he breaks the bow, and shatters the spear,
    and burns the shields with fire.

11 "Be still, then, and know that I am God; *
    I will be exalted among the nations;
    I will be exalted in the earth."

12 The LORD of hosts is with us; *
    the God of Jacob is our stronghold.

Antiphon I will dwell in your house for ever; I will take refuge under the cover of your wings.

Psalm 122 *Lætatus sum*

Antiphon Destroy this temple, and in three days I will raise it up. He was speaking of the temple of his body.

1 I was glad when they said to me, *
    "Let us go to the house of the LORD."

2 Now our feet are standing *
    within your gates, O Jerusalem.

3 Jerusalem is built as a city *
    that is at unity with itself;

4 To which the tribes go up,
    the tribes of the LORD, *
    the assembly of Israel,
    to praise the Name of the LORD.

5 For there are the thrones of judgment, *
    the thrones of the house of David.

6 Pray for the peace of Jerusalem: *
    "May they prosper who love you.

7 Peace be within your walls *
    and quietness within your towers.

8 For my brethren and companions' sake, *
    I pray for your prosperity.

9 Because of the house of the LORD our God, *
    I will seek to do you good."

Antiphon Destroy this temple, and in three days I will raise it up. He was speaking of the temple of his body.

Psalm 27 A *Dominus illuminatio*

Antiphon In Christ the whole structure is joined together and grows into a holy temple in the Lord.

1 The LORD is my light and my salvation;
   whom then shall I fear? *
       the LORD is the strength of my life;
       of whom then shall I be afraid?

2 When evildoers came upon me to eat up my flesh, *
       it was they, my foes and my adversaries,
       who stumbled and fell.

3 Though an army should encamp against me, *
       yet my heart shall not be afraid;

4 And though war should rise up against me, *
       yet will I put my trust in him.

5 One thing have I asked of the LORD;
   one thing I seek; *
       that I may dwell in the house of the LORD
       all the days of my life;

6 To behold the fair beauty of the LORD *
       and to seek him in his temple.

7 For in the day of trouble
   he shall keep me safe in his shelter; *
       he shall hide me in the secrecy of his dwelling
       and set me high upon a rock.

8 Even now he lifts up my head *
       above my enemies round about me.

Antiphon In Christ the whole structure is joined together and grows into a holy temple in the Lord.

Reading

Responsory (Rev. 21:2)
I saw the holy city, the new Jerusalem
    – coming down out of heaven from God.
She was prepared as a bride adorned for her husband
    – coming down out of heaven from God.
Glory to the Father and to the Son and to the Holy Spirit.
I saw the holy city, the new Jerusalem
    – coming down out of heaven from God.

Magnificat Antiphon They are before the throne of God, and worship him day and night within his temple, and the one who is seated on the throne will shelter them.

Litany
Christ Jesus, Living Temple, you provide a place for all people in your house of prayer; open your church to embrace all whom you welcome.
Lord, have mercy.
Christ Jesus, Foundation of the Church, you support all who are established on you; build us up into a living temple in you.
Christ, have mercy.
Christ Jesus, Keystone of the Universe, all creation finds its order in you; lead the dead to find themselves recreated in your image.
Lord, have mercy.

Invitation to the Lord's Prayer
As living stones built into Christ's temple, let us offer our sacrifice of praise to the Father.

Collect *From Evening Prayer I*

The Blessing
May we, who celebrate the mystery of the Church, the Bride of Christ, know ourselves to be loved and sanctified by Christ, our Bridegroom.
Amen.

Common of the Founding of the Community
Evening Prayer I

Hymn Rejoice, ye pure in heart! *Hymnal 556*

Antiphon 1 All who believed were together and had all things in common; they would sell their possessions and goods and distribute the proceeds to all, as any had need.
Psalms from Sunday Week One Evening Prayer I, page 130

Antiphon 2 Day by day, as they spent much time together in the temple, they broke bread at home and ate their food with glad and generous hearts.

Antiphon 3 They praised God and enjoyed the goodwill of all the people. Day by day the Lord added to their number those who were being saved.

Reading Luke 10: 38-42

Responsory (John 13: 34-35)
Just as I have loved you
> **– you also should love one another.**

I give you a new commandment
> **– you also should love one another.**

Glory to the Father and to the Son and to the Holy Spirit.
Just as I have loved you
> **– you also should love one another.**

Magnificat Antiphon If you have any encouragement from being united with Christ, then make my joy complete by being like-minded, having the same love, being one in spirit and of one mind.

Litany
You raised up this community in the power of the Holy Spirit; call women and men to follow you in the consecrated life.
Lord, have mercy.
You form your disciples in the pattern of contemplation and work; send your Spirit to sanctify monastics who live in the world.
Christ, have mercy.
You promise eternal life to all who faithfully follow you in the consecrated life; bring our departed brothers and sisters to your banquet in heaven.
Lord, have mercy.

Invitation to the Lord's Prayer
Faithful to the pledge we make of mutual forgiveness, let us ask God to cleanse our hearts as we pray with Christ.

Collect Gracious God, you raised up N. to be a religious community in the church. Help us to remain faithful to our charism until we dwell with you, O Father, and the Incarnate Word and the Holy Spirit in inexpressible joy, forever and ever. Amen.

The Blessing
May the word of Christ dwell in us richly as we teach and admonish one another in all wisdom. **Amen.**

Common of the Founding of the Community
Morning Prayer

Invitatory Christ calls to follow him in the common life: Come let us adore.

Hymn Over the chaos of the empty waters *Hymnal 176*

Antiphon 1 As God's chosen ones, holy and beloved, clothe yourselves with compassion, kindness, humility, meekness, and patience.
Psalms from Sunday Week 1 Morning Prayer, page 134
Antiphon 2 I have taught you the way of wisdom; I have led you in the paths of uprightness.
Antiphon 3 Who is wise and understanding among you? Let them show it by their good life, by deeds done in the humility that comes from wisdom.

Reading One Hosea 2: 14-23

Responsory One (Ps. 62:1, 6)
For God alone
　　　– my soul in silence waits.
My hope is in God
　　　– my soul in silence waits.
Glory to the Father and to the Son and to the Holy Spirit.
For God alone
　　　– my soul in silence waits.

Canticle You are God　　*Te Deum laudamus page 757*

Reading Two Acts 2: 37-47

Responsory Two (Ps. 133:1; Phil. 4:5)
How good and pleasant it is
　　　– when brethren live together in unity.
Let your gentleness be known to everyone
　　　– when brethren live together in unity.
Glory to the Father and to the Son and to the Holy Spirit.
How good and pleasant it is
　　　– when brethren live together in unity.

Benedictus Antiphon Those who love me will keep my word, and my Father will love them, and we will come to them and make our home with them.

Litany
Christ Jesus was obedient even to death on the cross; teach us obedience in our following the Gospel and the Rule.
Lord, have mercy.
Christ Jesus took on our human flesh and dwelled among us; support us in our stability to our sisters and brothers.
Christ, have mercy.
Christ Jesus preached a change of mind and heart; deepen our commitment to live the common life.
Lord, have mercy.

Invitation to the Lord's Prayer
In fellowship with consecrated women and men from centuries past and yet to come, let us approach the throne of grace and pray with Christ.

Collect *From Evening Prayer I*

The Blessing
May we prefer nothing whatever to Christ, and may he bring us all together to everlasting life. **Amen.**

Common of the Founding of the Community
Noonday Prayer
Hymn God of the prophets *Hymnal 359*

Antiphon One thing I asked of the Lord: to live in the house of the Lord all the days of my life, to behold the beauty of the Lord.
Psalms from Sunday Week 1 Noonday Prayer, page 138

Reading John 17: 14-19
I have given them your word, and the world has hated them because they do not belong to the world, just as I do not belong to the world. I am not asking you to take them out of the world, but I ask you to protect them from the evil one. They do not belong to the world, just as I do not belong to the world. Sanctify them in the truth; your word is truth. As you have sent me into the world, so I have sent them into the world. And for their sakes I sanctify myself, so that they also may be sanctified in truth.

Verse and Response

I made your name known to them, and I will make it known.
So that the love with which you have loved me may be in them, and I in them.

Collect *From Evening Prayer I*

Common of the Founding of the Community Evening Prayer II

Hymn God is Love, let heaven adore him *Hymnal 379*

Antiphon 1 All who believed were together and had all things in common; they would sell their possessions and goods and distribute the proceeds to all, as any had need.
Psalms from Sunday Evening Prayer II Week One, page 141
Antiphon 2 Day by day, as they spent much time together in the temple, they broke bread at home and ate their food with glad and generous hearts, praising God and having the goodwill of all the people.
Antiphon 3 For those who will follow this rule—peace be upon them, and mercy, and upon the Israel of God.

Reading John 17: 21b – 26

Responsory (John 13: 34-35)
Just as I have loved you
      – you also should love one another.
I give you a new commandment
      – you also should love one another.
Glory to the Father and to the Son and to the Holy Spirit.
Just as I have loved you
      – you also should love one another.

Magnificat Antiphon Peace be to the whole community, and love with faith, from God the Father and the Lord Jesus Christ. Grace be with all who have an undying love for our Lord Jesus Christ.

Litany
You raised up this community in the power of the Holy Spirit; call new women and men to follow you.
Lord, have mercy.
You form your disciples in the pattern of contemplation and work; send your Spirit to sanctify your people.
Christ, have mercy.

You promise eternal life to all who faithfully follow you in the monastic life; bring our departed sisters and brothers to your banquet in heaven. **Lord, have mercy.**

Invitation to the Lord's Prayer
Faithful to the pledge we make of mutual forgiveness, let us ask God to cleanse our hearts as we pray with Christ.

Collect *From Evening Prayer I*

The Blessing
May the word of Christ dwell in us richly as we teach and admonish one another in all wisdom. **Amen.**

Common of the Blessed Virgin Mary Evening Prayer I

Hymn The angel Gabriel from heaven came *Hymnal 265*

Psalm 113 *Laudate, pueri*

Antiphon Blessed are you among women, and blessed is the fruit of your womb.

1 Hallelujah!
Give praise, you servants of the LORD; *
praise the Name of the LORD.

2 Let the Name of the LORD be blessed, *
from this time forth for evermore.

3 From the rising of the sun to its going down *
let the Name of the LORD be praised.

4 The LORD is high above all nations, *
and his glory above the heavens.

5 Who is like the LORD our God, who sits enthroned on high, *
but stoops to behold the heavens and the earth?

6 He takes up the weak out of the dust *
and lifts up the poor from the ashes.

7 He sets them with the princes, *
with the princes of his people.

8 He makes the woman of a childless house *
to be a joyful mother of children.

Antiphon Blessed are you among women, and blessed is the fruit of your womb.

Psalm 45 B *Audi filia et vide*

Antiphon All glorious is the princess as she enters; her gown is cloth-of-gold.

11 "Hear, O daughter; consider and listen closely; *
    forget your people and your father's house.

12 The king will have pleasure in your beauty; *
    he is your master; therefore do him honor.

13 The people of Tyre are here with a gift; *
    the rich among the people seek your favor."

14 All glorious is the princess as she enters; *
    her gown is cloth of gold.

15 In embroidered apparel she is brought to the king; *
    after her the bridesmaids follow in procession.

16 With joy and gladness they are brought, *
    and enter into the palace of the king.

17 "In place of fathers, O king, you shall have sons; *
    you shall make them princes over all the earth.

18 I will make your name to be remembered
   from one generation to another; *
    therefore nations will praise you for ever and ever."

Antiphon All glorious is the princess as she enters; her gown is cloth-of-gold.

Psalm 145 *Exaltabo te, Deus*

Antiphon You are the glory of Jerusalem, the joy of Israel. You are the honor of our people.

1 I will exalt you, O God my King, *
    and bless your Name for ever and ever.

2 Every day will I bless you *
    and praise your Name for ever and ever.

3 Great is the LORD and greatly to be praised; *
    there is no end to his greatness.

4 One generation shall praise your works to another *
    and shall declare your power.

5 I will ponder the glorious splendor of your majesty *
    and all your marvelous works.

6 They shall speak of the might of your wondrous acts, *
    and I will tell of your greatness.

7 They shall publish the remembrance of your great goodness; *
    they shall sing of your righteous deeds.

8 The LORD is gracious and full of compassion, *
    slow to anger and of great kindness.

9 The LORD is loving to everyone *
    and his compassion is over all his works.

10 All your works praise you, O LORD, *
    and your faithful servants bless you.

11 They make known the glory of your kingdom *
    and speak of your power;

12 That the peoples may know of your power *
    and the glorious splendor of your kingdom.

13 Your kingdom is an everlasting kingdom; *
    your dominion endures throughout all ages.

14 The LORD is faithful in all his words *
    and merciful in all his deeds.

15 The LORD upholds all those who fall; *
    he lifts up those who are bowed down.

16 The eyes of all wait upon you, O LORD, *
    and you give them their food in due season.

17 You open wide your hand *
    and satisfy the needs of every living creature.

18 The LORD is righteous in all his ways *
    and loving in all his works.

19 The LORD is near to those who call upon him, *
    to all who call upon him faithfully.

20 He fulfills the desire of those who fear him; *
    he hears their cry and helps them.

21 The LORD preserves all those who love him, *
    but he destroys all the wicked.

22 My mouth shall speak the praise of the LORD; *
>   let all flesh bless his holy Name for ever and ever.

Antiphon You are the glory of Jerusalem, the joy of Israel. You are the honor of our people.

Reading *From the Proper of the Day*

Responsory (Gal. 4:4; Jn. 8:42)
When the fullness of time had come
>   **— God sent his Son, born of a woman.**

I came from God and now I am here
>   **— God sent his Son, born of a woman.**

Glory to the Father, and to the Son and to the Holy Spirit.
When the fullness of time had come
>   **— God sent his Son, born of a woman.**

Magnificat Antiphon *From the Proper of the Day*

Litany
You called Mary to be the Mother of your Incarnate Word; give insight and strength to all families who are raising children.
Lord, have mercy.
You taught Mary to see Jesus not only as her son but also as her Lord; deepen our discipleship of Christ, our Teacher.
Christ, have mercy.
You deepened Mary's faith by revealing to the Church the risen Christ; bring all the dead to share in Christ's risen life.
Lord, have mercy.

Invitation to the Lord's Prayer
As you called Mary to serve you as the Mother of Christ, may we answer your invitation to a more faithful following of Christ as we pray.

Collect *From the Proper of the Day*

The Blessing
May we who celebrate Mary whose womb bore Christ and whose breasts nursed Christ be more blessed in hearing the word of God and obeying it. **Amen.**

Common of the Blessed Virgin Mary
Morning Prayer

Invitatory The Word was made flesh: Come let us worship.

Hymn Praise we the Lord this day *Hymnal 267*

Antiphon 1 The Angel Gabriel was sent by God to a virgin engaged to a man whose name was Joseph of the house of David. The Virgin's name was Mary.

Psalms from Sunday of Week 1 Morning Prayer, page 134

Antiphon 2 Do not be afraid, Mary, for you have found favor with God. You will conceive in your womb and bear a son, and you will name him Jesus.

Antiphon 3 Here am I, the servant of the Lord; let it be with me according to your word.

Reading One *From the Proper of the Day*

Responsory (Zech. 2:10; Is. 12:6)
Sing and rejoice, O daughter Zion!
    − I will come and dwell in your midst.
Great in your midst is the Holy One of Israel
    − I will come and dwell in your midst.
Glory to the Father and to the Son and to the Holy Spirit.
Sing and rejoice, O daughter Zion!
    − I will come and dwell in your midst.

Canticle – Song of the Annunciation   *Ave gratia plena*
(Luke 1: 28, 30-33, 35, 38, 42, 45)

Antiphon Blessed is she who believed that there would be a fulfilment of what was spoken to her by the Lord.

Greetings, favored one! *
    The Lord is with you.'
    for you have found favor with God.

You will conceive in your womb and bear a son, *
    and you will name him Jesus.

He will be great, and will be called the Son of the Most High, *
    and the Lord God will give to him
    the throne of his ancestor David.

The Holy Spirit will come upon you, *
    and the power of the Most High will overshadow you;

Therefore the child to be born will be holy; *
  he will be called Son of God.

Here am I, the servant of the Lord; *
  let it be with me according to your word.

Blessed are you among women, *
  and blessed is the fruit of your womb.

Blessed is she who believed *
  that there would be a fulfilment
  of what was spoken to her by the Lord.

Antiphon Blessed is she who believed that there would be a fulfilment of what was spoken to her by the Lord.

Reading Two *From the Proper of the Day*

Responsory Two (Lk. 11:27; Lk. 1:45)
Blessed is the womb that bore you
  — Blessed are those who hear the word of God and obey it.
Blessed is she who believed
  — Blessed are those who hear the word of God and obey it.
Glory to the Father and to the Son and to the Holy Spirit.
Blessed is the womb that bore you
  — Blessed are those who hear the word of God and obey it.

Benedictus Antiphon *From the Proper of the Day*

Litany
Mary endured the estrangement of her unconventional motherhood; comfort all who are victims of sexual violence.
Lord, have mercy.
Mary followed your Son even in his agony; support all who endure the inequalities of our justice system.
Christ, have mercy.
Mary joined the disciples in prayer for the Spirit; deepen the prayer of all committed to contemplation.
Lord, have mercy.

Invitation to the Lord's Prayer As your Word took flesh from Blessed Mary, may you send us your Spirit that we may discern the Mystical Body of your Son as we pray to you.

Collect *From the Proper of the Day*

The Blessing
May we who believe that God sent his Son, born of a woman, born under the law, be blessed in our redemption and our adoption as children of God. **Amen.**

Common of the Blessed Virgin Mary
Noonday Prayer

Hymn Virgin Born, we bow before thee *Hymnal 258*

Antiphon Mary treasured all these words and pondered them in her heart.
Psalms from Sunday of Week One Noonday Prayer, page 138

Reading Zechariah 9:9
Rejoice greatly, O daughter Zion! Shout aloud, O daughter Jerusalem! Lo, your king comes to you.

Verse and Response
Blessed is the womb that bore you and the breasts that nursed you.
Blessed rather are those who hear the word of God and obey it.

Collect *From the Proper of the Day*

Common of the Blessed Virgin Mary
Evening Prayer II

Hymn Sing we of the Blessed Mother *Hymnal 278*

Psalm 113 *Laudate, pueri*

Antiphon Blessed are you among women, and blessed is the fruit of your womb.

1   Hallelujah!
    Give praise, you servants of the LORD; *
        praise the Name of the LORD.

2   Let the Name of the LORD be blessed, *
        from this time forth for evermore.

3   From the rising of the sun to its going down *
        let the Name of the LORD be praised.

4   The LORD is high above all nations, *
        and his glory above the heavens.

5   Who is like the LORD our God, who sits enthroned on high, *
        but stoops to behold the heavens and the earth?

6 He takes up the weak out of the dust *
     and lifts up the poor from the ashes.

7 He sets them with the princes, *
     with the princes of his people.

8 He makes the woman of a childless house *
     to be a joyful mother of children.

Antiphon Blessed are you among women, and blessed is the fruit of your womb.

Psalm 122 *Lætatus sum*

Antiphon All glorious is the princess as she enters; her gown is cloth-of-gold.

1 I was glad when they said to me, *
     "Let us go to the house of the LORD."

2 Now our feet are standing *
     within your gates, O Jerusalem.

3 Jerusalem is built as a city *
     that is at unity with itself;

4 To which the tribes go up,
   the tribes of the LORD, *
     the assembly of Israel,
     to praise the Name of the LORD.

5 For there are the thrones of judgment, *
     the thrones of the house of David.

6 Pray for the peace of Jerusalem: *
     "May they prosper who love you.

7 Peace be within your walls *
     and quietness within your towers.

8 For my brethren and companions' sake, *
     I pray for your prosperity.

9 Because of the house of the LORD our God, *
     I will seek to do you good."

Antiphon All glorious is the princess as she enters; her gown is cloth-of-gold.

Psalm 127 *Nisi Dominus*

Antiphon You are the glory of Jerusalem, the joy of Israel. You are the honor of our people.

1 Unless the LORD builds the house, *
   their labor is in vain who build it.

2 Unless the LORD watches over the city, *
   in vain the watchman keeps his vigil.

3 It is in vain that you rise so early and go to bed so late; *
   vain, too, to eat the bread of toil,
   for he gives to his beloved sleep.

4 Children are a heritage from the LORD, *
   and the fruit of the womb is a gift.

5 Like arrows in the hand of a warrior *
   are the children of one's youth.

6 Blessed is the man who has his quiver full of them! *
   he shall not be put to shame
   when he contends with his enemies in the gate.

Antiphon You are the glory of Jerusalem, the joy of Israel. You are the honor of our people.

Reading *From the Proper of the Day*

Responsory (Luke 1: 42; Luke 11: 28)
Blessed are you among women
   – blessed is the fruit of your womb.
Blessed are they who hear the word of God and keep it
   – blessed is the fruit of your womb.
Glory to the Father, and to the Son and to the Holy Spirit.
Blessed are you among women
   – blessed is the fruit of your womb.

Magnificat Antiphon *From the Proper of the Day*

Litany
The Father has chosen Mary to be the mother of his Son; let us rejoice with Christ in being called beloved children of God.
Lord have mercy.

Mary proclaimed that God would feed the hungry and lift the downtrodden; may we open our hands and our hearts to serve Christ in the hungry and oppressed.
Christ have mercy.
Mary has entered into the dwelling place prepared for her by Christ; may all the dead enter their heavenly home.
Lord have mercy.

Invitation to the Lord's Prayer
Rejoicing in our hope of sharing the glory of God, let us long for the kingdom of God in the words of Christ.

Collect *From the Proper of the Day*

Blessing
May we who celebrate Mary whose womb bore Christ and whose breasts nursed Christ be more blessed in hearing the word of God and obeying it. **Amen.**

Common of the Blessed Virgin Mary on Saturday Morning Prayer

Hymn Praise we the Lord this day *Hymnal 267*

Psalms from Saturday of the Current Week.

Benedictus Antiphon
Epiphany 1 On entering the house, they saw the child with Mary his mother; and they knelt down and paid him homage.
Epiphany 2 We seek your protection, O Holy Mother of God. Do not despise our petitions in our necessities, but deliver us always from all dangers, O Glorious and Blessed Virgin.
Pentecost 1 What the virgin Eve had bound fast through unbelief, this did the virgin Mary set free through faith.
Pentecost 2 Here am I, the servant of the Lord; let it be with me according to your word.
Pentecost 3 Blessed are you among women, and blessed is the fruit of your womb.
Pentecost 4 Mary treasured all these words and pondered them in her heart.
Pentecost 5 When the fullness of time had come, God sent his Son, born of a woman, born under the law, in order to redeem those who were under the law, so that we might receive adoption as children.

Pentecost 6 A great portent appeared in heaven: a woman clothed with the sun, with the moon under her feet, and on her head a crown of twelve stars.

Pentecost 7 Thou hast light in dark, and shutst in little room, immensity cloistered in thy dear womb.

Litany

Mary endured the estrangement of her unconventional motherhood; comfort all who are victims of sexual violence.

Lord, have mercy.

Mary followed your Son even in his agony; support all who endure the inequalities of our justice system.

Christ, have mercy.

Mary joined the disciples in prayer for the Spirit; deepen the prayer of all committed to contemplation.

Lord, have mercy.

Invitation to the Lord's Prayer As your Word took flesh from Blessed Mary, may you send us your Spirit that we may discern the Mystical Body of your Son as we pray to you.

Collect

Pour your grace into our hearts, O Lord, that we who have known the incarnation of your Son Jesus Christ, announced by an angel to the Virgin Mary, may by his cross and passion be brought to the glory of his resurrection; who lives and reigns with you, in the unity of the Holy Spirit, one God, now and for ever. Amen.

or

Father in heaven, by your grace the virgin mother of your incarnate Son was blessed in bearing him, but still more blessed in keeping your word: Grant us who honor the exaltation of her lowliness to follow the example of her devotion to your will; through Jesus Christ our Lord, who lives and reigns with you and the Holy Spirit, one God, for ever and ever. Amen.

or

O God, the King of saints, we praise and glorify your holy Name for all your servants who have finished their course in your faith and fear: for the blessed Virgin Mary; for the holy patriarchs, prophets, apostles, and martyrs; and for all your other righteous servants, known to us and unknown; and we pray that, encouraged by their examples, aided by their prayers, and strengthened by their fellowship, we also may be partakers of the inheritance of the saints in light; through the merits of your Son Jesus Christ our Lord. Amen.

The Blessing

May we who celebrate Mary whose womb bore Christ and whose breasts nursed Christ be more blessed in hearing the word of God and obeying it. **Amen.**

or

May we who believe that God sent his Son, born of a woman, born under the law, be blessed in our redemption and our adoption as children of God. **Amen.**

Common of the Blessed Virgin Mary on Saturday
Noonday Prayer

Hymn Virgin Born, we bow before thee *Hymnal 258*

Antiphon You are the glory of Jerusalem, the joy of Israel, the highest honor of our people.

Reading Zechariah 9:9
Rejoice greatly, O daughter Zion! Shout aloud, O daughter Jerusalem! Lo, your king comes to you.

Verse and Response
Blessed is the womb that bore you and the breasts that nursed you.
Blessed are those who hear the word of God and obey it.

Collect *From Morning Prayer*

Common of the Apostles
Evening Prayer I

Hymn The eternal gifts of Christ the King *Hymnal 233*

Antiphon 1 I give you a new commandment, that you love one another.
Psalms from Sunday Week 1 Evening Prayer I, page 130
or Sunday Evening Prayer I of the Current Week.
Antiphon 2 No one has greater love than this, to lay down one's life for one's friends.
Antiphon 3 You are my friends if you do what I command you.

Reading *From the Proper of the Day*

Responsory (Jn. 13:35)
By this everyone will know
　　　　— you are my disciples.
If you have love for one another
　　　　— you are my disciples.
Glory to the Father, and to the Son and to the Holy Spirit.

By this everyone will know
> – **you are my disciples.**

Magnificat Antiphon You did not choose me but I chose you. And I appointed you to go and bear fruit, fruit that will endure.

Litany
The apostles endured depravation and hardship; come to the aid of the hungry, the homeless and those in prison.
Lord, have mercy.
The apostles preached a gospel of peace; restore peace to those places torn by conflict.
Christ, have mercy.
The apostles proclaimed the Jesus was risen from the dead; bring all the departed into the light of your glory.
Lord, have mercy.

Invitation to the Lord's Prayer
Impelled by the Spirit to carry out Christ's mission to all people, let us pray that Christ restore all people to unity with God and one another in God's heavenly kingdom.

Collect *From the Proper of the Day*

The Blessing
Let us pray for one another that the word of the Lord may spread rapidly and be glorified everywhere, just as it is among us. **Amen.**

Common of the Apostles Morning Prayer
Invitatory Christ is the Lord of the Apostles: Come let us adore.

Hymn A mighty sound from heaven *Hymnal 230*

Antiphon 1 Go and make disciples of all nations, baptizing them and teaching them to obey everything that I have commanded you.
Psalms from Sunday Week 1 Morning Prayer, page 134
or Sunday Morning Prayer of the Current Week.
Antiphon 2 I am among you as one who serves.
Antiphon 3 Abide in me as I abide in you.

Reading One *From the Proper of the Day*

Responsory (1 Jn. 1:3)
We declare to you what we have seen and heard
> – **may you have fellowship with us.**

Our fellowship is with the Father and with his Son
— may you have fellowship with us.
Glory to the Father, and to the Son and to the Holy Spirit
We declare to you what we have seen and heard
— may you have fellowship with us.

Canticle – Song of the Apostles   *Vos sacerdotes Domini*
(Isaiah 61: 6-9)

Antiphon You are members of the household of God built upon the foundation of the apostles with Christ Jesus himself as the cornerstone.

You shall be called priests of the Lord, *
    you shall be named ministers of our God;

You shall enjoy the wealth of the nations, *
    and in their riches you shall glory.

Because their shame was double, *
    and dishonor was proclaimed as their lot,

Therefore they shall possess a double portion; *
    everlasting joy shall be theirs.

For I the Lord love justice, *
    I hate robbery and wrongdoing;

I will faithfully give them their recompense, *
    and I will make an everlasting covenant with them.

Their descendants shall be known among the nations, *
    and their offspring among the peoples;

All who see them shall acknowledge *
    that they are a people whom the Lord has blessed.

Antiphon You are members of the household of God built upon the foundation of the apostles with Christ Jesus himself as the cornerstone.

Reading Two *From the Proper of the Day*

Responsory (Jn. 13:34)
I give you a new commandment
        — love one another.
Just as I have loved you
        — love one another.
Glory to the Father and **to** the Son and to the Holy Spirit.
I give you a new commandment
        — love one another.

Benedictus Antiphon I do not call you servants; but I have called you friends, because I have made known to you everything that I have heard from my Father.

Litany
Strengthen us in the faith we have received that we may continue in the apostles' teaching and fellowship, in the breaking of bread and in the prayers.
Lord, have mercy.
Empower us in the faith we have received that we may proclaim by word and example the Good News of God in Christ.
Christ, have mercy.
Confirm us in the faith we have received that we may strive for justice and peace among all people and respect the dignity of every human being.
Lord, have mercy.

Invitation to the Lord's Prayer
Baptized into the faith we received from the apostles, let us open our hearts in prayer to our Father.

Collect *From the Proper of the Day*

The Blessing
May we rejoice that we are no longer strangers and aliens, but that we are citizens with the saints and members of the household of God, built upon the foundation of the apostles and prophets, with Christ Jesus himself as the cornerstone. **Amen.**

Common of the Apostles
Noonday Prayer

Hymn They cast their nets in Galilee *Hymnal 661*

Antiphon We preach Christ crucified, the power of God and the wisdom of God.
Psalms from Sunday Week 1 Noonday Prayer, page 138

Reading Acts 5:41-42
As they left the council, the apostles rejoiced that they were considered worthy to suffer dishonor for the sake of the name. And every day in the temple and at home they did not cease to teach and proclaim Jesus as the Messiah.

Verse and Response
Rejoice and be glad.
That your names are written in heaven.

Collect *From the Proper of the Day*

Common of the Apostles
Evening Prayer II

Hymn By all your saints still striving *Hymnal 231-232 (using the appropriate second verse)*

Psalm 112 *Beatus vir*

Antiphon No one has greater love than this, to lay down one's life for one's friends.

1 Hallelujah!
   Blessed are they who fear the Lord *
      and have great delight in his commandments!

2 Their descendants will be mighty in the land; *
      the generation of the upright will be blessed.

3 Wealth and riches will be in their house, *
      and their righteousness will last for ever.

4 Light shines in the darkness for the upright; *
      the righteous are merciful and full of compassion.

5 It is good for them to be generous in lending *
      and to manage their affairs with justice.

6 For they will never be shaken; *
      the righteous will be kept in everlasting remembrance.

7 They will not be afraid of any evil rumors; *
      their heart is right;
      they put their trust in the Lord.

8 Their heart is established and will not shrink, *
      until they see their desire upon their enemies.

9 They have given freely to the poor, *
      and their righteousness stands fast for ever;
      they will hold up their head with honor.

10 The wicked will see it and be angry;
      they will gnash their teeth and pine away; *
      the desires of the wicked will perish.

Antiphon No one has greater love than this, to lay down one's life for one's friends.

Psalm 115 *Non nobis, Domine*

Antiphon I have chosen you out of the world—therefore the world hates you.

1 Not to us, O LORD, not to us,
    but to your Name give glory; *
      because of your love and because of your faithfulness.

2 Why should the heathen say, *
      "Where then is their God?"

3 Our God is in heaven; *
      whatever he wills to do he does.

4 Their idols are silver and gold, *
      the work of human hands.

5 They have mouths, but they cannot speak; *
      eyes have they, but they cannot see;

6 They have ears, but they cannot hear; *
      noses, but they cannot smell;

7 They have hands, but they cannot feel;
    feet, but they cannot walk; *
      they make no sound with their throat.

8 Those who make them are like them, *
      and so are all who put their trust in them.

9 O Israel, trust in the LORD; *
      he is their help and their shield.

10 O house of Aaron, trust in the LORD; *
      he is their help and their shield.

11 You who fear the LORD, trust in the LORD; *
      he is their help and their shield.

12 The LORD has been mindful of us, and he will bless us; *
      he will bless the house of Israel;
      he will bless the house of Aaron;

13 He will bless those who fear the LORD, *
      both small and great together.

14 May the LORD increase you more and more, *
      you and your children after you.

15 May you be blessed by the LORD, *
    the maker of heaven and earth.

16 The heaven of heavens is the LORD's, *
    but he entrusted the earth to its peoples.

17 The dead do not praise the LORD, *
    nor all those who go down into silence;

18 But we will bless the LORD, *
    from this time forth for evermore.
    Hallelujah!

Antiphon I have chosen you out of the world—therefore the world hates you.

Psalm 138 *Confitebor tibi*

Antiphon Servants are not greater than their master. If they persecuted me, they will persecute you.

1   I will give thanks to you, O LORD, with my whole heart; *
    before the gods I will sing your praise.

2 I will bow down toward your holy temple
  and praise your Name, *
    because of your love and faithfulness;

3 For you have glorified your Name *
    and your word above all things.

4 When I called, you answered me; *
    you increased my strength within me.

5 All the kings of the earth will praise you, O LORD, *
    when they have heard the words of your mouth.

6 They will sing of the ways of the LORD, *
    that great is the glory of the LORD.

7 Though the LORD be high, he cares for the lowly; *
    he perceives the haughty from afar.

8 Though I walk in the midst of trouble, you keep me safe; *
    you stretch forth your hand against the fury of my enemies;
    your right hand shall save me.

9 The LORD will make good his purpose for me; *
    O LORD, your love endures for ever;
    do not abandon the works of your hands.

Antiphon Servants are not greater than their master. If they persecuted me, they will persecute you.

Reading *From the Proper of the Day*

Responsory (Ps. 96:3; Mk. 16:15)
Declare God's glory among the nations
    — the Lord's marvelous works among all the peoples.
Proclaim the good news to the whole creation
    — the Lord's marvelous works among all the peoples.
Glory to the Father and to the Son and to the Holy Spirit.
Declare God's glory among the nations
    — the Lord's marvelous works among all the peoples.

Magnificat Antiphon At the renewal of all things, when the Son of Man is seated on the throne of his glory, you who have followed me will also sit on twelve thrones, judging the twelve tribes of Israel.

Litany
The apostles endured depravation and hardship; come to the aid of the hungry, the homeless and those in prison.
Lord, have mercy.
The apostles preached a gospel of peace; restore peace to those places torn by conflict.
Christ, have mercy.
The apostles proclaimed that Jesus was raised from the dead; bring all the departed into the light of your glory.
Lord, have mercy.

Invitation to the Lord's Prayer
Since we share the apostles' mission as ambassadors of reconciliation, let us ask the Father to hasten the coming of the kingdom.

Collect *From the Proper of the Day*

The Blessing
Let us pray for one another that the word of the Lord may spread rapidly and be glorified everywhere, just as it is among us. **Amen.**

Common of Evangelists Evening Prayer I

Hymn Thanks be to God whose Word was spoken *Hymnal 630*

Psalm 110 *Dixit Dominus*

Antiphon The Gentiles have become fellow-heirs, members of the same body, through the gospel.

1 The LORD said to my Lord, "Sit at my right hand, *
  until I make your enemies your footstool."

2 The LORD will send the scepter of your power out of Zion, *
  saying, "Rule over your enemies round about you.

3 Princely state has been yours from the day of your birth; *
  in the beauty of holiness have I begotten you,
  like dew from the womb of the morning."

4 The LORD has sworn and he will not recant: *
  "You are a priest for ever after the order of Melchizedek."

5 The Lord who is at your right hand
  will smite kings in the day of his wrath; *
  he will rule over the nations.

6 He will heap high the corpses; *
  he will smash heads over the wide earth.

7 He will drink from the brook beside the road; *
  therefore he will lift high his head.

Antiphon The Gentiles have become fellow-heirs, members of the same body, through the gospel.

Psalm 96 *Cantate Domino*

Antiphon I do it all for the sake of the gospel, so that I may share in its blessings.

1 Sing to the LORD a new song; *
  sing to the LORD, all the whole earth.

2 Sing to the LORD and bless his Name; *
  proclaim the good news of his salvation from day to day.

3 Declare his glory among the nations *
  and his wonders among all peoples.

4 For great is the LORD and greatly to be praised; *
  he is more to be feared than all gods.

5 As for all the gods of the nations, they are but idols; *
 but it is the LORD who made the heavens.

6 Oh, the majesty and magnificence of his presence! *
 Oh, the power and the splendor of his sanctuary!

7 Ascribe to the LORD, you families of the peoples; *
 ascribe to the LORD honor and power.

8 Ascribe to the LORD the honor due his Name; *
 bring offerings and come into his courts.

9 Worship the LORD in the beauty of holiness; *
 let the whole earth tremble before him.

10 Tell it out among the nations: "The LORD is King! *
 he has made the world so firm that it cannot be moved;
 he will judge the peoples with equity."

11 Let the heavens rejoice, and let the earth be glad;
 let the sea thunder and all that is in it; *
 let the field be joyful and all that is therein.

12 Then shall all the trees of the wood shout for joy
 before the LORD when he comes, *
 when he comes to judge the earth.

13 He will judge the world with righteousness *
 and the peoples with his truth.

Antiphon I do it all for the sake of the gospel, so that I may share in its blessings.

Psalm 145 *Exaltabo te, Deus*

Antiphon We have heard of your faith in Christ Jesus because of the hope laid up for you in heaven. You have heard of this hope in the word of the truth, the gospel.

1 I will exalt you, O God my King, *
 and bless your Name for ever and ever.

2 Every day will I bless you *
 and praise your Name for ever and ever.

3 Great is the LORD and greatly to be praised; *
 there is no end to his greatness.

4 One generation shall praise your works to another *
 and shall declare your power.

5 I will ponder the glorious splendor of your majesty *
      and all your marvelous works.

6 They shall speak of the might of your wondrous acts, *
      and I will tell of your greatness.

7 They shall publish the remembrance of your great goodness; *
      they shall sing of your righteous deeds.

8 The LORD is gracious and full of compassion, *
      slow to anger and of great kindness.

9 The LORD is loving to everyone *
      and his compassion is over all his works.

10 All your works praise you, O LORD, *
      and your faithful servants bless you.

11 They make known the glory of your kingdom *
      and speak of your power;

12 That the peoples may know of your power *
      and the glorious splendor of your kingdom.

13 Your kingdom is an everlasting kingdom; *
      your dominion endures throughout all ages.

14 The LORD is faithful in all his words *
      and merciful in all his deeds.

15 The LORD upholds all those who fall; *
      he lifts up those who are bowed down.

16 The eyes of all wait upon you, O LORD, *
      and you give them their food in due season.

17 You open wide your hand *
      and satisfy the needs of every living creature.

18 The LORD is righteous in all his ways *
      and loving in all his works.

19 The LORD is near to those who call upon him, *
      to all who call upon him faithfully.

20 He fulfills the desire of those who fear him; *
      he hears their cry and helps them.

21 The LORD preserves all those who love him, *
      but he destroys all the wicked.

22 My mouth shall speak the praise of the LORD; *
   let all flesh bless his holy Name for ever and ever.

Antiphon We have heard of your faith in Christ Jesus because of the hope laid up for you in heaven. You have heard of this hope in the word of the truth, the gospel.

Reading *From the Proper of the Day*

Responsory (Is. 61:1; Lk. 4:18)
The Spirit of the Lord is upon me
   – to bring good news to the poor.
He has sent me to proclaim release to the captives
   – to bring good news to the poor.
Glory to the Father, and to the Son and to the Holy Spirit.
The Spirit of the Lord is upon me
   – to bring good news to the poor.

Magnificat Antiphon *From the Proper of the Day*

Litany
Father you revealed the mystery to bring all people together in Christ's body; manifest that mystery among those who are estranged.
Lord, have mercy.
You brought healing to a world broken by conflict and intolerance; restore those yearning for your word of grace and compassion. .
Christ, have mercy.
You gather into one the dispersed children of God; bring the dead to enjoy the light of your love.
Lord, have mercy.

Invitation to the Lord's Prayer We have received the word of truth in the Gospel so form us by the Spirit in the likeness of Christ as we pray.

Collect *From the Proper of the Day*

The Blessing
May we clothe ourselves with faith and the performance of good works and set out on the way, with the Gospel as our guide, that we may deserve to see him who has called us to his kingdom. **Amen.**

Common of Evangelists Morning Prayer

Invitatory Christ is the Lord and Teacher of the Evangelists: Come let us adore.

Hymn Lamp of our feet, whereby we trace *Hymnal 627*

Antiphon 1 God's grace has now been revealed through the appearing of our Savior Christ Jesus, who brought life and immortality to light through the gospel.
Psalms from Sunday Week 1 Morning Prayer, page 134
Antiphon 2 God is able to strengthen you according to my gospel and the proclamation of Jesus Christ.
Antiphon 3 I am not ashamed of the gospel; it is the power of God for salvation to everyone who has faith.

Reading One *From the Proper of the Day*

Responsory (1 Cor. 9:23; Rom. 1:9)
I do it all for the sake of the gospel
    – so that I may share in its blessings.
I serve God by announcing the gospel of his Son
    – so that I may share in its blessings.
Glory to the Father and to the Son and to the Holy Spirit.
I do it all for the sake of the gospel
    – so that I may share in its blessings.

Canticle – Song of the Mystery of Christ *In mysterio Christi*
(Ephesians 3: 5-10)
Antiphon I have become a servant of the Gospel according to the gift of God's grace.

The mystery of Christ was not made known to humankind *
    in former generations.

It has now been revealed *
    to his holy apostles and prophets by the Spirit.

The Gentiles have become fellow-heirs,
members of the same body, *
    and sharers in the promise in Christ Jesus through the gospel.

Of this gospel I have become a servant *
    according to the gift of God's grace.

The Gospel was given to me *
    by the working of God's power.

Although I am the very least of all the saints, *
    this grace was given to me:

To bring to the Gentiles the news
of the boundless riches of Christ, *
    and to make everyone see what is the plan of the mystery.

That mystery of Christ lay hidden for ages in God *
    who created all things;

So that through the church the wisdom of God in its rich variety *
    might now be made known
    to the rulers and authorities in the heavenly places.

Antiphon I have become a servant of the Gospel according to the gift of God's grace.

Reading Two *From the Proper of the Day*

Responsory Two (Eph. 3:5, 6)
In former times this mystery was not made known to humankind
    — as it has now been revealed by the Spirit.
Through the Gospel, the Gentiles become members of the same body.
    — as it has now been revealed by the Spirit.
Glory to the Father, and to the Son and to the Holy Spirit.
In former times this mystery was not made known to humankind
    — as it has now been revealed by the Spirit.

Benedictus Antiphon *From the Proper of the Day*

Litany
You called your holy evangelists to proclaim the good news of Jesus, your Son; continue to call faithful ministers of your word.
Lord, have mercy.
You manifested your healing to a broken world through the ministry of your beloved Son; continue your healing work through contemplative prayer.
Christ, have mercy.
You summoned the Gentiles to be joint heirs of the promises you gave to Abraham and Sarah; continue to call all people to share the table of your Holy Word.
Lord, have mercy.

Invitation to the Lord's Prayer We have received in the Gospel the full mystery of the Incarnate Word so we pray with Christ to the Father.

Collect *From the Proper of the Day*

The Blessing
May we do everything for the sake of the gospel, so that we may share in its blessings. **Amen.**

Common of Evangelists Noonday Prayer
Hymn Come sing, ye choirs exultant *Hymnal 235*

Antiphon Live your life in a manner worthy of the gospel of Christ.
Psalms from Sunday Week 1 Noonday Prayer, page 138

Reading Ephesians 4: 11-13
The gifts he gave were that some would be apostles, some prophets, some evangelists, some pastors and teachers, to equip the saints for the work of ministry, for building up the body of Christ, until all of us come to the unity of the faith and of the knowledge of the Son of God, to maturity, to the measure of the full stature of Christ.

Verse and Response
Our message of the gospel came to you not in word only.
But in power and in the Holy Spirit.

Collect *From the Proper of the Day*

Common of Evangelists Evening Prayer II
Hymn Spread, O spread, thou mighty word *Hymnal 530*

Psalm 116 *Dilexi, quoniam*
Antiphon The Gentiles have become fellow-heirs, members of the same body, through the gospel.

1 I love the LORD, because he has heard
the voice of my supplication, *
   because he has inclined his ear to me
   whenever I called upon him.

2 The cords of death entangled me;
the grip of the grave took hold of me; *
   I came to grief and sorrow.

3 Then I called upon the Name of the LORD: *
   "O LORD, I pray you, save my life."

4 Gracious is the LORD and righteous; *
   our God is full of compassion.

5   The LORD watches over the innocent; *
    I was brought very low, and he helped me.

6   Turn again to your rest, O my soul, *
    for the LORD has treated you well.

7   For you have rescued my life from death, *
    my eyes from tears, and my feet from stumbling.

8   I will walk in the presence of the LORD *
    in the land of the living.

9   I believed, even when I said,
    "I have been brought very low." *
    In my distress I said, "No one can be trusted."

10 How shall I repay the LORD *
    for all the good things he has done for me?

11 I will lift up the cup of salvation *
    and call upon the Name of the LORD.

12 I will fulfill my vows to the LORD *
    in the presence of all his people.

13 Precious in the sight of the LORD *
    is the death of his servants.

14 O LORD, I am your servant; *
    I am your servant and the child of your handmaid;
    you have freed me from my bonds.

15 I will offer you the sacrifice of thanksgiving *
    and call upon the Name of the LORD.

16 I will fulfill my vows to the LORD *
    in the presence of all his people,

17 In the courts of the LORD'S house, *
    in the midst of you, O Jerusalem.
    Hallelujah!

Antiphon The Gentiles have become fellow-heirs, members of the same body, through the gospel.

Psalm 126 *In convertendo*

Antiphon I do it all for the sake of the gospel, so that I may share in its blessings.

1 When the LORD restored the fortunes of Zion, *
 then were we like those who dream.

2 Then was our mouth filled with laughter, *
 and our tongue with shouts of joy.

3 Then they said among the nations, *
 "The LORD has done great things for them."

4 The LORD has done great things for us, *
 and we are glad indeed.

5 Restore our fortunes, O LORD, *
 like the watercourses of the Negev.

6 Those who sowed with tears *
 will reap with songs of joy.

7 Those who go out weeping, carrying the seed, *
 will come again with joy, shouldering their sheaves.

Antiphon I do it all for the sake of the gospel, so that I may share in its blessings.

Psalm 138 *Confitebor tibi*

Antiphon We have heard of your faith in Christ Jesus and of the love that you have for all the saints, because of the hope laid up for you in heaven. You have heard of this hope in the gospel.

1 I will give thanks to you, O LORD, with my whole heart; *
 before the gods I will sing your praise.

2 I will bow down toward your holy temple
and praise your Name, *
 because of your love and faithfulness;

3 For you have glorified your Name *
 and your word above all things.

4 When I called, you answered me; *
 you increased my strength within me.

5 All the kings of the earth will praise you, O LORD, *
 when they have heard the words of your mouth.

6 They will sing of the ways of the LORD, *
    that great is the glory of the LORD.

7 Though the LORD be high, he cares for the lowly; *
    he perceives the haughty from afar.

8 Though I walk in the midst of trouble, you keep me safe; *
    you stretch forth your hand against the fury of my enemies;
    your right hand shall save me.

9 The LORD will make good his purpose for me; *
    O LORD, your love endures for ever;
    do not abandon the works of your hands.

Antiphon We have heard of your faith in Christ Jesus and of the love that you have for all the saints, because of the hope laid up for you in heaven. You have heard of this hope in the gospel.

Reading *From the Proper of the Day*

Responsory (Is. 61:1; Lk. 4:18)
The Spirit of the Lord is upon me
        – to bring good news to the poor.
He has sent me to proclaim release to the captives
        – to bring good news to the poor.
Glory to the Father, and to the Son and to the Holy Spirit.
The Spirit of the Lord is upon me
        – to bring good news to the poor.

Magnificat Antiphon *From the Proper of the Day*

Litany
Father you revealed the mystery to bring all people together in Christ's body; manifest that mystery among those who are estranged.
Lord, have mercy.
You brought healing to a world broken by conflict and intolerance; restore those yearning for your word of grace and compassion. .
Christ, have mercy.
You gather into one the dispersed children of God; bring the dead to enjoy the light of your love.
Lord, have mercy.

Invitation to the Lord's Prayer In the Gospel, the Father reveals himself to us in Christ by the Spirit. In that Spirit, we pray with Christ to the Father.

Collect *From the Proper of the Day*

The Blessing

May we clothe ourselves with faith and the performance of good works and set out on the way, with the Gospel as our guide, that we may deserve to see God who has called us to his kingdom. **Amen.**

Common of Martyrs Morning Prayer

Invitatory Christ calls us to carry the cross: Come let us worship the King of Martyrs.

Hymn Let us now our voices raise *Hymnal 237*

Antiphon 1 Whoever acknowledges me before others, the Son of Man also will acknowledge before the angels of God.
Antiphon 2 We share abundantly in Christ's sufferings, so through Christ we share abundantly in his consolation.
Antiphon 3 If you would serve me, you must follow me; and where I am, there also shall my servant be.

Reading One *From the Proper of the Day*

Responsory One (Jn. 12:24; 1 Cor. 15:36)
If the grain of wheat dies
    — it bears much fruit.
What is sown is perishable, what is raised is imperishable
    — it bears much fruit.
Glory to the Father and to the Son and to the Holy Spirit.
If the grain of wheat dies
    — it bears much fruit.

Canticle — Song of the Martyrs   *Iustoium animae*
(Wisdom 3: 1-6)

Antiphon If any want to become my followers, let them deny themselves and take up their cross and follow me.

The souls of the righteous are in the hand of God, *
    and no torment will ever touch them.

In the eyes of the foolish they seemed to have died, *
    and their departure was thought to be a disaster.

Their going from us was considered to be their destruction; *
    but they are at peace.

For though in the sight of others they were punished, *
    their hope is full of immortality.

Having been disciplined a little, they will receive great good, *
    because God tested them and found them worthy of himself.

Like gold in the furnace he tried them, *
    and like a sacrificial burnt offering he accepted them.

Antiphon If any want to become my followers, let them deny
themselves and take up their cross and follow me.

Reading Two *From the Proper of the Day*

Responsory Two (Ps. 59:10, 11)
My eyes are fixed on you, O my Strength
    – for you, O God, are my stronghold.
My merciful God comes to meet me
    – for you, O God, are my stronghold.
Glory to the Father and to the Son and to the Holy Spirit.
My eyes are fixed on you, O my Strength
    – for you, O God, are my stronghold.

Benedictus Antiphon Those who hate their life in this world will keep
it for eternal life.

Litany
The martyrs show your strength made perfect in their weakness; support
us in our frailty.
Lord, have mercy.
The martyrs bore witness to you name by their death; let us proclaim
you in word and action.
Christ, have mercy.
The martyrs discovered your power coming to their aid in their
suffering; lift up all who experience pain and abandonment.
Lord, have mercy.

Invitation to the Lord's Prayer
As the martyrs gave their lives as an offering of love, forgiving those who
killed them, let us seek the image of God in those who offend us by asking
God to forgive us as we forgive others.

Collect *From the Proper of the Day*

The Blessing

May we always carry in our bodies the death of Jesus so that the life of Jesus may also be made visible in our bodies. **Amen.**

Common of Martyrs Noonday Prayer

Hymn King of the martyrs noble band *Hymnal 236*

Antiphon They have washed their robes and made them white in the blood of the Lamb.

Reading James 1: 12

Blessed is anyone who endures temptation. Such a one has stood the test and will receive the crown of life that the Lord has promised to those who love him.

Verse and Response

Be faithful until death.
And I will give you the crown of life.

Collect *From the Proper of the Day or one of the following*

Almighty God, who gave your servant N. boldness to confess the Name of our Savior Jesus Christ before the rulers of this world, and courage to die for this faith: Grant that we may always be ready to give a reason for the hope that is in us, and to suffer gladly for the sake of our Lord Jesus Christ; who lives and reigns with you and the Holy Spirit, one God, for ever and ever. Amen.

or this

Almighty God, by whose grace and power your holy martyr N. triumphed over suffering and was faithful even to death: Grant us, who now remember him in thanksgiving, to be so faithful in our witness to you in this world, that we may receive with him the crown of life; through Jesus Christ our Lord, who lives and reigns with you and the Holy Spirit, one God, for ever and ever. Amen.

or this (for a Virgin Martyr)

Almighty and everlasting God, who kindled the flame of your love in the heart of your holy martyr N.: Grant to us, your humble servants, a like faith and power of love, that we who rejoice in her triumph may profit by her example; through Jesus Christ our Lord, who lives and reigns with you and the Holy Spirit, one God, for ever and ever. Amen.

Common of Martyrs Evening Prayer

Hymn Blessed feasts of blessed martyrs *Hymnal 239*

Antiphon 1 You will be hated by all because of my name but the one who endures to the end will be saved.

Antiphon 2 I consider that the sufferings of this present time are not worth comparing with the glory about to be revealed to us.

Antiphon 3 Whoever follows me will never walk in darkness but will have the light of life.

Reading *From the Proper of the Day*

Responsory (Ps. 66:9,11)
You, O God, have proved us
> **− you have tried us just as silver is tried.**

You brought us out into a place of refreshment
> **− you have tried us just as silver is tried.**

Glory to the Father and to the Son and to the Holy Spirit.
You, O God, have proved us
> **− you have tried us just as silver is tried.**

Magnificat Antiphon The holy friends of Christ rejoice in heaven. They followed in his footsteps to the end. They have shed their blood for love of him and will reign with him forever.

Litany
By shedding their blood, the martyrs gave their greatest witness to Christ. Strengthen our faith by the example of the martyrs.
Lord, have mercy.
By shedding their blood, the martyrs surrendered all for love of you. Deepen our attachment to you and our detachment from passing things.
Christ, have mercy.
By shedding their blood, the martyrs were united with Christ in his self-offering. May the martyrs come to welcome all the dead and lead them to the holy city, the new and eternal Jerusalem.
Lord, have mercy.

Invitation to the Lord's Prayer
Christ joined the martyrs to himself in union with the Father. Let us pray to become one with the Father through prayer and holiness of life.

Collect *From the Proper of the Day*

The Blessing
May we rejoice in our sufferings for the church, for in our flesh we are completing what is lacking in Christ's afflictions for the sake of his body, that is, the church. **Amen.**

Common of Pastors Morning Prayer

Invitatory Christ is the Shepherd of the flock: Come let us adore.

Hymn Shepherd of souls, refresh and bless *Hymnal 343*

Antiphon 1 You are the light of the world. A city built on a hill cannot be hid.
Antiphon 2 Let your light shine before others, so that they may see your good works and give glory to your Father in heaven.
Antiphon 3 Whoever wishes to be great among you must be your servant.

Reading One *From the Proper of the Day*

Responsory (Ez. 34:15; Jn. 10:14)
I myself will be the shepherd of my sheep
— and I will make them lie down.
I know my sheep and my sheep know me
— and I will make them lie down
Glory to the Father and to the Son and to the Holy Spirit.
I myself will be the shepherd of my sheep
— and I will make them lie down.

Canticle – Song of the Learned *Beatus qui in sapientia*
(Sirach 14:22; 15:3.4.6b)
Antiphon Tend the flock of God that is in your charge, exercising the oversight, as God would have you do. Be examples to the flock.

Blessed are they who meditate on wisdom *
    and reason intelligently,

Who reflect in their hearts on her ways *
    and ponder her secrets,

She will feed them with the bread of learning, *
    and give them the water of wisdom to drink.

They will lean on her and not fall, *
    and they will rely on her and not be put to shame.

She will exalt them above their neighbors, *
    and will open their mouths in the midst of the assembly.

They will find gladness and a crown of rejoicing, *
    and will inherit an everlasting name.

Antiphon Tend the flock of God that is in your charge, exercising the oversight, as God would have you do. Be examples to the flock.

Reading Two *From the Proper of the Day*

Responsory Two (Ez. 3:17)
I have made you a watchman for the house of Israel
 — you shall give them warning from me.
Whenever you hear a word from my mouth
 — you shall give them warning from me.
Glory to the Father and to the Son and to the Holy Spirit.
I have made you a watchman for the house of Israel
 — you shall give them warning from me.

Benedictus Antiphon The Lord God will feed his flock like a shepherd, he will gather the lambs in his arms; he will carry them in his bosom, and gently lead those that are with young.

Litany
We thank you for raising up faithful pastors from among your people; give wisdom to our leaders that they may lead us in ways both new and old.
Lord, have mercy.
Your leaders championed the cause of the poor and alienated; open the ears of our leaders to hear your voice in the marginalized and outcast.
Christ, have mercy.
Your leaders spoke a word inspired by tradition in a language understood by the people of their day; open the minds and lips of our leaders to speak a faithful yet innovative word.
Lord, have mercy.

Invitation to the Lord's Prayer
You continue to call shepherds to pastor your flock so with our shepherds and all your faithful people we pray.

Collect *From the Proper of the Day*

The Blessing
May we remember our leaders, those who spoke the word of God to us; consider the outcome of their way of life, and imitate their faith. **Amen.**

Common of Pastors Noonday Prayer

Hymn Savior, like a shepherd lead us *Hymnal 708*

Antiphon As the Father has sent me, so I send you.

Reading 1 Tim. 1: 12
I am grateful to Christ Jesus our Lord, who has strengthened me, because he judged me faithful and appointed me to his service.

Verse and Response
Unless the Lord builds the house.
Their labor is in vain who build it.

Collect *From the Proper of the Day or the following*
Heavenly Father, Shepherd of your people, we thank you for your servant N., who was faithful in the care and nurture of your flock; and we pray that, following his example and the teaching of his holy life, we may by your grace grow into the stature of the fullness of our Lord and Savior Jesus Christ; who lives and reigns with you and the Holy Spirit, one God, for ever and ever. Amen.

Common of Pastors Evening Prayer
Hymn My Shepherd will supply my need *Hymnal 664*

Antiphon 1 Well done, good and trustworthy slave; enter into the joy of your master.
Antiphon 2 I am sending you out like sheep into the midst of wolves; so be wise as serpents and innocent as doves.
Antiphon 3 You received without paying, give without pay.

Reading *From the Proper of the Day*

Responsory (1 Pt. 4:5; Rev. 2:10)
When the chief shepherd appears
        − you will win the crown of glory.
Be faithful until death, and I will give you the crown of life
        − you will win the crown of glory.
Glory to the Father and to the Son and to the Holy Spirit.
When the chief shepherd appears
        − you will win the crown of glory.

Magnificat Antiphon How beautiful upon the mountains are the feet of the messenger who announces peace, who says to Zion, "Your God reigns."

Litany
Your pastors reconciled people in conflict; bring your harmony where there is discord.
Lord, have mercy.

Your pastors continued your ministry of healing; restore human frailty with your gentleness.
Christ, have mercy.
Your pastors comforted the dying and buried the dead; console those who mourn and lead the dead into your glory.
Lord, have mercy.

Invitation to the Lord's Prayer
Your pastors lead your people in fervent prayer so let us pray with Christ, the Shepherd of our souls.

Collect *From the Proper of the Day*

The Blessing
May we not quench the Spirit, not despise the words of prophets, but test everything, hold fast to what is good and abstain from every form of evil.
Amen.

Common of Theologians and Teachers Morning Prayer

Invitatory Christ alone is our Teacher: Come let us sit at his feet and worship.

Hymn We limit not the truth of God *Hymnal 629*

Antiphon 1 They are well instructed; their God teaches them.
Antiphon 2 Your ears shall hear a word behind you, saying, "This is the way; walk in it."
Antiphon 3 The beginning of wisdom is the most sincere desire for instruction, and concern for instruction is love of her.

Reading One *From the Proper of the Day*

Responsory One (Ps. 25:4; Ps. 43:3)
Lead me in your truth and teach me
        − for you are the God of my salvation.
Send out your light and your truth
        − for you are the God of my salvation.
Glory to the Father and to the Son and to the Holy Spirit.
Lead me in your truth and teach me
        − for you are the God of my salvation.

Canticle – Song of the Lord, our Rock *Audite caeli*
(Deuteronomy 32: 1-6)

Antiphon Let the earth hear the words of my mouth.

Give ear, O heavens, and I will speak; *
    let the earth hear the words of my mouth.

May my teaching drop like the rain, *
    my speech condense like the dew;

Like gentle rain on grass, *
    like showers on new growth.

For I will proclaim the name of the LORD; *
    ascribe greatness to our God!

The Rock, his work is perfect, *
    and all his ways are just.

A faithful God, without deceit, *
    just and upright is he.

Antiphon Let the earth hear the words of my mouth.

Reading Two *From the Proper of the Day*

Responsory Two (Eph. 4:11, 12; 1 Cor. 12:4)
The gifts he gave were that some would be pastors and teachers
    – to equip the saints for the work of ministry.
There are varieties of gifts
    – to equip the saints for the work of ministry.
Glory to the Father and to the Son and to the Holy Spirit.
The gifts he gave were that some would be pastors and teachers
    – to equip the saints for the work of ministry.

Benedictus Antiphon A disciple is not above the teacher, nor a slave above the master.

Litany
At the dawn of day, illumine our minds and hearts to understand your Word and follow your commands.
Lord, have mercy.
As you kindle your light among us, so shine in our minds that we may understand your teaching and put it into practice.
Christ, have mercy.

With your never failing wisdom, send your Spirit to all who teach, all who study and all who seek you.
Lord, have mercy.

Invitation to the Lord's Prayer
Since the Holy Spirit gives to some the word of wisdom, to others the word of knowledge, and to others the word of faith we praise God's Name for the gifts of grace in the church.

Collect *From the Proper of the Day*

The Blessing
May the God of our Lord Jesus Christ, the Father of glory, give us a spirit of wisdom and revelation that we may come to know God more deeply. **Amen.**

Common of Theologians and Teachers
Noonday Prayer
Hymn Lord be thy word my rule *Hymnal 626*

Antiphon The mouth of the righteous utters wisdom; the law of their God is in their heart.

Reading Isaiah 50: 4
The Lord God has given me the tongue of a teacher, that I may know how to sustain the weary with a word. Morning by morning he wakens—wakens my ear to listen as those who are taught.

Verse and Response
Out of Zion shall go forth instruction.
And the word of the Lord from Jerusalem.

Collect *From the Proper of the Day or one of the following*
O God, by your Holy Spirit you give to some the word of wisdom, to others the word of knowledge, and to others the word of faith: We praise your Name for the gifts of grace manifested in your servant N., and we pray that your Church may never be destitute of such gifts; through Jesus Christ our Lord, who with you and the Holy Spirit lives and reigns, one God, for ever and ever. Amen.
or
Almighty God, you gave to your servant N. special gifts of grace to understand and teach the truth as it is in Christ Jesus: Grant that by this teaching we may know you, the one true God, and Jesus Christ whom you have sent; who lives and reigns with you and the Holy Spirit, one God, for ever and ever. Amen.

Common of Theologians and Teachers Evening Prayer

Hymn Word of God come down on earth *Hymnal 633*

Antiphon 1 Teach them the statutes and instructions and make known to them the way they are to go.

Antiphon 2 As the Lord my God has charged me, I now teach you statutes and ordinances for you to observe.

Antiphon 3 Hear, my child, your father's instruction, and do not reject your mother's teaching.

Reading *From the Proper of the Day*

Responsory (Pro. 9:9; Pro. 6:23)
Give instruction to the wise, and they will become wiser still
     – teach the righteous and they will gain in learning.
The commandment is a lamp and the teaching a light
     – teach the righteous and they will gain in learning.
Glory to the Father and to the Son and to the Holy Spirit.
Give instruction to the wise, and they will become wiser still
     – teach the righteous and they will gain in learning.

Magnificat Antiphon You shall put these words of mine in your heart and soul, and you shall bind them as a sign on your hand, and fix them as an emblem on your forehead.

Litany
As the light moves into darkness, continue to shine in those places torn by misunderstanding.
Lord, have mercy.
With the approaching evening, give rest to our bodies and refreshment to our minds.
Christ, have mercy.
You alone are the rest of the dead, lead all the departed into your undying light.
Lord, have mercy.

Invitation to the Lord's Prayer
The Spirit bestows special gifts of grace to understand and teach the truth as it is in Christ Jesus: Grant that by this teaching we may know you, the one true God.

Collect *From the Proper of the Day*

The Blessing

May God become manifest in us, God who is the source of our life in Christ Jesus, who became for us wisdom from God, and righteousness and sanctification and redemption. **Amen.**

Common of Teacher of the Faith Morning Prayer

Invitatory The Lord is the fountain of wisdom: Come let us worship.

Hymn Praise To The Holiest In the Height *Hymnal 446*

Antiphon 1 The fear of the Lord is the beginning of wisdom.
Antiphon 2 Wisdom will come into your heart, and knowledge will be pleasant to your soul.
Antiphon 3 I love those who love me, and those who seek me diligently find me.

Reading One *From the Proper of the Day*

Responsory One (Prov. 9:10; Jas. 1:5)
The fear of the Lord is the beginning of wisdom
    – knowledge of the Holy One is insight.
If any of you lacks wisdom, let him ask God
    – knowledge of the Holy One is insight.
Glory to the Father and **to** the Son and to the Holy Spirit.
The fear of the Lord is the beginning of wisdom
    – knowledge of the Holy One is insight.

Canticle – Song of Wisdom's Feast   *Sapientia aedificavit*
(Proverbs 8: 1-6, 10-11)

Antiphon Give instruction to the wise, and they will become wiser still.

Wisdom has built her house, *
    she has hewn her seven pillars.

She has slaughtered her animals, she has mixed her wine, *
    she has also set her table.

She has sent out her servant-girls, she calls
from the highest places in the town. *
    "You that are simple, turn in here!"

To those without sense she says, *
    "Come, eat of my bread
    and drink of the wine I have mixed.

"Lay aside immaturity, and live, *
    and walk in the way of insight."

Give instruction to the wise, and they will become wiser still; *
    teach the righteous and they will gain in learning.

The fear of the Lord is the beginning of wisdom, *
    and the knowledge of the Holy One is insight.

For by me your days will be multiplied, *
    and years will be added to your life.

Antiphon Give instruction to the wise, and they will become wiser still.

Reading Two *From the Proper of the Day*

Responsory Two(Ps. 37:30; Ps. 51:6)
The mouths of the righteous utter wisdom
    – and their tongues speak justice.
You made them understand wisdom secretly
    – and their tongues speak justice.
Glory to the Father, and to the Son and to the Holy Spirit
The mouths of the righteous utter wisdom
    – and their tongues speak justice.

Benedictus Antiphon for a Female Teacher of the Faith In the midst of the church she spoke with great persuasion. The Lord filled her with the Spirit of wisdom and understanding.

Benedictus Antiphon for a Male Teacher of the Faith In the midst of the church he spoke with great persuasion. The Lord filled him with the Spirit of wisdom and understanding.

Litany
You illumine the minds and hearts of your holy teachers; let your Spirit kindle your truth in schools, colleges and universities.
Lord, have mercy.
You trained your holy teachers to speak your truth in their generation; let writers lead people to ever greater wisdom through fidelity to your Word.
Christ, have mercy.
You opened the mouth of your holy teachers to speak the truth in love; let us learn civility and graciousness in our dealings with one another.
Lord, have mercy.

Invitation to the Lord's Prayer
As the morning star illumines the earth, let us ask Christ, the Light of the world, to shine in our minds and hearts and lead us to the Father.

Collect *From the Proper of the Day*

The Blessing
May Christ, the Living Word and Wisdom of God, shine in us and through us. **Amen.**

Common of Teacher of the Faith Noonday Prayer
Hymn Can We By Searching Find Out God *Hymnal 476*

Antiphon Wisdom will come into your heart, and knowledge will be pleasant to your soul.

Reading Wisdom 7: 13-14
I learned without guile and I impart without grudging; I do not hide her wealth, for wisdom is an unfailing treasure for mortals; those who get it obtain friendship with God, commended for the gifts that come from instruction.

Verse and Response
They will pour forth their words of wisdom.
In prayer they will give thanks to the Lord.

Collect *From the Proper of the Day or the following*
Almighty God, you gave to your servant N. special gifts of grace to understand and teach the truth as it is in Christ Jesus: Grant that by this teaching we may know you, the one true God, and Jesus Christ whom you have sent; who lives and reigns with you and the Holy Spirit, one God, for ever and ever. Amen.

Common of Teacher of the Faith Evening Prayer
Hymn Praise To the Holiest In the Height *Hymnal 445 or 446*

Antiphon 1 Wisdom from above is first pure, then peaceable, gentle, willing to yield, full of mercy and good fruits
Antiphon 2 The mouth of the just tells of wisdom. The law of God is in their hearts.
Antiphon 3 In Christ are hidden all the treasures of wisdom and knowledge.

Reading *From the Proper of the Day*

Responsory (Sir. 15:5)
In the midst of the Church
          — they spoke with understanding.
The Lord filled them with a spirit of wisdom and insight
          — they spoke with understanding.
Glory to the Father and to the Son and to the Holy Spirit.
In the midst of the Church
          — they spoke with understanding.

Magnificat Antiphon O holy N. foremost teacher, light of the church, lover of the Gospel, pray for us to the Word of God.

- January 13 Hilary
- January 27 John Chrysostom
- January 28 Thomas Aquinas
- March 12 Gregory the Great
- March 18 Cyril of Jerusalem
- April 21 Anselm
- April 29, Catherine of Siena
- May 2 Athanasius
- May 9 Gregory of Nazianzus
- May 29 Bede, the Venerable
- June 10 Ephrem of Edessa
- June 14 Basil the Great
- August 20 Bernard
- August 28 Augustine
- September 17 Hildegard
- September 30 Jerome
- October 15 Teresa of Jesus
- November 10 Leo
- December 4 John of Damascus
- December 5 Clement of Alexandria
- December 7 Ambrose
- December 14 John of the Cross

Litany
Your wisdom led our teachers by the prompting of the Spirit; continue to guide scholars in their study and teaching.
Lord, have mercy.

Your wisdom embraced diverse forms of human understanding; make yourself known to us in ways that make sense in our generation.
Christ, have mercy.
Your wisdom is revealed in the mystery of Christ; lead all the dead who sought you to discover you in heaven.
Lord, have mercy.

Invitation to the Lord's Prayer
Let us pray to God, the source of all wisdom, in the words given to us by Christ, the Word of God.

Collect *From the Proper of the Day*

The Blessing
May the God of our Lord Jesus Christ, the Father of glory, give us a spirit of wisdom and revelation that we may come to know God more deeply. **Amen.**

Common of Missionaries Morning Prayer

Invitatory Christ sends disciples to the ends of the earth: Come, all nations, and worship God.

Hymn Christ for the world we sing *Hymnal 537*

Antiphon 1 I will give you as a light to the nations
Antiphon 2 Nations shall come to your light, and kings to the brightness of your dawn.
Antiphon 3 Let your light shine before others so that they may see your good works and give glory to your Father in heaven.

Reading One *From the Proper of the Day*

Responsory One (Ps. 67:5; Mk. 16:15)
Let the peoples praise you, O God
      – let the nations be glad and sing for joy.
Go out to all the world and proclaim the gospel
      – let the nations be glad and sing for joy.
Glory to the Father and to the Son and to the Holy Spirit.
Let the peoples praise you, O God
      – let the nations be glad and sing for joy.

Canticle – Song of the Evangelist *Quam pulchri super montes*
(Isaiah 52: 7–10)

Antiphon The herald of the Gospel brings good news and announces salvation.

How beautiful upon the mountains *
  are the feet of the messenger who announces peace.

The herald brings good news, *
  announces salvation,
  and says to Zion, "Your God reigns."

Listen! Your sentinels lift up their voices, *
  together they sing for joy.

In plain sight they see *
  the return of the LORD to Zion.

Break forth together into singing, *
  you ruins of Jerusalem.

The LORD has comforted his people, *
  he has redeemed Jerusalem.

The LORD has bared his holy arm *
  before the eyes of all the nations.

All the ends of the earth shall see *
  the salvation of our God.

Antiphon The herald of the Gospel brings good news and announces salvation.

Reading Two *From the Proper of the Day*

Responsory Two (Ps. 98:3; Rev. 7:9)
All the ends of the earth
    – have seen the victory of our God.
People from every tribe and tongue
    – have seen the victory of our God.
Glory to the Father and to the Son and to the Holy Spirit.
All the ends of the earth
    – have seen the victory of our God.

Benedictus Antiphon God will teach us his ways that we may walk in his paths.

Litany

You sent your disciples to the ends of the earth; send us out as heralds of the Gospel in our communities.
Lord, have mercy.
You stirred up missionaries in every age to discover your presence in different cultures; continue to reveal yourself in the patterns you inspire.
Christ, have mercy.
You draw all the world to yourself through the proclamation of your word; gather the scattered children of God into the fellowship of your church.
Lord, have mercy.

Invitation to the Lord's Prayer

Since the missionary impulse flows from the very nature of God who sends forth the Son and the Spirit, let us join in the prayer of Christ for the coming of God's reign.

Collect *From the Proper of the Day*

The Blessing

May God make known how great among us are the riches of the glory of this mystery, which is Christ in us, the hope of glory. **Amen.**

Common of Missionaries Noonday Prayer

Hymn When Jesus left his Father's throne *Hymnal 480*

Antiphon We must work the works of God who sent me while it is day.

Reading Matthew 26: 18-20

Jesus came and said to them, "All authority in heaven and on earth has been given to me. Go therefore and make disciples of all nations, baptizing them in the name of the Father and of the Son and of the Holy Spirit, and teaching them to obey everything that I have commanded you. And remember, I am with you always, to the end of the age."

Verse and Response

We declare to you what we have that you may have fellowship with us.
Our fellowship is with the Father and with his Son Jesus Christ.

Collect *From the Proper of the Day or the following*

Almighty God, whose will it is to be glorified in your saints, and who raised up your servant N. to be a light in the world: Shine, we pray, in our hearts, that we also in our generation may show forth your praise, who called us out of darkness into your marvelous light; through Jesus Christ our Lord, who lives and reigns with you and the Holy Spirit, one God, now and for ever. Amen.

Common of Missionaries Evening Prayer

Hymn Spread, O spread, thy mighty Word *Hymnal 530*

Antiphon 1 You will be my witnesses to the ends of the earth.
Antiphon 2 I appointed you a prophet to the nations.
Antiphon 3 Go and make disciples of all nations.

Reading *From the Proper of the Day*

Responsory (Is. 66:18; Mt. 5:6)
I am coming to gather all nations and tongues
   – and they shall see my glory.
Let your light shine before others
   – and they shall see my glory.
Glory to the Father and to the Son and to the Holy Spirit.
I am coming to gather all nations and tongues
   – and they shall see my glory.

Magnificat Antiphon Our Savior Christ Jesus abolished death and brought life and immortality to light through the gospel.

Litany
Raise up in this and every land evangelists and heralds of your gospel
Lord, have mercy.
Shine in the hearts of all who hear the Word of salvation.
Christ, have mercy.
Bring all the dead into the light of your peace.
Lord, have mercy.

Invitation to the Lord's Prayer
Since in you we live, move and have our being, draw us deeper into your life as we pray with Christ, the One whom you sent into the world.

Collect *From the Proper of the Day*

The Blessing
May the God of our Lord Jesus Christ, the Father of glory, may give us a spirit of wisdom and revelation as we come to know him. **Amen.**

Common of Prophetic Witnesses Morning Prayer

Invitatory Christ proclaims good news to the poor: Come let us worship.

Hymn When Christ was lifted from the earth *Hymnal 603*

Antiphon 1 Let justice roll down like waters, and righteousness like an ever-flowing stream.

Antiphon 2 Unarmed truth and unconditional love will have the final word.

Antiphon 3 Do no wrong or violence to the alien, the orphan, and the widow, or shed innocent blood in this place.

Reading One *From the Proper of the Day*

Responsory One (Is. 61:6; Jer. 26:12)
The Lord has sent me to bring good news to the oppressed
    – to proclaim liberty to the captives.
The Lord sent me to prophesy
    – to proclaim liberty to the captives.
Glory to the Father, and to the Son and to the Holy Spirit
The Lord has sent me to bring good news to the oppressed
    – to proclaim liberty to the captives.

Canticle – Song of the Servant of Light   *Ego Dominus vocavi*
(Isaiah 42: 6-9)

Antiphon I have given you as a covenant to the people, a light to the nations.

I am the LORD, I have called you in righteousness, *
    I have taken you by the hand and kept you.

I have given you as a covenant to the people, *
    a light to the nations,

To open the eyes that are blind, *
    to bring out the prisoners from the dungeon,
    from the prison those who sit in darkness.

I am the LORD, that is my name; *
    my glory I give to no other, nor my praise to idols.

See, the former things have come to pass,
and new things I now declare; *
    before they spring forth, I tell you of them.

Antiphon I have given you as a covenant to the people, a light to the nations.

Reading Two *From the Proper of the Day*

Responsory Two (Lev. 25:10; Is. 32:18)
You shall proclaim liberty throughout the land
        – it shall be a jubilee for you.
My people will abide in peace.
        – it shall be a jubilee for you.
Glory to the Father and **to** the Son and to the Holy Spirit.
You shall proclaim liberty throughout the land
        – it shall be a jubilee for you.

Benedictus Antiphon The Spirit of the Lord is upon me, because he has anointed me to bring good news to the poor.

Litany
Your servants were lights of justice in a dark world, make us heralds of right relations this day.
Lord, have mercy.
Your witnesses spoke a word of liberty to those who were held captive; let us work with you to free people confined in prisons of thought and prejudice.
Christ, have mercy.
Your prophets were anointed by the Spirit; strengthen us to be prophets in our communities.
Lord, have mercy.

Invitation to the Lord's Prayer
Your reign will dawn on us with justice and mercy so we implore you to shine your light in the world.

Collect *From the Proper of the Day*

The Blessing
May the very Lord of peace give you peace at all times in all ways.
Amen.

Common of Prophetic Witnesses Noonday Prayer

Hymn O Jesus Christ, may grateful hymns be rising *Hymnal 590*

Antiphon Justice, and only justice, you shall pursue, so that you may live and occupy the land that the Lord your God is giving you.

Reading Isaiah 58: 6-8

Is not this the fast that I choose: to loose the bonds of injustice, to undo the thongs of the yoke, to let the oppressed go free, and to break every yoke? Is it not to share your bread with the hungry, and bring the homeless poor into your house; when you see the naked, to cover them, and not to hide yourself from your own kin? Then your light shall break forth like the dawn, and your healing shall spring up quickly; your vindicator shall go before you, the glory of the Lord shall be your rear guard.

Verse and Response

For freedom Christ has set us free.

Stand firm, therefore, and do not submit again to a yoke of slavery.

Collect *From the Proper of the Day or the following*

Almighty God, whose prophets taught us righteousness in the care of your poor: By the guidance of your Holy Spirit, grant that we may do justice, love mercy, and walk humbly in your sight; through Jesus Christ, our Judge and Redeemer, who lives and reigns with you and the same Spirit, one God, now and for ever. Amen.

Common of Prophetic Witnesses Evening Prayer

Hymn Judge eternal clothed in splendor *Hymnal 596*

Antiphon 1 You will know the truth, and the truth will make you free.
Antiphon 2 Maintain justice, and do what is right, for soon my salvation will come.
Antiphon 3 You shall proclaim liberty throughout the land to all its inhabitants.

Reading *From the Proper of the Day*

Responsory (Is. 52:7; Is 33: 5)
Your messenger announces peace
        – brings good news and announces salvation.
The Lord fills Zion with justice
        – brings good news and announces salvation.
Glory to the Father and to the Son and to the Holy Spirit.
Your messenger announces peace
        – brings good news and announces salvation.

Magnificat Antiphon What does the Lord require of you but to do justice, and to love kindness, and to walk humbly with your God.

Litany

At the close of the day, forgive us for our lack of courage to witness to your justice and strengthen our resolve to relieve the needs of the poor.
Lord, have mercy.
In every age you have called brave souls to proclaim righteousness for the transformation of the world; may all people welcome the coming of your holy reign.
Christ, have mercy.
You fill us with hope for a world where mercy will embrace all people; welcome the dead into your loving arms.
Lord, have mercy.

Invitation to the Lord's Prayer

Yours is a rule of justice and peace so we pray with all who yearn for righteousness and pray for you to hasten the coming of your kingdom.

Collect *From the Proper of the Day*

The Blessing

May the God of peace himself sanctify you entirely; and may your spirit and soul and body be kept sound and blameless at the coming of our Lord Jesus Christ. **Amen.**

Common of Monastics Morning Prayer

Invitatory Christ became obedient unto death: Come let us worship.

Hymn O What Their Joy and Their Glory Must Be *Hymnal 623*

Antiphon 1 I saw a great multitude from every nation standing before the throne and before the Lamb.
Antiphon 2 Clothed in white garments, they follow the Lamb wherever he goes.
Antiphon 3 The Lord is righteous. The just shall see his face.

Reading One *From the Proper of the Day*

Responsory One (Ps. 62:1)
For God alone
　　– my soul in silence waits.
My hope is in God
　　– my soul in silence waits.
Glory to the Father and to the Son and to the Holy Spirit.
For God alone
　　– my soul in silence waits.

Canticle – Song of Betrothal *Ecce ego lactabo eam*
(Hosea 2: 14, 16, 18-19, 23)

Antiphon I will betroth you to me in righteousness and in justice, in steadfast love, and in mercy.

I will allure her, and bring her into the wilderness, *
> and speak tenderly to her.

"And in that day", says the LORD, *
> "you will call me, 'My beloved.'"

And I will make for you *
> a covenant on that day.

With the beasts of the field, the birds of the air, *
> and the creeping things of the ground.

I will abolish the bow, the sword, and war from the land; *
> and I will make you lie down in safety.

I will betroth you to me for ever; *
> I will betroth you to me in righteousness and in justice,
> in steadfast love, and in mercy.

I will betroth you to me in faithfulness; *
> and you shall know the LORD.

You will be my people, *
> and I will be your God.

Antiphon I will betroth you to me in righteousness and in justice, in steadfast love, and in mercy.

Reading Two *From the Proper of the Day*

Responsory Two (Ps. 119:116; Ps. 63:1)
Sustain me according to your promise, that I may live
> **– abandon me not in my hope.**
My soul thirsts for you
> **– abandon me not in my hope.**
Glory to the Father and to the Son and to the Holy Spirit.
Sustain me according to your promise, that I may live
> **– abandon me not in my hope.**

Benedictus Antiphon Those who love me will keep my word, and my Father will love them, and we will come to them and make our home with them.

Litany
You call your holy ones to forsake everything and follow you;
strengthen all who commit themselves to you in the monastic life.
Lord, have mercy.
You lead your holy ones to encounter you in prayer and sacred reading;
open our minds and hearts to meet you in worship and contemplation.
Christ, have mercy.
You set your holy ones as lights in their time; make us witnesses to you
in our generation.
Lord, have mercy.

Invitation to the Lord's Prayer
In fellowship with monks, nuns and oblates from centuries past and yet
to come, let us approach the throne of grace and pray with Christ.

Collect *From the Proper of the Day*

The Blessing
May we prefer nothing whatever to Christ, and may he bring us all
together to everlasting life. **Amen.**

Common of Monastics Noonday Prayer
Hymn Blest are the pure in heart *Hymnal 656*

Antiphon If you earnestly desire to be rich, then love true riches.

Reading Proverbs 4: 1-6
Listen, children, to a father's instruction, and be attentive, that you may
gain insight; for I give you good precepts: do not forsake my teaching.
When I was a son with my father, tender, and my mother's favorite, he
taught me, and said to me, "Let your heart hold fast my words; keep my
commandments, and live. Get wisdom; get insight: do not forget, nor turn
away from the words of my mouth. Do not forsake her, and she will keep
you; love her, and she will guard you.

Verse and Response
We shall run in the paths of God's commandments.
Our hearts overflowing with the inexpressible delight of love.

Collect *From the Proper of the Day or one of the following*
O God, whose blessed Son became poor that we through his poverty
might be rich: Deliver us from an inordinate love of this world, that we,
inspired by the devotion of your servant N., may serve you with singleness
of heart, and attain to the riches of the age to come; through Jesus Christ

our Lord, who lives and reigns with you, in the unity of the Holy Spirit, one God, now and for ever. Amen.
or this
O God, by whose grace your servant N., kindled with the flame of your love, became a burning and a shining light in your Church: Grant that we also may be aflame with the spirit of love and discipline, and walk before you as children of light; through Jesus Christ our Lord, who lives and reigns with you, in the unity of the Holy Spirit, one God, now and for ever. Amen.

Common of Monastics Evening Prayer

Hymn Jerusalem My Happy Home *Hymnal 620*

Antiphon 1 The just will shine like the sun in the kingdom of their Father.
Antiphon 2 The saints rejoice forever in heaven. They followed in Christ's footsteps and exult with Christ forever.
Antiphon 3 How glorious is that kingdom where all the saints rejoice with Christ.

Reading *From the Proper of the Day*

Responsory (Ps. 68:3)
Let the righteous be glad
    – and rejoice before God.
Let them be merry and joyful
    – and rejoice before God.
Glory to the Father and to the Son and to the Holy Spirit.
Let the righteous be glad
    – and rejoice before God.

Magnificat Antiphon
For Nuns Come, spouse of Christ, receive the crown prepared for you from all eternity.
For Monks You have died, and your life is hidden with Christ in God. When Christ who is your life is revealed, then you also will be revealed with him in glory.
For Oblates Let them prefer nothing whatever to Christ, and my he bring us all together to everlasting life.

Litany
Strengthen your monks, nuns and oblates, the soldiers of Christ, to take up obedience in the service of Christ the King.
Lord, have mercy.

Clothed with faith and good works, show them, in your love, the hidden way that leads to life.
Christ, have mercy.
Faithful to Christ's teaching until death, may we, with all the departed, deserve to share in Christ's kingdom.
Lord, have mercy.

Invitation to the Lord's Prayer
Faithful to the pledge we make of mutual forgiveness, let us ask God to cleanse our hearts as we pray with Christ.

Collect *From the Proper of the Day*

The Blessing
May we run in the path of God's commandments, our hearts overflowing with the inexpressible delight of love. **Amen.**

Common of Professed Religious Morning Prayer

Invitatory The Lord is glorious in his saints: Come, let us worship.

Hymn Rejoice, ye pure in heart *Hymnal 556*

Antiphon 1 If you would be perfect, go, sell what you possess and give to the poor, and you will have treasure in heaven; and come, follow me.
Antiphon 2 There are eunuchs who have made themselves eunuchs for the sake of the kingdom of heaven. Whoever is able to receive this, let them receive it.
Antiphon 3 My food is to do the will of him who sent me, and to accomplish his work.

Reading One *From the Proper of the Day*

Responsory One (Ps. 63:1; Rev. 21:6)
You are my God
      – **my soul thirsts for you.**
I will give them drink from the fountain of the water of life
      – **my soul thirsts for you.**
Glory to the Father and to the Son and to the Holy Spirit.
You are my God
      – **my soul thirsts for you.**

Canticle of Communion and Mission *Pater sanctifica eos*
(John 17: 17-26)
Antiphon Go, sell what you own, and give the money to the poor, and you will have treasure in heaven; then come, follow me.

Father, sanctify them in the truth; *
    your word is truth.

As you have sent me into the world, *
    so I have sent them into the world.

For their sakes I sanctify myself, *
    so that they also may be sanctified in truth.

I ask not only on behalf of these,*
    but also on behalf of those who will believe in me
    through their word.

May they all be one,
as you, Father, are in me and I am in you, *
    may they also be in us,
    so that the world may believe that you have sent me.

The glory that you have given me I have given them, *
    so that they may be one, as we are one,
    I in them and you in me.

May they become completely one, *
    so that the world may know that you have sent me
    and have loved them even as you have loved me.

Father, I desire that those also, whom you have given me, *
    may be with me where I am, to see my glory.

You have given me this glory *
    because you loved me before the foundation of the world.

Righteous Father, the world does not know you, *
    but I know you; and these know that you have sent me.

I made your name known to them, *
    and I will make it known.

So that the love with which you have loved me may be in them, *
    and I in them.

Antiphon Go, sell what you own, and give the money to the poor, and
you will have treasure in heaven; then come, follow me.

Reading Two *From the Proper of the Day*

Responsory Two (Ps. 116:18; Ps. 27:6)
I will offer my vows to the Lord
        – in the presence of all his people.

I will offer in his tent sacrifices with shouts of joy
   – **in the presence of all his people.**
Glory to the Father and to the Son and to the Holy Spirit.
I will offer my vows to the Lord
   – **in the presence of all his people.**

Benedictus Antiphon The Lord sanctified them by their faith and meekness. God manifested to them his glory.

Litany
Your holy ones left everything to follow Christ; lead us to live as the poor in spirit.
Lord, have mercy.
Your holy ones follow the Lamb wherever he goes; open our souls to purity of heart.
Christ, have mercy.
Your holy ones obeyed the voice of Christ; teach us obedience to your commands.
Lord, have mercy.

Introduction to the Lord's Prayer
In the company of faithful religious whose consecrated life prefigures the new life of God's reign let us pray that God may hasten the day of its fulfillment.

Collect *From the Proper of the Day*

The Blessing
May all who have freely vowed themselves in the religious live to the Lord diligently and faithfully conform themselves to the life they have promised. **Amen.**

Common of Professed Religious Noonday Prayer
Hymn Jerusalem the golden *Hymnal 624*

Antiphon You, O God, have heard my vows; you have granted me the heritage of those who fear your Name.

Reading Philippians 3: 8-10
I regard everything as loss because of the surpassing value of knowing Christ Jesus my Lord. For his sake I have suffered the loss of all things, and I regard them as rubbish, in order that I may gain Christ and be found in him, not having a righteousness of my own that comes from the law, but one that comes through faith in Christ, the righteousness from God

based on faith. I want to know Christ and the power of his resurrection and the sharing of his sufferings by becoming like him in his death.

Verse and Response
My soul clings to you.
Your right hand holds me fast.

Collect *From the Proper of the Day or the following*
O God, whose blessed Son became poor that we through his poverty might be rich: Deliver us from an inordinate love of this world, that we, inspired by the devotion of your servant N., may serve you with singleness of heart, and attain to the riches of the age to come; through Jesus Christ our Lord, who lives and reigns with you, in the unity of the Holy Spirit, one God, now and for ever. Amen.

Common of Professed Religious Evening Prayer
Hymn Sing alleluia forth in duteous praise *Hymnal 619*

Antiphon 1 Jesus called them; and they left their family and followed him.
Antiphon 2 I count everything as loss because of the surpassing worth of knowing Christ Jesus my Lord.
Antiphon 3 Every one who has left houses or brothers or sisters or father or mother or children or lands, for my name's sake, will receive a hundredfold, and inherit eternal life.

Reading *From the Proper of the Day*

Responsory (Ps. 116:14; Ps. 65:1)
I will fulfill my vows to the Lord
        ‒ in the presence of all God's people.
To you shall vows be performed in Jerusalem
        ‒ in the presence of all God's people.
Glory to the Father and to the Son and to the Holy Spirit.
I will fulfill my vows to the Lord
        ‒ in the presence of all God's people.

Magnificat Antiphon The Lord will espouse them forever in fidelity and mercy.

Litany
In response to your call, faithful men and women surrendered all things to serve your people, strengthen us in our care for the neglected among us.
Lord, have mercy.

In imitation of the apostolic church, they shared a common life of fellowship; open your church to receive people from different ways of life .
Christ, have mercy.
In anticipation of the resurrection, they lived for your alone; bring all the departed into the life you prepare for us.
Lord, have mercy.

Introduction to the Lord's Prayer
Faithful to the Spirit, who consecrates us in Baptism and deepens that holiness in Religious Profession, let us pray that the Spirit may draw us in the holy life of God.

Collect *From the Proper of the Day*

The Blessing
With the voice of thanksgiving may all professed religious sacrifice to you what they have vowed and be a sign of your presence in the church.
Amen.

Common of Holy Persons Morning Prayer

Invitatory The Lord is glorious in the saints: Come let us adore him.

Hymn Blest are the pure in heart *Hymnal 656*

Antiphon 1 You shall be for me a priestly kingdom and a holy nation.
Antiphon 2 The Lord set his heart in love on your ancestors alone and chose you, their descendants after them, out of all the peoples.
Antiphon 3 I have redeemed you; I have called you by name, you are mine.

Reading One *From the Proper of the Day*

Responsory (Ps. 32: 12; Ps. 100:1)
Be glad, you righteous
        – and rejoice in the Lord.
Serve the Lord with gladness
        – and rejoice in the Lord.
Glory to the Father, and to the Son and to the Holy Spirit.
Be glad, you righteous
        – and rejoice in the Lord.

<h2 style="text-align:center">Canticle – Song of the Beatitudes Beati pauperes spiritu</h2>
(Matthew 5: 3-12)

Antiphon Blessed are the pure in heart, for they will see God.

Blessed are the poor in spirit, *
  for theirs is the kingdom of heaven.

Blessed are those who mourn, *
  for they will be comforted.

Blessed are the meek, *
  for they will inherit the earth.

Blessed are those who hunger and thirst for righteousness, *
  for they will be filled.

Blessed are the merciful, *
  for they will receive mercy.

Blessed are the pure in heart, *
  for they will see God.

Blessed are the peacemakers, *
  for they will be called children of God.

Blessed are those who are persecuted for righteousness' sake, *
  for theirs is the kingdom of heaven.

Blessed are you when people revile you and persecute you *
  and utter all kinds of evil against you falsely on my account.

Rejoice and be glad, for your reward is great in heaven, *
  for in the same way they persecuted the prophets
  who were before you.

Antiphon Blessed are the pure in heart, for they will see God.

Reading Two *From the Proper of the Day*

Responsory (Ps. 37:31; Ps. 36: 10)
The law of their God is in their heart
  – their footsteps shall not falter.
You favor those who are true of heart
  – their footsteps shall not falter.
Glory to the Father and **to** the Son and to the Holy Spirit.
The law of their God is in their heart
  – their footsteps shall not falter.

Benedictus Antiphon Blessed are the poor in spirit, for theirs is the kingdom of heaven. Blessed are the pure in heart, for they will see God.

Litany
You set your holy ones apart as lights in their generation. Make us lights shining in a dark world.
Lord, have mercy.
Your holy ones bore witness to you by their faith and good works. Strengthen all people of faith to model their lives on the faith you have given them.
Christ, have mercy.
Your holy ones served you in their prayer and in their work. Deepen our prayer and sustain our works of service.
Lord, have mercy.

Introduction to the Lord's Prayer
Christ calls us to be a holy people consecrated by the Holy Spirit, so in the Spirit of holiness we pray.

Collect *From the Proper of the Day*

The Blessing
May God give us a spirit of wisdom and revelation as we come to know him, so that, with the eyes of our heart enlightened, we may know what are the riches of his glorious inheritance among the saints. **Amen.**

Common of Holy Persons Noonday Prayer
Hymn O what their joy and the glory must be *Hymnal 623*

Antiphon As God's chosen ones, holy and beloved, clothe yourselves with compassion, kindness, humility, meekness, and patience.

Reading Romans 8: 28-30
We know that all things work together for good for those who love God, who are called according to his purpose. For those whom he foreknew he also predestined to be conformed to the image of his Son, in order that he might be the firstborn within a large family. And those whom he predestined he also called; and those whom he called he also justified; and those whom he justified he also glorified.

Verse and Response
They shall receive a blessing from the Lord.
A just reward from the God of their salvation.

Collect *From the Proper of the Day or one of the following*

Almighty God, you have surrounded us with a great cloud of witnesses: Grant that we, encouraged by the good example of your servant N., may persevere in running the race that is set before us, until at last we may with him attain to your eternal joy; through Jesus Christ, the pioneer and perfecter of our faith, who lives and reigns with you and the Holy Spirit, one God, for ever and ever. Amen.

or this

O God, you have brought us near to an innumerable company of angels, and to the spirits of just men made perfect: Grant us during our earthly pilgrimage to abide in their fellowship, and in our heavenly country to become partakers of their joy; through Jesus Christ our Lord, who lives and reigns with you and the Holy Spirit, one God, now and for ever. Amen.

or this

Almighty God, by your Holy Spirit you have made us one with your saints in heaven and on earth: Grant that in our earthly pilgrimage we may always be supported by this fellowship of love and prayer, and know ourselves to be surrounded by their witness to your power and mercy. We ask this for the sake of Jesus Christ, in whom all our intercessions are acceptable through the Spirit, and who lives and reigns for ever and ever. Amen.

Common of Holy Persons Evening Prayer

Hymn Ye watchers and ye holy ones *Hymnal 618*

Antiphon 1 Well done, good and trustworthy slave; you have been trustworthy in a few things, I will put you in charge of many things; enter into the joy of your master.

Antiphon 2 Rejoice and be glad, for your reward is great in heaven.

Antiphon 3 If you have not been faithful with what belongs to another, who will give you what is your own?

Reading *From the Proper of the Day*

Responsory (Ps. 11:8)
The Lord is righteous
    − God delights in righteous deeds.
The just shall see God's face
    − God delights in righteous deeds.
Glory to the Father and to the Son and to the Holy Spirit.
The Lord is righteous
    − God delights in righteous deeds.

Magnificat Antiphon Come, you that are blessed by my Father, inherit the kingdom prepared for you from the foundation of the world.

Litany
You call your holy people to represent Christ and the Church; help us to bear witness to Christ wherever we may be.
Lord, have mercy.
You give your holy people gifts to carry on Christ's work of reconciliation in the world. Help them to take their place in the life, worship and governance of the church.
Christ, have mercy.
You call all Christians to follow Christ and to work, pray and give for the spread of your rule; bring the faithful departed and all the dead to the light of your life.
Lord, have mercy.

Collect *From the Proper of the Day*

The Blessing
May we agree with one another, live in peace; and the God of love and peace will be with us. **Amen.**

Common of Ember Days Morning Prayer

Invitatory Christ sends disciples to the ends of the earth: Come, all nations, and worship God.

Hymn God of the prophets, bless the prophets' heirs *Hymnal 359*

Antiphon 1 I will take some of the spirit that is on you and put it on them; and they shall bear the burden of the people along with you.
Antiphon 2 According to the grace of God given to me, like a skilled master builder I laid a foundation, and someone else is building on it.
Antiphon 3 I sent you to reap that for which you did not labor. Others have labored, and you have entered into their labor.

Reading One *From the Proper of the Day*

Responsory One (Ps. 43:4; Heb. 13:15)
I will go to the altar of God
　　　　– to the God of my joy and gladness.
Let us continually offer a sacrifice of praise to God
　　　　– to the God of my joy and gladness.
Glory to the Father and to the Son and to the Holy Spirit.
I will go to the altar of God
　　　　– to the God of my joy and gladness.

Canticle – Song of the Evangelist   *Quam pulchri super montes*
(Isaiah 52: 7–10)

Antiphon The herald of the Gospel brings good news and announces salvation.

How beautiful upon the mountains *
  are the feet of the messenger who announces peace.

The herald brings good news, *
  announces salvation,
  and says to Zion, "Your God reigns."

Listen! Your sentinels lift up their voices, *
  together they sing for joy.

In plain sight they see *
  the return of the LORD to Zion.

Break forth together into singing, *
  you ruins of Jerusalem.

The LORD has comforted his people, *
  he has redeemed Jerusalem.

The LORD has bared his holy arm *
  before the eyes of all the nations.

All the ends of the earth shall see *
  the salvation of our God.

Antiphon The herald of the Gospel brings good news and announces salvation.

Reading Two *From the Proper of the Day*

Responsory Two (Ps.132: 9, 17)
Let your priests be clothed with righteousness
    – let your faithful people sing with joy.
I will clothe her priests with salvation
    – let your faithful people sing with joy.
Glory to the Father and to the Son and to the Holy Spirit.
Let your priests be clothed with righteousness
    – let your faithful people sing with joy.

Benedictus Antiphon Select from among yourselves seven people of good standing, full of the Spirit and of wisdom, whom we may appoint to the ministry.

Litany

For all members of your Church in their vocation and ministry, that they may serve you in a true and godly life.
Lord, have mercy.
For all called to serve as bishops, priests and deacons in your church that they may faithfully fulfill the duties of their ministry, build up your Church, and glorify your Name.
Christ, have mercy.
For those who do not yet believe, and for those who have lost their faith, that they may receive the light of the Gospel.
Lord, have mercy.

Invitation to the Lord's Prayer

Let us pray that the Father bring the nations into his fold, pour out his Spirit on all flesh, and hasten the coming of his kingdom.

Collect Almighty God, the giver of all good gifts, in your divine providence you have appointed various orders in your Church: Give your grace, we humbly pray, to all who are [now] called to any office and ministry for your people; and so fill them with the truth of your doctrine and clothe them with holiness of life, that they may faithfully serve before you, to the glory of your great Name and for the benefit of your holy Church; through Jesus Christ our Lord, who lives and reigns with you, in the unity of the Holy Spirit, one God, now and for ever. Amen.

The Blessing

May the Lord see that the harvest is plentiful, but the laborers are few; and so send out laborers into his harvest. **Amen.**

Common of Ember Days Noonday Prayer

Hymn Strengthen for service *Hymnal 312*

Antiphon Ask the Lord of the harvest to send out laborers into his harvest.

Reading Matthew 26: 18-20

Jesus came and said to them, "All authority in heaven and on earth has been given to me. Go therefore and make disciples of all nations, baptizing them in the name of the Father and of the Son and of the Holy Spirit, and teaching them to obey everything that I have commanded you. And remember, I am with you always, to the end of the age."

Verse and Response
How beautiful upon the mountains.
Are the feet of the messenger who announces peace.

Collect O God, you led your holy apostles to ordain ministers in every place: Grant that your Church, under the guidance of the Holy Spirit, may choose suitable persons for the ministry of Word and Sacrament, and may uphold them in their work for the extension of your kingdom; through him who is the Shepherd and Bishop of our souls, Jesus Christ our Lord, who lives and reigns with you and the Holy Spirit, one God, for ever and ever. Amen.

Common of Ember Days Evening Prayer
Hymn Lead us, heavenly Father, lead us *Hymnal 559*

Antiphon 1 You shall be for me a priestly kingdom and a holy nation.
Antiphon 2 Serve one another with whatever gift each of you has received.
Antiphon 3 If any want to become my followers, let them deny themselves and take up their cross and follow me.

Reading *From the Proper of the Day*

Responsory (Is. 6:8; Ez. 3:4)
Whom shall I send, and who will go for us?
    – Here am I; send me.
Go to the house of Israel and speak my very words to them
    – Here am I; send me.
Glory to the Father and to the Son and to the Holy Spirit.
Whom shall I send, and who will go for us?
    – Here am I; send me.

Magnificat Antiphon Follow me and I will make you fish for people. And immediately they left their nets and followed him.

Litany
For the holy Church of God, that it may be filled with truth and love, and be found without fault at the Day of your Coming.
Lord, have mercy.
For all who fear God and believe in you, Lord Christ, that our divisions may cease and that all may be one as you and the Father are one.
Christ, have mercy.

For all who have died in the communion of your Church, and those whose faith is known to you alone, that, with the Blessed Virgin Mary and all the saints, they may have rest in that place where there is no pain or grief, but life eternal.
Lord, have mercy.

Invitation to the Lord's Prayer
O God of the nations of the earth, remember the multitudes who have been created in your image but have not known the redeeming work of our savior Jesus Christ as we pray.

Collect Almighty and everlasting God, by whose Spirit the whole body of your faithful people is governed and sanctified: Receive our supplications and prayers, which we offer before you for all members of your holy Church, that in their vocation and ministry they may truly and devoutly serve you; through our Lord and Savior Jesus Christ, who lives and reigns with you, in the unity of the Holy Spirit, one God, now and for ever. Amen.

The Blessing
May the Lord send ministers of Christ Jesus to the church in the priestly service of the gospel of God, so that the offering of all people may be acceptable, sanctified by the Holy Spirit. **Amen.**

Common of Rogation Days Morning Prayer

Invitatory God blesses our world with abundant bounty: Come let us worship.

Hymn O Jesus crowed with all renown *Hymnal 292*

Antiphon 1 The Lord God will give the rain for your land in its season and you will gather in your grain, your wine, and your oil.
Antiphon 2 Creation waits with eager longing for the revealing of the children of God.
Antiphon 3 You shall eat your fill and bless the Lord your God for the good land that he has given you.

Reading One *From the Proper of the Day*

Responsory One (Job 38: 12, 16)
Have you commanded the morning
        – and caused the dawn to know its place?
Have you entered into the springs of the sea
        – and caused the dawn to know its place?
Glory to the Father and to the Son and to the Holy Spirit.

Have you commanded the morning
  – and caused the dawn to know its place?

Canticle – Song of the Wilderness *Laetabitur deserta*
(Isaiah 35:1-7,10)

Antiphon The desert shall blossom abundantly, and rejoice with joy and singing.

The wilderness and the dry land shall be glad, *
  the desert shall rejoice and blossom;

It shall blossom abundantly, *
  and rejoice with joy and singing.

They shall see the glory of the LORD, *
  the majesty of our God.

Strengthen the weary hands, *
  and make firm the feeble knees.

Say to the anxious, "Be strong, do not fear! *
  Here is your God, coming with judgment to save you."

Then shall the eyes of the blind be opened, *
  and the ears of the deaf be unstopped.

Then shall the lame leap like a deer, *
  and the tongue of the speechless sing for joy.

For waters shall break forth in the wilderness *
  and streams in the desert;

The burning sand shall become a pool *
  and the thirsty ground, springs of water.

The ransomed of God shall return with singing, *
  with everlasting joy upon their heads.

Joy and gladness shall be theirs, *
  and sorrow and sighing shall flee away.

Antiphon The desert shall blossom abundantly, and rejoice with joy and singing.

Reading Two *From the Proper of the Day*

Responsory Two (Ps 107: 37, 38)
They sowed fields, and planted vineyards
  – and brought in a fruitful harvest.

The Lord blessed them, so that they increased greatly
   – and brought in a fruitful harvest.
Glory to the Father and to the Son and to the Holy Spirit.
They sowed fields, and planted vineyards
   – and brought in a fruitful harvest.

Benedictus Antiphon Consider the lilies of the field, how they grow; they neither toil nor spin, yet I tell you, even Solomon in all his glory was not clothed like one of these.

Litany
Walk with those who till, plant, and care for fields, pastures, gardens and orchards that they may be strengthened by your constant presence in all their labors.
Lord, have mercy.
Give us favorable weather and growing conditions that our farming efforts may not be in vain.
Christ, have mercy.
May the hungry be fed and may we always be mindful of their needs and wants. May governments around the world make good and wise decisions regarding their people and the food they need.
Lord, have mercy.

Invitation to the Lord's Prayer
Asking God's blessing on the work of farmers, industry and commerce, let us trust God to sustain their labor.

Collect Almighty God, Lord of heaven and earth: We humbly pray that your gracious providence may give and preserve to our use the harvests of the land and of the seas, and may prosper all who labor to gather them, that we, who are constantly receiving good things from your hand, may always give you thanks; through Jesus Christ our Lord, who lives and reigns with you and the Holy Spirit, one God, for ever and ever. Amen.

The Blessing
May the Lord command the blessing upon us in our barns and places of industry, and in all that we undertake. May God bless us in the land that the Lord our God is giving us. **Amen.**

Common of Rogation Days Noonday Prayer
Hymn For the beauty of the earth *Hymnal 416*

Antiphon Regard all utensils and goods of the monastery as sacred vessels of the altar.

Reading Sirach 38: 31, 32, 34

All artisans rely on their hands, and all are skillful in their own work. Without them no city can be inhabited, and wherever they live, they will not go hungry. They maintain the fabric of the world, and their concern is for the exercise of their trade.

Verse and Response
They set hearts on finishing their handiwork.
They are careful to complete its decoration.

Collect Almighty God, whose Son Jesus Christ in his earthly life shared our toil and hallowed our labor: Be present with your people where they work; make those who carry on the industries and commerce of this land responsive to your will; and give to us all a pride in what we do, and a just return for our labor; through Jesus Christ our Lord, who lives and reigns with you, in the unity of the Holy Spirit, one God, now and for ever. Amen.

Common of Rogation Days Evening Prayer

Hymn Earth and all stars *Hymnal 412*

Antiphon 1 Each builder must choose with care how to build on the foundation.
Antiphon 2 Those who want to be rich fall into temptation and are trapped by many senseless and harmful desires.
Antiphon 3 Do your work quietly and to earn your own living. Brothers and sisters, do not be weary in doing what is right.

Reading *From the Proper of the Day*

Responsory (Job 34: 29, 28)
From whose womb did the ice come forth
      – and who has given birth to the frost of heaven?
Has the rain a father?
      – and who has given birth to the hoarfrost of heaven?
Glory to the Father and to the Son and to the Holy Spirit.
From whose womb did the ice come forth
      – and who has given birth to the frost of heaven?

Magnificat Antiphon Take care! Be on your guard against all kinds of greed; for one's life does not consist in the abundance of possessions.

Litany

Keep us aware and sensitive to the needs of our farmers and their families. May they have a fair return for their efforts.
Lord, have mercy.
Bless all those who work in related agricultural businesses and those who are involved in the handling and sale of our agricultural products.
Christ, have mercy.
Give peace and strength to those who are bearing painful, heartbreaking burdens, and show us how we might be of assistance to them.
Lord, have mercy.

Invitation to the Lord's Prayer

Asking God's blessing on the work of farmers, industry and commerce, let us trust God to sustain their labor.

Collect O merciful Creator, your hand is open wide to satisfy the needs of every living creature: Make us always thankful for your loving providence; and grant that we, remembering the account that we must one day give, may be faithful stewards of your good gifts; through Jesus Christ our Lord, who with you and the Holy Spirit lives and reigns, one God, for ever and ever. Amen.

The Blessing

May the Almighty God, who provides us with every blessing in abundance, so that by always having enough of everything, we may share abundantly in every good work. **Amen.**

Common of National Holidays Morning Prayer

Invitatory The Lord is a God of justice and peace: Come let us worship.

Hymn God of our fathers *Hymnal 718*

Antiphon 1 God is not ashamed to be called their God; indeed, he has prepared a city for them.
Psalms are taken from the appointed day in the Psalter.
Antiphon 2 God is able to provide you with every blessing in abundance, so that by always having enough of everything, you may share abundantly.
Antiphon 3 Love your enemies and pray for those who persecute you.

Reading One *From the Proper of the Day*

Responsory One (Ps. 145: 8-9))

The Lord is gracious and full of compassion
> **– slow to anger and of great kindness.**

The Lord is loving to everyone
> **– slow to anger and of great kindness.**

Glory to the Father and to the Son and to the Holy Spirit.

The Lord is gracious and full of compassion
> **– slow to anger and of great kindness.**

Canticle – Song of the Trustful *Benedictus vir*
(Jeremiah 17: 7-8)

Antiphon Those of steadfast mind you keep in peace— in peace because they trust in you.

Blessed are those who trust in the LORD, *
> whose trust is the LORD.

They shall be like a tree planted by water, *
> sending out its roots by the stream.

It shall not fear when heat comes, *
> and its leaves shall stay green.

In the year of drought it is not anxious, *
> and it does not cease to bear fruit.

Antiphon Those of steadfast mind you keep in peace— in peace because they trust in you.

Reading Two *From the Proper of the Day*

Responsory Two (Ps 33:5, 1)

The Lord loves righteousness and justice
> **– the loving kindness of the Lord fills the whole earth.**

It is good for the just to sing praises
> **– the loving kindness of the Lord fills the whole earth.**

Glory to the Father and to the Son and to the Holy Spirit.

The Lord loves righteousness and justice
> **– the loving kindness of the Lord fills the whole earth.**

Benedictus Antiphon You have multiplied the nation, you have increased its joy; they rejoice before you as with joy at the harvest.

Litany

We thank you for the natural majesty and beauty of this land. They restore us, though we often destroy them.
Lord, have mercy.
We thank you for the great resources of this nation. They make us rich, though we often exploit them.
Christ, have mercy.
We thank you for the men and women who have made this country strong. They are models for us, though we often fall short of them.
Lord, have mercy.

Invitation to the Lord's Prayer

Let us pray with the Prince of Peace that we may reverently use our freedom, and that he help us to employ it in the maintenance of justice in our communities and among the nations.

Collect *From the Proper of the Day or one of the following*

For Social Justice

Almighty God, who created us in your own image: Grant us grace fearlessly to contend against evil and to make no peace with oppression; and, that we may reverently use our freedom, help us to employ it in the maintenance of justice in our communities and among the nations, to the glory of your holy Name; through Jesus Christ our Lord, who lives and reigns with you and the Holy Spirit, one God, now and for ever. Amen.

The Blessing

May we imitate our God who executes justice for the orphan and the widow, and who loves the strangers, providing them with food and clothing. **Amen.**

Common of National Holidays Noonday Prayer

Hymn God bless our native land *Hymnal 716*

Antiphon Proclaim liberty to the captives, and release to the prisoners.
Psalms are taken from the appointed day in the Psalter.

Reading John 14:27

Peace I leave with you; my peace I give to you. I do not give to you as the world gives. Do not let your hearts be troubled, and do not let them be afraid.

Verse and Response

O Lord, you will ordain peace for us.
For all that we have done, you have done for us.

Collect *From the Proper of the Day*

Common of National Holidays Evening Prayer

Hymn O day of peace *Hymnal 597*

Antiphon 1 You judge the peoples with equity and guide the nations upon earth.
Psalms are taken from the appointed day in the Psalter.
Antiphon 2 The Lord guards the paths of justice and preserves the way of his faithful ones.
Antiphon 3 Walk in the way of the good, and keep to the paths of the just.

Reading *From the Proper of the Day*

Responsory (Ps. 33:12, 8)
Blessed is the nation whose God is the Lord
 – blessed the people he has chosen to be his own.
Let all who dwell in the world stand in awe of the Lord
 – blessed the people he has chosen to be his own.
Glory to the Father and to the Son and to the Holy Spirit.
Blessed is the nation whose God is the Lord
 – blessed the people he has chosen to be his own.

Magnificat Antiphon They shall beat their swords into plowshares, and their spears into pruning hooks; nation shall not lift up sword against nation, neither shall they learn war any more.

Litany
We thank you for the torch of liberty which has been lit in this land. It has drawn people from every nation, though we have often hidden from its light.
Lord, have mercy.
We thank you for the faith we have inherited in all its rich variety. It sustains our life, though we have been faithless again and again.
Christ, have mercy.
We thank you for the lives of generations of people from diverse nations who contributed to this nation, grant them and all the departed a place of peace.
Lord, have mercy.

Invitation to the Lord's Prayer

Let us pray with the Prince of Peace that we may reverently use our freedom, and that he may help us to employ it in the maintenance of justice in our communities and among the nations.

Collect *From the Proper of the Day*

The Blessing

May God strengthen us to do justice, and to love kindness, and to walk humbly with our God. **Amen.**

Common of the Faithful Departed Morning Prayer

Invitatory Come let us worship God, for whom all are alive.

Hymn All my hope on God is founded *Hymnal 665*

Psalm 51   *Miserere mei, Deus*

Antiphon Make me hear of joy and gladness, that the body you have broken may rejoice.

1   Have mercy on me, O God,
      according to your loving-kindness; *
         in your great compassion blot out my offenses.

2   Wash me through and through from my wickedness *
         and cleanse me from my sin.

3   For I know my transgressions, *
         and my sin is ever before me..

4   Against you only have I sinned *
         and done what is evil in your sight.

5   And so you are justified when you speak *
         and upright in your judgment.

6   Indeed, I have been wicked from my birth, *
         a sinner from my mother's womb.

7   For behold, you look for truth deep within me, *
         and will make me understand wisdom secretly.

8   Purge me from my sin, and I shall be pure; *
         wash me, and I shall be clean indeed.

9   Make me hear of joy and gladness, *
         that the body you have broken may rejoice.

10 Hide your face from my sins *
    and blot out all my iniquities.

11 Create in me a clean heart, O God, *
    and renew a right spirit within me.

12 Cast me not away from your presence *
    and take not your holy Spirit from me.

13 Give me the joy of your saving help again *
    and sustain me with your bountiful Spirit.

14 I shall teach your ways to the wicked, *
    and sinners shall return to you.

15 Deliver me from death, O God, *
    and my tongue shall sing of your righteousness,
    O God of my salvation.

16 Open my lips, O Lord, *
    and my mouth shall proclaim your praise.

17 Had you desired it, I would have offered sacrifice, *
    but you take no delight in burnt-offerings.

18 The sacrifice of God is a troubled spirit; *
    a broken and contrite heart, O God, you will not despise.

19 Be favorable and gracious to Zion, *
    and rebuild the walls of Jerusalem.

20 Then you will be pleased with the appointed sacrifices,
    with burnt-offerings and oblations; *
    then shall they offer young bullocks upon your altar.

Antiphon Make me hear of joy and gladness, that the body you have broken may rejoice.

Psalm 65 *Te decet hymnus*

Antiphon To you that hear prayer shall all flesh come, because of their transgressions.

1 You are to be praised, O God, in Zion; *
    to you shall vows be performed in Jerusalem.

2 To you that hear prayer shall all flesh come, *
    because of their transgressions.

3 Our sins are stronger than we are, *
     but you will blot them out.

4 Blessed are they whom you choose
   and draw to your courts to dwell there! *
       they will be satisfied by the beauty of your house,
       by the holiness of your temple.

5 Awesome things will you show us in your righteousness,
   O God of our salvation, *
       O Hope of all the ends of the earth
       and of the seas that are far away.

6 You make fast the mountains by your power; *
     they are girded about with might.

7 You still the roaring of the seas, *
     the roaring of their waves,
     and the clamor of the peoples.

8 Those who dwell at the ends of the earth
   will tremble at your marvelous signs; *
       you make the dawn and the dusk to sing for joy.

9 You visit the earth and water it abundantly;
   you make it very plenteous; *
       the river of God is full of water.

10 You prepare the grain, *
     for so you provide for the earth.

11 You drench the furrows and smooth out the ridges; *
     with heavy rain you soften the ground and bless its increase.

12 You crown the year with your goodness, *
     and your paths overflow with plenty.

13 May the fields of the wilderness be rich for grazing, *
     and the hills be clothed with joy.

14 May the meadows cover themselves with flocks,
   and the valleys cloak themselves with grain; *
       let them shout for joy and sing.

Antiphon To you that hear prayer shall all flesh come, because of their transgressions.

Psalm 63 *Deus, Deus meus*

Antiphon My soul clings to you; your right hand holds me fast.

1 O God, you are my God; eagerly I seek you; *
     my soul thirsts for you, my flesh faints for you,
     as in a barren and dry land where there is no water.

2 Therefore I have gazed upon you in your holy place, *
     that I might behold your power and your glory.

3 For your loving-kindness is better than life itself; *
     my lips shall give you praise.

4 So will I bless you as long as I live *
     and lift up my hands in your Name.

5 My soul is content, as with marrow and fatness, *
     and my mouth praises you with joyful lips,

6 When I remember you upon my bed, *
     and meditate on you in the night watches.

7 For you have been my helper, *
     and under the shadow of your wings I will rejoice.

8 My soul clings to you; *
     your right hand holds me fast.

9 May those who seek my life to destroy it *
     go down into the depths of the earth;

10 Let them fall upon the edge of the sword, *
     and let them be food for jackals.

11 But the king will rejoice in God;
     all those who swear by him will be glad; *
     for the mouth of those who speak lies shall be stopped.

Antiphon My soul clings to you; your right hand holds me fast.

Reading One Isaiah 25: 6-9

Responsory One (Job 19:25-26)
I know that my Redeemer lives
        – In my body, I shall see God.
I myself shall see and my eyes behold him.
        – In my body, I shall see God.
Glory to the Father, and to the Son and to the Holy Spirit.

I know that my Redeemer lives
  – In my body, I shall see God.

Canticle – Song of The Resurrection *Nemo enim*
(Romans 14: 7-10)

Antiphon I am Resurrection and I am Life.

We do not live to ourselves, *
  and we do not die to ourselves.

If we live, we live to the Lord, *
  and if we die, we die to the Lord.

So then, whether we live or whether we die, *
  we are the Lord's.

For to this end Christ died and lived again, *
  so that he might be Lord of both the dead and the living.

Antiphon I am Resurrection and I am Life.

Reading Two John 11: 21-27

Responsory Two
You who raised Lazarus, already corrupted, from the grave
  – grant them rest, O Lord, and a place of forgiveness.
You shall come to judge the living and the dead and the world by fire
  – grant them rest, O Lord, and a place of forgiveness.
Glory to the Father, and to the Son and to the Holy Spirit.
You who raised Lazarus, already corrupted, from the grave
  – grant them rest, O Lord, and a place of forgiveness.

Benedictus Antiphon I am the resurrection and the life. Those who believe in me, even though they die, will live, and everyone who lives and believes in me will never die.

Litany
God of all light, at break of day, we rejoice in the resurrection of Christ; bring all the departed into the light of Christ's risen life.
Lord, have mercy.
Lord Christ, you wept at the tomb of your friend Lazarus; comfort all who mourn.
Christ have mercy.
You raised the dead to life; give eternal life to all the departed.
Lord, have mercy.

Invitation to the Lord's Prayer We pray with Christ, the Resurrection and the Life, to bring all the dead to behold the Father's face.

Collect O God, the Maker and Redeemer of all believers: Grant to the faithful departed the unsearchable benefits of the passion of your Son; that on the day of his appearing they may be manifested as your children; through Jesus Christ our Lord, who lives and reigns with you and the Holy Spirit, one God, now and for ever. Amen.

The Blessing
May the God of peace, who brought back from the dead our Lord Jesus, the great shepherd of the sheep, by the blood of the eternal covenant, make us perfect in everything good so that we may do his will, working among us that which is pleasing in his sight. **Amen.**

Common of the Faithful Departed Noonday Prayer
Hymn From glory to glory advancing *Hymnal 326*

Psalm 70 *Deus, in adjutorium*
Antiphon I am poor and needy; come to me speedily, O God.

1 Be pleased, O God, to deliver me; *
    O LORD, make haste to help me.

2 Let those who seek my life be ashamed
and altogether dismayed; *
    let those who take pleasure in my misfortune
    draw back and be disgraced.

3 Let those who say to me "Aha!" and gloat over me turn back, *
    because they are ashamed.

4 Let all who seek you rejoice and be glad in you; *
    let those who love your salvation say for ever,
    "Great is the LORD!"

5 But as for me, I am poor and needy; *
    come to me speedily, O God.

6 You are my helper and my deliverer; *
    O LORD, do not tarry.

Psalm 85 *Benedixisti, Domine*
1 You have been gracious to your land, O LORD, *
    you have restored the good fortune of Jacob.

2 You have forgiven the iniquity of your people *
    and blotted out all their sins.

3 You have withdrawn all your fury *
    and turned yourself from your wrathful indignation.

4 Restore us then, O God our Savior; *
    let your anger depart from us.

5 Will you be displeased with us for ever? *
    will you prolong your anger from age to age?

6 Will you not give us life again, *
    that your people may rejoice in you?

7 Show us your mercy, O LORD, *
    and grant us your salvation.

8 I will listen to what the LORD God is saying, *
    for he is speaking peace to his faithful people
    and to those who turn their hearts to him.

9 Truly, his salvation is very near to those who fear him, *
    that his glory may dwell in our land.

10 Mercy and truth have met together; *
    righteousness and peace have kissed each other.

11 Truth shall spring up from the earth, *
    and righteousness shall look down from heaven.

12 The LORD will indeed grant prosperity, *
    and our land will yield its increase.

13 Righteousness shall go before him, *
    and peace shall be a pathway for his feet.

Psalm 86 *Inclina, Domine*

1 Bow down your ear, O LORD, and answer me, *
    for I am poor and in misery.

2 Keep watch over my life, for I am faithful; *
    save your servant who puts his trust in you.

3 Be merciful to me, O LORD, for you are my God; *
    I call upon you all the day long.

4 Gladden the soul of your servant, *
    for to you, O LORD, I lift up my soul.

5 For you, O LORD, are good and forgiving, *
    and great is your love toward all who call upon you.

6 Give ear, O LORD, to my prayer, *
    and attend to the voice of my supplications.

7 In the time of my trouble I will call upon you, *
    for you will answer me.

8 Among the gods there is none like you, O LORD, *
    nor anything like your works.

9 All nations you have made will come
  and worship you, O LORD, *
    and glorify your Name.

10 For you are great;
  you do wondrous things; *
    and you alone are God.

11 Teach me your way, O LORD,
  and I will walk in your truth; *
    knit my heart to you that I may fear your Name.

12 I will thank you, O LORD my God, with all my heart, *
    and glorify your Name for evermore.

13 For great is your love toward me; *
    you have delivered me from the nethermost Pit.

14 The arrogant rise up against me, O God,
  and a band of violent men seeks my life; *
    they have not set you before their eyes.

15 But you, O LORD, are gracious and full of compassion, *
    slow to anger, and full of kindness and truth.

16 Turn to me and have mercy upon me; *
    give your strength to your servant;
    and save the child of your handmaid.

17 Show me a sign of your favor,
  so that those who hate me may see it and be ashamed; *
    because you, O LORD, have helped me and comforted me.

Antiphon I am poor and needy; come to me speedily, O God.

Reading 1 John 3: 1-2

See what love the Father has given us, that we should be called children of God; and that is what we are. The reason the world does not know us is that it did not know him. Beloved, we are God's children now; what we will be has not yet been revealed. What we do know is this: when he is revealed, we will be like him, for we will see him as he is.

Verse and Response

I believe that I shall see the goodness of the Lord.

In the land of the living.

Collect Lord Jesus Christ, by your death you took away the sting of death: Grant to us your servants so to follow in faith where you have led the way, that we may at length fall asleep peacefully in you and wake up in your likeness; for your tender mercies' sake. Amen.

Common of the Faithful Departed Evening Prayer

Hymn Christ the Victorious, give to your servants *Hymnal 358*

Psalm 116 *Dilexi, quoniam*

Antiphon I will walk in the presence of the Lord in the land of the living.

1 I love the LORD, because he has heard
    the voice of my supplication, *
        because he has inclined his ear to me
        whenever I called upon him.

2 The cords of death entangled me;
    the grip of the grave took hold of me; *
        I came to grief and sorrow.

3 Then I called upon the Name of the LORD: *
        "O LORD, I pray you, save my life."

4 Gracious is the LORD and righteous; *
        our God is full of compassion.

5 The LORD watches over the innocent; *
        I was brought very low, and he helped me.

6 Turn again to your rest, O my soul, *
        for the LORD has treated you well.

7 For you have rescued my life from death, *
        my eyes from tears, and my feet from stumbling.

8 I will walk in the presence of the LORD *
   in the land of the living.

9 I believed, even when I said,
   "I have been brought very low." *
      In my distress I said, "No one can be trusted."

10 How shall I repay the LORD *
    for all the good things he has done for me?

11 I will lift up the cup of salvation *
    and call upon the Name of the LORD.

12 I will fulfill my vows to the LORD *
    in the presence of all his people.

13 Precious in the sight of the LORD *
    is the death of his servants.

14 O LORD, I am your servant; *
    I am your servant and the child of your handmaid;
    you have freed me from my bonds.

15 I will offer you the sacrifice of thanksgiving *
    and call upon the Name of the LORD.

16 I will fulfill my vows to the LORD *
    in the presence of all his people,

17 In the courts of the LORD'S house, *
    in the midst of you, O Jerusalem.
    Hallelujah!

Antiphon I will walk in the presence of the Lord in the land of the
living.

Psalm 121 *Levavi oculos*

Antiphon The Lord shall preserve you from all evil; it is he who shall
keep you safe.

1 I lift up my eyes to the hills; *
   from where is my help to come?

2 My help comes from the LORD, *
   the maker of heaven and earth.

3 He will not let your foot be moved *
   and he who watches over you will not fall asleep.

4   Behold, he who keeps watch over Israel *
      shall neither slumber nor sleep;

5   The LORD himself watches over you; *
      the LORD is your shade at your right hand,

6   So that the sun shall not strike you by day, *
      nor the moon by night.

7   The LORD shall preserve you from all evil; *
      it is he who shall keep you safe.

8   The LORD shall watch over your going out
    and your coming in, *
      from this time forth for evermore.

Antiphon The Lord shall preserve you from all evil; it is he who shall
keep you safe.

Psalm 130 *De profundis*

Antiphon If you, Lord, were to note what is done amiss, O LORD,
who could stand?

1   Out of the depths have I called to you, O LORD;
    LORD, hear my voice; *
      let your ears consider well the voice of my supplication.

2   If you, LORD, were to note what is done amiss, *
      O LORD, who could stand?

3   For there is forgiveness with you; *
      therefore you shall be feared.

4   I wait for the LORD; my soul waits for him; *
      in his word is my hope.

5   My soul waits for the LORD,
    more than watchmen for the morning, *
      more than watchmen for the morning.

6   O Israel, wait for the LORD, *
      for with the LORD there is mercy;

7   With him there is plenteous redemption, *
      and he shall redeem Israel from all their sins.

Antiphon If you, Lord, were to note what is done amiss, O LORD,
who could stand?

Reading Revelation 7: 9-17

Responsory
Lord where shall I hide myself from you face?
  – For in my life I have greatly sinned.
I am afraid because of my transgressions.
  – For in my life I have greatly sinned.
Glory to the Father, and to the Son and to the Holy Spirit.
Lord where shall I hide myself from you face?
  – For in my life I have greatly sinned.

Magnificat Antiphon Blessed are the dead who from now on die in the Lord. They will rest from their labors, for their deeds follow them.

Litany
In the midst of life we are in death; from whom can we seek help?
From you alone, O Lord, who by our sins are justly angered.
Lord, have mercy.
Lord, you know the secrets of our hearts; shut not your ears to our prayers but spare us O Lord.
Christ, have mercy.
O worthy and eternal Judge, do not let the pains of death turn us away from you at our last hour.
Lord, have mercy.

Invitation to the Lord's Prayer We pray with Christ, the Resurrection and the Life, to bring all the dead to behold the Father's face.

Collect Lord Jesus Christ, Son of the living God, we pray you to set your passion, cross, and death between your judgment and our souls, now and in the hour of our death. Give mercy and grace to the living; pardon and rest to the dead; to your holy Church peace and concord; and to us sinners everlasting life and glory; for with the Father and the Holy Spirit you live and reign, one God, now and for ever. Amen.

The Blessing
May God, who is rich in mercy, out of the great love with which he loved us even when we were dead through our trespasses, make us alive together with Christ. **Amen.**

Lectionary for the Daily Office

Concerning the Daily Office Lectionary

The Daily Office Lectionary is arranged in a two-year cycle. Year One begins on the First Sunday of Advent preceding odd-numbered years, and Year Two begins on the First Sunday of Advent preceding even-numbered years. (Thus, on the First Sunday of Advent, 1976, the Lectionary for Year One is begun.) Three Readings are provided for each Sunday and weekday in each of the two years. Two of the Readings may be used in the morning and one in the evening; or, if the Office is read only once in the day, all three Readings may be used. When the Office is read twice in the day, it is suggested that the Gospel Reading be used in the evening in Year One, and in the morning in Year Two. If two Readings are desired at both Offices, the Old Testament Reading for the alternate year is used as the First Reading at Evening Prayer. When more than one Reading is used at an Office, the first is always from the Old Testament (or the Apocrypha). When a Major Feast interrupts the sequence of Readings, they may be re-ordered by lengthening, combining, or omitting some of them, to secure continuity or avoid repetition. Any Reading may be lengthened at discretion. Suggested lengthenings are shown in parentheses. In this Lectionary (except in the weeks from 4 Advent to 1 Epiphany, and Palm Sunday to 2 Easter), the Psalms are arranged in a seven-week pattern which recurs throughout the year, except for appropriate variations in Lent and Easter Season. In the citation of the Psalms, those for the morning are given first, and then those for the evening. At the discretion of the officiant, however, any of the Psalms appointed for a given day may be used in the morning or in the evening. Likewise, Psalms appointed for any day may be used on any other day in the same week, except on major Holy Days.

Year One

The Epiphany and Following

Epiphany 46, 97 □ 96, 100
Isa. 52:7-10 Rev. 21:22-27 Matt. 12:14-21
*The Psalms and Readings for the dated days after the Epiphany
are used only until the following Saturday Evening.*
Jan. 7 103 □ 114, 115
Isa. 52:3-6 Rev. 2:1-7 John 2:1-11
Jan. 8 117, 118 □ 112, 113
Isa. 59:15-21 Rev. 2:8-17 John 4:46-54
Jan. 9 121, 122, 123 □ 131, 132
Isa. 63:1-5 Rev. 2:18-29 John 5:1-15
Jan. 10 138, 139:1-17(18-23) □ 147
Isa. 65:1-9 Rev. 3:1-6 John 6:1-14
Jan. 11 148, 150 □ 91, 92
Isa. 65:13-16 Rev. 3:7-13 John 6:15-27
Jan. 12 98, 99, [100] □ ——
Isa. 66:1-2, 22-23 Rev. 3:14-22 John 9:1-12, 35-38

Eve of 1 Epiphany —— □ 104
Isa. 61:1-9 Gal. 3:23-29; 4:4-7

Week of 1 Epiphany

Sunday 146, 147 □ 111, 112, 113
Isa. 40:1-11 Heb. 1:1-12 John 1:1-7, 19-20, 29-34
Monday 1, 2, 3 □ 4, 7
Isa. 40:12-23 Eph. 1:1-14 Mark 1:1-13
Tuesday 5, 6 □ 10, 11
Isa. 40:25-31 Eph. 1:15-23 Mark 1:14-28
Wednesday 119:1-24 □ 12, 13, 14
Isa. 41:1-16 Eph. 2:1-10 Mark 1:29-45
Thursday 18:1-20 □ 18:21-50
Isa. 41:17-29 Eph. 2:11-22 Mark 2:1-12
Friday 16, 17 □ 22
Isa. 42:(1-9)10-17 Eph. 3:1-13 Mark 2:13-22
Saturday 20, 21:1-7(8-14) □ 110:1-5(6-7), 116, 117
Isa. 43:1-13 Eph. 3:14-21 Mark 2:23—3:6

Week of 2 Epiphany

Sunday 148, 149, 150 □ 114, 115
Isa. 43:14—44:5 Heb. 6:17—7:10 John 4:27-42
Monday 25 □ 9, 15
Isa. 44:6-8, 21-23 Eph. 4:1-16 Mark 3:7-19a
Tuesday 26, 28 □ 36, 39
Isa. 44:9-20 Eph. 4:17-32 Mark 3:19b-35
Wednesday 38 □ 119:25-48
Isa. 44:24—45:7 Eph. 5:1-14 Mark 4:1-20
Thursday 37:1-18 □ 37:19-42
Isa. 45:5-17 Eph. 5:15-33 Mark 4:21-34
Friday 31 □ 35
Isa. 45:18-25 Eph. 6:1-9 Mark 4:35-41
Saturday 30, 32 □ 42, 43
Isa. 46:1-13 Eph. 6:10-24 Mark 5:1-20

Week of 3 Epiphany

Sunday 63:1-8(9-11), 98 □ 103
Isa. 47:1-15 Heb. 10:19-31 John 5:2-18
Monday 41, 52 □ 44
Isa. 48:1-11 Gal. 1:1-17 Mark 5:21-43
Tuesday 45 □ 47, 48
Isa. 48:12-21 Gal. 1:18—2:10 Mark 6:1-13
Wednesday 119:49-72 □ 49, [53]
Isa. 49:1-12 Gal. 2:11-21 Mark 6:13-29
Thursday 50 □ [59, 60] or 118
Isa. 49:13-23 Gal. 3:1-14 Mark 6:30-46
Friday 40, 54 □ 51
Isa. 50:1-11 Gal. 3:15-22 Mark 6:47-56
Saturday 55 □ 138, 139:1-17(18-23)
Isa. 51:1-8 Gal. 3:23-29 Mark 7:1-23

Week of 4 Epiphany

Sunday 24, 29 □ 8, 84
Isa. 51:9-16 Heb. 11:8-16 John 7:14-31
Monday 56, 57, [58] □ 64, 65
Isa. 51:17-23 Gal. 4:1-11 Mark 7:24-37
Tuesday 61, 62 □ 68:1-20(21-23)24-36
Isa. 52:1-12 Gal. 4:12-20 Mark 8:1-10
Wednesday 72 □ 119:73-96
Isa. 54:1-10(11-17) Gal. 4:21-31 Mark 8:11-26
Thursday [70], 71 □ 74
Isa. 55:1-13 Gal. 5:1-15 Mark 8:27—9:1
Friday 69:1-23(24-30)31-38 □ 73
Isa. 56:1-8 Gal. 5:16-24 Mark 9:2-13
Saturday 75, 76 □ 23, 27
Isa. 57:3-13 Gal. 5:25—6:10 Mark 9:14-29

Week of 5 Epiphany

Sunday 93, 96 □ 34
Isa. 57:14-21 Heb. 12:1-6 John 7:37-46
Monday 80 □ 77, [79]
Isa. 58:1-12 Gal. 6:11-18 Mark 9:30-41
Tuesday 78:1-39 □ 78:40-72
Isa. 59:1-15a 2 Tim. 1:1-14 Mark 9:42-50
Wednesday 119:97-120 □ 81, 82
Isa. 59:15b-21 2 Tim. 1:15—2:13 Mark 10:1-16
Thursday [83] or 146, 147 □ 85, 86
Isa. 60:1-17 2 Tim. 2:14-26 Mark 10:17-31
Friday 88 □ 91, 92
Isa. 61:1-9 2 Tim. 3:1-17 Mark 10:32-45
Saturday 87, 90 □ 136
Isa. 61:10—62:5 2 Tim. 4:1-8 Mark 10:46-52

Week of 6 Epiphany
Sunday 66, 67 □ 19, 46
Isa. 62:6-12 1 John 2:3-11 John 8:12-19
Monday 89:1-18 □ 89:19-52
Isa. 63:1-6 1 Tim. 1:1-17 Mark 11:1-11
Tuesday 97, 99, [100] □ 94, [95]
Isa. 63:7-14 1 Tim. 1:18—2:8 Mark 11:12-26
Wednesday 101, 109:1-4(5-19)20-30 □ 119:121-144
Isa 63:15—64:9 1 Tim. 3:1-16 Mark 11:27—12:12
Thursday 105:1-22 □ 105:23-45
Isa. 65:1-12 1 Tim. 4:1-16 Mark 12:13-27
Friday 102 □ 107:1-32
Isa. 65:17-25 1 Tim 5:17-22(23-25) Mark 12:28-34
Saturday 107:33-43, 108:1-6(7-13) □ 33
Isa. 66:1-6 1 Tim. 6:6-21 Mark 12:35-44

Week of 7 Epiphany
Sunday 118 □ 145
Isa. 66:7-14 1 John 3:4-10 John 10:7-16
Monday 106:1-18 □ 106:19-48
Ruth 1:1-14 2 Cor. 1:1-11 Matt. 5:1-12
Tuesday [120], 121, 122, 123 □ 124, 125, 126, [127]
Ruth 1:15-22 2 Cor. 1:12-22 Matt. 5:13-20
Wednesday 119:145-176 □ 128, 129, 130
Ruth 2:1-13 2 Cor. 1:23—2:17 Matt. 5:21-26
Thursday 131, 132, [133] □ 134, 135
Ruth 2:14-23 2 Cor. 3:1-18 Matt. 5:27-37
Friday 140, 142 □ 141, 143:1-11(12)
Ruth 3:1-18 2 Cor. 4:1-12 Matt. 5:38-48
Saturday 137:1-6(7-9), 144 □ 104
Ruth 4:1-17 2 Cor. 4:13—5:10 Matt. 6:1-6

Week of 8 Epiphany
Sunday 146, 147 □ 111, 112, 113
Deut. 4:1-9 2 Tim. 4:1-8 John 12:1-8
Monday 1, 2, 3 □ 4, 7
Deut. 4:9-14 2 Cor. 10:1-18 Matt. 6:7-15
Tuesday 5, 6 □ 10, 11
Deut. 4:15-24 2 Cor. 11:1-21a Matt. 6:16-23
Wednesday 119:1-24 □ 12, 13, 14
Deut. 4:25-31 2 Cor. 11:21b-33 Matt. 6:24-34
Thursday 18:1-20 □ 18:21-50
Deut. 4:32-40 2 Cor. 12:1-10 Matt. 7:1-12
Friday 16, 17 □ 22
Deut. 5:1-22 2 Cor. 12:11-21 Matt. 7:13-21
Saturday 20, 21:1-7(8-14) □ 110:1-5(6-7), 116, 117
Deut. 5:22-33 2 Cor. 13:1-14 Matt. 7:22-29

Week of Last Epiphany
Sunday 148, 149, 150 □ 114, 115
 Deut. 6:1-9 Heb. 12:18-29 John 12:24-32
Monday 25 □ 9, 15
Deut. 6:10-15 Heb. 1:1-14 John 1:1-18
Tuesday 26, 28 □ 36, 39
Deut. 6:16-25 Heb. 2:1-10 John 1:19-28

The Season after Pentecost
Eve of Trinity Sunday ——— ☐ 104
Ecclus. 42:15-25 Eph. 3:14-21
Trinity Sunday 146, 147 ☐ 111, 112, 113
Ecclus. 43:1-12(27-33) Eph. 4:1-16 John 1:1-18
On the weekdays which follow, the Readings are taken from the numbered Proper (two through seven)
which corresponds most closely to the date of Trinity Sunday.
Proper 1 *Week of the Sunday closest to May 11*
Monday 106:1-18 ☐ 106:19-48
Isa. 63:7-14 2 Tim. 1:1-14 Luke 11:24-36
Tuesday [120], 121, 122, 123 ☐ 124, 125, 126, [127]
Isa. 63:15—64:9 2 Tim. 1:15—2:13 Luke 11:37-52
Wednesday 119:145-176 ☐ 128, 129, 130
Isa. 65:1-12 2 Tim. 2:14-26 Luke 11:53—12:12
Thursday 131, 132, [133] ☐ 134, 135
Isa. 65:17-25 2 Tim. 3:1-17 Luke 12:13-31
Friday 140, 142 ☐ 141, 143:1-11(12)
Isa. 66:1-6 2 Tim. 4:1-8 Luke 12:32-48
Saturday 137:1-6(7-9), 144 ☐ 104
Isa. 66:7-14 2 Tim. 4:9-22 Luke 12:49-59
Proper 2 *Week of the Sunday closest to May 18*
Monday 1, 2, 3 ☐ 4, 7
Ruth 1:1-18 1 Tim. 1:1-17 Luke 13:1-9
Tuesday 5, 6 ☐ 10, 11
Ruth 1:19—2:13 1 Tim. 1:18—2:8 Luke 13:10-17
Wednesday 119:1-24 ☐ 12, 13, 14
Ruth 2:14-23 1 Tim. 3:1-16 Luke 13:18-30
Thursday 18:1-20 ☐ 18:21-50
Ruth 3:1-18 1 Tim. 4:1-16 Luke 13:31-35
Friday 16, 17 ☐ 22
Ruth 4:1-17 1 Tim. 5:17-22(23-25) Luke 14:1-11
Saturday 20, 21:1-7(8-14) ☐ 110:1-5(6-7), 116, 117
Deut. 1:1-8 1 Tim. 6:6-21 Luke 14:12-24
Proper 3 *Week of the Sunday closest to May 25*
Sunday 148, 149, 150 ☐ 114, 115
Deut. 4:1-9 Rev. 7:1-4,9-17 Matt. 12:33-45
Monday 25 ☐ 9, 15
Deut. 4:9-14 2 Cor. 1:1-11 Luke 14:25-35
Tuesday 26, 28 ☐ 36, 39
Deut. 4:15-24 2 Cor. 1:12-22 Luke 15:1-10
Wednesday 38 ☐ 119:25-48
Deut. 4:25-31 2 Cor. 1:23—2:17 Luke 15:1-2,11-32
Thursday 37:1-18 ☐ 37:19-42
Deut. 4:32-40 2 Cor. 3:1-18 Luke 16:1-9
Friday 31 ☐ 35
Deut. 5:1-22 2 Cor. 4:1-12 Luke 16:10-17(18)
Saturday 30, 32 ☐ 42, 43
Deut. 5:22-33 2 Cor. 4:13—5:10 Luke 16:19-31

Proper 4 *Week of the Sunday closest to June 1*
Sunday 63:1-8(9-11),98 □ 103
Deut. 11:1-12 Rev. 10:1-11 Matt. 13:44-58
Monday 41,52 □ 44
Deut. 11:13-19 2 Cor 5:11—6:2 Luke 17:1-10
Tuesday 45 □ 47,48
Deut. 12:1-12 2 Cor. 6:3-13(14—7:1) Luke 17:11-19
Wednesday 119:49-72 □ 49,[53]
Deut. 13:1-11 2 Cor. 7:2-16 Luke 17:20-37
Thursday 50 □ [59,60] or 8, 84
Deut. 16:18-20, 17:14-20 2 Cor. 8:1-16 Luke 18:1-8
Friday 40, 54 □ 51
Deut. 26:1-11 2 Cor. 8:16-24 Luke 18:9-14
Saturday 55 □ 138,139:1-17(18-23)
Deut. 29:2-15 2 Cor. 9:1-15 Luke 18:15-30
Proper 5 *Week of the Sunday closest to June 8*
Sunday 24, 29 □ 8, 84
Deut. 29:16-29 Rev. 12:1-12 Matt. 15:29-39
Monday 56, 57, [58] □ 64, 65
Deut. 30:1-10 2 Cor. 10:1-18 Luke 18:31-43
Tuesday 61, 62 □ 68:1-20(21-23)24-36
Deut. 30:11-20 2 Cor. 11:1-21a Luke 19:1-10
Wednesday 72 □ 119:73-96
Deut. 31:30—32:14 2 Cor. 11:21b-33 Luke 19:11-27
Thursday [70], 71 □ 74
Ecclus. 44:19—45:5 2 Cor. 12:1-10 Luke 19:28-40
Friday 69:1-23(24-30)31-38 □ 73
Ecclus. 45:6-16 2 Cor. 12:11-21 Luke 19:41-48
Saturday 75, 76 □ 23, 27
Ecclus. 46:1-10 2 Cor. 13:1-14 Luke 20:1-8
Proper 6 *Week of the Sunday closest to June 15*
Sunday 93, 96 □ 34
Ecclus. 46:11-20 Rev. 15:1-8 Matt. 18:1-14
Monday 80 □ 77, [79]
1 Samuel 1:1-20 Acts 1:1-14 Luke 20:9-19
Tuesday 78:1-39 □ 78:40-72
1 Samuel 1:21—2:11 Acts 1:15-26 Luke 20:19-26
Wednesday 119:97-120 □ 81, 82
1 Samuel 2:12-26 Acts 2:1-21 Luke 20:27-40
Thursday [83] or 34 □ 85, 86
1 Samuel 2:27-36 Acts 2:22-36 Luke 20:41—21:4
Friday 88 □ 91, 92
1 Samuel 3:1-21 Acts 2:37-47 Luke 21:5-19
Saturday 87, 90 □ 136
1 Samuel 4:1b-11 Acts 4:32—5:11 Luke 21:20-28

Proper 7 *Week of the Sunday closest to June 22*
Sunday 66, 67 ☐ 19, 46
1 Samuel 4:12-22 James 1:1-18 Matt. 19:23-30
Monday 89:1-18 ☐ 89:19-52
1 Samuel 5:1-12 Acts 5:12-26 Luke 21:29-36
Tuesday 97, 99, [100] ☐ 94, [95]
1 Samuel 6:1-16 Acts 5:27-42 Luke 21:37—22:13
Wednesday 101, 109:1-4(5-19)20-30 ☐ 119:121-144
1 Samuel 7:2-17 Acts 6:1-15 Luke 22:14-23
Thursday 105:1-22 ☐ 105:23-45
1 Samuel 8:1-22 Acts 6:15—7:16 Luke 22:24-30
Friday 102 ☐ 107:1-32
1 Samuel 9:1-14 Acts 7:17-29 Luke 22:31-38
Saturday 107:33-43, 108:1-6(7-13) ☐ 33
1 Samuel 9:15—10:1 Acts 7:30-43 Luke 22:39-51
Proper 8 *Week of the Sunday closest to June 29*
Sunday 118 ☐ 145
1 Samuel 10:1-16 Rom. 4:13-25 Matt. 21:23-32
Monday 106:1-18 ☐ 106:19-48
1 Samuel 10:17-27 Acts 7:44—8:1a Luke 22:52-62
Tuesday [120], 121, 122, 123 ☐ 124, 125, 126, [127]
1 Samuel 11:1-15 Acts 8:1-13 Luke 22:63-71
Wednesday 119:145-176 ☐ 128, 129, 130
1 Samuel 12:1-6,16-25 Acts 8:14-25 Luke 23:1-12
Thursday 131, 132, [133] ☐ 134, 135
1 Samuel 13:5-18 Acts 8:26-40 Luke 23:13-25
Friday 140, 142 ☐ 141, 143:1-11(12)
1 Samuel 13:19—14:15 Acts 9:1-9 Luke 23:26-31
Saturday 137:1-6(7-9), 144 ☐ 104
1 Samuel 14:16-30 Acts 9:10-19a Luke 23:32-43
Proper 9 *Week of the Sunday closest to July 6*
Sunday 146, 147 ☐ 111, 112, 113
1 Samuel 14:36-45 Rom. 5:1-11 Matt. 22:1-14
Monday 1, 2, 3 ☐ 4, 7
1 Samuel 15:1-3,7-23 Acts 9:19b-31 Luke 23:44-56a
Tuesday 5, 6 ☐ 10, 11
1 Samuel 15:24-35 Acts 9:32-43 Luke 23:56b—24:11
Wednesday 119:1-24 ☐ 12, 13, 14
1 Samuel 16:1-13 Acts 10:1-16 Luke 24:12-35
Thursday 18:1-20 ☐ 18:21-50
1 Samuel 16:14—17:11 Acts 10:17-33 Luke 24:36-53
Friday 16, 17 ☐ 22
1 Samuel 17:17-30 Acts 10:34-48 Mark 1:1-13
Saturday 20, 21:1-7(8-14) ☐ 110:1-5(6-7), 116, 117
1 Samuel 17:31-49 Acts 11:1-18 Mark 1:14-28

Proper 10 *Week of the Sunday closest to July 13*
Sunday 148, 149, 150 □ 114, 115
1 Samuel 17:50—18:4 Rom. 10:4-17 Matt. 23:29-39
Monday 25 □ 9, 15
1 Samuel 18:5-16,27b-30 Acts 11:19-30 Mark 1:29-45
Tuesday 26, 28 □ 36, 39
1 Samuel 19:1-18 Acts 12:1-17 Mark 2:1-12
Wednesday 38 □ 119:25-48
1 Samuel 20:1-23 Acts 12:18-25 Mark 2:13-22
Thursday 37:1-18 □ 37:19-42
1 Samuel 20:24-42 Acts 13:1-12 Mark 2:23—3:6
Friday 31 □ 35
1 Samuel 21:1-15 Acts 13:13-25 Mark 3:7-19a
Saturday 30, 32 □ 42, 43
1 Samuel 22:1-23 Acts 13:26-43 Mark 3:19b-35
Proper 11 *Week of the Sunday closest to July 20*
Sunday 63:1-8(9-11),98 □ 103
1 Samuel 23:7-18 Rom. 11:33—12:2 Matt. 25:14-30
Monday 41,52 □ 44
1 Samuel 24:1-22 Acts 13:44-52 Mark 4:1-20
Tuesday 45 □ 47,48
1 Samuel 25:1-22 Acts 14:1-18 Mark 4:21-34
Wednesday 119:49-72 □ 49,[53]
1 Samuel 25:23-44 Acts 14:19-28 Mark 4:35-41
Thursday 50 □ [59,60] or 66, 67
1 Samuel 28:3-20 Acts 15:1-11 Mark 5:1-20
Friday 40,54 □ 51
1 Samuel 31:1-13 Acts 15:12-21 Mark 5:21-43
Saturday 55 □ 138,139:1-17(18-23)
2 Samuel 1:1-16 Acts 15:22-35 Mark 6:1-13
Proper 12 *Week of the Sunday closest to July 27*
Sunday 24, 29 □ 8, 84
2 Samuel 1:17-27 Rom. 12:9-21 Matt. 25:31-46
Monday 56, 57, [58] □ 64, 65
2 Samuel 2:1-11 Acts 15:36—16:5 Mark 6:14-29
Tuesday 61, 62 □ 68:1-20(21-23)24-36
2 Samuel 3:6-21 Acts 16:6-15 Mark 6:30-46
Wednesday 72 □ 119:73-96
2 Samuel 3:22-39 Acts 16:16-24 Mark 6:47-56
Thursday [70], 71 □ 74
2 Samuel 4:1-12 Acts 16:25-40 Mark 7:1-23
Friday 69:1-23(24-30)31-38 □ 73
2 Samuel 5:1-12 Acts 17:1-15 Mark 7:24-37
Saturday 75, 76 □ 23, 27
2Samuel 5:22—6:11 Acts 17:16-34 Mark 8:1-10

Proper 13 *Week of the Sunday closest to August 3*
Sunday 93, 96 ☐ 34
2 Samuel 6:12-23 Rom. 4:7-12 John 1:43-51
Monday 80 ☐ 77, [79]
2 Samuel 7:1-17 Acts 18:1-11 Mark 8:11-21
Tuesday 78:1-39 ☐ 78:40-72
2 Samuel 7:18-29 Acts 18:12-28 Mark 8:22-33
Wednesday 119:97-120 ☐ 81, 82
2 Samuel 9:1-13 Acts 19:1-10 Mark 8:34—9:1
Thursday [83] or 145 ☐ 85, 86
2 Samuel 11:1-27 Acts 19:11-20 Mark 9:2-13
Friday 88 ☐ 91, 92
2 Samuel 12:1-14 Acts 19:21-41 Mark 9:14-29
Saturday 87, 90 ☐ 136
2 Samuel 12:15-31 Acts 20:1-16 Mark 9:30-41
Proper 14 *Week of the Sunday closest to August 10*
Sunday 66, 67 ☐ 19, 46
2 Samuel 13:1-22 Rom. 15:1-13 John 3:22-36
Monday 89:1-18 ☐ 89:19-52
2 Samuel 13:23-39 Acts 20:17-38 Mark 9:42-50
Tuesday 97, 99, [100] ☐ 94, [95]
2 Samuel 14:1-20 Acts 21:1-14 Mark 10:1-16
Wednesday 101, 109:1-4(5-19)20-30 ☐ 119:121-144
2 Samuel 14:21-33 Acts 21:15-26 Mark 10:17-31
Thursday 105:1-22 ☐ 105:23-45
2 Samuel 15:1-18 Acts 21:27-36 Mark 10:32-45
Friday 102 ☐ 107:1-32
2 Samuel 15:19-37 Acts 21:37—22:16 Mark 10:46-52
Saturday 107:33-43, 108:1-6(7-13) ☐ 33
2Samuel 16:1-23 Acts 22:17-29 Mark 11:1-11
Proper 15 *Week of the Sunday closest to August 17*
Sunday 118 ☐ 145
2 Samuel 17:1-23 Gal. 3:6-14 John 5:30-47
Monday 106:1-18 ☐ 106:19-48
2 Samuel 17:24—18:8 Acts 22:30—23:11 Mark 11:12-26
Tuesday [120], 121, 122, 123 ☐ 124, 125, 126, [127]
2 Samuel 18:9-18 Acts 23:12-24 Mark 11:27—12:12
Wednesday 119:145-176 ☐ 128, 129, 130
2 Samuel 18:19-23 Acts 23:23-35 Mark 12:13-27
Thursday 131, 132, [133] ☐ 134, 135
2 Samuel 19:1-23 Acts 24:1-23 Mark 12:28-34
Friday 140, 142 ☐ 141, 143:1-11(12)
2 Samuel 19:24-43 Acts 24:24—25:12 Mark 12:35-44
Saturday 137:1-6(7-9), 144 ☐ 104
2 Samuel 23:1-17,13-17 Acts 25:13-27 Mark 13:1-13

Proper 16 *Week of the Sunday closest to August 24*
Sunday 146, 147 □ 111, 112, 113
2 Samuel 24:1-2,10-25 Gal. 3:23—4:7 John 8:12-20
Monday 1, 2, 3 □ 4, 7
1 Kings 1:5-31 Acts 26:1-23 Mark 13:14-27
Tuesday 5, 6 □ 10, 11
1 Kings 1:38—2:4 Acts 26:24—27:8 Mark 13:28-37
Wednesday 119:1-24 □ 12, 13, 14
1 Kings 3:1-15 Acts 27:9-26 Mark 14:1-11
Thursday 18:1-20 □ 18:21-50
1 Kings 3:16-28 Acts 27:27-44 Mark 14:12-26
Friday 16, 17 □ 22
1 Kings 5:1—6:1,7 Acts 28:1-16 Mark 14:27-42
Saturday 20, 21:1-7(8-14) □ 110:1-5(6-7), 116, 117
1 Kings 7:51—8:21 Acts 28:17-31 Mark 14:43-52
Proper 17 *Week of the Sunday closest to August 31*
Sunday 148, 149, 150 □ 114, 115
1 Kings 8:22-30(31-40) 1 Tim. 4:7b-16 John 8:47-59
Monday 25 □ 9, 15
2 Chron. 6:32—7:7 James 2:1-13 Mark 14:53-65
Tuesday 26, 28 □ 36, 39
1 Kings 8:65—9:9 James 2:14-26 Mark 14:66-72
Wednesday 38 □ 119:25-48
1 Kings 9:24—10:13 James 3:1-12 Mark 15:1-11
Thursday 37:1-18 □ 37:19-42
1 Kings 11:1-13 James 3:13—4:12 Mark 15:12-21
Friday 31 □ 35
1 Kings 11:26-43 James 4:13—5:6 Mark 15:22-32
Saturday 30, 32 □ 42, 43
1 Kings 12:1-20 James 5:7-12,19-20 Mark 15:33-39
Proper 18 *Week of the Sunday closest to September 7*
Sunday 63:1-8(9-11), 98 □ 103
1 Kings 12:21-33 Acts 4:18-31 John 10:31-42
Monday 41, 52 □ 44
1 Kings 13:1-10 Phil. 1:1-11 Mark 15:40-47
Tuesday 45 □ 47, 48
1 Kings 16:23-34 Phil. 1:12-30 Mark 16:1-8(9-20)
Wednesday 119:49-72 □ 49,[53]
1 Kings 17:1-24 Phil. 2:1-11 Matt. 2:1-12
Thursday 50 □ [59,60] or 93, 96
1 Kings 18:1-19 Phil. 2:12-30 Matt. 2:13-23
Friday 40,54 □ 51
1 Kings 18:20-40 Phil. 3:1-16 Matt. 3:1-12
Saturday 55 □ 138,139:1-17(18-23)
1 Kings 18:41—19:8 Phil. 3:17—4:7 Matt. 3:13-17

Proper 19 *Week of the Sunday closest to September 14*
Sunday 24, 29 ☐ 8, 84
1 Kings 19:8-21 Acts 5:34-42 John 11:45-47
Monday 56, 57, [58] ☐ 64, 65
1 Kings 21:1-16 1 Cor. 1:1-19 Matt. 4:1-11
Tuesday 61, 62 ☐ 68:1-20(21-23)24-36
1 Kings 21:17-29 1 Cor. 1:20-31 Matt. 4:12-17
Wednesday 72 ☐ 119:73-96
1 Kings 22:1-28 1 Cor. 2:1-13 Matt. 4:18-25
Thursday [70], 71 ☐ 74
1 Kings 22:29-45 1 Cor. 2:14—3:15 Matt. 5:1-10
Friday 69:1-23(24-30)31-38 ☐ 73
2 Kings 1:2-17 1 Cor. 3:16-23 Matt. 5:11-16
Saturday 75, 76 ☐ 23, 27
2 Kings 2:1-18 1 Cor. 4:1-7 Matt. 5:17-20
Proper 20 *Week of the Sunday closest to September 21*
Sunday 93, 96 ☐ 34
2 Kings 4:8-37 Acts 9:10-31 Luke 3:7-18
Monday 80 ☐ 77, [79]
2 Kings 5:1-19 1 Cor. 4:8-21 Matt. 5:21-26
Tuesday 78:1-39 ☐ 78:40-72
2 Kings 5:19-27 1 Cor. 5:1-8 Matt. 5:27-37
Wednesday 119:97-120 ☐ 81, 82
2 Kings 6:1-23 1 Cor. 5:9—6:8 Matt. 5:38-48
Thursday [83] or 146, 147 ☐ 85, 86
2 *Kings* 9:1-16 1 Cor. 6:12-20 Matt. 6:1-6,16-18
Friday 88 ☐ 91, 92
2 Kings 9:17-37 1 Cor. 7:1-9 Matt. 6:7-15
Saturday 87, 90 ☐ 136
2Kings 11:1-20a 1 Cor. 7:10-24 Matt. 6:19-24
Proper 21 *Week of the Sunday closest to September 28*
Sunday 66, 67 ☐ 19, 46
2 Kings 17:1-18 Acts 9:36-43 Luke 5:1-11
Monday 89:1-18 ☐ 89:19-52
2 Kings 17:24-41 1 Cor. 7:25-31 Matt. 6:25-34
Tuesday 97, 99, [100] ☐ 94, [95]
2 Chron. 29:1-3; 1 Cor. 7:32-40 Matt. 7:1-12
 30:1(2-9)10-27
Wednesday 101, 109:1-4(5-19)20-30 ☐ 119:121-144
2 Kings 18:9-25 1 Cor. 8:1-13 Matt. 7:13-21
Thursday 105:1-22 ☐ 105:23-45
2 Kings 18:28-37 1 Cor. 9:1-15 Matt. 7:22-29
Friday 102 ☐ 107:1-32
2 Kings 19:1-20 1 Cor. 9:16-27 Matt. 8:1-17
Saturday 107:33-43, 108:1-6(7-13) ☐ 33
2 Kings 19:21-36 1 Cor. 10:1-13 Matt:8:18-27

Proper 22 *Week of the Sunday closest to October 5*
Sunday 118 ☐ 145
2 Kings 20:1-21 Acts 12:1-17 Luke 7:11-17
Monday 106:1-18 ☐ 106:19-48
2 Kings 21:1-18 1 Cor. 10:14—11:1 Matt. 8:28-34
Tuesday [120], 121, 122, 123 ☐ 124, 125, 126, [127]
2 Kings 22:1-13 1 Cor. 11:2,17-22 Matt. 9:1-8
Wednesday 119:145-176 ☐ 128, 129, 130
2 Kings 22:14—23:3 1 Cor. 11:23-34 Matt. 9:9-17
Thursday 131, 132, [133] ☐ 134, 135
2 Kings 23:4-25 1 Cor. 12:1-11 Matt. 9:18-26
Friday 140, 142 ☐ 141, 143:1-11(12)
2 Kings 23:36—24:17 1 Cor. 12:12-26 Matt. 9:27-34
Saturday 137:1-6(7-9), 144 ☐ 104
Jer. 35:1-19 1 Cor. 12:27—13:3 Matt. 9:35—10:4
Proper 23 *Week of the Sunday closest to October 12*
Sunday 146, 147 ☐ 111, 112, 113
Jer. 36:1-10 Acts 14:8-18 Luke 7:36-50
Monday 1, 2, 3 ☐ 4, 7
Jer. 36:11-26 1 Cor. 13:(1-3)4-13 Matt. 10:5-15
Tuesday 5, 6 ☐ 10, 11
Jer. 36:27—37:2 1 Cor. 14:1-12 Matt. 10:16-23
Wednesday 119:1-24 ☐ 12, 13, 14
Jer. 37:3-21 1 Cor. 14:13-25 Matt. 10:24-33
Thursday 18:1-20 ☐ 18:21-50
Jer. 38:1-13 1 Cor. 14:26-33a, 37-40 Matt. 10:34-42
Friday 16, 17 ☐ 22
Jer. 38:14-28 1 Cor. 15:1-11 Matt. 11:1-6
Saturday 20, 21:1-7(8-14) ☐ 110:1-5(6-7), 116, 117
2 Kings 25:8-12, 22-26 1 Cor. 15:12-29 Matt. 11:7-15
Proper 24 *Week of the Sunday closest to October 19*
Sunday 148, 149, 150 ☐ 114, 115
Jer. 29:1,4-14 Acts 16:6-15 Luke 10:1-12,17-20
Monday 25 ☐ 9, 15
Jer. 44:1-14 1 Cor. 15:30-41 Matt. 11:16-24
Tuesday 26, 28 ☐ 36, 39
Lam. 1:1-5(6-9)10-12 1 Cor. 15:41-50 Matt. 11:25-30
Wednesday 38 ☐ 119:25-48
Lam. 2:8-15 1 Cor. 15:51-58 Matt. 12:1-14
Thursday 37:1-18 ☐ 37:19-42
Ezra 1:1-11 1 Cor. 16:1-9 Matt. 12:15-21
Friday 31 ☐ 35
Ezra 3:1-13 1 Cor. 16:10-24 Matt. 12:22-32
Saturday 30, 32 ☐ 42, 43
Ezra 4:7,11-24 Philemon 1-25 Matt. 12:33-42

Proper 25 *Week of the Sunday closest to October 26*
Sunday 63:1-8(9-11),98 ☐ 103
Haggai 1:1—2:9 Acts 18:24—19:7 Luke 10:25-37
Monday 41,52 ☐ 44
Zech. 1:7-17 Rev. 1:4-20 Matt. 12:43-50
Tuesday 45 ☐ 47,48
Ezra 5:1-17 Rev. 4:1-11 Matt. 13:1-9
Wednesday 119:49-72 ☐ 49,[53]
Ezra 6:1-22 Rev. 5:1-10 Matt. 13:10-17
Thursday 50 ☐ [59,60] or 33
Neh. 1-1:11 Rev. 5:11—6:11 Matt. 13:18-23
Friday 40,54 ☐ 51
Neh. 2:1-20 Rev. 6:12—7:4 Matt. 13:24-30
Saturday 55 ☐ 138,139:1-17(18-23)
Neh. 4:1-23 Rev. 7:(4-8)9-17 Matt. 13:31-35
Proper 26 *Week of the Sunday closest to November 2*
Sunday 24, 29 ☐ 8, 84
Neh. 5:1-19 Acts 20:7-12 Luke 12:22-31
Monday 56, 57, [58] ☐ 64, 65
Neh. 6:1-19 Rev. 10:1-11 Matt. 13:36-43
Tuesday 61, 62 ☐ 68:1-20(21-23)24-36
Neh. 12:27-31a,42b-47 Rev. 11:1-19 Matt. 13:44-52
Wednesday 72 ☐ 119:73-96
Neh. 13:4-22 Rev. 12:1-12 Matt. 13:53-58
Thursday [70], 71 ☐ 74
Ezra 7:(1-10)11-26 Rev. 14:1-13 Matt. 14:1-12
Friday 69:1-23(24-30)31-38 ☐ 73
Ezra 7:27-28, 8:21-36 Rev. 15:1-8 Matt. 14:13-21
Saturday 75, 76 ☐ 23, 27
Ezra 9:1-15 Rev. 17:1-14 Matt. 14:22-36
Proper 27 *Week of the Sunday closest to November 9*
Sunday 93, 96 ☐ 34
Ezra 10:1-17 Acts 24:10-21 Luke 14:12-24
Monday 80 ☐ 77, [79]
Neh. 9:1-15(16-25) Rev. 18:1-8 Matt. 15:1-20
Tuesday 78:1-39 ☐ 78:40-72
Neh. 9:26-38 Rev. 18:9-20 Matt. 15:21-28
Wednesday 119:97-120 ☐ 81, 82
Neh. 7:73b—8:3,5-18 Rev. 18:21-24 Matt. 15:29-39
Thursday [83] or 23,27 ☐ 85, 86
1 Macc. 1:1-28 Rev. 19:1-10 Matt. 16:1-12
Friday 88 ☐ 91, 92
1 Macc. 1:41-63 Rev. 19:11-16 Matt. 16:13-20
Saturday 87, 90 ☐ 136
1 Macc. 2:1-28 Rev. 20:1-6 Matt. 16:21-28

Proper 28 *Week of the Sunday closest to November 16*
Sunday 66, 67 □ 19, 46
1 Macc. 2:29-43,49-50 Acts 28:14b-23 Luke 16:1-13
Monday 89:1-18 □ 89:19-52
1 Macc. 3:1-24 Rev. 20:7-15 Matt. 17:1-13
Tuesday 97, 99, [100] □ 94, [95]
1 Macc. 3:25-41 Rev. 21:1-8 Matt. 17:14-21
Wednesday 101, 109:1-4(5-19)20-30 □ 119:121-144
1 Macc. 3:42-60 Rev. 21:9-21 Matt. 17:22-27
Thursday 105:1-22 □ 105:23-45
1 Macc. 4:1-25 Rev. 21:22—22:5 Matt. 18:1-9
Friday 102 □ 107:1-32
1 Macc. 4:36-59 Rev. 22:6-13 Matt. 18:10-20
Saturday 107:33-43, 108:1-6(7-13) □ 33
Isa. 65:17-25 Rev. 22:14-21 Matt. 18:21-35
Proper 29 *Week of the Sunday closest to November 23*
Sunday 118 □ 145
Isa. 19:19-25 Rom. 15:5-13 Luke 19:11-27
Monday 106:1-18 □ 106:19-48
Joel 3:1-2,9-17 1 Pet. 1:1-12 Matt. 19:1-12
Tuesday [120], 121, 122, 123 □ 124, 125, 126, [127]
Nahum 1:1-13 1 Pet. 1:13-25 Matt. 19:13-22
Wednesday 119:145-176 □ 128, 129, 130
Obadiah 15-21 1 Pet. 2:1-10 Matt. 19:23-30
Thursday 131, 132, [133] □ 134, 135
Zeph. 3:1-13 1 Pet. 2:11-25 Matt. 20:1-16
Friday 140, 142 □ 141, 143:1-11(12)
Isa. 24:14-23 1 Pet. 3:13—4:6 Matt. 20:17-28
Saturday 137:1-6(7-9), 144 □ 104
Micah 7:11-20 1 Pet. 4:7-19 Matt. 20:29-34

Year Two

The Epiphany and Following
Epiphany 46, 97 □ 96, 100
Isa. 49:1-7 Rev. 21:22-27 Matt. 12:14-21
The Psalms and Readings for the dated days after the Epiphany
are used only until the following Saturday evening.
Jan. 7 103 □ 114, 115
Deut. 8:1-3 Col. 1:1-14 John 6:30-33,48-51
Jan. 8 117, 118 □ 112, 113
Exod. 17:1-7 Col. 1:15-23 John 7:37-52
Jan. 9 121, 122, 123 □ 131, 132
Isa. 45:14-19 Col. 1:24—2:7 John 8:12-19
Jan. 10 138, 139:1-17(18-23) □ 147
Jer. 23:1-8 Col. 2:8-23 John 10:7-17
Jan. 11 148, 150 □ 91, 92
Isa. 55:3-9 Col. 3:1-17 John 14:6-14
Jan. 12 98, 99, [100] □ ——
Gen. 49:1-2,8-12 Col 3:18—4:6 John 15:1-16
Eve of 1 Epiphany —— □ 104
Isa. 61:1-9 Gal. 3:23-29; 4:4-7

Week of 1 Epiphany
Sunday 146, 147 □ 111, 112, 113
Gen. 1:1—2:3 Eph. 1:3-14 John 1:29-34
Monday 1, 2, 3 □ 4, 7
Gen. 2:4-9(10-15)16-25 Heb. 1:1-14 John 1:1-18
Tuesday 5, 6 □ 10, 11
Gen. 3:1-24 Heb. 2:1-10 John 1:19-28
Wednesday 119:1-24 □ 12, 13, 14
Gen. 4:1-16 Heb. 2:11-18 John 1:(29-34)35-42
Thursday 18:1-20 □ 18:21-50
Gen. 4:17-26 Heb. 3:1-11 John 1:43-51
Friday 16, 17 □ 22
Gen. 6:1-8 Heb. 3:12-19 John 2:1-12
Saturday 20, 21:1-7(8-14) □ 110:1-5(6-7), 116, 117
Gen. 6:9-22 Heb. 4:1-13 John 2:13-22

Week of 2 Epiphany
Sunday 148, 149, 150 □ 114, 115
Gen. 7:1-10,17-23 Eph. 4:1-16 Mark 3:7-19
Monday 25 □ 9, 15
Gen. 8:6-22 Heb. 4:14—5:6 John 2:23—3:15
Tuesday 26, 28 □ 36, 39
Gen. 9:1-17 Heb. 5:7-14 John 3:16-21
Wednesday 38 □ 119:25-48
Gen. 9:18-29 Heb. 6:1-12 John 3:22-36
Thursday 37:1-18 □ 37:19-42
Gen. 11:1-9 Heb. 6:13-20 John 4:1-15
Friday 31 □ 35
Gen. 11:27—12:8 Heb. 7:1-17 John 4:16-26
Saturday 30, 32 □ 42, 43
Gen. 12:9—13:1 Heb. 7:18-28 John 4:27-42

Week of 3 Epiphany
Sunday 63:1-8(9-11), 98 ☐ 103
Gen. 13:2-18 Gal. 2:1-10 Mark 7:31-37
Monday 41, 52 ☐ 44
Gen. 14:(1-7)8-24 Heb. 8:1-13 John 4:43-54
Tuesday 45 ☐ 47, 48
Gen. 15:1-11,17-21 Heb. 9:1-14 John 5:1-18
Wednesday 119:49-72 ☐ 49, [53]
Gen. 16:1-14 Heb. 9:15-28 John 5:19-29
Thursday 50 ☐ [59, 60] or 118
Gen. 16:15—17:14 Heb. 10:1-10 John 5:30-47
Friday 40, 54 ☐ 51
Gen. 17:15-27 Heb. 10:11-25 John 6:1-15
Saturday 55 ☐ 138, 139:1-17(18-23)
Gen. 18:1-16 Heb. 10:26-39 John 6:16-27

Week of 4 Epiphany
Sunday 24, 29 ☐ 8, 84
Gen. 18:16-33 Gal. 5:13-25 Mark 8:22-30
Monday 56, 57, [58] ☐ 64, 65
Gen. 19:1-17(18-23)24-29 Heb. 11:1-12 John 6:27-40
Tuesday 61, 62 ☐ 68:1-20(21-23)24-36
Gen. 21:1-21 Heb. 11:13-22 John 6:41-51
Wednesday 72 ☐ 119:73-96
Gen. 22:1-18 Heb. 11:23-31 John 6:52-59
Thursday [70], 71 ☐ 74
Gen. 23:1-20 Heb. 11:32—12:2 John 6:60-71
Friday 69:1-23(24-30)31-38 ☐ 73
Gen. 24:1-27 Heb. 12:3-11 John 7:1-13
Saturday 75, 76 ☐ 23, 27
Gen. 24:28-38,49-51 Heb. 12:12-29 John 7:14-36

Week of 5 Epiphany
Sunday 93, 96 ☐ 34
Gen. 24:50-67 2 Tim. 2:14-21 Mark 10:13-22
Monday 80 ☐ 77, [79]
Gen. 25:19-34 Heb. 13:1-16 John 7:37-52
Tuesday 78:1-39 ☐ 78:40-72
Gen. 26:1-6,12-33 Heb. 13:17-25 John 7:53—8:11
Wednesday 119:97-120 ☐ 81, 82
Gen. 27:1-29 Rom. 12:1-8 John 8:12-20
Thursday [83] or 146, 147 ☐ 85, 86
Gen. 27:30-45 Rom. 12:9-21 John 8:21-32
Friday 88 ☐ 91, 92
Gen. 27:46—28:4,10-22 Rom. 13:1-14 John 8:33-47
Saturday 87, 90 ☐ 136
Gen. 29:1-20 Rom. 14:1-23 John 8:47-59

Week of 6 Epiphany
Sunday 66, 67 ☐ 19, 46
Gen. 29:20-35 1 Tim. 3:14—4:10 Mark 10:23-31
Monday 89:1-18 ☐ 89:19-52
Gen. 30:1-24 1 John 1:1-10 John 9:1-17
Tuesday 97, 99, [100] ☐ 94, [95]
Gen. 31:1-24 1 John 2:1-11 John 9:18-41
Wednesday 101, 109:1-4(5-19)20-30 ☐ 119:121-144
Gen. 31:25-50 1 John 2:12-17 John 10:1-18
Thursday 105:1-22 ☐ 105:23-45
Gen. 32:3-21 1 John 2:18-29 John 10:19-30
Friday 102 ☐ 107:1-32
Gen. 32:22—33:17 1 John 3:1-10 John 10:31-42
Saturday 107:33-43, 108:1-6(7-13) ☐ 33
Gen. 35:1-20 1 John 3:11-18 John 11:1-16

Week of 7 Epiphany
Sunday 118 ☐ 145
Prov. 1:20-33 2 Cor. 5:11-21 Mark 10:35-45
Monday 106:1-18 ☐ 106:19-48
Prov. 3:11-20 1 John 3:18—4:6 John 11:17-29
Tuesday [120], 121, 122, 123 ☐ 124, 125, 126, [127]
Prov. 4:1-27 1 John 4:7-21 John 11:30-44
Wednesday 119:145-176 ☐ 128, 129, 130
Prov. 6:1-19 1 John 5:1-12 John 11:45-54
Thursday 131, 132, [133] ☐ 134, 135
Prov. 7:1-27 1 John 5:13-21 John 11:55—12:8
Friday 140, 142 ☐ 141, 143:1-11(12)
Prov. 8:1-21 Philemon 1-25 John 12:9-19
Saturday 137:1-6(7-9), 144 ☐ 104
Prov. 8:22-36 2 Tim. 1:1-14 John 12:20-26

Week of 8 Epiphany
Sunday 146, 147 ☐ 111, 112, 113
Prov. 9:1-12 2 Cor. 9.6b-15 Mark 10:46-52
Monday 1, 2, 3 ☐ 4, 7
Prov. 10:1-12 2 Tim. 1:15—2:13 John 12:27-36a
Tuesday 5, 6 ☐ 10, 11
Prov. 15:16-33 2 Tim. 2:14-26 John 12:36b-50
Wednesday 119:1-24 ☐ 12, 13, 14
Prov. 17:1-20 2 Tim. 3:1-17 John 13:1-20
Thursday 18:1-20 ☐ 18:21-50
Prov. 21:30—22:6 2 Tim. 4:1-8 John 13:21-30
Friday 16, 17 ☐ 22
Prov. 23:19-21,29—24:2 2 Tim. 4:9-22 John 13:31-38
Saturday 20, 21:1-7(8-14) ☐ 110:1-5(6-7), 116, 117
Prov. 25:15-28 Phil. 1:1-11 John 18:1-14

Week of Last Epiphany

Sunday 148, 149, 150 □ 114, 115
Ecclus. 48:1-11 2 Cor. 3:7-18 Luke 9:18-27
Monday 25 □ 9, 15
Prov. 27:1-6,10-12 Phil. 2:1-13 John 18:15-18,25-27
Tuesday 26, 28 □ 36, 39 Prov. 30:1-4,24-33 Phil. 3:1-11 John 18:28-38

The Season after Pentecost
Eve of Trinity Sunday ——— □ 104
Ecclus. 42:15-25 Eph. 3:14-21
Trinity Sunday 146, 147 □ 111, 112, 113
Job 38:1-11,42:1-5 Rev. 19:4-16 John 1:29-34
On the weekdays which follow, the Readings are taken from the numbered Proper (two through seven)
which corresponds most closely to the date of Trinity Sunday
Proper 1 *Week of the Sunday closest to May 11*
Monday 106:1-18 □ 106:19-48
Ezek. 33:1-11 1 John 1:1-10 Matt. 9:27-34
Tuesday [120], 121, 122, 123 □ 124, 125, 126, [127]
Ezek. 33:21-33 1 John 2:1-11 Matt. 9:35—10:4
Wednesday 119:145-176 □ 128, 129, 130
Ezek. 34:1-16 1 John 2:12-17 Matt. 10:5-15
Thursday 131, 132, [133] □ 134, 135
Ezek. 37:21b-28 1 John 2:18-29 Matt. 10:16-23
Friday 140, 142 □ 141, 143:1-11(12)
Ezek. 39:21-29 1 John 3:1-10 Matt. 10:24-33
Saturday 137:1-6(7-9), 144 □ 104
Ezek. 47:1-12 1 John 3:11-18 Matt. 10:34-42
Proper 2 *Week of the Sunday closest to May 18*
Monday 1, 2, 3 □ 4, 7
Prov. 3:11-20 1 John 3:18—4:6 Matt. 11:1-6
Tuesday 5, 6 □ 10, 11
Prov. 4:1-27 1 John 4:7-21 Matt. 11:7-15
Wednesday 119:1-24 □ 12, 13, 14
Prov. 6:1-19 1 John 5:1-12 Matt. 11:16-24
Thursday 18:1-20 □ 18:21-50
Prov. 7:1-27 1 John 5:13-21 Matt. 11:25-30
Friday 16, 17 □ 22
Prov. 8:1-21 2 John 1-13 Matt. 12:1-14
Saturday 20, 21:1-7(8-14) □ 110:1-5(6-7), 116, 117
Prov. 8:22-36 3 John 1-15 Matt. 12:15-21
Proper 3 *Week of the Sunday closest to May 25*
Sunday 148, 149, 150 □ 114, 115
Prov. 9:1-12 Acts 8:14-25 Luke 10:25-28,38-42
Monday 25 □ 9, 15
Prov. 10:1-12 1 Tim. 1:1-17 Matt. 12:22-32
Tuesday 26, 28 □ 36, 39
Prov. 15:16-33 1 Tim. 1:18—2:8 Matt. 12:33-42
Wednesday 38 □ 119:25-48
Prov. 17:1-20 1 Tim. 3:1-16 Matt. 12:43-50
Thursday 37:1-18 □ 37:19-42
Prov. 21:30—22:6 1 Tim. 4:1-16 Matt. 13:24-30
Friday 31 □ 35
Prov. 23:19-21,29—24:2 1 Tim. 5:17-22(23-25) Matt. 13:31-35
Saturday 30, 32 □ 42, 43
Prov. 25:15-28 1 Tim. 6:6-21 Matt. 13:36-43

Proper 4 *Week of the Sunday closest to June 1*
Sunday 63:1-8(9-11),98 □ 103
Eccles. 1:1-11 Acts 8:26-40 Luke 11:1-13
Monday 41,52 □ 44
Eccles. 2:1-15 Gal. 1:1-17 Matt. 13:44-52
Tuesday 45 □ 47,48
Eccles. 2:16-26 Gal. 1:18—2:10 Matt. 13:53-58
Wednesday 119:49-72 □ 49,[53]
Eccles. 3:1-15 Gal. 2:11-21 Matt. 14:1-12
Thursday 50 □ [59,60] or 8, 84
Eccles. 3:16—4:3 Gal. 3:1-14 Mat. 14:13-21
Friday 40, 54 □ 51
Eccles. 5:1-7 Gal. 3:15-22 Matt. 14:22-36
Saturday 55 □ 138,139:1-17(18-23)
Eccles. 5:8-20 Gal. 3:23—4:11 Matt. 15:1-20
Proper 5 *Week of the Sunday closest to June 8*
Sunday 24, 29 □ 8, 84
Eccles. 6:1-12 Acts 10:9-23 Luke 12:32-40
Monday 56, 57, [58] □ 64, 65
Eccles. 7:1-14 Gal. 4:12-20 Matt. 15:21-28
Tuesday 61, 62 □ 68:1-20(21-23)24-36
Eccles. 8:14—9:10 Gal. 4:21-31 Matt. 15:29-39
Wednesday 72 □ 119:73-96
Eccles. 9:11-18 Gal. 5:1-15 Matt. 16:1-12
Thursday [70], 71 □ 74
Eccles. 11:1-8 Gal. 5:16-24 Matt. 16:13-20
Friday 69:1-23(24-30)31-38 □ 73
Eccles. 11:9—12:14 Gal. 5:25—6:10 Matt. 16:21-28
Saturday 75, 76 □ 23, 27
Num. 3:1-13 Gal. 6:11-18 Matt. 17:1-13
Proper 6 *Week of the Sunday closest to June 15*
Sunday 93, 96 □ 34
Num. 6:22-27 Acts 13:1-12 Luke 12:41-48
Monday 80 □ 77, [79]
Num. 9:15-23,10:29-36 Rom. 1:1-15 Matt. 17:14-21
Tuesday 78:1-39 □ 78:40-72
Num. 11:1-23 Rom. 1:16-25 Matt. 17:22-27
Wednesday 119:97-120 □ 81, 82
Num. 11:24-33(34-35) Rom. 1:28—2:11 Matt. 18:1-9
Thursday [83] or 34 □ 85, 86
Num. 12:1-16 Rom. 2:12-24 Matt. 18:10-20
Friday 88 □ 91, 92
Num. 13:1-3,21-30 Rom. 2:25—3:8 Matt. 18:21-35
Saturday 87, 90 □ 136
Num. 13:31—14:25 Rom. 3:9-20 Matt. 19:1-12

Proper 7 *Week of the Sunday closest to June 22*
Sunday 66, 67 □ 19, 46
Num. 14:26-45 Acts 15:1-12 Luke 12:49-56
Monday 89:1-18 □ 89:19-52
Num. 16:1-19 Rom. 3:21-31 Matt. 19:13-22
Tuesday 97, 99, [100] □ 94, [95]
Num. 16:20-35 Rom. 4:1-12 Matt. 19:23-30
Wednesday 101, 109:1-4(5-19)20-30 □ 119:121-144
Num. 16:36-50 Rom. 4:13-25 Matt. 20:1-16
Thursday 105:1-22 □ 105:23-45
Num. 17:1-11 Rom. 5:1-11 Matt. 20:17-28
Friday 102 □ 107:1-32
Num. 20:1-13 Rom. 5:12-21 Matt. 20:29-34
Saturday 107:33-43, 108:1-6(7-13) □ 33
Num. 20:14-29 Rom. 6:1-11 Matt. 21:1-11
Proper 8 *Week of the Sunday closest to June 29*
Sunday 118 □ 145
Num. 21:4-9,21-35 Acts 17:(12-21)22-34 Luke 13:10-17
Monday 106:1-18 □ 106:19-48
Num. 22:1-21 Rom. 6:12-23 Matt. 21:12-22
Tuesday [120], 121, 122, 123 □ 124, 125, 126, [127]
Num. 22:21-38 Rom. 7:1-12 Matt. 21:23-32
Wednesday 119:145-176 □ 128, 129, 130
Num. 22:41—23:12 Rom. 7:13-25 Matt. 21:33-46
Thursday 131, 132, [133] □ 134, 135
Num. 23:11-26 Rom. 8:1-11 Matt. 22:1-14
Friday 140, 142 □ 141, 143:1-11(12)
Num. 24:1-13 Rom. 8:12-17 Matt. 22:15-22
Saturday 137:1-6(7-9), 144 □ 104
Num. 24:12-25 Rom. 8:18-25 Matt. 22:23-40
Proper 9 *Week of the Sunday closest to July 6*
Sunday 146, 147 □ 111, 112, 113
Num. 27:12-23 Acts 19:11-20 Mark 1:14-20
Monday 1, 2, 3 □ 4, 7
Num. 32:1-6,16-27 Rom. 8:26-30 Matt. 23:1-12
Tuesday 5, 6 □ 10, 11
Num. 35:1-3,9-15,30-34 Rom. 8:31-39 Matt. 23:13-26
Wednesday 119:1-24 □ 12, 13, 14
Deut. 1:1-18 Rom. 9:1-18 Matt. 23:27-39
Thursday 18:1-20 □ 18:21-50
Deut. 3:18-28 Rom. 9:19-33 Matt. 24:1-14
Friday 16, 17 □ 22
Deut. 31:7-13, 24—32:4 Rom. 10:1-13 Matt. 24:15-31
Saturday 20, 21:1-7(8-14) □ 110:1-5(6-7), 116, 117
Deut. 34:1-12 Rom. 10:14-21 Matt. 24:32-51

Proper 10 *Week of the Sunday closest to July 13*
Sunday 148, 149, 150 ☐ 114, 115
Joshua 1:1-18 Acts 21:3-15 Mark 1:21-27
Monday 25 ☐ 9, 15
Joshua 2:1-14 Rom. 11:1-12 Matt. 25:1-13
Tuesday 26, 28 ☐ 36, 39
Joshua 2:15-24 Rom. 11:13-24 Matt. 25:14-30
Wednesday 38 ☐ 119:25-48
Joshua 3:1-13 Rom. 11:25-36 Matt. 25:31-46
Thursday 37:1-18 ☐ 37:19-42
Joshua 3:14—4:7 Rom. 12:1-8 Matt. 26:1-16
Friday 31 ☐ 35
Joshua 4:19—5:1,10-15 Rom. 12:9-21 Matt. 26:17-25
Saturday 30, 32 ☐ 42, 43
Joshua 6:1-14 Rom. 13:1-7 Matt. 26:26-35
Proper 11 *Week of the Sunday closest to July 20*
Sunday 63:1-8(9-11),98 ☐ 103
Joshua 6:15-27 Acts 22:30—23:11 Mark 2:1-12
Monday 41,52 ☐ 44
Joshua 7:1-13 Rom. 13:8-14 Matt. 26:36-46
Tuesday 45 ☐ 47,48
Joshua 8:1-22 Rom. 14:1-12 Matt. 26:47-56
Wednesday 119:49-72 ☐ 49,[53]
Joshua 8:30-35 Rom. 14:13-23 Matt. 26:57-68
Thursday 50 ☐ [59,60] or 66, 67
Joshua 9:3-21 Rom. 15:1-13 Matt. 26:69-75
Friday 40,54 ☐ 51
Joshua 9:22—10:15 Rom. 15:14-24 Matt. 27:1-10
Saturday 55 ☐ 138,139:1-17(18-23)
Joshua 23:1-16 Rom. 15:25-33 Matt. 27:11-23
Proper 12 *Week of the Sunday closest to July 27*
Sunday 24, 29 ☐ 8, 84
Joshua 24:1-15 Acts 28:23-31 Mark 2:23-28
Monday 56, 57, [58] ☐ 64, 65
Joshua 24:16-33 Rom. 16:1-16 Matt. 27:24-31
Tuesday 61, 62 ☐ 68:1-20(21-23)24-36
Judges 2:1-5,11-23 Rom. 16:17-27 Matt. 27:32-44
Wednesday 72 ☐ 119:73-96
Judges 3:12-30 Acts 1:1-14 Matt. 27:45-54
Thursday [70], 71 ☐ 74
Judges 4:4-23 Acts 1:15-26 Matt. 27:55-66
Friday 69:1-23(24-30)31-38 ☐ 73
Judges 5:1-18 Acts 2:1-21 Matt. 28:1-10
Saturday 75, 76 ☐ 23, 27
Judges 5:19-31 Acts 2:22-36 Matt. 28:11-20

Proper 13 *Week of the Sunday closest to August 3*
Sunday 93, 96 □ 34
Judges 6:1-24 2 Cor. 9:6-15 Mark 3:20-30
Monday 80 □ 77, [79]
Judges 6:25-40 Acts 2:37-47 John 1:1-18
Tuesday 78:1-39 □ 78:40-72
Judges 7:1-18 Acts 3:1-11 John 1:19-28
Wednesday 119:97-120 □ 81, 82
Judges 7:19—8:12 Acts 3:12-26 John 1:29-42
Thursday [83] or 145 □ 85, 86
Judges 8:22-35 Acts 4:1-12 John 1:43-51
Friday 88 □ 91, 92
Judges 9:1-16,19-21 Acts 4:13-31 John 2:1-12
Saturday 87, 90 □ 136
Judges 9:22-25,50-57 Acts 4:32—5:11 John 2:13-25
Proper 14 *Week of the Sunday closest to August 10*
Sunday 66, 67 □ 19, 46
Judges 11:1-11,29-40 2 Cor. 11:21b-31 Mark 4:35-41
Monday 89:1-18 □ 89:19-52
Judges 12:1-7 Acts 5:12-26 John 3:1-21
Tuesday 97, 99, [100] □ 94, [95]
Judges 13:1-15 Acts 5:27-42 John 3:22-36
Wednesday 101, 109:1-4(5-19)20-30 □ 119:121-144
Judges 13:15-24 Acts 6:1-15 John 4:1-26
Thursday 105:1-22 □ 105:23-45
Judges 14:1-19 Acts 6:15—7:16 John 4:27-42
Friday 102 □ 107:1-32
Judges 14:20—15:20 Acts 7:17-29 John 4:43-54
Saturday 107:33-43, 108:1-6(7-13) □ 33
Judges 16:1-14 Acts 7:30-43 John 5:1-18
Proper 15 *Week of the Sunday closest to August 17*
Sunday 118 □ 145
Judges 16:15-31 2 Cor. 13:1-11 Mark 5:25-34
Monday 106:1-18 □ 106:19-48
Judges 17:1-13 Acts 7:44—8:1a John 5:19-29
Tuesday [120], 121, 122, 123 □ 124, 125, 126, [127]
Judges 18:1-15 Acts 8:1-13 John 5:30-47
Wednesday 119:145-176 □ 128, 129, 130
Judges 18:16-31 Acts 8:14-25 John 6:1-15
Thursday 131, 132, [133] □ 134, 135
Job 1:1-22 Acts 8:26-40 John 6:16-27
Friday 140, 142 □ 141, 143:1-11(12)
Job 2:1-13 Acts 9:1-9 John 6:27-40
Saturday 137:1-6(7-9), 144 □ 104
Job 3:1-26 Acts 9:10-19a John 6:41-51

Proper 16 *Week of the Sunday closest to August 24*
Sunday 146, 147 □ 111, 112, 113
Job 4:1-6,12-21 Rev. 4:1-11 Mark 6:1-6a
Monday 1, 2, 3 □ 4, 7
Job 4:1,5:1-11,17-21,26-27 Acts 9:19b-31 John 6:52-59
Tuesday 5, 6 □ 10, 11
Job 6:1-4,8-15,21 Acts 9:32-43 John 6:60-71
Wednesday 119:1-24 □ 12, 13, 14
Job 6:1,7:1-21 Acts 10:1-16 John 7:1-13
Thursday 18:1-20 □ 18:21-50
Job 6:1,7:1-21 Acts 10:17-33 John 7:14-36
Friday 16, 17 □ 22
Job 9:1-15,32-35 Acts 10:34-48 John 7:37-52
Saturday 20, 21:1-7(8-14) □ 110:1-5(6-7), 116, 117
Job 9:1,10:1-9,16-22 Acts 11:1-18 John 8:12-20

Proper 17 *Week of the Sunday closest to August 31*
Sunday 148, 149, 150 □ 114, 115
Job 11:1-9,13-20 Rev. 5:1-14 Matt. 5:1-12
Monday 25 □ 9, 15
Job 12:1-6,13-25 Acts 11:19-30 John 8:21-32
Tuesday 26, 28 □ 36, 39
Job 12:1,13:3-17,21-27 Acts 12:1-17 John 8:33-47
Wednesday 38 □ 119:25-48
Job 12:1,14:1-22 Acts 12:18-25 John 8:47-59
Thursday 37:1-18 □ 37:19-42
Job 16:16-22,17:1,13-16 Acts 13:1-12 John 9:1-17
Friday 31 □ 35
Job 19:1-7,14-27 Acts 13:13-25 John 9:18-41
Saturday 30, 32 □ 42, 43
Job 22:1-4,21—23:7 Acts 13:26-43 John 10:1-18

Proper 18 *Week of the Sunday closest to September 7*
Sunday 63:1-8(9-11), 98 □ 103
Job 25:1-6,27:1-6 Rev. 14:1-7,13 Matt. 5:13-20
Monday 41, 52 □ 44
Job 32:1-10,19—33:1,19-28 Acts 13:44-52 John 10:19-30
Tuesday 45 □ 47, 48
Job 29:1-20 Acts 14:1-18 John 10:31-42
Wednesday 119:49-72 □ 49,[53]
Job 29:1,30:1-2,16-31 Acts 14:19-28 John 11:1-16
Thursday 50 □ [59,60] or 93, 96
Job 29:1,31:1-23 Acts 15:1-11 John 11:17-29
Friday 40,54 □ 51
Job 29:1,31:24-40 Acts 15:12-21 John 11:30-44
Saturday 55 □ 138,139:1-17(18-23)
Job 38:1-17 Acts 15:22-35 John 11:45-54

Proper 19 *Week of the Sunday closest to September 14*
Sunday 24, 29 ☐ 8, 84
Job 38:1,18-41 Rev. 18:1-8 Matt. 5:21-26
Monday 56, 57, [58] ☐ 64, 65
Job 40:1-24 Acts 15:36—16:5 John 11:55—12:8
Tuesday 61, 62 ☐ 68:1-20(21-23)24-36
Job 40:1,41:1-11 Acts 16:6-15 John 12:9-19
Wednesday 72 ☐ 119:73-96
Job 42:1-17 Acts 16:16-24 John 12:20-26
Thursday [70], 71 ☐ 74
Job 28:1-28 Acts 16:25-40 John 12:27-36a
Friday 69:1-23(24-30)31-38 ☐ 73
Esther 1:1-4,10-19* Acts 17:1-15 John 12:36b-43
Saturday 75, 76 ☐ 23, 27
Esther 2:5-8,15-23* Acts 17:16-34 John 12:44-50
Proper 20 *Week of the Sunday closest to September 21*
Sunday 93, 96 ☐ 34
Esther 3:1—4:3* James 1:19-27 Matt. 6:1-6,16-18
Monday 80 ☐ 77, [79]
Esther 4:4-17* Acts 18:1-11 Luke (1:1-4),3:1-14
Tuesday 78:1-39 ☐ 78:40-72
Esther 5:1-14* Acts 18:12-28 Luke 3:15-22
Wednesday 119:97-120 ☐ 81, 82
Esther 6:1-14* Acts 19:1-10 Luke 4:1-13
Thursday [83] or 146, 147 ☐ 85, 86
Esther 7:1-10* Acts 19:11-20 Luke 4:14-30
Friday 88 ☐ 91, 92
Esther 8:1-8,15-17* Acts 19:21-41 Luke 4:31-37
Saturday 87, 90 ☐ 136
Hosea 1:1—2:1 Acts 20:1-16 Luke 4:38-44
* *In place of Esther may be read Judith:*
F 4:1-15 Su 5:22–6:4, 10-21 Tu 8:9-17; 9:1,7-10 Th 12:1-20
Sa 5:1-21 M 7:1-7, 19-32 W 10:1-23 F 13:1-20
Proper 21 *Week of the Sunday closest to September 28*
Sunday 66, 67 ☐ 19, 46
Hosea 2:2-14 James 3:1-13 Matt. 13:44-52
Monday 89:1-18 ☐ 89:19-52
Hosea 2:14-23 Acts 20:17-38 Luke 5:1-11
Tuesday 97, 99, [100] ☐ 94, [95]
Hosea 4:1-10 Acts 21:1-14 Luke 5:12-26
Wednesday 101, 109:1-4(5-19)20-30 ☐ 119:121-144
Hosea 4:11-19 Acts 21:15-26 Luke 5:27-39
Thursday 105:1-22 ☐ 105:23-45
Hosea 5:8—6:6 Acts 21:27-36 Luke 6:1-11
Friday 102 ☐ 107:1-32
Hosea 10:1-15 Acts 21:37—22:16 Luke 6:12-26
Saturday 107:33-43, 108:1-6(7-13) ☐ 33
Hosea 11:1-9 Acts 22:17-29 Luke 6:27-38

Proper 22 *Week of the Sunday closest to October 5*
Sunday 118 □ 145
Hosea 13:4-14 1 Cor. 2:6-16 Matt. 14:1-12
Monday 106:1-18 □ 106:19-48
Hosea 14:1-9 Acts 22:30—23:11 Luke 6:39-49
Tuesday [120], 121, 122, 123 □ 124, 125, 126, [127]
Micah 1:1-9 Acts 23:12-24 Luke 7:1-17
Wednesday 119:145-176 □ 128, 129, 130
Micah 2:1-13 Acts 23:23-35 Luke 7:18-35
Thursday 131, 132, [133] □ 134, 135
Micah 3:1-8 Acts 24:1-23 Luke 7:36-50
Friday 140, 142 □ 141, 143:1-11(12)
Micah 3:9—4:5 Acts 24:24—25:12 Luke 8:1-15
Saturday 137:1-6(7-9), 144 □ 104
Micah 5:1-4,10-15 Acts 25:13-27 Luke 8:16-25
Proper 23 *Week of the Sunday closest to October 12*
Sunday 146, 147 □ 111, 112, 113
Micah 6:1-8 1 Cor. 4:9-16 Matt. 15:21-28
Monday 1, 2, 3 □ 4, 7
Micah 7:1-7 Acts 26:1-23 Luke 8:26-39
Tuesday 5, 6 □ 10, 11
Jonah 1:1-17a Acts 26:24—27:8 Luke 8:40-56
Wednesday 119:1-24 □ 12, 13, 14
Jonah 1:17—2:10 Acts 27:9-26 Luke 9:1-17
Thursday 18:1-20 □ 18:21-50
Jonah 3:1—4:11 Acts 27:27-44 Luke 9:18-27
Friday 16, 17 □ 22
Ecclus. 1:1-10,18-27 Acts 28:1-16 Luke 9:28-36
Saturday 20, 21:1-7(8-14) □ 110:1-5(6-7), 116, 117
Ecclus. 3:17-31 Acts 28:17-31 Luke 9:37-50
Proper 24 *Week of the Sunday closest to October 19*
Sunday 148, 149, 150 □ 114, 115
Ecclus. 4:1-10 1 Cor. 10:1-13 Matt. 16:13-20
Monday 25 □ 9, 15
Ecclus. 4:20—5:7 Rev. 7:1-8 Luke 9:51-62
Tuesday 26, 28 □ 36, 39
Ecclus. 6:5-17 Rev. 7:9-17 Luke 10:1-16
Wednesday 38 □ 119:25-48
Ecclus. 7:4-14 Rev. 8:1-13 Luke 10:17-24
Thursday 37:1-18 □ 37:19-42
Ecclus. 10:1-18 Rev. 9:1-12 Luke 10:25-37
Friday 31 □ 35
Ecclus. 11:2-20 Rev. 9:13-21 Luke 10:38-42
Saturday 30, 32 □ 42, 43
Ecclus. 15:9-20 Rev. 10:1-11 Luke 11:1-13

Proper 25 *Week of the Sunday closest to October 26*
Sunday 63:1-8(9-11),98 □ 103
Ecclus. 18:19-33 1 Cor. 10:15-24 Matt. 18:15-20
Monday 41,52 □ 44
Ecclus. 19:4-17 Rev. 11:1-14 Luke 11:14-26
Tuesday 45 □ 47,48
Ecclus. 24:1-12 Rev. 11:14-19 Luke 11:27-36
Wednesday 119:49-72 □ 49,[53]
Ecclus. 28:14-26 Rev. 12:1-6 Luke 11:37-52
Thursday 50 □ [59,60] or 33
Ecclus. 31:12-18,25—32:2 Rev. 12:7-17 Luke 11:53—12:12
Friday 40,54 □ 51
Ecclus. 34:1-8,18-22 Rev. 13:1-10 Luke 12:13-31
Saturday 55 □ 138,139:1-17(18-23)
Ecclus. 35:1-17 Rev. 13:11-18 Luke 12:32-48
Proper 26 *Week of the Sunday closest to November 2*
Sunday 24, 29 □ 8, 84
Ecclus. 36:1-17 1 Cor. 12:27—13:13 Matt. 18:21-35
Monday 56, 57, [58] □ 64, 65
Ecclus. 38:24-34 Rev. 14:1-13 Luke 12:49-59
Tuesday 61, 62 □ 68:1-20(21-23)24-36
Ecclus. 43:1-22 Rev. 14:14—15:8 Luke 13:1-9
Wednesday 72 □ 119:73-96
Ecclus. 43:23-33 Rev. 16:1-11 Luke 13:10-17
Thursday [70], 71 □ 74
Ecclus. 44:1-15 Rev. 16:12-21 Luke 14:18-30
Friday 69:1-23(24-30)31-38 □ 73
Ecclus. 50:1,11-24 Rev. 17:1-18 Luke 13:31-35
Saturday 75, 76 □ 23, 27
Ecclus. 51:1-12 Rev. 18:1-14 Luke 14:1-11
Proper 27 *Week of the Sunday closest to November 9*
Sunday 93, 96 □ 34
Ecclus. 51:13-22 1 Cor. 14:1-12 Matt. 20:1-16
Monday 80 □ 77, [79]
Joel 1:1-13 Rev. 18:15-24 Luke 14:12-24
Tuesday 78:1-39 □ 78:40-72
Joel 1:15—2:2(3-11) Rev. 19:1-10 Luke 14:25-35
Wednesday 119:97-120 □ 81, 82
Joel 2:12-19 Rev. 19:11-21 Luke 15:1-10
Thursday [83] or 23,27 □ 85, 86
Joel 2:21-27 James 1:1-15 Luke 15:1-2,11-32
Friday 88 □ 91, 92
Joel 2:28—3:8 James 1:16-27 Luke 16:1-9
Saturday 87, 90 □ 136
Joel 3:9-17 James 2:1-13 Luke 16:10-17(18)

Proper 28 *Week of the Sunday closest to November 16*
Sunday 66, 67 ☐ 19, 46
Hab. 1:1-4(5-11)12—2:1 Phil. 3:13—4:1 Matt. 23:13-24
Monday 89:1-18 ☐ 89:19-52
Hab. 2:1-4,9-20 James 2:14-26 Luke 16:19-31
Tuesday 97, 99, [100] ☐ 94, [95]
Hab. 3:1-10(11-15)16-18 James 3:1-12 Luke 17:1-10
Wednesday 101, 109:1-4(5-19)20-30 ☐ 119:121-144
Mal. 1:1,6-14 James 3:13—4:12 Luke 17:11-19
Thursday 105:1-22 ☐ 105:23-45
Mal. 2:1-16 James 4:13—5:6 Luke 17:20-37
Friday 102 ☐ 107:1-32
Mal. 3:1-12 James 5:7-12 Luke 18:1-8
Saturday 107:33-43, 108:1-6(7-13) ☐ 33
Mal. 3:13—4:6 James 5:13-20 Luke 18:9-14
Proper 29 *Week of the Sunday closest to November 23*
Sunday 118 ☐ 145
Isa. 19:19-25 Rom. 15:5-13 Luke 19:11-27
Monday 106:1-18 ☐ 106:19-48
Joel 3:1-2,9-17 1 Pet. 1:1-12 Matt. 19:1-12
Tuesday [120], 121, 122, 123 ☐ 124, 125, 126, [127]
Nahum 1:1-13 1 Pet. 1:13-25 Matt. 19:13-22
Wednesday 119:145-176 ☐ 128, 129, 130
Obadiah 15-21 1 Pet. 2:1-10 Matt. 19:23-30
Thursday 131, 132, [133] ☐ 134, 135
Zeph. 3:1-13 1 Pet. 2:11-25 Matt. 20:1-16
Friday 140, 142 ☐ 141, 143:1-11(12)
Isa. 24:14-23 1 Pet. 3:13—4:6 Matt. 20:17-28
Saturday 137:1-6(7-9), 144 ☐ 104
Micah 7:11-20 1 Pet. 4:7-19 Matt. 20:29-34

Holy Days

	Morning Prayer	Evening Prayer
St. Andrew November 30	34 Isaiah 49:1-6 1 Corinthians 4:1-16 42	96,100 Isaiah 55:1-5 John 1:35-42
St. Thomas December 21	23,121 Job 42:1-6 1 Peter 1:3-9	27 Isaiah 43: 8-13 John 14:1-7
St. Stephen December 26	28,30 2 Chronicles 24:17-22 Acts 6:1-7	118 Wisdom 4:7-15 Acts 7:59—8:8
St. John December 27	97,98 Proverbs 8:22-30 John 13:20-35	145 Isaiah 44:1-8 1 John 5:1-12
Holy Innocents December 28	2,26 Isaiah 49:13-23 Matthew 18:1-14	19,126 Isaiah 54:1-13 Mark 10:13-16
Confession of St. Peter January 18	66,67 Ezekiel 3:4-11 Acts 10:34-44	118 Ezekiel 34:11-16 John 21:15-22
Conversion of St. Paul January 25	19 Isaiah 45:18-25 Philippians 3:4b-11	119:89-112 Ecclesiasticus 39:1-10 Acts 9:1-22
Eve of the Presentation		113,122 1 Samuel 1:20-28a Romans 8:14-21
The Presentation February 2	42, 43 1 Samuel 2:1-10 John 8:31-36	48,87 Haggai 2:1-9 1 John 3:1-8
St. Matthias February 24	80 1 Samuel 16:1-13 1 John 2:18-25	33 1 Samuel 12:1-5 Acts 20:17-35
St. Joseph March 19	132 Isaiah 63:7-16 Matthew 1:18-25	34 2 Chronicles 6:12-17 Ephesians 3:14-21
Eve of the Annunciation		8, 138 Genesis 3:1-15 Romans 5:12-21 or Galatians 4:1-7

	Morning Prayer	**Evening Prayer**
The Annunciation March 25	85, 87 Isaiah 52:7-12 Hebrews 2:5-10	110:1-5(6-7),132 Wisdom 9:1-12 John 1:9-14
St. Mark April 25	145 Ecclesiasticus 2:1-11 Acts 12:25—13:3	67, 96 Isaiah 62:6-12 2 Timothy 4:1-11
SS. Philip & James May 1	119:137-160 Job 23:1-12 John 1:43-51	139 Proverbs 4:7-18 John 12:20-26
Eve of the Visitation		132 Isaiah 11:1-10 Hebrews 2:11-18
The Visitation May 31	72 1 Samuel 1:1-20 Hebrews 3:1-6	146,147 Zechariah 2:10-13 John 3:25-30
St. Barnabas June 11	15, 67 Ecclesiasticus 31:3-11 Acts 4:32-37	19, 146 Job 29:1-16 Acts 9:26-31
Eve of St. John the Baptist		103 Ecclesiasticus 48:1-11 Luke 1:5-23
Nativity of St. John the Baptist June 24	82, 98 Malachi 3:1-5 John 3:22-30	80 Malachi 4:1-6 Matthew 11:2-19
SS. Peter & Paul June 29	66 Ezekiel 2:1-7 Acts 11:1-18	97, 138 Isaiah 49:1-6 Galatians 2:1-9
Independence Day July 4	33 Ecclesiasticus 10:1-8,12-18 James 5:7-10	107:1-32 Micah 4:1-5 Revelation 21:1-7
St. Mary Magdalene July 22	116 Zephaniah 3:14-20 Mark 15:47—16:7	30, 149 Exodus 15:19-21 2 Corinthians 1:3-7
St. James July 25	34 Jeremiah 16:14-21 Mark 1:14-20	33 Jeremiah 26:1-15 Matthew 10:16-32

	Morning Prayer	**Evening Prayer**
Eve of the Transfiguration		84 1 Kings 19:1-12 2 Corinthians 3:1-9,18
The Transfiguration August 6	2, 24 Exodus 24:12-18 2 Corinthians 4:1-6	72 Daniel 7:9-10,13-14 John 12:27-36a
St. Mary **the Virgin** August 15	113, 115 1 Samuel 2:1-10 John 2:1-12	45, or 138, 149 Jeremiah 31:1-14 or Zechariah 2:10-13 John 19:23-27 or Acts 1:6-14
St. Bartholomew August 24	86 Genesis 28:10-17 John 1:43-51	15, 67 Isaiah 66:1-2,18-23 1 Peter 5:1-11
Eve of Holy Cross		46, 87 1 Kings 8:22-30 Ephesians 2:11-22
Holy Cross Day September 14	66 Numbers 21:4-9 John 3:11-17	118 Genesis 3:1-15 1 Peter 3:17-22
St. Matthew September 21	119:41-64 Isaiah 8:11-20 Romans 10:1-15	19, 112 Job 28:12-28 Matthew 13:44-52
St. Michael & **All Angels** September 29	8, 148 Job 38:1-7 Hebrews 1:1-14	34, 150, or 104 Daniel 12:1-3 or 2 Kings 6:8-17 Mark 13:21-27 or Revelation 5:1-14
St. Luke October 18	103 Ezekiel 47:1-12 Luke 1:1-4	67, 96 Isaiah 52:7-10 Acts 1:1-8
St. James **of Jerusalem** October 23	119:145-168 Jeremiah 11:18-23 Matthew 10:16-22	122,125 Isaiah 65:17-25 Hebrews 12:12-24
SS. Simon & Jude October 28	· 66 Isaiah 28:9-16 Ephesians 4:1-16	116,117 Isaiah 4:2-6 John 14:15-31

	Morning Prayer	Evening Prayer
Eve of All Saints		34 Wisdom 3:1-9 Revelation 19:1, 4-10
All Saints' Day November 1 2	111,112 Esdras 2:42-47 Hebrews 11:32—12:2	148,150 Wisdom 5:1-5, 14-16 Revelation 21:1-4, 22—22:5
Thanksgiving Day	147 Deuteronomy 26:1-11 John 6:26-35	145 Joel 2:21-27 1 Thessalonians 5:12-24
Special Occasions **Eve of the** **Dedication**		48,122 Haggai 2:1-9 1 Corinthians 3:9-17
Anniversary **of the** **Dedication** **of a Church**	132 1 Kings 8:1-13 John 10:22-30	29, 46 1 Kings 8:54-62 Hebrews 10:19-25
Eve of the **Patronal Feast**		27, or 116,117 Isaiah 49:1-13 or Ecclesiasticus 51:6b-12 Ephesians 4:1-13 or Revelation 7:9-17 or Luke 10:38-42
The Patronal **Feast**	92,93, or 148, 149 Isaiah 52:7-10 or Job 5:8-21 Acts 4:5-13 or Luke 12:1-12	96,97 or 111,112 Jeremiah 31:10-14 or Ecclesiasticus 2:7-18 Romans 12:1-21 or Luke 21:10-19
Eves of **Apostles and** **Evangelists**		48, 122, or 84, 150 Isaiah 43:10-15* or Isaiah 52:7-10** Revelation 21:1-4,9-14 or Matthew 9:35—10:4

Devotional Prayers

The Angelus

The Angel of the Lord announced to Mary
And she conceived by the Holy Spirit.
Hail Mary, full of grace, the Lord is with you. Blessed are you among women, and blessed is the fruit of your womb, Jesus
Holy Mary, Mother of God, pray for us sinners, now and at the hour of our death. Amen.

Behold the handmaid of the Lord
Be it unto me according to your word
Hail Mary, full of grace, the Lord is with you. Blessed are you among women, and blessed is the fruit of your womb, Jesus
Holy Mary, Mother of God, pray for us sinners, now and at the hour of our death. Amen.

And the Word was made flesh.
And dwelled among us.
Hail Mary, full of grace, the Lord is with you. Blessed are you among women, and blessed is the fruit of your womb, Jesus
Holy Mary, Mother of God, pray for us sinners, now and at the hour of our death. Amen.

V: Pray for us, O holy Mother of God.
R: *That we may be made worthy of the promises of Christ.*
Let us pray:
Pour your grace into our hearts, O Lord, that we who have known the incarnation of your Son Jesus Christ, announced by an angel to the Virgin Mary, may by his cross and passion be brought to the glory of his resurrection; through Jesus Christ our Lord. *Amen.*

The General Thanksgiving

Almighty God, Father of all mercies,
we your unworthy servants give you humble thanks
for all your goodness and loving-kindness
to us and to all whom you have made.
We bless you for our creation, preservation,
and all the blessings of this life;
but above all for your immeasurable love
in the redemption of the world by our Lord Jesus Christ;
for the means of grace, and for the hope of glory.
And, we pray, give us such an awareness of your mercies,
that with truly thankful hearts we may show forth your praise,
not only with our lips, but in our lives,
by giving up our selves to your service,
and by walking before you
in holiness and righteousness all our days;
through Jesus Christ our Lord,
to whom, with you and the Holy Spirit,
be honor and glory throughout all ages. Amen.

A Prayer of St. Chrysostom

Almighty God, you have given us grace at this time with one
accord to make our common supplication to you; and you
have promised through your well-beloved Son that when two
or three are gathered together in his Name you will be in the
midst of them: Fulfill now, O Lord, our desires and petitions
as may be best for us; granting us in this world knowledge of
your truth, and in the age to come life everlasting. Amen.

A General Thanksgiving

Accept, O Lord, our thanks and praise for all that you have done for us. We thank you for the splendor of the whole creation, for the beauty of this world, for the wonder of life, and for the mystery of love.

We thank you for the blessing of family and friends, and for the loving care which surrounds us on every side.

We thank you for setting us at tasks which demand our best efforts, and for leading us to accomplishments which satisfy and delight us.

We thank you also for those disappointments and failures that lead us to acknowledge our dependence on you alone.

Above all, we thank you for your Son Jesus Christ; for the truth of his Word and the example of his life; for his steadfast obedience, by which he overcame temptation; for his dying, through which he overcame death; and for his rising to life again, in which we are raised to the life of your kingdom.

Grant us the gift of your Spirit, that we may know him and make him known; and through him, at all times and in all places, may give thanks to you in all things. Amen.

Acknowledgements

Litany
The Rogation Day litanies from The Diocese of Saskatoon of the Anglican Church of Canada.

Collects
Benedictine Sanctoral
March 21 Transitus of our Holy Father St. Benedict
July 11 Our Holy Father Saint Benedict of Nursia
November 14 All Souls of the Benedictine Order

Monastery of the Glorious Cross, Branfort, Ct.
February 10 Scholastica Evening Prayer I, Morning Prayer,

Scholastica Project of the Monastic Liturgy Forum
February 10 Scholastica Evening Prayer II

Trappist Sanctoral
April 30 The Holy Abbots of Cluny:
May 15 Pachomius
November 13 All Saints of the Benedictine Order
November 19 Mechtild

Original Compositions
August 16 Roger Schutz
August 26 Raimon Panikkar

Canticles for Daily or Weekly Use

You are God   *Te Deum laudamus*

You are God: we praise you;
You are the Lord: we acclaim you;
You are the eternal Father:
All creation worships you.
To you all angels, all the powers of heaven,
Cherubim and Seraphim, sing in endless praise:
   Holy, holy, holy Lord, God of power and might,
   heaven and earth are full of your glory.
The glorious company of apostles praise you.
The noble fellowship of prophets praise you.
The white-robed army of martyrs praise you.
Throughout the world the holy Church acclaims you;
   Father, of majesty unbounded,
   your true and only Son, worthy of all worship,
   and the Holy Spirit, advocate and guide.
You, Christ, are the king of glory,
the eternal Son of the Father.
When you became man to set us free
you did not shun the Virgin's womb.
You overcame the sting of death
and opened the kingdom of heaven to all believers.
You are seated at God's right hand in glory.
We believe that you will come and be our judge.
   Come then, Lord, and help your people,
   bought with the price of your own blood,
   and bring us with your saints
   to glory everlasting.

The Song of Zechariah *Benedictus Dominus Deus*

Luke 1: 68-79

Blessed be the Lord, the God of Israel; *
    he has come to his people and set them free.
He has raised up for us a mighty savior, *
    born of the house of his servant David.
Through his holy prophets he promised of old,
 that he would save us from our enemies, *
    from the hands of all who hate us.
He promised to show mercy to our fathers *
    and to remember his holy covenant.
This was the oath he swore to our father Abraham, *
    to set us free from the hands of our enemies,
Free to worship him without fear, *
    holy and righteous in his sight
    all the days of our life.
You, my child, shall be called the prophet of the Most High, *
    for you will go before the Lord to prepare his way,
To give his people knowledge of salvation *
    by the forgiveness of their sins.
In the tender compassion of our God *
    the dawn from on high shall break upon us,
To shine on those who dwell in darkness
and the shadow of death, *
    and to guide our feet into the way of peace.
Glory to the Father, and to the Son, and to the Holy Spirit: *
    as it was in the beginning, is now, and will be for ever. Amen.

The Song of Mary *Magnificat*

Luke 1:46-55

My soul proclaims the greatness of the Lord,
my spirit rejoices in God my Savior; *
    for he has looked with favor on his lowly servant.
From this day all generations will call me blessed: *
    the Almighty has done great things for me,
    and holy is his Name.
He has mercy on those who fear him *
    in every generation.
He has shown the strength of his arm, *
    he has scattered the proud in their conceit.
He has cast down the mighty from their thrones, *
    and has lifted up the lowly.
He has filled the hungry with good things, *
    and the rich he has sent away empty.
He has come to the help of his servant Israel, *
    for he has remembered his promise of mercy,
The promise he made to our fathers, *
    to Abraham and his children for ever.
Glory to the Father, and to the Son, and to the Holy Spirit: *
    as it was in the beginning, is now, and will be for ever. Amen.